Policy Making in China
Leaders, Structures, and Processes

Policy Making in China
Leaders, Structures, and
Processes

• • •

KENNETH LIEBERTHAL
AND
MICHEL OKSENBERG

Princeton University Press

PRINCETON, NEW JERSEY

This book has been composed in Linotron Aldus
Clothbound editions of Princeton University Press books are
printed on acid-free paper, and binding materials are
chosen for strength and durability.
Paperbacks, although satisfactory for personal collections,
are not usually suitable for library rebinding

Printed in the United States of America
by Princeton University Press
Princeton, New Jersey

Library of Congress Cataloging-in-Publication Data
Lieberthal, Kenneth.
Policy making in China.
Bibliography: p.
Includes index.
1. China—Politics and government—1976-
I. Oksenberg, Michel, 1938-   . II. Title.
JQ1512.L564 1988   320   88-7202
ISBN 0-691-05668-4 (alk. paper)

9 8 7 6 5 4 3 2

We dedicate this book to our wives
Jane and Lois
with much love and appreciation

CONTENTS

CONTENTS

CONTENTS

ACKNOWLEDGMENTS

This volume revises a study done under a contract with the United States Department of Commerce: *Bureaucratic Politics and Chinese Energy Development* (Washington: Government Printing Office, August 1986). The Commerce Department felt that a deeper understanding of the bureaucratic structures and the policy processes of energy development in China would enable American firms to work more effectively with the People's Republic of China (PRC). We shared this conviction and oriented the original volume toward the business community.

In undertaking our revisions, we believed that our research shed light on important aspects of the policy-making process in China that would be of more general interest. We therefore have substantially revised the original study for publication by Princeton University Press. Our revisions include writing two new chapters (Chapters One and Eight), deleting material of interest primarily to businessmen, adding footnotes and integrating the volume around the themes articulated in the new introductory and concluding chapters. The present study corrects errors in the original volume.

We envisioned this study to be pathbreaking in its combination of documentary sources and extensive interviews with Chinese, Americans, Europeans, and Japanese who have been involved in developing China's energy industries. We have promised absolute confidentially to each of these individuals, and thus we cannot thank people by name. Suffice it to make two points to indicate the size of our debt to our sources. First, every non-Chinese that we approached for an interview agreed to our request, and most were very generous with their time and their wisdom. Second, we received extraordinary cooperation in several research trips to China in 1984, 1985, and 1986. The Chinese People's Institute for Foreign Affairs (CPIFA) hosted the major part of this research, and we are especially appreciative of its energetic assistance. We also express our special thanks to the several score Chinese officials in Beijing, Guangdong, Shanxi, Hubei, and Hong Kong who helped us understand their policy process.

Most of the information contained in the sketches of bureaucratic units presented in Chapter Three comes from our interviews specifically for this project in China. We have also, however, drawn from other sources for these sketches and have freely expressed our own judgments, too. We sent the initial drafts of these sketches back to some of the people we interviewed for review. Typically, their responses reflected a careful reading of the text, and a number of details were corrected or updated as a result. At the same time, every unit that responded indicated that, while it did not agree with all our judgments, it would not note the areas of disagreement unless they were purely of a factual nature. While other chapters also draw some information from these interviews, they are based primarily on other materials. Our Chinese interlocutors did not see the drafts of these other chapters in advance of publication. While we hope they find them insightful, we know that they may take exception to certain of the comments we have made in them.

Indeed, this entire volume is infused with perspectives and information that we have developed over a period of years that extends well beyond the research specifically for this book. This book has benefitted to an unusual extent not only from the interviewing done directly for this project during 1984-86, but more generally from our personal exposure to China since 1972, when China opened to American academics. In subsequent years we have been in meetings with many of China's top leaders, interviewed Beijing officials in virtually all of the numerous bureaucracies mentioned in this volume, travelled to most of China's provincial capitals, and hosted numerous visiting Chinese officials and scholars in the United States. Although we are indebted to an extraordinary range of individuals and organizations on both the Chinese and American sides for these opportunities, we especially note the invaluable role of the Committee on Scholarly Communications with the People's Republic of China and of the National Committee on US-China Relations, Inc. in facilitating contact of American scholars with Chinese officials. Chapters Two, Four, and Seven draw especially heavily from this larger set of experiences.

At the U.S. Department of Commerce, Eugene K. Lawson was the Deputy Assistant Secretary of Commerce for East Asia and the Pacific at the time we initiated our project. As our contract officer until he left the government he encouraged and facilitated our work wherever possible. His successors as our contract officers, Mr. Roger D. Severance and Mr. Melvin W. Searls, Jr., along with Mrs. Myna Stoltz, continued Dr. Lawson's approach of encouragement and flexibility. Former Commerce Department staff members David Denny and Dan Stein also provided valuable ideas as we formulated our research design.

We also benefitted from the help of several other individuals who assisted this project. Stephanie R. Green was our associate in interviewing in the United States and Hong Kong. Her diligence, knowledge, and judgment gave the effort needed direction and energy in the early stages.

Heidi Proegler was outstanding in developing and maintaining appropriate computer files and rendering other research assistance. Yoshihide Soeya capably assisted our interviewing in Japan and summarized Japanese language materials for us. Patricia Preston, David Patterson, Fred Zimmerman, Ena Schlorff, and the Center for Chinese Studies at the University of Michigan also contributed in various ways to the project. We thank them all.

Finally, one's colleagues are always important sources of insight and wisdom in thinking through a book, and we have learned much from the comments received when we presented portions of this study in many seminars with students and scholars (at Berkeley, Columbia, Harvard, Michigan, Washington, and SAIS), businessmen, and officials in the US government and in international organizations. We received very helpful written comments on various chapters from A. Doak Barnett, Matthew Evangelista, Zvi Gitelman, Steven Goldstein, Nina Halpern, David M. Lampton, Melanie Manion, Lester Ross, Gilbert Rozman, Dorothy Solinger, Richard Suttmeier, Michael Swayne, Ezra Vogel, and Kim Woodard. We also thank Margaret Case of Princeton University Press for her support and patience. For the remaining faults and errors in this study, we must assume sole responsibility.

KENNETH LIEBERTHAL
MICHEL OKSENBERG
May 1, 1987

ABBREVIATIONS

BOC	Bank of China
CAAC	Civil Aviation Administration of China
CAS	Chinese Academy of Sciences
CASS	Chinese Academy of Social Sciences
CCP	Chinese Communist Party
CCPIT	China Commission for the Promotion of International Trade
CEO	Chief Executive Officer
CITIC	China International Trust and Investment Corporation
CGG	Compagnie General de Geophysique
CMSNC	China Merchant Steam Navigation Company
CNCDC	China National Coal Development Corporation
CNCIEC	China National Coal Import and Export Corporation
CNODC	China National Oil Development Corporation
CNOGEDC	China National Oil and Gas Exploration and Development Corporation
CNOJSC	China Nanhai Oil Joint Services Company
CNOOC	China National Offshore Oil Corporation
COCOM	Coordinating Committee (on sales to communist countries)
COOS	China Offshore Oil Services
CPIFA	Chinese People's Institute for Foreign Affairs
CRMC	Coal Resources Management Committee
CTC	(UN) Center for Transnational Corporations
CTSC	Coal Transport and Sales Corporation
ECAFE	Economic Commission for Asia and the Far East
FBIS	Foreign Broadcast Information Service—China Daily Report
FEC	Finance and Economics Committee
FICC	Foreign Investment Control Commission
FIMB	Foreign Investment Management Bureau
GGA	Geological General Administration
GMRB	Guangming ribao
JMC	Joint Management Committee
JNOC	Japan National Oil Company
JPC	Joint Procurement Committee

JPRS	Joint Publications Research Service
JTC	Joint Technical Committee
LCMB	Local Coal Management Bureau
LTTA	(Sino-Japanese) Long Term Trade Agreement
MCI	Ministry of Coal Industry
MITI	Ministry of International Trade and Industry
MMT	Million Metric Tons
MOF	Ministry of Finance
MOFERT	Ministry of Foreign Economic Relations and Trade
MOG	Ministry of Geology
MPI	Ministry of Petroleum Industry
MR	Military Region
MWREP	Ministry of Water Resources and Electric Power
NCUSCT	National Council on US-China Trade
NEP	New Economic Policy
NPC	National People's Congress
PLA	People's Liberation Army
PRC	Peoples Republic of China
RMB	Renminbi (the Chinese dollar)
RMRB	Renmin ribao (People's Daily)
SCBDO	Shanxi Coal Base Development Office
SCC	Safe Channel Capacity
SCCC	State Capital Construction Commission
SCMP	Survey of China Mainland Press
SDI	Shenyang Design Institute
SEC	State Economic Commission
SEZ	Special Economic Zone
SINOPEC	Chinese Petrochemical Corporation
SPC	State Planning Commission
SSB	State Statistical Bureau
SSTC	State Science and Technology Commission
USBR	United States Bureau of Reclamation
USLO	United States Liaison Office
YVPO	Yangtze Valley Planning Office

Policy Making in China
Leaders, Structures and Processes

· 1 ·

STRUCTURE AND PROCESS: AN OVERVIEW

This book has a simple purpose: to illuminate how the bureaucratic structure of the state, policy processes, and outcomes are interrelated in contemporary China. The processes through which large-scale energy development projects are decided reveal that the fragmented, segmented, and stratified structure of the state promotes a system of negotiations, bargaining, and the seeking of consensus among affected bureaucracies. The policy process in this sphere is disjointed, protracted, and incremental.

To many students of politics, our effort to relate structure, process, and outcome would appear to be an elaboration of the obvious. Certainly the writings on American politics have long recognized that, for example, the making of American foreign policy can only be understood in the context of the powers and perspectives of the President, the role of Congress, and the interests and involvement of the National Security Council, the State Department, the Defense Department, and the Central Intelligence Agency. But in the case of China, scholars to date have tended to neglect the complex structure of the state itself as a significant determinant of the political process and policy outcomes. The competing explanations for the proclamation of a policy in China usually have taken one of the following forms: 1. policy X was adopted pragmatically to solve new policy problems pressing upon the leaders; 2. policy X was promulgated in order to keep alive the ideological vision of its proponents; 3. policy X was adopted as a tactical ploy of one or several temporarily allied leaders to rebuff a challenge from rivals; or 4. policy X was adopted by a dominant and enduring faction for the rewards it bestows upon its network of loyalists. The first two explanations assert that policies are reasoned responses to perceived policy problems; the latter two attribute policies to the struggle for power among the top leaders or factions into which they coalesce. None of these explanations incorporates structural dimensions of the Chinese bureaucracy into the explanation.

This volume suggests that an additional hypothesis should regularly be added to these alternative explanations for a policy outcome: Policy X resulted from a bargain among Ministries A, B, and C and Province D either 1. brokered by one or more top leaders, 2. arranged by coordinating staffs acting in the name of one or more top leaders, or 3. negotiated by the supra-ministry coordinating agency, and ratified through routine procedures by the top leaders. Disgruntled Ministries E and F, losers in the deal, planned to pursue strategies to erode the agreement. The bargain sought to reconcile the conflicting organizational missions, ethos, structure, and resource allocations of the ministries involved. Thus, policies are not necessarily either coherent and integrated responses to perceived problems or part of a logical strategy of a leader or faction to advance power and principle. For analytical purposes, a package or bundle of policies is best disaggregated into its individual or separate policies. While some of those policies may result from the initiative of top leaders, others are best seen as a temporary agreement arranged by the top leaders among contending and powerful bureaucracies with diverse purposes, experiences, and resources.

THE WESTERN LITERATURE ON THE CHINESE POLICY PROCESS

Before summarizing our principal findings and providing a road map to this book, it seems appropriate to sketch the development of Western analyses of the Chinese policy process and to indicate how this study seeks to join the existing literature.

Analysis to the Late 1960's

In the years immediately prior to the start of the Cultural Revolution (1966), Western analysts had achieved a broad consensus concerning the major characteristics of the Chinese state that had emerged in the wake of the communist revolution. The Chinese state included the government, the Chinese Communist Party (CCP), the People's Liberation Army (PLA), the smaller surviving parties of the *ancien régime*, and the organizations which mobilize the populace. This system, whose structural features were similar to those of the Soviet Union and Eastern Europe, was authoritarian and highly coercive. It was dominated by a single party formally organized on Marxist-Leninist principles and had a socialist or Soviet-type economy. So went the conventional description of the core features of the Chinese system. Its authoritarian or totalitarian features merited stress due to the alleged firm grasp of the state over society, the absence of the rule of law, and the hierarchical structure of power. Compared to most other countries, the top leaders wielded enormous power, and few if any institutional checks existed to guard against the exercise and abuse of this power. The central role of the public security apparatus in the relationship between the elite and the masses underscored the salience of coercion in the system. In no small measure,

4

order was maintained in society through the threat and use of force as well as through automatic deference to authority.

The socialist economy particularly deserved emphasis due to the role of the state in the management of the economy. The state owned and managed the major means of production. Private property was strictly limited, and the allocation of strategically significant resources occurred through state command rather than in the market place. The state sought to regulate the economy through five year and annual plans rather than through monetary and fiscal instruments of control. Prices of key commodities were bureaucratically administered rather than set impersonally in the market.

No portrayal could overlook the fact that the Chinese Communist Party dominated the state apparatus through its control of personnel appointments, its setting of policy guidelines which Party members everywhere were expected to obey, and its control of the media through which it shaped the ideological climate in which the entire populace lived. The adherence of the leaders to Marxist-Leninist ideology constituted another core feature, not only because of the organizational consequences which flowed from their beliefs but because the goals which the leaders set for the nation, the methods they employed to analyze problems, and the perceptual lenses through which they filtered information about their environment were all significantly influenced by their formal ideology.

In the mid-1960's, several major books were published which elaborated on these core features. To varying degrees, the authors had combined interviews of lower level former Chinese officials with extensive readings of the Chinese press to reach their conclusions. In *Cadres, Bureaucracy, and Political Power in China*,[1] A. Doak Barnett drew upon interviews to detail the hierarchical structure of the state and describe how the Party penetrated and controlled the government apparatus. *Leadership in Communist China*[2] by John Lewis also illuminated the formal structure and ideology of the Party. Jerome Cohen examined the coercive dimension of communist rule in *The Criminal System in the People's Republic of China*.[3] *The Chinese Economic System* by Audrey Donnithorne provided an encyclopedic account of the bureaucratic structures which controlled the economy,[4] while *Market Control and Planning in Communist China* by Dwight Perkins analyzed state control of the market.[5] In his classic *Ideology and Organization in Communist*

[1] New York: Columbia University Press, 1967.
[2] Ithaca, N.Y.: Cornell University Press, 1963.
[3] Cambridge: Harvard University Press, 1968.
[4] New York: Praeger Publishers, 1967.
[5] Cambridge: Harvard University Press, 1966.

China,[6] Franz Schurmann argued that the penetration of society and the Chinese Communist Party and its Marxist-Leninist ideology had reunified a nation previously fragmented by foreign aggression, civil war, and loss of a value consensus.[7] In *Mao Tse-tung: A Political Biography*, Stuart Schram demonstrated how the thought of Mao prompted his specific policy preferences.[8] Finally, in *Political Participation in Communist China*, James Townsend stressed that the populace was involved in the implementation of policy at the choice of the rulers, but ordinary citizens lacked meaningful opportunity to influence the process.[9]

The major discordant theme was struck by Lucian Pye. He advanced a particularly controversial cultural interpretation of the Chinese politics in *The Spirit of Chinese Politics*,[10] and his student Richard Solomon refined and elaborated upon this approach in his seminal *Mao's Revolution and the Chinese Political Culture*.[11] To Pye and Solomon, the communist system was unmistakably *Chinese*. Certain cultural traits infused and were core to the system, especially the importance of personal relations, the allure of patrimonialism and patron-client ties, and the deep-seated fear of disorder (*luan*). They argued that, for cultural reasons, the organizational apparatus which so impressed most analysts was vulnerable to rapid breakdown. They claimed that from birth, Chinese are taught to enter into and exploit patron-client relations. Subordinates place excessive faith in the capacity of their patrons, whether familial or political, and when hopes are dashed, anger comes to the fore. Chinese are not taught to handle conflict well, according to the Pye-Solomon interpretation. As a result the structure of political authority, built upon clientist ties, is easily susceptible to rupture either when the leaders engage in their inevitable factional struggles at the top or when patrons prove unable to protect their clients.

The Effect of the Cultural Revolution upon Analysis

For several reasons, the Cultural Revolution and its aftermath from 1966 to 1976 eroded the emerging consensus and appeared to validate the insights of Pye and Solomon. For the most part, the previous description

---

[6] First edition, Berkeley: University of California Press, 1966.

[7] In the second edition, published by the University of California Press in 1968, Schurmann *inter alia* built the military far more prominently into his model of the Chinese power structure.

[8] New York: Simon and Schuster, 1966.

[9] Berkeley and Los Angeles: University of California Press, 1967.

[10] Cambridge, Mass.: MIT Press, 1968.

[11] Berkeley and Los Angeles: University of California Press, 1971.

of the core features of the regime did not enable Western analysts to anticipate or explain the Cultural Revolution. While not overturning the insights of the earlier landmark studies, therefore, political developments during that tumultuous decade raised new questions and posed new challenges to the mid-1960's portrayal of the system. The original Schurmann argument underwent a significant metamorphosis. Previously he had argued that ideology and organization were mutually reenforcing, but with the attack by Mao Zedong upon the Party, in the revised edition of his book,[12] Schurmann observed that the relationship between beliefs and institutions could become tension ridden. Schurmann, as many others, concluded the Cultural Revolution in part was a conflict between defenders of the faith and defenders of the institutions. Equally significantly, Schurmann as others concluded that the Cultural Revolution revealed the continued vitality of Chinese traditions and social organizations beneath the formal organizational overlay. In a sense, this conclusion reenforced the theme of Pye and Solomon, a message long proclaimed by historian John Fairbank: a valid interpretation of Chinese politics must be rooted in an understanding of its cultural and intellectual roots.[13]

The deep differences among the top leaders called into question the previous assertions that they adhered to a single, unifying ideology. Marxism-Leninism clearly permitted a diversity of views on goals, epistemology, and policies. The previous portrayal of a cohesive leadership group in smooth control of its society clearly had to be modified, and henceforth no portrayal could ignore the political conflict and tension seemingly endemic to the system. Indeed, explaining the sources of conflict became a new, major analytical task.

The rise of the People's Liberation Army and Lin Biao during 1965-1971 and the subsequent role of several top PLA commanders in helping Deng Xiaoping to become the successor to Mao also had several implications. The PLA surpassed the public security apparatus as the coercive instrument meriting foreign attention; scholars had previously tended to neglect its domestic role. Further, the PLA not only played a role in maintaining order in society, but was intimately involved in elite level political struggles. The role of coercion in Chinese politics extended to the apex of the system.[14]

---

[12] Second edition, enlarged, Berkeley and Los Angeles: University of California Press, 1968.

[13] John Fairbank, *The United States and China*, 4th ed., enlarged (Cambridge: Harvard University Press, 1983).

[14] See, e.g., Michael Ying-mao Kao, *The People's Liberation Army and China's Nation Building* (White Plains, N.Y.: International Arts and Sciences Press, 1973); Kao (ed.), *The*

The Red Guard movement revealed that under certain circumstances, political involvement of the populace could escape the confines of the leadership, and some spontaneity in participation could occur, with considerable influence upon policy, although the effect was not necessarily what the populace intended. The previous image of a state in control of society yielded to a more complex portrayal of interaction between the leaders and the led.[15] This issue stimulated some scholars to modify and apply "interest group" theory developed in the United States to the Chinese case, as Sovietologists were also then doing in the Soviet case.[16] Other scholars began to examine in depth how particular sectors of society sought to influence the system,[17] and yet others began to examine carefully the interaction of state and society at the lowest levels. Interesting for our purposes, this literature in recent years has persuasively traced the relationship between structure and process in such diverse work units as rural villages, hospitals, and factories.[18] In all locales, the

Lin Piao Affair: Power, Politics and Military Coup (White Plains, N.Y.: M. E. Sharpe, 1975); William Whitson (ed.), *The Military and Political Power in China in the 1970's* (New York: Praeger, 1972); Whitson, *The Chinese High Command: A History of Communist Military Politics, 1927-71* (New York: Praeger, 1973); Thomas Robinson, "The Wuhan Incident," *China Quarterly*, No. 47 (July-September, 1971), pp. 413-438; Andres Onate, "Hua Kuo-feng and the Arrest of the 'Gang of Four,' " *China Quarterly*, No. 70 (September, 1979), pp. 540-565; *Nie Rongzhen huiyi lu* (Reminisces of Nie Rongzhen) (Beijing: Liberation Army Press, 1984), pp. 842-869; Harvey Nelson, *The Chinese Military System: An Organizational Study of the People's Liberation Army* (Boulder: Westview Press, 1977); Lowell Dittmer, "Bases of Power in Chinese Politics: A Theory of Analysis of the Fall of the Gang of Four," *World Politics*, (October 1978), pp. 26-60.

[15] See Hong Yung Lee, *The Politics of the Chinese Cultural Revolution* (Berkeley and Los Angeles: University of California Press, 1978); Stanley Rosen, *Red Guard Factionalism and the Cultural Revolution in Guangzhou* (Boulder: Westview Press, 1981); Susan Shirk, *Competitive Comrades* (Berkeley and Los Angeles: University of California Press, 1982); David Zweig, *Agrarian Radicalism in China: 1968-78; The Search for a Social Base*, Ph.D. thesis (Ann Arbor: University of Michigan, 1983).

[16] See David S. Goodman (ed.), *Groups and Politics in the People's Republic of China* (Armonk, N.Y.: M. E. Sharpe, 1984); Victor Falkenheim (ed.), *Citizens and Groups in Contemporary China* (Ann Arbor: University of Michigan's Center for Chinese Studies), 1987; Michel Oksenberg, "Occupations and Groups in Chinese Society and the Cultural Revolution," *The Cultural Revolution: 1967 in Review*, eds. Michel Oksenberg, *et al.*, Michigan Papers in Chinese Studies, No. 2 (Ann Arbor: University of Michigan's Center for Chinese Studies, 1968), pp. 1-39.

[17] See, for example, John Burns, *Chinese Peasant Interest Articulation: 1949-1974*, Ph.D. thesis (New York: Columbia University, 1978); Gordon White, *Party and Professionals: The Political Role of Teachers in Contemporary China* (Armonk, N.Y.: M. E. Sharpe, 1981); Lynn White, "Workers Politics in Shanghai," *Journal of Asian Studies*, No. 36 (November, 1976), pp. 99-116.

[18] See Jean Chun Oi, *State and Peasant in Contemporary China: The Politics of Grain Procurement*, Ph.D. thesis (Ann Arbor: University of Michigan, 1983); Gail Henderson

researchers have found, the political structure fosters dependency and patrimonialism. In a sense, our study discovers the same phenomenon at the bureaucratic and higher levels.

Finally, documents released during the Cultural Revolution, as well as changes in the structure of the Chinese state, especially the attacks upon Party and government bureaucracies in 1966-68, raised questions about the efficacy, discipline, and coherence of Chinese organizations. A debate emerged between some scholars who argued the system was centralized and others who contended the system was cellular, with either the provinces or local units enjoying considerable autonomy and a capacity to resist the upper levels.[19] Our study joins this debate as well.

Two Models of the Policy Process Emerge

In short, the core features of the system which were elaborated in the early and mid-1960's provided a static picture which proved unable to explain political change or the dynamics of the system. The Cultural Revolution and its aftermath stimulated many new questions and approaches to the study of Chinese politics. Nowhere was this invigoration more evident than in the analysis of the policy process: how decisions are made and why particular policies are adopted.[20] In fact, two different approaches emerged in the 1970's in the common effort to illuminate the policy process. One approach focused on the evolution of policy in particular areas: agriculture,[21] science,[22] public health,[23] education,[24] agri-

---

and Myron Cohen, *The Chinese Hospital* (New Haven: Yale University Press, 1984); Andrew G. Walder, *Communist Neo-Traditionalism: Work and Authority in Chinese Industry* (Berkeley and Los Angeles: University of California Press, 1986).

[19] Audrey Donnithorne, "China's Cellular Economy: Some Economic Trends Since the Cultural Revolution," *China Quarterly*, No. 52 (October-December, 1972), pp. 605-619; Donnithorne and Nicholas Lardy, "Comment: Centralization and Decentralization in China's Fiscal Management," and "Reply," *China Quarterly*, No. 66 (June, 1976), pp. 328-354.

[20] Two early studies were Parris Chang, *Power and Policy in China* (University Park: Pennsylvania State University Press, 1976); and Byong-joon Ahn, *Chinese Politics and the Cultural Revolution* (Seattle: University of Washington Press, 1976).

[21] Kang Chao, *Agricultural Production in Communist China, 1949-1985* (Madison: University of Wisconsin Press, 1970).

[22] Richard P. Suttmeier, *Research and Revolution: Scientific Policy and Societal Change in China* (Lexington, Mass.: Lexington Books, 1974).

[23] David M. Lampton, *Health, Conflict, and the Chinese Political System* (Ann Arbor: University of Michigan's Center for Chinese Studies, 1974).

[24] Joel Glassman, "Change and Continuity in Chinese Communist Education Policy," *Contemporary China*, Vol. 2, No. 2 (September, 1978), pp. 847-890.

cultural mechanization,[25] and so on. The second focused on the elite political strife which produced major policy departures: the Hundred Flowers campaign, the Great Leap Forward,[26] the Cultural Revolution,[27] or the post-Mao reforms.[28] For understandable reasons, given the limitations of the previous emphasis upon the totalitarian features of the system and the seeming weakening of organizations in China from 1966 to 1976, a third approach received only muted emphasis: to examine structure and bureaucratic politics.[29]

The selection of a research topic inescapably reveals the assumptions of the analyst about the dynamics of the system. To sharpen the differences between the two dominant emphases—one initially focused on policy analysis and the other on personal politics at the top—we suggest the first stems from an implicit "rationality model" of the policy process while the second arises from an individual or factional "power model." To the former, reasoned debates by the leaders over substantive issues are primary in Chinese politics, while to the latter, the struggle for power among contending leaders supercedes other considerations. The "rationality model" focuses upon the response of the leaders to changing economic and foreign policy environments, while the "power model" attributes the stimulus for policy changes to the perpetual jockeying for position among the leaders.

In reality, most analysts of a policy issue also draw upon the "power" model, while many studies of elite strife incorporate aspects of the "ra-

[25] Benedict Stavis, *Making Green Revolution: The Politics of Agricultural Development in China, Rural Development Monograph*, No. 1 (Ithaca: Cornell University Press, 1974); Benedict Stavis, *The Politics of Agricultural Mechanization in China* (Ithaca: Cornell University Press, 1978).

[26] Roderick MacFarquhar, *The Origins of the Cultural Revolution*, 2 vols. (New York: Columbia University Press, 1974 and 1983); Parris Chang, *Power and Policy in China*.

[27] Edwin Rice, *Mao's Way* (Berkeley: University of California Press, 1972); Roderick MacFarquhar, *The Origins of the Cultural Revolution*; Merle Goldman, *China's Intellectuals: Advise and Dissent* (Cambridge: Harvard University Press, 1981).

[28] Jurgen Domes, *The Government and Politics of the PRC: A Time of Transition* (Boulder: Westview Press, 1985).

[29] Exceptions were Victor Falkenheim, *Provincial Administration in Fukien, 1949-1966*, Ph.D. thesis (New York: Columbia University, 1972); David M. Lampton, *The Politics of Medicine in China: The Policy Process, 1949-1977* (Boulder: Westview Press, 1975); Kenneth Lieberthal with James Tong and Sai-cheung Yeung, *Central Documents and Politburo Politics in China* (Ann Arbor: University of Michigan's Center for Chinese Studies, 1978); Kenneth Lieberthal, *A Research Guide to Central Party and Government Meetings in China, 1949-75* (White Plains, N.Y.: International Arts and Sciences Press, 1976); Michel Oksenberg, "Methods of Communication Within the Chinese Bureaucracy," *China Quarterly*, No. 57 (January-March, 1974), pp. 1-39; Michel Oksenberg, "The Chinese Policy Process and the Public Health Issue: An Arena Approach," *Studies in Comparative Communism* (Winter, 1974), Vol. VII, No. 4, pp. 375-408.

tionality" approach. The analysts of policy issues recognize that the resolution of policy disputes depends, in part, upon the power of the various
contending schools, while the adherents of the "power model" acknowledge that most leaders pursue power as a means to attain policy objectives. Yet, it is worth elaborating upon pure versions of the two models
in order to illuminate the strengths and limitations of each, especially
since this study seeks in self-conscious fashion to incorporate both
models and add a third ingredient—the interaction of the elite with the
bureaucracies, the relations within and among bureaucracies, and the
role of bureaucracies in the policy process. With some exceptions, neither the policy analyses undertaken to date and the "rationality model"
which they embody nor the studies of elite politics and the "power"
model on which they are primarily based investigate bureaucratic politics
in depth or recognize that in many instances policy outcomes are in substantial part the product of ubiquitous inter-agency competition.

POLICY ANALYSIS AND THE RATIONALITY MODEL

The original rationality model posits that policy outcomes are the result
of an evaluation of choices by a coherent group with shared perceptions
of the values to be maximized in response to a perceived problem. The
overarching concern of the group is to advance the national interest. The
model originates with Western notions about how policy ideally ought
to be made: a problem triggers a search for the appropriate solution. Data
are gathered about the nature of the problem. Pragmatic officials, motivated primarily by the desire to advance the public good, evaluate alternative solutions in light of their respective costs and benefits, and finally,
after reasoned debate, the best solution is selected.[30]

While no analyst of politics is so naive as to accept this portrayal as
representing all of reality,[31] the model has had its impact in subtle but

[30] This model and its applications are perhaps most clearly explicated in Graham T. Allison's discussion of the "rational policy paradigm" in his *Essence of Decision: Explaining
the Cuban Missile Crisis* (Boston: Little, Brown, 1971).

[31] Students of Western decision making have critiqued this model, questioning both its
plausibility as description and usefulness as prescription, and substituting instead a model
of decision making that is "boundedly rational" from a variety of perspectives. See, in
particular: Richard M. Cyert and James G. March, *A Behavioral Theory of the Firm* (Englewood Cliffs, N.J.: Prentice-Hall, 1963); Charles E. Lindblom, "The Science of Muddling
Through," *Public Administration Review* (Spring 1959), pp. 79-88; James G. March,
"Bounded Rationality, Ambiguity, and the Engineering of Choice," *Bell Journal of Economics* (Autumn 1978), pp. 587-608; James G. March and Herbert A. Simon, *Organizations* (New York: John Wiley, 1958); Herbert A. Simon, "A Behavioral Model of Rational
Choice," in *Models of Man: Social and Rational* (New York: John Wiley, 1957), pp. 241-
260; Herbert A. Simon, *Administrative Behavior*, 2d ed. (New York: Macmillan, 1957);

important ways. Scholars implicitly influenced by the "rationality model" in the study of Chinese politics believe Chinese politics are rooted in reasoned debates over perceived policy problems. Such analysts devote their energy to explicating the inner logic and coherence of each viewpoint in a particular policy debate. The differences among Chinese leaders are explained in terms of their distinctive values and preferences for the nation. The contending solutions to a problem are each the result of relating means to ends, with proponents advocating different objectives. Policy alternatives are articulated by contending schools of thought, and policy outcomes are the result of either a victory of one policy line over another or a compromise. The "rationality model" researchers tend to portray outcomes as coordinated responses to perceived policy problems, in light of the ideological proclivities of the prevailing policy makers.

Examples of policy studies which implicitly draw heavily upon the rationality model are *Uncertain Passage* by A. Doak Barnett,[32] *Organizing China* by Harry Harding,[33] and *Chinese Business under Socialism* by Dorothy Solinger.[34] Although he has also pioneered institutional studies, through the years Doak Barnett has perhaps been the leading political analyst to detail the objective environment within which policy is shaped and the range of rational responses the leaders enjoy to the problems that press upon them. He believes the primary way to identify long-term trends is to illuminate the parameters which the leaders perceive and in which they inescapably work.

Several sentences in the opening pages of *Organizing China* reveal Harding's similar underlying assumptions: "[The] aim is to examine the problems Chinese leaders have encountered in building and maintaining effective administrative organizations. The book examines Chinese organizations through the eyes of China's leaders, seeking to understand their diagnoses of their country's organizational problems, the debates they have conducted on organizational questions, and the programs they have adopted. . . . Chinese leaders have experimented with a wide range of organizational programs and structures, seeking at some times to rationalize their bureaucracy, at other times to subject it to external supervision, and at still other times to replace it with more participatory forms of organization. . . . The Chinese communists have realized that political organization is an essential mechanism. . . . Because of the importance

---

and John D. Steinbruner, *The Cybernetic Theory of Decision: New Dimensions of Political Analysis* (Princeton: Princeton University Press, 1974).

[32] Washington: Brookings, 1974. *See also his China's Economy in Global Perspective* (Washington: Brookings, 1981).

[33] Stanford: Stanford University Press, 1981.

[34] Berkeley: University of California Press, 1984.

assigned to organizations, discussions of this administrative apparatus have occupied a [high] place on the Chinese political agenda."[35] These sentences embody a strong underlying assumption of rationality in the policy process. *Organizing China* implicitly assumes a connection among what it terms the "diagnoses," "debate," and "program" stages of the policy process.

Nor is the Harding volume alone in the rationality that it assumes inheres in the Chinese policy process. In the introduction to her informative work on the politics over domestic commercial systems, Solinger suggests that conflict among the Chinese elite over the organization of domestic trade "revolves around the question of the proper scope for the market under socialism. . . . This controversy has its roots in conflicting ideals within the philosophy of Marxism, each of which is relatively more important to some members of the elite than to others."[36] *Chinese Business Under Socialism* identifies these conflicting values as maximizing equity, preserving order, and increasing productivity. It concludes that the "repeated reorganizations of the processes for handling consumer goods is in large part the product of sharp clashes among the elite over the priorities in these values."[37]

LIMITATIONS OF THE "RATIONALITY" MODEL.

Those who utilize an underlying "rationality model," in short, believe Chinese policies result from an effort of the leaders to match national resources to national objectives and to relate national means to national ends. The theoretical literature on decision making enumerates the requisites for this "rationality model" to prevail. The decision makers must have available the relevant information, they must have a clearly ordered set of priorities, they must have sufficient time to define and evaluate their choices, and the reasons they consciously offer for their choices must be the operative considerations that govern their behavior. Western scholars who implicitly accept the rationality model, however, have generally not explored the constraints upon China's top leaders which may preclude their attaining the rationality which the scholars assume. Thus, the policy analysts tend not to probe decisional constraints upon the leaders due to the limited information available to them, the ambiguities and ambivalences in the minds of the leaders concerning their hierarchy of value preferences, and the time pressures they confront in comprehensively evaluating their alternatives.

Further, the analysts of Chinese policy issues frequently accept the rationale for policy choices which the leaders offer, instead of asking

---

[35] Harding, *Organizing China.*
[36] Solinger, *Chinese Business Under Socialism*, p. 6.
[37] *Ibid.*

whether the real motivations of the decision makers differed from stated rationales. They do not explore the possibility that policy was no more than an uninformed and unconsidered impulse which powerful leaders then instructed their idealogues to cloak in ideologically justifiable garb. Moreover, while policy analysts such as Harding and Solinger recognize there are competing solutions to policy problems, they tend to portray each solution as equally rational, coherent, and reasoned in relating national resources and objectives. They frequently do not consider that the views of one group may indeed be the product of a rational calculus, while a second view may be simple whim, and a third may be the product of yet another decisional process.

The policy analysts also tend to assume that there is a direct relationship between the problem and the solution, and that the policy is an actual response to the problem that triggered the decisional process. But organizational theorists suggest even this assumption merits scrutiny. The connection between the original stimulus, the process, and the response may be very complex, loose, and nearly random.[38] In the American case, at least, policies can be adopted not so much actually to solve the perceived problem of the moment but because the leaders wish to appear to be grappling with the problem at hand. They accept as the purported "solution" a policy which specialists had devised as a preferred response to a previous policy problem. Unable to market their recommendations on the last occasion, these specialists then seize upon the new opportunity to repackage and sell their "solution" to the leaders.[39] Given all the processes that demonstrably arise in other bureaucratic systems, a sophisticated approach to the Chinese political process cannot be safely rooted in assumptions that the "rationality model" has sufficiently powerful explanatory value to be used in isolation from other approaches.[40]

POWER MODEL

The second frequently employed model of the Chinese policy process is the "power" one. Policy outcomes result from struggles among the top leaders who are quite sensitive to the implications of alternative policy choices upon their stature and power. Issues are not just or even largely decided on their merits in terms of promoting the national interest.

---

[38] See Michael D. Cohen, James G. March, and Johan P. Olsen, "A Garbage Can Model of Organizational Choice," *Administrative Science Quarterly* (March 1972), pp. 1-25; and James G. March and Johan P. Olsen, eds., *Ambiguity and Choice in Organizations* (Bergen: Universitetsforlaget, 1976).

[39] See John W. Kingdon, *Agendas, Alternatives, and Public Policies* (Boston: Little, Brown, 1984).

[40] See in particular Nina Halpern, "Policy Communities, Garbage Cans, and the Chinese Economic Policy Process," manuscript, 1984.

Rather, they are evaluated in terms of the personal consequences of the decision upon the individual policy maker or faction. To label one approach the "rationality model" and the second a "power model" does not imply that the adherents of the "power model" necessarily portray the individual leaders of China as irrational. To the contrary, from their individual or factional perspectives, given their individual or factional means and ends, the behavior of the leaders may be quite rational. But the policies which result from the struggle over power cannot be said to be either rational or irrational. Rather, policy is the aggregate response of leaders or factions to problems they perceive and this response reflects the relative power of the participants, their strategies for advancing their beliefs and political interests, and their differentiated understanding of the problem at hand.

Several sophisticated studies have appeared in recent years employing this framework, among them *The Origins of the Cultural Revolution* by Roderick MacFarquhar, and *The Dynamics of Chinese Politics* by Lucian Pye.[41] MacFarquhar succinctly described his approach, which seeks to combine principles and power, in this fashion:

The official explanation of the cultural revolution is that it was . . . a long term struggle between two [policy] lines. . . . But a careful examination of the evidence suggests that neither Mao nor Liu was consistent; that Mao and Liu were not always opponents. . . . Use of the term "two lines" implies that the issues were of fundamental importance, and this is certainly true in large part. . . . But as always in the affairs of men there were also bitter feuds over power and status. The cultural revolution was rooted in both principled and personal disputes.[42]

Attributing his interpretation to cultural influences, Lucian Pye justifies his focus on factionalism at the top in this way:

The fundamental dynamic of Chinese politics is a continuous tension between the imperative of consensus and conformity on the one hand, and the belief, on the other hand, that one can find security only in special, particularistic relationships, which by their very nature tend to threaten the principle of consensus. These particularistic ties tend to produce factions.[43]

[41] Roderick MacFarquhar, *The Origins of the Cultural Revolution*; Lucien Pye, *The Dynamics of Chinese Politics* (Cambridge: Oelgeschlager, Gunn, and Hain, 1981); other pertinent studies include: Jurgen Domes, *The Government and the Politics of the PRC: A Time of Transition*; Byung-joon Ahn, *Chinese Politics and the Cultural Revolution*; Parris Chang, *Power and Policy in China*; Edwin Rice, *Mao's Way*.

[42] Roderick MacFarquhar, *Origins of the Cultural Revolution*, Vol. 1, pp. 2-3.

[43] Lucian Pye, *The Dynamics of Chinese Politics*, p. 4.

Pye goes on to argue that "factions rarely, if ever, represent clearly defined institutional, geographical, or generational interest." Rather, the
bases of factions are shared trust and loyalties, perceived common foes,
and mutual career self-interest. Nor, says Pye, are factions formed in
response to shared policy preferences. Pye asserts, "Those who are actively engaged in [Chinese politics] do not have the luxury of deciding
their stand on new issues on the basis of an objective weighing of all the
pros and cons."[44] Pye then asserts, "There are no fixed rules in the relationship between policy and factional politics."[45]

Most China specialists propounding the "power model" have not
placed their analysis in a comparative framework.[46] Yet, several theorists
of Western organizations have featured prominently the struggle for
power among competing individuals and factions.[47] As well, some of the
underlying dynamics of the "power model" have been captured by those
who use game theoretic concepts to study conflict and cooperation. They
focus on motivations, payoff matrices, constraints, and the resulting
strategies to influence the behavior of others. Decisional outcomes are
the result of strategies pursued by rational actors facing different payoff
matrices. Outcomes occur at the point where different strategies inter-
sect, and the game of politics involves trying to encourage the other players to alter their strategies so that the point of intersection will change to
a more favorable payoff point to oneself.[48] The choices of rational individuals are governed by the structure of the situation which they confront.

INTRODUCING BUREAUCRATIC STRUCTURE

The contrast between the "power" and the "policy" models is considerable. Their most significant difference is that the policy analysts believe
the top leaders of China evaluate policy choices in terms of their percep-

---

[44] Lucian Pye, *The Dynamics of Chinese Politics*, p. 7.

[45] Lucian Pye, *The Dynamics of Chinese Politics*, p. 12.

[46] Exceptions are Andrew Nathan, "A Factionalism Model for Chinese Communist Party
Politics," *China Quarterly*, No. 53 (January-March, 1973), pp. 1-33; and Tang Tsou, "Pro-
legomenon to the Study of Informal Groups in Chinese Communist Party Politics," *China
Quarterly*, No. 65 (March, 1976), pp. 98-114.

[47] The best studies of this are Michel Crozier, *The Bureaucratic Phenomenon* (Chicago:
University of Chicago Press, 1964) and Melville Dalton, *Men Who Manage* (New York:
John Wiley, 1959).

[48] See especially the seminal work of Thomas C. Schelling, *The Strategy of Conflict*
(Cambridge: Harvard University Press, 1960) and, for an application to the dynamics of
conflict and cooperation in a range of settings, Robert Axelrod, *The Evolution of Cooperation* (New York: Basic Books, 1984).

tions of the national interest, while the power analysts stress that the choices are evaluated in terms of individual or factional interests. A second difference is that the policy analysts tend to neglect the pursuit of and struggle over power as a core interest in politics, while the "power" analysts usually do not dwell in depth on the substantive issues at stake. Yet, both models accept the notion that policy is shaped primarily at the top and that the leaders seek a purposeful outcome. While both approaches recognize that bureaucratic structure often creates or compounds the problems demanding political decisions, neither approach considers the structure of the bureaucracy as a necessary ingredient for understanding typical policy outcomes. Neither approach examines the ways in which bureaucracies alter, bend, or distort the external impulses—such as information about economic development or foreign affairs—which they channel to the top leaders. With rare exception, the policy analysts do not detail the formal structures, the different organizational missions, or the ethos of each bureaucracy involved in handling the particular issues they study. The "power" analysts, while cognizant of the formal procedures at the apex, neither carefully examine the differentiated linkages between each of the top leaders and the bureaucracies they lead nor fully explore the extent to which some leaders reflect the views of the bureaucracies for which they are responsible. Both MacFarquhar and Pye acknowledge the importance of this dimension but do not extensively pursue it.

The neglect of bureaucratic structure frequently leads to dubious assumptions about the policy process. For example, both the policy and power analysts search for logical coherence in policy and assume it must have an underlying, logical consistency. Or, they attribute evident discrepancies—such as contradictory paragraphs in a policy document—to differences among the elite. Another possibility—that semi-autonomous bureaucracies are pursuing different policies and that inconsistencies in a single policy statement are the effort of the top leaders to satisfy competing agencies—tends to be insufficiently explored. Neither the rationality model nor the power model adequately considers that leaders might propound the views of the bureaucracies over which they preside, and that elite contention over policy and/or power might be a manifestation of bureaucratic conflict. Nor do either of these models leave much room for the ubiquitous bureaucratic struggles over the transformation of policy decisions into detailed administrative directives, the incorporation of the directives into budgetary expenditures, and the jurisdictions for implementing the directives.

Recognizing the considerable advances made by the adherents of both the "rationality" and the "power" models, this monograph seeks to wed

17

those two approaches while introducing and emphasizing the bureaucratic structure in which the policy process is embedded. Our effort parallels work of several other scholars who stress the importance of the bureaucratic structure in understanding Chinese politics.[49] Our own focus on structure, process, and outcomes reveals the potential relevance of yet another body of literature—theories of decision making or problem solving in complex organizations. The structural evolution posited in our concluding chapter and the policy processes in the sphere of energy development appear to resonate with a number of competing, abstract models of decision making that have been derived from observing how individuals reach decisions in large bureaucracies.[50] In recent years, organizational theorists have developed many different abstract models of the decisional process: "garbage can," "satisficing," "evolutionary," or "incremental," to name a few. Our information does not allow our identifying one model as the most powerful analytical tool from among the alternatives, all of which place boundaries on the explanatory power of the "rationality" or "game theoretic" models. Many of these organizational decision making models recognize that policy outcomes in large organizations do not reach or are not even intended to seek the "best" outcome. Rather, drawing upon the pioneering work of Herbert Simon, many analysts stress that decisional processes permit the attainment of "acceptable" or "satisfying" outcomes, with the participants employing a number of alternative criteria to identify acceptability.[51] As informa-

[49] David M. Lampton, *Policy Implementation in the People's Republic of China* (Berkeley: University of California Press, 1987); Susan Shirk, "The Politics of Industrial Reform," in Elizabeth Perry and Christine Wong, *The Political Economy of Reform in Post-Mao China* (Cambridge: Harvard, 1985), pp. 195-222; Lester Ross, *Environmental Policy in China* (Bloomington: Indiana University Press, forthcoming); Barry McCormick, *Political Reform in Post-Mao China: Democracy and Due Process in the Leninist State*, Ph.D. thesis (Madison: University of Wisconsin, 1985); Nina Halpern, *Economic Specialists and the Making of Chinese Economic Policy, 1955-1983*, Ph.D. thesis (Ann Arbor: University of Michigan, 1985); David Bachman, *To Leap Forward: Chinese Policy-Making, 1956-57*, Ph.D. thesis (Stanford: Stanford University, 1984).

[50] For reviews of the early evolution of this literature, see: Joseph Bower, "Descriptive Decision Theory From the 'Administrative' Viewpoint," in Raymond Bauer and Kenneth Gergen (eds.), *The Study of Policy Formulation* (New York: The Free Press, 1968), pp. 103-148; and Donald W. Taylor, "Decision Making and Problem Solving," in James G. March (ed.), *Handbook of Organizations* (New York: John Wiley & Sons, 1959). On a somewhat more descriptive level, *see*: Anthony Downs, *Inside Bureaucracy* (Boston: Little, Brown and Company, 1967).

[51] In writing about the Soviet Union, Donald Kelley has also questioned whether the essence of Soviet decision making is the search for an optimum response to a policy problem. Instead, he posits a quest for a solution that nurtures an organization or a network of relationships. See: Donald R. Kelley, "Toward a Model of Soviet Decision Making: A Research Note," *American Political Science Review*, vol. 68 (1974), pp. 701-706.

tion about Chinese decision making becomes more available, insights of this theoretical literature will prove valuable in developing a more refined sense of policy processes in China.

New Sources

To repeat, we do not denigrate the contribution of the "policy" or "power" approaches or the models which they implicitly embody. Those approaches were an improvement over and built upon the earlier static descriptions of the core features of the Chinese state. As both the "policy" and "power" analysts recognized, their studies were constrained by the sources available to them, and they did not have direct access to Chinese bureaucracies.[52] They could not probe the organizational dimension of the process as fully as they might have wished.

It has recently become possible to advance one step further: to place Chinese politics more firmly in its bureaucratic setting and to explore how the structure affects the policy process and elite struggles over power and principle. The opening of China in the post-Mao era to foreign scholars, businessmen, diplomats, journalists, and philanthropists permits this progress, as does the presence abroad of Chinese officials, scholars, and visiting dignitaries who are willing to describe the process from their vantage. Beginning in the early 1980's, it became possible to interview Chinese officials systematically in different ministries and research institutes.[53] No longer were Chinese organizations abstract entities to the analysts. The Ministry of Finance, the State Science and Technology Commission, the Ministry of Education, and other agencies became peopled by human beings working in dank, ill-lit office buildings. Researchers could begin to identify the mandates, spirit, and histories of different agencies.

Not only did foreign scholars gain access to Chinese organizations in the early 1980's, but foreign businessmen began to invest in China, undertake joint ventures, and establish permanent offices in Beijing, Shanghai, and Guangzhou. Foreign journalists developed their own con-

[52] For discussions of the effect of the data base upon analytical perspective in Chinese politics, see Michel Oksenberg, "Sources and Methodological Problems in the Study of Contemporary China," in A. Doak Barnett (ed.), *Chinese Communist Politics in Action* (Seattle: University of Washington Press, 1969); and Michel Oksenberg, "The Literature on Post-1949 China: An Interpretive Essay," in John Fairbank and Roderick MacFarquhar (eds.), *The Cambridge History of China*, Vol. 13, Part One (Cambridge: Cambridge University Press, 1987).

[53] E.g., David M. Lampton's chapter on management of water resources in David M. Lampton (ed.), *Policy Implementation*. See also: Michel Oksenberg, "Economic Policy-Making in China: Summer 1981," *China Quarterly*, No. 90 (June 1982), pp. 165-194.

tacts with individual Chinese. Foundation officials and international civil servants began to cooperate with Chinese in development projects involving many Chinese ministries. Many foreigners, in short, began to acquire insight into diverse parts of the Chinese system, especially its economic dimension. Through interviews, scholars could combine this disparate knowledge into a coherent interpretation of the system.

In addition, the Chinese government resumed its habit of the 1950's of publishing some administrative regulations, statistics, yearbooks, and organizational handbooks which revealed new information about administrative procedures and the state structure. These new materials did not obviate the utility of the previous sources: deciphering of the *People's Daily* and other major newspapers and journals, interviewing in Hong Kong, reading of fiction, and so on. But the newly available sources of the early 1980's, combined with the evident need to go beyond policy studies and reconstructions of elite struggles, provided the impetus for this monograph. We seek to build upon previous approaches, not to discard them, while drawing upon the new sources of information.

LIMITATIONS OF THE STUDY

Our data concerns China's energy policy decision making, including the structures and processes of Chinese energy bureaucracies and their influence on energy policy outcomes. More precisely, we focus on the initial development of large-scale energy projects. We gathered information on this sector because the energy bureaucracies—petroleum, coal, and hydroelectric—have developed extensive contact with the outside world, and officials in these bureaucracies were willing to assist our study. They, as we, believed that an enhanced Western understanding of their structures and processes would facilitate the cooperation they sought.

We recognize that the decisions concerning energy development projects are not "typical" or "representative" of all decision making in China. Indeed, this study examines only *one* sector of a complex and varied system, and the extent to which its specific findings apply to other sectors awaits subsequent research.

In several respects, the policy process for large-scale energy development projects is distinctive. First, feasibility studies, financial calculations, and measurement of output are somewhat easier to undertake in evaluating alternatives in the economic sector than, say, in the educational or military sphere. Thus, the criteria for decisions in this sphere may differ from those employed elsewhere. Second, development projects are part of the capital investment decision process, in which the State Planning Commission—even under the reforms—plays an especially important role. This study does not dwell on structures and processes in the on-stream production and allocation of energy or in the setting and implementation of the annual energy plan. Such a focus would have led to greater attention to the State Economic Commission, the General Administration of State Supplies, and the mechanisms for resolving disputes over contracts.

Third, the large projects on which we focus—the exploration for off-shore oil, the Three Gorges hydroelectric project, and large scale coal mines in Shanxi province—are not representative of the full range of energy projects. Most investment projects in the energy sphere are much smaller than these giant undertakings, and the procedures for inclusion of small projects in the state plan are different, with less detailed involvement of the central government and greater initiative residing at local levels. Indeed, during the 1980's, a growing portion of small-scale investments was financed outside the traditional planning and budgeting process described in this monograph. Finally, our selection of projects with a foreign involvement introduces another distinctive factor. It probably means that to some extent the criteria for evaluating the merits of the project reflect foreign influence, with price, output, and profit considerations receiving heightened attention. The role of the foreigner also probably encourages high level officials to become involved in the decision.

It is also likely that the role of the Chinese Communist Party is more limited in the politics of large-scale energy development projects than, for instance, in the formation and implementation of agricultural policy, cultural policy, or personnel decisions. Not only does the sector we study lead to a portrayal of the Party as less central than usually is assumed to be the case, but our written sources and Chinese informants revealed little about the role of the Party: the role of the Party Committees and Party core groups within the Ministry, the chain-of-command from the Party organizations within government agencies to their supervisory CCP bodies (these chains-of-command do not completely coincide with the government chains-of-command), and the roles of provincial Party committees and Central Committee organs in the setting of energy policy. This is the single most serious limitation to the study, but the problem is not so severe as to drain all value from the findings.

We suspect that in fact many of our generalizations about the government energy bureaucracies would apply to the Party in energy policy decision making as well. The CCP and government are, after all, deeply intertwined. For example, in major economic ministries the Party core group usually consists of the minister and vice-ministers. These individuals make the key decisions on professional matters in the ministry re-

21

gardless of whether they are wearing their Party or their government hats. Thus, our portrayal of the core features of the decision making process probably would remain basically the same if we knew more about the Party, at least in this major sector. Moreover, since we portray the Chinese bureaucracy as fragmented, we contend that in the post-Mao era, at least, the Party is not effectively performing one of its major roles: to bridge the natural divisions in the government bureaucracy and to perform an integrating or unifying function in the formulation and implementation of policy.

PRINCIPAL FINDINGS

Our study reveals a fragmented bureaucratic structure of authority, decision making in which consensus building is central, and a policy process that is protracted, disjointed, and incremental. We summarize these findings here, rather than in our conclusion, because these characteristics of the Chinese state prompted the sequence of chapters in this book: detailed analysis of formal organizations and informal processes, followed by three case studies of energy policy making.

A Fragmented Structure of Authority

The structure of authority within the Beijing leadership (what the Chinese term the "Center") consists of four tiers: 1. the core group of twenty-five to thirty-five top leaders who articulate national policy; 2. the layer of staff, leadership groups, research centers, and institutes which link the elite to and buffer them from the bureaucracy; 3. State Council commissions and ministries that have supra-ministerial status and coordinate activities of line ministries and provinces; and 4. line ministries which implement policy. Different pressures and influences shape the behavior of officials at each level. Chapters Two through Four explore the factors at play in each sphere, noting the importance of personal considerations at the elite level and the different organizational missions and ethos at the ministerial level.

The structure of the energy sector highlights the fragmentation of authority. Put simply, the structure of authority requires that any major project or policy initiative gains the active cooperation of many bureaucratic units that are themselves nested in distinct chains of authority. This, in broad terms, has three operational consequences. First, issues tend to rise to higher levels in the system, where appropriate coordinating bodies (such as the State Planning Commission or, at the highest level in the government, the State Council Standing Committee) possess leverage over numerous bureaucratic hierarchies and can bring together the various parties. In other words, a single ministry or province usually lacks the clout by itself to launch or sustain a large project or major new policy. Rather, that ministry or province will have to obtain the active cooperation of others, and this in turn may require that the appropriate coordinating body exercise considerable effort to sustain momentum. Second, the fragmentation of authority demands that elaborate efforts be made at each stage of the decision making process to create and maintain a basic consensus to move forward with the effort at hand. The fault lines in the structure of authority essentially contour the opportunities of each of many different units to obstruct adoption and implementation of a major project. Finally, the fragmentation of authority requires that one or more top leaders enthusiastically support the initiation of a major project or policy in order to overcome bureaucratic impasses at lower levels.

Consensus Building

Consensus building is thus central to the policy process. It is a subtle and complex matter in practice. The Chinese system, after all, does permit the top leaders to bring enormous pressure to bear to advance a project over the objections of key participants. Yet, progress can easily bog down in the bowels of China's various bureaucracies, and most top leaders recognize the great advantages that are to be gained from obtaining the active cooperation of all the major parties concerned. This has, moreover, become increasingly important as a result of the reforms of the system that have occurred to date. For example, the top leaders are more reluctant to employ the tools that Mao and his colleagues wielded in the past to overcome bureaucratic lethargy and resistance—political campaigns, ideological broadsides, suppression of dissent, purge of recalcitrant individuals, deification of the top leader, and so forth. Relatedly, the reforms have increased the financial resources available for various units to undertake activities outside of the state plan. This has increased the opportunities for units to use their resources for their own benefit instead of concentrating their efforts on state-mandated activities. The reforms, therefore, have increased the importance of a consultative process in making decisions on large energy projects.

A consensus must thus be sought both vertically and horizontally in the system. Lower level units have important resources they can bring to bear, and wide ranging efforts are, therefore, made to strike balances that permit each major actor to support an effort or project with some enthusiasm. To an extent, as the case studies in Chapters Five, Six, and

Seven reveal, energy policy results from an ongoing process of bargaining among units at all levels of the bureaucratic hierarchy. The territory available for cooperative development with foreign firms at the Antaibao coal field in Shanxi province, for example, was delineated in a complex deal struck between Shanxi and the Center. The arrangements available to foreign firms for servicing of the offshore oil exploration effort in the South China Sea arose from the bargaining between the Center and Guangdong province. The height of the proposed Three Gorges dam is affected by the bargaining among Sichuan province, Hubei province, other units, and the Center. Each of these provincial units, in turn, must strike deals with their own relevant prefectures, counties and municipalities.[54] Understanding energy policy decision making is, therefore, in substantial part a task of identifying and understanding the resources, arguments, and specifics of the pertinent bargains that are made to permit policies to be adopted and implemented.

A Diffuse Policy Process

Partly as a result of the segmentation, bargaining, and consensus building, the policy processes in energy development are quite diffuse.[55] That is, the process is *protracted*, with most policies shaped over a long period and acquiring a considerable history that is well known to many of the participants. It is *disjointed*, with key decisions made in a number of different and only loosely coordinated agencies and inter-agency decisional bodies. And it is *incremental*, with policy in reality usually changing gradually.

This diffuseness is manifest in four ways. First, the press of events and the pursuit of particular missions by different bureaucracies have precluded the formation and implementation of a single, coherent national "energy policy" and produced instead a plethora of distinct and somewhat contradictory policies to deal with various dimensions of the energy issue. Second, the development plans and investment budgets of the different energy ministries are, in the main, considered separately. The basic expectation in the Chinese budgetary process—and our interviews confirmed this repeatedly—is that a ministry would receive at least what it obtained the previous year for its operating expenses. However, investment allocations can vary significantly from year to year, and the alternative energy ministries therefore compete primarily over the

[54] Details are provided in Chapters Seven, Five, and Six respectively.

[55] An earlier study also argued that the Chinese policy process was disjointed and incremental. See Michel Oksenberg, *Policy Formulation in China: The Case of the 1957-58 Water Conservancy Campaign*, Ph.D. thesis (N.Y.: Columbia University, 1969).

changes in investment funds. Third, for the typical policy or initiative there is no single "decision" that determines the issue. Rather, a whole string of mutually reinforcing "decisions" are required in order to keep any one initiative on track—and the announcement of a "decision" in the national media tends to cloak this protracted process. A major "decision," in brief, does not by itself ensure that the substance of the decision will be implemented. Relatedly, the search for the timing of a particular decision is often misplaced, for the process of making a decision is protracted, as a consensus for it is built. Indeed, on occasion, one or another leader will try to push forward the decision making process and mobilize support by announcing that a major decision has been made when in fact no such thing has occurred.[56] Fourth, the fragmentation of authority in China has important operational consequences for the way policies work their way through the system—and for the capacity of the system to handle different types of issues effectively. Thus, energy *policy* is subdivided into sectoral and particular issues; a *decision* itself is composed of a series of reinforcing decisions; and *authority* is fragmented in ways that produce substantial operational consequences for the decision making process.

The lack of a cohesive, consistent national energy development policy is quite evident. For example, there have been continual changes in the priorities to be accorded to the development of coal, petroleum, nuclear, and hydropower resources respectively. Comparable changes have taken place, moreover, within at least the coal and hydropower sectors. The mid 1980's shift away from the development of large, open pit coal mines in favor of local mines, for instance, changed priorities that had been set as recently as the end of the 1970's. With a commodity as critically important as energy, not surprisingly the national leadership has been unable to specify and sustain a single strategic plan for development. In this, the Chinese experience is reminiscent of that of most other major countries.[57] But any analysis of how policy is made in the energy sector must take into account the multiplicity of such policies and the almost constant contention over energy-related investment priorities.

[56] In yet another variant, sometimes a "decision" will be leaked prematurely by an in-house opponent of the policy in order to mobilize opposition to an initiative before the leadership has formally given its imprimatur to it. For examples, see: Kenneth Lieberthal, *Central Documents.*

[57] See Thomas Fingar, "Implementing Energy Policy: The Rise and Demise of the State Energy Commission," in David Lampton, *Policy Implementation.* Also Thomas Fingar, "Overview: Energy in China," in Joint Economic Committee of Congress of the United States, *China's Economy Looks to the Year 2000* (Washington: Government Printing Office, 1986), Vol. 2, pp. 1-21.

The lack of a single "decision point" perhaps requires additional explanation. Any important policy requires a *series* of "decisions" in order to move it along. Even when the top twenty-five to thirty-five leaders launch a bold initiative, the document proclaiming it typically results from considerable staff work and prior circulation among the leaders. Frequently, the document is issued nationwide in classified form as a "draft" directive, which is then promulgated in final form months later, after national debate and the mobilization of support. With considerable publicity, the Center then announces its bold "decision" to move ahead in a particular direction or to undertake a major project. Such a decision to move in a given direction, which is called a *fangzhen*, serves important purposes. Studies can then be conducted to decide how best to implement the *fangzhen*, and supporters of the policy will be able to point to the high-level "decision" to help them overcome remaining bureaucratic obstacles. Nevertheless, a *fangzhen*—a decision on the general direction of bureaucratic activity—is not in itself sufficient to produce concrete results.

Actual activities are the result of *concrete* policies (*zhengce*) that are adopted in support of the general decision. These concrete decisions may take the form of including certain projects in the State Plan, adopting particular sets of implementing regulations, passing down specific orders for action, and so forth. There is usually a series of iterations of this process, where the initial *zhengce* prove inadequate and are supplemented by ever more refined administrative orders, regulations, directives, and instructions to achieve the broad task that has been articulated.[58]

There are, then, important differences among "decisions": to consider an initiative among the leaders; to announce the initiative; to enter the actual allocation of funds and commitment of material resources into the plan; and then to approve the pertinent construction schedules, regulations, and concrete measures to make the initial decision produce the desired outcome. Many of these subsequent steps require extensive bargaining among involved units. Any major project, for example, currently requires separate approvals of a feasibility study, a general design study, a technical design study, the construction plan, annual appropriations of funds and materials for construction, and so forth. The range of actors participating, moreover, varies according to the nature of the particular decision at issue. In this, the process resembles in some fashion that of

---

[58] For a Chinese account of the range of types of concrete decisions, see Yang Guanghan, et al., *Mishu xue yu mishu gongzuo* (Beijing: Guangming ribao chubanshe, 1984), pp. 115-166.

the American Congress, where many major "decisions" must clear hurdles first in House and Senate Committees, then on the full floor of the House and of the Senate, then a joint conference, and then repeat this whole series in the appropriations process, to say nothing of the roles of the Executive and Judicial Branches. Certainly the nature and bases of these hurdles differ fundamentally between China and the United States. But in Beijing as much as in Washington, it is simply unrealistic to view a single act as constituting the sum and substance of the "decision" on a major issue or project.

The central leadership obviously is aware of this dynamic, and many central "decisions," therefore, are evidently quite consciously viewed as steps in a process of mobilizing bureaucratic resources in a protracted effort to tackle a problem. Thus, central decisions often only set forth goals or prescriptions on what should be done. They do not bear close resemblance to the types of detailed implementing and regulating documents that frequently accompany high level decision making in the United States. In their scope and language, they may mislead foreigners into believing that the Central leaders in fact have more latitude on an issue than the leaders themselves know to be the case. The protracted bureaucratic negotiations that ensue from high level "decisions" often transform these bold initiatives into modest programs or turn them, in reality, into non-decisions.

Sometimes the essentially tentative nature of most "decisions" stands out in fairly bold relief. For example, as explained in Chapter Six, in both 1958 and 1984 the top leadership "decided" to build the Three Gorges Dam, but the supplementary decisions necessary to turn these major "decisions" into actual dam construction have not yet been forthcoming. And Chapters Five and Seven detail how the 1979 decision to enter into production sharing and risk contracts with foreign oil firms initiated a protracted process to give specificity to a new orientation in policy. In the past, the detailed information has been lacking to remind analysts of this fundamentally incremental dimension of the Chinese policy process.

Variation in Perspective and the
Locus of Decision

We have already noted that a four tiered structure exists at the national level: the top 25 to 35 leaders; the personal staffs, leadership groups, research centers, and institutes that link the leaders to the bureaucracies; the supra-ministerial commissions which coordinate policy; and line ministries. Energy decisions can be made at any of these levels, with considerable consequence for the range of considerations that are taken

27

into account. Two major analytical questions, then, concern the differ-ences in perspectives among these levels—especially between the top leaders or the commission and ministerial level—and the factors which determine the locus of specific decisions.

The literature on national decision making in the United States has posited several distinctions that are pertinent to these questions.[59] Ac-cording to this literature, the perspectives on a policy of importance to an official arise from a variety of sources. One is the bureaucratic posi-tion of the individual, a perspective summed up by the phrase "where you stand [on an issue] depends on where you sit [in the bureaucracy]." This is the influence of current role: the official's responsibilities and the ethos of his organization. A second major influence is the past experi-ences of the official, as these may have led him to some basic conclusions about risk taking, the reliability of certain kinds of information, the ef-ficacy of various types of initiatives, and so forth, that can play a major role in shaping his views on the matter at hand. This is the effect of background. A third influence is the standard operating procedures of the organization, and a fourth influence is the shared definition in the na-tional capital of the national interest. A fifth influence is the game of political power itself, stemming from the fact that political leaders deal with a wide range of issues and must employ tactics that permit them to retain the resources they consider necessary over the long run, often at the cost of advancing their preferred choice on a particular policy issue.

In China, these various determinants of perspective appear to vary in relative importance according to the level of the hierarchy. For the top 25 to 35 leaders, and especially for the preeminent leader, the generalists, and the elders (these terms are explained in Chapter Two), past experi-ence, the game of politics, and concerns with the national interest have greater salience. Their roles as preeminent leaders, generalists, or elders necessitate their casting their policy preferences in national interest terms and expose them to conflicting bureaucratic positions. Here is where the "policy" and "power" approaches to Chinese politics acquire their rationale. For example, the past experiences of Chen Yun and his view of the national interest have led him to embrace quite strong and consistent views concerning the danger of deficits, the importance of holding the line on inflation, the utility of local markets, and the best means by which to obtain Party discipline, among other issues.[60] Peng

[59] Graham Allison made the classic statement of the following analysis in his *Essence of Decision*, esp. pp. 162-184. We are consciously using Allison's categories for purposes other than those he intended, and we do not use his three-model framework of analysis.

[60] On the first three of these issues, see: Nicholas Lardy and Kenneth Lieberthal (eds.), *Chen Yun's Strategy for China's Development* (Armonk, N.Y.: M. E. Sharpe, 1983).

Zhen has long had similarly strong views on social order and the legal system.[61] At this very high level, moreover, each person must deal with a wide range of issues in a fluid political environment. Therefore, the tactical need to retain power and influence becomes important to decision making at this level. One cannot understand the views on literature, art, and dissent of Deng Xiaoping, for example, without taking this consideration into account. Deng is very much concerned with maintaining a working consensus to nurture the basic thrusts of his reforms, and this concern imposes important tactical demands on his policy positions. The functional specialists among the top leaders, however, command a somewhat more parochial perspective. They are responsible for a limited number of specialized ministries, and appear more likely to reflect partial, bureaucratic perspectives and be less compelled to remain sensitive to a "national interest" perspective.

At the level of State Council ministries and commissions (and especially the former), the current role of the official and the operating procedures of the organization become very powerful in shaping behavior. Two basic factors contribute to this. First, the system is designed to have this effect. Rhetoric aside, the entire decision making process at this level is premised on the notions that: ministries and bureaus have particular missions that they should pursue with zeal; ministers and bureau chiefs should represent and articulate the views of their units; economic ministries and bureaus should seek additional investment capital so as to better carry out their mandates; ministries should push hard to make the top leaders understand and appreciate the ministry's expertise and potential contributions, and bureau chiefs should behave similarly toward their ministries. The structure of the system (with National Planning Conferences, feasibility studies, National Economic Work Conferences, National Finance Conferences, Central Work Conferences, and so forth) is then organized so as to adjudicate the resulting conflicting ministerial demands. Second, while China's reforms of the 1980's encompass efforts that both strengthen and inhibit the tendency of officials in ministries to adopt substantive policy positions that reflect the tasks of their units, the net effect seems to have been to strengthen this influence on decision making. Relevant reforms include: reducing the role of ideology as an integrative mechanism; encouraging each unit involved in a potential project to voice its views; making fuller use of technical specialists to help

---

[61] On Peng Zhen, see *Zhongyang, he Zhongyang lingdao tongzhi guanyu shehui zhuyi minzhu, shehui zhuyi fazhi he renmin daibiao dahui zhidu de lunshu* (Commentary of Center and Leadership Comrades on Socialist Democracy, Socialist Legality, and People's Congress System), Beijing: Standing Committee of Beijing Municipal Assembly, 1984.

develop ministerial positions; and judging the performance of economic line ministries by the revenue they generate.

Naturally, the top leaders may be influenced by a "bureaucratic" perspective on particular decisions. As previously noted, the Chinese system now virtually requires the enthusiastic support of at least one major leader in order for a very large project to be approved. Ministry officials turn first either to the top leader who has had historic ties with that ministry or who has current supervisory responsibilities over it to elicit his interest and enthusiasm, and this may produce the desired response. Nevertheless, there does appear to be a significant difference between the top leaders and the State Council ministers in the extent to which bureaucratic responsibilities and organizational rules shape formal positions on policies.

Thus, the level of the political system at which an issue is decided affects the mix of considerations that goes into the decision. At the apex, the prior personal experiences of individual leaders and the need to think in tactical terms about an ongoing political game exert a major influence. At the bureaucratic level, the official position is more significant. Unfortunately, the data are not available to analyze more precisely the consequences of these differences upon policy outcomes. This may turn out to be one of the frontier areas for research in the coming years.

What, then, determines whether a particular policy will be decided within the State Council bureaucratic apparatus or by the top 25 to 35 leaders? Several factors can propel an issue onto the agenda of the top leaders.

The particular interests of individual top leaders explain many instances of problems being brought to this high level. Members of the core group of the top 25 to 35 leaders can find ways to bring project decisions to the attention of their colleagues if they so desire. Deng Xiaoping, for example, clearly brought the Antaibao project with Occidental Petroleum onto the agenda of the top leaders.[62]

Chinese bureaucrats can try to force an issue onto the agenda of the highest leaders. As noted in Chapter Three, for instance, the State Science and Technology Commission encouraged broad gauged studies of the energy situation in China so as to produce reports that would command the attention of the national authorities. If an impasse is reached at the annual planning conference, as another example, the contending ministers may take the issues or projects at stake to the top leaders for resolution.

The emergence of a critical problem may capture the attention of the top leaders and force decisions to be made. The 1981 flooding in Sichuan

---

[62] See Chapter Seven.

province made the issue of aforestation in the region of critical and immediate importance, requiring highest level action. These floods on the Yangtze then drew the attention of the leaders to the whole problem of the basin, flood control, and the role of the Three Gorges project. Similarly, our account in Chapter Five of the evolution of policy toward foreign involvement in offshore petroleum developments reveals how the agenda of the top leaders was shaped by such developments as the Sino-Soviet dispute, the rise in world energy prices in the 1970's, and the peaking of production at Daqing.

Foreigners may force an issue onto the agenda of the highest level leaders. Foreign firms, for example, may require very high level assurances that the Chinese government stands fully behind a project before they will commit themselves to the effort.[63] The heads of major foreign firms can obtain audiences with the highest level Chinese leaders, and this then provides an occasion to involve these leaders directly in the project. In this way, foreigners may in fact push an initiative into the top leadership arena. Perhaps of equal importance, the impending visit by a foreign corporate head provides pertinent bureaucrats with an opportunity to brief the member of the core leadership group, thus focusing his attention on the issues of concern to them. Foreign visits can, therefore, be highly instrumental in raising the level at which an issue is deliberated in the Chinese system. Indeed, Japan's crucial roles in shaping China's energy policies in 1973 and 1977-78 highlight the important influence that foreigners on occasion actually exercise.[64]

Procedural Requirements. Administrative regulations also can affect the locus of decision. If the project exceeds a certain level of budgetary commitment, for example, it automatically must be considered by the State Council. The planning cycles for the annual and five-year plans also bring items onto the agenda of the top 25 to 35 leaders, as these documents must be approved by the highest level Party and State leadership. Thus, there are triggering mechanisms within the system which will route a project to a particular decisional body.

OUTLINE OF THE STUDY

These themes and findings are developed throughout the text. We do not develop each finding in a separate chapter. Rather, given our emphasis

[63] Reportedly, for example, several major oil companies required such assurances from Premier Zhao Ziyang before they would commit themselves to a full program of offshore exploration.

[64] As explained in Chapter Five, the Nakasone visit in 1973 and the Inayama initiative (leading to the long-term Sino-Japanese trade agreement) in 1978 had major influences on China's energy policy and related issue areas.

on structure, the monograph begins with the institutional arrangements for energy development. Chapter Two illuminates the organization of political power at the very top of the Chinese system, among the twenty-five to thirty-five individuals who lead China. It traces the linkages of the leaders with the energy policy bureaucracies and provides biographical sketches of several leaders to illuminate the complex interplay of background and role in shaping the views of an official. Chapter Three surveys the "energy" bureaucracies, including not only the three key line ministries (Petroleum, Coal, and Water Resources and Electric Power), but also the other commissions, ministries, and "interface organizations" (such as the China National Offshore Oil Corporation). This chapter specifies each unit's roles, structure, activities, ethos, and mission and outlines how these units relate to each other in handling major energy development issues. While China's table of organization undergoes continual change (as in 1982), analysts must grasp the system in this detail to understand policy making at any given moment.

Chapter Four then analyzes the way in which the structures and processes described in the preceding two chapters shape the perspectives and actual behavior of Chinese bureaucrats in general and in the energy sector in particular. The chapter grapples with a paradox. The formal organizational charts and the structure of authority suggest the top leaders are efficiently in command of the bureaucracies and the policy process. But at the provincial and local levels, the reality frequently diverges sharply from the policies proclaimed in Beijing, and orders from the Center often are not scrupulously implemented in the provinces. Each bureaucracy and local unit commands some resources of its own and enjoys a measure of *de facto* and/or *de jure* autonomy. The fragmentation is overcome through negotiations, bargains, and exchanges that are struck among the parts of the system. China is held together by the formal structure of authority, by the networks of individuals bound by mutual obligations and loyalties who are embedded in the formal organizations, and by the total web of bargains among hundreds of thousands of units which comprise the system. The way these bargains are struck and the purposes behind them go to the heart of organizational practice. Constant and protracted haggling, side exchanges, and inclusion of tangential units in bargains in order to produce a consensus are core features of Chinese bureaucratic politics. This is the way an energy development project is launched and, when completed, is lodged in the system.

Chapters Five through Seven present three strategically selected case studies that illuminate different facets of the relationship among structure, process, and outcome. Chapter Five explores the evolution of policy at an elite level. Specifically, it traces the origins of the foreign involvement in the exploration and development of the South China Sea petro-leum reserves. Policy evolved gradually but significantly from the com-mitment in the 1960's to self-reliance in the development of the Daqing oil fields to an invitation in 1979 for the international oil companies to invest in the development of offshore oil on a risk basis. The case study illuminates the complex relationship among elite politics, the interna-tional arena, and the organizational mission and evolving ethos of the Ministry of Petroleum. The evolution of policy resulted from the inter-action between the top leaders, who themselves were engaged in political struggles over energy policy, and the pertinent ministries in a context of changing domestic energy production and opportunities for access to for-eign technology, capital, and equipment. The case especially illuminates the incremental evolution of policy at an elite level.

Chapter Six traces the evolution of the long contemplated, mammoth Three Gorges Dam project on the Yangtze River. This is primarily a story, especially in more recent years, of bureaucratic politics among ministries and provinces with contrasting interests in the project, al-though the top leaders are inescapably drawn into the policy debate. The project has not been launched to date because of the resources that would be devoured during its construction, because of the political difficulty in building a consensus for the project, and because no top leader has yet stepped forward to propel the project through the obstacles it faces. The case particularly illuminates the organizational mission and consensus-building dimensions of the policy process at the provincial and ministe-rial levels. The chapter concludes by examining the effects of Deng's re-forms in the 1980's upon the state's ability to launch a project of this magnitude.

Chapter Seven focuses specifically on relations between the Center and the provinces to better understand the resources and tactics each uses to deal with the other. The Chapter specifically examines the attempts to achieve cooperation between the Center and Guangdong province in sup-port of the oil efforts off the coast of Guangdong; and the relations be-tween Beijing and Shanxi province in the development of the enor-mously rich coal basin that is centered in Shanxi. It confirms that neither the center-in-command nor the cellular image of the system is accurate. Rather, the cases show that both the center and the provinces have re-sources the other needs. Mutual dependence best captures the relation-ship between the two, with the result that this chapter particularly illu-minates the central-provincial bargaining aspect of the policy process.

Chapter Eight, the concluding chapter, draws upon the findings about bureaucratic structures, processes, and outcomes in Chinese energy de-velopment to address several interrelated questions. What are the implications of this study for research on the bureaucracies in Soviet-type political systems more generally? How do our data illuminate topics of recurring interest to scholars of comparative communism, such as the allocation of authority between center and locality in those systems and the representation of interests? More speculatively, what does our study contribute to understanding the seemingly inescapable transformation of communist regimes from revolutionary or mobilization regimes to highly bureaucratic systems? Finally, what do our findings suggest about the capacity of the top leaders in communist states to undertake major reforms of their system?

On the latter points, the concluding chapter offers a tentative interpretation of the evolution of the state structure in communist systems, centering on the initial centralization of power in the immediate aftermath of revolution; the subsequent fragmentation of authority as individual bureaucracies acquire "proprietary" claims upon resources; next, the ever more desperate search for measures by the top leaders to discipline their bureaucracies; then, the emergence of tactics among the bureaucracies to evade the control mechanisms; and finally, the emergence of a mature communist system in which top leader-bureaucracy relations achieve an uneasy equilibrium.

Reformers who seek to transform this economically inefficient and hidebound system face enormous challenges. The far flung bureaucracies defy sudden change, unless the leader dares launch a Cultural Revolution or a Great Purge with all the costs involved, and even such massive onslaughts do not necessarily produce the leader's desired results. Gradual reform has its own dangers, since some seemingly attractive initial steps in reform—such as increasing the authority of lower level units—may actually inhibit subsequent steps in reform. However, our data show that it may indeed be possible to reform communist systems if the top leaders—as Deng Xiaoping and his associates—weaken the monopoly grip of bureaucracies upon resources by gradually expanding the role of the market place, create new bureaucracies which have an interest in reform, and carefully forge links with the external world that reenforce domestic reformist inclinations. At this writing, it is impossible to forecast the outcome of the reforms now underway in several communist countries, but given the theme of this book, one thing is certain. The bureaucratic structure of a mature Soviet-type state in large measure determines the outcome of massive reform efforts, and extraordinary political leadership is required to overcome the constraints this structure imposes on reform.

· 2 ·

AT THE TOP

The Chinese energy industry is part of the complex, hierarchical, Chinese political-economic system. In overly simple terms, the Chinese system in its upper reaches comprises several levels: 1. the roughly 25 to 35 top policy makers: the preeminent leader, elder advisers, a small number of generalists, plus several clusters of specialists; 2. the personal staff, leadership groups, research institutes, and research centers which assist the top leaders and link the top leaders to the bureaucracy; 3. the overarching or comprehensive commissions and ministries which integrate the activities of functionally and territorially specific bureaucracies; and (4) the functionally and territorially specific ministries, provinces and, more recently, corporations. We take up the first two of these in this chapter and examine the latter two in the following chapter.

The Top Leadership

At any moment in time, approximately 25 to 35 people constitute China's top leadership. This group is roughly the equivalent of the Board of Directors and the Management/Executive Committee of an American corporate hierarchy. The group is partly defined by the positions its members hold: most of the Politburo and Secretariat of the Chinese Communist Party and of the Standing Committee of the State Council, the top commanders of the military, and the leaders of the wealthiest and largest cities and provinces.[1]

The group is not defined only by formal position. Indeed, on occasion, some Politburo members are in sufficient political disgrace that they are not considered members of the top power elite even though they retain formal titles. In addition to official position, then, membership in the top group stems from a combination of intangible attributes: one's standing with the preeminent leader of the country, the respect and influence one has with one's colleagues, the network of personal ties one commands in the country at large, and the attractiveness and seeming pertinence of one's ideas and vision.

---

[1] A number of people hold more than one of these posts simultaneously. The State Council consists of the heads of all government ministerial agencies, the Premier, Vice Premiers, and State Councillors, while the Standing Committee consists of only the latter three officials.

These 25 to 35 people preside over special channels of information. They enjoy access to high level decisional meetings and can comment on circulating draft directives through which national policy is formulated. They enjoy extraordinary deference and command many special perquisites. They have their own staffs. In the case of Politburo members, the staff constitutes a small personal office, while the others enjoy more limited service of several personal secretaries, administrative assistants, and aides. They are able to enhance their coterie of advisors and staff either formally—through the formation of offices, research centers, or committees—or informally, through the cultivation of professionals in units like the Chinese Academy of Social Sciences. They are the leaders physically ensconced in the Zhongnanhai complex—the command headquarters of the far flung Chinese Communist Party and government apparatus.[2]

The 25 to 35 top leaders, in sum, constitute China's power elite. They consist of several types of leaders. First is the *preeminent leader*: Mao Zedong until 1976 and, after a brief interregnum, Deng Xiaoping from 1978 to the present. The precise role of the preeminent leader has varied considerably over time, but his core tasks have included personnel appointments at the highest levels, enunciation of ideological principles, and—usually after extensive discussion with colleagues—the identification of the primary tasks confronting the nation. Second, there are typically between four and seven *elders*: highly respected and influential semi-retired leaders who command the loyalty of select bureaucrats—their former staff aides, subordinates, associates, and ideological allies—throughout the nation. In late 1985, the elders included Chen Yun, Li Xiannian, Peng Zhen, and Ye Jianying. These elders have a stature independent of the preeminent leader and therefore are capable, within limits, of challenging his initiatives.

Third are a few *generalists* whose responsibilities are widespread, who serve as the chief lieutenants or "prime ministers" of the preeminent leader, and who seek to integrate the activities of the diverse Chinese bureaucracy into a coherent whole. These leaders bear a special burden for resolving major bureaucratic conflicts and deciding upon major policy issues. Since 1949, such leaders as Zhou Enlai, Liu Shaoqi, Li Xiannian, Deng Xiaoping, and Lin Biao have played this role. In late 1985, the generalists were Zhao Ziyang, Hu Yaobang, Wan Li, Hu Qili, and Li Peng, with Tian Jiyun apparently beginning to acquire a broad range of responsibilities.

[2] Some of these individuals actually live in the Zhongnanhai, while others simply have offices there.

Fourth are the *functional specialists*. They assume responsibility for managing foreign affairs; the economy; military affairs; the ideology, culture, and propaganda sphere; science and technology; agriculture; core Party affairs including personnel management; and the legal, judicial, and public security sector. Each of these spheres, in other words, is directed by a formally designated committee or an informally constituted sub-group of the top 25 to 35 leaders. On occasion, in some functional areas, this committee system is two-tiered, consisting of an upper tier, small committee of very senior leaders—including some of the generalists—who set broad policy guidelines and another cluster of slightly lower ranking officials who are in charge of day-to-day policy direction of that sphere. This lower tier of specialists, in addition to members of the top leadership group, may include some who are just outside that leadership core. These various levels, in other words, merge into each other with occasional overlapping of personnel and tasks.

One dimension of this scheme that is often confusing to foreign observers, therefore, is that a single individual may in fact function simultaneously at several different levels of the hierarchy. For example, Li Peng as of late 1985 functioned both increasingly as a generalist (with Zhao Ziyang, Hu Yaobang, Hu Qili, and Wan Li) and as a specialist responsible for energy. This phenomenon can occur because as an individual moves quickly up to a top leadership position, he may retain for some time the specific portfolio(s) he had acquired along the way. In late 1985, the economic specialists among the top leaders included Gu Mu, Yao Yilin, Bo Yibo, Wang Bingqian, Kang Shien, Song Ping, Zhang Jingfu, Chen Muhua, and Lu Dong. This cluster looked to generalists Zhao Ziyang and Li Peng as the highest active leaders who were responsible for their sector, while Deng Xiaoping, Chen Yun, and Li Xiannian were the senior leaders with particular interest in economics. Further, some of the economic specialists among the top leaders head government commissions,[3] while each of them assumes responsibility for a specific set of ministries, provinces, and/or issues. That is, a division of labor exists among the top economic specialists. In the energy sphere, Li Peng and Kang Shien were the key actors in late 1985. The key energy ministries—Petroleum (MPI), Coal (MCI), Water Resources and Electric Power (MWREP), and Nuclear Energy as well as the key energy corporations—China National Coal Development Corporation (CNCDC),[4] China National Offshore Oil Corporation (CNOOC), and China Na-

[3] As of late 1985, Song Ping headed the State Planning Commission and Lu Dong headed the State Economic Commission.

[4] And this corporation's other guise, the China National Coal Import and Export Corporation (CNCIEC).

tional Oil Development Corporation (CNODC)—depended upon Li and Kang to be their voice among the 25 to 35 top policy makers, and those 25 to 35 in turn looked to Li and Kang as their key links to the energy bureaucracies.

In the 1970's and 1980's, three economic specialists among the 25 to 35 top leaders have had primary responsibility for energy: Yu Qiuli (until 1982), Kang Shien, and Li Peng (from 1983). Their responsibilities have been sufficiently great that, as with other functional specialists among the top leaders, they have usually had as their associates a handful of even more specialized high level officials in their sector. These other officials, typically Ministers, Vice Ministers, or heads of corporations, are also frequently on the Central Committee of the Communist Party. In the energy sphere, these latter have included Tang Ke, Song Jingwen and Wang Tao from the Ministry of Petroleum; Qian Zhengying from the Ministry of Water Resources and Electric Power; Gao Yangwen and Yu Hongen from the Ministry of Coal; and Qin Wencai from the China National Offshore Oil Corporation. Such individuals are brought into the deliberations at the highest level on a selective basis, when their subject matter is on the agenda of the Chinese Communist Party or State Council bodies (the Politburo, Secretariat, and Standing Committee of the State Council). They and their aides brief such top leaders as Deng Xiaoping, Zhao Ziyang, or Li Peng before the latter meet with foreign delegations. Chart 2-1 portrays the general relationships discussed to this point.

Thus at any moment in time, there are a cluster of five to eight top officials in the energy sphere. One or two of these are among the economic specialists within the 25 to 35 top leaders of the country, and the remainder are the leaders of the energy bureaucracies. The chain-of-command, therefore, goes from Deng Xiaoping (with the elders looking over his shoulder) to generalists to the economic specialists among the 25 to 35 top leaders (who must coordinate their policies with the other broad policy sectors such as public security and the military), one or two of whom are responsible for energy matters, to the cluster of top officials in the energy sector who lead the energy bureaucracies themselves. This last group must coordinate its policies with the other groups managing different parts of the economic sector: communications and transportation, heavy industry, light industry, and so on.

In this as at other levels of the Chinese hierarchy, the range of activities and influence of an official reflects his intangible stature as well as his formal bureaucratic position. Stature apparently stems from a number of factors: his seniority in the Party and accomplishments during the revolution, his record after 1949, his ties with the preeminent leader, and

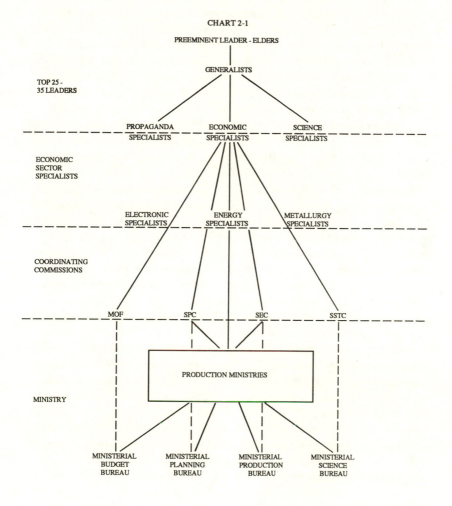

CHART 2-1

PREEMINENT LEADER - ELDERS

GENERALISTS

TOP 25 -
35 LEADERS

PROPAGANDA   ECONOMIC   SCIENCE
SPECIALISTS   SPECIALISTS   SPECIALISTS

ECONOMIC
SECTOR
SPECIALISTS

ELECTRONIC   ENERGY   METALLURGY
SPECIALISTS   SPECIALISTS   SPECIALISTS

COORDINATING
COMMISSIONS

MOF   SPC   SEC   SSTC

PRODUCTION MINISTRIES

MINISTRY

MINISTERIAL   MINISTERIAL   MINISTERIAL   MINISTERIAL
BUDGET   PLANNING   PRODUCTION   SCIENCE
BUREAU   BUREAU   BUREAU   BUREAU

the network of individuals scattered among the bureaucracies who owe him loyalty and look to him for guidance. The importance of stature as well as formal position was exemplified in the petroleum sector as of the end of 1985. The new Minister, Wang Tao, had risen swiftly to his position in the middle of the year from heading the Nanhai East subdivision of CNOOC, jumping over several more senior people in the ministry. The formal post brought with it the responsibility for briefing the top leaders when petroleum issues came directly onto their agendas, but most observers felt he still had to acquire the stature—and thus the degree of easy access to and ease with the top elite—that his predecessors evidently enjoyed. Thus, ministerial changes can affect the clout of key ministries, at least over the short term. The coal ministry also witnessed this type of change in 1985, with veteran Minister Gao Yangwen yielding his position to a younger Minister, Yu Hongen. Yu had long experience in this ministry but lacked the higher level ties that Gao brought to the position.

The usual table-of-organization for China stresses the division between the Party and government, while our portrayal is of a unified chain-of-command. We adopt this approach in part because the top leaders of the government also hold high Party rank. Further, top government and Party organs are both housed within the same compound. Party core groups are nested within—and lead—each government ministry. The funds for running the Party apparatus come from the government.[5] Thus, while efforts have been made to separate the Party from the government, at least at the apex the chains of authority appear to converge upon a single command structure.

The top 25 to 35 leaders meet in several overlapping decision making bodies: the Politburo of the CCP, the Secretariat of the CCP, the Standing Committee of the State Council, and the Military Affairs Commission. A very rough division-of-labor exists among these bodies. The Politburo, which meets infrequently, charts broad policy guidelines.[6] The Secretariat refines those guidelines and supervises the activities of CCP Committees (especially at the provincial level) and such central organs of the Party as the Organization Department (which manages personnel assignments), the Propaganda Department (which manages ideological,

---

[5] Based on interviews, but see also reference to government appropriation to the Party in *Zhongyang Caizheng Fagui Huibian, 1956* (1956 Central Finance Legal Compendium), Beijing: Finance Press, 1957.

[6] This is true for the Politburo in the mid 1980s; See: A. Doak Barnett, *The Making of Foreign Policy in China: Structure and Process* (Boulder: Westview Press, 1985). In the 1950's the Politburo appears to have met more frequently and regularly: Kenneth Lieberthal, *Research Guide*.

cultural, and educational affairs), and the United Front Department (in charge of relations with non-communist groups in China). The Military Affairs Commission supervises the army and its many affiliated organizations, while the Standing Committee of the State Council directs the activities of the government ministries. In fact, these four organizations are interrelated, and documents frequently circulate among the members of most of them. Repeatedly, indeed, the Chinese system has gone through periods in which actual policy process has defied any neatly drawn scheme based on institutional responsibilities at the very top.

Staff, Research, and Coordinating Offices

The chain-of-command sketched above—preeminent leader, generalists, economic specialists, top officials of the energy industry—is oversimplified because, by rules we do not fully understand, top leaders are able to create bureaucratic units to serve their policy needs. As a result, embedded in the structure at the apex are a number of staff offices, research institutes, research centers, and "leadership small groups" (*lingdao xiaozu*), either inside or immediately subordinate to the Zhongnanhai, which perform a wide range of functions for the top leaders. The institutes basically carry out policy-relevant research, investigating the feasibility of initiatives which their patrons might wish to introduce. They also can investigate the implementation of policies currently in effect, thereby performing a monitoring role through the papers they prepare for their principals. They may, too, engage in long-term forecasting and identify looming issues. Given the enormous time pressures on the top 25 to 35 individuals, these institutes, centers, and groups may even acquire responsibilities to resolve problems and mediate bureaucratic disputes in the name of the leaders.[7]

Given the segmented nature of the Chinese bureaucracy discussed in greater detail below, in the economic sphere substantial use is made of "leadership small groups" to help the top leaders coordinate the activities of their myriad bureaucracies. Typically, each "small group" is led directly by one of the top leaders, and each includes some economic specialists pertinent to the task area of the small group. These "small groups" also develop their own staffs. An incomplete list in the energy area in late 1985 included the following such groups: Nuclear Power; Rural Energy; Offshore Oil Rigs;[8] Shanxi Coal; and the Three Gorges

---

[7] For additional discussion, see Nina Halpern, " 'Scientific Decision Making': The Organization of Expert Advice in Post-Mao China," unpublished manuscript.

[8] This was different in that it was actually under Fan Muhan and nested in the State Economic Commission.

41

project. These "small groups" appear to be necessary because the more formal coordinating mechanisms, such as the State Planning Commission, the State Economic Commission, and other bodies[9] cannot adequately mesh the wide range of activities that energy policy entails. In the energy field, for example, coordination is necessary among suppliers, producers, consumers, designers, planners, financiers, importers, and so on. As implied above, in some instances top leaders also may form "leadership small groups" as a way of exerting increased personal leverage over an issue area—and of developing the personal staff resources necessary to accomplish this goal.

These various staff offices play crucial but as yet not well understood roles linking the top leaders to the bureaucracy. They are the Chinese equivalent to the various White House staffs in the United States government: the Council of Economic Advisors, the Domestic Council Staff, the National Security Council Staff, and various *ad hoc* commissions and study groups. When top leaders assign one of these bodies a task—to draft a directive, to engage in a study and make policy recommendations, to resolve an interagency dispute—typically the body will form a team which includes members from line agencies and from specialized research institutes and universities. These units are usually eager to dispatch one or more of their officials to become part of the study team as a way of keeping informed and influencing the outcome. Over a period of years, the repeated formation of such teams probably builds a sense of community among the professionals in a particular area.[10] This crucial staff level, then, links the top leaders to the bureaucracies, creates channels for intellectuals to influence the policy process, generates a pool of ideas which can be drawn upon as the opportunities arise, and forms a network of individuals working on common issues across the otherwise segmented bureaucratic structure.

THREE ENERGY SECTOR LEADERS

We have implicitly stressed the highly personalized nature of the system at the apex rather than focusing on the key decision making institutions at the top. We have highlighted the 25 to 35 leading *individuals* whose authority only partly rests on the formal positions they hold. Given the

[9] All of these are described in detail below.

[10] Nina Halpern uses the term "policy community" in her *Economic Specialists*, esp. pp. 44-52. The concept of policy communities comes from students of American politics. See Jack L. Walker, "The Diffusion of Knowledge, Policy Committees, and Agenda Setting," in John E. Tropman, *et al.*, *New Strategic Perspectives on Social Policy* (New York: Pergamon Press, 1981), and John W. Kingdon, *Agendas*, pp. 123-146.

importance of individuals, it seems appropriate both to profile several top energy personnel to illuminate their personalities and styles and to discuss questions of factionalism among these top leaders.

Our research included gathering available biographical information on the leaders of the energy sector: the energy specialists among the top 25 to 35 leaders, and the officials actually in charge of the energy ministries. Interviews and search of the usual biographical sources yielded detailed profiles of: petroleum leaders Yu Qiuli, Kang Shien, Tang Ke, Qin Wencai, Song Jingwen, and Sun Zhenmin; hydroelectric power leaders Qian Zhengying, and Li Peng; and coal leaders Gao Yangwen and Kong Xun.[11] The material we were able to generate on other key figures—Wang Tao at MCI, Lin Yishan of the Yangtze Valley Planning Office (YVPO)—was less extensive.

Data on individual careers and personalities illuminate these questions: First, what is the basis of political struggles at the top: factional, institutional, ideological, or some combination of these three? Second, to what extent does personality come into play? Are the leaders at the top a rather similar group in terms of their individual characteristics? Can their viewpoints and leadership styles be ascertained simply through knowing their career patterns and current bureaucratic responsibilities? Or, do idiosyncratic considerations—their innate boldness, imagination, and dynamism, for example—make a difference? Third, what attributes explain the rise of officials to be among the top leaders?

Before addressing these questions, let us sketch three contrasting energy leaders. Two of these energy sector leaders, Kang Shien and Tang Ke, represent the older generation that contributed mightily to the rapid growth of China's petroleum production from the end of the 1950's to the 1980's. Kang and Tang come from very different educational and social backgrounds, and yet each played a major role in bringing about China's increasing cooperation with foreign firms in development of the country's petroleum resources. Their backgrounds and careers provide testimony to the need for considerable caution in making assumptions about an official's substantive policy positions based on his educational or other background characteristics.

The third leader whose biography we present here is Li Peng. Li rep-

---

[11] See especially Donald Klein and Anne B. Clarke, *Biographical Dictionary of Chinese Communism, 1921-1965* (Cambridge: Harvard Press, 1971); Wolfgang Bartke, *Who's Who in the People's Republic of China* (Armonk, N.Y.: M. E. Sharpe, 1981); Kasumigaseki Society, *Gendai Chugoku jimmei jiten, 1982* (Tokyo: Konan Shoin, 1982). See also Donald Klein, "Sources for Elite Studies and Biographical Materials on China," in Robert Scalapino, ed., *Elites in the People's Republic of China* (Seattle: University of Washington Press, 1962), pp. 609-656.

resents the younger generation, currently in their fifties, that is entering the core political elite from an energy-based background. Li's career and his working style, as explained below, provide a textbook case of the types of attributes that should spell success in China over the coming decade. All three of these personal sketches convey a sense of the diversity, willfulness, and the range of competencies and connections that leaders at the apex of the Chinese system bring to their tasks.

Kang Shien: Patriotic Technocrat[12]

Kang Shien, a native of Hebei province, was a geology major at the prestigious Qinghua University. The university, founded with the Boxer Indemnity Fund which the United States had received from the Qing dynasty (1644-1911), was an institution where foreign influence was strong, and most students had some fluency in English. Its student body came largely from wealthy and privileged families. The growing humiliation of China at the hands of the Japanese in the 1930's led to an increasingly fervent and militant student movement (named the December 9th Movement after a key date in its development), and Qinghua University students were at the forefront. Communist Party underground workers encouraged the movement, though how pivotal they were remains a matter of debate. In any case, by 1936, the Party underground had begun to recruit successfully among the December 9th student leaders, enlisting them to join guerrilla forces in newly created base areas in the desolate mountainous regions well over 100 miles west of Beijing.

Kang was precisely such a student leader, along with such future communist leaders as State Planning Commission (SPC) Chairmen Yao Yilin and Song Ping and Foreign Minister Huang Hua. During the war against Japan Kang served in a number of administrative posts at the county level, including positions in the Party Organization and United Front Departments. One reliable foreign source asserts Kang first met and worked with Yu Qiuli during this time. During the 1946-49 civil war, he was promoted to be head of the political department of the Yenan Military Region and head of the political department of the Ninth Division in the First Field Army.

The First Field Army captured the northwest region of China, and after 1949 Kang became the chief military representative at the Yumen Oil Fields and the Secretary of its Party Committee. Kang's background in geology at Qinghua may have determined this assignment. By 1952

---

[12] For biographical information on Kang, see Bartke, *Who's Who*; Kasumigaseki; United States Government, *Directory of Chinese Communist Officials*, 1963 (n.p.); United States Government, *Appearances and Activities of Chinese Communist Officials*, 1966 (n.p.).

he had been promoted to head the Petroleum Management Bureau of the entire Northwest, then China's most productive and promising petroleum region. Next, he moved to Beijing to head the Beijing Municipal Petroleum Management General Bureau, and in July 1953, at the age of 38, he was appointed director of the Petroleum Management Bureau in the Ministry of Fuel Industry. The ministry included coal, electric power, and hydropower under its wings, and this assignment indicates Kang was the chief civilian bureaucrat charged with the development and production of petroleum. He continued to mount the bureaucratic hierarchy, being promoted to the rank of Assistant Minister when the Ministry of Petroleum was established as a separate entity in July 1955, becoming Vice Minister in October 1956. There is no evidence that he received sustained, formal education in petroleum engineering, however, and he probably acquired his knowledge through on-the-job training.

His first known foreign travel occurred in 1955, when at the age of 40 he travelled to the Soviet Union. In 1960 he went to Daqing, where, upon the return of Yu Qiuli to Beijing in 1961, he became the First Party Secretary. After Yu Qiuli became *de facto* head of China's planning apparatus in late 1964,[13] Kang became acting Minister of Petroleum. During the Cultural Revolution, Kang—as Yu Qiuli—came under severe attack, particularly for the priority he allegedly attached to production and expertise. He was labelled as Yu's henchman and—as all other disgraced ministers—was said to be a collaborator of Liu Shaoqi and Deng Xiaoping. Red Guards accused him of making Daqing a "sham" model and asserted that the oil field's management ideology had in fact been a good deal less egalitarian and Spartan than the propaganda had made it appear.[14] Kang was purged in May 1967.

Kang's disgrace was, however, apparently less severe and prolonged than that of many others. In 1969, he became Deputy Director of the Jianghan oil field. With the reorganization of the various energy industries in June 1970, during which the Ministry of Petroleum was combined with the Ministries of Coal and Chemical Industries to form the Ministry of Fuel and Chemical Industries, Kang Shien soon became the ranking Vice Minister and deputy head of the Party "small group" in the new ministry.[15] Kang seems to have been acting head from January 1972

---

[13] For details, see Chapter Five.

[14] For Red Guard accusations against Kang, see for example three articles in *Jinggangshan*, March 18, 1967, p. 3. One of these articles is translated in *Supplement to Survey of China Mainland Press*, No. 238 (November 8, 1968). See also *Daqing gongshe*, May 7, 1967; May 19, 1967, p. 3; *Hongse gongjiao*, April 14, 1967.

[15] The formal head of the ministry from June 1970 to January 1975, according to an authoritative PRC publication, was Yi Wen. Yi, evidently a military official dispatched to

on and was formally named Minister of Petroleum in January 1975, as well as head of the Party small group. To this point, Kang had been a leader of the petroleum industry for nearly two decades. He was the person whom the 25 to 35 highest leaders turned to for guidance in this specific sector.

Kang rose quickly in the years of transition from Mao to Deng. In early 1978 he became a Vice Premier and, probably with the support of his patron Yu Qiuli, he also became head of the State Economic Commission (SEC). He was also made a member of the pivotal Financial and Economic Commission under the State Council in July 1979.

In this immediate post-Mao era, many Chinese and outside observers began to speak of a "petroleum clique" (*shiyou pai*) headed by Yu Qiuli. This group traced its origins to the individuals who developed the Daqing oil field and/or who had gathered around Yu Qiuli in 1964-66 as the new, or "small," planning commission. As of early 1980, Kang Shien was perceived to be a member of this group, as was State Capital Construction Commission and Foreign Investment Control Commission Chairman Gu Mu, Minister of Coal Gao Yangwen, Minister of Metallurgy Tang Ke, Minister of Petroleum Song Zhenming, Minister of Chemical Industries Sun Jingwen, Minister of the Fifth Ministry of Machine Building (Ordnance) Zhang Zhen, and Beijing Mayor Lin Hujia. Our interviews suggest that these individuals did not constitute a highly cohesive, purposeful group in the eyes of these officials, and there is good anecdotal evidence of conflicts and tensions among them. Nonetheless, others in China—especially middle-level bureaucrats—perceived them as a group who had benefited from the successes of the Ministry of Petroleum. They were seen as arrogant, assertive, and seeking to extend their influence into other agencies. In the eyes of others, with Yu Qiuli at the SPC and Kang Shien at the SEC, the "clique" was trying to place its own followers throughout the economic system.

The years 1979-80 saw Kang at the pinnacle of his career. In effect, he was China's energy czar during the crucial period when the top leaders decided that foreign energy firms would be allowed equity holdings on a joint venture basis.[16] The leaders concluded that this form of cooperation was appropriate to elicit foreign involvement in the surveying, exploration, and development of China's energy resources, especially for off-shore petroleum. Kang met many foreign officials and businessmen

---

the ministry to help restore order, probably left the ministry substantially before 1975, indeed probably as early as 1972. See China Revolutionary Museum, *Zhonghua Renmin Gongheguo quanguo renda, zhongyang he difang zhengfu, quanguo zhengxie lijie fuzeren renminglu* (Beijing: People's Daily Press, 1984), p. 57.

[16] See Chapter Five below.

during this period. He was involved in the negotiations with the multi-national oil companies for development of Bohai and South Sea oil. He began to travel abroad.[17]

He consistently impressed his foreign interlocutors with his intellectual curiosity, precision, and cultured demeanor. Some found him to be a wily negotiator, while others judged him to be straightforward. All judged him to be conversant with the details of the oil business. At the beginning, he was not very knowledgeable about international practices, but he quickly learned. Further, he was able to educate his interlocutors about the beliefs and difficulties of the Chinese in a patient and dignified way. All of his known involvements in policy suggest he strongly believed in the modernization and technological transformation of China.

Kang ran afoul of the same political problems that affected Yu Qiuli and others in the so called "Petroleum Faction" in 1980. Kang received an official reprimand for his conduct during the Bohai oil rig incident.[18] In March 1981, he left his higher ranking position at the SEC to resume his position as Minister of Petroleum. The Ministry was without a formally designated head from August 1980 until Kang's appointment. In May 1982, he ceased being Minister. His replacement was Tang Ke (see below). Kang Shien became a State Councillor (the equivalent of "Vice Premier" status), and until 1983 he was the vice premier-level official generally responsible for the energy sector. With the promotion of Li Peng to Vice Premier (see below), Kang lost that all-energy portfolio, retaining only special responsibility for petroleum. Some observers believe he retained that responsibility in part because of the confidence and esteem which foreign oil men had for him.

His eclipse in the mid-1980's, no doubt, was partly due to the eroded influence of the petroleum group generally, but the main factor was his severe illness. Kang developed cancer of the pancreas, for which he received treatment in the United States. The disease weakened him. He appeared to recover somewhat in 1985, and his presence was immediately more noticeable in oil matters.

Kang, like his fellow December 9th movement activists, is thus a man with a good education and technological background who became a technocrat in the new regime. As might well have been expected in 1949, he mounted a career ladder within China's growing industrial base. Kang

---

[17] Kang visited the United States in May-June, 1979, meeting President Carter in Washington, visiting coal mines, hydraulic power plants, and oil refineries in Alaska, Pennsylvania, and Texas, and negotiating in Houston with several companies for surveying South Sea.

[18] For the reprimand, see Beijing Xinhua, August 25, 1980, in FBIS, No. 166 (August 25, 1980), pp. L1-2.

found his niche in petroleum, and he rose both as petroleum prospered and his superior, Yu Qiuli, rose. He became an advocate of technological innovation and of expanding contact with the outside world to develop China's resources. His move toward wider responsibilities, however, was cut short by illness and by the political setbacks of the petroleum group.

Tang Ke: Energetic Politician[19]

Tang Ke is roughly the same generation as Kang Shien (Tang is five years younger than Kang). He, too, eventually played a key role as an advocate of greater Chinese involvement with the international arena. Unlike Kang, however, Tang lacked a technical education and a cosmopolitan background. As previously noted, his career demonstrates that inferences about an official's policy preferences based on personal background may be unwarranted.

Tang Ke served as Minister of Petroleum from May 1982 to July 1985, a crucial time in the development of China's relations with the multinational oil companies. He presided over the oil industry during the negotiations with the companies and when the joint ventures began the exploration phase in the South China Sea. Along with CNOOC head Qin Wencai, Tang had extensive dealings with the leaders of petroleum exploration and drilling companies, as well as the producers, throughout the world. Many of these came to consider him a genuine friend and respected advocate and defender of China's interests. In 1985, he gave way to a younger Minister, Wang Tao, the first minister with extensive, formal training in petroleum engineering.

Tang was born in 1918 in Jiangsu province. He joined local communist guerrilla forces in northern Jiangsu sometime in late 1936 or early 1937, and he fought at the local level through much of the war. Tang may also have been a leader of the ordnance industry in a base area. Tang served in PLA units transferred to the Northeast upon the defeat of Japan. In a process and for reasons that are unclear, Tang soon transferred to the heavy industry department of the Northeast Government. Then, in 1950, he was assigned to Beijing. After receiving technical training in Czechoslovakia and East Germany for a short period of time—not exceeding a year—Tang began his work in China's energy industry. By 1951, he was deputy director of the Petroleum Management Bureau of the Ministry of Fuel Industry. Hence, his presence in this core bureau antedated that of Kang Shien, who became director of the bureau in 1953,

---

[19] For biographies of Tang Ke, see footnote 11 above.

and of Yu Qiuli, with whom he first established links when Yu began to be involved in petroleum in 1957-58.

Tang joined Yu and Kang at Daqing, and Tang clearly played a major role in supervising development of the field through the early 1960's. In April 1964, Tang was promoted to head the China National Oil and Gas Exploration and Development Corporation (CNOGEDC), and in February 1965 he became Vice Minister of Petroleum. His responsibilities and rank were growing with the successful record of his industry.

Tang came under Red Guard attack during the Cultural Revolution, condemned as an associate of Yu Qiuli.[20] By 1970 he was back at work, and in 1971 it was revealed that he was Vice Minister of Fuel and Chemical Industries. From 1970 to 1975, he travelled widely. He had already visited France and Algeria from November 1963 to April 1964, a trip that apparently had a significant effect upon him. Then, he travelled to Canada and France in fall, 1972, and in late 1974 to early 1975 he went to Venezuela and Mexico. During his 1972 Canadian trip, testing the limits of his instructions, he came in direct contact with American oil men. In both his 1972 and 1974-75 journeys, he eagerly sought foreign advice and cooperation to develop China's off shore deposits.

In October 1975, he became Vice Minister of Metallurgy, and in June 1977 he became the Minister. As we already noted, the appointment reflected the spread of petroleum officials to several economic ministries, probably under the aegis of Yu Qiuli. Tang was an active minister. He spent nearly two months in Western Europe from May to July, 1978, and visited the United States in spring, 1979. The decision to construct the controversial foreign built Baoshan Iron and Steel works was made while he was Minister. On his visit to Western Europe, he displayed lively interest in various methods to finance the ambitious projects he had in mind for China's metallurgy industry. With Tang's encouragement, several American firms, such as Alcoa, Reynolds Aluminum, Bethlehem Steel, and US Steel, became deeply involved in planning huge projects in China. The record unmistakably reveals Tang to have been an enthusiastic supporter—indeed, an instigator—of China's exuberant turn to the outside world in 1978-79.

However, as Baoshan encountered severe engineering problems, Tang Ke soon came under fire. He fought back, defending the Baoshan project. But in the August-September 1980 National People's Congress, precisely when Kang Shien was criticized for the Bohai Gulf oil rig accident, Tang

[20] See *Hongse zaofanbao*, February 19, 1967, in *Supplement to* SCMP, No. 238 (November 8, 1968), p. 16.

Ke had to make amends for shortcomings in the Baoshan project.[21] The gregarious Minister, who had been appearing frequently in public and at private banquets, was seen less frequently after October 1980. In fact, during 1981 he only made three appearances reported in the Chinese media.[22] According to one source, he went to the Taiyuan Iron and Steel Mill to help solve practical problems.[23]

His eclipse ended with his May 1982 appointment as Minister of Petroleum. As at the Metallurgical Ministry, he was an active Minister. Western oil executives, for example, believed that he was more willing to assert himself in the domain of Qin Wencai, their chief Chinese counterpart, than Kang Shien had been. While Tang was Minister, the Beijing representatives of several multinational corporations had easy access to Tang, and they would draw their problems in the South Sea exploration to his attention. He was willing to give orders on the spot to help settle various small problems which had become entangled in bureaucratic delays. However, Tang did not appear to be the final authority in the offshore negotiations. The significant issues clearly were decided above the Ministry level.

Westerners uniformly believe Tang was not as knowledgeable about the technical aspects of the oil business as was Kang Shien, nor did he immerse himself as deeply in the details of negotiations as did CNOOC-head Qin Wencai. Rather, he was an activist who apparently relied on competent technicians to advise him on details. His career suggests that he enjoyed the confidence of several high level officials; Western observers speculate alternatively that Deng Xiaoping, Hu Yaobang, and/or Li Xiannian were among his supporters. His enthusiasm, his determination and courage, and his imposing physical appearance—at 6'1", he is quite tall among Chinese—made him a dynamic leader. The record also strongly suggests that he was effective in the Chinese organizational context during the Mao and Deng eras. In three instances—Daqing, Baoshan, and South Sea oil—he was at the helm as organizations were put together to undertake major development projects.

In many respects, then, Tang Ke embodied the attributes of many successful Chinese officials: skilled in interpersonal relations, availing themselves of sponsors and cultivating their own clients. He rose as his organization and his patron prospered. At the same time, Tang stands out in several ways. First, he was outspoken and more clearly identified

[21] For criticism of Tang, see FBIS, September 25, 1980, p. L-5; September 18, 1980, p. L-13; September 19, 1980, pp. L-18-21; September 11, 1980, pp. L-28-29.

[22] He made fifteen such appearances in 1980. These data are recorded in FBIS.

[23] Beijing Domestic Service, September 26, 1981, in FBIS, No. 188 (September 29, 1981), p. K-22.

himself with a policy position than the typical, more cautious leader does. He strongly advocated involving foreigners in China's resource development. Second, and relatedly, he became one of the more accessible Chinese leaders to foreigners at the Minister level and above. He sought the education which extensive foreign travel yields. He was an eager questioner. In spite of his friendliness and renowned hospitality at banquets, he revealed surprisingly little to foreigners about his own background and personal life. This suggests that a disciplined sense of purpose accompanied his openness. Third, he was willing to take risks, both personally and for the organizations he headed. Other leaders no doubt harbor a courageous and innovative spirit, but few exhibit it as clearly as did Tang. In mid-1985 Tang left the Ministry at an earlier date than observers expected. The torch at MPI passed to a younger generation.

Li Peng: Successor Generation

Li Peng is a member of the successor generation who as of 1985 had risen to a position within the elite core of 25 to 35 people. He is not an old revolutionary—indeed, he was only twenty-one when the People's Republic of China was established in 1949. He nevertheless was associated with the communist movement almost literally from birth. He is among a number of younger people assuming positions of authority in the 1980's who have close blood or other relations with the old revolutionaries of the communist movement's top elite.

Li Peng was born in 1928 in Chengdu, Sichuan. His father, a member of the Communist Party, died a martyr's death at the hands of the Guomindang in 1931. No information is available on Li's childhood until he turned eleven years old. At that time, in 1939, Li was "adopted" by Zhou Enlai and his wife Deng Yingchao.[24] Zhou and Deng had arrived in Chongqing in the fall of 1938 as liaison to the Nationalist government. Both of them left for the Soviet Union in the summer of 1939, however, and it is not clear at what point they took the young Li Peng under wing. Zhou returned to Chongqing for the period of mid-1940 to mid-1943, while Deng may have gotten back to Chongqing somewhat earlier than Zhou. Both of them moved to Yan'an in 1943 for the duration of the war.

No concrete information is available on the precise nature of Zhou's and Deng's relationship with Li Peng. Official comments from Beijing in the 1980's have indicated that Zhou and Deng became, essentially, Li's

[24] This and many other details in this biographical sketch are taken from "Ji Li Peng," *Liaowang* (November 20, 1983), pp. 6-8.

foster parents, but no details have been given and the relationship was probably less close than the Beijing media subsequently implied. Zhou and Deng in fact "adopted" scores of children of revolutionary martyrs over the years. Typically, this provided those individuals with some special access to Zhou and Deng, but very few of these people seem to have developed very close ties with Zhou and Deng themselves. Li was sent to live in Yan'an in 1941, two years before Zhou and Deng went there. Li graduated from middle school in Yan'an and attended the Institute of Natural Sciences and the Zhangjiakou Technical Middle School.[25]

Li's activities from 1945 to 1949 suggest that he already was seen as someone who would play a major role as he grew older. He officially joined the Chinese Communist Party in 1945, at age 16.[26] During the following two years, he moved to the Northeast, where major communist forces had moved in behind the protection of Soviet occupation troops directly following Japan's surrender. Li Peng first served as a technician at the Shanxi-Chahar-Hebei Electric Company. He soon, however, became the assistant manager and Party branch secretary at the Harbin Oils and Fats Corporation.

In 1948, at about age 20, Li was sent off for his university training at the Moscow Power Institute in the USSR. This positioned Li to become over the long run one of the leading figures on the PRC's electric power sector. It also put him in the first substantial wave of Chinese students going to Moscow in the early 1950's for advanced technical training. Li became the head of the Chinese student association formed in the Soviet Union, a position that brought him into contact with a number of others who also came back to successful careers in the state sector in China. As indicated below, Li Peng has maintained close relations with at least some of the students with whom he became acquainted during his Moscow days.

His final months in the USSR proved important in Li's career. Liu Lanbo, who was in charge of electric power in the Ministry of Fuel Industry, travelled to the Soviet Union for four months with Li Rui and a group of hydropower specialists to study Soviet experience in hydro-

[25] Many schools moved to Yan'an from other areas during the war, and this was the case with the Zhangjiakou school. Li is mistakenly said by the usually reliable *Liaowang* to have attended technical middle school in the city of Zhangjiakou—a city never captured by the communists during the war—for a period in the early 1940's: *Liaowang* (November 20, 1983), pp. 6-8. On Zhou's and Deng's "adoption" of scores of orphaned children, see: Kathryn Minnick, "The Development of Chinese Nuclear Energy Policy," M.A. thesis (Ann Arbor: University of Michigan Center for Chinese Studies, 1987), p. 65.

[26] It was unusual for someone to achieve full Party membership at such a young age, as the Party had also organized separate mass organizations for youths.

power development. Li Rui had since 1952 assumed responsibility for hydropower under Liu, and Li Rui convinced Liu to make this trip so as to familiarize himself with hydropower affairs. There, Liu and Li Rui linked up with a group of Chinese hydropower students who had just completed their studies in Moscow, and they all travelled together for several months during the winter of 1954-55. Subsequently, Liu took special care to train and protect these people. He paid particular attention to Li Peng, and during the ensuing years he had Li Peng assigned to positions at each succeeding rung of the Chinese electric power bureaucracy so as to groom him for future leadership. Since Liu Lanbo's personal base was in Liaoning province, Liu had Li spend his career in Liaoning (until Liu himself was purged during the Cultural Revolution).[27]

Liaoning was a region that had been developed primarily by the Japanese and then stripped by the Soviets during their occupation at the end of World War II. During the 1950's, it was the site of many of the key plants that were being built (or rebuilt) with Soviet aid. Li's first assignment, not surprisingly, was to one of these enterprises in the hydropower sector: the Fengman Power station, a keypoint project in Soviet assistance that was being constructed with a substantial number of Soviet advisors. Li was one of the key liaison people with the Soviet experts there. Li was first the deputy director and then the chief engineer at this power station.

Li left Fengman and then successively held two other positions in the Northeast electric power sector before the outbreak of the Cultural Revolution. Unfortunately, information on the specific timing of these job changes is not available. From Fengman, Li became chief engineer of the Northeast China Electric Power Administration, an administrative unit directly under the Ministry of Water Resources and Electric Power at the time that Li must have served in it. Li was also director of the Distribution Department for this Power Administration. From there, Li Peng became director of the Fuxin Power Plant in Liaoning Province.

The Cultural Revolution itself benefited Li's career rather than hurt it—a fact that probably makes him quite atypical among officials who received technical training in the Soviet Union during the 1950's. Li Peng's career during the Cultural Revolution suggests that he remained under the protection of powerful patrons. When Liu Lanbo came under attack and thus was no longer able to control assignments in Liaoning, Li was transferred to the capital, where he held a succession of top Party and Government posts in the Beijing Power Supply Bureau and the Beijing Electric Power Administration. He first became the acting secretary

[27] Li Rui (ed.), *Huainian shi pian* (Renmin chubanshe, 1983), esp. pp. 88-89.

53

of the Party Committee of the Beijing Power Supply Bureau and chairman of its Revolutionary Committee. This made him the top leader in this municipal office. He also held other posts, although it is not clear to what extent (if any) these overlapped with his tenure at the Power Supply Bureau. The other positions were at the Beijing Electric Power Administration, the equivalent body to the Northeast Electric Power Administration that Li had headed at an earlier stage in his career. Again, specific information on dates that Li held different positions in the Beijing Power Administration are not available. He did, however, serve as acting secretary of its Party Committee and as secretary of the Party Core Group (the real center of power within the unit). He also served successively as vice chairman of its Revolutionary Committee, deputy director (the post-Cultural Revolution equivalent to the vice chairman position), and then as director. Thus, by the late 1970's, Li was the leading Party and Government person in the Power Administration that controlled the provision of electric power to the vital Beijing-Tianjin-Tangshan grid.[28] Premier Zhou Enlai reportedly arranged for Li's Beijing positions early in the Cultural Revolution to make sure that the power supply for the critical Beijing-Tianjin-Tangshan area was not disrupted by the political anarchy of these years.[29]

Li acquitted himself so well in these difficult circumstances that he was appointed Vice Minister of Electric Power when the Ministry of Water Resources and Electric Power was divided into its constituent ministries in early 1979. As related in the Three Gorges case study in Chapter Six below, this redivision of the ministry may have been connected to an effort by pro-Three Gorges dam people on the water resources side of the ministry to enhance their position. While Li Peng served in the independent Ministry of Electric Power he on at least several occasions voiced his opposition to this mammoth and controversial project.

Liu Lanbo had himself been rehabilitated and was appointed Minister of Electric Power at that time. Liu, however, was ill, and two years later he recommended that Li Peng succeed him as Minister. This recommendation reportedly received enthusiastic endorsement from "central leading cadres."[30] At the same time, an article that Liu wrote in *Hongqi* on explaining his approach to choosing a successor implied quite strongly that many within the ministry had opposed Li Peng's promotion on the ground that he was too arrogant.[31]

[28] Xinhua in English, June 20, 1983—in FBIS, June 21, 1983, p. K-17.

[29] Christopher Clarke, "China's Third Generation," *China Business Review* (March-April 1984), pp. 36-38.

[30] Li Rui, *Huainian shi pian*, pp. 88-89.

[31] *Hongqi*, No. 23 (1981), pp. 44-45.

Li was briefly reduced again to vice ministerial status in early 1982, when the Electric Power Ministry was again folded into a reconstituted MWREP. This probably did not amount to a significant diminution in his authority over the electric power sector itself, however. Qian Zhengying, who was more senior and who had headed the MWREP before it was divided in 1979, was given back her previous portfolio. Li became the Vice Minister with primary responsibility for electric power in a ministry in which overall the electric power side tended to be stronger than the water resources component.

Li, in any case, did not remain at the Vice Minister level for long. He swiftly rose to the highest levels of power with his election to the Central Committee in September 1982 and his appointment as Vice Premier in June 1983. When in 1983 Li Peng moved his office into the Zhongnanhai compound to take up his duties as vice premier, Deng Yingchao reportedly personally stopped by to warn him against arrogant behavior.[32] As Vice Premier, Li initially assumed responsibility for energy, communications, and keypoint construction. By the summer of 1984 he had also become the head of a small leadership group that had been established to deal with the proposed Three Gorges project.[33] He also became the head of "leadership small groups" in charge of rural energy and nuclear energy.

After 1983 Li Peng rapidly broadened his areas of responsibility beyond the energy and communications sectors. In 1984 he began playing an increasingly active role in China's diplomacy toward the Soviet Union and Eastern Europe. Li Peng's promotion to the Politburo and the Secretariat in September 1985 made him one of only two State Council vice premiers[34] to hold simultaneous membership on the powerful Party Politburo and Central Committee Secretariat. With these additional positions, Li gained solid entry into the core leadership group of 25 to 35 individuals who form China's central power elite. By late 1985, he had become well positioned to become China's next premier.

Li thus became one of the two or three most successful men of his generation in China. What were the ingredients of this extraordinary record of rapid advancement? His relationship with Premier Zhou Enlai and with Zhou's wife Deng Yingchao[35] must have been helpful. Through

[32] *Liaowang*, (November 20, 1983), p. 8.

[33] Chapter Six provides details.

[34] The other was Wan Li.

[35] Deng herself is a Long March veteran and an important figure in her own right. She was a member of the Politburo until September 1985 and thus remained in a position to help Li Peng long after Zhou himself passed away. Zhou and Deng had no children of their own.

this tie, Li almost certainly became acquainted with the leaders of the revolution in his youth. Li was given unusual early opportunities, such as his training in the Soviet Union starting in the late 1940's and being made the head of the Chinese student association while there. Liu Lanbo then became his personal patron. Liu, of course, may have been encouraged to play this role by Zhou Enlai and Deng Yingchao.

In any case, Zhou personally felt comfortable in entrusting Li Peng with key political and technical tasks during the turbulent Cultural Revolution. After 1976, moreover, Zhou's generally favorable treatment in the Chinese media probably helped Li Peng's career as a person who in some fashion provided a link to the former Premier. More broadly, ties to members of the old guard proved increasingly important in determining who would advance in China of the 1980's.

Li did not, however, move ahead only because of his martyred father and illustrious patrons. Foreigners who dealt with him were very impressed with several of Li's qualities. He time and again exhibited good technical mastery over his field. Visits to power stations and dam sites produced detailed questions that revealed a person well briefed and highly competent in his field. Li tended, moreover, to be quite direct, even blunt, in pressing a line of questioning. He created the impression of being comfortable in the exercise of authority, an impression bolstered by his good grooming and the high quality of his personal accoutrements. Overall, he impressed Westerners as "sharp," "sophisticated," and very much in control of the issues for which he held responsibility. Li exhibited little tolerance for puffery and a considerable capacity for hard work and for detail.

On domestic matters, Li followed a tradition very much favored in China by making frequent inspection trips to various locales to gain first-hand exposure to problems. Chinese accounts of these trips tended to emphasize the decisions Li made on the trips and the problems he confronted. They did not make a point, as they sometimes do with the travels of other leaders, of describing Li's efforts to keep his entourage simple and to share the hardships of the local people.[36] Conversations with knowledgeable Chinese have brought forth anecdotes of times when Li Peng has taken a decisive stand against the pet projects of powerful local leaders while on the road.

For all his authoritative style, people who know him indicate that Li Peng has numerous friends and is able to get along well with people. Li also appears to be well schooled in the types of loyalty that contribute to success in China. For example, as noted above, he developed lasting ties

---

[36] Coverage of Hu Yaobang's travels, for example, often included this latter dimension.

to people with whom he came in contact during his student days in Moscow, and many of these individuals in the mid-1980's assumed key positions in the State Council. A tentative list of these would include Song Jian, head of the State Science and Technology Commission; Huang Yicheng, Vice Minister of the State Planning Commission; Lin Zongtang, Vice Minister of the State Economic Commission; Peng Shilu, Vice Minister of the MWREP; Zheng Guangdi, Vice Minister of Communications; and Wang Pingqing, Special Assistant to the Minister of Foreign Economic Relations and Trade. Wang Tao (Minister of Petroleum Industry) and Li Tieying (Minister of Electronics) may also belong to this group, as both also studied in the USSR when Li was there. Li often included several members of this group in his entourage when he traveled in China. In addition, several new appointees at the provincial level worked in the Soviet Union while Li was there. The reported fact that Li's wife and children all work in the electric power sector which he headed also suggests that he has a keen sense of personal and unit identification and loyalty.

That Li was more than merely a good technocrat is also indicated by the succession of Party posts he held that are noted above. He throughout his career held positions that required political as well as technical skills.

Li Peng's substantive views as of 1985 were beginning to come into sharper focus. He appeared to be a supporter of the economic reforms, but in a very cautious and pragmatic way. Li did not believe in the magic of the market place. Rather, he advocated that reforms be implemented only where they could be controlled and used effectively. He thus appeared to believe in the use of the market only in a very limited sense. In these matters, his overall views seemed to be closest to those of Chen Yun among the Party elders. Within the energy sphere itself, Li was a strong advocate of the development of nuclear power.[37] He also, as noted above, opposed commencing the Three Gorges dam project when he was Minister of Electric Power in the early 1980's. His views on this project may have shifted in the middle 1980's as his responsibilities and political position rapidly grew.[38]

On a international level, Li's active role in diplomacy toward the Soviet Union in the mid-1980's built on his earlier experience in dealing with the Soviets. Li's position as head of the Chinese student association in the USSR in the early 1950's must have brought him into frequent

[37] The best available account of Li Peng's involvement with China's nuclear industry is Minnick, "The Development of Chinese Nuclear Energy Policy," pp. 64-126.
[38] Minnick provides a credible political rationale for this shift. See: *Ibid.*

contact with Soviet authorities on political, cultural, and administrative issues. His position at the Fengman Power Station after his return to China included substantial liaison work with the Soviet advisors there. Indeed, Liaoning retained very heavy Soviet influence throughout the 1950's, and Li Peng probably played a role in dealing with the Russians on electric power industry matters throughout the latter part of that decade. Li speaks Russian fluently, and used this language facility effectively on diplomatic forays to the Soviet Union in the 1980's (where, for example, he talked with Gorbachev without bothering to use an interpreter). Also perhaps reflecting his political acumen, he reportedly began studying English in his spare time in 1973, shortly after the Nixon visit opened up the possibility of extensive future relations between China and the United States.

In sum, Li Peng was a sharp, technically competent, new member of the top leadership core in the mid-1980's. He was responsible for energy policy and a rapidly expanding list of other issues (Li assumed leadership of the newly established State Education Commission in June 1985, for example). He enjoyed what almost amounted to lifelong contact with the key leaders of the older generation, and he also took care to cultivate his own style and following. Indeed, his whole career to 1985 marked him as the type of person likely to provide the core leadership for the coming one or two decades in China: technically competent, politically well connected with the older generation, sensitive to the importance of developing his own group of supporters, experienced at both technical and political tasks, and temperamentally suited to exercising strong authority.

THE QUESTION OF FACTIONALISM AMONG THE LEADERS

The above sketches of Kang Shien, Tang Ke, and Li Peng portray strong-willed individuals from varied backgrounds with quite distinctive personalities. Within the elite circle of the top 25 to 35 leaders, the dynamics of interpersonal relations are important factors in determining the tenor and capacity of the system. How do these top 25 to 35 leaders relate to one another? Does the preeminent leader totally dominate the top leaders? Or, is he constrained by the opinions and alignments among the top leaders? Are the top leaders permanently subdivided into two or more contending factions, or is the situation more fluid—with shifting alliances from issue to issue? And is the struggle at the top governed by rules and shared norms, or is the struggle a free-for-all? Few questions have so engrossed outside observers of Chinese politics as these, yet on few issues is there as little certainty. The biographies of Kang, Tang, and

Li, as well as other biographical data, do shed some light on these questions, however.[39]

Naturally, the adherents of the "power" model have addressed these issues with particular care, but the policy analysts have also sought to elucidate the cleavages delineating the various opinion groupings among the leaders.[40] Pivotal to most such analyses is the concept of "faction," and conceptual clarity is necessary to address this issue. Analysts usually define a faction or clique—*pai* in Chinese—as a group bound by shared background, intertwined careers, and current bureaucratic responsibilities whose members evidently feel some loyalty and obligation toward one another and who have a common destiny. A faction rises and falls together. Although a faction may share similar policy orientations on at least some major issues, its members attach primacy to promoting the political fortunes of one another rather than advancing their policy preference.

Some analysts have portrayed the top 25 to 35 leaders as essentially subdivided into several contending factions.[41] These analysts argue that, either for cultural or structural reasons, Chinese politics at the apex is inescapably one of factional strife, with the boundaries among factions rather tightly and permanently drawn.

Such observers frequently cite four examples of factions at the top in recent decades: 1. the idealogues who initiated the Cultural Revolution and whose survivors ultimately became known as the "Gang of Four;" 2. certain military people around Lin Biao; 3. some of the neo-Maoist bureaucrats around Hua Guofeng who rose to the top 25 to 35 during the Cultural Revolution and who helped in the 1976-77 interregnum between Mao Zedong and Deng Xiaoping; and 4. the petroleum faction. Each of these clusterings was distinctive in terms of its cohesiveness, previous shared experience, and commitment to an identifiable set of policies.[42]

Other analysts portray a more fluid situation, contending that the lines of conflict vary over time and from issue to issue. Such analysts tend to see politics as a struggle among a number of strong willed indi-

[39] See also David M. Lampton, *Paths to Power* (Ann Arbor: University of Michigan Center for Chinese Studies, 1986).

[40] This analysis benefits from Jurgen Domes, *Government and Politics of the PRC*, pp. 80-84.

[41] See Andrew Nathan, "Factionalism Model," and Lucian Pye, *Dynamics*. Also see Tang Tsou, "Prologemenon."

[42] This, of course, does not exhaust the list of elite factions discussed by foreign analysts. Others have identified a security faction in the mid 1970's, a heavy industry faction in the mid 1950's, and so forth.

viduals, each of whom has his distinctive vision of the appropriate route to modernity. *Clusters* of such leaders come together because of their shared views on one or several issues. The group is not highly cohesive and not bound by personal ties.[43]

As the biographies of Kang Shien, Tang Ke, and Li Peng suggest, and as subsequent chapters will demonstrate, such clusters do indeed exist. But their nature is quite complicated, and they may not be "factions" in the sense described above. The officials who developed Daqing oilfield in the early 1960's and whom Mao assembled in 1964-65 to run the economy became known in China as the "petroleum faction." Centered around Yu Qiuli and including Kang Shien, Gu Mu, and Tang Ke, by the early 1970's its members controlled the energy sector and headed several principal economic agencies in China: the SPC, SEC, and State Capital Construction Commission (SCCC). Beginning in 1979 its members came under concerted attack, and by 1985 their influence had been reduced primarily to the petroleum sphere.

This group may not have been representative of all elite factions in China. Nevertheless, its development and dynamics provide some useful cautions to overly-simplified and rigid notions of factions. For much of the time it commanded the economic sector, this group did exhibit some common policy preferences, especially for high rates of capital accumulation, for high growth rates, for attaching priority to heavy industry, and for turning to the outside world to hasten China's growth. They exhibited extraordinary confidence in their ability to increase petroleum production rapidly and to finance imports through expanded exports. They essentially brought an optimistic, expansive, "can do" attitude to the management of the Chinese economy.

But, as we noted previously, the members of the petroleum group—we do not call them a "faction"—initially were viewed as a faction more in the eyes of their non-members than of their members. Their identity was bestowed upon them rather than being self-assumed. It is not clear how cohesive the cluster felt until it acquired a label and began to be perceived by others as a group. At that point they began to share a common destiny and therefore had to act on each other's behalf. Further, significant differences and even personal rivalries existed within the cluster. Its boundary was ill-defined, and its members owed obligations and loyalties to patrons and peers outside the cluster as well as within it. For

[43] For such analyses, see Frederick Teiwes, *Leadership, Legitimacy, and Conflict in China* (New York: M. E. Sharpe, 1984). He and other analysts differ over the extent to which the preeminent leader dominates the nature of the debate, the degree to which the unwritten rules actually regulate the competition, and exactly when the system began to deteriorate in its Cultural Revolution phase.

example, Gu Mu and Kang Shien had close links with many top officials outside the energy sphere. Finally, while the group shared some common views, those views evolved over time, not simply out of power considerations but because of changes in the policy environment. Thus, in the early 1960's, the petroleum group appeared committed to the virtues of self-reliance and mobilizational techniques for policy implementation, but by the early 1970's they had modified their views as opportunities and requirements had changed. They became proponents of importing technology and exporting petroleum to hasten economic development. To this group, at least, the substantive issues did matter. Yet, the group did prosper and suffer together. They were the patrons of larger networks of individuals within MPI and other agencies who looked to them for protection, advancement, and rewards. They clearly were bound by personal ties rooted in much more than common policy preferences and transitory bureaucratic responsibilities. One is almost tempted to call such a group a "near-faction or "semi-faction."

Not all 25 to 35 top leaders are members of such clusters, nor do politics at the top consist strictly of factional strife. To be sure, from the late 1960's through Mao's death, the increasingly polarized and violent nature of political struggle drove the vast majority of the top leaders into one cluster or another, and politics became almost entirely factionally based. With the exception of that era, while one or two such clusters may exist at any moment in time, the remaining leaders are divided over specific policy issues and bureaucratic concerns, and these divisions appear to vary from issue to issue. Thus, as our case studies of the Three Gorges dam and offshore oil reveal, policy is not exclusively the product of factional strife, with the issues simply being used for tactical purposes.

The biographical information suggests that personal characteristics do count in the Chinese process. Tang Ke did provide a certain drive and vigor which greatly facilitated the launching of the joint effort with foreign firms to explore and develop offshore petroleum. Kang Shien brought to the negotiations a caution and thoroughness which required his negotiators to be particularly tough-minded and careful. Our case studies will reveal other instances of the views and styles of individual leaders affecting the pace and outcome of decisions: the ingratiating style of Yu Qiuli facilitating the efficacy of the Ministry of Petroleum under varying preeminent leaders and generalists; the determination of Qian Zhengying to pursue the Three Gorges project; and so on.

Finally, our biographical data underscore the patrimonial quality of Chinese politics. To be sure, leaders rise to the top for a variety of reasons: their talent, vision, ability to articulate a convincing rationale for a particular set of policies; bureaucratic skills, and so on. But few people rise in the Chinese system without the protection and assistance of one or more patrons. Kang Shien had a long relationship with Yu Qiuli; Li Peng enjoyed the backing of Liu Lanbo and Zhou Enlai. Moreover, as leaders rise, they tend to pull others up with them and to cultivate their own network of clients. Radiating out from the top 25 to 35 leaders, then, are not only the bureaucracies under their formal command but the networks of individuals lodged in those bureaucracies who look to them for protection and advancement.

· 3 ·

COMMISSIONS AND MINISTRIES

We now transit from the level of the top leaders and their *ad hoc* coordinating agencies to the realm of bureaucracy and institutionalized power. This is not to demean the extent to which rules govern the way policy is shaped within the deliberative bodies on which the top 25 to 35 leaders sit: rather, it recognizes that at the apex, in many respects power is vested more in individuals than in specific institutions. No matter how powerful these individuals appear, however, they lack the time, interest, and knowledge to manage and coordinate all the activities in the energy sphere. Not even the handful of top energy specialists can manage the vast, sprawling petroleum, coal, and electric power industries. Inevitably, much of the critical activity in the shaping and implementing of policy takes place within the bureaucracies at the national level.

Central level bureaucracies consist of two tiers: *commissions (wei-yuanhui)*, which integrate energy policies with other facets of the economy; and *ministries (bu)*, which manage specific aspects of the economy. Many issues are decided at this level: feasibility studies are conducted, a consensus is constructed, appropriate funding is allocated, necessary resources are coordinated, the major options are elucidated, and energy policy decisions are implemented. While all of this can be affected by the top leaders, much of it in fact goes on without their active and sustained intervention. To understand the policy process in the energy sector, therefore, it is as necessary to appreciate the structure and processes in the relevant portions of this central bureaucratic system as it is to appreciate the dynamics of the Zhongnanhai complex in which the top leaders work.

The commissions are at a higher bureaucratic level than are ministries.[1] Within their respective spheres of competence, therefore, commissions can give instructions to ministries. The commissions are supposed to take a more comprehensive view of things than do the more narrowly focused line ministries, thereby striking balances among competing efforts that the overall national situation requires. One ministry, though, the Ministry of Finance, is also considered to be a relatively "comprehensive" organ.

The core units involved in energy development just below the top leaders, their research institutes, and "small leadership groups" are thus:

[1] Chapter Four explains the influence of bureaucratic rank on the structure of authority.

the comprehensive organs (the SPC, SEC, State Science and Technology Commission [SSTC], and Ministry of Finance [MOF]), the energy line ministries (MPI, MCI, and MWREP), and a few other related organs (Ministry of Foreign Economic Relations and Trade [MOFERT], the Bank of China, corporations such as CNOOC, and other units depending on the particular project concerned). Provinces, which have the bureaucratic rank of ministries, also can play critically important roles in this process.[2] The principal central bureaucracies—their individual missions, resources, personnel, and styles—are key to understanding decision making in the PRC's energy sector. The following sketches of each of the key bureaucratic bodies are based in large part on interviewing officials in these bodies (supplemented by documentary sources). We have included in these sketches what may seem to be numbing detail because it is precisely this complexity of bureaucratic structure that produces such a strong effect on policy process in the energy sphere.

STATE PLANNING COMMISSION

Since it was established in 1952, the State Planning Commission has played a crucial role in the management of China's centrally planned economy as the politically prominent figures who have headed this commission[3] testify. The SPC seeks to guide and organize the production and distribution of major commodities as well as the construction of significant capital projects. It is the key body for working out the Five Year Plan, and the annual plan which it sets has a certain legal status (but not the full force of law that the Soviet plan enjoys).[4] The SPC is expected to approach its task from a long term, strategic, and comprehensive viewpoint; that is, its views are expected to mesh with the state's long term interests.[5]

Concretely, the SPC plays a key all-around role in the development of the national economy. It primarily focuses on macro-economic management and on achieving basic balances among three segments of the national economy: finance; material supplies; and the labor force. Through

[2] Indeed, as the case study on coal in Chapter Seven details, even subprovincial units can become very important actors in this drama. The players outside of Beijing are taken up in subsequent chapters.

[3] Gao Gang, Li Fuchun, Yu Qiuli, Yao Yilin, and Song Ping.

[4] The concluding section of this chapter provides details on the planning process for both the Five Year Plan and the annual plan.

[5] The documentary sources on the SPC and the SEC are not as revealing as are those on the financial organs and the line ministries. On the SPC and its role, see: He Jianzhang and Wang Zhiye (eds.), *Zhongguo jihua guanli wenti* (Beijing: Zhongguo shehui kexue chubanshe, 1984).

manipulation of these basic factors, the SPC tries to determine the speed and contours of national economic development. In fulfilling this wide-ranging mandate, the SPC investigates key issues such as prices, bank credit, and salaries.

Specifically, the SPC tries to control the balance between industry and agriculture. It also plays a crucial role in selecting which among the numerous proposed capital construction projects will be accepted and acted upon. In considering new investments, the SPC determines not only the size of the investment funds but also their overall geographical and sectoral distributions and the key projects for the investment budget in the national economy as a whole. As a supra-ministerial body, it also directs the activities of a range of ministries and other bodies in bringing new projects to fruition. The SPC attempts to strike the balance between investment and personal consumption. Finally, it also stipulates the balances to be struck between domestic and foreign trade, and it makes provision for personnel training. All of this is done in accordance with the policies of the Party Center and the State Council.

The State Planning Commission not only sets the concrete targets for the annual plan but also plans for the core tasks for medium and long term plans, although both are subject to ongoing revision as events mandate adjustments. These targets concern both new project development and production levels for certain commodities.[6] All commodities are placed into one of three categories. The SPC has directly controlled the production and allocation of Category I goods, which are considered either crucial for national economic growth (such as petroleum, electricity, cement, and steel) or of critical political importance (such as certain consumption items).[7] The central ministries directly control Category II items and report on the details to the SPC. The SPC simply disregards Category III items, which are controlled by the locales. There has been a marked trend during the 1980's to shift commodities from Category I to Category II and from the latter to Category III. As of late 1984, approximately sixty-five items remained in Category I.

As explained below, the SPC relies on a network of planning organs embedded in the ministries and the provincial governments to perform these tasks. It also must consult with the Ministry of Finance over the annual and long term financial balances, with the Ministry of Foreign

[6] In the 1980's the SPC has also been involved in issues such as the number of university graduates and their post-graduation distribution among jobs.

[7] The SPC does not control production or allocation of Category I goods which exceed the plan. That is, factories must meet quotas, the goods produced within the target are part of the plan and must be allocated and delivered through state-directed mechanisms, and above-quota goods can be sold by the enterprise.

Economic Relations and Trade (formerly the Ministry of Trade) for the foreign trade balance, and with the People's Bank for the monetary dimensions. In addition, the SPC must coordinate closely with the State Economic Commission in determining the plan.[8] Projects of sufficiently large scale are transmitted to the State Council for decision, while those smaller than a certain scale can be initiated by the line ministries or local governments without item approval by the SPC. Thus, the SPC is part of a large web of relationships. In important energy planning and projects, as of the mid-1980's it was closer to the center of that web than was any other organ.

The SPC in the Energy Sector

The State Planning Commission during the period under review played three major roles in energy development: it formulated mid-term and long-term energy plans that included construction, production, and conservation; it decided which projects to construct, conducted appropriate technical and other feasibility studies, and determined the project's size, its speed of development, and the year in which each effort should begin; and it coordinated the actual construction of energy-related projects. The planning effort itself required that the SPC forecast future energy supplies and demands, both sectorally and geographically. For example, the Ministry of Coal Industry and the Ministry of Water Resources and Electric Power separately plan the development of their sectors. But since most of China's electricity is generated in coal-fired thermal plants, the development of both sectors must be closely coordinated, based on the future need for electricity. The SPC performed this task.

In this as in its other endeavors, the SPC could draw on the expertise available in related bureaucracies. For example, during 1979-1982 the SPC cooperated with the State Science and Technology Commission and the former State Energy Commission to draft a long term set of projections of China's energy supply and demand up to the year 2000. This effort also brought in more than 500 technical specialists, professors, and management specialists from 170 units representing concerned departments, science and technology organs, and universities. It produced a final volume of over 500,000 characters that outlined the overall energy situation and policy recommendations for the country.[9] While this proj-

---

[8] The SEC has responsibility for organizing and guiding the implementation of the production plan for key commodities, and it resolves problems in the production of these goods. It also resolves problems in the operation (as versus construction) of major projects where the difficulties involve more than one ministry or province.

[9] *Guangming Ribao*, November 8, 1982.

ect was unusual in its scope and the length of the final product, it reflects a typical approach to planning, in which the SPC draws on relevant experts from other units.

SPC plans include stipulations on the use of foreign funds. The SPC-developed national plan also specifies the major joint ventures to be signed, which then become targets for the appropriate ministries (the SPC itself typically does not send representatives to participate in the negotiations for these ventures). The size of a joint venture necessary to trigger direct SPC involvement has varied by time and locale. During 1981-84, in most locales energy projects that cost more than US $10 million were included in the SPC-stipulated national plan, but the trend was toward raising this "trigger" figure.[10]

The State Planning Commission uses its long term projections of energy supplies and demands to guide specific decision making on the priorities for different types of concrete investment projects. In translating these general guidelines into specific decisions, though, the SPC has not been able to rely on a complete input-output table of the energy sector of China's economy. As of 1984, it had a partial table and was working on developing a more complete one, along with other economic models. In addition, SPC decisions must be responsive to the overall political guidelines it receives from Politburo leaders and the Central Committee of the Chinese Communist Party.

Within the energy sector, the SPC relies on the line ministries and the provincial bodies to generate most requests for new projects and the studies to buttress those requests.[11] These requests are part of the plans that each of the four energy-sector line ministries (Ministry of Coal Industry, Ministry of Petroleum Industry, Ministry of Water Resources and Electric Power, and Ministry of Nuclear Industry) and the provinces submit to the SPC. These plans are supposed to be based on the broad guidelines for long term development promulgated by the SPC. Still, though, requests far outstrip the country's capacities for new construction, and thus the SPC must determine which proposals are desirable and both technically and economically feasible. In addition, the SPC may find that it differs from an energy line ministry in its judgment about the best strategy for development of a particular sector. For example, the SPC may differ from the Ministry of Coal concerning the relative em-

---

[10] See: Luo Long, "Project Approval," *MOR China Newsletter* (April/May 1987), pp. 6-7.

[11] The overall guidance the SPC provides, which in turn influences these requests, is itself reflective of priorities set at the State Council (and Politburo) level. Clearly, these higher level bodies can also place a specific project on the SPC's agenda, but this evidently rarely occurs.

phasis to be given to large, medium, and small mines. In such a case, the SPC can refuse the line ministry's requests that depart from the SPC's preferred development strategy. The SPC finally draws up an overall balance based on repeated consultations with the ministries and provinces in the process of turning their aspirations into a national plan. When the draft of the final plan is completed, it is sent to the State Council for approval.[12]

Within a province or a line ministry, proposals to the SPC must obtain the approval of the head of the unit and be presented to the State Planning Commission as a request from that unit as a whole. Beginning in the early 1980's, each major request had to be accompanied by a feasibility study. The line ministry or province making the request must consult with the relevant other units in the process of drawing up this feasibility study. The SPC then could decide to conduct its own feasibility study. Whatever the SPC's course of action, it often drew on expertise both in the proposing unit and elsewhere to bolster the effort.

Once a project is put into the official plan, the SPC then coordinates the work of the various relevant ministries during the construction of the project. The SPC's Fuel and Power Bureau focuses on energy development and related construction and production. It thus makes the initial decisions on all aspects of energy development. Which SPC bureau then assumes charge of implementing the decision of the Fuel and Power Bureau depends on the nature and importance of the project involved. The Fuel and Power Bureau itself assumes this responsibility for most energy projects. Conservation projects that involve large-scale construction are generally given to the Energy Conservation Bureau.[13] A few major projects of critical national importance come under the aegis of the First Bureau of Key Projects Construction.[14]

Coordination of construction is a critical task because all ministries have the same rank and therefore do not have formal leverage over each other. It requires either the State Council itself or a commission,[15] which

---

[12] The State Council in turn submits it to the National People's Congress for examination and approval. This gives the plan a legal character.

[13] The State Economic Commission's Energy Bureau assumes a greater role in projects that amount primarily to upgrading energy conservation technology at existing facilities.

[14] It assumed charge of the petroleum bases for the search for offshore oil, the Pingshuo mining project, and the Gezhouba and (prospectively) Three Gorges hydropower projects on the Yangtze River. This bureau, like most in the SPC, has 20-30 people in it. The Second Bureau of Key Projects Construction is in charge of major communications projects.

[15] As of the end of 1985 there were the following commissions: Planning; Economic; Science and Technology; Science, Technology, and Industry for National Defense; Restructuring the National Economy; Education; Family Planning; Nationalities Affairs; and Physical Culture and Sports.

is a half-note higher than a ministry, to make various ministries and provinces coordinate their efforts.[16] Thus, for example, in the construction of the open pit mine at Antaibao involving Occidental Petroleum and the Ministry of Coal Industry, the SPC had to direct the Ministry of Railways and other ministries to meet their obligations on the project. Although the Ministry of Coal Industry alone deals with Occidental on all material and personnel dimensions of the project, that Ministry must in turn work through the State Planning Commission to resolve problems it may encounter with the Ministry of Railways, etc.[17]

For a very small number of truly key projects (such as the Baoshan steel complex), the SPC continues to play a crucial role once the project has been completed in that it has the final voice on setting the annual plan targets for the project.[18] Problems that require inter-ministerial coordination once a plant has begun production, however, go to the State Economic Commission, not to the State Planning Commission.

In sum, the State Planning Commission in many ways makes the crucial decisions that either permit or block construction of major energy development projects. It does not make these decisions alone, and indeed the small size of its staff assures that considerable use must be made of "outside" expertise. In addition, the SPC has lacked input-output tables for the energy sector which could put its decision making on a more scientific basis. SPC decisions to go ahead with a proposed project produce enforceable obligations for the various Chinese ministries and other units to do their respective parts. During the construction phase, the SPC continues to provide the leverage required to assure coordination among the otherwise coequal ministerial and provincial units.

SPC decisions on project feasibility and appropriateness are based primarily on consideration of the need for the product and on the technical and economic feasibility of accomplishing the construction task. The State Planning Commission also provides for domestic project financing, as China's Construction Bank releases investment funds according to the national plan that has been set by the SPC.[19] But the SPC is not primarily responsible for assuring that the government in fact has sufficient funds or supplies to cover the cost of the projects in the plan. These tasks fall

---

[16] As noted above, provinces have the same rank as ministries.

[17] On some financial dimensions, Occidental could deal directly with the Bank of China.

[18] More typically, however, the SPC merely sets the overall level of output for a sector and permits the relevant line ministry to allocate that production among different plants. The feasibility study conducted by the SPC when the initial decision to build the plant was made includes projections of future levels of production and the necessary inputs for this.

[19] The Construction Bank also investigates the economic results of the construction project and provides the SPC with information on these.

instead to the Material Supply Bureau and the Ministry of Finance.[20] The latter does not always agree with the SPC over investment levels. Meetings between these two ministries to coordinate their decisions are often quite heated.

Organizational Network

Its position as the spearhead organization in the planned economy of China has not protected the State Planning Commission from fluctuations in its role since 1949.[21] The organization played a critical role during the First Five Year Plan (1953-57), the heyday of emulation of the Soviet model. The Great Leap Forward's (1958-61) emphasis on decentralized initiative and use of plan targets primarily for purposes of mobilization sharply reduced the concrete ability of the SPC to guide the economy during these years. The Great Leap also created pressures that essentially robbed the central planners of the accurate statistics they needed in order to do their work. Planning began to revive during 1962-65, and by mid-1964 the SPC had developed the control figures for the Third Five Year Plan. Mao Zedong, who at all times exercised enormous influence over plan targets, then intervened to change these numbers and to shift responsibility for setting overall policy in planning work to the "small planning commission" that he had formed under Yu Qiuli.[22]

The Cultural Revolution undermined the ability of the State Planning Commission to play a guiding role in the economy. By March 1967, Yu Qiuli was under Red Guard attack, and no annual plan was adopted for 1967. In addition, the statistical system that the SPC requires in order to perform its work deteriorated dramatically. The plan for 1968 was incomplete. As of December 1968, indeed, the State Planning Commission itself had only sixteen people remaining at its central offices. These sixteen produced the plan for 1969 which, not surprisingly, was not very detailed. The SPC thus *de facto* played a far less important role in the economy. All of this turned around beginning in the early 1970's, and after 1976 the SPC was fully rehabilitated and strengthened.

The State Planning Commission is internally divided into a number of bureaus, and these in turn are grouped together functionally under different deputy Commission heads. As of mid-1985, Huang Yicheng was

---

[20] See the section on the Ministry of Finance below.

[21] On these, see: He Jianzhang and Wang Zhiye (eds.), *Zhongguo jihua guanli wenti*.

[22] See: Fang Weizhong (ed.), *Zhonghua Renmin Gongheguo jingji dashiji* (Beijing: Zhongguo shehui kexue chubanshe, 1984). At all times, the "small planning commission" used the bureaus and staff of the SPC for its work.

the deputy head responsible for energy and communications.[23] The two key bureaus dealing exclusively with energy under Huang were the Fuel and Power Bureau and the Energy Conservation Bureau. The Fuel and Power Bureau is concerned primarily with producing the energy development plan. The Energy Conservation Bureau focuses on the conservation plan.[24] Other bureaus in the SPC also play important roles in energy affairs. The Investment Bureau has a few energy specialists in it, and it takes care of investment matters. The First Bureau of Key Projects Construction,[25] as noted above, plays a critical role in the construction of certain major projects, including several in the energy sector.

For most planning purposes, the SPC's Fuel and Power Bureau is a relatively important body.[26] This bureau was created in the early 1950's and recruited most of the personnel it had as of 1985 by 1959. About 90 percent of these came out of technical training in the universities, most of whom then went through the line ministries in the energy sector. The Bureau as of 1985 had about thirty-five staff members organized into four divisions (*chu*): comprehensive, oil, coal, and electricity. The comprehensive *chu* was established in 1978. The other three existed continuously since the 1950's. There has been great continuity of technical personnel in these divisions.

Most of the contact between the SPC and the energy line ministries and provinces goes via the people in these SPC Fuel and Power *chu*. Each *chu* has contact with the pertinent ministries. Within each ministry there is a planning bureau, and this is the primary (but not the exclusive) body through which these contacts are maintained. The other pertinent state commissions—the State Economic Commission and the State Science and Technology Commission—also have energy bureaus, with which the Fuel and Power Bureau remains in close contact.

Similarly, each province has a provincial planning bureau, and all of these provincial planning units have at least one person primarily re-

---

[23] Specifically, Huang Yicheng was the vice-minister of the SPC responsible for the Fuel and Power Bureau, the Energy Conservation Bureau, the Communications Bureau, and the two Key Projects Construction Bureaus.

[24] Specifically, the SPC Energy Conservation Bureau drafts long term goals and the annual plan for energy conservation, organizes the construction of the major energy conservation projects, initiates relevant medium and long term research projects, and implements the general mid-1980's policy of substituting coal for oil.

[25] This bureau in 1982 was absorbed into the SPC. Previously, it was in the State Capital Construction Commission.

[26] The National Economy Comprehensive Bureau (*guomin jingji zonghe ju*) could be considered more important in that this bureau determines the overall role that energy should play in the national plan. The Fuel and Power Bureau then takes this general guideline and implements it.

sponsible for energy affairs.[27] The pertinent divisions in the SPC Fuel and Power Bureau maintain close contact with these provincial planning individuals and tap their expertise on the feasibility of doing projects in that locale. For example, the SPC may ask the pertinent provincial planning bureau for relevant information on the displacement of people, utilization of land, and so forth in the construction of a hydropower project in the area.

Thus, the State Planning Commission has its own organizational network that provides it with its "reach" into ministries and provincial governments. As noted above, not all communications go via this network. For many items, the SPC must deal directly with the non-planning bureaus and other bodies in the line ministries and provinces. Similarly, only the minister can represent the ministry as a whole in proposing the ministry's economic plan to the SPC. But the links between the SPC and the planning bureaus is significant, and many SPC personnel have come up through the ranks of the planning bureaus at provincial and ministerial level through the years.

State Economic Commission

The core task of the State Economic Commission is to organize the implementation of the production plans made by the State Planning Commission. The SEC uses its position as a supraministerial organization to solve problems that require coordination among ministries in the process of plan fulfillment. This central concern with production in the mid-1980's drew the SEC into the related areas of technological improvement, management reform, and assuring that adequate raw materials and energy were available to meet plan demands. These latter issues in turn made the SEC an advocate of setting exports of energy and raw materials at a level that permitted meeting domestic production targets. In sum, the SEC became involved in a significant range of issues as an integral part of its mandate to assure that the state plan concerning industrial production was fulfilled.

In general, the SEC is not deeply involved in planning or coordinating the construction phase of plan projects, although some consultations do take place with the State Planning Commission during the course of the planning process. For example, the SEC's Energy Research Institute (formerly under the now defunct State Energy Commission) has participated in long term energy planning and forecasting. It works with the SPC's Bureau of Fuel and Power to forecast energy output targets for the an-

---

[27] Each province decides on the internal organization of its own planning bureau.

nual and five year plans.[28] When the construction phase of a new project is completed, though, assuring the up-to-standard operation of the project is the responsibility of the SEC, working through the appropriate line ministries.[29] Likewise, in foreign trade the major responsibility falls to MOFERT, although the SEC as of 1985 was on the distribution list for preliminary contract terms for major joint venture projects.[30] The SEC becomes more heavily involved only where the matter has direct repercussions for current production, such as is the case with the renovation and technological upgrading of plants done with foreign assistance. The SEC also monitors the export of a raw material to ensure the state plan for the use of that material has been fulfilled. In this latter role, the SEC sometimes found itself in conflict with both MOFERT and the relevant line ministry, which tended to prefer higher levels of exports.

Structure

The internal structure of the SEC changed considerably over time, with the last major organizational change relevant to energy made in 1982. In that year, the State Energy Commission was abolished as an independent organ, and many of its staff of more than 100 moved to the SEC.[31] At that time the SEC created a new Energy Bureau.

Within the SEC, as of 1985 two bureaus dealt primarily with energy. The first was the Production Management Bureau (*shengchan diaodu ju*), which had twenty to thirty people in it. This Bureau directed the entire energy production process on the basis of daily reports. Internally, the bureau had three Divisions (*chu*): coal, electric power, and petroleum. These Divisions settled problems that were basically difficulties in interministerial coordination, for example when questions between the Ministry of Coal Industry and the Ministry of Railways prevented coal from being transported efficiently.[32] Such problems always concern sev-

---

[28] This Institute has also been asked to analyze and make recommendations on energy conservation; to research alternative sources of energy; and to provide information and statistics on the country's energy situation (*China Business Review*, January-February 1985, p. 143).

[29] China in the 1980's began making increasing use of corporations that operate under ministries, a trend strongly endorsed by the SEC.

[30] In the mid 1980's all joint ventures that had more than 100 million U.S. dollars in capital were decided upon jointly by the SPC, the SEC, and MOFERT's Foreign Investment Management Bureau. The SPC played the major role in these deliberations, though, and ventures of this size also had to receive the approval of the State Council.

[31] The State Energy Commission had been housed at the Ministry of Petroleum Industry's building.

[32] This particular aspect of the SEC's work was highlighted when it organized and led an

eral ministries, and the bureau only came in when, for example, the coal ministry could not solve the problem itself. The Production Management Bureau was on call 24 hours a day, and only the toughest problems went there. It had the power to issue instructions to correct a situation.

The second major energy related bureau in the SEC, the Energy Bureau (*nengyuan ju*), was more concerned with policy issues. This bureau worked closely with the SPC's Fuel and Power Bureau, and it gave advice on annual plan formulation. It, in turn, was divided into two parts: production and conservation. The production side had three divisions (*chu*): coal, electric power, and petroleum. These had almost half of the thirty people working in the Energy Bureau as a whole, and they primarily conducted research and investigations on how to push forward policy in energy. For example, they worked on how to raise efficiency, how to lower production costs, and so forth. They worked most closely with the planning, production, and management bureaus (*ju* and *si*) in the Ministries of Coal, Petroleum, and Electric Power. When the three energy line ministries had problems, they reported to the SEC to make an appropriate decision. If it were a policy issue, it went to the Energy Bureau; if a production problem, it went to the Production Management Bureau.

The Energy Bureau's conservation side was in charge of organizing the effort for national energy conservation. Because there are separate ministries of coal, water resources and electric power, and petroleum, however, the SEC need not control everything. The conservation side worked both through the line ministries and through the provincial SEC's to carry out its policies. It had three divisions (*chu*) concerned, respectively, with planning, control (*guanli*), and technology.[33]

In the Energy Bureau, most of the people in the oil, coal, and electric power divisions originally came from the line ministries, where they typically worked for more than ten years before being transferred to the SEC. The ministries want to send persons to the SEC so that they have sympathetic and understanding people there. These people often have worked not only in the ministries but also in actual production. Only a small number of them ever return to the ministries from which they came.[34]

The SEC's Economic Comprehensive Bureau (*jingji zonghe ju*) is also related to energy but does not directly control energy. Rather, it analyzes

---

interministerial delegation to the United States in February 1980 to study how to improve the SEC's ability to coordinate coal production, rail transport, and shipping: *China Business Review* (May-June 1980), pp. 47-48.

[33] The Energy Bureau also had a "comprehensive" section.

[34] The usual career paths of the staff for the Production Management Bureau are not clear.

how to implement the national economic plan, both monthly and quarterly. It works with the State Statistical Bureau to publish economic statistics monthly, quarterly, and annually. Through this work, it also highlights problems in the energy area, as energy constraints are one of the most critical bottlenecks in plan fulfillment.

Outside of Beijing, every province has the equivalent of the energy bureau of the SEC. These are called energy "divisions" (*chu*) or "offices" (*bangongshi*). These have responsibility for both production and conservation. Some have a separate conservation division, but most do not. Different provinces have somewhat different arrangements, depending on how important energy production is in the province. For example, as of 1985 Shanxi province's SEC had an energy division that took charge of all aspects of energy production. Its tasks included production, allocation, sales, transportation, and conservation. On all substantive matters, this provincial energy division looked to the State Economic Commission for leadership. The Shanxi provincial government only made decisions on administrative matters concerning the provincial SEC.

The SEC and Energy Production

As the above overview suggests, the SEC does not play as central a role as does the SPC in the overall determination of energy policy and in the approval and construction phases for new major energy ventures. Nevertheless, the SEC is often of critical importance for enabling an energy project to function effectively, and in addition the SEC does manage to play some well-defined and significant roles in energy policy itself. A review of the SEC's impact on China's energy industry indicates the following areas where the SEC's impact is substantial.

First, once an energy project comes on line, the SEC is the most important body for coordinating efforts among the various ministries to make the project work. In the coal industry, this inevitably involves coordination of production and transport, but it can also entail other matters, such as the assignment of critical equipment to a mine to enable production to proceed smoothly. If necessary, the SEC can order the import of equipment to meet this kind of need. In offshore oil, the SEC (like the Bank of China) has at most only a minor consultative role to play until commercially viable oil is found and the development stage begins. From that point on, however, the SEC is the Chinese unit that assures that adequate cooperation from other ministries is obtained for the oil development effort. In rig construction under joint venture arrangements, however, the SEC formed an Offshore Oil Rig Leadership Group (*haiyang shiyou pingtai lingdao xiaozu*) headed in 1985 by Fan

Muhan to coordinate the work of various units that must contribute to this production effort. Both Ministry of Petroleum Industry and CNOOC representatives participated in this leadership group, as did the other related ministries. The Group brought together all necessary units to map out a plan for the rig construction, and then it helped manage the coordination among these units during the construction process. This Group did not, however, have direct contact with the foreign partner in rig construction.[35]

Given its division of labor with the SPC, therefore, the SEC would not be centrally involved in the Occidental-China National Coal Development Corporation project at Pingshuo, for the Gezhouba and Three Gorges dam projects, or for the offshore oil activities (other than in joint ventures already established to produce offshore rigs and other products for the offshore effort), until each of these projects entered into actual production. Once that point has been reached, however, the nature of the Chinese system is such that none of these projects would be able to operate efficiently without the assistance of the Production Management Bureau of the SEC.[36]

Second, the SEC in the mid-1980's played a significant role in the effort to invigorate Chinese enterprises, and this had potentially important spinoffs for energy. A key element in this effort was to create industrial enterprises in place of the former units which were subordinate parts of ministries and to invest these enterprises with increased autonomy from higher administrative control.[37] In the energy area, concretely this set of policies mandated the SEC to devise ways to increase the authority and autonomy for oil fields vis-à-vis the Ministry of Petroleum Industry and for coal fields with respect to the Ministry of Coal. In oil, the SEC advanced the idea of establishing a national petroleum corporation, with a branch corporation for each oil field. In coal, it supported the conversion of the former coal fields (an administrative level called *kuanwu ju*) to enterprises. The electric power industry is, for technological reasons, inherently more centralized, but even here the SEC became an advocate of greater managerial autonomy at local levels. The SEC is not responsible for deciding the ultimate mix of centralization and decentralization in China's energy sector; that key decision rests with the highest level leaders in the Zhongnanhai. But in the ongoing analysis of these complex

---

[35] This same leadership group played an equivalent role in domestic rig construction.

[36] Chapters Five through Seven provide information on these projects.

[37] The idea was not to create fully autonomous economic organizations, but rather to enhance initiative at the enterprise level without sacrificing the ability of higher administrative levels to control the overall directions of the enterprise.

issues, the SEC during the mid-1980's was responsible for devising ways to increase local initiative and efficiency through decentralization.

Third, the SEC plays a key role in both the technological upgrading of plants and in energy conservation,[38] two efforts that are often closely related. In this capacity, it sets appropriate standards and has an important voice in deciding what equipment and services to import for these purposes. Foreign cooperation in technological upgrading and in energy conservation efforts is more likely to be the result of SEC acquiescence than is the case where foreign firms are seeking to help construct new facilities, which would fall under the responsibility of the SPC.[39]

Fourth, the SEC is centrally concerned with managing production in the face of energy shortages in the country. On the one hand, this makes the SEC sensitive to the need to construct additional energy producing facilities. On the other hand, it also leads the SEC to appreciate the costs of Chinese energy exports. The SEC thus helps to make sure that the Ministry of Coal Industry (or, more concretely, the China National Coal Import and Export Corporation) does not export coal before domestic obligations have been satisfied, and the SEC was likely to argue the Chinese should retain as much oil as possible from any petroleum that is produced jointly with foreign firms.

In sum, the SEC plays a relatively marginal role in the decisions to create new energy-related facilities, but a major role once those facilities come on line. Relatedly, its core tasks of fulfilling the plan and increasing economic efficiency have produced direct involvement with energy-related issues from conservation, to export policy, to management reform, to technology imports, and so forth. In the 1980's, the SEC increased its ability to deal with energy issues since it inherited much of the staff from the former State Energy Commission.[40] At the same time, the SEC's overall approach to its job gradually evolved away from detailed interference in day-to-day operations to more general methods of influencing outcomes.[41] But even with this evolution, the SEC is the single most

---

[38] The SPC is also involved in energy conservation. As noted above, it drafts long term goals and the annual plan for energy conservation, organizes the construction of the major energy conservation projects, initiates relevant medium and long term research projects, and implements the general policy of substituting coal for oil.

[39] The SEC has a Technological Renovation Division (*jishu gaizao chu*) that manages projects to upgrade older plants.

[40] When the Energy Commission was established in 1980, it had drawn most of its staff from the three energy line ministries. The net effect of these bureaucratic changes, therefore, was to move a group of good, experienced cadres from the energy ministries to the SEC.

[41] This evolution was reflected, for example, in the change in policy toward enterprise depreciation funds in the early 1980's. As of 1983, 30% of the depreciation funds went to

important organ for quickly resolving production problems that arise through conflicts among different ministries.

STATE SCIENCE AND TECHNOLOGY COMMISSION

The State Science and Technology Commission has two broad missions: to illuminate the scientific and technological dimensions of the choices confronting China's leaders; and to raise China's own science and technology standards to world levels. With a staff in 1985 of 300 and responsibility for the entire sphere of planning in science and technology, the Commission encourages and uses studies by academic experts and the research institutes of the Chinese Academy of Sciences and the ministries in pursuit of these goals. The SSTC also has a professional relationship with the Science and Technology Bureau that exists in almost every production ministry. Thus, this Commission has a network of relationships which give it great potential in the formulation and implementation of China's energy policy.

The SSTC played a discernible role in energy planning in post-Third Plenum (December 1978) China, with its overall importance gradually increasing. But the SSTC traditionally lacked strong links to the production process, and thus its part in actual energy policy is more modest than that of the SPC, the SEC, and the relevant line ministries (including, apparently, the Ministry of Finance).

The lack of integration of science and technology with production has roots going back at least to the early 1950's, when the SSTC was established on the model of its Soviet counterpart.[42] While it planned research in science and technology, it played little role in turning research results into production processes. This was partly because most new technology in the 1950's came from the Soviet Union, and thus China did not yet rely seriously on its indigenous scientific capabilities for technological advancement. It also stemmed from the fact that the SSTC lacked the funds necessary to set up pilot projects to turn scientific discoveries into economically viable industrial processes.

During the early phase of the Cultural Revolution, the SSTC merged

---

the SEC in Beijing, 20% went to the provincial SEC's, and 50% was retained by the enterprises. In 1984 this formula changed to leave 70% of the depreciation funds in the hands of an enterprise and the remaining 30% with its provincial SEC. This effectively reduced the level of detailed involvement of the SEC in Beijing in enterprise renovation and removed a major monetary resource from the central SEC.

[42] At that time, it was called the State Scientific Planning Commission, which was merged in 1958 with the State Technological Commission to form the State Science and Technology Commission.

with the Chinese Academy of Sciences (CAS). CAS was itself heavily politicized, and in many areas scientific research and development ceased or was seriously impaired. This period witnessed a low point of integration of science and technology and production. The SSTC was only re-established in October 1977. During the following years, however, the top Chinese leadership turned to science and technology as potential keys to rapid economic growth, and the SSTC took on a rapidly increasing burden of responsibilities.

China had no coherent national energy policy during the 1970's. The government, rather, propagated the view that the world energy crisis was a product of capitalist modes of organization and that China could pursue a path of self-reliance in this sphere. A number of scientists working in this area, however, recognized flaws in this approach, and the SSTC provided them with a series of national energy symposia in 1979-1983 by which they brought this more sober analysis to the attention of the highest levels.[43]

The first of these symposia was announced in May 1979 and actually convened that December in Hangzhou, where over 100 experts from various sectors[44] focused on the energy situation. The experts presented data and statistics that essentially detailed the misconceptions that had guided China's leaders on energy policy in the previous few years and made the leadership aware that the country faced potentially serious, imminent energy constraints. A second meeting, attended by more than 270 experts from various government agencies and from 27 provincial level units, convened in December 1980. This meeting focused on the actions that should be taken to meet the country's newly appreciated energy problems. This meeting decided to establish the Chinese Energy Research Association as a non-governmental, professional society that would organize experts from many sectors and disciplines to make proposals on energy policy. This Association was formally sponsored by the SEC and was headed by Lin Hanxiong.[45] A third nationwide symposium met in January 1982 in Zhengzhou, with more than 500 people participating. This meeting considered a broader range of questions, including energy forecasting and planning to the year 2000.

[43] It is not clear to what extent the energy line ministries promoted this effort. As indicated in Chapter Five, at least the Ministry of Petroleum Industry had by this time already decided in favor of seeking substantial help abroad for development of offshore oil.

[44] The main body came from universities and research institutes, although there were also representatives from all major areas of energy production and use.

[45] Lin had been Director of the SSTC's bureau responsible for energy. He then moved over to the SEC, where he again assumed responsibility for energy. He also became head of the Rural Energy Leading Group of the State Council.

The key individual in this effort at basic education and long term planning was Wu Mingyu, who headed the SSTC's Science Policy Research Office and served as Director of the National Research Center for Science and Technology Development. All the detailed work in the series of conferences mentioned above was done under Wu's direction. This effort led to yet another meeting, this one lasting for ten days in March 1983, for which Wu asked more than 200 ministries and independent scholars to submit their proposals. Follow-up work after the meeting produced revised drafts and papers, and these were then forwarded to the State Council's Science and Technology Leading Group.[46] The energy policy paper at this meeting was the responsibility of the Division of Technology Policy of Wu's National Research Center for Science and Technology Development. Finally, in the summer of 1984 the Energy Subgroup of Wu Mingyu's Technology Policy Group of the Science and Technology Office of the SSTC completed a formal draft document for China's long term national energy policy. This group, which was formed in March 1983, reportedly enjoyed excellent access to the highest level political leaders, and the group's leaders used this access to provide overall guidance on national energy strategy.[47]

Through this series of meetings, the SSTC had a role in shaping the perceptions of the leaders and China's overall approach to energy policy during the late 1970's and early 1980's. In addition, during the early 1980's the SSTC became embedded in a web of committees that provided some basis for continuing input into energy decision making, but specific cases of meaningful influence by the SSTC on concrete decisions remained difficult to find. For example, in 1982 the State Council organized a Science and Technology Leading Group with an office in the State Council's Secretariat. While Zhao Ziyang headed this group, the SSTC's Zhao Dongwan took charge of its office. The following year, an attempt was made to overcome the traditional problems of integrating science and technology with actual economic plans by merging the planning bureaus of the SPC and the SSTC. Zhao Dongwan also took charge of this merged bureau, and he became Vice Minister of the SPC as well as Vice Minister of the SSTC. The actual staff of this combined planning bureau, however, moved to the SPC, and on balance this effort did not produce the wedding of science and technology to economic planning that had been hoped.

The SSTC also moved in the direction of exerting some influence on policy toward technology imports, but again concrete results in energy

[46] Details on this Leading Group are provided below.
[47] As of 1985, Wu was a Vice Minister of the SSTC.

development are difficult to identify. Before 1983, the SEC largely controlled technology imports, but in 1983 the government stated that technology imports should become an integral part of China's science and technology policy. The SSTC responded by forming a small group under its Bureau of Development Forecasting to work out the role that the SSTC should play in technology imports. The most likely potential roles were to become actively involved in the formulation of general technology import policy, and to review the importation of some specific key items at MOFERT's request. But neither of these possibilities had been realized as of 1985.

The SSTC did not play a research or policy role in the development of offshore oil. Rather, the China National Offshore Oil Company took charge of the science and technology studies done in this area. Similarly, the SSTC did not play an active role in energy price issues, even though the former SSTC head, Tong Dalin, joined the State Commission on Restructuring the Economic System, which became an important actor on this issue. Nevertheless, the SSTC can undertake studies of issues if major problems arise. In 1984 it utilized this prerogative to begin a feasibility study on the Three Gorges dam, one of a number of feasibility studies on this mammoth project. A vice chairman of the SSTC requested the SSTC's Department of Development Forecasting to do the Three Gorges study. Limited staff facilities in this department made it difficult for a full study to be done expeditiously, but this example illustrates the SSTC's ability to become involved in key energy issue debates if it has the staff time and expertise to do so.

In the early spring of 1985 during the debate over the Three Gorge project that preceeded the National People's Congress (NPC),[48] Vice Premier Li Peng requested the SSTC's Industry Technical Department to undertake a feasibility study of the technical aspects of the Three Gorge project. The SSTC formed a group to do this study with representatives from the Ministry of Water Resources and Electric Power, the Communications Ministry, the Ministry of Agriculture, Animal Husbandry and Fishery, and the Ministry of Machine Building. The plan was to have each of the individual organs participating write up its part of the final report, with the SSTC collating these and discussing them in plenary session. The approved report would then go to Li Peng's Leading Group on the Three Gorges,[49] with any dissenting units permitted to send their separate views directly to the Vice Premier.

In sum, the SSTC is able to mobilize considerable scientific talent and

[48] For details, see Chapter Six.
[49] For details on this body, see the Three Gorges case study in Chapter Six.

is positioned to produce policy-relevant research on important energy issues. The SSTC has, however, remained hampered by difficulties in bridging the gap between research and production, and this has limited its impact on concrete energy decisions. Differences in style and in tasks have also made it difficult for the SSTC to cooperate effectively with the (more powerful) SPC and SEC. Thus, on balance, the SSTC is the weakest of these three commissions in large part because it deals in knowledge rather than material resources. Therefore, the SSTC exercised its greatest influence in terms of affecting the basic perspectives of the leaders about the country's energy position and prospects, thereby having an impact on the PRC's basic energy agenda. The SSTC does participate in discussions of more concrete energy related problems,[50] however, although in most cases no information is available to understand just how influential this effort has been.

Ministry of Petroleum

Few ministries have been as successful, influential, and publicized as the Ministry of Petroleum. Its story from 1960 to the late 1970's was dramatic. Charged with exploring, developing, and producing petroleum and natural gas, it expanded production of this vital resource from 5.2 MMT (*million metric tons*) in 1960 to 104.1 MMT in 1978. This performance was a significant factor in China's overall, impressive industrial growth rate during the 1960's and 1970's. Without it, China's industrialization and drive to modernity would have been severely impaired. It achieved this record through development of the massive Daqing field in Heilongjiang province and the Dagang and Shengli fields in Hebei and Shandong.

Not only did this Ministry turn China from an oil importer into an oil exporter, but its profits enriched the state coffers. From 1960 to 1984, the huge Daqing field, which accounted for well over fifty percent of annual production during that period, turned over 68.1 *billion* RMB in profits and taxes to the state.[51] This was roughly 20 times the value of state investment in Daqing. Since 1966, Daqing led the nation as the factory, mine, or enterprise with the largest finanical payment to the state. As of the mid-1980's, no less than three percent of total revenue which the state earns from all enterprise profits and taxes—the largest single source of state revenue—came from Daqing.

Petroleum exports also became a major source of foreign currency

[50] E.g., on the relative merits of increasing methanol production from coal.
[51] Yao Mingli, "The Past, Present, and Future of Daqing, China," *China Oil*, Vol. 2, No. 1 (Spring, 1985), p. 43.

earnings. In 1960, China spent roughly $150-175 million or about 10% of its total foreign expenditures on petroleum imports.[52] In 1978, it exported 13.6 MMT of petroleum and petroleum products, earning US $1.3 billion or 11% of its total foreign exchange earnings, and in 1985, these figures grew to 29 MMT, US $6.4 billion, 23% of foreign earnings.

Its record from 1960 to the late 1970's and beyond generated an unmistakable sense of elan and confidence within MPI. With its production growing nearly 20 times, its ranks also grew dramatically. Many of its recruits came from the army. Others came from technical schools, and the MPI ran its own petroleum engineering institute. Its newness, rapid growth, and high circulation of leaders and technicians through Daqing and then to other fields made MPI appear less plagued by deeply rooted groupings and cleavages than other ministries.

Through the mid-1980's, MPI was thought to be a good place to work. It reportedly attracted the best and the brightest. As an expanding organization, it offered opportunities for mobility that other agencies lacked. Further, since wages were held constant in the Maoist era, dynamic organizations sought to compensate their employees and to develop an esprit in other ways, especially by providing better services than other agencies. Bureaucrats in Beijing, for example, secure their housing from their Ministry, they take their showers and eat many meals in the canteen at the Ministry, and the Ministry provides access to scarce commodities—television sets, theater tickets, and so on. Since MPI was earning considerable money for the state and was able to retain a portion of its revenue, it was able to provide its employees both in Beijing and outside with somewhat better services.[53]

History

Although the Nationalists had developed a small petroleum industry before 1949, the new communist regime sought to expand production at the Yumen and Karamay fields in the northwest. It also sought to carry out geological surveys to identify other reserves. (Many foreign geologists asserted China was unlikely to have major oil reserves, but Chinese

[52] This crude estimate is based on A. Doak Barnett, *China's Economy*, pp. 459-460 and p. 152.

[53] The life of the workers in the oil fields, however, was harsh and even primitive. Working conditions yielded to the drive for production. Further, the principles governing labor at Daqing in the Maoist era—minimizing the differences between mental and physical labor and between industry and agriculture—meant the staff and workers lived in peasant-type accommodations. The houses did have heat, however, and food apparently was in adequate supply.

geologists disagreed and persisted.) Initially, the petroleum industry was sufficiently small that, as previously noted, it was included as a bureau within the Ministry of Fuel and Power. Not until 1955 was a separate Ministry of Petroleum Industry created. Mao apparently decided to give greater priority to attaining self-sufficiency in this area in 1958 and assigned Deng Xiaoping to be the Vice Premier with special responsibility in this sphere.[54] While the Ministry thus formally grew from the Petroleum Bureau in the Ministry of Fuel and Power, it also drew heavily from the PLA, and its links to the Logistics Department were intimate. The PLA had what is now referred to as the "Petroleum Division" (*shiyou shi*), a unit of about 30,000 troops from which a large number of MPI leaders came.

With the discovery and development of Daqing from 1959 to 1963, the Ministry came into its own. Minister of Petroleum Yu Qiuli, a Long March veteran and long-time soldier, personally led work at Daqing during the winter of 1959-60. He and the others who pioneered the project—such as Kang Shien, Tang Ke, and Song Zhenming—became the leaders of the entire industry. Their political acumen was undergirded by the support of several extremely capable engineers who guided technical activities in the 1960's and 1970's. Yu soon won plaudits from Mao Zedong, and the Chairman encouraged the entire nation to emulate the organizational principles of Daqing. When Mao became disenchanted with the way the SPC was drafting the Third Five Year Plan, he turned to Yu Qiuli to head a new planning group, and Kang Shien was named a member.

The fate of the Ministry and its pre-Cultural Revolution leaders during the tumultuous 1966-69 era is unclear. Yu Qiuli and the other developers of Daqing came under severe attack, and a new set of officials took charge. Zhou Enlai played a major role in protecting Yu from humiliating purge and incarceration, arguing that Yu enjoyed Mao's confidence. We believe the Ministry, as many others, fell under the control of the PLA, with the Logistics Department playing a prominent leadership role. As the power of Lin Biao ebbed, the group around Yu Qiuli reasserted itself, suggesting that Yu had ties with personal networks in the PLA that were rivals of the network led by Lin Biao. In general, it appears that MPI did not suffer as severely during the Cultural Revolution and its aftermath as most other ministries. It appears to have been less plagued by the intense factional strife which plagued other minis-

[54] This information comes from a very knowledgeable Chinese official. Deng reportedly held this responsibility until the Cultural Revolution. Confirmation of Deng's role is in Ministry of Petroleum Industry, "Zhongguo shiyou gongye de jueqi," in *Guanghui de chengjiu* (Beijing: People's Press, 1984).

tries. The precise reasons for its comparatively more fortunate fate are unclear. Possibly its newness, prior success, and esprit made the Ministry less vulnerable to the fragmentation that affected others. In 1966-69, the Ministry was not riven by groups who had risen from different locales of Ministry activity, a source of intra-ministerial factionalism which plagued other ministries. Its prior, intimate relations with the PLA may have been helpful. That it enjoyed Mao's prior blessing no doubt was a factor, as was the strategic importance of its product. MPI still suffered from the Cultural Revolution, but because it proved to be more cohesive, it was able to recover from the turmoil of that period with greater rapidity.

In any case, by 1971-72, the pre-Cultural Revolution leaders of MPI had more than recouped their losses. The Ministries of Coal and of Chemical Industries had been merged with the MPI, with petroleum officials dominating the conglomerate ministry. Moreover, Yu Qiuli became head of the SPC. Until early 1979, the Chinese economy essentially was led by former officials of the Ministry of Petroleum and by former associates of Yu Qiuli, after which their influence began to diminish. By late 1985, the group only retained a strong grip over the Ministry of Petroleum, and its influence had eroded in such ministries as Chemical Industries, Metallurgy and Coal and in the comprehensive commissions.

During the period of its ascendancy, the Ministry exhibited a robust spirit. In the 1960's, it was at the forefront of the policy of national self-reliance. In the 1970's, it spearheaded policies aimed at high growth rates. From the mid-1970's through the 1980's, it pioneered the policies of importing foreign technology and equipment, exporting natural resources, and forming joint ventures. Paralleling developments in Western countries, though for somewhat different reasons, the Ministry exerted enormous influence over the entire economy and, as its production soared and world prices rose, it extended its control over other industries. But when in the mid-1980's prices softened and production levelled, its position weakened.

Structure

Compared to most other ministries, MPI is highly centralized.[55] At headquarters, it has the usual staff bureaus of finance, foreign affairs, planning, capital construction, personnel, education, and science and technology which have liaison with the relevant commissions and ministries.

[55] For an excellent description of MPI's structure, see David Denny, "China's On-Land Oil and Gas Organizations," *The China Business Review* (January-February, 1985), pp. 30-36.

It also has such operative bureaus as transportation and marketing, supplies, drilling and engineering equipment manufacturing, oilfield development, and geological exploration. These bureaus directly lead subordinate units in various oil and natural gas fields.

The fields themselves are obviously large units. MPI as of 1985 had at least ten oilfields with bureau-level status (Dagang, Daqing, Jianghan, Karamay, Liaohe, Renqiu, Shengli, Sichuan, Yumen, and Zhongyuan). The heads of such fields report directly to the Minister or Vice Minister. While for some issues, such as personnel decisions, the oilfields enjoy some administrative autonomy, and while as of the mid-1980's the oilfields seemed to be gaining additional authority, on most matters, the oilfields operated under tight central control. With some variance from field to field, MPI retains particularly tight reins on equipment purchases and production targets. In its assessment of the structure of MPI, the influential World Bank report gently recommended, "Greater autonomy for regional companies may need to be considered, including increased flexibility for exploration, development, and production activities and for contracting of domestic and foreign services."[56]

MPI as of 1985 had several corporations under its leadership which could deal directly with foreign companies: the China National Oil and Gas Exploration and Development Corporation, the China National Oil Development Corporation (CNODC), and the China National Offshore Oil Company. All had intimate relations with MPI. They shared personnel and used some of the same services, such as a data processing center. CNOGEDC, the oldest of the three, purchased equipment and services for onshore survey and development. Quite active in the 1970's, it was heavily intertwined with MPI and in some respects served as a front for it. Its leaders at that time, especially Zhang Wenbin and Qin Wencai, pioneered its cooperation with the outside world. Initially, CNOGEDC was the lead Chinese agency in negotiating various cooperative arrangements with the outside world for offshore activity, including the signing of contracts with Japanese and French consortia and with ARCO for exploration in the Bohai and Yinggehai. With the creation of CNOOC in 1982, these contracts were transferred to the new body. In fact, a substantial portion of CNOGEDC personnel and bureaus were moved to CNOOC. In the mid-1980's, however, CNOGEDC renewed activity in connection with exploration and development of reserves in northwest China. The China National Oil Development Company was created specifically to engage in joint ventures in ten southern provinces onshore,

<hr>

[56] World Bank, *China: Long Term Development Issues and Options* (Washington, D.C.: Johns Hopkins University Press, 1985), Annex Three: The Energy Sector, p. 48.

while CNOOC (described separately below) was established for the off-shore joint ventures.

Organizational Locus

The organizational locus of MPI determines some of its natural bureaucratic rivalries. MPI shares with the Ministry of Geology (MOG) the responsibility for seismic surveys and gathering of geological data. The boundary between these two ministries is not clearly drawn, and the jealousies between them are considerable. Each hoards data from the other. The MOG is understandably proud of its accomplishments and capacity, and it resented the curtailment of its seismic exploration responsibilities in the offshore areas with the turn to the foreign oil companies to undertake this work. In the mid-1980's, it began to establish its own commercial links with foreign businesses. MOG has also been at the forefront in pioneering scientific exchanges with foreign geologists. It is not a nativistic organization.

MPI depends upon the Ministry of Machine Building as a major supplier of equipment. MPI has become an arbiter between its oilfields, which frequently prefer more sophisticated and higher quality foreign equipment, and the Ministry of Machine Building and the trade companies under the Ministry of Foreign Economic Relations and Trade, which seek to preserve the domestic market for indigenous products and thus to minimize foreign imports. As of 1985, MPI had a list of petroleum equipment for which it could authorize foreign purchases; MOFERT had a list for other equipment under its control. The Ministry of Machine Building tended to claim that it could supply equipment of comparable quality, although it, too, on occasion imported manufacturing technology for key oilfield equipment.

To a limited extent, MPI competes with alternative energy ministries for budgetary allocations and project authorization, but the SPC and MOF make such adjustments incrementally and at the margins. MPI, the Ministry of Water Resources and Electric Power, and the Ministry of Coal expect to obtain the same spending authorization as the previous year, plus some growth, and the competition among the three largely is over the allocation of the increment.[57] This competition among competing energy projects is not just an issue of developing alternative energy sources. At stake too is the spatial development of the nation, as the

---

[57] The narrow annual fluctuations in the percentage of the state budget devoted to capital investments in petroleum is in *Zhongguo tongji nianjian 1984* (Beijing: Chinese Statistical Press, 1985), p. 311. About 11% of total state investment in industry was devoted to petroleum. The high was 12.9% in 1981, and the low was 9.7% in 1982.

alternative energy projects in coal, oil, and hydroelectric power usually are in different provinces and benefit different regions. The choices are fought out among provinces as much as among MOC, MPI, and MWREP.

The most important downstream consumers of MPI as of 1985 were MOFERT, which handles the export of petroleum, the military, the Ministry of Chemical Industry and SINOPEC, the vertically integrated petrochemical corporation, and the MWREP. MPI does not decide on the allocation of its product, however. Basically, this is a decision of the State Council and the SPC.

Finally, MPI depends upon the Ministry of Communications and the Ministry of Railroads to transport its product. The Ministry of Communications is responsible for pipeline construction, harbor facilities, and shipping. However, the decisions about whether petroleum will be processed near the oilfield or will be shipped—and if so, by rail or pipeline—are not made exclusively within MPI. These are primarily SPC decisions.

Thus, the SPC looms large in determining the fate of the MPI. Yet, we sense that the Ministry has a different relationship with the SPC than does the Ministry of Coal. Our research has identified instances where the SPC has overturned proposals from MCI, but we have not identified a case where MPI was as clearly rebuffed. Within its web of organizational connections, MPI must be seen as a ministry that at least through the mid-1980's wielded clout and influence.

Issues

The Ministry must wrestle with a number of technologically complex issues that fall within its domain. Perhaps the nature of these issues helps to explain the reluctance of the non-experts to intrude on its domain. These issues include:

— which promising geological formations to explore through test drilling;
— which proven reserves to develop on a priority basis;
— how to develop a proven reserve, particularly balancing the rate of recovery against the total recovery;
— what balance to strike between exploration and development of new fields vs. secondary and tertiary recovery of existing fields.
— what price to charge for crude petroleum and what depreciation allowances to permit in calculating the cost of extracting this non-renewable resource;

— what role to permit foreign governments, oil companies, and banks to play in developing and producing oil in China;

— what priority to give to development and use of natural gas resources;

— what use to make of crude petroleum—plastics, synthetic fibers, fertilizer, fuel, generation of electricity, etc.

Each of these issues is both highly technical and highly political. This means MPI is involved in the decisions, but ultimately, the SPC and the State Council decide the issues. We have already touched upon the most important of these issues—how much to invest in the survey, exploration, and development of reserves. Foreign observers uniformly believed annual investments, which averaged about $2 billion per year through the mid-1980's, would have to double or even triple in order to meet production requirements in the future. This is a decision for the State Council.

MINISTRY OF COAL

Probably no ministry is more important to the economic development of China than is the Ministry of Coal. The reason for its centrality is simple: coal is China's leading fuel, providing nearly 75% of China's inanimate energy supply. Roughly 75% of electricity is generated in coal-fired thermal plants. China's huge, proven coal reserves mean that into the 1990's and beyond the energy industry will continue to be based primarily on coal, and as scientists improve techniques for employing coal hydro-carbons as feed stock for the chemical industry, the importance of coal is likely to increase.

Mission and Spirit

The objectives of the Ministry are easily stated.[58] It is responsible for the survey, exploration, development, and production of coal. Given the nature of coal—in scattered deposits, neither easily extracted from the earth nor a uniform substance, possessing many impurities (such as ash and sulphur), bulky and difficult to transport—the mission of the Ministry is formidable. Probably few economic ministries face as nettlesome a set of issues as does the MCI. Also, few equal the MCI in total size and in extent of involvement in many provinces.

The MCI is a ministry with diverse tasks and skills, and its "spirit" or

[58] Perhaps the best single source on the Ministry of Coal Industry is *China Coal Industry Yearbook* (Hong Kong: Economic Information and Agency, 1985).

ethos is therefore not easily summarized. It sets policy guidelines for thousands of small-scale coal mines, where conditions are primitive, and it directs large-scale mines with modern technology. As of the mid-1980's it was in the process of developing open pit coal mines of huge size and also ran underground mines that date back to the 1800's. Its leading technicians mirror the history of modern China: some elderly technicians trained either in the West or in Western-influenced universities in China before 1949; others trained in Japan or under Japanese tutelage in Manchuria; yet others trained in the Soviet Union and Eastern Europe in the 1950's and 1960's; still others trained in Chinese institutions in the 1960's; and a few more were exposed to the West and Japan in the 1970's. Its mine districts are total societies, not only managing coal mines and designing, testing, and participating in the manufacture of mining equipment but running schools, hospitals, housing projects and providing services to staff and miners.

To judge from the mainland press, the Ministry suffered from intense factional strife during the Cultural Revolution. Production fluctuated from 1966 to 1976. Apparently, the "Gang of Four" perceived the Ministry to be heavily influenced by Liu Shaoqi and his associates, and it felt the intense scrutiny and wrath of the radicals. Suicides were not uncommon within the MCI, apparently including the Minister. The central Ministry headquarters in Beijing were closed. The Ministry merged with the Ministry of Petroleum and Electric Power to form the Ministry of Fuel and Power located in the building of the former Ministry of Petroleum. The disruptions, deep divisions and scars of those years healed slowly.

Adding to the distinctiveness of the Ministry is its age. The Ministry was newly created in 1949, but the coal industry itself is of ancient vintage, with a rapid expansion under British and Belgian aegis at the Kailuan mines in Hebei and Japanese-directed mines in Manchuria. Customs and practices probably arose from that era which have been the object of change under communist rule but which partially persist to the present day.

In short, the Ministry is best characterized as diverse: serving many external agencies, embodying many traditions of different origin, pursuing many tasks, and containing many types of units within. It is therefore not an easy ministry to unify and lead. These characteristics make its production record all the more impressive. Coal production grew from 32 million metric tons in 1949 and 66 million metric tons in 1952 to 354 million metric tons in 1970, 482 million metric tons in 1975, and over 800 million metric tons in 1985. Indeed, one suspects the diversity of the Ministry helps explain this success, for the Ministry must encompass the ability to advance coal production under widely differing geological and economic circumstances.

Setting in the System

Formally—as with all ministries—the Coal Ministry is under the State Council, and its Party Group is under the Central Committee. The Vice Premier who as of 1985 included the MCI in his domain was Li Peng. Various facets of the Ministry's economic activities must be coordinated with the State Planning Commission (concerning setting the five-year and annual plans and initiating and pacing the construction of major capital construction projects), the State Economic Commission (concerning implementation of the annual plan), the Ministry of Finance (concerning setting the budget), the Ministry of Foreign Economic Relations and Trade (concerning import of foreign equipment and technology and arranging joint ventures with foreign firms), and the People's Bank and the Bank of China (concerning credit and obtaining foreign currency). Within each of these agencies are specialists who deal with MCI matters, while the MCI has its specialists who are familiar with the relevant external agencies. In many instances, these agencies must concur in the plans of the MCI. If irreconcilable differences emerge, the MCI and the contending agency can appeal to the State Council for resolution of the issue. In this, the MCI is similar to the other energy line ministries.

The Ministry is nestled within the web of ministries on which it depends and which, in turn, depend on it. The boundaries between these adjacent ministries are not clearly drawn, and these ministries are thus both natural allies and sources of annoying difficulties. The Ministry of Geology is responsible for broad geological survey work, identifying areas for more intense coal survey. MCI relies on the Ministry of Railways to transport the bulk of coal. In many places, particularly Shanxi, the existing railway network as of the 1980's is severely stretched to move coal. Both the existing tracks and coal cars are insufficient, and the competition among mines for the available space is intense.

Thus, MCI looks to the Ministry of Railways (and the SPC) to expand its capacity to move coal. Meanwhile, the Ministry, its provincial departments, and locally run mines also use trucks and highways to deliver some coal. For example, it is economical to move a portion of Shanxi coal to nearby provinces by truck, thereby generating links between the MCI and its subunits, the Ministry of Communications and its subunits (which are responsible for expanding the nation's highways), and the truck manufacturing industry. Planning and coordination between the MCI and the transportation sector, however, is not always adequate.

The chief consumers of coal are the Ministry of Railways and its bureaus (to fuel locomotives), the Ministry of Metallurgy and its corporations (primarily for coking coal), and the Ministry of Water Resources and Electric Power (for coal-fired thermal plants—the single largest consumer of MCI production). At local levels, coal is consumed in large quantity by various small-scale industries and in household heating.

Within such a complex setting, the success of the Ministry depends upon maintaining successful relations with its many partners and upon retaining the confidence of the top leaders. In this regard, the Ministry on balance has been rather successful.

Provincial cooperation is necessary to develop a major field and maintain its production. Obtaining the land, providing services, and securing some unskilled labor require cooperation between the MCI and the province, and the province in return secures some revenue from the field.[59]

Issues

The Ministry has consistently confronted a number of substantive, interrelated issues which are worth enumerating. Policy on these issues has varied considerably through time, and these issues are likely to remain on the agenda for the foreseeable future. Policy is not exclusively set by MCI, although the Ministry participates in the policy making process. Rather, most of these issues have been decided at the State Council or Party Central Committee level. Such agencies as the SPC, SEC, Ministry of Finance, and MOFERT have significant voices in the setting of these policies:

1. The *administered price* of coal, which has remained basically constant since the mid-1950's, and which many Western observers believe is too low;
2. The relative emphasis and priority to be given to the development of large, medium, and small-scale mines; relatedly, the priority to be attached to mechanization and mine safety;
3. The administrative and financial control over mines, particularly whether certain large mines are primarily under central or provincial leadership;
4. The relative emphasis to be given to tunneling and opening of new mines versus production in existing mines;
5. The extent to which mining equipment should be internally produced versus purchased abroad, and if purchased abroad, what

[59] See Chapter Seven for details.

types of technology and what country's equipment should be purchased;

6. Where the relative emphasis should be placed in development of coal: the northeast, the northwest, the east, or the south, and how much importance should be attached to development of coal versus other energy resources;

7. How labor in the mines should be organized and how wages should be paid;

8. What flexibility should be incorporated into the plan, how much autonomy mine and district managers should have, and to what extent coal can be produced outside the plan and sold at negotiated prices;

9. How much attention should be given to coal preparation—washing and cleaning of coal—in order to enhance energy yields and to reduce pollution.

In fact, this is only a partial and simplistic listing of the issues contained in the newspapers and journals of the coal mining industry. There is no "ideal" solution to these issues. Any particular policy has both beneficial and harmful consequences, and, as the objective situation changes, policies on these different issues evolve. What can be said, however, is that the policies on these many, diverse issues have considerable consequences for the internal structure of the MCI and/or for its relations with other ministries. For example, any decision to increase the administered price of coal produced in the large scale, centrally controlled mines would immediately and adversely affect the profit margins of the MCI's main consumers; or an emphasis on expanding production in small-scale, locally controlled mines would adversely affect China's effort to improve environmental standards (since scattered mines make coal preparation more difficult), but this emphasis would also yield more revenue to county and township governments. To understand China's coal industry therefore requires tracing the organizational implications of policies in each of the issues listed above.

Internal Organization

There is basic division of responsibility among Vice Ministers, but this is not rigid. Frequently, Vice Ministers travel to mines on business. While one Vice Minister is gone, another covers his field. As of 1985 there was one Vice Minister in charge of management: this includes material supplies, finance, coal distribution, wages, and labor. A second Vice Minister took charge of production and sources: this specifically includes production, science and technology, machine building, and coal processing. A third Vice Minister controlled construction: including survey design, capital construction, geological surveys, and coal mine construction. The fourth Vice Minister was in charge of planning, education, and the internal organization of the Ministry. In addition, organizational reforms in the early 1980's resulted in appointing one chief engineer and three deputy chief engineers for the Ministry as a whole.

In addition to the usual bureaus within the central ministry (Personnel, Planning, Finance, and Foreign Affairs), the MCI contains several important functional bureaus: Capital Construction, Locally run Mines, Mechanized Mines, Coal Utilization, Safety Supervision, Production, and Machine Building. As of the mid-1980's it directly led over twenty large coal mining districts such as Kailuan in Hebei, Datong in Shanxi, Fushun in Liaoning, and Pingdingshan in Henan, and exercised professional guidance over the Departments of Coal in the provinces. It runs a Planning and Design Institute in Beijing and shares in the leadership of eight other design institutes with the Provincial Coal Departments. It sponsors the Central Coal Mining Research Institute with eleven research institutes and staff of 5,000. It directly operates twelve institutions of higher learning and twelve secondary technical schools. It is, by any definition, a huge ministry.

MINISTRY OF WATER RESOURCES AND ELECTRIC POWER

The Ministry of Water Resources and Electric Power embodies two quite different types of agencies which coexist within one ministry. The electric power side exerts close operational control over the vast majority of electricity production in the country. It runs both the generating plants and the major power grids and thereby produces revenue for the state budget. The water resources side, by contrast, vests a large part of both design and operating responsibilities in local units. The ministerial level concerns itself more with matters of broad policy and with pursuing its mandate within the politics of the capital. This portion of the ministry does not have large production enterprises, employing thousands, under its direct control, nor is it a major revenue earner. It does, however, direct the work of large construction agencies which employ tens of thousands of people.

The MWREP is also a special amalgam in that the two aspects of the Ministry have contact with different portions of the Chinese bureaucracy. Most of the electricity in China is generated in coal (the vast majority) or oil-fired thermal plants. Hydropower accounts for a relatively small percent of the country's electric generation. Hence, the electric power agencies have close liaison with the coal and petroleum industries, as well as the transportation agencies which move those commodities (especially the Ministry of Railways).

The water resources people have a mandate that extends well beyond construction and supervision of hydroelectric projects. The water resources system is responsible for flood control, irrigation, drainage, and—in some instances—transportation, as well as hydropower, and these tasks bring the water resources people into close contact with the Ministry of Agriculture[60] and Ministry of Communications (which supervises river transport). Moreover, the major locus of concern of the two agencies is significantly different: the water resources people concentrate on harnessing China's major rivers, while the electric power people are pressed to supply adequate electricity to the industrial centers of the country.

Further, dam design, construction, and utilization involve striking a balance among these different but interrelated end uses. For example, the water resources people may advocate an accelerated discharge of water stored in upstream reservoirs so as to leave ample capacity to store water in case of flood. This, however, risks leaving an inadequate supply of water for electric power generation from these hydropower facilities. This tension is also brought out in different attitudes toward the construction of the Three Gorges dam on the Yangtze above Yichang. This dam would serve a major role in flood control but would take at least fifteen years to complete. Many electric power people as of the mid-1980's preferred initial construction of smaller dams on tributaries to the Yangtze. These would have far less impact on flood control, but they would generate some badly needed new electric power far more quickly (although some areas would not be beneficiaries of the upstream dams).[61] Thus, the 1982 marriage of the water resources and the electric power bureaucracies produced a hybrid ministry with what the Chinese would term unusually prominent "contradictions" within it.

Why, then, were these contending units thrown together? Twice since 1949, first in 1958 and then again in 1982, this hybrid ministry was constructed out of the previously existing separate Ministries of Water Resources[62] and of Electric Power.[63] The decision to amalgamate different

[60] Since 1982, formally called the Ministry of Agriculture, Animal Husbandry, and Fishery.

[61] See Chapter Six for details.

[62] The name of this ministry was officially translated as the Ministry of Water Conservancy. When it was merged with the Ministry of Electric Power, the official translation changed to "Water Resources" (without any corresponding change in the Chinese term,

ministries almost always is the result of complex considerations, and no single reason can explain it all.

One contributing factor in both 1958 and 1982 may have been the notion by top leaders that more resources should be poured into hydropower development. The 1958 merger came at a moment when major hydropower projects were being planned on the Yangtze River, the Yellow River, and the Han River, and it was thought that hydropower would eventually produce more than half of the country's overall power by 1972.[64] These projects highlighted the importance of integrating planning for water resources and for hydropower development. In reality, however, the initial hope to increase substantially the percentage of electric power generated by hydropower was dashed with the problems encountered in the operation of some key projects,[65] long delays in the completion of other key projects due to shoddy workmanship during the Great Leap Forward,[66] and the inability to reach final agreement to proceed on still other core projects.[67] In the December 1981 Fourth Session of the Fifth NPC, just two months before the second merger of these ministries, Premier Zhao Ziyang announced that China should "gradually place its emphasis on hydropower."[68]

---

shuili, involved). We use the term "Water Resources" throughout here, as the ministry's functions have all along gone beyond the flood control that the original translation implies.

[63] The first joining of these ministries ended in February 1979 for reasons that are examined in detail in Chapter Six. One element in this change was that the water resources people chafed under the dominance of the electric power side. That dominance, in turn, probably stemmed from two sources: the above noted fact that the electric power side exercised operational control over subordinate units while the water resources side played more of a strictly policy role; and the fact that the electric power side generated a great deal of revenue, while the water resources side did not.

[64] Li Rui, "It is Necessary to Develop Hydropower on a Priority Basis," *Renmin Ribao,* (March 6, 1980).

[65] E.g., Sanmenxia on the Yellow River, which ran into such severe silting problems that eventually some of its generators were transferred to other dams: Barry Naughton, "The Economy of the Cultural Revolution: Military Preparation, Decentralization, and Leaps Forward" (Paper prepared for the "New Perspectives on the Cultural Revolution" Conference, Harvard University, May 15-17, 1987), p. 9.

[66] E.g., Danjiangkou on the Han River, whose completion was delayed more than ten years because of the poor quality of concrete used during construction in 1958-61. See Hong Qingyu, "Dui Danjiangkou shuili shuniu ruogan wenti de kanfa," *Renmin Changjiang,* No. 4 (1982).

[67] Most notably, the Three Gorges on the Yangtze River.

[68] *Shuili fadian,* No. 8 (August 12, 1982). This stricture was reflected in plans to have hydropower account for roughly half of the new electric power generating capacity brought on line during the 6th and 7th Five Year Plans. Hydropower would, according to plan, grow to about 25% of total electrical power generation by the year 2000. A knowledgeable Chinese official attributed the 1982 merger to another factor: the persistent bickering be-

In the re-amalgamation of the ministries, a delicate balancing act was performed. Qian Zhengying, the highly respected and well connected former Minister of Water Resources, became the head of the new ministry. Li Peng, who had headed the Ministry of Electric Power, within a little over a year was promoted from Vice Minister of the MWREP to Vice Premier, with responsibility for (among other things) the work of the new MWREP. Of the five Vice Ministers as of mid-1985, the first ranking Vice Minister (responsible for providing overall assistance to the Minister) was Zhao Qingfu, from the electric power side; and the second ranking Vice Minister (in charge of water resources) was Yang Zhenhuai, from the water resources side.[69] The various bureaus generally remained unchanged, and only the bureaus concerned with such matters as personnel and welfare were actually merged.

In sum, the MWREP's two basic component parts have both overlapping and somewhat competing operational missions, different types of relations with subordinate units, different financial profiles, and different career paths for their officials. The resulting internal tensions are a natural outgrowth of these fundamental features.

The electric power sphere, and especially its hydropower component, presents particularly contentious issues in any case in China. One major issue in electric power concerns the allocation of the grossly inadequate electrical output. In broad terms, electrical output as of 1985 could meet only eighty percent of the needs of the country's industrial plant, and therefore power shortages forced significant underutilization of industrial facilities. The meetings held each year to set priorities for allocation of electrical power during the following year are reportedly exceptionally contentious. Few resources that the central government distributes are as important to the provinces and the industrial ministries as is electric power.

Within the realm of electric power generation, hydropower presents

---

tween the Ministry of Water Resources and the Ministry of Electric Power during 1979-81 that had to be resolved at the State Council level. The State Council reportedly eventually became so annoyed at this constant irritation that it put the two ministries back together so that future disputes would have to be decided within the merged ministry. A ministry is supposed to present a unified "ministerial" position to the State Council in the Chinese system. In any case, this second merger coincided with a more widespread effort to merge ministries (and reduce the number of coordinating State Council Commissions). The Ministries of Water Resources and of Electric Power must have seemed natural candidates for merger, given their previous history and plans to try again to increase the percentage of electricity generated by hydropower.

[69] The other three vice-ministers, in order of rank were: Lu Youmei, responsible for hydropower; Zhang Fengxiang, in charge of thermal power; and Yao Zhenyan, who oversaw capital construction.

particular problems. Construction of a hydroelectric dam displaces the population above the dam, with a higher dam resulting in more displacement and more loss of arable land. The MWREP itself, however, cannot undertake the resettlement work, as it is not equipped to do so. Rather, this onerous task falls on the province(s) where the people formerly lived. But often these provinces are not themselves the primary beneficiaries of either the electrical power or the flood control benefits of the hydropower project. Given their critical role in resettlement of population, however, they have a major voice in new dam construction.

Other concerns are also involved in major dam development. The Ministry of Communications may be affected by the temporary disruptions in the river transport system (although it may welcome improved upstream navigation after the dam is completed), and it often also has ideas about the specifications for the new locks which differ from those of the water resources planners. The reservoirs created by dams often submerge more than agricultural land, and these other losses affect additional ministries (with their particular responsibilities).[70] Indeed, the MWREP is dependent on cooperation from many other ministerial and provincial units for progress in hydropower development. The list of such units typically includes the provincial and local governments where the dam will be constructed; the Ministry of Communications, which must work out transport problems; the Engineering Corps of the PLA, which assists in construction; the Ministry of Machine Building Industry, for machine design for the interior of power plants; the Ministry of Geology and Minerals for geological studies; the State Seismological Bureau for seismological studies; other state agencies for data on flooding, hydrology, and meteorology; and other ministries, determined by the resources in the area that is to be submerged by the dam's reservoir.[71] In addition, the acquiescence of the Ministry of Agriculture and of the local Bureau of Fisheries should be obtained.[72]

[70] For example, the MWREP's plan for construction of the Shuikou Hydropower Station in Fujian would submerge a rail line, among other things. The State Planning Commission therefore ordered the Ministry of Railways to work out plans and budget estimates to relocate the railroad and to submit these as part of the planning for this project. The SPC also asked Fujian province to plan and make budget estimates for the relocation of the populace necessitated by this project. See *Fujian Ribao*, September 7, 1983.

[71] This list is incomplete in that it leaves out the other units, such as the State Planning Commission or the Ministry of Finance, which must provide support for *any* large construction project. The size and location of a dam project substantially affect the number and range of ministries and other units whose cooperation is required.

[72] On the latter, Anhui's Fishery Bureau managed to create a significant obstacle to progress on the Three Gorges project in the early 1980's because it felt that construction of a fish ladder would be needed to preserve the Yangtze River sturgeon in the face of this dam

In short, the development of hydropower is inherently a highly complex and often controversial undertaking. Both benefits and costs are high, and, typically, long lead times are involved before any of the benefits become available. In China's accounting system as of the mid-1980's, all costs for a new dam (including those for communications and other aspects of a multi-use approach to the dam) were charged to the MWREP for the dam construction, which added to the potential tensions inherent in deciding when, where, and how to build a major new dam.

The above factors combine to give the MWREP a distinctive set of challenges. MWREP decision makers face competing interests, reconcile contradictory responsibilities, and establish difficult balances and trade-offs, and officials there speak more readily in terms of problems and tensions than do officials in other ministries. Given the range of concerns which must be accommodated, many major decisions in the MWREP are not decided easily or smoothly. It is, in this sense,[73] a highly political ministry.

The water resources and the electric power sides of the MWREP differ sufficiently to warrant providing a separate description of each.

MWREP's Water Resources Component

The water resources side of the MWREP takes the coordination, guidance, and encouragement of the national effort to prevent floods, improve drainage, provide steady water supplies, and reduce vulnerability to drought as its major priorities. These efforts are managed in a decentralized fashion, as the two major "legs" of the water resources side of the MWREP are outside of Beijing. The first of these "legs" is the river valley commissions. The other is the design institutes.[74]

The river commissions work out overall plans for the development of river valleys. As of the mid-1980's, six such commissions existed, responsible respectively for the Changjiang (Yangtze),[75] Pearl, Yellow, Hai, Songliao and Liao (combined commission), and the Huai Rivers. Of these, the first three commissions were the most famous. The initial task of each such commission is to develop an overall plan for the whole river

---

construction. The step ladder idea was dropped only when it was determined that this would not be an efficacious way to accomplish this goal. New dams also sometimes create opportunities to develop new fish breeding industries.

[73] Not in the sense of being highly factionalized or very leftist.

[74] Although the former Ministry of Electric Power also had design institutes, these remained separate under the merged ministry.

[75] The body responsible for overall planning for the Yangtze was unique in that it was an "office" rather than a "commission." The history behind this anomaly is provided in Chapter Six.

basin. At the same time, each commission has a design capability, and the commission may itself do the design work for a few of the major projects it recommends.

For example, the Yangtze Valley Planning Office, in its earlier incarnation as the Yangtze Valley Water Conservancy Commission, during 1955-57 surveyed the entire length of the river and developed an outline plan for the several-stage development of the Yangtze and its major tributaries. Informed Western observers report that these commissions see their tasks primarily in terms of flood control. Since proposals for specific dam projects do not originate with the MWREP in Beijing but rather come from the plans developed by these commissions, the commissions' emphasis on flood control is reflected in the views of the water resources people of the MWREP.

The water resources side of the MWREP also has regional design institutes (called the "Hydropower Investigation and Design Institutes") in the Northeast (Changchun), East (Hangzhou), Northwest (Xian), Central-South (Wuhan), and Southwest (institutes in both Chengdu and Kunming). These institutes belong to the Water Resources and Hydroelectric Power Construction Corporation under the MWREP, which is the body actually responsible for most hydropower dam construction.[76] These design institutes undertake work related to construction of hydropower projects anywhere in the country. Their work is assigned to them by the MWREP. These are the core bodies for planning and designing a hydroelectric project.[77] The design institutes make the site selection, undertake initial designs, and carry out the feasibility studies. Once the State Planning Commission has approved the feasibility study, the pertinent design institute begins to develop final blueprints.[78] One design institute assumes responsibility for any given dam, but it may contract out part of the work to other design institutes.[79] These design institutes are staffed primarily by engineers, and they do not consider the financial dimensions of the projects they propose to be their central responsibility.[80]

---

[76] This Corporation also has fourteen hydropower construction bureaus under it.

[77] The same is true for the role of the design institutes on the electric power side in terms of thermal power plants. There are "Electric Power Planning and Engineering Institutes" under the Central Electric Power Planning and Design Institute in North China as well as in the other five regions (the East China institute is located in Shanghai rather than in Hangzhou; all the others are in the same cities as are their hydropower counterparts).

[78] Actual construction of the dam may begin before these final blueprints have been drawn up if investment funds for the project are released.

[79] For example, the Chengdu Institute had overall responsibility for the Ertan dam on the Yalong River, but it utilized the Nanjing Institute for work on the hydraulic gates for this project. The Nanjing Institute is particularly strong in hydraulics.

[80] In addition, there are several Hydrology Engineering Research Institutes under the

Overall, the MWREP and the design institutes are generally effective in planning flood control projects. But this same structure makes multi-use planning for river development quite difficult. For that, the State Planning Commission must arrange for input from each of the relevant ministries. Not surprisingly, it is difficult to obtain results that optimize the various potential uses of a river through this type of process.

The construction of a hydropower project is organized at the Center by the MWREP's China Water Resources and Hydroelectric Power Construction Corporation, and actual dam construction involves organizing a complex institution. Since dam construction often involves very large numbers of workers on the site for a long period of time,[81] the MWREP often must provide housing, schooling, medical facilities, and other support services to supplement what local authorities can provide. To carry this out, the MWREP both uses its own construction bureaus and calls on construction teams from the PLA for much of this work.[82]

Funding for dam construction is provided in annual installments according to a schedule determined by the SPC. While this funding schedule is worked out on the basis of the project-specific construction timetables proposed by the MWREP, the MWREP nevertheless is permitted to shift money among different construction projects as it sees fit. The MWREP finds that this annual disbursement often creates problems because its funds frequently become available at a rate that differs from the optimal rate of construction. The MWREP would thus prefer for the Ministry of Finance to pay out the entire funds for the project at the commencement of the effort.[83]

MWREP's Electric Power Component

As noted above, the electric power component of the MWREP is far more centralized than is the water resources side. China as of 1985 had thirteen power grids, of which six major ones were under the direct control of the MWREP and seven smaller ones were under provincial control. Each province has its own Electric Power Bureau, which is under the dual leadership of the provincial government and the MWREP's power grid that

---

MWREP—the two most prominent of which as of 1985 were located in Beijing and Nanjing. Also, every province and regional power grid has its own research facilities.

[81] The Chinese tend to use larger construction corps than would American firms doing comparable projects. For example, the Gezhouba Dam project in the middle reaches of the Yangtze involved nearly 50,000 Chinese workers and dependents during the early 1980's, a multiple of the number that would build such a dam in the United States.

[82] See, e.g., Hu Yaobang's remarks in *Sichuan ribao*, October 9, 1982.

[83] The Ministry of Finance has opposed this method, for it would thereby relinquish its control over the pacing of construction.

encompasses that province. This dual structure is necessary because many provinces feed local power into the MWREP's main grids.[84]

The electric power side of the MWREP is basically responsible for producing the vast majority of the inanimate energy which is consumed in China. This includes not only hydropower but also power generated by burning coal and oil. The ten electric power design institutes under the MWREP do essentially the kind of work on thermal power plants that their counterparts on the water side do for hydropower projects.

The electric power side of MWREP generates a great deal of revenue, and it is under constant pressure to increase the amount of electricity it can deliver to end users. This involves both new construction and efforts to improve the electrical transmission system, which currently loses excessive amounts of current.

In general, the electric power people often prefer thermal plants to hydroelectric ones and smaller hydropower stations to larger ones. These preferences stem from cost and time factors. Thermal plants are less expensive to build than are dams, and they come on line more quickly. Smaller dams have these same advantages over larger dams. Also, thermal plants are preferable to hydropower because the facility is solely dedicated to electricity generation, and thus its output is relatively reliable and controllable. Hydropower projects suffer in several respects. Their water levels may have to be manipulated for flood control purposes, with adverse effects on electricity generation. Also, changes in water availability and the need to leave room for additional water storage both mean that the facility often performs at less than its maximum capability. Very large hydropower facilities, moreover, may require generators that are so large that they cannot be used effectively in the rapid and finely tuned way that is necessary to meet peak load demands in a complex set of power grids. All of these factors tend to mean that the views of the electrical power people depart somewhat from those of the water resources people.[85]

Conclusion

The above analysis highlights the challenges which are inherent in the MWREP, and make the many achievements of the Ministry even more noteworthy. Differences between the water resources and the electric

---

[84] As of 1984, altogether 1,574 of China's 2,137 counties had built their own small hydroelectric power generating stations, and 774 of them relied primarily on small power stations for electricity. Many counties formed their own electric power grids (Xinhua, April 6, 1984).

[85] Including those who specialize in hydropower.

power people typically cannot be resolved on technical grounds alone. This stems in part from the administered price system which reduces the efficacy of cost-benefit analysis of competing alternatives in power supply. The prices for electric power were set region by region in China in the 1950's, based on the mix of power generating facilities then available. As a result, prices in the 1980's do not accurately reflect either the cost of power production or the real mix of sources available for power generation in each region. Beyond this, of course, as in any country, cost estimates for hydroelectric power projects are difficult to make due to the long investment lead times, the uncertainties of future prices, and the unknown problems that can be encountered during construction. A result of this difficulty in resolving matters on technical grounds is that the non-technical people within the MWREP play a very strong role in decision making there.

Another important aspect of the MWREP is that the water resources side is highly decentralized. The strong role and geographical identification of the design institutes and river valley commissions mean that authority often resides outside Beijing, and foreign observers have reported that the various institutes and commissions sometimes do not cooperate well together. The fact that large hydropower projects inevitably require the active (and often reluctant) cooperation both of other ministries and of a number of local governments simply multiplies the problems. The result is that very often the SPC or the MWREP must form *ad hoc* "small groups" that cut across normal administrative boundaries in order to plan for and undertake large scale projects.

The typical policy cycle in the development of a hydroelectric project is as follows. A river valley commission or a design institute is asked to work out a plan for the overall development of a river.[86] That body then proposes an overall development plan, which is sent to the MWREP—and from there to the SPC and, possibly, the State Council—for approval. This is called the *guihua*, or long term planning, stage. Next, the design institute proposes specific construction projects. For each of these, the initial design is sent to the MWREP and from there goes to the SPC. This organ then conducts a feasibility study, which may entail asking related organs to do necessary studies.[87] Approval for the project brings

---

[86] At the same time, the Ministry of Communications and other organs may be asked to work out their own plans for the river.

[87] A good illustration of this stage was provided by *Fujian ribao* on September 7, 1983: "In order to complete the preparatory work for the initial construction stage of this large-scale, broad-scope hydroelectric power station, the State Planning Commission recently issued a notice calling on all involved departments and Fujian Province to determine, according to the relevant State regulations, an economic responsibility system and divisions

with it preliminary funding. This is called the concrete planning, or *jihua*, stage. At this point, actual construction may begin, while the design institute works up the final design blueprints. This final design proposal again goes back through the MWREP to the SPC for approval, in the *sheji*, or design, stage. The design institute then works out a detailed plan for actual construction, which again goes through the MWREP to the SPC. During these last two phases, the MWREP has arranged for

---

of labor with individual responsibilities. The notice made clear delineations: The Ministry of Water Resources and Electric Power will be responsible for surveys and designs, the quality of construction and progress of the work, overall project budget estimates, and the economic results; the Fujian Provincial People's Government will be responsible for planning and making budget estimates for the flooding of the reservoir area and the relocation of the populace, coordinating these efforts with the aforementioned ministry; working out the plans and budget estimates to relocate the railroad within the reservoir area and the construction work involved will be the responsibility of the Ministry of Railways; preliminary designs for the Shuikou Hydroelectric Power Station, plans to relocate the railroad, models and designs for dams to accommodate shipping and log rafts, overall project budget estimates, etc., must be submitted to the State Planning Commission for review and approval. No construction personnel will be dispatched until the proposed item has been placed officially on the agenda.

The notice calls upon the Ministry of Water Resources and Electric Power, the Ministry of Railways, the Ministry of Communications, the Ministry of Posts and Telecommunications, the Ministry of Forestry, and the Fujian Provincial People's Government to make careful examinations and strict budgetary studies. Initial phase work on the power station will be undertaken with a view to conserving funds, reducing the construction time, and pooling experience and resources with priority given to project quality and safety."

Another example, concerning the Yantan power project on the Hongshui, was presented as follows: "Under direction of the State Planning Commission, a meeting to appraise the preliminary plan for the Hongshui He Yantan Hydropower Station was held in Nanning September 9-16, 1983 with participation by the Ministry of Water Resources and Electric Power, the Guangxi Zhuang Autonomous Region, and other related departments. Specialists, professors, and engineering and technical personnel from Qinghua University, the Ministry of Geology and Mineral Resources, and the Geological Research Institute of the Chinese Academy of Sciences were also invited to the meeting. After listening to reports, making on-the-spot surveys and holding group discussions, the conference felt that the Guangxi Electric Power Bureau Survey and Design Academy had done a great deal of work and that the proposed achievements basically suited preliminary design requirements. The conference basically agreed with the revisions of the preliminary design for the Yantan Hydropower Station proposed by the Guangxi Academy and the pivotal overall arrangements and organizational plans for construction that were made by the Bureau of Water Conservancy and Hydropower Construction and the Planning and Design Academy in April-June 1983, and examined the overall budget estimates, the plans for moving people from the reservoir area and other special topics. The comrades at the meeting felt that the Yantan Hydropower Station should be made a project for development in the near future according to the plans for the Hongshui He that were approved by the State Council. The construction conditions are now mature, and based on the needs of electrical power development in the South China region, the power station will be included in 1984 state plans and construction will formally begin," *Shuili fadian* no. 2 (February 12, 1984).

work to start on the project by engaging an MWREP construction bureau, a provincial construction company, and/or the services of a construction corps from the PLA. The SPC continues to release funds in annual installments for the project. While the design institute leads the work at the site, the SPC continues to play an active role in coordinating the many non-MWREP units that must cooperate to bring the project to fruition. This is all part of the *shigong*, or construction, stage.[88] Each of these project stages brings into play a somewhat different set of interests and policy dynamics.

For all of its difficulties and complexities, the MWREP is a very important ministry. Its leaders are competent and influential. Of great importance, both the water resources and the electric power components of this ministry are engaged in activities that are recognized as being of central importance to China's economic growth. The fact that the electric power side makes this contribution in a more direct, day-to-day way and that it is also a major revenue generator for the central government probably helps make this the stronger of the two MWREP components.

This ministry is constrained in its dealings with foreigners because it does not earn foreign exchange from its domestic activities.[89] It has, therefore, limited authority to engage services and purchase equipment from abroad without approval from other agencies. This situation may ease slightly in the 1990's, as China begins to sell electricity to Hong Kong. Also, in May 1985 the State Council decided to permit private development of electric power generating facilities, with variable rates to reflect market forces being charged for the resulting electricity. This decision was very likely made in part with a view to creating a framework for foreign equity participation in power generation.[90] The Ministry benefited during the mid-1980's, in any case, from the considerable foreign interest and willingness to extend loans and project assistance for construction of hydroelectric and thermal power plants. Nonetheless, the problem of a lack of foreign exchange precludes having this ministry interact with foreign interests to the extent that the Ministry of Petroleum Industry has done so.

[88] These various stages are detailed in Chapter Six on the Three Gorges Dam project.

[89] The MWREP does have a China International Water and Electric Corporation that earns some foreign exchange through technical consulting and the export of skilled workers abroad, especially to the Middle East, Africa, and Southeast Asia. These activities do earn some foreign exchange. It has, therefore, limited authority to engage services and purchase equipment from abroad without approval from other agencies. This situation may ease slightly in the 1990's, as China begins to sell electricity to Hong Kong.

[90] Xinhua, June 4, 1985.

MINISTRY OF FINANCE

The Ministry of Finance grew from a small organization of fifty to sixty cadres drawn from the pre-1949 Finance Department of the North China People's Government to a unit that plays a vital role in revenue generation, budgetary expenditures, and planning for the entire economy.[91] It has functioned for most of the time since the early 1950's under the influence of five key individuals: Chen Yun, Li Xiannian, Yao Yilin, Wang Bingqian and Wu Bo.[92] As of 1985, Chen Yun remained an important presence in finance work, but Yao Yilin and Li Xiannian turned largely to other matters, while Wu Bo had retired. Nevertheless, the guiding philosophy and priorities of these five individuals provided a strong center of gravity for the Ministry as it tried to guide the financial side of China's economic development.[93]

The core principle of this guiding philosophy can be summed up as the need to ensure an ongoing set of three balances: between financial revenues and expenditures; between credit allocations and receipts; and between supply of and demand for materials. As a recent volume edited by two authors from the Ministry of Finance summed up, "Our country's historical experience proves that balance in revenue and expenditure is an indicator of national economic stability, and without a balance in revenues and expenditures there will not be sustained stable development of the national economy."[94]

The Ministry of Finance has seen itself as the guardian of the state's ability to maintain the above three balances in the face of multifaceted

[91] A brief organizational history of the Ministry of Finance is available in Li Cha, *Zhonggong shuishou zhidu* (Kowloon: Union Research Institute, 1969), pp. 70-76.

[92] Chen Yun has had a consistent interest in finance and has been the highest ranking of these five individuals. Li Xiannian from 1954 to 1975 was the leader primarily concerned with operational management of finance in his concurrent roles as Minister of Finance and (until the Cultural Revolution) as head of the State Council's Fifth Staff Office (in charge of finance, trade, and food). Yao Yilin is close to Chen Yun and as of 1964 headed the Central Committee's Finance and Trade Political Department. Wang Bingqian was identified as director of the Budget Bureau of the Ministry as early as 1963. In 1968, when the Logistics Department of the PLA took over control of the Ministry of Finance, the Military Control Commission in the Ministry had to rely heavily on Wang's expertise. Wang had become vice minister by 1973 and served as minister starting in 1980. Wu Bo became Vice Minister of Finance in 1954, was the ranking Vice Minister for many years, and was Minister of Finance in 1979-80.

[93] Li Xiannian, it should be noted, was perhaps less firm in his commitment to the principles enumerated below than were Chen Yun, Yao Yilin, Wang Bingqian and Wu Bo, as suggested by Li's continued political strength even during periods of Mao's most radical policies.

[94] Xu Yi and Chen Baosen, eds., *Caizheng xue* (Beijing: Chinese Finance and Economics Publishing Company, 1984), p. 279.

challenges. This has made the Ministry *de facto* a strong supporter of maintaining a key role for the centrally planned sector of the economy and perhaps produced less enthusiasm at the Ministry than has been evident elsewhere for foreign borrowing, decentralization of foreign trade, and rapid expansion of foreign trade.[95] Large energy projects are, by their nature, the types of undertakings that usually fall within the state plan, and the Ministry has an interest in seeing China's energy bottleneck overcome. Thus, the Ministry has no evident reason to oppose either large investments in energy development or the utilization of foreign capital and technology in this sphere. It does, however, approach this issue from the perspective of the guiding philosophy just outlined.

Structure

The internal organization of the Ministry of Finance conveys the scope of its operational responsibilities and provides a guide to the ways in which it becomes directly involved in energy policy deliberations. As of the mid-1980's, the key relevant bureaus (*ju* and *si*) within the Ministry are:

— Basic Construction Finance Bureau (*jiben jianshe caiwu ju*): takes charge of funding for planned capital construction. Funds for construction are actually distributed by the Construction Bank, but this bank is under the Ministry of Finance and allocates funds according to the state plan.
— Offshore Tax Bureau: in charge of developing the taxation system for offshore oil.
— Budget Bureau (*yusuan si*): divided into sections that handle, respectively, the central government and the provincial budgets. The staff of each of these sections is, in turn, functionally divided along ministerial or provincial lines.
— External Finance Bureau (*waishi caiwu si*): established in 1978, this bureau obtains foreign credits from the World Bank or other sources.[96]
— Industrial Finance Bureau (*gongye caiwu ju*): administers all fi-

[95] Trade with other socialist countries does not pose the same problems for the Ministry, as this trade is normally done on a barter basis and is controlled by the central trading organizations. It is also carried out according to annual and longer term plans.

[96] The MOFERT's No. 4 Division under its Foreign Investment Management Bureau then implements the World Bank loans within China in terms of putting items for procurement under these loans out for bids, typically through China Technical Import Corporation (Techimport). The Bank Of China then takes care of actual disbursements of World Bank funds to various Chinese agencies.

nancial transactions among the industrial ministries. This bureau is internally organized by ministry. One division (*chu*) within this bureau is in charge of coal, oil, and electric power. It has fifteen people and deals directly with the pertinent line ministries, not the provinces.

— Administrative Finance Bureau (*xingzheng caiwu ju*): takes charge of governmental administrative expenses.

— Comprehensive Balance Bureau: makes recommendations to the Minister of Finance on the overall balance that should be struck among the various proposals from different industrial ministries.

— Law and Contracts Bureau: scope of responsibilities unclear.[97]

In addition to these constituent bureaus within the Ministry, there are other "independent" organs that operate under the direct leadership of the Ministry. The most important of these in terms of energy policy is the Taxation General Administration (*shuiwu zongju*), which is responsible for tax policy. This unit also works out the expected revenues based on the SPC plans, and figures out how much revenue should come from each ministry and province during a plan year.

Like the State Planning Commission, moreover, the Ministry of Finance has its own network of bureaus embedded in other central ministries. Thus, each ministry has a Finance Bureau, and this bureau maintains close contacts with the Ministry of Finance. The Ministry of Finance can be in direct touch with other bureaus in another ministry, but for most purposes the pertinent Finance Bureau provides the channel for communications and information. There are also Finance Departments (*ting*) under each provincial government, which again provide points of contact between the central ministry and the provincial units. These provincial finance bureaus are generally organized along the lines of the Ministry of Finance, with modifications and simplifications in accordance with local economic conditions and needs.[98]

The above brief organizational data are sufficient to highlight the extraordinarily wide scope of the Ministry of Finance's responsibilities. The Ministry is the only organ that has solid information on the availability of revenues, and this puts it in an important position when funding for new projects is being discussed.[99] Ventures that come on stream are

---

[97] There are also other bureaus in the Ministry of Finance that are less pertinent to this discussion, such as those in charge of financial affairs regarding agriculture, accounting systems, culture and education, and so forth.

[98] For an example, see: Li Cha, *Zhonggong shuishou zhidu*, p. 76.

[99] China's Ministry of Finance does not, however, have nearly the power attributed to

subject to taxation according to the regulations drawn up by the General Tax Administration under the Ministry's aegis. This has been an important factor in energy policy in the mid-1980's, as attested to by the delicate discussions required to develop tax laws for offshore oil that would permit American companies to credit these taxes against their US tax obligations.[100] Pertinent officials from the Ministry of Finance, therefore, participated in the China National Offshore Oil Corporation's negotiations with foreign firms that led to the contracts for exploratory drilling off the China coast. The Ministry's External Finance Bureau is the body assigned to raise credit from abroad, and its World Bank Division has the legal responsibility to supervise the use of World Bank funds, including those for energy projects. This division as of late 1985 was understaffed, but it (along with the pertinent line ministries) monitors the Bank's projects and maintains contact with the Bank on them. Finally, the Ministry of Finance exercises ongoing control over budget expenditures and plays a major role in the annual budget debates that produce the yearly fiscal budget and material allocations plan.

Financial Planning

In broad terms, China's planning process requires judgments on both physical capabilities and budgetary possibilities. The SPC is the key body in charge of the former and tries to determine which projects are both desirable and within the country's ability to construct. As explained in the section on the SPC, that organ then also plays a critical role in coordinating the actual construction of major projects.

Because it manages the state's revenues and expenditures, the Ministry of Finance's central concern in the planning of new projects is to gauge the project's effects on the national economy and to ensure that the state's limited funds are adequate to meet the plan objectives. While the SPC attempts to establish overall plan priorities, the Ministry of Finance is responsible for determining how much money will be available for plan implementation. This determination in turn affects the judgments about priorities themselves.

Feasibility studies were added to this process in the early 1980's, when the experience with the Baoshan steel mill, the problems associated with

---

most such ministries by Aaron Wildavsky in his cross national study, *Budgeting: A Comparative Theory of Budgetary Processes* (Boston: Little, Brown and Company, 1975). This *relative* weakness of China's finance ministry probably reflects the preference the top leaders have given to central planning in physical commodities.

[100] *See*, for example, the seminar the Ministry's Offshore Oil Tax Bureau convened in Beijing with foreign specialists in October 1984 (Xinhua, October 15, 1984).

upgrading the Wuhan steel complex, and the construction of Gezhouba, combined with foreign encouragement, convinced the top leaders of the need for such analyses. The country's price system makes conduct of financial feasibility studies a difficult and uncertain task at best.[101] Nevertheless, increased attention to both physical and financial feasibility studies inevitably injected the Ministry of Finance more directly into deliberations over key energy projects.

For example, the Three Gorges project has been debated since the mid-1950's, but it was only in 1982 that the Ministry of Finance was asked to undertake a financial feasibility study for this huge item. The resulting study, still in progress as of 1985, made use of several sets of prices and complex calculations to analyze the ramifications of the Three Gorges dam for the national economy, including such concerns as its effects on regional economic development. On balance, however, the central concern of the Ministry in this study appeared to be to the effects on the entire economy of committing such large sums of investment capital to one project that would not begin to pay back the investment for at least ten years.

The actual economic plan that emerges is the product of a complex process. Generally, most line ministries and provinces tend to portray their needs for funds as pressing, their ability to use new funds as strong, and their capacity to generate funds as limited. They develop project proposals and submit them to the SPC for analysis and approval. The Ministry of Finance, though, must go over the draft plan from the SPC with a view to its financial feasibility and implications. Not surprisingly, the perspectives of the three major participants in this process (the line ministries and provinces; the SPC; and the Ministry of Finance) often differ as to both the revenue and expenditure implications of their proposals. Typically, moreover, the economic norms and models available to the planners are not sufficiently refined to permit these differences to be resolved on the basis of purely technical criteria.

In the Maoist era,[102] the key forums for resolving the differences among these various groups in the annual planning cycle were generally the National Planning Conference and the National Finance Conference that were usually held in the late fall, often simultaneously (and with some representatives from each sitting in on the other). Since not all problems could be solved at these meetings, a central work conference

[101] This is, of course, to some extent true in all countries, regardless of the pricing system. In major dam projects, for example, a financial feasibility study must monetize such items as reduction in loss of life from flooding. The resulting figures are necessarily somewhat arbitrary.

[102] But not at times of the greatest leftist radicalism during Mao's reign.

that brought together provincial Party first secretaries as well as Politburo members and other key officials usually met to reach final decisions on particularly contentious issues. The Politburo itself met separately to determine its position, where necessary. There is some evidence that under Zhao Ziyang the National Planning Conference began to convene earlier in the year, but otherwise this process remained largely unchanged. Therefore, the final balance to be struck in the plan is worked out at a political level (a central work conference or the Politburo), with the fate of individual projects determined by the level dictated by the importance and scale of the project.

The Ministry of Finance and Energy Policy

Given its responsibilities and organizational structure, in concrete terms how has the Ministry of Finance become involved in energy policy? There are several channels through which it plays an important role in energy-related matters.

On the broadest level, the Minister himself has on occasion exercised major influence in nudging the general thrust of China's economic policy in directions that had important implications for energy policy. The Ministry of Finance also enters into energy policy decision making directly in a range of more specific ways. First, as of the mid-1980's major projects must receive the approval of several different organs, the exact list varying with the scale and substance of the project. All large-scale energy projects include the Ministry of Finance on this approval list, as the Ministry must assure that adequate funds are available to enable the project to be completed and operated successfully. Where there is foreign involvement in the project, MOFERT asks the Ministry of Finance for its opinion on the proposed undertaking. In this capacity, the Ministry of Finance has been one of the critical organs that bring domestic economic considerations to bear in judging the value of a potential foreign investment in China.

On a policy level, also, the Ministry of Finance in the early 1980's took a strong position on the need for China to understand the costs associated with absorption of foreign technology. Its own studies of the country's experience in the late 1970's indicated that China would have to be prepared to spend four *renminbi* in the process of utilizing every U.S. dollar worth of technology and equipment it imported. In addition, the Ministry focused attention on the importance of having projects generate adequate foreign exchange to repay hard currency debts that had been incurred in constructing the project. The Ministry's position on these issues evidently contributed significantly to China's backing away from the expansion of imports that had occurred in 1978-79.

The Ministry of Finance is important in a range of ways in foreign energy-related investments. As noted above, the Ministry assumes responsibility for raising foreign credits from international financial institutions where these are appropriate. The amount of foreign credit needed is, of course, a function of the projects approved in the state plan, and actual administration of the foreign loan is generally undertaken either by MOFERT or by the Bank of China.[103] But as of the mid-1980's it was the Finance Ministry that actually acquired foreign credits from the World Bank and other external funding sources. The External Finance Bureau of the Ministry, established in late 1978, became the specific unit in charge of this.

As noted above, the 1980 Baoshan steel experience combined with other issues to make China's leaders place great stress on conducting feasibility studies for proposed projects. This move toward feasibility studies had the effect of broadening the number of participants with potentially significant input into decisions on major projects, and the Ministry of Finance began to play a larger role in project deliberations as a result of this development. Within the Ministry, the Comprehensive Balance Bureau and the Finance Research Institute often are the key organs that organize these feasibility studies. They may draw on the expertise of other relevant bureaus in the Ministry, and they report their recommendations to the Minister to act upon. The Comprehensive Balance Bureau, rather than the Industrial Finance Bureau, is put in charge of this because, unlike the specialized bureaus, its staff members are not closely linked to the line ministries. It is therefore more able to make overall judgments about the appropriateness of a project supported by one of these ministries.

The Ministry's impact on energy policy is, of course, not limited to projects involving foreign cooperation. The Ministry's responsibility for the budget implications of policy give it a potentially important role to play in price decisions on category I goods (goods whose production and distribution are determined by the state plan). Typically, the Ministry is asked to produce an analysis of the direct and indirect effects of changes in price on these goods. For example, energy products such as coal from the centrally-run mines are on the category I list. Informed Westerners believe the Ministry of Finance during the mid-1980's opposed price increase requests by the Ministry of Coal Industry. The Coal Ministry

---

[103] The authors have received somewhat conflicting information on this point from the two organizations concerned.

argued that it should be granted a price increase because the price of coal in most other countries was rising. The Finance Ministry insisted that the Coal Ministry, instead, justify its case based on its own cost and production data, which the Coal Ministry was unwilling to do. The resulting standoff produced a continuation of the low price of "central" coal.

As indicated above, during the construction phase of a project on the state plan, the Construction Bank under the Ministry of Finance controls the flow of investment funds for the project. During the 1950's the Bank released all project funds right at the start, but by the mid-1980's it had adopted a posture of paying out funds in coordination with the construction schedule itself. Once an energy project comes on stream, its financial operations come under the jurisdiction of the Industrial Finance Bureau of the Ministry of Finance. As noted above, this Bureau's staff members are subdivided into divisions, one of which is concerned with coal, oil, and electric power. The fifteen staff members of this bureau deal directly with the finance bureau people in the relevant line ministries. They do not, though, deal directly with finance bureau staff in the provinces. Rather, these provincial financial staff are divided along functional lines, and they deal with the relevant line ministry rather than with the Ministry of Finance's Industrial Finance Bureau itself. Finally, the Ministry of Finance's role in tax policy and in the development of the state plan obviously affects the fate of domestic energy projects as well as that of energy projects involving foreign cooperation.

To sum up, in a broad sense the Ministry's overall fiscal caution provides part of the policy framework within which energy development efforts must take place. On balance, then, the Ministry of Finance has been a force that encourages a larger role for the state planned sector of the economy and a cautious approach to the use of deficits and imports of technology and capital from abroad. In a range of ways, the Ministry of Finance's considerable authority and responsibilities have enabled it to ensure that these general preferences have affected China's energy policy.

MINISTRY OF FOREIGN ECONOMIC RELATIONS AND TRADE

The Ministry of Foreign Economic Relations and Trade was established in March 1982 out of a merger of the State Import and Export Control Commission, the Foreign Investment Control Commission, the Ministry of Foreign Trade, and the Ministry of Economic Relations With Foreign Countries. The consolidation of these units brought the major components of China's dealings with the international economy under one bureaucratic roof. After its inception, however, MOFERT existed in a rap-

113

idly changing policy environment, with many central ministries, provincial governments, and national corporations increasingly claiming independent authority to work in the international economic arena.

MOFERT Responsibilities

MOFERT perceives its mandate to be to implement the policies of the Central Committee of the Chinese Communist Party and the State Council concerning China's economic relations with the outside world. Important principles of that policy since 1949, in spite of the vicissitudes in Chinese foreign trade, have included ensuring that China's trade, aid, and joint ventures serve the national interest (instead of particularist interests within China), assisting China's economic development, and not leading China to be subservient to foreign countries. More specifically, the leaders of China have sought, as an ideal, a rough balance of trade with each of their trading partners and the minimum necessary dependence on externally supplied raw materials and commodities. The Ministry believes that to attain this mandate, Chinese trade, aid, and joint ventures must develop in an orderly, coordinated, and well supervised fashion. Competition and price-cutting among provinces over scarce foreign markets which MOFERT believes reduce Chinese profits and the purchase of foreign equipment when perfectly adequate domestic supplies exist are two practices, for example, which MOFERT considers undesirable.

MOFERT's formal responsibilities encompass seven broad areas. First, it implements the state plan with respect to foreign trade. To carry out this task, MOFERT mostly relies on the specialized trading corporations (such as Machimpex and Techimport) that it inherited from the Ministry of Foreign Trade. These corporations negotiate and sign contracts with foreign buyers and sellers on behalf of Chinese producers and end users. These contracts are sought in accordance with categories and items on the annual state plan, and the necessary foreign currency and bureaucratic approvals are ensured because of this fact.[104]

Second, in addition to the state plan, MOFERT tries to enhance the overall size of China's foreign trade along the general lines of current policy (such as to promote exports over imports). In short, MOFERT engages in trade promotion activity as well as working to implement purchases and sales mandated by the state plan.

Third, MOFERT's Foreign Investment Management Bureau (*waiguo touzi guanli ju*) manages both foreign direct investment in China and

---

[104] This state plan for foreign purchases and sales is not made public.

loans from foreign governments and from mixed government and private sources. It also plays a role in supervising the bidding process through which Techimport purchases goods on World Bank loans.

Fourth, the import and export of all items that require licenses are handled by MOFERT, via its Foreign Trade Control Bureau.

Fifth, MOFERT plays a role in the development of foreign trade rules and regulations as well as in the implementation of these requirements.

Sixth, MOFERT provides a range of expertise and advice pertinent to the implementation of China's international economic dealings. In this, the pertinent bureaus of MOFERT seem to function in much the same capacity as U.S. State Department regional bureaus might when they provide expertise necessary to the development and execution of American foreign policy. MOFERT's three regional bureaus[105] provide advice on geographical strategies in trade. They also give advice to other MOFERT units on specific trading partners and conditions in the countries under their respective jurisdictions. MOFERT's Technology Import and Export Bureau provides policy oriented advice on technological matters. Through its studies, it makes judgments on whether China needs to import a particular technology, whether the PRC is capable of absorbing the technology, and which sources of the technology should be sought out. MOFERT's Treaty and Law Bureau provides advice on pertinent regulations and legal issues. MOFERT's International Trade Research Institute and its International Economics Institute undertake policy relevant studies.

Finally, MOFERT is involved directly in a range of discrete activities such as dispensing foreign aid[106] and contracting with foreign countries for the use of Chinese labor abroad.[107] China's leaders, through a series of economic reforms in the 1980's, sought to reduce the scope of the central plan, to alter the administrative authority of many central level ministries (curtailing their internal powers but occasionally expanding their foreign trade authority), to encourage local bureaucratic initiative, and to increase the use of market forces. This produced a great deal of uncertainty among the agencies involved, with the result that MOFERT's trading corporations, to some extent, compete with various local bodies (both government bureaus and enterprises) and with the corporations under other ministries for control over trade and investment ac-

---

[105] As of 1985, the First Regional Bureau dealt with the USSR, East Europe, North Korea, and Indochina; the Second Regional Bureau dealt with Africa, West Asia, non-communist Southeast Asia, and Japan; and the Third Regional Bureau dealt with the Americas, West Europe, and Australia and New Zealand.

[106] Via MOFERT's Bureau of Foreign Aid.

[107] Via the Foreign Contract Labor Cooperation Bureau.

tivities. In a few clear instances, trade authority was transferred from MOFERT to other agencies. For example, after a period of contention, in 1982 the Ministry of Coal Industry's Coal National Import and Export Corporation was granted the exclusive right to import and export coal.

In most other instances, however, the boundaries remained unclear. For example, oil fields under the Ministry of Petroleum Industry began trying either to purchase equipment directly from foreign suppliers or to make such purchases through non-MOFERT organizations, such as the Everbright Corporation based in Hong Kong. MOFERT's Machimpex, however, as of 1985 still controlled a major share of the business in this rapidly changing sector. Similar tensions occurred in many areas, and policy—probably reflecting the differing inclinations of national leaders—continually shifted between greater centralization (under MOFERT trading corporations) and more decentralization (to the other units) during the mid 1980's.

In the area of managing foreign loans and financing for joint venture projects, there appears to be some overlap, and, according to foreign observers, some competition among organizations. Here, the Bank of China and MOFERT's Foreign Investment Management Bureau are two key actors.

MOFERT and Energy Policy

With these responsibilities MOFERT affects that portion of China's energy policy which involves foreigners. The Vice Minister in charge of energy matters at MOFERT as of 1985 was Wei Yuming. The regional, technical, and legal advisory bureaus may steer the PRC's business toward one or another supplier or market or may raise legal and technical issues that affect particular transactions. The ability of MOFERT's trading corporations to survive and prosper during the decentralizing reforms affects the channels and personnel used by the Chinese side in energy-related trade activities. MOFERT's management of the international bidding for World Bank financed energy projects (and any bidding for other projects financed by foreign government loans and aid, such as the Tianshengqiao dam project on the Hongshui River) give MOFERT an important role to play in the allocation of these energy-related funds.

MOFERT is also involved with direct foreign investment in China's energy development. The major portion of MOFERT's activities dealing with direct foreign investment is undertaken by its Foreign Investment Management Bureau (FIMB), whose approximately eighty staff members as of 1985 largely came from the former State Foreign Investment Control Commission. The FIMB has two parts. One manages foreign government, mixed public and private, and international agency loans. The other investigates, approves, and to some extent oversees joint ventures involving private foreign corporations.

The second part of the FIMB helps organize the Chinese units to negotiate a project that involves direct foreign investment. It may participate in the negotiations itself.[108] In any case, the FIMB investigates a joint venture contract to make sure it meets all Chinese policy and legal requirements. FIMB approval (including approval for any loans that are a part of the project financing) is necessary for all projects above a value that varies from province to province. As indicated above, under certain circumstances MOFERT might also become directly involved in project financing itself. The FIMB plays a role in monitoring a project to make sure it works well and conforms to original contract terms.

The 5 March 1983 24th Meeting of the Standing Committee of the National People's Congress made MOFERT responsible for investigating and approving all aspects of joint ventures.[109] Concretely, before a contract is signed the FIMB studies the contract terms and circulates twenty to thirty copies of the contract both to other pertinent MOFERT bureaus and to relevant non-MOFERT bodies. For large projects, these latter typically include the SPC, SEC, Bank of China, Ministry of Finance, the relevant line ministries, the Law Department of Peking University, and other units. The FIMB stipulates a date by which they must have reviewed the proposed contract, and then they attend a meeting to discuss any problems they have with it. Although the FIMB is responsible for arranging this meeting, it does not always attend it.

The meeting of interested parties provides a forum for each unit to raise its concerns about the proposed contract, but in the final analysis it is the FIMB that has the responsibility to approve the contract or demand specific changes in its terms. The FIMB bases its decision on whether the terms, conditions, arbitration language, etc. of the contract comply with China's applicable laws, regulations, and current policy. The FIMB often turns to the services of MOFERT's Treaties and Law Bureau and of its

---

[108] The FIMB as of 1985 typically did not participate in negotiations for projects under ten million US dollars. Its participation in negotiations for projects worth ten to one hundred million US dollars depended on whether the project involved very advanced technology or was of particular importance for some other reason. The FIMB, along with the SPC, participated in negotiations for projects worth over one-hundred million US dollars, but in these it was the SPC that had the greater authority to approve or turn down the draft contract.

[109] Actually, this NPC decision only gave all the powers regarding joint ventures of the former State Foreign Investment Control Commission to MOFERT to exercise (*FBIS*, March 7, 1983, p. K-6). But MOFERT understood this to encompass the right to investigate and approve or turn down all aspects of any joint venture arrangement.

117

Technology Import and Export Bureau in its investigation of a proposed contract. FIMB far less frequently has occasion to draw on the services of the three regional bureaus in MOFERT.

If any of the participants in the large meeting continues to take strong exception to the FIMB decision on an important matter regarding the contract, the other party may appeal against the FIMB directly to the State Council. As of 1985, Zhao Ziyang was the person on the State Council responsible for foreign investment. Chen Muhua, Gu Mu, and Li Peng could also be brought in, and they in turn might convene a meeting of the pertinent State Councillors and Vice Premiers who had some responsibility for the particular project concerned. They could also organize special meetings of relevant units to handle this situation. But this appeal process rarely was utilized.

Once the terms of a proposed contract have been approved, the FIMB informs the line ministry concerned that it (or its subordinate corporation) may sign the contract. Alternately, the FIMB may instruct the line ministry that particular clauses must be renegotiated before the contract can be approved. In this case, the foreign firm is likely to find that issues that it thought had been settled are now again opened up for discussion.[110]

There have been instances where the Chinese side has sought to revise clauses in a joint venture contract even after the contract had been formally signed. For example, there have been instances when a Chinese unit has signed a joint venture contract with a foreign firm without having secured the necessary FIMB approval, essentially trying to "box in" the FIMB so that it could not require changes in the contract without embarassing the PRC. In these circumstances, however, the FIMB still could demand that the Chinese unit obtain *ex post facto* changes in contract terms. The FIMB exercised this right on several occasions. Again, the foreign firm usually was not informed of the bureaucratic procedures behind the Chinese partner's insistence that a signed contract be renegotiated. Another example of contract revision occurs when FIMB, having approved a draft contract, finds the Chinese side agrees to subsequent changes without FIMB endorsement.

The above procedures apply in general to energy joint ventures. Within the FIMB as of 1985 there were six divisions (*chu*), of which the First Division was responsible for energy, including coal, hydroelectric power, nuclear power, and petroleum.[111] The negotiations for coopera-

---

[110] Typically, interviews with foreign businessmen reveal, the foreign firm remains ignorant of the MOFERT role in reopening discussion on these issues.

[111] The First Division also had responsibility for transportation, metallurgy, non-ferrous metals, machinery, chemicals, and geology. The other five divisions and their spheres of

118

tion with foreign firms to explore for oil offshore, however, were handled somewhat differently. The model contract that was used as the basis for almost all of the joint venture exploration contracts was worked out within China during late 1980 and 1981, before the various foreign trade units were drawn together to form MOFERT. The Ministry of Petroleum Industry took the leading role in developing this model contract, and in the course of the drafting process it widely solicited advice from foreign companies and experts. Within China, FIMB's predecessor, the State Foreign Investment Control Commission, had frequent contact with the Ministry of Petroleum Industry throughout the drafting process. During the course of 1981 the model contract went through eleven drafts. At the vice-premier level, Chen Muhua[112] and Kang Shien[113] were kept closely informed of the drafting process. When complicated issues arose, the Ministry of Petroleum Industry and the State Foreign Investment Control Commission appealed for guidance to higher levels.[114]

In November or December 1981 this drafting process culminated in a national meeting which lasted for a week and produced the final model contract. The Foreign Investment Control Commission approved of this model contract, and thus neither it nor its successor (MOFERT's FIMB) subsequently became involved in the actual contract negotiations with the foreign firms on a day-to-day basis. This same type of procedure was utilized for the second round of offshore bidding.

MOFERT evidently also plays some role in overseeing the implementation of joint venture projects. In so doing, it relies on the various ministerial Foreign Affairs or Foreign Trade departments to monitor the situation and call its attention to difficulties. MOFERT tries to be in a position to act when problems arise.

Summary

The Ministry of Foreign Economic Relations and Trade's activities significantly affect both traders and investors in China's energy sector. On

---

responsibility as of 1985 were as follows: Second Division: light industry, textiles, chemicals such as medicines, building materials, space and aviation, telecommunications, and weaponry; Third Division: tourism, culture and education, health, agriculture and forestry, lumber, rubber, and food processing; Fourth Division: loans from the World Bank and U.N. agencies such as the Food and Agriculture Organization; Fifth Division: loans from Japan, Australia, and New Zealand; Sixth Division: loans from governments other than those covered by the Fifth Division.

[112] At that time, the Minister of Economic Relations With Foreign Countries.

[113] Who was Minister of Petroleum.

[114] In 1981, Gu Mu, who was also a Vice Premier, headed the Foreign Investment Control Commission.

the trading side, the Ministry wishes to ensure that China's imports and exports are conducted in an orderly fashion, which its officials tend to believe best occurs under its firm aegis. Since this has the effect of interposing the Ministry's trading corporations between the Chinese end user and the foreign vendor, many foreigners would prefer a more decentralized system. The MOFERT trading corporations are a holdover from the pre-1978 period of tight controls over foreign trade, and in the 1980's they are experiencing some internal changes as well as having to operate in a generally more confusing and competitive environment. These internal changes entail loosening the administrative constraints so that these corporations compete more with each other and act increasingly as enterprises rather than government bureaus. Official policy in this sphere remained uncertain and fluid throughout the mid-1980's, allowing MOFERT's trading corporations on balance to maintain a substantial role in energy-related imports and exports but not to monopolize business in either of these spheres.

MOFERT plays a pivotal role in the process by which joint venture agreements are concluded, including those dealing with energy. While the decision to undertake a joint venture is typically made by a line ministry or lower level government body in cooperation with the SPC or SEC, the contract and financing terms for the venture must obtain MOFERT's approval. MOFERT also oversees the process by which other units comment on the proposed contract terms. As is often the case given the structure of authority in China, therefore, MOFERT cannot of itself create a joint venture, but MOFERT opposition (and specifically that of its Foreign Investment Management Bureau) would prevent a joint venture contract from being signed and implemented.

In sum, MOFERT is very much a part of the country's policy of opening up to the international economy. This same ministry, though, also reflects the faith Beijing's leaders put into centralized administrative guidance over China's economic activity.

Bank of China

The Bank of China (BOC) differs from commissions and ministries but is still very much a part of the Chinese government. Its operational principles, unlike those of the organs discussed above, make it centrally concerned with the *fiscal soundness* of the projects it supports. The BOC is the key Chinese financial institution when foreign exchange is involved in a project. For projects that derive all of their funding from domestic sources, the Bank remains uninvolved. Projects requiring foreign exchange, however, bring in the BOC in a range of ways: as a financial consultant; as a direct lender, an arranger of loan consortia, or a guarantor of loans from other sources; as an allocator of foreign funds; as a manager of loans; and as the organ responsible for loan repayment. As of 1985, the BOC claimed it had played a direct role in organizing, using, and repaying some eighty percent of the foreign exchange available for use in China.

The BOC's key role in dealing with foreign sources of funds has made it careful to maintain its image of fiscal integrity and responsibility. It runs a very centralized organization within China,[115] and it can refuse to finance (or arrange financing for) a project if it concludes that the project is not fully credit worthy. If it has doubts about a project that the government instructs it to support, it can (and does) require that the state through the SPC effectively guarantee the loan from the state budget.

Specifically, the BOC usually initially becomes involved in a major project after the line ministry proposing the undertaking has made a formal project request to the State Planning Commission.[116] The SPC decides whether the project requires participation by the BOC. If BOC participation is anticipated, the SPC usually asks the BOC to become involved in the feasibility study conducted under the aegis of the SPC. The BOC's role in this study is to present its views about the financial feasibility of the project. For a large project, the SPC then makes a recommendation to the State Council. The State Council approves the project and makes basic decisions about site location, scale, and so forth. It then hands the project back to the SPC for implementation and the SPC in turn assigns the relevant units their responsibilities. The SPC may at this point ask the BOC to develop a way to raise the funds for the project.

Where the project involves a joint venture type arrangement with a foreign firm, the BOC keeps informed about the negotiations with the foreign partner that then ensue, and often the BOC has a representative at the negotiating table itself. Where the BOC is playing an important role in project financing (as a source of funds or as a guarantor), it can exercise what may amount to an effective veto over the contract terms.

Structure

The BOC is a complex organization with dozens of foreign branches as well as branches throughout China. We are concerned here, however, only with the central office in Beijing. Within that headquarters, it is the

[115] The BOC gives each of its domestic branches a line of credit to loan foreign currency. The size of this line depends on the size of the branch concerned—in the mid 1980's Shanghai's and Tianjin's were large, while Kunming's and Guiyang's were small. Branch bank lending beyond the credit limit requires direct approval by the head office in Beijing.

[116] Since a foreign initiated proposal of any magnitude must be put into the state plan, it goes through essentially this same sequence of steps.

Second Credit Department that as of 1985 took charge of most work on energy projects. This department was established in early 1983, and as of 1984 it had only eleven staff members (but had plans to build up its staff to several dozen people). Among the 1984 staff were some recent university graduates as well as people who had spent long careers in the Bank already. At least one staff member formerly worked at the Ministry of Petroleum Industry. None had come from the other energy line ministries. This Department is able to seek advice from individuals at universities, research institutes, and other state organs when the need arises. The Second Credit Department is responsible for analyzing the best mix of funds to use to finance the projects in which it is involved. It then reports its conclusions to the General Manager of the BOC. Thus, formally, the Second Credit Department reports to the General Manager of the BOC, who in turn maintains direct contact with the SPC. In reality, though, it is often the Second Credit Department that represents the Bank in interagency meetings related to projects under its jurisdiction.

Other units within the BOC also become involved in energy-related projects. The Foreign Exchange and Funds Department, for example, floats bonds and notes in the world market, and it, therefore, becomes involved when this method of financing is utilized in support of an energy undertaking. It is the Second Credit Department, however, that was involved in the Pingshuo open pit coal mine project with Occidental Petroleum, the offshore oil ventures, and the Daya Bay nuclear power plant project for Guangdong. The lion's share of staff work on energy project financing, therefore, appears to fall into the bailiwick of the Second Credit Department.

Summary

The BOC commitment to keep its risks low and its credibility high has made it a sometimes difficult participant in the negotiations on some major energy projects. The Bank is often an active participant in the project planning and negotiations on the Chinese side long before the foreign firms have direct negotiations with Bank officials. This earlier role begins with the feasibility study and sometimes has the Bank serve as a consultant throughout the negotiations. At a later stage, the Bank can greatly facilitate a project by providing either a source of financing or the confidence that comes with loan guarantees. When the Bank becomes a finance source itself, it in some respects becomes a silent partner of the venture.

The Bank has a strong interest in promoting the development of major energy ventures, and the establishment of the Second Credit Department in early 1983 facilitated this by enhancing the Bank's staff capabilities in this specialized area. Still, though, the Bank on occasion raises questions that have the effect of substantially stretching out the negotiating period for key energy contracts. Some foreign observers have felt that some of these delays have stemmed from inadequate expertise at the Bank.[117] The Bank's own basic operating philosophy, however, appears to be a strong force in making the Bank proceed at a very deliberate pace in large energy ventures.

China National Offshore Oil Corporation

The China National Offshore Oil Corporation is an example of the type of interface organizations the Chinese have established to broker the country's relations with foreigners in the energy area. Thus, unlike those units discussed above, CNOOC is a state corporation, not an administrative unit of the national government. CNOOC formally came into being on 25 February 1982 as a corporation formed under the Ministry of Petroleum Industry with the task of exercising exclusive control over the negotiations and bidding, exploration, development and marketing of all oil resources within offshore areas designated by the Chinese government. Its formal establishment came in the fourth year of China's discussions with Western oil companies concerning their possible participation in offshore oil development. The company was an outgrowth in part of China's learning from the experiences of other countries about how best to organize this kind of effort.[118] It also reflected China's response to the urgings of Western firms that the PRC establish a legal entity with clearly defined jurisdiction with which the foreign firms could sign contracts that would govern the cooperative oil effort.

CNOOC grew out of discussions and activities between foreign firms and the Ministry of Petroleum Industry from 1978 to 1982. These years had witnessed progress from initial exploratory discussions concerning the extent and modalities of a cooperative effort through agreement on geophysical survey work done by the foreign firms to discussions of a model contract that would provide the framework for specific bids to explore and develop individual offshore blocs. During these years, the foreign firms negotiated with teams put forward by the China National Oil

[117] Several of these elements were manifested in the Sino-British-French negotiations over the financing of a nuclear plant at Daya Bay: *South China Morning Post*, July 29, 1985, in FBIS, August 2, 1985, p. W-1.

[118] Norway's Statoil played a significant role in shaping China's thinking on this issue, but the MPI also studied the experiences of England, Indonesia, and other places. See Chapter Five for details.

and Gas Exploration and Development Company. As noted previously, these negotiations also brought in, as necessary, representatives from other organs, such as the Ministry of Finance (on taxation issues).

Foreign firms in general were impressed by the rapidity with which the Chinese learned what they needed to know about the international oil business and by the skills of the Chinese in negotiations. They also became concerned, however, about the range of potential actors and the difficulty of determining the real authority of any one of them. These concerns were heightened by incidents such as an evident misunderstanding about the Ministry of Geology sinking wells in an area that had been granted "exclusively" by the Ministry of Petroleum to a foreign firm to survey. Western firms thus wanted a single entity to deal with— one that clearly had the legal authority to make and abide by long term cooperative contracts with foreign firms.

On the Chinese side, Vice Minister of Petroleum Industry Qin Wencai had been put in charge of the cooperative efforts with foreign firms for offshore work at least by October 1980, and probably earlier. Qin was the first-ranking vice minister in the MPI, and he began to sketch out the framework for a separate organization that he would head to take charge of this effort. He started putting this organization together in 1980, and it appears that it was *de facto* almost fully in place by the spring 1981. The nearly one-year delay in formally announcing its establishment resulted at least in part from uncertainty as to what the stature of the new organization would be. It could have been assigned to any of three levels: that of a bureau; that of a general bureau; or that of a ministry. After many months of uncertainty, the newly-formed CNOOC was designated as an independent corporation with the status of a general bureau (*zongju*), higher than a bureau but lower than a ministry. The offshore petroleum regulations issued on 12 January 1982 made clear that CNOOC would have *exclusive* jurisdiction over oil work done in the offshore areas assigned to it.

By the time CNOOC's formation was announced, the organization had already been functioning for some time. Foreign firms noticed, in most instances, only a small change in the cast of characters with whom they dealt. CNOOC sought to gain the full confidence of the foreign firms. This required efforts on a number of fronts. During its first year CNOOC had the central government make several pronouncements that effectively gave it a stronger legal underpinning. For example, it formally registered as a legal entity on 1 September 1982 and it received an official business license on 25 February 1983. In broad terms, CNOOC sought to protect its prerogatives and remained sensitive to encroachments on its authority. It had to fend off many other Chinese organizations that wanted to participate in the potentially lucrative offshore oil effort.

CNOOC is formally responsible for all policy matters relating to off-shore oil activities in the areas under its jurisdiction. This includes carrying out the bidding and contract negotiations and ruling on any issues of contract interpretation that arise. CNOOC is also the agent through which China would assume an equity position in the development stage, should commercially viable quantities of oil be found off shore. Indeed, in the case of ARCO's discovery of a gas field in the Yinggehai, CNOOC agreed to form a joint equity venture with ARCO and with Santa Fe Minerals Asia (owned by Kuwait) to develop this field. While CNOOC is the key organization with which the foreign firms deal on these issues, CNOOC itself must go to the Ministry of Petroleum Industry or to the State Council on all major policy (as versus operational and technical) issues.[119] For example, as of 1985 CNOOC did not have the right to decide which offshore oil areas could be opened to foreigners, how much acreage to make available, or the terms for foreign participation. CNOOC could formulate proposals for these items, but they would then be submitted to higher levels for government approval. CNOOC could, however, procure foreign equipment listed on a schedule of permitted procurement items. It could also procure foreign exchange loans directly, either from the Bank of China or from foreign banks.[120] CNOOC as of 1985 planned to use foreign loans as a significant part of its financing in the development stage of its projects. Additionally, unlike most Chinese corporations, CNOOC has the right to use any foreign exchange that it earns. It also retains all of its after-tax profits.

Naturally, contract implementation in the Beibuwan, the Yinggehai, the Pearl River mouth, the South Yellow Sea, the East China Sea, and the Bohai requires that numerous operational details be handled on the spot. Many of these, moreover, necessarily involve the local and provincial governments in providing essential support services. The fact that several dozen foreign firms are involved in the effort complicates matters still further. To manage this difficult set of operational demands, a relatively simple formula was developed. CNOOC created four operating companies, each taking the form of a CNOOC branch corporation and having the rank of a ministerial bureau (*ju*). These companies took

[119] According to some foreign sources, by the spring of 1984 CNOOC's position had risen somewhat so that on some issues it could go straight to the State Council (as a ministry level organization can do), while on others it still had to go to the Ministry of Petroleum Industry.

[120] For loans from the Bank of China, CNOOC puts up its own resources as collateral. For loans from foreign banks, the Bank of China guarantees the loan if the Ministry of Petroleum Industry approves of this arrangement.

charge of implementing the contracts in cooperation with the foreign firms, with the Chinese companies assuming the task of managing the operational details (for customs, housing, coordination with local Chinese agencies and with the navy, and so forth) that are integral to contract fulfillment. The local companies formed Joint Management Committees (JMC's) with the foreign firms that provide the organizational vehicle for this cooperation and decide on the program that each foreign operator should follow to explore his tract.[121] All issues of contract interpretation and of the actual terms for foreign and Chinese cooperation, however, go back to CNOOC headquarters in Beijing for decision.

In 1984 CNOOC set up a new subsidiary, the Gas Utilization Corporation (GUC), with headquarters in Guangzhou. On 28 September 1984 this new corporation signed an agreement that commits it as of 1989 to purchase the gas produced from the ARCO field in the Yinggehai. The GUC as of 1985 planned to construct a pipeline from Sanya (the location on Hainan Island to which the joint venture producing the gas will pipe it) to Guangzhou, Shenzhen, and possibly eventually to Hong Kong. The GUC would become the sole vendor for this gas in China. All of this was planned under the CNOOC business license, which permits the firm not only to explore for and develop resources in the offshore areas under its aegis but also to sell those resources in China.

While the above structure is simple in outline, it is in fact quite complex in implementation. Indeed, the four branch operating companies differ greatly among themselves, and cooperation either among them or between them and CNOOC headquarters was not always smooth. Provincial and local authorities, moreover, sometimes raised additional problems. For example, CNOOC itself, the branch companies, provincial bodies, other national ministries, and local authorities have all tried to provide supplies and support services, such as transportation, and in many areas they are doing so in competition with foreign firms that are also seeking this business. Details on some of these issues are provided below.

Structure

CNOOC as of 1985 had about 200 professional staff members, but this was only a partial indicator of its real staff strength. It could borrow additional staff relatively freely from the Ministry of Petroleum Industry, and it also used the resources of a research facility in Zhou Xian, in

---

[121] While the JMC's discuss where to drill each well and when to abandon a test well, the ultimate decision on these issues belongs to the foreign operator.

the southwest suburbs of Beijing. As noted above, it also formally established four branch corporations as operating companies to implement the contracts that it signed with the foreign firms and entered into joint ventures with more than ten domestic Chinese firms as part of an effort to involve these firms in the offshore oil activities. Thus, although CNOOC has a relatively small staff core, its reach extends quite some distance via its various branches and joint ventures.

CNOOC as of 1985 had a president (Qin Wencai)[122] and five vice-presidents: Zhong Yiming, who had long experience in offshore oil drilling and served concurrently on the board of the China National Offshore Joint Services Company (CNOJSC); You Dehua, a Qinghua University graduate and an intellectual who played a leading role in negotiations with foreign firms before 1982; Zhao Shengzhen, long involved in negotiations with foreign firms and a technically competent individual; Liu Dongming, on whom we have no available biographical information; and Tang Zhenhua, who also has an engineering background and was in charge of operations and procurement.

The key departments at CNOOC's headquarters as of late 1985 were: Liaison, for reception of foreigners, contacts with oil companies, and work concerning foreign experts; Finance, for accounting and finance; Contract and Legislation (formerly Cooperation), for contract negotiation and signing, amendments and supplements to the contracts, and management of legislation in CNOOC; Exploration and Development, for contract execution; Operational Services (formerly Production Operations), for implementation of production aspects of the contract, production status reports, environmental protection, and safety of offshore operations; Planning, for long term planning; Personnel, for training and personnel assignments; Engineering, for design, manufacture, and installation of platforms and equipment; Marketing and Procurement (formerly Procurement and Marketing), for marketing crude, procurement, and purchasing; Science and Technology Development (formerly Technical Development and Training); Audit (formerly a part of the Finance Department), established in 1984; and Service, for meals, cars, and chauffeurs.[123] CNOOC had by 1985 established offices in Houston, London, Tokyo, and Hong Kong.

Conclusion

CNOOC has functioned effectively as a state oil company for the Chinese. It has encountered strains in coordination with its branch com-

---

[122] Qin relinquished his post as Vice Minister of MPI when he took charge of CNOOC.
[123] Other standard departments also existed, such as the General Office.

panies and in dealing with other Chinese units that want to benefit from the oil effort, but this is unavoidable in any such undertaking. It is clear, on balance, that the people working both there and in the branch companies quickly travelled an impressive way down a learning curve.

Several factors could affect the mid-1980's relationships in the future. One, mentioned above, is the changes that must inevitably occur either when oil and gas in substantial quantities are found off shore or when they are not. In the former case, many new issues would have to be faced, as the nature of operations and of cash flows change dramatically. In the latter case, CNOOC would perforce cease to be the spearhead of a major initiative that it now is.

Another potential element of change involves China's decision to involve foreign oil companies in equity participation for onshore exploration and development. This effort as of 1985 was in too early a stage to anticipate its eventual consequences. But the Ministry of Petroleum Industry created a new corporation, the China National Oil Development Corporation, to handle this effort. As previously noted, the CNODC, like CNOOC, is an independent company with the status of a general bureau (*zongju*). The further development of CNODC and the movement of the foreign participation into onshore activities in a significant way would undoubtedly affect the relationships sketched out here and in the summary on the Ministry of Petroleum Industry.

Formal Policy Process

We have now introduced the principal bureaucratic actors in the extremely complex world of Chinese energy development. The next step in the analysis is to understand the process of interaction. How do the pieces fit together, for example, when the issue is whether to approve and construct a major new energy project? As is often the case in China, the *outline* of the process by which major energy projects are approved and constructed is reasonably simple. The possible variations on this outline in the real world, however, are almost endless. Even a brief overview of the basic outline can be important, though, as it indicates the key steps and hurdles that any large project must navigate in order to gain approval.

There are two broad dimensions to the policy process for major project approval and implementation. The first concerns the general rhythm of the planning process, which has both annual and five year cycles. The second is the specific sequence of actions that must occur to bring any single project to fruition within the context of this larger planning effort.

The overall planning cycle has received attention from Western scholars in the past. China has both Five Year Plans and annual plans. The former have not been rigid prescriptions that have laid out in binding detail the key economic activities over the ensuing five year period. Rather, they have been more general, setting goals and directing rather than offering detailed and concrete planning. Even at this broad level, they have often been adopted well after the start of the actual five year period and been modified considerably during the course of the plan. These are, thus, rolling plans rather than static documents. For all this flexibility they are, nevertheless, important breakpoints in the economic policy cycle and warrant attention.[124]

The Five Year Plan serves a number of important purposes, not the least of which is that it forces the leaders and the bureaucratic apparatus to look at medium term economic trends and goals in a serious, operational way. A project that has been put into the plan may still possibly be delayed or dropped, as unforeseen circumstances force cutbacks or the reallocation of resources. What is of great importance to project advocates, however, is that until the Seventh Five Year Plan (1986-90) a large project that had not been put into a Five Year Plan generally could not begin construction during the tenure of that plan. The Seventh Five Year Plan made a partial exception to this rule because the central leadership was unable to reach full agreement on several major projects (including the Three Gorges Dam project and the Sunan nuclear power project). A sum of money was, therefore, kept separate from the plan to cover start-up costs during this plan period on any of these projects on which agreement could be obtained.[125] Overall, the great difficulty of initiating construction during a plan period on a major project not included in the plan means that enormous effort is expended to win a place in the five year plan for each bureaucracy's highest priority projects.

The five year cycle leaves considerable room for decisions to be made on an annual basis, even for major projects. Some of these decisions concern questions of timing, as circumstances force significant modifications in the longer term plan. Others deal with actual project approvals themselves. Only the very largest projects are actually listed as separate items in the Five Year Plan. Otherwise, the plan specifies overall targets and figures on investment levels and the sectoral distribution of planned investments. Within these broad guidelines, various ministries and their

---

[124] An overview of Chinese economic planning is available in: He Jianzhang and Zhang Zhiye (eds.), and in Zhou Taihe (ed.), *Dangdai Zhongguo de jingji tizhi gaige* (Beijing: Zhongguo shehui kexue chubanshe, 1984), pp. 213-248.

[125] This special arrangement in the Seventh Five Year Plan may indicate a growing difficulty in the Chinese system as a whole in initiating very large projects. This possibility is explored in Chapters Six and Eight.

subordinate units struggle to obtain approval for specific expenditures on their own priority proposals. These proposals in aggregate regularly far exceed the resources available in the system. The battle over the distribution of resources therefore is very much affected by the cycle of the annual plan.

The timing of the drafting of each annual plan has varied a good deal since the early 1950's, but the basic process has remained reasonably constant. Essentially, three efforts come together to produce the annual plan. These are: the collection of project proposals; the determination of overall needs and capabilities for the coming year; and the assessment of the budgetary situation and possibilities.

Each ministry and province puts forward a list of the priority project proposals that it would like to see in the annual plan. In this, the ministry or province must itself go through the process of working up the proposal to an acceptable level of detail. Since organs below the ministerial and provincial levels cannot submit proposals to the planning authorities directly, the ministries and provinces themselves must do some of the sifting to produce a final list that it is willing to support fully. This procedure is thus designed, among other things, to prevent lower level bodies from flooding the top leaders with projects that cannot win the support of either the appropriate ministry or province. Nevertheless, the top planning officials are in fact always in a position of having to decide among far more proposals than the economy can bear.

It falls to the State Planning Commission to work through these proposals to determine a final short list. The SPC keeps track of the situation throughout the year, touching base with each ministry and province to understand both the economy's performance to date and the types of project proposals that are likely to be put forward. When the SPC receives specific proposals, moreover, it reviews the major ones in detail to determine their feasibility. Once a year the SPC convenes a National Planning Conference that brings together all the key participants in order to make up a relatively final list of projects and priorities for the ensuing annual plan.

The Ministry of Finance also plays a role in this annual planning process. Like the SPC, it monitors the economic situation during the course of the year and then tries to anticipate the budgetary consequences for the coming year. Within this framework, each year the Ministry convenes a National Finance Conference. There is much communication between the budget makers in the Ministry of Finance and the Planners in the SPC. Nevertheless, they have somewhat different priorities, as the planners are primarily concerned with what the country needs and whether the physical means are available to satisfy these needs, while the budgetary people are more concerned with what the country can afford without producing large budget deficits and possible bouts of inflation. Similar tensions—between the process of adopting projects and the process of producing a budget—exist in most countries.[126]

Inevitably, the overload of demands from the ministries and provinces combines with the relatively cautious budgetary strictures from the Ministry of Finance to produce conflicts over some projects that cannot be resolved at the level of the SPC itself. These conflicts are then brought to the highest political level for decision. The national political leadership also ratifies the decisions that were reached at the National Finance and Planning Conferences before these decisions are reported to the National People's Congress for formal adoption.[127]

The above annual cycle requires almost constant related activity from the ministries and provinces. They are always in the process of receiving new project proposals from their subordinate organs, developing those proposals through consultations and pertinent studies, discussing the possibilities with the planning and budgetary authorities, and lobbying for the proposals once they have been submitted to higher levels. Nevertheless, the annual planning and finance meetings do structure the timing and intensity of many of these activities. Even with the efforts during the 1980's to reduce the role of the plan in the country's overall economic activities, moreover, the major projects in the energy sector are of sufficient importance and magnitude that virtually without exception they must make it through the hurdles of the five year and/or annual planning process in order to go from the drawing boards to actual construction.

Looked at from the point of view of a single project, the basic process from initial idea to final construction is thus as follows. The original impetus for a project may come from almost any source from a high level leader to a ministerial official to a provincial government to a foreign contact. No matter what the origins of the idea, however, it is the pertinent line ministry or province that must assume responsibility for actually working up the initial project proposal. To simplify, the following discussion takes the line ministry as the key organ, as most large energy projects seem to follow a ministerial rather than provincial route.

The line ministry involved must consult with other relevant ministries and related bodies in the course of drafting its proposal. Any large project inevitably requires the active cooperation of other bodies, and the process of building a consensus begins early. During this initial drafting stage,

---

[126] Wildavsky, *Budgeting.*

[127] The Planning and Finance Conferences themselves convene under the policy guidelines articulated by the national political leadership.

the ministry typically seeks the advice of these other bodies and attempts to shape the proposal so as to take into consideration any strong objections raised. As the case study on the Three Gorges project[128] demonstrates, the reforms since 1978 have been increasing the importance of consensus building as part of the policy process in the energy sector. Having worked up its proposal (and in the process tried to develop at least a basic consensus on it), the ministry forwards it to the State Planning Commission for consideration.

The SPC can simply accept the feasibility work on the project done by the ministry, but on large projects the SPC increasingly is inclined to conduct its own feasibility studies on ministerial proposals.[129] Often, especially for a major undertaking, the SPC draws upon expertise that resides in the ministries, research institutes, and universities in the course of its feasibility study. This feasibility study provides yet another opportunity to develop a working consensus in favor of a new project. If the project is of sufficient scale and expense, the Ministry of Finance may also study its financial feasibility, and the MOF and SPC have to resolve any differences they have over the project. The SPC can send a project back to the line ministry for additional work and subsequent resubmission.

Some projects are of a magnitude such that the SPC alone cannot approve the effort. These are reported to the State Council, along with the SPC recommendation on them. Formally, the State Council then decides whether or not to construct the project, in which case it is submitted to the National People's Congress as part of the coming Five Year Plan. Actually, projects of this magnitude are also individually considered at the highest Party levels before final approval is given.

In sum, projects may be approved at different levels, depending on their size, expense, and importance. Some can be done largely at the discretion of the ministry within its budgetary allocations. Others must go to the SPC for its review and approval. And a few are sent up to the top leadership core group itself. What are termed "keypoint" projects become individual items in the Five Year Plan (and they are also, of

---

[128] Chapter Six.

[129] In February 1986 Beijing gave publicity to the China International Engineering Consulting Corporation which, it said, would henceforth examine on behalf of the SPC and the SEC all major construction and technical transformation projects to determine their technical feasibility. Presumably, many of the points made in the text about the SPC-directed feasibility studies would henceforth apply to the feasibility reviews conducted by the China International Engineering Consulting Corporation. This corporation has been doing technical consulting work since its establishment in 1982. It may seek to employ foreign specialists, and it reportedly counts more than three thousand engineers among its staff: *Renmin ribao*, February 8, 1986—FBIS, February 21, 1986, pp. K11-13.

course, listed in each of the pertinent annual plans). Important projects below the "keypoint" level must be provided for individually in the annual plan. (Still smaller projects may be constructed with discretionary funds available to the ministries and provinces.) In any case, a process of consensus building is begun in the initial drafting stage, and the SPC-directed feasibility study furthers this process.

If the project involves foreign participation, in theory it is at this stage that the ministry should enter into negotiations with a foreign firm that can actually lead to a binding contract. In reality, the ministry and the firm usually have begun negotiations much earlier in the process, before the project has been approved and therefore before a binding contract could be signed. These premature negotiations, however, may assist the ministry in building its case internally.[130] Foreign firms typically have not understood this sequence and have mistaken initial negotiations for the later talks that ensue when a ministry has obtained the approvals necessary to actually sign a contract.

These negotiations with the foreign firm may include participation by representatives of MOFERT and/or the Bank of China. As often as not, these trade and financial representatives are not explicitly identified as such to the foreign negotiators, but their participation is an important part of the continuing effort to construct the internal consensus that will be necessary to undertake the project.

Once a contract has been negotiated (but before it is actually signed), MOFERT assumes responsibility for scrutinizing the agreement for consistency with Chinese law and policy. At this point, if the project is a joint venture, MOFERT circulates the proposed contract to the relevant bodies to solicit their opinions. MOFERT's approval, given once this process has been completed, is required for joint ventures of any size in the energy sector. When the Ministry concerned has received MOFERT's approval, it may then proceed to sign the contract. MOFERT then again scrutinizes the contract and reaffirms its approval.[131]

The Bank of China plays a role if financing terms become a part of the negotiation. The Bank can participate in a number of ways: by becoming a direct source of financing; by guaranteeing loans made to the project; by arranging for financing; by serving as a financial advisor to the Chinese negotiators; and so forth. Unlike the other units discussed to this point, the Bank's major concern typically lies strictly in the financial

[130] The foreign firm may provide a feasibility study, it may lobby on behalf of the project at higher levels, it may secure access to foreign capital, and it often enables the ministry to obtain a firmer idea of the cost of the project.

[131] At any of the stages of its involvement, MOFERT can require that specific clauses in the contract be renegotiated to meet its concerns.

133

soundness of the project concerned. It has an independent capability to refuse participation in the project unless the financial terms it seeks are adopted by the participants. As explained above, the Bank can also be ordered by the government to support a project over the Bank's own reservations, but in this instance arrangements are made to back up the Bank with government budgetary funds. Bank of China objections occasionally cause substantial delays in completing negotiations for major projects, such as those for the Daya Bay nuclear plant.

Once the contract has been signed and reconfirmed, the SPC or SEC (largely depending on whether this is a new project or a renovation of an existing facility) takes over responsibility for coordinating the implementation of the contract. The foreign firm continues to deal only with the line ministry with which it signed the contract, but internally that ministry lacks the power to compel other organizations to provide the necessary resources and facilities for contract implementation. Therefore, the supraministerial commissions have a crucial role to play here.

As should be evident from the above sketches of the individual organizations, each of the major bureaucratic units in this process has its own mission, resources, personnel, and style, and these individual characteristics of the units are extremely important in shaping the dynamics of decision making in the energy sector. The above overview of the policy process notes the basic progression for a project and the minimum set of hurdles that must be cleared. It does not attempt either to explain or to convey an appreciation of the variations on this basic process that in fact often occur.

· 4 ·

SALIENT CHARACTERISTICS OF THE
STRUCTURE OF POWER

Chapter One analyzed two contrasting images of the Chinese policy process found in the Western literature. Both of these—the rational problem solving model and the power politics model—focused on the motivations of decision makers at the highest levels. The shared underlying assumption, as pointed out in that chapter, is that because these top leaders exercise centralized control over the system it is vitally important to understand why and how they reach their decisions. Chapter Two then detailed the division of responsibility among the top twenty-five to thirty-five leaders, and Chapter Three introduced the formal structure and policy process of the Chinese energy bureaucracy so as to elucidate the bureaucratic apparatus through which the top leaders rule the country.

In the present chapter we provide a conceptual framework that bridges a second set of contrasting images of the Chinese political system found in much of the literature to date. This latter set of images concerns the allocation of authority in the system. Many scholars, as explained in Chapter One, picture the country as effectively organized and led. According to this view, the top political leaders have sufficient power to elicit compliance from lower levels on almost any issue at any time. This perspective focuses on the top leaders and the bureaucratic apparatus at their command. The essence of Chinese politics, according to this view, is to be found in Beijing, or more precisely in the Zhongnanhai. Leaders like Deng Xiaoping or Mao Zedong before him have been able to obtain the desired response from officials throughout the vast Chinese Party and government apparatuses.[1]

The second and contradictory image is that the policies proclaimed in Beijing bear little resemblance to the reality at lower levels. According to this "cellular" perspective, there is a great concentration of power in the hands of provincial level officials and leaders of lower level units (*danwei*). China is thus a cellular economy and polity, with the territorial components of the system surprisingly self-sufficient and capable of thwarting and subverting Beijing's demands.[2] Far from being an efficient

[1] Roderick MacFarquhar presents a rigorous and sophisticated example of this approach in his *Origins of the Cultural Revolution*.

[2] For a vigorous advocacy of this view, see: Audrey Donnithorne, "China's Cellular Economy."

system controlled from the top, then, this view considers the Chinese chain of command inefficient, largely ineffective, and—to the extent it works—laboriously slow.

Since 1978, foreign businessmen who have worked in China have frequently experienced the ability of local officials to torpedo agreements reached in Beijing. They also have witnessed the refusal of Beijing to endorse agreements which provinces have assured them were authoritative. From the viewpoint of the foreign businessman, top level policy often amounts to little more than a rhetorical flourish that is ignored or blunted in the middle and lower reaches of officialdom. Thus, for example, Central declarations to stop imports of Japanese electronic consumer goods, permit foreign firms in joint ventures to repatriate their profits, constrain local governments from undertaking off-plan capital construction on too large a scale, and so forth are simply flouted throughout much of the country. The experience of foreign businessmen to date suggests that in some respects the top leaders exert only very limited control over the activities of the Party and government apparatuses. The opening of China, if anything, enhanced the attractiveness of the second, cellular image.[3]

In fact, the available evidence supports both perspectives. Neither perspective alone suffices. Abundant evidence points to the strength of the Center. The top leaders have guided the energy sector through major changes in policy (such as the decision to approach offshore oil via risk contracts with foreign firms) and marshalled the resources and local cooperation necessary to achieve impressive results. They have opened four special economic zones. They have transformed agriculture. Indeed, the list of successful initiatives is a rather long one.[4] At the same time, foreigners who deal with China repeatedly encounter instances where central policy has had little effect on the activities and incentives of local officials. A careful examination of the reforms reveals the considerable extent to which local levels have been able to alter policy initiatives from above.[5]

This chapter seeks to reconcile these contrasting images of the system through a careful analysis of the components of power in China and the

[3] Harry Harding provides a summary and analysis of some of the pertinent literature in his, "From China With Disdain: New Trends in the Study of China," *Asian Survey* (October 1982), pp. 934-958.

[4] See, for example: A. Doak Barnett and Ralph Clough (eds.), *Modernizing China*, (Boulder: Westview, 1986); and The World Bank, *China: Long-Term Development Issues*, and the six annex volumes to this report.

[5] David M. Lampton (ed.), *Policy Implementation*; and Elizabeth Perry and Christine Wong, *Political Economy of Reform* (Cambridge: Harvard University Press, 1985).

ways in which power is accumulated and utilized. Any such analysis must convey how Chinese officials themselves view their own system and the resources that units at various levels of the national hierarchy can bring into play to achieve their goals in the political arena. This analysis must also examine how these different resources are brought to bear—that is, the ongoing bargaining between units that is crucial to the functioning of the Chinese political system. In this chapter, therefore, we first highlight the cleavages and sources of fragmentation that shape the way policies are fought over and implemented. The fragmented nature of the system undergirds the second, cellular image. We then present the linkages in the system that help to overcome its fragmentation and analyze how these have changed over the years. These linkages undergird the first, control image. Finally, we reconcile the two perspectives by analyzing how officials develop the power necessary to be effective within the system.

FRAGMENTED STRUCTURE OF AUTHORITY

The formal table of organization conveys an impression of a complex but nationally unified, disciplined system radiating out in a clearly defined hierarchy of authority from Beijing. It suggests a system with a core top leadership, linked by key responsible individuals to large vertical ministries that control units from the center to the local levels. Commissions responsible for coordination sit atop these ministerial pyramids. Each of these hierarchies perceives itself as having a mission, to which it attaches great importance. Obviously, the formal structure generates interagency competition and problems of coordination, but the table of organization suggests that the central leaders should have a substantial ability to dictate the national agenda and to make the various bureaucracies work effectively together.

While the formal system does to an extent work as expected, tables of organization are only partial guides to the real authority relations in the Chinese polity. What on paper appears to be a unified, hierarchical chain of command turns out in reality to be divided, segmented, and stratified. Indeed, the *fragmentation* of authority is a core dimension of the Chinese system. The fault lines in China's bureaucratic structure require elucidation, therefore, if the policy process in the energy sector is to be understood in a realistic way.

Understanding the world of Chinese officials illuminates their ability—or frequently their inability—to meet obligations to which they have committed themselves. As this chapter indicates, there is no way precisely to measure the real authority of any particular group of offi-

137

cials, but it is possible to make informed estimates based on the formal structure of authority (described in Chapters Two and Three) and the more subtle, informal considerations we introduce in this chapter. Too often, long delays have attended the resolution of what appear to be minor issues. Even more disturbingly, decisions that appeared to entail firm commitments have subsequently been reversed or modified while obtaining necessary approvals. In one major instance, for example, an American company believed it had a firm commitment from the Ministry of Coal Industry to proceed with an open pit coal mine, only to learn that the State Planning Commission would not approve the project. The explanations for such phenomena lie in an understanding of the cleavages in China's structure of power.

The vocabulary of Chinese leaders and bureaucrats is rich in the distinctions it permits them to use in describing the organizations that inhabit their world. This vocabulary and the underlying perceptions it reveals suggest the participants consider themselves both enmeshed in a unified hierarchical system and operating in a loosely integrated world of competing agencies. We draw upon the vocabulary of the Chinese bureaucrats to portray the principal distinctions and boundaries they perceive among the different types of organizations in China.

Center and Locale

One significant fault line is that between the "center" (*zhongyang*) and the "locale" (*difang*)—or the national level on the one hand and the provinces, municipalities, and counties on the other. The distinction is similar to that in American corporate life between headquarters and regional offices. The "center" includes the State Council and its commissions, ministries, and leadership small groups in Beijing, as well as the Party Politburo, Secretariat, and the organs of the Central Committee.[6] The "locales" consist of the provinces but also include lower level units. Chinese officials often speak in terms of whether a decision or action was done at the "center" or carries the authority of the "center."

The relationship between the Center and the provinces is the object of continual reform, as the leaders of China seek an appropriate blend of national uniformity and provincial autonomy. Excessive centralization stifles local initiative, the leaders believe, while excessive decentralization produces chaos and detracts from pursuit of the national interest. As noted above, outside analysts frequently argue over whether the Center

---

[6] The same term for Center also refers to the Central Committee itself and to the preeminent leader. Context usually makes clear which "center" is meant.

dominates the provinces or the provinces are, in fact, relatively independent and possess great autonomy. Our research rejects both interpretations and suggests each has resources the other needs.

Central-provincial relations are characterized by intense bargaining, with neither capable of totally disregarding the interests and needs of the other. The changes in center-provincial relations usually are marginal adjustments which typically affect the overall balance less dramatically than the publicity announcing the change suggests. Frequently, a publicized grant of increased authority to the provinces, for example, is accompanied by a quiet, off-setting change in favor of the Center. Moreover, the national government differs greatly in the degree of control it exerts over different provinces, and provinces differ among themselves in their bargaining leverage over the Center, depending upon such factors as their wealth, strategic significance, and the personal connections, ambition, and acumen of their leaders.

A crucial dimension of central-provincial relations revolves around finances: the budgetary process and the national banking system. Both of these have undergone substantial reforms since the late 1970's, and on balance these reforms have strengthened the provincial and lower level territorial components of this structure and placed a smaller percentage of the country's monetary and fiscal resources under the direct control of the Center.[7] The budgetary reform has permitted provinces to retain increasing portions of the revenues they generate. The Chinese budget obscures this trend, as it aggregates the local and central budgets into a total state budget. Revenues and expenditures are itemized in functional categories rather than by territorial unit. In reality, according to several financial officials, the major portion of the central government's revenues now comes from negotiated agreements with each province as to how much revenue it will submit to the Center.[8] These agreements are renegotiated periodically. Their overall effect since the late 1970's has been to leave more funds under the control of the locales.

The reforms have also expanded the role of the banks. During the mid 1980's, they became a major additional source of investment capital. This development created new sources of funds that localities tapped to promote projects not approved at the Center. In addition, various enterprises and local government units have long had pockets of money over which they themselves retained control, and the reforms have increased sub-

[7] See, e.g.: Xu Yi and Chen Baosen, *Zhongguo de caizheng, 1977-80* (Beijing: Renmin chubanshe), esp. chaps. 3-4. More generally, see: Xu Yi and Chen Baosen (eds.), *Caizheng xue*, esp. chaps. 10 and 13.

[8] The proportion turned over to the Center varies by province, and as of 1985 about 13 or 14 provinces actually received subsidies from the Center.

139

stantially the revenues that fall into this category. These additional funds come from a bewildering variety of sources, such as retained profits, depreciation funds, special fees, and so forth.[9] Their magnitude grew during the 1980's to the point where they became a significant source of investment capital.[10]

These budgetary and other changes enhanced the ability of various provincial and lower level units (including both official offices and corporations) to make their own decisions. As the Chinese media made plain, localities exercised some of their increased autonomy in ways that ran against the broad policy priorities favored by the Center.[11] Increasing economic independence for local units thus accentuated the gap between Center and locality.

In addition to budgetary and credit controls, the opening to the outside world made the management of foreign currency an increasingly important ingredient in shaping central-provincial relations. The central government in the latter half of the 1980's derives a significant portion of its investment funds from foreign sources, such as World Bank loans, which it carefully channels through Central units. This presumably strengthens the Center vis-à-vis the provinces. The Bank of China also controls the bulk of China's foreign currency holdings. However, in two other respects management of foreign currency has increased the strength of the provinces. To stimulate exports, the Center has allowed provinces to retain and spend within set limits a portion of the foreign currency which they earn.[12] The Center can unilaterally and suddenly curtail this autonomy, as in late 1980 and again in 1985, in reaction to an eroding trade balance. In addition, a foreign currency black market began to grow, beyond the reach of the central government, which local officials (among others) used to make foreign purchases against the wishes of the top leaders.[13]

[9] For example, in the mid-1980's the enterprises for the first time were permitted to retain their depreciation funds to use them as they wish. See Barry Naughton, "The Decline of Central Control Over Investment in Post Mao China," in David M. Lampton, *Policy Implementation.*

[10] See, for example, *Shijie jingji daobao*, December 2, 1985—trans. in *FBIS*, December 23, 1985, pp. K8-10; and Katsuhiko Hama, "Systemic Reforms and Financial Problems—The 'Investment Fever' Mechanism," *China Newsletter*, no. 47 (November-December 1983), pp. 7-14.

[11] See, e.g.: Tian Jiyun's speech to a conference of cadres of central organs on January 6, 1986: Xinhua domestic, January 11, 1986—trans. in *FBIS*, January 13, 1986, esp. pp. K11-12.

[12] Provinces enjoy differing degrees of autonomy in their access to and use of foreign currency. As of mid 1985, Guangdong and Fujian in particular enjoyed a privileged position, followed by such cities as Beijing, Tianjin, and Shanghai.

[13] On the overall foreign exchange issue, see: John Stuermer, "The Foreign Exchange Situation," *China Business Review*, (January-February 1986), pp. 14-17.

Vertical Systems and Dual Leadership

Another key organizing concept for the Chinese bureaucrat is the *xitong*, or "system." *Xitong* in essence refers to the vertical functional hierarchies described in Chapter Three. They stretch from Beijing to the local units. Each central ministry or State Council commission heads its own *xitong*, which consists at its core of the hierarchy of bureaus and lower level units that are directly under that ministry or commission. But the concept of *xitong* is somewhat more inclusive than an organizational chart of, say, the Ministry of Finance reveals. As explained in Chapter Three, this ministry keeps in close contact with the financial offices in other government agencies. The Ministry of Finance considers these financial offices to be part of its own financial *xitong*, even though they also are a part of the *xitong* of the ministry or other body in which each is directly nested. A number of other ministries and State Council commissions in similar fashion deal with particular specialized offices in other government units, and they, too, regard these offices as part of their own "systems." Thus, the idea of "systems" is a central organizing concept in the minds of Chinese bureaucrats and policy makers.[14]

One major issue concerns the relationship of these vertical functional systems to the horizontal territorial governing bodies.[15] The Chinese express this problem in terms of whether *tiao tiao* (a "line," referring to a vertical system) serves *kuai kuai* (a "piece," referring to a territorial authority such as a provincial, municipal, or county government) or vice versa. Policy on this issue has varied enormously over the years, and actual policy differs at any given time as one goes from one system to another. Within the energy sector in the mid-1980's, for example, the petroleum and electric power elements gave relatively strong priority to the vertical functional lines of control as versus the territorial units, while in the water resources and the coal spheres the emphasis was more on the territorial dimension.

Another major issue generated by the country's bureaucratic structure concerns the extent to which units in different ministries and/or functional systems cooperate with each other. Formal lines of authority and communication are channeled either within the vertical hierarchy of a ministry or "system" (for example, from a municipal coal department to a provincial coal bureau to the central coal ministry) or within the territorially defined chain-of-command (such as between the Guangdong Coal Department and the Guangdong Provincial People's Government).

This arrangement inhibits direct communication and cooperation be-

[14] A. Doak Barnett, *Cadres*, esp. Part IV and pp. 6-9, 456-457.

[15] H. Franz Schurmann provided the classic statement of this issue in his *Ideology and Organization* chap. 3.

tween functional units under different ministries, as these units are parts of different *xitong*. For example, the Guangdong Electric Power Bureau finds it difficult to establish formal, direct ties with the local railway district or the Guangdong Coal Department, as these are part of different ministerial hierarchies. The planning and economic commissions of the Guangdong Provincial People's Government coordinate intra-provincial economic activities, but each of the economic departments within the province is also part of a vertical hierarchy that the provincial government does not fully control. The ability to elicit voluntary cooperation from specific units in the province depends in part on how centralized their individual "systems" are. In brief, only at the State Council level do all the lines of authority come together, and short of referring interagency disputes to the State Council for resolution, a great deal of time and effort must be expended on trying to achieve a working consensus among the various involved units.

As a result, major projects cannot be initiated or pursued with dispatch and decisiveness. Any major project requires extensive, active cooperation among people in different functional systems (such as railways, electric power, coal, and agriculture), as well as among different levels of government and, often, different governments at the same level of the national political hierarchy (e.g., different counties or provinces). Since leaders in different ministries have no direct authority over each other, the system enables one or a few affected units to delay a project for substantial periods of time. Rather than producing total paralysis, however, this situation has bred a wide range of measures to enhance coordination and overcome the fragmentation of authority, as detailed below.

Bureaucratic Ranks

Every unit in China—whether it be a governmental, Party, or corporate body or a sub-unit of any of these—has a rank. This system enables each unit to appraise its status with respect to all other units. For example, a ministry, a provincial government, and certain State corporations (such as SINOPEC and the China International Trust and Investment Corporation (CITIC)) have the same rank. In like fashion, a provincial government department and a ministerial bureau also have the same rank. This rank system is thus embedded in the hierarchy of formal levels of government that ascends from villages and cities through counties, prefectures, and provinces up to the national government (the "center") itself, and it makes real authority relations differ from the impression that might be gained from simply looking at an organizational chart that shows the national hierarchy of territorial units. Table 4-1 outlines the major equivalent positions in this national system of bureaucratic ranks.

As this table shows, ministries and provinces are of equal rank, as are ministerial bureaus and provincial departments. As explained below, units of equal rank cannot issue binding orders to each other, and thus a basic knowledge of this table is critical for understanding what is difficult to accomplish and what can be done more easily in terms of policy process in the energy sector.

It is pertinent to our story about the energy sector to note that municipalities and state corporations can be assigned to any one of several possible ranks, depending on circumstances. Municipalities are given ranks according to their size and importance. Beijing, Tianjin, and Shanghai are the only municipalities which fully enjoy the rank of a province; other municipalities may be regarded as the equivalents of prefectures, counties, or sub-county units. Anhui province, for example, as of 1985 had eight county level cities and eight prefectural level cities. A state corporation can be regarded as being the equivalent of a general bureau,[16] a bureau,[17] or virtually any other rank in the system. Indeed, as indicated above, SINOPEC and CITIC have ministerial rank and are directly under the State Council.

Because units with equal rank have no formal authority over each other, only a higher ranking unit can bring coequals together, elicit decisions, and enforce plans. Thus, only various Commissions under the

TABLE 4-1
Rank Equivalents among Government Organizations

Center	Province	County
Ministry (Bu)	Province (Sheng) Centrally Administered City (Beijing; Tianjin; Shanghai)	
General Bureau (Zongju)	Commission	
Bureau (Ju AND Si)	Provincial Department (Ting or Ju) Prefecture	
Division (Chu)		County (Xian) County Level Municipality
Section (Ke)		County Department

[16] CNOOC has this rank.
[17] The Capital Iron and Steel Corporation has this rank.

State Council have the authority to issue instructions to ministries to cooperate, and this is a crucial reason for the Commissions' existence and pivotal role.[18] The decision in 1985 to establish a State Educational Commission arose partly from this consideration. Many ministries run their own institutions of higher education. These fell outside the jurisdiction of the Ministry of Education, since other ministries have the same rank as the Ministry of Education. By turning the old Ministry of Education into a Commission in 1985 (and naming a Vice Premier as its head), the State Council created a structure that permits the top educational authorities to issue instructions to other ministries concerning the institutions of higher education in their "system."[19]

Although corporations (*zong gongsi*) and companies (*gongsi*) are assigned bureaucratic ranks, they are not formally a part of the government hierarchy, and therefore they cannot issue instructions to lower level government bodies.[20] Nevertheless, the level at which they fit into the bureaucracy, the official rank of their top officers, and other ways in which they deal with the state *are* affected by their bureaucratic ranks, and thus there is great sensitivity to this issue. Much energy may be spent to secure a higher rank. For example, as previously noted, for many months prior to its official establishment in 1982, the founders of CNOOC waged a quiet struggle over its rank. According to informed Western sources, the delay in the formal announcement of its existence was also due to a related disagreement over what body should make the announcement of its formation. If the Ministry of Petroleum Industry were to make the formal announcement, this would make clear that the CNOOC was at a lower bureaucratic rank than the ministry itself. If another body, such as the State Council, issued the announcement, then CNOOC might have full ministerial status.

Yet another complication arises because government institutions have Party organizations within them. It is, therefore, necessary to look at the relationships among the various Party organizations within government organs as well as the relations among government organs themselves to fully understand the authority relations.[21] Nanhai-West Oil Company,

---

[18] The ministries do have the right to appeal such instructions to the State Council, but this right evidently is not exercised frequently—presumably because the Commission has closer direct ties with the State Council than does the pertinent ministry in most cases.

[19] This authority does not, however, extend to the educational system within the People's Liberation Army.

[20] In Chinese jargon, corporations are "enterprises" (*qiye*) rather than "administrative organs" (*xingzheng jigou*).

[21] The Party side, for example, is critical for personnel appointments to positions of authority within the government organ.

one of the four operating companies under CNOOC, illustrates the complexities. In the formal table of organization, the Company is subordinate to CNOOC. Since Nanhai-West is located in Zhanjiang Municipality, the Zhanjiang Municipal Party Committee is in charge of the "Party life" activities (political study groups, political campaigns, etc.) of Party members in the Company, thereby enabling the municipality and its superior, the Guangdong Party Committee, to reach into the Company. However, the Party Committee of CNOOC in Beijing is in charge of the *professional* activities, including personnel appointments, for the Nanhai-West Party organization. In most cases outsiders simply lack the necessary information on Party leadership relations and formal government ranks to fully comprehend the lines of authority in the energy-related organs of government in China. Nevertheless, even at the above very general level an appreciation of the formal hierarchy of ranks does explain some of the major characteristics of China's policy process that are discussed in the remainder of this report.

Individual Rank and Stature

The bureaucratic ranking system is not the sole indicator of the authority of a particular unit. Another major factor is the rank and status of the individuals who lead the unit. Chinese officials in turn derive their status from the formal ranks they hold and the informal sources of infuence at their command. Most high level officials actually have three formal ranks: their formal government and/or Party title; their civil service grade; and their position in the Communist Party. These together determine their real stature when they deal with others. These three components of personal stature usually roughly correlate with each other. First, the rank of the leader of a unit—minister, governor, vice minister, bureau chief—usually is related to the unit itself, but this is not a rigid rule and there are quite a few exceptions. Officials usually retain the highest rank they have attained. Thus, the head as of 1986 of the China National Oil Development Corporation, Song Zhenming, was Minister of Petroleum from 1978 to 1980, and many Chinese still defer to him as a minister, even though CNODC has a General Bureau rank. Similarly, Chinese always recall that Qin Wencai was a Vice Minister of Petroleum before becoming head of CNOOC. Each official rank for individuals carries with it specific perquisites—such as access to cars, standards of housing accomodations, and fare at banquets—as well as a certain degree of prestige, and thus differences in these personal position-based ranks can be important.

Underlying this system of rank is a system of civil service grades. The

Chinese have developed a civil service system that includes more than twenty grades, with each grade specifying a salary range for the individuals in that grade. Generally speaking, a particular span of civil service grades is considered appropriate for each rank.[22]

While the above two types of ranks for individuals have their analogues in the American system, the third component of the personal stature of a Chinese official has no direct American counterpart. For unlike in America, in China for most purposes *Party* status is more significant than *government* rank as an indicator of real power. Party status derives both from the time the individual joined the revolution,[23] and from the career followed once in the Party. Party status is thus based primarily on prestige within the Party. Unfortunately, since internal Party affairs are considered privileged, data on a person's Party status are usually not available. Occasionally, the most powerful individual within a ministry or other organ is not the person who formally heads that unit but rather is a "subordinate" official who is the leading member of the Party group within the unit. Moreover, when two officials of equal government standing deal with a matter, the Party status of each can significantly affect their perceptions of each other.

With three components of personal stature plus a ranking system for government and corporate units operating simultaneously, calculations of real authority inevitably are complex and often cannot be arrived at by mechanically applying a set of rules. Indeed, different rank systems may have greater importance for different issues or transactions, and how officials interact is a function of both the relative personal status of the parties concerned and the relative ranks in the national political hierarchy of the organizations involved. Two examples illustrate the subtleties of the resulting situation.

First, the State Council established an Adjustment Office[24] within the Zhongnanhai in the mid-1980's. This office was put together primarily to better coordinate policy among the SPC, SEC, and Ministry of Finance. It became necessary to establish this office in part because since June of 1983 the SPC, SEC, and Ministry of Finance had all been headed

---

[22] For details on the civil service grade system, see: *Zhongyang caizheng fagui huibian*, 1957; and Barnett, *Cadres*, pp. 41-43.

[23] Indeed, Party cadres are often informally referred to by the date they joined the revolution: "Long March" cadres are those who participated in that epic event; Anti-Japanese war cadres joined during 1938-1945; civil war cadres joined during 1946-1948; and so forth; See Barnett, *Cadres*, pp. 43-45. The importance of the date of joining the revolution is also explored by William Whitson, "Organizational Perspectives and Decision Making in the Chinese Communist High Command," in Robert Scalapino (ed.), *Elites in the People's Republic of China* (Seattle: University of Washington Press, 1972), pp. 384-389.

[24] The Chinese name is *tiaojie bangongshi*.

by State Councillors.[25] The fact that all three heads held the same official rank (even though the Ministry of Finance as a unit had a lower rank than did the SPC or SEC) made it more difficult to coordinate policy among them. The Readjustment Office itself was headed by a Vice Minister of the SEC, but since the office formally represents the Premier, it could issue instructions to the SPC, SEC, and the Ministry of Finance.

Second, as previously noted, the establishment of CNOOC raised a sensitive question in terms of the relative ranks of the organization itself and of its new head, Qin Wencai. Qin had been the highest ranking Vice Minister of Petroleum before he had to resign that position in order to move to the CNOOC. A Vice Minister, however, has a personal official rank above that of a bureau head and typically would be loath to be put in charge of an organization that merely had the rank of a bureau. In the final analysis, CNOOC was given a rank—*zongju*, or "general bureau"—just below that of a ministry but above that of other bureaus. When the China National Oil Development Corporation was formed in 1985 to handle foreign participation in onshore exploration and development, therefore, this corporation was also assigned the rank of "general bureau"—even though, as noted above, it was headed by a man who is the former Minister of Petroleum and who personally retained the official rank of Minister.[26] The China National Coal Development Corporation, like CNOOC, was initially headed by a former Vice Minister and was assigned a "general bureau" rank.

These brief examples highlight both the subtleties of the interactions of the various ranking systems and the fact that these systems in reality do play a major role in decision making. The system of ranks is thus extremely important to the way the Chinese view and handle each other, both formally and informally. On a formal level, the ability of officials to gain access to others is structured by the rank system.[27] Also, as noted above, explicit guidelines stipulate the amenities that should be accorded individuals of each rank. Informally, one's rank both reflects and plays a

[25] This occurred when Minister of Finance Wang Bingqian became a State Councillor in June 1983.

[26] The former minister, Song Zhenming, had been disgraced in the Bohai oil rig disaster and assigned to a bureau level position as head of the Zhongyuan oil field since the beginning of the 1980's. Therefore, it was possible to assign him to a "general bureau" status position without undue problems in 1985, even though he retained the rank of Minister. One knowledgeable source commented that an individual's personal official rank is never reduced, even if that person assumes an actual position that normally confers a lower rank than the one he previously enjoyed.

[27] Personal contacts and informal relationships also, of course, play a role in obtaining access to individuals.

part in determining one's prestige and ability to be helpful to supporters, and these are core ingredients of power in any political system.[28]

This system of ranks extends to foreign individuals and firms themselves. The Chinese may conclude that a particular foreign firm is roughly the rank, for example, of a division (*chu*) in a central ministry, and its subordinate representative office in Beijing will be treated accordingly in terms of access and amenities. When the head of such a firm visits China, however, he may be given a higher rank, with appropriate changes in treatment. While Chinese never directly inform foreigners of their rank, a sensitive observer can assess his standing based on the access and treatment he receives. One Westerner indicated that his firm had initially received a lower rank than he thought appropriate, and he spent considerable time to ensure his very large corporation was reassigned to a higher rank.

Two points about this complex and highly formalized system of ranks bear repeating. First, ranks play an extremely important role in structuring authority relations, and much of the routing of an issue in the policy process reflects the fact that the bureaucratic terrain is contoured by this system. Second, formal ranks are not the sole determinants of how individuals and offices deal with each other. Actual behavior is also a function of many other factors. Two among these stand out: the bureaucratic divisions along functional lines described in the previous section; and on a less formal level, the influence of personal ties and the power of political networks based on those ties. This latter topic is taken up at the end of this chapter.

Interagency Relations

As already noted, most agencies are simultaneously subordinate to several other units. For example, a functional department in a provincial government is usually subordinate both to the provincial government itself and to the pertinent central ministry. This system of overlapping authority has generated a rich vocabulary to describe the formal relations between one separate unit and another. Perhaps the most fundamental distinction in this lexicon is that concerning "leadership" relations as versus "professional/business" relations.

Where "leadership relations" (*lingdao guanxi*) apply, the higher ranking unit can issue binding orders to its subordinate. Typically, this will also give the superior unit a powerful voice in such things as personnel appointments and major budget decisions for the subordinate organ.

[28] See below for details.

"Professional/business relations" (*yewu guanxi*) exist among agencies in interrelated areas of activity. In some instances, *yewu guanxi* refers to a relationship between a superior and a subordinate. In such instances, the superior agency issues guidelines, instructions, opinions, or non-binding directives to the subordinate agency, while recognizing these documents are for reference and can be modified or neglected. An obligation exists to take these documents into account, and the system works in a way that ensures the obligation is taken seriously. Yet, discretion exists at the lower level. This is one of the more confusing aspects of Chinese bureaucratic practice. The outsider is told by the superior agency that it has issued a directive, but is not told that there is no assurance the directive will be obeyed.[29]

Yewu guanxi also exist between agencies without formal channels between them but whose activities require frequent consultation and cooperation. Beijing's state wholesale companies, for example, have "professional/business relations" with the city's major government run retail department stores. The former cannot dictate what the latter should purchase, but all concerned recognize that substantial efforts to work closely together are in order.[30]

Typically, administrative guidelines specify "leadership relations" and the "professional relations" of an agency. These specifications are not always what outside observers might anticipate. For example, as of 1985 the MPI had "leadership" over all oil fields, but the Ministry of Coal Industry had only "professional/business" relations with provincial coal departments.[31]

Unfortunately, the "leadership" and "professional/business" distinction does not exhaust the list of important types of relationships between units in China. Participants in the world's largest bureaucracies, heirs to the world's oldest bureaucratic tradition, have devised a considerable list of additional terms that describe and prescribe formal relations among organs. Indeed, even within the "leadership–professional/business" sphere, there are refinements not captured in these brief observations. For example, the Party units embedded within two government organs or corporations may have relations that differ from the relations of the government/corporate units themselves. In addition, as explained in the illustration about leadership over the Communist Party organization in

---

[29] This problem exists for Chinese citizens as well as for foreigners.

[30] Kenneth Lieberthal, "Beijing's Consumer Market," *China Business Review* (September-October 1981).

[31] These provincial coal departments are "led" by the governments of the provinces in which they are located.

the Nanhai-West Oil Company provided above, one superior unit may lead part of the activity while another may lead a different part.[32]

Units jealously protect their ranks and the prerogatives that go with them. They tend to disregard requests from units with which they have no defined relationship, particularly if the request comes in the form of a formal directive or instruction. To illustrate this type of problem from the energy sector, in 1971-72 the South Sea Branch (SSB) of the China Petroleum Corporation[33] sought to build a large base at the port city of Zhanjiang. At the time, the main petroleum activities in Guangdong province were at Maoming. Zhanjiang municipality encompassed four regions: an old city; a large undeveloped area stretching five miles along the waterfront; a new town in the southeast part; and undeveloped land on the far side of Potou Bay. The Ministry of Fuel and Chemical Industries[34] in Beijing endorsed the SSB's plan to establish a Zhanjiang base. For reasons that are not clear, however, the Ministry did not communicate directly with the Zhanjiang municipal authorities, nor did it enlist Guangdong province in the negotiating process. Instead, Maoming municipality and the Maoming Oil Company pressed the case on behalf of the Ministry and the SSB. Maoming had a direct stake in the outcome because the SSB base might well develop a refinery that would handle Maoming crude.

The SSB wanted to establish its facilities on the strip of land between Zhanjiang's old city and new town. Zhanjiang's authorities opposed the SSB's plans for several seemingly rational reasons. They had hopes of developing the strip between the two built up areas of the city to make the municipality a more unified whole. They also did not want the pollution from a refinery. And they feared that they would have to give up some of their valuable wharf facilities without receiving comparable benefits in return. But, as one Zhanjiang native later confided, the city also opposed this proposal for another reason. The Zhanjiang leaders jealously protected their status, and they did not wish to make it appear they were subordinate to Maoming by taking orders from that city's leadership.

Zhanjiang's solution was to offer the poorer location on the far side of the Bay to the SSB. The SSB strongly opposed this decision but, working through Maoming, it could do nothing about it. Zhanjiang would almost

[32] As a reminder, in this case Nanhai-West's operations are subordinate to the Party Committee in CNOOC, while the "Party life" for Party members in Nanhai-West is under the leadership of the Zhanjiang Municipal Party Committee.

[33] The SSB later became Nanhai-West Oil Corporation.

[34] Which included what both previously and subsequently was the Ministry of Petroleum Industry.

certainly have had to yield if the Ministry of Fuel and Chemicals itself had directly pulled rank.[35] But Maoming's bureaucratic rank was no higher than that of Zhanjiang municipality itself. In the words of a Zhanjiang municipal official, "Maoming had no authority to lead Zhanjiang."[36]

The above analysis introduces some of the most basic fault lines in China's bureaucratic structure. As in all large scale organizations, there are tensions between vertical/functional and horizontal/territorial lines of authority. In addition, a complex group of unit and personal ranking systems seriously affects the way officials deal with each other. This set of circumstances produces twofold effects. Factors other than the substantive issue at stake influence the interaction among officials. Further, as the case of Maoming and Zhanjiang illustrates, the fragmentation of authority makes it potentially very difficult to reach satisfactory decisions and to implement those decisions in a coordinated fashion.

THE INTEGRATIVE MECHANISMS

To review, based on formal tables of organization, Chapter Three portrayed a highly complex but basically coordinated, hierarchical system. The preceding section, drawing on the perceptions and language of Chinese officials, portrayed the system as more fragmented, segmented, and stratified. This section seeks to reconcile these contrasting images. It illuminates the ties that bind the disparate parts of the Chinese system loosely together. Several major integrative mechanisms—in addition to the coordinating organs (SPC, SEC, SSTC, and MOF)—help bring a measure of unity and coherence to the Chinese bureaucratic system. Two mechanisms are the formal communication channels—document flows and meetings—that transcend the normal bureaucratic fault lines. In addition, adaptive, informal mechanisms have developed to facilitate cooperation among agencies: organizational stability, personal ties, and interagency bargains and exchange. Finally, a major integrative mechanism which the leaders attempted to use in the Mao era—ideology—is yielding to an effort to establish more effective methods for analyzing policy.

[35] This calculation is made somewhat complicated by the fact that the Ministry is a functional organ and the municipality is a territorial body, and 1972 was a period in which Beijing was giving relatively greater latitude to local territorial units. Still, the Ministry could have brought enormous pressure to bear.

[36] As of 1985, Zhanjiang had cause to regret its treatment of the SSB request. By then, Nanhai-West on the far side of Potou Bay was busily engaged in cooperative activities with foreign firms exploring for oil offshore—and Nanhai-West took care to limit the benefits that Zhanjiang municipality could reap from this potential windfall.

The Meeting System

Regularly convened national meetings bring together officials from diverse localities and hierarchical systems.[37] The leaders communicate their policies at these meetings, mobilize support, respond to criticism, and seek to cultivate a consensus over the proper direction of economic, ideological, and foreign policies. These meetings include formal plenums of the approximately 400 member Central Committee[38] of the CCP and secret gatherings of roughly the same group (called Central Work Conferences). At least one or two of these meetings are held each year. The several thousand member National People's Congress convenes once a year for one to two weeks. It brings together high and middle ranking officials from throughout China in government, industry, education, the military, research institutes, and so on to hear and comment upon a "state-of-the-union" address by the Premier, the annual plan and (when appropriate) the Five Year Plan, and the budget. The CCP gathers a similar group, but less frequently, in a National Party Congress or a National Party Conference. There were such Party gatherings, for example, in 1977, 1982, and 1985. The annual National Planning Conference convened by the SPC brings together officials from every ministry and province to set the annual plan, and the annual National Finance Conference convened by the MOF also assembles officials from every ministry and province to set the annual budget. These meetings can last up to a month or more and involve considerable bargaining.

Each of these types of meetings is convened according to detailed administrative rules. Their participants perceive them as a major way of overcoming the fragmentation of authority. At the same time, the voicing of different viewpoints and exposure of conflicting interests can be deeply divisive. As a result, the leaders spend a great deal of time preparing for these meetings, drafting the documents which are circulated at these meetings with considerable care and seeking to ensure the meetings will proceed smoothly.

The Document System

Most official communications take place *within* functional and territorial bureaucratic subsystems, thus reenforcing the structural fragmentation of the political apparatus. Each ministry, for example, has its own document series that it circulates to its subordinate organs. Ministerial jour-

---

[37] On national Party and government meetings, *see*: Kenneth Lieberthal, *Research Guide*.

[38] Including alternate members.

nals are also intended primarily for internal consumption. The country's excessive sense of secrecy, which was only beginning to lift under the reforms in the 1980's, contributed further to this compartmentalization of documentation and information.[39]

Some types of official documents, nevertheless, are specifically intended to overcome this compartmentalization. The most important of these are issued in the name of the Communist Party's Central Committee[40] and are called "central documents" (in Chinese, *zhongfa*). These documents may take many forms: direct orders; expressions of opinion; circulars that provide information on some issue; and so forth. They are sent to diverse units at several levels throughout the bureaucratic hierarchy,[41] and there is an elaborate system for further disseminating their contents to designated audiences.

The Politburo deliberately uses "central documents" to overcome the inherent functional and territorial compartmentalization of information that the system produces. For example, a "central document" may distribute a report on an important development or a successful example of policy implementation that has come to the attention of the leaders through the normal, segmented channels of communication. In such a case, the leaders issue a covering document on the report, indicating why it merits nationwide study, and append a copy of the report. Or, the leaders may decide that a directive which initially affects a limited portion of the population should come to the attention of the nation. Directives pertaining to agricultural organization, for example, frequently take the form of "central documents" and are disseminated outside the rural sector. Speeches of top leaders may also be the object of a "central document." Thus, a number of issues are handled via "central documents" precisely because the issues themselves cross the narrower functional and geographical boundaries that fragment authority in the Chinese system. The Party Secretariat and the State Council have their own document series that can be circulated to a wide range of receiving organs.[42]

Organizational Stability and Policy Communities

At the Central level, at least, greater organizational stability exists than the history of China's numerous bureaucratic reorganizations would

---

[39] See: Michel Oksenberg, "Methods of Communication."
[40] Although these are actually initiated by the Politburo.
[41] The specific receiving units vary with the document.
[42] See: Kenneth Lieberthal, *Central Documents and Politburo Politics in China.*

suggest. This organizational stability, moreover, has enabled extensive informal ties to develop that partially bridge the gaps in authority that separate functional units. At the Center, one very important level at which this continuity and "networking" occurs is that of the bureau (*ju* or *si*).[43] While the configurations of the ministries themselves within the energy sector have changed in almost every mathematically feasible way since the early 1950's, for example,[44] the changes at the functional bureau level within this sector have been far less frequent or dramatic. Indeed, more often than not, when ministries and commissions are merged or split, most of the bureaus concerned remain basically untouched, with the same responsibilities after the change that they had before.

The fate of the bureau in charge of key projects at the State Capital Construction Commission illustrates the phenomenon of having bureau level units survive through periods of major bureaucratic reshuffling. This unit simply became the Key Projects Construction Bureau of the SPC when the Capital Construction Commission was abolished in 1982, and its employees continued to work in the very same office space that they had used before. Similar cases abound. The abolition of the State Energy Commission, as noted in Chapter Three, basically saw its personnel become a bureau in the State Economic Commission even though it physically remained located in the Ministry of Petroleum Industry compound. The merger of the Ministry of Water Resources with the Ministry of Electric Power produced changes in only a few bureaus, such as personnel, that serve the entire ministry. All other bureaus remained the same, with the water resources offices on one side of a large compound in southwest Beijing and the electric power offices on the other side. The Foreign Investment Management Bureau of MOFERT was formerly the Foreign Investment Control Commission. When the Commission was abolished, the people moved intact into MOFERT.

Personnel changes at the bureau level have also tended, on the basis of the limited empirical evidence available, to occur very slowly: China's top leaders have found it relatively easy to change people at the Vice Minister level or higher but generally have not been able to make sweeping personnel changes at the bureau level and below. For example, when

[43] See Michel Oksenberg, "Economic Policy-Making." Similar networking may also characterize the system at the "department" (*chu*) level.

[44] The Ministries of Water Resources and of Electric Power have combined, split, and combined again as noted in Chapter Three. From 1949-1955 the electric power, coal, and petroleum bureaucracies were all combined into a single Ministry of Fuel Industry. The Ministry of Petroleum Industry united with the Ministry of Chemicals for 1970-1978. The Ministry of Coal Industry combined with Petroleum and Chemicals in 1970, only to split off again in 1975.

Yu Qiuli brought in a new team to head the State Planning Commission,[45] he still had to rely on the former SPC staff. As of the 1980's, these same people (who had been recruited to their jobs as young men by either Gao Gang or Li Fuchun in the 1950's) remained the dominant portion of the SPC staff.

The continuity at the bureau level becomes more significant when one considers that certain bureaus in different ministries and commissions have had to deal with each other regularly for decades.[46] With continuity both of personnel and of cooperative activities, considerable mutual knowledge and understanding are developed that cross current ministerial boundaries. Indeed, interviewing suggests that in some instances interrelated bureaus in two different ministries know more about the development of a particular policy than do their counterparts within either of the ministries. Within the MWREP, SPC, SSTC, and Ministry of Communications in Beijing, for example, exists a community of people who have analyzed and debated the Three Gorges project for over thirty years. They are more knowledgeable about the project and where it stands bureaucratically than are, say, bureau chiefs and vice ministers within the MWREP who are not involved in the Three Gorges plan. Similarly, a community of experts at the MPI, CNOOC, MOFERT, the Ministries of Geology and Communications, the SPC, SEC, and the Bank of China have been working on the offshore oil issue for nearly twenty years. This does not mean the members of a "policy community" share a common perspective on the problem. Indeed, our interviews suggest perspectives are largely shaped by people's primary organizational responsibilities. Nonetheless, while formal functional divisions remain important, bureau level networks cross organizational boundaries and are a key feature of the bureaucratic terrain.[47]

Personal Ties and Networks

Embedded within Chinese organizations and totally missing from the formal organizational charts are the personal ties which bind different agencies together. Indeed, many informed foreign and Chinese observers believe these bonds of mutual obligation—*guanxi* in Chinese—constitute the single most important ingredient which integrates the system

---

[45] See Chapter Five for details.

[46] This is also true for relations between central level bureaus and certain lower level bureaucratic units and large state enterprises.

[47] Almost certainly, moreover, a parallel situation exists at lower levels of the national hierarchy.

and enables it to function.[48] While not denigrating the significance of *guanxi*, other observers stress its relative importance has fluctuated over time and attach great weight as well to the formal channels of authority.[49]

In any case, *guanxi* is a concept deeply rooted in Chinese culture, as is the related notion of *ganqing*, or sentiment and affect.[50] Bonds of *guanxi* entail mutual obligation. These bonds arise from family connections, common geographical origin, shared experience (school or military service ties), or shared loyalty toward the same patron or commander (such as having served Zhou Enlai or Liu Shaoqi).

Politically ambitious patrons and cliques seek to place people with whom they have *guanxi* in other agencies to extend their influence. We have already noted how the petroleum group at its height had placed people loyal to it at various levels in the SPC, SEC, the Ministries of Finance, Coal, Chemical Industries, and Metallurgy, as well as in the State Council. Madame Mao and her associates placed people with whom they had *guanxi* throughout the bureaucracy during the Cultural Revolution era. In the mid-1980's, people associated with the Communist Youth League in the 1950's—which Hu Yaobang headed—and who were trained in Moscow in the 1950's—where Li Peng was active—were winning positions throughout the bureaucracy.[51] This was thought to accrue to the benefit of Hu and Li. Efforts are also made to cultivate *guanxi* where little or none exists, in order to have sympathetic personnel in other agencies.

Several qualifications must be noted, however. Individuals have *guanxi* with many people and owe obligations to more than one patron. Groups who share *guanxi* are not totally cohesive; they are marked by internal rivalries. Loyalties may change, and clients of one patron may

[48] This underlying notion structures the work by Lucien Pye; See, e.g., his *Dynamics*. See also John Wilson Lewis, *Political Networks and the Chinese Policy Process* (Stanford: Northeast Asia-United States Forum on International Policy, 1986).

[49] See, e.g.: Harry Harding, *Organizing China*; Kenneth Lieberthal, *Revolution and Tradition in Tientsin, 1949-52* (Stanford: Stanford University Press, 1980), esp. pp. 180-196; Ezra Vogel, "From Friendship to Comradeship," *China Quarterly*, No. 21 (January-March 1965), pp. 46-60; and Frederick Teiwes, *Politics and Purges in China* (New York: M. E. Sharpe, 1979).

[50] See: Morton Fried, *Fabric of Chinese Society: A Study of the Social Life of a Chinese County Seat* (New York: 1969); and Andrew Nathan, *Peking Politics, 1918-1923* (Berkeley: University of California Press, 1976), esp. pp. 47-58.

[51] On Li Peng, *see*: Dong Xusheng, "Zhongguo weilai: liu Su pai yu liu Mei pai de bodou," *Zhongguo zhi chun* (November 1985), pp. 10-16. On Hu Yaobang, *see*: William Mills, "Generational Change in China," *Problems of Communism*, (November-December, 1983), esp. pp. 33-35.

shift to others if the client believes the first patron is losing his capacity to fulfill his obligations. *Guanxi* and the cliques built upon it are therefore subtle and potentially fragile. Nonetheless, Chinese strongly prefer to initiate contact across bureaucratic boundaries through someone with whom they have *guanxi*. That person serves as the entree into another organization, providing information about the lay of the land, who counts, how to get things done, and so on. That person also acts as the guarantor, so to speak, of one's merit and seriousness. In short, Chinese culture attaches great importance to human relations; such virtues as loyalty, mutual trust, and fulfillment of personal obligations are core to Confucian civilization. Personal networks based on traditional values continue to exist within the framework of fragmented organizations and are essential to surmounting the barriers among them.

Bargains and Exchange

The existence of policy communities and groups bound by *guanxi* enable bureaucrats to strike credible deals between different agencies. In fact, relations among units are governed by wide-ranging, complex agreements that have been negotiated over a period of months and years. In effect, the leaders of each province have struck their deal with the Center. A package has been worked out concerning the revenue flow between the two, the amount the Center will invest in the province, the amount of foreign currency at the disposal of the province, the amount of scarce centrally controlled material resources (such as electricity) the Center will allocate to the province, and so on. The package is subject to an annual review and marginal adjustment.

Both provinces and counties strike deals as well, swapping scarce commodities each needs. Shanxi province, for example, negotiates many agreements with units outside the province to supply Shanxi coal for a wide range of materials Shanxi needs,[52] as do counties within the provinces. In fact, bargains and deals are struck at all levels of the hierarchy.[53]

A substantial portion of the transactions into which an agency enters are legal and encouraged by the state. However, other transactions are only semi-legal or illegal, such as, for example, trading in centrally-allocated commodities outside the state plan. Yet, these latter dealings also play an important role in making the economy work.

Bargaining and ancillary agreements are essential in initiating major

[52] For details, see Chapter Seven.

[53] David M. Lampton presents a broadly similar view of the prevalence of intra-bureaucratic bargaining in the Chinese system in "Chinese Politics: The Bargaining Treadmill," *Issues and Studies* vol. 23, no. 3 (1987), pp. 11-41.

capital construction projects. This bargaining process is necessary because any major construction project requires the active cooperation of the local officials in the province(s) concerned. Local officials cannot openly refuse a demand from the Center. All parties concerned, nevertheless, recognize that the locales must be enticed into cooperation because otherwise they are capable of producing interminable delays during the construction of the project.

The relative bargaining leverage of each party depends on a range of matters, including the extent to which the proposed project is intrusive and disruptive in the locale(s) concerned. In this regard, for example, oil exploration (which is often done in remote areas) should be politically "easier" than development of major coal fields (which may require relocation of population and substantial environmental degradation). Hydropower dam construction should be the most difficult of all, as it not only requires relocation of people who lived in the reservoir area and changes in transport systems, but also its major benefits (flood control and electric power) often accrue disproportionately to those who did not have to pay the greatest price (i.e., the people who live upstream of the dam).

From Ideology to Policy Analysis

Slogans buttressed by ideological sanctions have been an important force for overcoming the natural fragmentation of the system. Under Mao Zedong, the central leadership often adopted a basic stance, such as to stress self-reliance or to develop small-scale industry, that would be encapsulated in appropriate slogans and made the basic thrust of national policy. Bureaucrats in various units would then have to justify their policies in terms of the ideologically sanctioned slogan of the moment. This made units in different functional spheres march to the same drummer, if not always in perfect step.[54] Believing that simple-minded sloganeering and the ideological dogmatism behind it helped bring on the disasters of the Great Leap Forward and the Cultural Revolution, Deng Xiaoping and his associates deliberately rejected the Maoist heavy reliance upon unifying slogans as a mechanism for achieving policy coherence.

In place of slogans, the Deng leadership has attempted to forge an empirically-based policy process, in which coherence is attained through a process of consensus building and consultations. To overcome fragmentation of authority, the leaders have introduced or strengthened mecha-

[54] See, for example: Michel Oksenberg, *Policy Formulation.*

nisms which have less deleterious consequences.[55] The goal is to to forge nationally accepted, more rigorous methods for analyzing policy choices and for decentralizing the decision-making process. Four measures along these lines warrant brief mention.

First, in the 1980's an effort is being made to foster a sense of professionalism. The Chinese Academy of Social Sciences (CASS) and the Chinese Academy of Sciences have fleshed out their organizations, established new research institutes, enhanced their library holdings, and begun to publish a substantial number of professional journals and volumes. Also, professional societies have been established that hold periodic meetings and, in some instances, issue publications. Some of these societies have regional branch associations. These professional organizations and their activities help to bring together people in disparate units and facilitate communication among them. In the energy area, for example, the China Energy Research Society (*Zhongguo nengyuan yanjiu hui*), organized in 1981, helps energy specialists from various sectors coordinate research in energy policy and technology. Communities of experts which cut across bureaucratic divisions, in short, are emerging at the initiative of the leaders.

Second, a concerted effort has been made in the 1980's to improve the quality of data on which decisions are based. Key to this has been the expanded scope and improved quality of statistics collected by the State Statistical Bureau. A great deal of the statistical collection effort in China before the 1980's was done by ministries themselves. The ministries maintained their information in a way that often made it very difficult for other pertinent units to obtain necessary data, thus contributing to the fragmentation of the system. The 1980's efforts to increase the power of the SSB and to disseminate its results more widely are reducing the extent to which ministries act as independent empires that do not communicate effectively with each other.[56]

Third, the stress since the early 1980's on feasibility studies[57] has provided a strong organizational impetus toward greater consultation and cooperation in the planning stages of major projects. As explained in

[55] The use of slogans produced a number of undesirable effects, including an inappropriate degree of uniformity across different issue areas, unwillingness of experts to voice their views for fear of reprisals, a tendency toward big pushes rather than the sustained attention that many issues required, and so forth.

[56] The State Statistical Bureau, for example, now publishes an annual statistical yearbook, and in mid-1985 it commenced open publication of a wide-ranging monthly statistical bulletin. Both of these types of publication are available for purchase in China's book stores.

[57] In Chinese, *kexing xing de yanjiu baogao.*

Chapter Three, the State Planning Commission not only commissions specialized studies pertinent to major project proposals, but since the early 1980's has also convened conferences of the key specialists from many pertinent units to go over the proposals in detail to determine their feasibility.[58] This process of determining project feasibility thus attempts to compensate for the inherent fragmentation in authority and communications in earlier stages of the policy process.

Fourth, China's reformers are trying to move the entire economic system in a direction that would increasingly base transactions on market activities rather than on bureaucratic actions. This effort in effect amounts to yet another way to navigate around the "great walls" that tend to separate bureaucratic entities in different functional hierarchies. They wish to diminish the importance of personal ties and bureaucratic deals and to expand the role of the market place in integrating the economy. This shift toward the use of economic ties and market relationships had not as of 1985, however, gone very far in the energy sector.[59]

A wide range of mechanisms, therefore, enable energy bureaucrats to meet the objectives which their leaders and they have set, to cooperate with one another, and to achieve some coherence and consistency in policy implementation. The actual system does not correspond with the prescribed one, however, and units cooperate for reasons other than ones which the top leaders desire. Put another way, the system works in general, but this is not due primarily to the formal authority relations which we outlined in Chapters Two and Three. Rather, it works because it is usually in the interest of middle and lower level officials to respond to and strike deals with their superiors. Therefore, one has to understand what bureaucratic considerations drive the leaders of individual agencies in China.

BEHAVIORAL CONSEQUENCES

A key question is what resources leaders of a unit seek to accrue either for themselves or for the unit in order to strike effective bargains. The answer to this question must vary somewhat with the motivations of the leader involved. Some leaders, after all, seek to advance further in the system. Others give higher priority to increasing the security of their current position. Still others gain their greatest satisfaction from winning approval from their subordinates. These various goals are, of course, somewhat overlapping, and the strategies to pursue each are not

---

[58] A detailed description of one of these conferences, convened in May 1983, is presented in Chapter Six on the Three Gorges dam.

[59] The case studies in Chapters Five through Seven buttress this general assertion.

mutually exclusive. Indeed, similar choices confront middle-level managers in any bureaucratic hierarchy. But the strategies of Chinese officials to achieve varying mixes of these goals exhibit some distinctive features.

A Chinese unit leader's strategy generally must make major provision for: obtaining access to scarce resources that he can distribute to individuals in his own organization; protecting his organization from the uncertainties of an external environment in which top leaders can act capriciously and bureaucratic authority is fragmented; and developing goods and services within his organization which he can use to strike his bargains with the external environment. These different components of a strategy are, moreover, to some extent interrelated. An element that is core to all three is the need to build up a collection of followers and to cultivate one or more patrons who can provide protection and benefits.

For the first strategy to work, a successful leader must provide his followers with access to resources—including everything from opportunities for advanced study or promotion to the access necessary to acquire goods that are not otherwise available. This strategy in China of the 1980's increasingly encourages obtaining resources from the international arena, as foreign connections have become of growing importance as a way to create opportunities for supporters to obtain foreign exchange and/or to travel abroad. The ability to secure advanced study and training abroad is highly prized (often in part for the additional foreign connections it can generate), and an official who can generate these opportunities for his supporters increases his own standing not only with his followers but also with many of his peers.

The foreign connection thus became a highly valued resource among Chinese officials by the mid-1980's.[60] There also remained ambivalence about close dealings with foreigners, who many Chinese believe may corrupt and exploit China. Close contacts with foreigners thus became simultaneously a source of strength and vulnerability for the key individuals concerned. Officials who are not successful in drawing resources from the international arena may be prepared to adopt a very critical attitude toward those who do. Many people who *are* able to broker relations with the international arena find, moreover, that they are under constant pressure to *increase* the resources they obtain so as to maintain their status by meeting the rapidly growing demands of their own constituents.

The second basic element of strategy—devising means to protect one's

[60] Probably a similar dynamic developed with regard to opportunities to go to the Soviet Union in the heyday of Sino-Soviet cooperation in the 1950's.

own unit from an uncertain external environment—grows out of the basic nature of the system itself. Given sharp changes in policy and the fragmentation of bureaucratic authority, it is not surprising that a demonstrated ability to protect one's own organization and its prerogatives has become a key way to generate respect. This factor may help to explain, for example, why Nanhai-West fought tenaciously against dividing up its territory and authority with Nanhai-East, even though both were operating companies under CNOOC. Originally, Nanhai-West had responsibility for all of the offshore effort[61] off the coast of Guangdong province. When Nanhai-East was first formed it assumed control over a slice of this territory that was then reduced in several stages under pressure from Nanhai-West.

Hence, the demonstrated ability to employ a large staff and to keep them working is a major ingredient of influence; it secures *guanxi* and generates loyalty. Leaders of organizations know that many of the people upon whom they depend measure their accomplishments more in terms of their success in employing and taking care of additional people than in terms of their efficiency in completing a job. The key reformers in China's current power elite, it should be noted, want to assign efficiency a higher priority than employment. But there is ample evidence that the previous norms continue to govern the thoughts and actions of a large percentage of both cadres and workers.

Examples of this priority on employment over efficiency abound. In 1984 Nanhai-West was reportedly preparing to add another 4,000 members to its staff, even though it already had about 10,000 people on its payroll and no commercial oil had yet been found in areas under its jurisdiction. The fact that as of late 1985 these additional personnel had not been allocated may well have been interpreted among some bureaucrats in China as suggesting that Nanhai-West's power had not grown over the intervening year. The relatively disappointing results of the offshore exploration effort in the areas under Nanhai-West's jurisdiction would itself have warranted keeping the company's staff from growing. Significant staff additions even in the face of these results would, however, have contributed to the prestige of the head of Nanhai-West among his colleagues and followers.

Relatedly, in the hydropower sector, 35,000 to 50,000 people (including dependents) were engaged in building the Gezhouba dam on the Yangtze River. Foreign specialists, as explained in Chapter Six, believe that the much larger Three Gorges Dam farther upstream on the Yangtze

---

[61] With the exception of some preliminary exploratory drilling done by the Ministry of Geology.

could be built most efficiently with a small fraction of this work force.[62] Nevertheless, the Chinese as of 1985 planned to assign the entire Gezhouba construction force to work on the Three Gorges project. While the design people may well recognize the desirability of sharply reducing the size of this construction contingent, the construction units themselves would fight any such attempt, as it would greatly diminish the power of the cadres involved. Since the construction forces have the same bureaucratic rank as the design units, moreover, the design specialists lack the authority to enforce their preferences on the construction units.

This desire to protect one's organization from the uncertainties of an external environment finds its most striking manifestation in the strategy that the Chinese call "creating your own society." This has the organ concerned provide not only wages and insurance/pension benefits but also housing, education, health facilities, and other things. When major new projects are undertaken (such as opening a new coal mine, developing a new oil supply base, building a new dam, and so forth), typically the project people do not rely on the local government authorities for housing, education, health facilities, and related amenities. Instead, they develop their own duplicate facilities, and these then remain in place for as long as the project people are there.

There are many examples of the "own society" approach in the energy sector. The Yangtze Valley Planning Office[63] in Wuhan, for instance, provides its employees housing, health and recreational facilities, and education (including, until the Cultural Revolution, its own university). This unit is a permanent government facility, with some 12,000 staff as of 1985. As explained above, Nanhai-West grew out of the former South Sea Branch of the China Petroleum Corporation. When it began to develop land across Potou Bay from the built-up section of the city of Zhanjiang in the early 1970's, it also constructed the educational, housing, and other facilities its staff required. This is reflected in its administrative structure, which includes individual departments in charge of education, technology development and training, scientific research, public security, car services, and a technical school, workers' hospital, and daily life service company. Other Nanhai-West departments, such as those involved in construction, build office space, living quarters, and guest quarters as well as undertaking construction work directly involved in offshore oil exploration and development.

While the YVPO represents a permanent government organ and Nan-

---

[62] This type of dam construction inherently requires the use of large, complex machinery and is not amenable to the type of mass mobilization of relatively unskilled labor that may be effective in other types of construction.

[63] Chapter Six deals with this unit in detail.

hai-West typifies a large government corporation, the Gezhouba dam site illustrates that this same strategy has been implemented on a project-specific basis. An entire small city was built to house and educate the dependents of the workers at Gezhouba. During the nearly two decades that it will take to build the Three Gorges Dam, the workers and their families will continue to live in this city and will commute to the construction site more than forty kilometers away. Again, it is the dam construction units that are responsible for building this support city and for maintaining its services.[64]

Indeed, the strategy of "creating your own society" is so fundamental that it arouses comment when the leader of an important organization chooses *not* to follow this approach. Wang Tao, who headed Nanhai-East, did this, as did the leadership of the South Yellow Sea Oil Corporation. The fact that Wang Tao was promoted to Minister of Petroleum Industry in 1985 may have been in some measure due to his eschewing the path of "creating one's own society." But the political and bureaucratic factors that led so many officials to utilize the "own society" strategy in the past do not change easily or quickly, and Wang Tao's very different approach should remain atypical. For solid reasons "creating one's own society" should continue to be the preferred strategy, and the ability to attain it is likely for years to remain one measure of a leader's success in the eyes of most of his colleagues and followers.[65]

Obtaining resources from the external environment and protecting the unit from the uncertainties of that environment are thus basic strategies pursued by most bureaucratic leaders to solidify their positions. But an ambitious official also wants to enhance his own and his unit's position in the system. Many tactics can contribute to meeting this goal. Leaders who want to move up almost certainly will cultivate patrons at higher levels, in which case those patrons will come under pressure to provide both protection and access to resources to their followers. In addition, successful leaders in the past have sometimes worked hard to have their own units recognized as official models for others to emulate in accomplishing one or another national task. Given the nature of the system, which requires that units engage in an almost constant process of bargaining and exchange, an additional critical concern for an ambitious of-

[64] Nicholas H. Ludlow, "Three Gorges Project: Harnessing the Yangzi." *China Business Review* (May-June 1980), pp. 16-21.

[65] A separate but related issue is whether the policy of "creating your own society" means that major projects can be constructed and run without extensive cooperation from local governing authorities. The answer is "no," and Chapter Seven, on central-local relations, details the ways in which such local cooperation remains critical even where a unit follows an "own society" policy.

ficial must be to try to develop within the unit resources that can be used in bargaining with others. A major resource, in this regard, is the ability to generate revenues for the Center.

At the central level, the ability of a ministry to generate funds affects its power, prestige, and, in circular fashion, its ability to obtain additional funding. Within the energy sector, the Ministry of Petroleum Industry has held a very strong position in the system in part because from the early 1960's to the late 1970's its performance in rapidly increasing oil production made it a major revenue earner.[66] Financial reforms in the 1980's, moreover, made petroleum—along with electric power—two of the four sectors whose taxes flow to the central level (versus the provinces and lower levels) in a higher percentage than is the case for other production ministries.[67] Also, the offshore effort during the 1980's was structured in a way that contributed to this revenue flow from the petroleum sector.[68] The MPI was thus regarded as a particularly strong ministry, and this strength was reflected in a number of areas. For example, the MPI was able to negotiate a depletion allowance with the Ministry of Finance that substantially increased its funds.[69] It was also more successful than other energy ministries in placing its people onto the staffs of, for example, the Ministry of Finance and the Bank of China. And people who joined this ministry straight out of the university reportedly have enjoyed relatively rapid promotions and good career opportunities.

The Ministry of Coal Industry, by contrast, is not a major revenue earner. In part, this stems from the low prices that are stipulated for coal produced by the major mines. In addition, most tax revenues from the mines go to the local authorities rather than to the central ministry.[70] Coal's low revenue status has perhaps, again in circular fashion, been a factor in its not being able to garner the power and prestige at the Center needed to obtain an increase in coal prices.[71] This may also have affected career advancement, which has tended to be slow and erratic, within this highly factionalized ministry. Thus, the coal ministry currently lacks the

[66] Chapter Five provides details.

[67] On a fixed basis, as of 1985 seventy percent of these taxes went to the Center. The other two, according to interview data, are nonferrous metals and petrochemicals.

[68] See Chapter Five for details.

[69] The MPI used these funds, in part, to enhance the welfare of its employees. For example, it constructed a huge cold storage facility for storage of perishable commodities.

[70] This is the case for mines run directly by the Center as well as for mines administered at a provincial level. Chapter Seven explains some of the complexities of levels of ownership, administration, and finance in the coal sector.

[71] If so, this is not the only factor but may be an important contributing element. Certainly the importance of coal in the pricing of a wide range of industrial products also produces caution in raising the price of this core resource.

bureaucratic clout of its petroleum counterpart even though it plays a far more important role in the country's overall energy picture.

The MWREP falls somewhere in between. As noted in Chapter Three, the cost allocation in dam development is structured in such a way that the MWREP is charged with the full cost of a dam, even when a good part of that cost is generated by the needs of the Ministry of Communications, environmental authorities, agricultural interests, and other beneficiaries of a multi-purpose facility. The water resources people in the MWREP, therefore, cannot show a positive balance sheet, and their position is affected accordingly.[72] The electric power people within the MWREP, by contrast, preside over a very profitable segment of the energy sector, and one in which, as noted above, seventy percent of the tax revenues go directly to the Center. This contributes to their relative dominance of the MWREP itself.[73]

As these very quick summaries suggest, the ability to generate revenues for the Center is a very important factor in determining power and prestige. Thus, calculations of the power of a ministry (and its leaders) must combine consideration of the volume of production and the importance of that production to the national economy with analysis of related prices, production costs, and the distribution of tax revenues, product by product. It is these latter factors that dictate the extent to which the Ministry can contribute to the coffers of the Center.

One component of power, of course, is the ability to oppose a policy or project. Given the nature of the Chinese system, rarely is open opposition either tolerated or effective. Indeed, when the "wind" of a policy is blowing strongly (to use a Chinese metaphor), opponents usually quietly seek cover to ride out the tempest rather than try more overt protest actions. When a policy wind is blowing more gently, however, officials may voice dissenting opinions more directly.

Chinese officials have utilized a wide range of subtle strategies to lessen the impact of policies with which they disagree. Many of these strategies take advantage of the relatively self-contained nature of Chinese units to try to blunt the effects of an offending policy. One time honored strategy of opposition, for example, has been to proclaim one's support of the offending policy while not in fact carrying it out in one's unit. When the policy eventually begins to change, the unit can then

---

[72] This financial weakness is, however, partly counterbalanced by the very large number of people employed by this section of the MWREP and the enormous contributions the MWREP makes to improving the lives of China's peasants through flood prevention.

[73] As explained in Chapter Three, the relative centralization of the electric power side and decentralization of the water resources side also affects power relationships within the MWREP.

emerge as a pace setter in support of the new policy trend. Thus, one of the factors contributing to the tendency of Chinese officials to seek autarky for their units is connected to strategies of opposition and of self-protection. In this regard, it bears stressing that a number of reforms in the fiscal and personnel systems during the early 1980's had the effect of further encapsulating individual units, making them more opaque to observation from outside the unit.

During the Maoist era, defensive strategies often also included political name calling that sought to tarnish the reputation of an opposing unit's leaders. The post-Mao reforms generally reduced the political temperature in China to the extent that labelling opponents as class enemies and capitulationists fell out of vogue. These same reforms, however, enhanced the utility of other weapons in the arsenals available to officials. For example, during the 1980's those opposed to the Three Gorges project called for additional feasibility studies to be done "so as to make sure that the dam will fully meet expectations." Opponents of this dam also cited the views of foreign experts where these raised doubts about the feasibility of the project. The reforms generally stress technical evaluation and utilizing foreign expertise, and they thus made these ploys more effective and therefore more popular in the 1980's. The rapidly growing concern over corruption in the mid-1980's also produced its own incentives. Whereas under Mao character assassination often took the form of questioning a person's political "stance," in the mid-1980's the more frequent charge was that of pursuing private interests over the public good. In both cases, the object was to tarnish a policy through questioning the probity of its advocates.

SUMMARY

Having teased out pertinent models in the literature on China and provided an overview of the formal and informal structures and practices in the energy sector, we now turn to concrete case studies. These studies in the next three chapters explore the dynamics of energy policy making in greater depth. Understanding the basic structure and political processes of this sector, we can probe the factors which determine specific energy policies and capture the interplay among the concerns and vision of the leaders, the behavior of the energy sector bureaucracies, and the interests and resources of the provinces. The first study (Chapter Five), of the gradual expansion of foreign participation in China's petroleum development, focuses attention primarily on the leadership level. The second case (Chapter Six), concerning the debate over whether to construct the

Three Gorges dam, highlights more the importance of bureaucratic interests and politics, especially in the 1980's. And the third and fourth cases (Chapter Seven), the development of the Shanxi coal basin and the relations between Beijing and Guangdong in the offshore oil saga, concentrate on the bargaining inherent in central-provincial relations.

· 5 ·

CHINA'S INVOLVEMENT WITH THE OUTSIDE WORLD:
THE CASE OF PETROLEUM, 1959-84

From the late 1950's to the mid-1980's, China's petroleum industry underwent a dramatic transformation. An industry which produced five million metric tons of crude petroleum in 1960 pumped 126 MMT from the earth in 1985. Dependent upon oil imports in its first decade, the People's Republic became self-sufficient in petroleum production in the mid-1960's, began to export modest amounts in the early 1970's, and in 1985, it exported over 25% of its petroleum production and earned over 20% of its foreign currency through the export of crude petroleum and petroleum products. In 1963, Mao Zedong proclaimed that the Ministry of Petroleum Industry embodied his principles of self-reliance and economic development through reliance of mobilization of the masses. By the mid-1970's, the Ministry epitomized China's thirst for foreign technology and equipment and willingness to sell natural resources to finance the desired imports. By the early 1980's, the Ministry was at the forefront of forming joint ventures with foreign firms in which the foreigners obtained equity holdings in China.

Remarkable individuals—the so-called "petroleum group"—spearheaded these changes. Yu Qiuli, Kang Shien, Tang Ke, and Song Zhenming led the development of the Daqing oilfield in the early 1960's. The group expanded to embrace economic officials whom Mao designated to take charge of the Chinese economy under the leadership of Yu Qiuli in 1963-65: Gu Mu, Sun Jingwen, Lin Hujia and others. By the mid-1970's, several of these individuals (Yu, Kang, and Gu) were the principal economic specialists among the top 25 to 35 leaders of the country—while others such as Tang, Song, and Sun led key ministries and linked the top leaders to the bureaucracies. In less than 25 years, these individuals went from well-drilling in remote Heilongjiang province and from middle level positions in the Maoist bureaucracy to membership in the cosmopolitan and complicated international petroleum industry. Many came from humble peasant backgrounds, and their story parallels the rise of successful oilmen who began their lives in the Saudi Arabian desert, the Sumatran jungles, and the Texas plains, and who manage the world's future in this vital resource.

Chinese policy toward development of its petroleum resources evolved incrementally from the original commitment to self-reliance. This chapter traces the various steps along the way: the rise of the petroleum group to national prominence; the 1972 readiness to import foreign equipment; the 1973 decision to export substantial amounts of oil to pay for imported technology; the 1974 acceptance of disguised credit to finance purchases; the political strife of the mid-1970's among the top leaders in opposition to these trends; the 1977 decision rapidly to expand petroleum production; the 1978 willingness to enter into cooperative arrangements with multinational corporations to survey, explore, and develop offshore petroleum reserves; the major 1979 decision that the multinational corporations would be allowed equity holdings offshore on a joint venture basis; the 1980-83 decisions shaping the nature of the joint ventures; and finally the significant 1984 decision to invite the multinationals to participate in the development of China's onshore resources on a joint venture basis. Our focus is upon the evolution of policy toward the outside world; this is not a comprehensive political history of the Ministry.

At each juncture along the way, the top 25 to 35 leaders confronted major dilemmas concerning their strategy for economic development and their relations with the outside world. And at each juncture, their petroleum specialists offered bold solutions to the problems which the top leaders then accepted. In a sense, this is a story of how a group rode the wave of increasing domestic petroleum production (until 1978), rising world petroleum prices (until 1981), and improving relations between China and the industrial democracies of Western Europe, the United States, and Japan. These trends enabled the group to propose policies which promised to solve the problems of the moment. Each solution entailed an additional step away from the principles which initially attracted Mao's praise of the group. Each step placed the group in a more exposed position, as it entailed the group's making additional commitments for the petroleum industry to expand production and increase the foreign revenue it would earn through exports.

This chapter, then, seeks to integrate the three perspectives developed in earlier chapters: 1. *rationality perspective*: the economic and foreign policy problems and opportunities which the top leaders perceive the nation confronts, the resources they believe the nation enjoys to cope with these problems, and their reasoned effort on behalf of the nation to relate means to ends; 2. *elite power perspective*: the power needs and calculations of individual interests of the top leaders; 3. *bureaucratic perspective*: the actions, programs, and missions of the large ministries in Beijing and provincial and local governments around the country. Combining these three perspectives, this chapter concludes that petroleum policy was shaped through the ability of the economic specialists in charge of this sector to propose convincing solutions which appeared to meet a changing combination of the power and policy needs of the top leaders.

Over the long run, the understanding which the top leaders had of their foreign policy and economic environment determined the direction of policy. China's leaders increasingly perceived two overpowering realities: foreign equipment, technology, and capital would greatly facilitate the rapid and effective development of China's petroleum resources, especially offshore; and oil exports could help finance imports which would accelerate China's industrialization. The ideological preference of the top leaders to minimize reliance on the outside world delayed their response, particularly while Mao was China's preeminent leader. To this extent, the data support the rationality model.

A reasoned response to economic pressures and opportunities was not the sole source of policy, however. Calculations of individual interest and power also came into play. Economic specialists chose not to voice their views, lest they suffer politically for challenging the predispositions of the top leaders. Almost every step outward appears to have been contested, taken with reluctance, and subject to challenge and reversal as the implementation of the new policy commenced.

However, the interplay occurred within the evolving, complex Chinese bureaucratic framework. Many of the stimuli demanding a response from the top leaders—the changing conditions in Chinese petroleum production, the evolving availability and pertinence of foreign technology, new assessments of Chinese offshore petroleum reserves—reached the top leaders through the Ministry of Petroleum, and officals in the Ministry sought to couch these developments in terms that assisted the Ministry in pursuit of its mission and that accorded with the political tenor of the time. Moreover, once the top leaders had decided on new departures in petroleum policy, the relevant ministries had to implement the instructions of their leaders. Bureaucratic considerations repeatedly affected the pace of cooperation with the outside world, as well as its form. Chinese bureaucracy was sluggish; Chinese bureaucrats did not equate time with money. As a result, the pace was frequently slow, as the top leaders laboriously elicited a response from the myriad bureaucracies involved. In this case, at least, the understanding which the top leaders had of their environment was the best guide to the long-term direction of policy; high level politics best explain the timing of major innovations and retreats in policy, and the specific pace and organizational forms of cooperation with the outside world were largely the product of China's bureaucratic structure and processes.

STAGE ONE: THE DAQING YEARS, 1960-63

The Perceived Problem

The problems which the top leaders confronted in the early 1960's were largely self-induced. For a number of reasons, largely brought on by Mao Zedong, Sino-Soviet relations worsened in 1958 and 1959.[1] The descending spiral prompted Mao to call for (among other measures) an accelerated effort to become self-sufficient in petroleum. By the spring of 1960, China and the Soviet Union were clashing heatedly in various international gatherings of communist nations, and their polemical attacks upon one another in the media were only thinly disguised. In the summer, the Soviet Union withdrew its advisors from China, and making a virtue of necessity, China's leaders proclaimed a policy of self-reliance in economic development.

Meanwhile, by mid-1959 several Chinese leaders understood that the Great Leap Forward was bringing economic disaster to China. The widespread consequences included severe problems in energy supplies.[2] Mao rebuffed his critics at a crucial Party meeting in July-August, 1959, and Great Leap programs intensified in the winter of 1959-60. The massive effort swiftly to transform the economy through massive mobilization of labor, however, plunged the nation into a deep depression, and by mid-1960, the top leaders—including Mao—recognized that most economic indicators were plummeting. Among the falling industries, the drop in coal production was particularly pronounced.

The twin disasters of loss of Soviet assistance and economic collapse induced a national security crisis in 1961-62, as Chinese leaders perceived military pressure upon them from the east (Taiwan), the south (India), and the north and west (the Soviet Union).[3] The military keenly felt shortages in fuel supplies at this time.

The Solution: Develop Daqing Rapidly Along Maoist Lines

In these dire circumstances, the petroleum group offered a solution to one need that the leaders perceived. They brought in a large oil field at Daqing, and did so in a way that appeared to conform to the ideological predispositions of the preeminent leader Mao Zedong. The key policy

---

[1] The classic account of Sino-Soviet relations during these years is Donald Zagoria, *The Sino-Soviet Conflict, 1956-1961* (New Jersey: Princeton University Press, 1962).

[2] For accounts of high level Chinese politics at this time, see Roderick MacFarquhar, *Origins*, Vol. Two.

[3] See Allen Whiting, *The Chinese Calculus of Deterrence* (Ann Arbor: University of Michigan Press, 1975), Chap. Five.

decisions during the period from early 1960 to late 1963 were to develop the field at a maximum rate and to do so without reliance on foreign technicians, capital, and equipment. The Paris-based Coordinating Committee (COCOM) composed of the United States and its allies, which controls exports to communist countries, would not have permitted the export of advanced petroleum equipment and technologies to China at that time. There was, nonetheless, an indirect foreign involvement. The Chinese technicians applied technology they had learned from the Soviets, they drew upon pertinent articles in American petroleum engineering journals, and they may have marginally benefitted from Romanian assistance. Nonetheless, the Chinese proceeded largely on their own: foreign advisors did not assist in any major way in the early development stage.

EXPLORATION IN THE SONGLIAO SEDIMENTARY BASIN

In May, 1959, the Ministry of Petroleum and the Ministry of Geology publicized their decision to give highest priority to exploration for oil in the Songliao plain, a region in Manchuria in the western portions of Heilongjiang and Jilin provinces.[4] Testing was to be concentrated in the most promising areas in order to ascertain swiftly their value. The Northeast Petroleum Exploration Brigade of the Ministry of Geology, the Songliao Petroleum Exploration Bureau of the Ministry of Petroleum, and the Songliao Petroleum Investigation Brigade of the Jilin Provincial Bureau of Petroleum jointly had undertaken a comprehensive survey during the previous three years, the article revealed, with the assistance of Soviet and Hungarian advisors, and the results were judged to be most promising.[5] An exploration plan had already been completed. The dispatch

[4] "Petroleum Exploration in the Eastern Industrial Area; Several Thousand Exploration Personnel Converge on the Songliao Plain," Renmin ribao, May 6, 1959, p. 5.

[5] There is some evidence that as early as 1957, not long after the survey commenced, Chinese geologists concluded the Songliao plain contained commercial petroleum deposits. Soviet geologists played a major role assisting the survey. The journal Geological Knowledge in mid-1957 reported, "Many concealed structures, oil fields, and gas fields were discovered in the eastern part of China, such as the Songliao plain, North China, and south of the Changjiang." Further, the Ministry of Geology stated in its report on work in 1957 and tasks for 1958 that 105 possible oil bearing structures had been discovered throughout eastern China in 1957. See Akio Akagi and Morihiko Sato, "Taching Oil Fields and China's Industrial Technology," Shizhen, May 1974, pp. 62-73, translated in Joint Publication Research Service, Translations on the People's Republic of China, No. 305 (JPRS 64466), April 2, 1975, p. 19. The Great Leap Forward greatly accelerated surveying activity in China, as thousands of personnel were organized into survey teams under the direction of geological personnel. The bulk of activity in the northeast in 1958 appears to have focused on promising structures in Jilin province. See Renmin ribao, May 1, 1958, p. 1, and June 26, 1958, p. 3, and Shiyu kantan, 1959, no. 9, p. 43, all cited in H.C. Ling, The Petroleum

disclosed that exploration personnel were converging upon the Songliao plain from Xinjiang and the Beijing Petroleum Research Institute, and a large amount of exploration equipment had already arrived at the work site, shipped by air and surface transportation. The drilling equipment was Soviet in origin.[6] Air freight was not highly developed in China in the late 1950's, and its use highlighted the priority which the government had clearly assigned to this effort.

One spot was in Heilongjiang province, near the small railroad depot at Anda, on the railroad line from Harbin to Qiqihar. Sites with convenient communication facilities enjoyed priority. On September 9, 1959, the drillers struck oil beneath the swampy, mosquito-infested grasslands.[7] Seventeen days later, test well number three came in, this one revealing a commercially viable structure.[8] In the following months, the Chinese drilled 22 test wells to delimit the rough size of the oil area, which was determined to be roughly 200 square kilometers. Earlier geological surveys had suggested that the area actually consisted of seven separate fields or trap structures. The site soon acquired a name: Daqing, Great Celebration, a name chosen out of recognition that the discovery occurred on the eve of the widely celebrated tenth anniversary of the founding of the People's Republic. News of the strike swiftly reached the Zhongnanhai and received oblique mention during the National Day celebrations. Vice Minister of Geology He Changgong probably had Daqing in mind when he disclosed, "In the Great Leap Forward, we greatly strengthened work in the Northeast, especially in the discovery of oil in the Songliao area. The discovery of this oilfield will be very important for the development of our country's petroleum industry."[9]

By February 13, 1960, the Party Committee in the Ministry of Petroleum felt sufficiently confident and knowledgeable to report formally to the Central Committee of the Chinese Communist Party and to recom-

---

Industry of the People's Republic of China (Stanford: Hoover Institution Press, 1975), p. 127. Without identifying the precise location, *Peking Review* announced in August 1958 that two oil strata had been discovered in the Songliao plain. See Chu Chi-lin, "China's Skyrocketing Oil Output," in *Peking Review*, No. 23 (August 5, 1958), pp. 9-11, reprinted in H.C. Ling, *The Petroleum Industry*, p. 143.

[6] Unpublished notes from Senator Henry Jackson trip to China, summer 1983. See also "China's Taching Oilfield," *Current Scene*, Vol. VI, No. 16 (September 17, 1968), p. 2.

[7] Jackson trip notes.

[8] See the Ministry of Petroleum, "Zhongguo shiyou," p. 356. See also the credits given for the photo of this third well in *Daqing* (Beijing: People's Fine Arts Press, 1970); no page citation, see photo 16 and the credit. The same information is given in *Dui Daqing jingyan de zhengzhi jingji xue gaocha* (People's Press, 1979), p. 15.

[9] He Changgong, "A Glorious Road for Our Country's Geological Work," in *Renmin ribao*, October 11, 1959, p. 6, in H.C. Ling, *The Petroleum Industry*, p. 127.

mend specific action.[10] The MPI Party Committee notified the Central Committee that the site had as much potential as Karamai, a major field in northwest China which had recently commenced production. Further, it requested that the territory designated for Ministry activity be expanded from 200 to 2,000 square kilometers, embracing some of the additional fields, and that 2,000 technical workers be transferred to the site to initiate the development process. One week later, on February 20th, the Central Committee responded favorably, authorizing the drawing of technicians from petroleum and natural gas fields at Yumen, Xinjiang, Qinghai, and Sichuan.[11] In addition, two days later the Central Committee ordered the People's Liberation Army to transfer 30,000 personnel to the Ministry of Petroleum: 15,000 from the Shenyang Military Region (MR), 10,000 from the Nanjing MR, and 5,000 from the Jinan MR.[12] Zhou Enlai soon departed for Harbin, where he gathered personnel from the Ministry of Petroleum and the Heilongjiang Party Committee to make concrete plans.[13] While some contingents arrived as early as March, personnel began to arrive in large numbers in May 1960, and within months, 40,000 people were amassed at the site. Many would die under the harsh climate and even harsher working conditions.

Drilling of a large, productive well was completed on 14 April 1960, and the first shipment of crude petroleum left Daqing by rail in June.[14] The first year was primarily devoted to a more precise delineation of the geographic size, geological composition, and reserves, and during the three years from 1961 to 1963 the field was brought into production.[15]

DEVELOPING DAQING

The extent to which Daqing was indigenously designed and developed is unclear. According to Chinese claims, seven Soviet advisors spent a

[10] Photocopies of the report and the central committee directives were on display at the Exhibition Hall in Daqing in August 1983.

[11] While the February 20, 1960, decision was in the name of the Central Committee, one Chinese source attributes the decision to Chairman Mao, indicating that Mao personally approved the Ministry of Petroleum report. *Dui Daqing jingyan*, p. 25.

[12] *Dui Daqing jingyan*, p. 25.

[13] On Zhou's 1960 trip, see *Dui Daqing jingyan*, p. 25. According to a Western account, Zhou Enlai visited the site sometime in 1959, after which it was decided to accelerate development of the field. See "The Taching Oilfield: Triumph and Troubles," *China Topics*, YB 533 (August 15, 1969), p. 3. However, in a talk to Red Guards, Zhou did not recall visiting Daqing either in 1959 or 1960. He remembered visits on three occasions: in 1962, 1963, and 1966. See "Zhou Enlai Speech to Rebels of the Departments of Industry and Communications," in *Hongse zaofanbao*, February 19, 1967, in *SCMP Supplement*, No. 238 (November 8, 1968), p. 14.

[14] Akagi and Sato, "Taching Oil Fields," p. 25.

[15] Ministry of Petroleum, "Zhongguo shiyou."

175

month at the site in 1960, just prior to Khrushchev's withdrawal of all advisors in July 1960.[16] They counseled against attempting to exploit the site, according to later Chinese recollections, but the Chinese persisted, their confidence buoyed because the discovery itself resulted from reliance upon indigenously developed geological theories concerning the likely location of petroleum deposits in China. Some Western experts believe that Soviet advisors deserve more credit for assisting in the exploration stage and that, had not Khrushchev withdrawn then, Soviet advisors would have been fully involved in the development stage.[17]

The First Party Secretary at Daqing during that first, difficult year was also the Minister of Petroleum, Yu Qiuli. The 45-year-old, one-armed Long March veteran had moved to the site to direct the work in person. Among his chief lieutenants were 44-year-old Kang Shien, 38-year-old Tang Ke, and 34-year-old Song Zhenming—people who would become familiar to politicians and bureaucrats throughout Beijing and to oilmen throughout the world in the coming 25 years.[18]

Daqing attracted the personal attention of additional members of the top 25 to 35 leaders by 1961. Liu Shaoqi and Deng Xiaoping, for example, visited the field on August 9, 1961, and received a briefing from Kang Shien, who had replaced Yu Qiuli as the Daqing Party First Secretary sometime in late 1960 or early 1961.[19] Premier Zhou Enlai, as noted above, visited Daqing in 1962 and again in 1963.[20]

Production rose quickly in Daqing from 1960 to 1963. Even more significant, with the peaking of the Yumen field during this period and the reduction in imports from the Soviet Union, the role of Daqing in China's overall petroleum situation had become crucial by the end of 1963. (See Table One, Column Six.)

An unmistakable conclusion emerges from Table One. Expressed as a percentage of the total availability of petroleum—both of domestic production and imports—Daqing crude rose from roughly 9% of the total in its first year of operation—no small achievement in itself—to 46 percent in 1963. As a percentage of China's domestic crude production, Daqing rose from 15% in 1960, to 19% in 1961, 47% in 1962, and 68% in 1963.[21] Daqing's record assumes even greater significance when one

[16] Jackson trip notes.

[17] Based on interview.

[18] For biographies of Kang and Tang, see Chapter Two. For Yu Qiuli, see David M. Lampton, *Paths to Power*, Chapter Five.

[19] Jackson trip notes.

[20] See Note 13 above.

[21] These figures may even understate Daqing's growing importance. Chinese statistics released after Barnett's estimates used in Table 5-1 reveal crude petroleum imports from

TABLE 5-1
Daqing's Role in National Petroleum Supply
Availability of Crude Petroleum and Petroleum Products, 1960–63
(Million Metric Tons)

	1 Domestic Crude Petroleum Production	2 Petroleum Imports from USSR	3 Imports from Other Countries	4 Total Petroleum Supply	5 Daqing Production	6 % of Total Supply
1960	5.20	2.96	.91	9.07	.79	8.7
1961	5.31	2.93	.46	8.70	(1.02)	12.7
1962	5.75	1.86	1.14	8.75	(2.73)	31.2
1963	6.48	1.41	1.60	9.49	4.40	46.3

SOURCES: Column One is derived from State Statistical Bureau, ed., *Zhongguo tongji nianjian* (*China Statistical Yearbook*) (Beijing: Chinese Statistical Press, 1983), p. 245. Columns Two, Three, and Five are from A. Doak Barnett, *China's Economy*, p. 459 and pp. 436-437. The Daqing estimates originate with CIA, *China: Oil Production Prospects*, ER 77-100 OU (June 1977), p. 9. These CIA estimates merit confidence, since the CIA estimates of total production have proven to be remarkably close to subsequent Chinese disclosures. The CIA series is within two percent of the Chinese production figure for each year from 1960 through 1963. Column Four is the sum of Columns One, Two, and Three. Petroleum exports during 1960-63 were negligible and had minimal effect on total domestic supply. See *Zhongguo dui wai jingji maoyi nianjian, 1984*, (Beijing: Chinese Foreign Economic Trade Press, 1984), pp. IV, 105.

takes into account plummeting production of coal during these same years: 369 MMT in 1959, 397 in 1960, 278 in 1961, 220 in 1962, and 217 MMT in 1963.[22] Put simply, Daqing became a rare bright spot during those bleak years in the Chinese economy.

Under the harsh conditions, such a record required extraordinary dedication from those who opened the field. Even allowing for hyperbole, portrayals of the pioneers are worth noting:

> The natural environment and material conditions confronting the people of Daqing were most unfavorable. . . . Equipment was inadequate, motor vehicles few, and there were no roads to speak of. . . . There were no houses, so they pitched tents. . . . In 1960,

the Soviet Union dropped precipitously from 1960 to 1963, thereby making Daqing's share even larger. See *Zhongguo dui wai jingji maoyi nianjian, 1984* (Beijing: Chinese Foreign Trade Press, 1984), p. IV, p. 114.

[22] State Statistical Bureau (ed.), *Zhongguo tongji nianjian* (Beijing: Chinese Statistical Press, 1983), p. 244. The Great Leap figures for 1959-1961 are unreliable, but the underlying point is clear. Measured in BTU equivalents, Daqing's role in China's *total* energy production from 1960 to 1963 skyrocketed, although given the predominance of coal in the overall energy picture, it still provided a small percentage of this total.

everyone, men and women, old and young, from leading cadres and experts to technicians and ordinary workers, helped to build large numbers of mud houses. These served as shelter for the first winter. . . . It is a continuation and development of the revolutionary spirit of Yenan where people lived in caves during the War of Resistance against Japan (1937-1945). . . . Means of transport were limited, so they used shoulder poles to carry the rigs. When there was no running water for drilling they fetched it basin by basin from a small lake one mile away.[23]

Here is how an oil rigger described moving a drill in 1960 to the site from the railway which traverses Daqing, before spur lines were built:

Dragging with ropes, prizing with crowbars, and easing it along on wooden logs, we moved the 60-ton driller inch by inch, yard by yard, to the site and set it up. It was a real battle, lasting three days and nights.[24]

Without such heroism Daqing would not have achieved its success.

CREATING THE MYTH OF DAQING

Mao Zedong and his ideological supporters, as well as the architects of Daqing, soon began to develop an official explanation for the remarkable success of the oil field. Key to the explanation was that Daqing was not just an oil field. It was a total society, with its own ethos and identity, which allegedly exemplified the commitments Mao was seeking from the entire populace. Self-reliance, a leadership style in which leaders and led lived together with minimum status differences, a division of labor in which the families of the industrial workers tilled the land, thereby narrowing the differences between town and countryside, and the solving of technical problems through dialectical reasoning were some of the concepts said to be at the heart of Daqing's accomplishments. Certainly the high motivation of the Daqing pioneers stemmed from their patriotism, their dedication to Mao Zedong and the other leaders of the country, their confidence in the Communist Party, and their belief that human will could triumph over all difficulties. In a very real sense, Daqing witnessed the successful application of Maoist doctrines of the PLA to problems of industrialization.

While Mao Zedong focused on the organizational and ideological aspects of Daqing in understanding and explaining its achievements, however, the rapid exploitation of the field had technical explanations as

[23] *China Pictorial*, no. 7, 1966.
[24] *Ibid.*

well.[25] The technicians and the administrators who understood the reality of the field apparently chose to obfuscate these technical considerations, instead playing to Mao's search for a political model he could place before the country. In essence, the field was exploited through a more rapid and earlier injection of water into the oil-bearing strata than would have occurred through the usual techniques employed in Western countries. The heavy dosages of water drove the oil more rapidly toward the wells from which the oil was pumped, and the heavy dosages of water also sustained the pressure for a longer period of time. A row of water injection wells alternated with a row of producing wells. But the price of this extraction technique—a method favored by Soviet engineers and called the "line drive" technique—was the rapid accumulation of water in the oil reservoirs, so that after a few years, a high and increasing percentage of the liquid pumped to the surface was water, not crude petroleum. The line drive method, in other words, maximized rapid recovery at the probable cost of long term, total recovery of a field. An alternate technique would have been to inject water more gradually into a field, with the ratio between pumping and injection wells much higher than the line drive method.

At least one article suggests the adoption of the line drive method had been debated in 1960-61, with some technicians arguing that "the problems in injecting water into the formations are well known and insoluble."[26] The opponents, it seems, argued that the line drive method would produce early waterlogging and make it particularly difficult to sustain appropriate pressure in the small and highly fractured structures that comprise the Daqing field. The proponents claimed that technological innovations developed at Daqing would enable them to avoid the pitfalls experienced elsewhere. Especially, some Daqing technicians wished to inject water at different rates depending upon the permeability of the various structures, and they developed various devices to implant underground, such as casing hangers and pipes, to prevent the injected water from seeping from one oil-bearing stratum into another and thus contaminating it. These innovations which they proposed depended upon an

[25] This discussion is based on Kim Woodard, *The International Energy Relations of China* (Stanford: Stanford University Press, 1980), pp. 306-308; The World Bank, *China: Socialist Economic Development, The Energy Sector*, Annex E (Washington: World Bank, June 1, 1981), pp. 38-39; and Akagi and Sato, "Taching Oil Fields," especially pp. 28-33.

[26] "Oil Production Technology" (Peking: NCNA, January 2, 1966), reprinted in H. C. Ling, *The Petroleum Industry*, p. 149. Another article referring to the injection method is Min Yu, "The Daqing Oil Field Developed Under the Direction of the Thought of Mao Zedong," *Hongqi*, No. 13 (December 6, 1965), translated in *Survey of China Mainland Press*, No. 505 (January 3, 1966), especially pp. 38-39.

unusually detailed geological exploration of the field. Put simply, the advocates of the line drive method claimed to have made improvements which enabled them to inject water in a carefully controlled and directed fashion, in keeping with the differentiated structure of the field. The chief architect of this strategy was Liu Wenzhang, Assistant Chief Engineer of Daqing and Director of the Oil Drilling Technology Institute.[27]

Apparently, the two views were presented to the Daqing Party Committee for decision, and it selected the modified and improved line drive approach.[28] Thus, Yu Qiuli, Kang Shien, Tang Ke, and the other top leaders probably proceeded with some awareness of the possible pitfalls of their approach. There is no evidence, however, that they had any real latitude in their choice. Alternate technologies may not have been available to the leaders of Daqing, either because their technicians were more familiar with Soviet line drive techniques as the basic approach or because of COCOM restrictions on technology transfer to China. Further, the developers of Daqing undoubtedly were under intense political pressure to expand production rapidly, which the line drive method best enabled. In any case, whether out of confidence in their technology or in order to make a virtue of necessity, the developers of Daqing focused primarily upon motivational and organizational factors in explaining their success, and when they did feature technological issues, they presented an optimistic picture of innovation, creativity, and scientific advance. No hint of possible risks and future difficulties was contained in the articles about Daqing that began to appear after 1963.[29]

In two important ways, the official descriptions of Daqing's development were not totally accurate. First, technicians played a crucial part in the survey, exploration, and development. Amateurs did not bring a field of this magnitude into production. However, in the propaganda about Daqing, the role of technicians was understated. Technological innovation did receive emphasis, to be sure, but the innovation frequently was attributed to the "masses" or to workers. The model heroes were the well drillers, especially Iron Man Wang Jinxi and the 1205 drilling team. One searches in vain for model technicians and laboratory teams.

Second, although "self-reliance" was its watchword and the basic reality, in fact the success of the petroleum industry was partly attributable

[27] Akagi and Sato, "Taching Oil Fields," p. 32.

[28] "Oil Production Technology," in Ling, *The Petroleum Industry*, p. 149.

[29] See, for example, "Daqing Oilfield Achieves High Standards" (Beijing: NCNA English, September 29, 1969), in *Translations on Communist China*, No. 74 (JPRS 49030, 10 October 1969), pp. 33-34, or Xu Jinqiang, "Basic Experience in Revolutionizing Daqing Oil Field," *Jingji Yanjiu*, No. 4 (April 20, 1956), in *SCMM*, No. 538 (August 22, 1966), pp. 8-27, or Min Yu, "The Daqing Oil Field."

to the outside world. Soviet and Hungarian geologists had assisted in surveying the Songliao basin. Although not mentioned in subsequent years, the line drive extraction technology was Soviet in origin. Further, imports of petroleum continued to constitute an important source of supply throughout the 1960-63 era, in spite of the sloganeering. Most significantly, the increase in domestic petroleum production meant that by 1962-63, China's refining capacity and petrochemical industry needed expansion. While self-reliance was the watchword for development and production of crude petroleum, China had to turn outward to purchase equipment to process the greater quantities of crude petroleum. A refinery was built in Daqing in 1962-63, utilizing foreign equipment.

In these two important respects, therefore, the publicity about Daqing and the petroleum industry did not accord entirely with reality. It is not clear whether officials within the petroleum sector or propagandists and idealogues were primarily responsible for the creation of an image that conformed with the predispositions of Mao and his associates. But the result was to enhance the political standing of the petroleum officials in Mao's eyes. They had served his needs well in the dark aftermath of the Great Leap Forward, configuring their accomplishments to accord with Mao's vision, and the Chairman would turn to them and elevate them as he perceived new needs in 1964-65.

The Context Changes, 1963-64

By 1963-64, the policy environment had changed in several important ways. The economic recovery enabled the top leaders to turn from immediate issues of survival to development of longer term plans. Specifically, drafting of the Third Five Year Plan was on the agenda of the top leaders in 1964, raising the inevitable questions of priorities, pace of development, and spatial location of investments. By August, 1964, Mao wanted to emphasize military preparedness, accelerate the rate of growth, and create new industrial complexes in the interior. When the entrenched planners responded slowly, he began to look for new allies.

The foreign policy environment had also changed in 1963-64. The Sino-Soviet dispute had worsened, with each side now lambasting the other in acerbic, open polemics.[30] But China had made an opening to Japan and the West.[31] Sino-Japanese unofficial trade resumed following the disruptions of the Great Leap era. A breakthrough also occurred with the recognition of the PRC by Charles de Gaulle in 1964. The opportu-

[30] See William Griffith, *Albania and the Sino-Soviet Rift* (Cambridge: MIT Press, 1963).
[31] See Samuel Ho and Ralph Heunemann, *China's Open Door Policy* (Vancouver: University of British Columbia Press, 1984).

nity presented itself to expand commerical relations with Western Europe. More ominously, the expanding American involvement in Vietnam raised the danger of a Sino-American confrontation, a danger which the top leaders assessed especially in the days and months following the Tonkin Gulf incident in August, 1964.[32]

Tours abroad gave China's petroleum leaders and specialists their first direct exposure to Western petroleum technology and equipment at various exhibitions in 1963-64. As one of these individuals later recalled, it became evident that this technology and equipment would be very useful to China. Moreover, it was obvious that the leading technology was American in origin. This Chinese claimed that more than one influential official in the petroleum sector who travelled abroad returned to China in the mid-1960's convinced of the desirability of obtaining foreign equipment and technology not just for downstream processing, but for exploration and development. According to this individual, the idea of fostering contacts with the outside world, specifically with such companies as Schlumberger, which had American technology, began to develop in 1963-64. This official apparently discussed with a few of his colleagues the advisability of reporting their views and recommending a more energetic effort to obtain foreign technology, perhaps by sending petroleum engineers abroad for study. They noted that their report would go first to Nie Rongzhen, the leader of the State Science and Technology Commission, and they guessed Nie would support them. The recommendation would then need the endorsement of Premier Zhou Enlai, whose reaction would be uncertain since Zhou would have to submit such an idea to Mao Zedong for his approval. Mao not only probably would react negatively to the idea, but might criticize the initiators of the proposal. Thus, precisely at the time that Daqing was emerging as a model of self-reliant development, some of the leaders in the petroleum exploration and development sector were beginning to harbor private thoughts about the advisability of increasing contacts with the outside world. But they withheld their views from the top 25 to 35 leaders because they feared an unfavorable response.

In one area—petroleum refining—the top leaders perceived the need for equipment and technology to be so pressing that they were willing to turn to the outside world to alleviate the problem. From the fall of 1962 to the outbreak of the Cultural Revolution, China embarked on a wave of whole plant and equipment imports, many of which were petroleum related. Between 1963 and 1966, the Chinese signed contracts to purchase 46 plants from ten Western European countries and Japan. For ex-

---

[32] See Allen Whiting, *Chinese Calculus*, Chapter Seven.

ample, China purchased two synthetic fiber textile plants from Japan, two oil refineries from Italy, chemical fertilizer plants, and petro-chemical plants, all of which used petroleum-derived feedstock.[33]

By late 1963, the petroleum situation itself had evolved considerably from 1960. Not only had Daqing been developed in the northeast, but a new oilfield at Shengli, adjacent to the Bohai south of Tianjin, had begun production in 1962. The successes of the petroleum sector contrasted sharply with other portions of the economy, including coal. Finally, the projected organizational ethos at Daqing—with its understating of the role of technicians, of foreign involvement, and of the perils of the line drive method of exploitation—was in keeping with the leadership doctrine of the PLA then being espoused by Lin Biao. The stage was set for the emergence of Daqing's developers onto China's national scene.

STAGE TWO: THE PETROLEUM GROUP EMERGES ON THE NATIONAL SCENE, 1964-71

Mao Perceives New Problems, 1963-64

Increasingly from 1962 on, Mao Zedong brooded over the likely destiny of China after his death.[34] He feared that a fate awaited China similar to that of the Soviet Union after Stalin. Namely, revolutionary fervor would be lost, an entrenched class would dominate the Communist Party and perpetuate its rule, and the quest for a communist society would be abandoned. Mao sought to reinstill ideological vigor in the Party and society following the debacle of the Great Leap. He scrutinized the generalists and functional specialists among the top leaders with skeptical eyes, testing to see who among them were loyal to his vision. He searched restlessly for individuals who appeared to exhibit his values, and he sought to identify policies and organizational units which exemplified his ideas in practice.

---

[33] For a brief reference to this wave of imports, see Ho and Heunemann, p. 15. For a more detailed study of the early 1960's imports, see Robert Dernberger, "The Resurgence of 'Chung-hsueh wei-t'i, hsi-hsueh wei-yung' in Contemporary China: The Transfer of Technology to the PRC," paper prepared for Conference on Technology and Communist Culture, Villa Serbelloni, August 22-28, 1975, pp. 46-51 and Table A-5.

[34] For lengthier treatments of Mao's concerns at this time, see Stuart Schram (ed.), *Authority, Participation and Cultural Change in China* (England: Cambridge University Press, 1973); Benjamin Schwartz, *Communism and China; Ideology in Flux* (Cambridge: Harvard University Press, 1968); and Maurice Meisner, *Mao's China: A History of the People's Republic of China* (New York: Free Press, 1977).

CHAPTER FIVE

The Solution: "In Industry, Study Daqing"

The petroleum group offered a solution to Mao's problem: turn Daqing into a national model. Mao not only did this, but he grew discontent with the sluggishness and inflexibility of the economic specialists among the top leaders. In late 1964, Mao called for significant changes in the drafts of the Third Five Year Plan, but his suggestions received only a partial response. Feeling rebuffed, he set aside these specialists and called upon Yu Qiuli, Kang Shien, and others to head a new planning body. The developers of Daqing emerged on the national scene as economic specialists with broad responsibilities for the entire sector, not just for the petroleum industry. In more detail, this period unfolded as follows.

MAO PRAISES THE PETROLEUM INDUSTRY

The Fourth Session of the Second National People's Congress met from November 17 to December 3, 1963. The meeting occurred during a period of intense secrecy. For three years, no comprehensive statistics had been published on the economy, and the media had ceased the 1950's practices of publishing speeches of the top leaders to national meetings. Thus, the Chinese public had yet to read in the open media about the accomplishments at Daqing. While the speeches delivered at the NPC meeting were not released, a summary communique published in the *People's Daily* on December 4th tersely revealed this intriguing news: "The variety of petroleum products produced in our country doubled from 1957 to 1962. . . . In the past, our country relied upon imports for a great portion of the petroleum we required. Now we have attained basic self-sufficiency."[35]

Also in December 1963, Yu Qiuli and Kang Shien reported on the basic experience of Daqing to a large gathering of cadres of central organs and Beijing municipality.[36] This December 1963 meeting of the bureaucratic establishment in the capital meant the nation's top leaders were now prepared to give Daqing widespread publicity. Yu and Kang informed the audience during the secret gathering that a large oil field had been brought into production.[37] They claimed it had reserves in place of over 2.67 billion tons, and was currently producing at the rate of 6 million tons per year.[38] The state investment of 7.01 billion *yuan* had already

---

[35] *People's Daily*, December 4, 1963, in *Renmin Shouce* (Beijing: Dagongbao Press, 1964), p. 7.

[36] Fang Weizhong, ed., *Jingji dashiji*, p. 373.

[37] *Ibid.*

[38] Yu and Kang did not mention and perhaps did not understand that the reserves-in-place or the "total reserves" in the producing area were not the "ultimately recoverable"

184

been recovered, and the field had already accumulated 3.05 billion *yuan* for the state. Yu and Kang claimed that Daqing had also trained forces for the petroleum industry with a certain technological level, organization, discipline, daring, and capacity to endure hardship. On December 26, 1963—either at this gathering or commenting upon it—Mao Zedong raised the slogan "Industry Study Daqing."[39]

On February 5, 1964, the Party Central Committee disseminated a classified circular to lower level committees which contained a report from the Ministry of Petroleum concerning Daqing. The report summarized the December 1963 speeches by Yu and Kang. Pointing out that Daqing was a model of "more, faster, better, and more economical" development, the Central Committee informed its lower level committees that Daqing had systematically applied the experience of political work in the PLA and had closely integrated political thought, revolutionary ardor, and scientific management. Further, the Central Committee observed that Daqing's experience was applicable to industry and units in transportation, finance, culture, and education, and even organs at various levels within the Party, government, military, and mass organizations could apply its methods or at least use them for reference. After this circular was issued, a national movement to study Daqing began among industrial and communications units.

While no available evidence directly links the February 5th circular with Mao Zedong, his December 26, 1963, statement probably provided inspiration for the campaign. More generally, by late 1963 and early 1964, Mao was concerned with identifying units that reflected his core values, that met his desire to combat revisionism, and that were training "revolutionary successors." Probably in a related development, five days after the Party circular on Daqing, on February 10, 1964, *Renmin ribao* publicized its counterpart in agricultural production, Dazhai brigade.[40] The two production units which would epitomize Maoist values for more than the coming decade had now been identified.

Daqing remained very much on Mao's mind throughout 1964, as reflected in his available speeches from this time. Speaking at the Spring Festival on February 13th, eight days after the Party circular on Daqing, Mao noted that in order to remedy certain deficiencies in industrial work, "We must study the PLA and study Daqing of the Ministry of Petro-

---

reserves. Typically, recoverable reserves are about 30-35% of reserves-in-place. Yu and Kang used the higher figure.

[39] The date of this Mao slogan is in *Dui Daqing jingyan*, p. 3. No currently available selection of Mao's statements contains this particular saying attributed to this date.

[40] Fang Weizhong, ed., *Jingji dashiji*, p. 374. The Renmin ribao editorial of February 10 is translated in SCMP 3171, p. 1.

leum."[41] After mentioning the relatively low investment in Daqing and noting it produced considerable oil after three years of development, Mao succinctly praised the oil field: "The investment was little, the time was short, and the effectiveness was high." He repeated himself: "Every ministry ought to study the Ministry of Petroleum, study the PLA, and grasp good experience."

In March, at a report meeting, Mao again heaped praise on the Ministry of Petroleum.[42] Commenting upon the Socialist Education Campaign, an ideological campaign then underway at Mao's instigation, and upon capital construction in heavy industry, Mao chastised unnamed provinces and industries for proceeding in hasty and superficial fashion.[43] Once again, he said, "Study the PLA, study the Ministry of Petroleum." He called for leadership that did not neglect class struggle, scientific experimentation, or production. He continued, "I say that the great achievements of the Ministry of Petroleum are attributable to its cultivation of people's revolutionary spirit." He went on to note that the Ministry not only had reached record levels of production but had also constructed a refinery "of high quality, of international standards." "Only in this way can you convince someone," Mao concluded. Clearly, the Ministry had convinced the Chairman.

THE THIRD FIVE YEAR PLAN AND THE VIETNAM WAR IMPINGE

Two developments outside the energy sector in the second half of 1964 further propelled Mao to look with favor upon the leaders of the petroleum industry: the drafting of the Third Five Year Plan and the growing American presence in Vietnam. The drafting of the plan, scheduled to go into effect in 1966, formally began in February, 1964.[44] At a preliminary meeting focusing on long term plans in industry and communications, weapons manufacture and grain production were singled out as the foci for national development from 1966 to 1970. These in turn depended on rapid expansion of the chemical and fertilizer industries. From February to May, the rough parameters and balances for the Third FYP were set, leading to a May-June 1964 Central Work Conference in Beijing. Among

[41] "A Record of Talk at the Spring Festival," February 13, 1964, in *Mao Zedong sixiang wansui* (NP, ND), p. 456.

[42] "Comments at a Report Meeting," March 1964, *ibid.*, pp. 475-476.

[43] The Socialist Education Campaign is discussed in Richard Baum, "Revolution and Reaction in the Chinese Countryside: The Socialist Education Movement in Cultural Revolutionary Perspective," *China Quarterly* No. 38 (April-June, 1969), pp. 92-119; Richard Baum and Frederick C. Teiwes, *Ssu-Ch'ing: The Socialist Education Movement of 1962-1966*, China Research Monograph, No. 2 (Berkeley: University of California Press, 1968); and Byung-joon Ahn, *Chinese Politics*.

[44] Fang Weizhong, ed., *Jingji dashiji*, p. 374.

the preliminary targets which the SPC presented to the Conference was to produce 16.5 to 18 million metric tons of crude oil in 1970. (Planned production for 1964 was 7.6 million metric tons.)[45] Sometime in June, following discussion of these figures at the Work Conference, Mao responded to a briefing from the State Planning Commission concerning the Third Five Year Plan.[46]

While agreeing with its emphasis on agriculture and national defense, evidently Mao was not totally pleased with the initial casting of the Five Year Plan. In particular he delivered instructions to create what he termed a "third front," that is, to develop an industrial base in the southwest. He also called for a somewhat faster pace of development than the SPC had presented to the May-June work conference, while simultaneously stressing the need to raise quality and increase the supply of deficient commodities. Further, he supported various measures to increase agricultural production, so that grain imports could be gradually reduced and imports of new technologies could therefore be increased. This conference, it is worth noting, addressed a wide range of issues, including agricultural planning, ideological matters, educational policy, the posture toward the Soviet Union, finance and trade concerns, and cultivating successors to the revolutionary generation. Mao emerged from this meeting with considerable political momentum, and the ideological tenor of the country—particularly in the urban areas—moved leftward in the subsequent months.

Mao became increasingly vexed with his top planners, and the next few months proved to be turbulent ones for the economic specialists on the Politburo and State Planning Commission as they sought to complete the 1965 plan and continue drafting the Third Five Year Plan.[47] In mid-August, the Party Secretariat convened a protracted meeting to discuss the Chairman's suggestion concerning capital construction in the interior. On August 17 and 20, immediately following the Tonkin Gulf incident and perhaps in reaction to it, Mao addressed the meeting. He pointed out that China must prepare for the possibility that the United States would undertake an aggressive war and that the concentration of

[45] *See* Fang Weizhong, ed., *Jingji dashiji*, pp. 377-378. A lengthier description of this work conference, convened from mid-May to June 17, is in *Zhonggong dangshi dashi nianbiao* (N.P., People's Press, 1981), p. 141.

[46] The following reconstruction interweaves Fang Weizhong, ed., *Jingji dashiji*, p. 379; *Zhonggong dangshi dashi*, p. 141; Liu Suinian, et al., *Liushi niandai guomin jingji tiaozheng de huigu* (Beijing: Finance and Economic Press, 1983), p. 208; *Zhongguo gongchandang lizi zhongyao huiyi ji* (Shanghai: People's Press, 1983, p. 202; and Naughton, "Economy of the Cultural Revolution."

[47] This paragraph is based on Fang Weizhong, ed., *Jingji dashiji*, pp. 379-383 and interviews in China.

factories in cities and the coastal region was not conducive to preparation for war. He stated that the geographical emphasis of economic development should be upon the interior and called upon individual plants, schools, scientific institutes, design institutes, and Beijing University to move a portion of their activities to the interior. On the basis of Mao's instructions, the Secretariat ordered that capital construction projects which were being included in the Third Five Year Plan be located in the interior when possible.

MAO ELEVATES THE PETROLEUM GROUP

Mao's focus upon the planning system persisted. On the 27th of August, he wrote comments on a letter from Chen Boda: "The methods of planning work must undergo change this year and next. If it is not changed, then it would be best to abolish the current SPC and establish another organ." In response to Mao's blast, a national planning conference was convened from September 21 to October 19.[48] In addition to setting the 1965 annual plan (draft), the month long meeting decided upon a long list of measures to simplify and decentralize the Chinese planning system. Most significantly for our purposes, the meeting endorsed the idea of the center to establish a "national economy supreme command" (*guomin jingji tongsibu*) directly under the leadership of Mao Zedong and Liu Shaoqi.[49] The new office was to give the highest levels—in Chinese parlance, the "Center"—"a high degree of concentrated leadership over planning and economic work." Unmistakably, Mao was seeking to strengthen his control over a sector whose leadership he found wanting.

Mao's vigorous involvement in economic policy and his criticism of the State Planning Commission—a body which had drawn his ire on earlier occasions—necessitated creating alternative bodies and identifying leaders in this sphere who enjoyed his confidence and upon whom he could rely. The alternate to the SPC which Mao had created—the National Economic Supreme Command—apparently soon became known as the "small planning commission" (*xiao jiwei*).[50] Quite naturally, he turned to his successful Minister of Petroleum Yu Qiuli to play the leading role in this new body. Its existence was secret and only came to public

---

[48] Fang Weizhong, ed., *Jingji dashiji*, p. 382; Liu Suinian, et al., p. 210; Zhou Taihe, ed., *Dangdai Zhongguo de jingji tizhi gaige* (Beijing: Social Sciences Press, 1984), pp. 121 and 772.

[49] Fang Weizhong, ed., *Jingji dashiji*, p. 382. The connotation is that the idea for the supreme command came from elsewhere, possibly from Mao.

[50] There is no direct evidence indicating the "*xiao jiwei*" was the same as the National Economy Supreme Command, but circumstantial evidence points in this direction.

light through Red Guard publications several years later. Ostensibly, Yu Qiuli acquired a position as Vice Chairman of the SPC, and even this was not publically and formally announced until November 13, 1965. As is often the case in China, the public announcement lagged behind the reality. As Zhou Enlai recalled, "Yu Qiuli was transferred to the Planning Commission in 1964 and in two years he worked out the third-front plan (i.e., the plan to develop the interior, especially Sichuan) and the Third Five Year Plan.[51] Others who joined him on the Small Planning Commission included Vice Chairman of the State Economic Commission Gu Mu, Beijing Vice Mayor Jia Tingsan, and Zhejiang Party official Lin Hujia.

Mao soon began to receive the response he sought from his economic specialists. On October 30, the Center had approved and disseminated the 1965 annual plan. It reflected Mao's concerns, even before Yu Qiuli was well inserted into the planning apparatus. Its guiding principle was to prepare for the possibility that the imperialists would launch an aggressive war against China and hence energetically to construct a strategic rear base. Petroleum continued to be a pace-setting sector of growth. Production of crude petroleum for 1964, according to statistics available to the leaders in late December, was 8.48 million metric tons, surpassing the plan target of 7.6 million metric tons by 12%. The 1965 plan called for production of 9.7 million metric tons, a 14% increase for the year.

Then, in early December, after securing the approval of Chairman Mao, the State Planning Commission distributed to the Politburo, Secretariat, and Party groups within the relevant commissions and ministries the procedures (*chengzu*) for long term planning. In the document, the SPC acknowledged the inadequacies in its preliminary thinking in the spring about the Third Five Year Plan and the insufficient attention it devoted to capital construction in the interior. Mao's intervention also had altered the content of the Five Year Plan targets, significantly increasing the rate of investment in defense industries, metallurgy, chemical industries, and transportation, while reducing expenditures in agriculture, education, urban housing, and light industry. Investment in Sichuan—the third front—was to rise dramatically.[52] The document raised the slogan, "In industry, rely upon the spirit of Daqing."

The rise of Yu Qiuli evidently engendered some initial opposition, not surprisingly since the Small Planning Commission soon surplanted the old SPC leaders as the group in charge of the SPC bureaucracy. At least,

[51] *Supplement to SCMP*, No. 238, p. 14.
[52] For the impact on Sichuan, see Zhou Taihe, ed., *Dangdai Zhongguo*, pp. 588-592.

a brief exchange between Mao and Premier Zhou in December, 1964 points in this direction:

> Mao: You mean it will not do for Yu Qiuli to become Vice Chairman of the SPC? He only is a valiant general, a daring general? The Ministry of Petroleum also does planning work! It is that I want him to take a new work style there.
>
> Zhou: To go and break through a pool of stagnant water.[53]

Years later, upon being asked how Mao could have intervened and in effect dismiss the entire leadership of the SPC, a Chinese official swiftly laughed and recalled: "What do you think? He dismissed the entire State Council a year later!" Indeed, Mao did have his way, and his chief briefers on economic matters in 1965 no longer were the prior heads of the SPC and SEC, Li Fuqun and Bo Yibo; Yu Qiuli and Gu Mu took their place. Thus, in January, 1965, Yu and Gu reported to the Chairman on planning work, and on June 16, the twosome journeyed to Mao's Hangzhou retreat to report on the Third Five Year Plan.[54]

Yu Qiuli and his associates continued to pledge rapid increases in petroleum production, and the industry met its commitments. The September, 1965, final Third Five Year Plan document established a 1970 target of 18.5 MMT, an increase over the initial target of 16.5 to 18 MMT set in the May, 1964 draft. Actual production in 1965 totalled 11.3 million metric tons, a 36% increase over 1964 and 16% above the plan. The target for 1966, set in October, 1965, called for production of 13.0 MMT, and actual production reached 14.5 MMT in spite of the harmful consequences of the Cultural Revolution in the last quarter of the year.

This detail illustrates the political interaction that occurred between the preeminent leader and the economic specialists in the Maoist era. The specialists prospered when their performance demonstrated the validity of the views of the leader. This capricious ability of Mao decisively and willfully to intervene in the planning process became precisely the object of post-Mao reforms. Yu Qiuli emerged as a major figure in the economic sphere not during the Cultural Revolution, as many outside observers believe, but by late 1964. While not yet one of the top 25 to 35 leaders, he had become a principal figure among the economic specialists. Mao rewarded him because the policies implemented in his sector corre-

---

[53] "Summary of Central Work Symposium," December 20, 1964, in *Mao Zedong sixiang wansui*, p. 579.

[54] *Mao Zedong sixiang wansui*, p. 605 and Fang Weizhong, ed., *Jingji dashiji*, p. 395. Other evidence of Mao's reliance upon Yu and the Small Planning Commission came in March, 1966, when he designated the Committee and Yu and Lin Hujia specifically to handle the agricultural mechanization issue. See *Mao Zedong sixiang wansui*, p. 633.

sponded with Mao's perception of what the objective situation demanded and permitted. During the coming two decades, Yu and his associates in turn used their enhanced position to advance the mission of the organization in which their power was rooted: the Ministry of Petroleum. The stage was set for the Ministry to be at the cutting edge of Chinese economic policy. But first, its leaders had to survive the Cultural Revolution.

The Cultural Revolution Breaks: 1966

From 1964 through mid-1966, Mao became increasingly alarmed by, among other things, the policies which many among the top 25 to 35 leaders were pursuing in the educational, cultural, public health, ideological, and rural realms.[55] Perceiving problems extending far beyond the economic and foreign policy realms, he concluded that most among the top 25 to 35 leaders did not merit being his successors, and he set about to purge them. More than that, he concluded that the entire Party apparatus was infested with members who had a "capitalist" or "bourgeois" mentality. He turned to the PLA as the organization committed to his principles. Minister of Defense Lin Biao and a group of "leftist" idealogues encouraged and aided Mao out of conviction and a sense they would benefit from the purge. Mao sought to conduct his purge in a way that would instill his values in the populace, and therefore he called upon the populace to help him save his revolution. In the summer of 1966, he mobilized the youth, in the form of Red Guards, as a new instrument of rule, and he launched the Cultural Revolution. The Red Guard movement soon escaped his precise control, and the nation was engulfed in strife.[56] The fragile structure of authority crumbled, and pent up tensions within bureaucracies and local units erupted into often violent factional struggles.

The Petroleum Group Seeks to Survive

The turmoil and strife engulfed Yu Qiuli and the Ministry of Petroleum and soon extended to Daqing. While the entire petroleum group came

[55] At this writing, the most detailed account of the political origins of the Cultural Revolution remains Edwin Rice, *Mao's Way*. See also Lowell Dittmer, *Liu Shao-ch'i and the Chinese Cultural Revolution: The Politics of Mass Criticism* (Berkeley: University of California Press, 1975); and Kenneth Lieberthal, "The Great Leap Forward and the Split in the Yenan Leadership," in John K. Fairbank and Roderick MacFarquhar (eds.), *The Cambridge History of China*, Vol. XIV (Cambridge: Cambridge University Press, 1987).

[56] The Red Guard movement is analyzed in Hong-yung Lee, *Politics*; and Stanley Rosen, *Red Guard Factionalism*.

under Red Guard attack, Yu Qiuli apparently was the object of particular emnity from Mao's wife. The discrepancies between the reality and the propaganda which the chapter noted earlier became a focus of Red Guard criticism. Daqing ceased receiving national praise in early 1967 and did not resume its position as a national model until early 1969, and even then its stated principles differed from the 1963-65 publicity. Egalitarian values, self-reliance, and the primacy of politics received even greater stress. Yu Qiuli himself was sufficiently hard pressed in 1967-68 that Li Fuqun resumed command of a national production and supply meeting which the SPC convened in 1967.[57] The status of Yu remained shaky until 1969-70, when he was named to the CCP Central Committee (April, 1969) and became formal head of the reorganized State Planning Commission (June, 1970).

During the 1966-69 era, in short, the petroleum group did not have a relevant answer to the specific concerns which gripped Mao and his new-found allies. The top leaders focused on issues for which the petroleum industry had little responsibility. The petroleum group became marginal to Mao's concerns, and hence in his eyes they became potentially dispensable. During this political storm, the only solution for the group was to seek shelter elsewhere and attempt to survive. The scanty available evidence does not enable a judgment as to whether the strategy was purposeful or instinctual, but it appears to have encompassed three elements: 1. to seek the protection of Zhou Enlai, who repeatedly came to the defense of Yu Qiuli; 2. to reach some sort of accommodation with the PLA, which dispatched personnel into the Ministry; and 3. to maintain production at Daqing.

Despite the political turmoil, the record of petroleum production was remarkably good after the turmoil of 1967. Production fell in 1967 to 13.9 MMT, a drop from the 14.5 figure of 1966, but the subsequent three years saw extraordinary gains: 16.0 in 1968, 21.7 in 1969, and 30.7 in 1970.[58] This exceeded the Third Five Year Plan target of 18.5 MMT by a whopping 66 percent. Even more important, the central government increasingly depended upon revenue earned in the petroleum sector. Once again, as in 1960-62, the petroleum sector contrasted with many others, especially coal and electric power, which were more adversely affected by Cultural Revolution turmoil.

Several factors help to explain this remarkable record.[59] Oil fields tend

---

[57] Fang Weizhong, ed., *Jingji dashiji*, p. 430.

[58] State Statistical Bureau, *Zhongguo tongji nianjian, 1983*, p. 244.

[59] This paragraph is based on Jackson trip notes and Li Chengrui, "An Analysis of China's Economic Situation during the Period of Ten Years of Internal Disorder," *Jingji yanjiu*, No. 1, January, 1984, pp. 23-31, translated in FBIS, Vol. I, No. 46 (March 7, 1984), esp. p. K-8.

to go through a natural cycle, and at this point, Daqing was in its expanding phase. Moreover, after 1967, the remnant personnel managing the industry from Beijing, in cooperation with the PLA, devised ways to maintain some tranquility. At Daqing, for example, several thousand soldiers arrived in February, 1967 and did not leave until spring, 1971. By late 1967, they had brought some order to the previously chaotic situation. The oil field was, for all practical purposes, under military control. The military personnel, drawn mainly from the Shenyang Military Region and its Heilongjiang Military District, remained at the administrative headquarters. They tended not to go to the basic levels, where cadres continued to work as before, even if they had been criticized. The PLA dispatched many of the previous leading Daqing officials to nearby May 7th cadre schools and kept the "revolutionary rebels" in offices at headquarters, where they received formal positions of responsibility but were constrained in their actual duties. In reality, the previous officials at the nearby May 7th schools were available for frequent consultations with the military and the regular engineers and technicians working at the well sites and with the drilling teams. Production did not suffer under this arrangement, but surveying and exploration were seriously neglected. More generally, the rapid growth of Daqing and the initiation of production at new fields (Shengli in 1962 and Dagang in 1968) resulted, to a considerable extent, from investments made before the Cultural Revolution. Further, production equipment and material were used at accelerated rates, with inadequate attention to maintenance or depreciation. As one Chinese summarized it, the record was accomplished by "eating stored food" and "eating next year's food."

New Problems Confront Petroleum Officials

By the early 1970's the petroleum sector was confronting an emerging dilemma. On the one hand, not only was the demand for petroleum increasing rapidly, but the central government wished to increase the revenue it was deriving from the oil bonanza. The draft Fourth Five Year Plan, which was discussed at a national planning conference in February-March, 1970, anticipated that in 1975 petroleum, natural gas, and hydropower would supply 31% to 38% of the total energy supply derived from natural resources, a dramatic jump from the 17% they provided in 1969. Coal would drop in the same period from 83% to 62%-69%. With the long lead times required for hydropower construction and the technological challenges in using natural gas, clearly petroleum was to be the fuel sustaining the industrial growth of the early 1970's.[60] On the other hand,

---

[60] Fang Weizhong, ed., *Jingji dashiji*, p. 462.

the sector was neither spending adequate sums nor developing indigenous technologies to sustain production increases beyond a limited future. Thoughtful petroleum experts in China understood the need to find successor fields to Daqing, Shengli, and Dagang. Meanwhile, these three fields would have to be exploited in ways that maximized short term returns.

In short, how to sustain the expansion in petroleum production became the major question the leaders of the petroleum industry confronted in 1970-71. Their answer to this question was soon affected by foreign assessments that the continental shelf of China probably contained vast oil deposits.[61] The Economic Commission for Asia and the Far East (ECAFE), a United Nations organization headquartered in Bangkok, initiated a major effort in 1966 to assess the potential mineral resources in the East Asian sea bed. Under contract to ECAFE and a multinational committee ECAFE organized, the United States Navy conducted airborne and seaborne surveys of the continental shelf in 1968, and the data were analyzed in 1969. The first report based on these preliminary surveys concluded, "A high probability exists that the continental shelf between Taiwan and Japan may be one of the most prolific oil reservoirs in the world." Another US team surveyed the South China Sea and the Gulf of Thailand in 1969. One of the most promising areas was reported to be the continental shelf of China from the southern tip of Taiwan to Hainan Island. The Dagang field itself was located on the marshes edging the Gulf of Bohai, and petroleum engineers believed that the oil-bearing structures probably stretched under its shallow waters. Thus, by 1970-71, offshore oil increasingly loomed as the likely next spot for major finds. But, the Chinese lacked the technology and equipment needed to develop offshore petroleum reserves—especially in the typhoon-prone, moderate to deep waters off the southern coast. Inexorably, China's search for energy was literally and figuratively propelling policy into new waters.

STAGE THREE: THE PETROLEUM GROUP TURNS OUTWARD, 1972-77

Harbingers of the Turn Outward: 1964-70

The origins of most policies in China frequently can be traced to periods when the political climate supposedly would have precluded such policies. This is certainly the case with the policy of seeking foreign technol-

---

[61] This paragraph is based on Woodard, *International Energy Relations*, pp. 150-153. See also Selig Harrison, *China, Oil, and Asia: Conflict Ahead*, (New York: Columbia, 1977).

ogy to facilitate exploitation and development of offshore oil reserves. We have already noted that the development of Daqing did entail the indigenous application of foreign technology, that China embarked upon a wave of foreign imports in refining equipment in 1963-65, and that the exploration and development people came in contact with Western technology with the establishment of diplomatic relations with France in 1964. When the Chinese began prospecting for oil in the Bohai Gulf in 1964, pressures increased for foreign technology and equipment, and for the rest of the decade—even as the storm clouds of the Cultural Revolution gathered and broke—MPI initiated sporadic contacts with the outside world. The first technological exchanges with Japan began in June, 1964, when a delegation from Nippon Mining and Teikoku Oil visited the PRC. A delegation of the China National Oil and Gas Exploration and Development Corporation visited Japan in 1966 or 1967 to learn about and acquire offshore survey and drilling technology.[62] Members of the delegation allegedly included MPI officials Zhang Wenbin and Zhao Shengzhen, who later were at the forefront of the turn to the outside world. In 1966-67, the Chinese purchased equipment from France for geophysical surveys which it used in the Bohai.[63] By 1969, it had successfully and secretly bought an $11 million drill ship from Japan.[64] In 1969-70, the Chinese initiated efforts to purchase a drilling ship and a rig from Japan, but these deals foundered due to political problems in the Sino-Japanese relationship and COCOM denials.[65] These probes did not add up to a policy, but they were harbingers of future developments. They revealed a Chinese interest in exploring its offshore reserves.

However, the political climate both within China and internationally did not permit a genuine opening to the outside world. Especially from 1966 to 1970, the Cultural Revolution turmoil, the Vietnam War, Sino-American animosity and the trade restrictions which the United States imposed through COCOM precluded imports of advanced survey, drilling, and extraction equipment and technology. The adherence to a strict policy of self-reliance by Mao's Cultural Revolution supporters also continued to make it politically risky for MPI officials to advocate extensive purchase of foreign goods. The guidelines for the annual plans and Fourth Five Year Plan which Mao endorsed in 1969-70 emphasized decentralization and called for development projects that were "small scale,

---

[62] A Japanese source dated this visit as 1967, while Selig Harrison dates it as summer, 1966. The visit was kept secret to avoid criticism from the United States. See *Ibid.*

[63] *Ibid.*, p. 74.

[64] *Ibid.*, p. 62.

[65] Japanese sources and *Ibid.*

indigenous, and labor intensive" rather than "large scale, foreign, and capital intensive."

A Changed Policy Environment, 1970-72

Several developments came together in 1970-72 to alter the situation. Some of the most enthusiastic supporters of self-reliance and isolation, especially the influential ideologue Chen Boda, suffered political reversals at Mao's hand in several high level meetings in 1969-71.[66] The September, 1971 demise of Lin Biao, Mao's annointed successor, brought an end to the national security strategy of high defense budgets and militant opposition to both the Soviet Union and the United States. The petroleum group was restored to good graces by early 1970, and Yu Qiuli and his associates resumed their leadership of the principal economic agencies. Yu was confirmed as head of the SPC in June, 1970, while Tang Ke made his first public appearance since 1967 in February, 1971 and Kang Shien appeared in May, 1971. Kang and Tang were in the Ministry of Fuel and Chemical Industry, then headed by Yin Wen—a cultural revolution appointment who subsequently disappeared from official namelists. Finally, the breakthrough in Sino-American relations in 1971, highlighted by the July visit of Henry Kissinger, the admission to the United Nations, and the visits of Richard Nixon and Kakuei Tanaka to Beijing in 1972 promised an end to China's isolation. New opportunities beckoned for access to foreign equipment and technology.

The climate toward foreign involvement in China's economic development had definitely begun to change. The February, 1972 Shanghai Communique and the September, 1972 establishment of diplomatic relations with Japan enabled leaders from the Ministry of Fuel and Chemical Industries to have direct meetings with Americans, to broaden contacts with the Japanese, and to travel more widely. Zhang Wenbin, one of the most senior petroleum officials at the time, was part of a prestigious ten member Chinese economic mission to Japan in March, 1972. Zhang joined Zhao Shengzhen, the Chief Drilling Engineer in the Ministry and a particularly knowledgeable technician, on a visit to Iran in April, 1972. By the end of the year, Exxon, Mobil, Gulf, and Getty had initiated meetings with Chinese officials at various levels in Hong Kong, Canton, or while the Chinese were on tour. The visit of Song Zhenming, Tang Ke, and other high level petroleum officials to Canada and France

[66] See especially references to meetings of February 16-March 24, 1969 (Fang Weizhong, ed., *Jingji dashiji*, pp. 450-453); February 15-March 21, 1970 (*Ibid.*, pp. 460-463), and December 15, 1970-February 19, 1971 (*Ibid.*, pp. 470-471). See also Mao's interview with Yaya Kahn of November 13, 1971 in *Ibid.*, p. 470.

from September to November was particularly important. Several Chinese officials dated their interest in some kind of joint venture arrangement to that extensive exposure to Western oil companies. For example, Mobil made direct contact with the delegation, and several officials from the exploration division flew from corporate headquarters to Toronto for a meeting. Using Canton as the contact point, Getty submitted a proposal for a production-sharing contract in the Bohai and Yellow Sea. While such proposals were not yet feasible in the political climate of the time, the idea now was planted in the minds of MPI officials.

Meanwhile, at the higher levels, the top 25 to 35 leaders began to explore and initiate expanded commercial dealings with the West. A major development came in October, 1972, when the State Council finally approved a 1971 request from the Ministry of Metallurgy, which the SPC had endorsed, to purchase from West Germany and Japan a steel rolling mill capable of producing 1.7 meter plates. On two previous occasions, in 1959 and 1964, the Ministry of Metallurgy had suggested to add such a mill to the Wuhan iron and steel complex, and the third time the proposal was put forth, it was approved.[67] Another important step came in early January, 1973, when, on the basis of instructions from Zhou Enlai, Yu Qiuli's SPC submitted a written report to the State Council.[68] The document, entitled "A Request to Increase the Import of Equipment and Expand Economic Exchange," apparently set forth an integrated plan to import US $4.3 billion worth of equipment and whole plants. Soon known as the "4-3 program," the State Council accepted the proposal. Some of the projects had already been approved, and it seems an important aspect of this decision was for the Politburo and State Council leaders to bestow legitimacy and coherence to the policy of foreign purchases. After its adoption, additional items were added, so that the program eventually called for the purchase of US $5.14 billion worth of goods. Many of the items used crude petroleum and natural gas feed stock and would be under Kang Shien's Ministry of Fuel and Chemical Industry: thirteen large-scale fertilizer plants, four large chemical fibre plants, three petro-chemical plants, and one alkyl-benzene plant. The Chinese also began to enter the world market for various types of offshore drilling ships and rigs. The internal forces which in 1963-65 had produced similar purchases were again making themselves felt. The political generalists were accepting proposals from the petroleum bureaucracy, transmitted to them by the former leaders of this sector who now

---

[67] Fang Weizhong, ed., *Jingji dashiji*, p. 497.

[68] See Fang Weizhong, ed., *Jingji dashiji*, p. 505. This information is also in Ho and Huenemann, pp. 15-17.

were the leaders of the entire economic sector. The top leaders had decided to purchase foreign technology and equipment to accelerate the development of China's petro-chemical industry.

The New Problem and the Proposed Solution: Export Petroleum and Import Equipment and Techology

The ambitious "4-3 program" raised a new problem: How would China pay for these massive imports? The State Council had received the "4-3 program" on the eve of the January 17-21, 1973, trip to Beijing by Minister of International Trade and Industry (MITI) Yashuhiro Nakasone. Following the establishment of formal Sino-Japanese diplomatic relations, MITI had replaced the previous non-governmental agencies in Japan directing trade between the two countries, necessitating the Nakasone visit. The new issue concerned how to finance the imports. Already in 1972, there were indications that China was interested in increasing its oil exports, primarily to Japan and also to Thailand and the Philippines. In August, 1972, Yoshio Inayama, the head of Nippon Steel and one of the architects of Sino-Japanese economic relations, had proposed to the Chinese that commercial ties be rooted, in essence, in an "oil-for-steel" exchange. When Nakasone met Zhou in January, Zhou Enlai apparently tacitly accepted the Inayama formulation. Zhou offered one million metric tons of petroleum for 1973. MITI swiftly organized a Japanese consortium, which then signed a contract in April, and the first tanker arrived in Japan under the agreement in September.

Optimistic assessments of China's offshore potential persisted throughout the early 1970's, encouraged by successful test wells in the Bohai. The Chinese, therefore, included petroleum technology and equipment in their 1973-74 foreign purchases to enable development of the Bohai and to survey their continental shelf on their own.[69] The effort was multi-pronged. First, the Chinese entered the world market for a wide range of drilling rigs: ships, platforms, and semi-submersibles. Second, the Chinese purchased oceanographic vessels from Japan and France. Third, they signed contracts with two American companies for computers and related equipment that would permit analysis of the seismic equipment. Fourth, they commissioned a French geophysical company, Compagnie Générale de Geophysique (CGG), to undertake a survey of the Bohai. Fifth, they sought out pipeline technology and equipment, primarily from Japan. Sixth, they ordered equipment to improve their

---

[69] This paragraph is based on Harrison, *China, Oil, and Asia*, Chap. Four, and Woodard, *International Energy Relations*.

onshore operations, especially at Daqing. Initially, in most of these areas, the Chinese seemed to attach priority to Japanese sources, but by 1974, their attention was increasingly devoted to the United States, Canada, and select Western European countries. According to one estimate, for the entire period from 1972 through mid-1970, total purchases for all six categories totaled $400 million.[70]

The decision to finance imports through increased oil exports seemed prescient following the 1973 Yom Kippur War and the ensuing Arab oil embargo. World oil prices soared and Chinese prices accompanied them. Daqing crude which fetched US $4.59 in late 1973 skyrocketed to $14.80 in January, 1974, dropping slightly to $12.85 by July. With the world facing bleak energy prospects, the Chinese eagerly promised more oil. In January, 1974, Zhou pressed the issue with visiting Japanese Foreign Minister Ohira, and the 1974 contract called for Chinese sales of 4.8 million metric tons, while the 1975 contract provided for sales of 7.5 million metric tons. China entered a two-year agreement in September, 1974 to barter oil to Thailand. In October, 1974, Deng Xiaoping continued to express optimism about the expanding export of crude.

In this environment, purchases of foreign plants and equipment more generally reached a new high in 1974. The picture was not entirely rosy, however. Imports grew more rapidly than exports, and China began to confront balance-of-payment difficulties. Ever since China completed repayment of its loans from the Soviet Union, its leaders had trumpeted that China was a nation without debt. The ideology of the Cultural Revolution scorned entangling relations with and dependency upon the developed, capitalist world. The cultural revolutionaries perceived interest payments on loans and sale of natural resources to be forms of exploitation. If trade were necessary, at least it should be balanced.

The policies of 1972-74 challenged these principles. To circumvent the injunction against foreign debts and interest payments, foreign venders had to arrange their own financing, and contracts enabled the Chinese to pay over a protracted period of time. The Chinese did not pay interest. Instead, the vender included its interest payments in the price which it charged. The euphemism for these practices was "deferred payment."

The Solution under Attack

Predictably, these policies—seemingly rational and driven by economic necessity—soon came under attack from cultural revolution ideo-

[70] Barnett, *China's Economy*, p. 480.

logues.[71] The chief architect of the 1972-73 turn outward and of the "4-3 program" was Zhou Enlai. Probably more crucially, he had engendered the wrath of pro-Cultural Revolutionaries for his effort to roll back their policies in the educational and cultural spheres. Mao made the Premier fair game and emboldened Zhou's opponents when, in April of 1973, he criticized the Ministry of Foreign Affairs, a ministry synonymous with Zhou, and in November, on his instructions, the Politburo convened a meeting to criticize the Premier.[72] The fate of the nation seemingly turned upon such pronouncements from the increasingly mercurial Chairman.

The late 1973-early 1974 campaign to criticize Confucius and Lin Biao, as it unfolded in the hands of Cultural Revolution ideologues, became a campaign against Zhou Enlai and the moderate policies he had introduced.[73] In March, the Premier was criticized by name in wall posters put up within the Ministry of Fuels and Chemical Industry for encouraging imports and for increasing dependency upon the outside world. Disruptions in production throughout the country brought an end to the campaign by mid-1974 but Zhou, already suffering from cancer, was losing his political initiative. The Cultural Revolution ideologues seemed ready to reverse the policies which Zhou had introduced from 1970 on. As the year wore on, however, Mao wearied of the machinations of his radical supporters. Seeking a credible alternative to them, he had already restored the purged Deng Xiaoping to his post as Vice Premier in March, 1973, and appointed him PLA Chief of Staff in December, 1973. Prevailing over opposition from his more radical supporters, Mao then named Deng in December, 1974 as his ranking Vice Premier. In January, due to Zhou's illness, Mao placed Deng in charge of daily work of the Party, thereby making Deng the leading generalist among the top leaders and at least temporarily, the challenge from the "left" abated.

Thus, on balance the political tensions among the top leaders in 1973-74 did not significantly disrupt the turn outward in the petroleum sphere. Objective economic conditions and foreign policy opportunities, coupled with activism of the economic bureaucracies on this occasion constrained factional strife among the top leaders. The cultural revolutionaries had served notice of their willingness to struggle against the prevailing policies, but Zhou and Deng were determined to push ahead. Under their aegis, the opening to the outside accelerated in 1975. High

[71] See *Zhonggong dangshi dashi*, pp. 162-172.

[72] See Hao Mengbi and Duan Gaoran, eds., *Zhongguo gongchandang liushi nian* (Beijing: PLA Press, 1984), vol. two, p. 632.

[73] On the intricacies of this campaign, see Merle Goldman, *China's Intellectuals: Advise and Dissent*.

level petroleum delegations visited Mexico, Venezuela, the United States, and Norway. Discussions were held with Royal Dutch Shell concerning Chinese interest in its offshore drilling and technology. Most significantly, Deng commissioned major studies to examine policies in three areas: industry, science, and the Party. Among the recommendations in these studies which later surfaced outside China was this passage in a September, 1975 secret document:

> If we are to import more advanced technologies from abroad, we must increase exports and raise the proportion of industrial and mineral products among export commodities. . . . We must not consider only our import requirements without considering the need to increase export resources.
>
> In order to accelerate the exploitation of our coal and petroleum, it is possible that on the condition of equality and mutual benefit and in accordance with accepted practices of international trade such as deferred payment and installment payment, we may sign long-term contracts with foreign countries and designate several production points, where they will supply complete sets of modern equipment required by us and then we will pay for them with the coal and oil we produce.[74]

Apparently guided by this policy, Vice Premier and leading economic specialist Yao Yilin nonetheless muted the message when discussing cooperation in petroleum development with an American delegation in October, 1975, when he stated:

> China would import advanced technology and advanced, sophisticated equipment from the United States, and imports for the exploration and exploitation of oil would not be excluded. China does not seek cooperation with foreign firms or countries in the development of its oil, and there will be no joint development of China's oil industry. China will not become a major exporter of oil.[75]

The cautionary concluding sentences of Yao's remarks indicate either that he personally harbored some reservations about the policy or, more likely, that he thought it politically wise to indicate the policy had its limits. For, by late 1975, the "4-3 program," the "oil for steel" policy, and the tentative steps to explore the Bohai and other regions within the framework of "self reliance" were again encountering substantive and

---

[74] "Some Questions on Accelerating the Development of Industry" (discussion draft), September 2, 1975, in Kenneth Lieberthal, *Central Documents*, p. 134.

[75] Notes from World Affairs Delegation of the National Committee on US-China Relations.

political difficulties.[76] In the south, as of late 1975, prospecting in the promising Maoming region had been unsuccessful, and exploration activities in the Guangdong region moved to the more difficult Yinggehai off the shores of Hainan Island. In the north, the Chinese were having trouble in the Shengli field securing the offshore platforms to the ocean floor. In addition to problems in exploration and development, the rate of increase in the Chinese production of crude began to slow.

Exports continued to grow rapidly, however, jumping from 3.0 million metric tons in 1973 to 12.0 million metric tons in 1975. As a result, exports constituted 16% of production, compared to only 6% in 1973. Petroleum deficient industries and regions would certainly complain. In addition, the world price for crude petroleum began to drift downward in 1975, and Japanese refiners no longer felt any urgency to avail themselves of Daqing crude, with its high parafin content. The Japanese began

TABLE 5-2
Petroleum Production, Export, and Consumption

	A Total Production Crude Petroleum in Metric Tons	B Growth over Previous Year, MMT	C % Growth over Previous Year	D Exports MMT	E Exports as % of Total Production
1969	21.7	5.8	36%	.2	1%
1970	30.6	8.9	41%	.4	1%
1971	39.4	8.8	29%	.6	2%
1972	45.7	6.3	16%	1.5	3%
1973	53.6	7.9	17%	3.0	6%
1974	64.8	10.8	20%	6.5	10%
1975	77.1	12.3	19%	12.0	16%
1976	87.2	10.1	13%	10.4	12%
1977	93.6	6.4	7%	11.1	12%
1978	104.0	10.4	11%	13.5	13%

SOURCE: This table is derived from State Statistical Bureau, *Zhongquo tongji nianjian, 1982*, pp. 244 and 249, and *Zhongquo dui wai jingji maoyi nianjian, 1984*, p. IV-105. These statistics were not available to Barnett or Woodard when they sought to illuminate the same set of issues, drawing on CIA estimates. Nonetheless, their findings are close to our data. See especially Barnett, *China's Economy*, p. 463; and Woodard, *International Energy Relations*, p. 538. Column D adds together exports of crude petroleum and petroleum products.

[76] The following depends upon American interviews and Woodard, *International Energy Relations*, p. 180.

to press for price concessions. Moreover, the entire "4-3 program" was encountering trouble.[77] China was experiencing serious problems in putting the turn-key plants into full production in timely fashion. Many of the projects, especially the Wuhan rolled steel mill, suffered cost overruns and protracted delays. In addition, in 1975 and 1976, funds for imported items constituted 14% and 21% of total national investments that were financed through the state budget.[78] This drain on capital generated indignation and opposition in those locales and industries which were not beneficiaries of the new projects.

While these problems were neither the catalyst nor the primary cause, they were used by the cultural revolutionaries among the top leaders to flail Deng Xiaoping, Yu Qiuli, Kang Shien, and their associates in 1975-76. Beginning in November, 1975, apparently taking advantage of Mao's increasing frailty and securing his approval through various machinations, the advocates of Cultural Revolution policies renewed their attack on Deng Xiaoping. Following Zhou Enlai's death on January 8, 1976, they were able to prevent Deng from succeeding Zhou as premier. In April, they removed Deng from office, and in the months until Mao's death in September and their own arrest in October, this group desperately sought to reverse the policies of the previous four years. They openly attacked Deng's three policy documents of 1975, hitting particularly hard on his petroleum policy.[79] Addressing a February 10, 1976, meeting to notify responsible officials from provinces, municipalities, and military regions (literally a "serve notice meeting"—da zhaohu huiyi), Zhang Chunqiao and his Shanghai supporter Ma Tianshui criticized the purchases of foreign plants and the export of petroleum and described Deng Xiaoping as a "comprador bourgeosie" and "more noxious than Chiang Kai-shek." Joining the chorus, Jiang Qing asserted that China's petroleum was "all being taken off to other countries."

From February to June, 1976, in fact, Jiang Qing and her three principal allies on the Politburo, Wang Hongwen, Zhang Chunqiao, and Yao Wenyuan convened several national conferences, intervened in Politburo meetings, and voiced their views when the SPC reported to the Politburo concerning the economy. The media, where the influence of the Cultural Revolutionaries was strong, reflected the inner-Party deliberations and hammered at the policy of exporting oil and importing technology and

---

[77] See Fang Weizhong, ed., Jingji dashiji, p. 505 and Ho and Huenemann, pp. 15-17.

[78] See Fang Weizhong, ed., Jingji dashiji, pp. 505-506.

[79] See Fang Weizhong, ed., Jingji dashiji, p. 559, and Kuo Chi, "Foreign Trade: Why the 'Gang of Four' Created Confusion," Peking Review, vol. 20, no. 9 (February 25, 1977), p. 16.

equipment.[80] Deng Xiaoping, Yu Qiuli, Kang Shien, and possibly Li Xiannian and Ye Jianying[81] were among the recipients of these barbs:

By exporting petroleum, China is shifting the international energy crisis on to the Chinese people and has saved the first and second worlds, i.e., the US, Japan, and Western Europe. The State Council is leasing China's natural resources to foreign countries and is engaged in national betrayal.

We are importing too many major items, a whole bunch of things at once.

The Ministry of Foreign Trade has unrestrainedly imported what China can produce, and limitlessly exported what is badly need at home.

The Ministry has conceded sovereignty over the exploitation of mines and resources to others and tried to turn China into the dumping ground, raw material base, repair workshop, and outlet for investment of the imperialist countries.[82]

The vehement indignation of these remarks was, in part, theatrical and opportunistic. Evidently, at an earlier time, Jiang Qing and her allies had professed agreement with the plan to export fuel and raw materials.[83] They also allegedly knew that the plan, while proposed by Premier Zhou, had been approved by Chairman Mao himself. Further, the tight national supply of fuel in 1976—especially of coal and petroleum—could neither be solely attributed to the export of petroleum, as Madame Mao and her allies charged in 1976, nor just to the disruptions in transportation induced by "Gang of Four" factionalism, as their opponents charged in 1977-78. Rather, while each charge had some basis in fact, shortages in oil supplies were largely attributable to the rapid growth in domestic demand, brought on by high growth rates in heavy industry, the profligate use of cheap energy, and the conversion from coal- to oil-fired thermal power plants, as envisioned in the Fourth Five Year Plan.

In sum, Jiang Qing and her allies used the 1976 energy crunch as one of several issues to stave off their opponents. Their intervention had

---

[80] See Barnett, *China's Economy*, pp. 122-126, and Allen Whiting, *Chinese Domestic Politics and Foreign Policy in the 1970's* (Ann Arbor: University of Michigan Center for Chinese Studies, 1979).

[81] We believe Ye may have been a target in light of his action at the time of the removal of Deng Xiaoping in February, 1976. In response, Ye pleaded illness, and Mao designated Chen Xilian to take charge of the work of the Military Affairs Commission. See Fang Weizhong, ed., *Jingji dashiji*, p. 559.

[82] Kuo Chi, "Foreign Trade."

[83] *Ibid.*

temporary effect. The 1976 deliveries of 6.2 MMT to Japan fell short of China's contract obligations to deliver 6.8 MMT during the year, a commitment which in any case was substantially lower than either the 1975 commitment of 7.8 MMT or 1975 actual deliveries of 8.1 MMT. The wave of foreign purchases and contracts swiftly ebbed in 1976, and the petroleum group faded from public view during the interval between the removal of Deng Xiaoping in April and the death of Mao in September. The hiatus proved only temporary, and the political landscape changed dramatically with the death of Mao and the subsequent incarceration of Jiang Qing and her allies.

Summary

In terms of our analytical framework, the evolution of policy from 1972 to 1977 offers striking instances of the interplay of power concerns of the top leaders, bureaucratic politics, and developments in the economy and foreign affairs which the top leaders perceived to require a response. Decisions in fall, 1972, to purchase foreign equipment to develop an indigenous petro-chemical industry and to sell petroleum were responses of the top leaders to changing conditions. Their perceptions of these developments were shaped by the bureaucracies responsible for this sphere of activity, especially the Ministry of Fuel and Chemical Industry. Further, the ascendency of Zhou Enlai, temporarily enjoying support of Mao, and the return of the petroleum group to the command of the Chinese economy provided the political setting conducive to bold decisions. SPC Chairman Yu Qiuli had the responsibility of transmitting the views of Kang Shien and Tang Ke to the top leaders. In addition, achieving the diplomatic breakthroughs with the United States and Japan fell to Zhou's bureaucratic base at the Ministry of Foreign Affairs. This further strengthened Zhou's hand.

However, these and other policies which Zhou, Yu Qiuli, and their allies pursued challenged both the power and ideological inclinations of Mao's wife and her important allies. Able to secure support from Mao in 1973 and 1976 but rebuffed by him in 1974-75, the Cultural Revolutionaries twice mounted severe challenges to the 1972 decisions and forced a retreat from them. Assisting their effort to challenge Zhou were bureaucratic considerations. The foreign purchases of petroleum, which the producing and trading ministries supported so they could afford to purchase necessary foreign equipment, came at the discernible cost of certain regions and bureaucracies whom Jiang could then recruit into their alliance. Further, the bureaucracies importing the whole plants—such as the Ministry of Metallurgy with the Wuhan complex—encountered delays and cost overruns, and the slow pace of these projects strengthened the arguments of Jiang Qing and her supporters. Their demise in October, 1976, opened a new chapter where the top leaders were less bound by ideological constraints.

Stage Four: Foreign Equity Holdings Will Be Permitted, 1977-79

The core problems which the top leaders perceived from late 1976 to late 1978 were the disorder in the country, the uncertain legacy of Mao and his ideology, the disenchantment among the populace with the political system, the wounds of the Cultural Revolution, and the erratic economic performance. Restoring order, instilling confidence in communist rule, and hastening economic growth became the primary objectives of the post-Mao leaders. Economic projects which had been shelved for a decade were taken off the shelf; specific economic issues which had been ignored for a decade began to be debated. The top leaders were by no means unified on these issues. Some advocated neo-Maoist policies—Maoism without the extremism and interference of the Gang of Four. Others sought a return to the policies of the early 1960's which enabled the rapid recovery from the Great Leap, and yet others supported a return to the orderly era of the First Five Year Plan. In a sense, an underlying issue of the 1976-78 period concerned the appropriate strategy for economic growth.[84]

Circumstantial evidence suggests that, as in the mid-1960's and in the early 1970's, the influence of the petroleum group was again crucial in developing the response to these issues. Development of the petroleum industry became a focal point of the development strategy as it unfolded in 1977-78. Moreover, the thrust of policy coincided with the solution that Yu Qiuli and his associates encouraged from 1972 to 1975: financing imports through increased oil exports and accelerating development of petroleum fields through intensified cooperation with the outside world. In the context of 1976-78 politics, moreover, the solution had wide appeal. To the neo-Maoists, the petroleum group could recall the endorsement which Mao had made of Daqing. They only had to resurrect the model and the slogans that went with it, as they did in early 1977. To those who looked with favor on the early 1960's, the solution entailed a resumption of those early imports of equipment from the outside. And to those who remembered the 1950's fondly, the solution entailed an

[84] For discussions of politics at this time, see Jurgen Domes, *China After the Cultural Revolution: Politics Between Two Party Congresses* (London: C. Hurst and Company, 1976); and Barnett, *China's Economy*.

emphasis on heavy industry—metallurgy and machine building as well as the energy sector—and on high rates of capital accumulation.

The Risk Contract

Perhaps the most significant solution which bears the imprint of the petroleum group was a series of decisions from late 1977 through mid-1979 that led China to enter into joint venture agreements with foreign oil companies to survey, explore, and develop China's offshore potential. Crossing ideological barriers, the decisions permitted the foreign firms to invest in China and to own a percentage of any petroleum discovered in the exploration. In the jargon of the oil business, this arrangement entails a "risk contract." That is, the foreign oil firm invests a negotiated portion of the cost for surveying, exploring, and developing the field. The foreign partner then has a claim upon—in a sense, it owns—a negotiated portion of any discovered petroleum. The foreign company assumes a risk; if no oil is discovered, it leaves empty handed. Alternatives are the "no risk" contract and the "service" contract. In the latter, the host country simply purchases the services of the foreign company to survey, explore, and/or develop the field. In the former, the foreign company obtains right to a portion of petroleum if it is discovered and developed, but if the effort yields no commercial oil, the host country is obligated under the contract either to pay a fee or provide an agreed amount of petroleum from some other source. This arrangement entails "no risk" to the foreign company.

Multinational oil companies prefer the risk contracts. Precisely because of the risk, the rate-of-return is higher. The venture makes them either the sole operator (under a concession agreement), an operator (under some production-sharing arrangements), or joint operator (under a joint venture agreement) in the production phase, and increases their management role over the life of the project. And, they participate in decisions about production of the natural resource which they discover. The "risk contract" also offers benefits to the host country. The most obvious is the lower cost at the outset. The host country puts up less capital and has a reduced financial obligation should the venture fail. The protracted cooperation between the foreign producer and the host country also usually results in a more substantial transfer of technology over the long run. Since a genuine partnership is formed, the foreign firms are somewhat more willing to assist their partner in acquiring the requisite skills to run the project well.

Until 1977, with the exception of the 1974 service contract with CGG, the Chinese generally eschewed risk, no risk, or service contracts. The policy of self-reliance favored purchase of whole plants, equipment, or technology on a cash basis; it precluded any form of cooperation that implied a long-term presence and perceived dependence upon multinational oil companies. Nonetheless, throughout the 1970's, several people in the petroleum sector at the Minister and Vice Minister levels had begun to familiarize themselves with the complexities of various forms of cooperation: Kang Shien, Sun Jingwen, Song Zhenming, Zhang Wenbin, and Qin Wencai; and below that rank, such top aides as Zhao Shengzhen, Li Jingxin, Zhong Yiming, and You Dehua. These officials spearheaded the change in policy.

The evolution of petroleum policy from 1977 to 1979 occurred in three incremental steps. First came the full restoration of the policy to import foreign technology and to finance it through increased exports of petroleum. This policy was in place by late summer, 1977, and was part of the effort to restore order to the country and remove the influences of the so-called Gang of Four. Then came the second significant decision that China would avail itself of foreign capital, a decision made by early 1978. This decision came in a bullish environment, when the leaders envisioned high growth rates, a rapid increase of exports, and hence an ability to repay loans. The leaders needed to fund their large capital investment projects and with the many foreign countries and banks pressing credit upon them, they enjoyed an unprecedented opportunity to borrow from abroad. Finally, the third decision for "no risk" contracts came in the first half of 1979, under conditions of retrenchment and perceived financial stringency when the leaders of China were searching for ways to reduce their own immediate financial burden to fund the nation's development.

The First Step: Calling for a New Great Leap,
January 1977-October 1978

The immediate origins of these pathbreaking decisions can be traced to the full return of Yu Qiuli and Gu Mu to the economic helm under the leadership of Hua Guofeng and Li Xiannian in late 1976, soon after Mao's death; to the high targets for increasing petroleum production which were set in spring 1977; to the revival of the 1975 industrial development program in mid-1977; and to the return of Deng Xiaoping at about the same time. In effect, Hua Guofeng and the senior Party leaders around him presided over a transitional era.

Three months after the imprisonment of Jiang Qing and her associates, the top leaders were able to begin seriously to address economic issues. They convened a series of meetings under Party and government aegis both at the top level and at the bureaucratic level, beginning with a preparatory work conference from January 12 to 24, 1977, to discuss the 1977 economic plan.[85] Drawing on this meeting, the appropriate bureaucracy, the SPC, drafted a summary report which it submitted to the Politburo. The top leaders in turn disseminated this document on March 3 for implementation and submitted it to a March Central Party Work Conference for further discussion. Simultaneously, the 1977 National Planning Conference met from March 3 to 17, and considered the same document. Among its main actions was to resurrect the 1975 industrial program which advocated increased imports of foreign technology and equipment and exports of natural resources. The National Planning Conference addressed ten issues which, it claimed, had been handled inadequately during the 1966 to 1976 era. It identified the need to import advanced foreign technology as one such issue. The meeting also set a 1977 target for crude petroleum of 93-95 MMT, compared to 87.2 MMT in 1976.

The top leaders then convened the April-May, 1977 National Conference on Industry to disseminate their new policy orientation (fangzhen), which inter alia reestablished Daqing as a model unit and confirmed the great influence of the petroleum group. Members of the group gave major addresses to the meeting and recapped the lessons of Daqing during the previous 17 years, placing a somewhat greater emphasis on the role of technology in its exploits than in the past.[86] The tone of the meeting, nonetheless, echoed the style of the Maoist era: sloganeering and emphasizing self-reliance. The underlying message was that the "overthrow of the Gang of Four" had opened a new era, and now all things were possible. An era of realism had not yet replaced ideological faith. Premier Hua Guofeng spoke to the participants of this conference on April 18. Based on tenuous geological data, Hua nonetheless stated that for the petroleum industry to have one Daqing was not good enough; it must and could create ten oil fields such as Daqing. He also called for more energetic exploration of offshore petroleum reserves. In the months that followed, other industrial sectors such as metallurgy and coal began either voluntarily or under pressure from Hua, SPC Commissioner Yu Qiuli, and other leaders to set equally ambitious and unrealistic goals.

On July 17, 1977, the SPC submitted a plan to the State Council concerning the import of technology and equipment during the coming eight

---

[85] The following paragraph is based on Fang Weizhong, ed., Jingji dashiji, pp. 576-579.

[86] "Chairman Hua Kuo-feng's Speech at the National Conference on Learning," Peking Review, May 20, 1977, pp. 7-14.

years. The State Council submitted the Plan to the Politburo, which approved the plan in principle. It called for a swift completion of the projects envisioned under the 1973 "4-3" plan and for undertaking another round of imports. Once again, the emphasis was on imports of whole plants in metallurgy and petro-chemicals (fertilizer plants, synthetic fiber plants, refineries, and so on). In order to increase exports of natural resources, imports would also have to include new technology and pivotal equipment for the extractive industries, such as geo-survey ships and petroleum drilling equipment. The plan envisioned that China's imports from 1977 to 1985 would total US $6.5 billion. Total internal Chinese investments for the projects using these imports would total an additional 40 billion RMB. The plan anticipated that roughly 20% of annual capital investments from 1977 to 1985 would be devoted to these projects. In expectation of swift growth in petroleum production, the Chinese also made plans for rapid increases in exports. A high level Japanese trade delegation announced in early November, 1977, that China was prepared to export 15 MMT of petroleum to Japan by 1982.[87]

Next in this series of escalating targets and growing aspirations was the November 24 to December 11, 1977, National Planning Conference which studied long-term plans and the 1978 plan. A preparatory meeting had already begun deliberations on October 17 and two weeks later, this meeting submitted a report to the Politburo. The November-December Planning Conference discussed and endorsed the document which the Politburo was considering, and on February 5, 1978, the Politburo approved and disseminated the 1978 annual plan and the long-term (1978-1985) projections. The long-term projections called for production of 205 MMT of crude petroleum by 1985, which necessitated the development of ten large oil fields. The role of the petroleum sector in these grandiose plans was evident in other ways. Among the 120 large capital construction projects to be undertaken from 1978 to 1985 were ten large oil refineries, over ten fertilizer plants, and ten synthetic fiber plants. The targets, encompassing the Fifth and Sixth Five Year Plans, were more ambitious than those envisioned in the 1975 projections. The plan was then unveiled at the First Session of the Fifth National People's Congress which met in Beijing from February 26 to March 5, 1978. The targets were published in the newspapers and became the vague goals shaping policy for the next several months. In fact, the document was hastily assembled and unbalanced. The entire plan was never openly published nor fully disseminated to lower levels, but it established a framework for

[87] *Petroleum News* (January 1978).

evaluating specific projects; it defined the climate and established the direction of policy through October, 1978.

The State Council convened a series of meetings from July 6 to September 9, 1978, to discuss issues of principle and ideological guidelines (*wuxu hui*) in economic planning. This meeting proposed that a new Great Leap Forward be organized to accelerate national economic growth. It also strongly advocated relaxing restrictions over (*fang shou*, literally "letting go one's hold over") use of foreign capital and importing advanced foreign technology and equipment in large quantities. Overlapping this series of meetings, the State Council convened the annual National Planning Conference to discuss the 1979 and 1980 plans. Provincial planning commission heads and finance bureau chiefs attended the preparatory meeting that began on September 5, and the provincial Party secretaries responsible for economic affairs arrived on September 24, when the full meeting formally began. This meeting decided that the economic front must carry out three transformations: scientific advance; managerial reform; and turn to the outside world. It called for a turn away from the mentality of "closing the door to international intercourse" (*biguan zishou*). Instead, the Planning Conference called for actively importing foreign equipment, using foreign capital, and actively entering foreign markets. The State Council formally approved the SPC report on September 10, 1978, even before the formal meeting began. It decided to increase the targets for the 1978 plan and to increase capital expenditures in the last quarter by 4.8 billion yuan. The decision was based on a very optimistic assessment of the 1978 growth rate.

To summarize, during the hectic months from January, 1977, to September, 1978, the top leaders made a number of interrelated decisions in which petroleum production played a central part: to increase petroleum exports significantly, to use foreign capital, to pursue a strategy of rapid economic growth through high rates of capital accumulation, and to set high planning targets. The process leading to these decisions revealed the effort of the top leaders to reestablish orderly procedures at the apex. Thus, documents passed from a revived SPC to the top leaders and thence were disseminated nationally for discussion. The National Planning Conference coincided with a Party Work Conference, so the planners and the politicans could work in tandem. The bureaucracies reasserted themselves, and the initiatives for many projects incorporated in the 1978-85 plan came from ministries who had long harbored hopes to launch them.

To an extent, the new orientation of the top leaders was their reasoned response to perceived problems and new opportunities—especially for expanded trade with Japan. Yet, the top leaders had also initiated a dynamic process reminiscent of the Maoist era. The top leaders had convened at least one conference, the National Conference on Industry, to mobilize lower level officials in support of their initatives, and they convened meetings of ideologues to develop an ideological rationale for their policies. Time pressures induced by these eager leaders precluded gathering adequate information and carefully evaluating the feasibility of projects. The policy debates at the bureaucratic level took place in an ideologically charged environment. The lower officials felt under pressure to respond enthusiastically and uncritically to instructions from above, and when the top leaders elicited this positive response, they became even more convinced that their course was well chosen and merited rapid pursuit. In sum, the policy process during this period is best understood neither in terms exclusively of elite nor bureaucratic politics but rather as involving a rapid interaction between the two.

The Second Step: Deciding to Accept Foreign Loans and Enter into Cooperative Agreements, 1977-78

The 1977-78 decisions raised new issues for Chinese leaders. How, in the short run, would China finance these imports? How, in the long run, would China pay for them? To the extent petroleum would be a major source for foreign exchange, how could this natural resource be developed in an expeditious fashion? Would the rise of petroleum as a major Chinese export require that alternative fuels—especially coal—be substituted as a domestic energy source, thereby altering the 1966-1975 trend toward increased domestic reliance upon petroleum, rather than coal? Finally, in what form would China seek to avail itself of foreign capital: strictly through loans or also through involvement of foreign firms in China? In contrast to the mid-1970's, however, the domestic political climate and the expanded state of Sino-American and Sino-Japanese relations enabled a more frank and vigorous exploration of the choices available to China's leaders.

Petroleum policies toward the United States and Japan, while clearly related, were somewhat disjointed, as the policy toward each country was also closely integrated into the overall policy the top leaders were pursuing toward each country. Thus, progress in the Sino-American petroleum relationship became part of the 1977-78 movement toward normalization, while on the Japanese side, developments were nested in the negotiations for a long term trade agreement and a Peace and Friendship Treaty. The following pages trace the twin negotiations in three sections: Sino-American progress, 1977 to February, 1978; Sino-Japanese relations, 1977-78; and Sino-American developments, February-December, 1978.

Once again, members of the petroleum group responded with vigor to the political environment. They reenforced the optimism of 1977-78 by pledging rapid increases in petroleum exports even as they harbored private concerns about their ability to sustain expansion in production in the early 1980's. They seized upon the willingness of the top leaders to borrow capital from Japan to enter into negotiations with Japanese petroleum companies to cooperate in the development of the Bohai. They were at the cutting edge of the diplomatic opening which Deng Xiaoping pursued toward Tokyo and Washington. The convergence of interests among the top leaders, the petroleum bureaucracy, and the foreign powers prompted rapid movement.

SINO-AMERICAN PETROLEUM DEVELOPMENTS, 1977—FEBRUARY, 1978

The second half of 1977 saw renewed Sino-American exchanges in the petroleum realm after the 1976 slowdown. The National Council on US-China Trade (NCUSCT) hosted a delegation from China National Oil and Gas Exploration and Development Corporation which met with many leading oil companies; in turn, the NCUSCT sent a petroleum industry delegation to China, hosted by the Chinese Commission for the Promotion of International Trade (CCPIT). The policies of 1972-75 which Jiang Qing and company had disrupted in 1976 were basically back in place. Deng Xiaoping, having emerged as the preeminent leader in July, began to meet and discuss petroleum issues with visiting Americans. In response to a question about Chinese potential for oil exports posed by the Chairman of the National Committee on US-China Relations, Charles Yost, on October 23, 1977, Deng replied,

> We are prepared to export more oil products. We can do that. According to our own statistics, we have large oil deposits. We are basically able to solve the exploration problem ourselves. In order to introduce technology from other countries, we must export more. Oil is the main product. We are trying to export more, but this must be increased step-by-step. The Japanese have told us we have 55 billion tons in oil reserves.[88]

The former head of the United States Liason office in China (USLO), Ambassador George Bush, also visited China in November.[89] Bush visited China with Pennzoil Chairman Hugh Liedtke. The group met with Deng Xiaoping, and suggested the Chinese meet with US oil firms to

[88] From the notes of the meeting between Deng Xiaoping and the Board of Directors of the National Committee on US-China Relations.

[89] The effect of the George Bush visit is discussed in James Tanner, "Promise of Finds Draws Oil Firms to China," *Wall Street Journal*, October 19, 1978.

discuss offshore oil production. In fact, the Bush meeting swiftly led to invitations to Pennzoil and possibly a second American oil company to begin discussions on cooperation offshore. Next, the head of the USLO, Ambassador Leonard Woodcock, called upon Minister of Petroleum and Chemical Industries, Kang Shien, in December. The meeting marked the first time the USLO head called upon a ministry other than Foreign Affairs and Foreign Trade.

The next breakthrough occurred when Secretary of Energy James Schlesinger, long admired by the Chinese for his global strategic views, invited the Ministry of Petroleum to send a delegation to the United States. Schlesinger's old friend Henry Jackson along with George Bush, upon his return from China, had encouraged Schlesinger to issue the invitation; the Chinese accepted, marking the first time the Chinese were willing to have the American government, rather than a private body, host a Chinese delegation. The absence of diplomatic relations was no longer a total barrier to official exchanges in the energy realm, although Deng Xiaoping had told one distinguished visitor,

> After normalization, cooperation can be bigger. If progress toward normalization is slow, this would somehow or other be limited. . . . As to our cooperation in oil, we will have to impose some conditions.

The high ranking delegation, which arrived in the United States in January, 1978, focused on petrochemical refinery processes and offshore development. The delegation traveled to Houston, New Orleans, California, and the east coast, and it had contact with many multinational petroleum companies. The delegation sought, in the subsequent words of one participant, "to explore how the US had accumulated offshore experience and to establish a basis for further cooperation." Upon returning to China after its Japan tour, the group met with Kang Shien and his senior advisors for three days in February.[90] They identified technology for immediate import and for import somewhat later. The record clearly reveals that high level discussions between Chinese and American leaders, which placed Sino-American cooperation in development of Chinese petroleum resources in a broader strategic context, helped to provide momentum in 1977.

SINO-JAPANESE PETROLEUM EXCHANGE, 1977-78

More significant developments had begun to unfold with Japan in the second half of 1977. According to a knowledgeable Japanese source, Jap-

---

[90] *FBIS*, February 28, 1979, pp. E 17-18; 28 March 1978, pp. E 15-16.

anese petroleum industrialists had initiated contact with Qin Wencai and Zhao Shengzhen at MPI in 1976-77.[91] After the defeat of the South Vietnam government in 1975, the Japanese National Oil Company (JNOC) sought to revitalize its previous exploration contracts in South Vietnam by contacting Hanoi. JNOC delegations traveled to Hanoi via Beijing on a few occasions in 1976-77, and used the occasion to begin discussions with the Chinese. These had made little progress.

However, other aspects of Sino-Japanese relations developed rapidly in 1977. Yoshihiro Inayama, the President of Nippon Steel who had played a pivotal role in the "oil-for-steel" agreements of 1972-73, returned to China in February, 1977, and revived his earlier proposal for long-term trade relations. Inayama returned to China in March as the head of a *Keidanren* delegation which met Hua Guofeng. This delegation reached an agreement-in-principle calling for long-term Chinese exports of oil and coal in exchange for imports of plants, machinery, and steel. They set the target for Chinese petroleum exports by 1982-83 at 50 MMT a year. The Chinese designated Vice Minister of Foreign Trade Liu Xiwen to be Inayama's counterpart. During the following months, Inayama and Liu hammered out a long-term trade agreement and organized associations within their respective countries to sustain Sino-Japanese trade. The Japanese group included prominent industrialists, financiers, and traders, while the Chinese formed an inter-ministerial committee.

Key meetings between Liu and Inayama took place in Japan in late September, when both sides concluded the 50 million ton figure was highly unrealistic. China lacked the ability to expand its exports that rapidly, and Japanese oil importers were not eager to make themselves dependent on Chinese high-wax crude, which requires special refining equipment. The September talks reaffirmed the March agreement that the amount of Japanese oil and petroleum imports would largely determine Chinese imports. While the total trade during the envisioned eight-year period would be balanced, Chinese imports would begin at a high level, while its exports would build more slowly. In the September meetings, Liu Xiwen requested the Japanese to consider offering China low-interest credit with long-term repayment. Inayama promised to consider the request, noting that Japan operated under the constraints of the November, 1975 Rambouillet agreement of the industrial democracies.

[91] This section is based on interviews with knowledgeable Japanese. See also Chae-Jin Lee, *China and Japan: New Economic Diplomacy* (Stanford: Hoover Institution, 1984); *Jetro China Newsletter*, No. 16 (January, 1978), and No. 18 (June, 1978); and Yoshi Soeya, *Japan's Postwar Economic Diplomacy with China: Three Decades of Non-Governmental Experience*, Ph.D. thesis (Ann Arbor: University of Michigan, 1987).

However, Inayama indicated the Japanese government might be willing to extend low-interest loans for export of petroleum drilling equipment and other similiar equipment eligible for "development finance" outside the Rambouillet accords.

The next step came in negotiations from November 26 to 30, 1977, in Beijing. MITI and Natural Resources and Energy Agency officials joined Inayama, giving the Japanese delegation an official cast. After some bargaining, with the Chinese pressing for higher figures and assuring the Japanese of their ability to deliver, the two sides agreed that total Japanese petroleum imports from 1978 to 1982 would be between 45.5 and 51.1 MMT, with the total reaching 15 MMT in 1982. Detailed discussions were also held on how Japanese loans would actually be made. The November meetings basically completed the negotiations, and Inayama and Liu Xiwen signed the Long Term Trade Agreement (LTTA) on February 16, 1978. Its length coincided with the economic program then being enunciated by Hua Guofeng, 1978 to 1985, and the two plans were closely related. The LTTA called for a total trade of $20 billion, with Japan exporting $7-8 billion in plants and technology in the first five years. In principle, China had not abandoned its commitment to avoiding foreign debt since trade would be balanced over the lifetime of the agreement. In reality, China had crossed the Rubicon when it had committed itself to obtain loans from the Japanese Eximbank. The issue left to subsequent negotiation was the interest rate.

As a follow-up to the February, 1978 Sino-Japanese Long Term Trade Agreement, a large Chinese economic delegation visited Japan in March-April, 1978. The group leader was Lin Hujia, then a leading Shanghai official and, relevant for our narrative, a member of the Small Planning Commission in 1964-65. (Japanese sources also suggest Lin is the son-in-law of Yu Qiuli.) A main purpose of the visit was to prepare for purchase of the Baoshan Iron and Steel Mill to be located in Shanghai (hence, presumably, Lin's involvement as head of the delegation).[92] The group also toured petroleum and chemical industry complexes. During his March-April visit, Lin Hujia revealed a Chinese interest in cooperative efforts to develop Chinese petroleum reserves. The Japanese concluded that the Chinese—at least the petroleum group—had decided, following the Song Zhenming visit of February to the US and Japan and the signing of the LTTA, to seek cooperative arrangements.

In effect, the petroleum group was now in the exposed position, having

[92] The State Council approved the report of the SPC, SCC, SEC, Shanghai Municipality, and Ministry of Metallurgy on March 11, 1978, requesting permission to proceed with the Baoshan project. Fang Weizhong, ed., *Jingji dashiji*, p. 597.

promised rapid increases in production and export, while sensing that their goals were highly unrealistic. At least, several of the top officials at MPI had privately confided to foreigners in early 1978 that the "ten oil field" goal then being proclaimed was propaganda, a rallying cry, but not the enunciation of a realistic goal. These leading experts within MPI believed that Chinese output would not appreciably increase from 1978 to 1985. Sustaining annual production at 100 MMT was attainable, these officials believed, but that would necessitate foreign technology. Chinese drilling techniques were outmoded, they noted, but to surmount their obstacles, China would attempt to improve its own drilling industry, purchasing foreign equipment and technology and copying it.

In his May, 1978, meeting with the Chairman of the Japanese Commission for Economic Development Tadashi Sasaki, Kang Shien reenforced the message which Lin Hujia had carried. Kang indicated that China would welcome a delegation of Japanese oilmen and that China preferred joint development arrangements to a technological agreement for oil prospecting.[93] That is, by May, Kang seemed to be expressing a preference for a no-risk rather than a service contract.

Then, in May, 1978, the Chinese Geological General Administration (GGA) requested the JNOC to send a delegation to China.[94] The delegation arrived on June 28; its head was JNOC Vice President Jin Miyazaki. With the GGA as the host (except for the tour of the Bohai, where the MPI was the host), the JNOC group visited oilfields throughout the country. The Chinese requested the Japanese to develop whatever offshore field they preferred. Toward the end of its visit, the JNOC group met with Kang Shien and Li Xiannian. Kang sought a ten-year agreement with the JNOC, during which the JNOC would provide technology, machinery, and services in return for natural gas and petroleum. Mirroring the internal State Council discussions then taking place, Li Xiannian alluded to a Chinese desire to obtain loans from Japan while China and Japan cooperated to develop offshore gas and oil. The Chinese envisioned a $10 billion investment. On July 24, 1978, the Chinese and Japanese agreed to cooperate in the development of the Bohai. The two sides agreed on two items: that specialists would meet in Beijing in September and that the cooperation would take the form of a joint venture between China National Oil and Gas Exploration and Development Corporation and the JNOC. Although the July 24 agreement used the phrase "joint venture," the Japanese participants understood this to mean cooperation, perhaps no more than a service contract, financed through loans, with

---

[93] *Survey of the Chinese Mainland Press*, July 18, 1978.
[94] This paragraph draws on interviews in Japan.

the Chinese absorbing the long-term risks. At the time, Japanese sources indicate, the Chinese sought a method of cooperation that would prevent foreigners from gaining all the profit.

The second JNOC delegation visited Beijing in October, 1978. It was headed by the experienced negotiator Akira Matsuzawa. The MPI had replaced GGA as the Chinese host organization, and the JNOC was informed that henceforth the MPI would be in charge of all negotiations. The change was significant. A ministry generally in favor of expanded cooperation with the outside world had wrested control over the negotiations from an agency more deeply embued with the spirit of self-reliance. Li Jingxin became the principal interlocutor; he had long specialized in Japanese affairs within his Ministry. During the October visit, the two sides agreed that the form of Sino-Japanese cooperation would be a no-risk contract. Repayment of Japanese investment in the exploration and development of fields in the Bohai would be in the form of crude petroleum either from the Bohai or—in the event no commercial petroleum was produced—from other fields in China.

The route toward an agreement appeared quick and relatively easy. When Li Jingxin arrived in Tokyo for the third round of negotiations on January 16, 1979, both sides believed that a contract was in the offing. For this round, MITI joined JNOC in the talks, for the Japanese had concluded that a new public-private company would have to be created to undertake Japanese oil operations in the Bohai. The negotiations opened with the outline of a "no risk" contract. Under the contract, the JNOC would provide the new company with capital at 6.25% interest with an 18-year repayment period. China obligated itself to repay the loan in oil, priced at international levels, with an additional 3-4% of production given to Japan *as profit*. (Hence, even if the contemplated contract was "no risk," it contained a clause which included an element of risk and acknowledged the Japanese right to profit.) The Japanese investment was to total 400 billion *yen* (or roughly US $2 billion), with further discussions to be held between the Bank of China and the Japanese Import-Export Bank concerning the loan provisions.

The third round of negotiations proceeded smoothly from mid-January to February 15. At that point, with only a few items left undecided, the two sides believed a February 25 signing was possible. Modifications were made in the contract which introduced a measure of risk to the Japanese and decreased the Chinese obligation to pay in crude oil from other fields in the event of failure. The trend, in short, was toward a risk contract, but as of February 15, the contract essentially was a "no risk" one. As the Chinese departed the negotiating room on the fifteenth, they indicated they would continue the next day. On the sixteenth, however, the Chinese team announced that, for reasons they did not know, they had received an order to return to China, and Li Jingxin and his team departed on the seventeenth. Clearly something had gone awry in Beijing. We trace the source of the discomfiture after examining developments on the Sino-American petroleum front in 1978.

SINO-AMERICAN PETROLEUM EXCHANGES, 1978[95]

American multinational firms were quite active in 1978 as well. ARCO, Pennzoil, Exxon (Esso Exploration), Union, Phillips, and Mobil all sent delegations in the second half of 1978, and Texaco joined the list in January, 1979. Our interviews with officials from many of these companies reveal the Chinese strategy: to draw out each of these companies, to stimulate their interest in China, and to play off one against the other. The multinationals were, of course, not new to such a situation; and they approached the Chinese as veterans of efforts in Indonesia, Malaysia, Nigeria, Saudi Arabia, and so on. Discerning as the Americans were, they were willing to accept Chinese claims of ignorance and naiveté. That is, four of the companies which we interviewed asserted that it alone was the first to detail for the Chinese precisely what concessions, production sharing arrangements, and risk-contracts entailed. Our interviews reveal, in other words, that the same group of Chinese told each company that its presentation was new, frank, and established the basis for a special relationship. Early on, the Chinese revealed an ability to encourage several foreign interlocutors to believe they were favored and had earned particular confidence and friendship. Moreover, precisely when Japanese negotiators were being told in June, 1978 that the Chinese preferred Japan to take the lead in the Bohai, the same group of officials were seeking to entice an American firm to enter the Bohai on a service contract. As another example, even as the Chinese were professing total ignorance about various forms of cooperation, they knew enough to seek advice from the very best officials of other governments who had negotiated with multinational oil companies, especially Norway.

The American multinationals approached the Chinese with their own postures and strategies. Although the Americans differed among themselves in style, the issues to which they attached priority, and their long-term assessments of the risks and opportunities at stake, their separate approaches in 1978 shared some common attributes. They felt that a job of education lay ahead. That is, while the Chinese seem to have been in

---

[95] This section draws on interviews with the leading executives of American corporations involved in the seismic surveys and in the negotiations leading to joint venture exploration of the South China and South Yellow Seas.

a semi-negotiating posture from the outset—probing, adopting a posture, enunciating principles—the Americans wished to discuss alternative approaches and concepts. The Americans also approached the Chinese with confidence and patience. The multinationals knew they owned the capital and technology which the Chinese needed, especially for deep offshore surveys and explorations. At the same time, by late 1978, the deteriorating situation in Iran reminded the multinationals of the need to diversify oil sources—a message that was underlined as the Iranian revolution unfolded in 1979. The chief negotiators of the multinationals also believed that to engage their companies in China involved an undertaking of historic and strategic significance, and they were attracted to the challenge. At least three companies—Pennzoil, ARCO, and Occidental—developed their initial contacts with Deng Xiaoping and Li Xiannian through the political activities of their Chairman, Chief Executive Officer (CEO), and/or Boards of Directors, rather than through their exploration or sales divisions. Finally, their competitive urge against their rivals also came into play. One higher ranking official, for example, could not interest his CEO in China, despite a strenuous effort, until the CEO read a front page newspaper story that Exxon, Pennzoil, and others were going to China. Down came the phone call: "Let's go."

The initial American approaches, then, tended to be interested, cautious, and patient. With rare exception, the Americans preferred "risk" contracts, and they wanted to learn more about the Chinese terrain—both geologically and politically—before concluding the "risk" was acceptable. Meanwhile, the Chinese cloaked their eagerness to get started and configured themselves as the willing pupil, ready to consider proposals the multinationals might offer. They were not yet ready to enter into risk contracts, however.

One American company, ARCO, adopted a somewhat different stance. ARCO Chairman Robert Anderson went to China in June, 1978, as Chairman of the Aspen Institute, and his delegation met with Li Xiannian.[96] Just before Anderson was leaving, Li asked Anderson, "Would you be interested in helping us develop our offshore potential?" Anderson responded positively, ultimately leading to an October, 1978 visit to China by an ARCO delegation that went to China prepared to negotiate a contract. The company had selected a block south of Hainan Island in which it wished to work, and therefore ARCO was prepared when the Chinese asked what area they would like to develop in the offshore areas.

---

[96] The ARCO negotiations from the Chinese perspective are described in an interview with Zhang Wenbin. See *The China Business Review*, Vol. 8, No. 6 (Nov.-Dec., 1981), pp. 24-25.

(When the Chinese asked some other American companies this question, their response was to ask for seismic survey data—which proved to be unavailable—or to recommend that a seismic survey be undertaken.) The Chinese initially responded that they would have to study the request, but in a few days they agreed. CNOGEDC officials and the ARCO delegation then negotiated a fifteen-page agreement. ARCO introduced the concept of "production sharing," with which the Chinese claimed to be unfamiliar, but at the end of the ten-day negotiations, according to ARCO officials, CNOGEDC officials apparently understood and accepted the idea. Prior to returning to the United States, ARCO and the Chinese negotiators had reached basic agreement on such matters as the split of oil, training, preference for purchase of Chinese equipment, and so on. However, when ARCO officials returned in January, 1979, to complete the negotiations, the Chinese were no longer willing to move swiftly ahead. You Dehua indicated the Chinese wished to divide the contract into two phases—the seismic survey phase and the exploration and development phase. As with the JNOC negotiations in Tokyo a week later, the ARCO negotiations ground to a halt.

Nor was the petroleum sector the only one experiencing such disruptions in negotiations in January-February, 1979. For example, an American metallurgy firm was making steady progress in its negotiations to rennovate a major Chinese steel mill. This progress continued until January 15, at which point the Chinese informed the American firm "procedural problems" had developed on the Chinese side which would have to be resolved internally. Although the Chinese claimed the problem would be resolved shortly, by mid-February, the American side had concluded the problems were complicated and involved a decision by the Chinese government to review its financial commitments. The American firm sensed that the Chinese negotiators had been instructed not to conclude any contract involving commitments of funds until national level decisions were made. This assessment by the American firm was shrewd and, we now know, correct.

The Third Step: Deciding to Permit Foreign Equity Holdings
in China, 1979

Sometime between late fall, 1978, and March, 1979, and most likely between the eve of the mid-February rupture of negotiations with JNOC and the early March departure of a petroleum delegation to the United States, the top 25 to 35 leaders made a decision to proceed with foreign companies in the development of offshore petroleum through "joint venture" risk contracts. We are unable to say precisely on what date the

221

relevant bodies—MPI, State Council, and the Politburo—endorsed the "risk" form of cooperation. The MPI probably recommended such a decision to the top leaders by August, 1978. At that time, MPI officials began to tell foreign companies such as Exxon and BP that foreign risk capital would be welcomed in offshore oil exploration, and the notion of risk was introduced into the French contract negotiations in the fall of 1978. But MPI, as other Ministries at this time, may have been exceeding its mandate. The absence of a top-level decision was indicated when Minister of Foreign Trade Li Qiang contraindicated MPI statements and said that under no circumstances would China consider joint ventures.[97] Further evidence that the issue was on the agenda of the top leaders was a *Guangming Ribao* (GMRB) article of August 18, 1978 describing the New Economic Policy (NEP) of Lenin. GMRB was used frequently at the time to generate support for proposals being considered at higher levels. This particular article noted that NEP policies included organizing joint ventures and offering foreign firms long-term concessions in such endeavors as petroleum development.

The first sign that a firm decision had been made came in March. A risk contract was implicit in the agreement which CNOGEDC Vice President Zhang Wenbin signed with Arco in Los Angeles on March 19, 1979. While that agreement only called for a seismic survey of a large block south of Hainan Island, it gave Arco the right of first refusal to undertake exploration and development of this area on a risk basis. On the same March trip to the United States, the CNOGEDC team—including You Dehua, Zhao Shengzhen, and Tang Changxu—met with several American oil companies. The group clearly indicated that the Chinese wished to enter into negotiations for risk contracts and wished to entice American petroleum companies to undertake seismic surveys. The principle was also well embodied in the draft contract which Matsuzawa negotiated in the fourth round of Sino-Japanese talks in July, 1979. Thus, it appears that roughly between mid-February, 1979, when Li Jingxin left the Tokyo negotiations, and mid-March, 1979, when the Arco contract was signed, the top leaders made the decision that risk contracts were acceptable in principle.

Two other developments in early 1979 suggest a decision had been made to permit foreign equity holdings in China. This was the time when it became widely known that the Chinese government was drafting general regulations for joint ventures (not limited to petroleum).[98] At the same time, the Chinese government dispatched a number of teams

---

[97] *The Financial Times*, August 10, 1978, p. 28, in FBIS, August 11, 1978, p. A-12.
[98] Ho and Huenemann, p. 73.

of planners and economists to study "export" or "free trade" zones in other countries.[99] As part of this policy, on February 15, 1979, the State Council approved the proposal of Baoan county adjacent to Hong Kong and Zhuhai county adjacent to Macao to establish foreign trade bases in these two counties and appropriated 150 million RMB (about US $75 million in 1979) for this purpose. This, of course, is the genesis of the special economic zones.

Our ability to pinpoint the timing of the "risk contract" decision is important to our narrative. Many foreign observers have been inclined to believe that the petroleum group were enthusiastic advocates of the idea, and that they had to overcome opposition of more cautious economic planners. Many observers also believe that the policy can be traced to Deng Xiaoping; this inference is based on his 1975 position advocating petroleum exports and his 1978 offer to foreigners to develop coal mines for export. Our narrative suggests, however, a more complicated situation. While opposition to risk contracts did exist, cautious economic planners such as Chen Yun explicitly endorsed this form of foreign involvement, as we demonstrate below. Thus, the decision came when both Deng Xiaoping and the petroleum group were encountering difficulties and tempering their policies in other areas. (Deng's problems in spring, 1979 were attributable to the high cost of the Chinese incursion into Vietnam and ideological challenges arising from popular opinions expressed during the Democracy Wall movement.)

We have already mentioned the problems in economic affairs which some leaders perceived by late 1978. The year had been one of a "great leap outward," with Chinese having signed contracts for close to $7 billion in purchase of complete plants.[100] The November 11-December 13, 1978, Central Work Conference and the December 18-22, 1978, Third Plenum of the Eleventh Central Committee began to question the expansionist economic policies of 1978, and in the weeks thereafter, this concern was pressed within the Politburo. In February, 1979, the Chinese at least temporarily suspended many of the contracts signed in 1978, including the large Baoshan Steel project. On precisely the same day, February 16, that Li Jingxin terminated the negotiations in Tokyo, the Ministry of Finance in Beijing informed some Japanese that the Bank of China had not approved the financial terms for the Baoshan project.[101] These initiatives reflected a growing sense of urgency to establish control

[99] Michael Moser, "Law and Investment in the Guangdong Special Economic Zones," in Moser, ed., *Foreign Trade, Investment and the Law in the People's Republic of China*, (Oxford: Oxford University Press, 1984), p. 143.

[100] Barnett, *China's Economy*, p. 133.

[101] Date is in Ho and Huenemann, p. 151.

over a deteriorating situation. While 1978 had been a solid year in economic growth, the government had generated a substantial deficit, and the high growth was purchased through the highest rate of capital investment since the Great Leap Forward. In fact, in many respects, with the important exception of extensive foreign imports, the economic growth strategy of 1977-1978 had not departed dramatically from the approach of the Maoist era: high rates of saving; priority to metallurgy and machine building; and a general neglect of the collectivized agricultural sector and of education and science. Indeed, the political management of the economy in 1978 had resembled the Great Leap Forward, with the setting of unrealistic plans early in the year and the raising of these to even higher levels in the latter half of the year.

The November-December, 1978 Party meetings called for revisions in the draft 1979 and 1980 plans before their submission to the National People's Congress.[102] More importantly, they established a political framework for challenging the economic strategy of the previous two years. The ambitious calls of early 1978, including the target of creating ten Daqings by 1985, were abandoned. The meetings called for a comprehensive balance in economic development instead of "rushing things, wasting manpower and material."[103] Accepting ideas advanced earlier in the year, these meetings concluded that massive structural changes were necessary for China's modernization. Policies toward agriculture and intellectuals required major adjustments. The meetings ushered in an era of innovation, experimentation, and change. Neo-Maoism was out; reform and readjustment became the watchwords of the day. Politically, moreover, the meetings weakened those on the Politburo whose authority was rooted in praise and endorsements by Mao. The meetings restored to full honor many who had opposed Mao and been purged by him, including several officials who had been influential in the economic sphere before the Cultural Revolution. Hua Guofeng and several on the Politburo closely identified with him emerged from the meetings greatly weakened. The stage was also set for an erosion in the influence of the petroleum group, i.e., of those who came to the fore since 1963-64 via Daqing and the small planning commission, and who were, in late 1978, running the Chinese economy as heads of the SPC, SEC, State Capital Construction Commission, and Ministries of Petroleum, Metallurgy, and Chemical Industries.

One of the first to take advantage of the new environment was Chen

---

[102] Fang Weizhong, ed., *Jingji dashiji*, p. 611. See also *Zhengming* (May, 1979), pp. 9-13.

[103] See the Communique of the Third Plenum of the Central Committee in *Peking Review*, No. 52 (December 29, 1978), pp. 11-12.

Yun, a respected Politburo elder and economic figure who had never been enamored with Maoist economic strategies.[104] Chen favored balanced and steady growth: a planned economy which, nonetheless, had important residual room for market forces to meet consumer demand particularly in the countryside; limited decentralization to stimulate local initiative without surrendering central control over the provinces; and commercial and technological exchanges with the outside in ways that would not disrupt the political and ideological essence of China. Chen abhorred inflation, government deficits, and foreign debts that would risk China's hard-won independence in world affairs. The November-December Party meetings, in effect, unleashed Chen; and he soon made his presence felt.

On January 1 and 5, Chen criticized the draft 1979 plan.[105] He noted that the draft plan acknowledged that certain materials would be lacking and that there were many gaps in the plan. Chen wrote, "I believe we must not leave gaps. I prefer that we reduce our targets. I would rather reduce some projects." He also observed, "If material supplies are to be lacking, then we do not have a truly reliable plan." Chen's two comments—presumably circulated to other Politburo officials—elicited a directive from Deng Xiaoping on January 6: "In our general orientation (*fangzhen*), we must have a readjustment (*tiaozheng*). We must give priority to projects that are relatively easy to manage, can be completed swiftly, and can earn a profit. We should reduce some steel mills and some large projects. The emphasis in imports should be on projects that are effective and can earn money. This year's plan must reduce some targets." On the basis of this directive the SPC began to readjust the plan.

One of the major deficiencies in the plan and one of the major anticipated shortfalls in supply was energy.[106] Fully 20% of industrial capacity went unused in 1978 due to shortages in electricity and coal. Coal-using industries were growing more rapidly than was the production of coal. Energy shortages were not the only factor producing the retrenchment, but it is important to note that the 1979 plan called for 101 MMT production of crude petroleum compared to 1978 production of 104 MMT. For the first time since 1960, the Ministry of Petroleum could not promise a substantial increase in supply. One could easily imagine the temptation

---

[104] For more extended discussions of Chen Yun, see Lardy and Lieberthal, eds., *Chen Yun's Strategy*; Solinger, *Chinese Business*, pp. 77-81; and David Bachman, *Chen Yun and the Chinese Political System* (Berkeley: University of California Press, 1985).

[105] This paragraph is based on Fang Weizhong, ed., *Jingji dashiji*, p. 614.

[106] This paragraph is based on Fang Weizhong, ed., *Jingji dashiji*, p. 619, and Zhou Taihe, ed., *Dangdai zhongguo*, p. 169.

to reverse the 1972 decision, endorsed again in 1975 and 1977, to export petroleum, using it instead for domestic purposes. But, that option did not tempt the leaders. To the contrary, in the midst of formulating the retrenchment policies, and under the leadership of cautious economic planners, the leaders reaffirmed their commitment to use oil as a major source of foreign revenues.

The Politburo and State Council, as well as two national conferences (a March 3-25 meeting convened by the SPC and an April 5-28 Central Work Conference), discussed foreign loans, the retrenchment, and its relationship to energy policy.[107] Chen Yun elaborated his position in his March 21 talk to the Politburo. Chen criticized the Ministry of Metallurgy for not calculating carefully in its foreign purchases. The nation lacked the electricity, coal, and petroleum, Chen noted, to sustain all the steel mills under construction. Further, the rate of borrowing in 1977 which the Ministry planned would create a large debt which could plague China in 8 to 10 years. Finally, external borrowing for projects still demanded internal investments, and this had not been carefully considered. Chen recalled that the State Council had carefully considered foreign borrowing last year, and that after people sent abroad to study this problem had returned, they advocated borrowing billions. Chen noted that some people may have been opposed to this policy, but they did not speak up. Chen said that in his opinion, the decision of the Center to borrow from abroad was correct, but China has only a limited capacity to absorb foreign capital.

Chen summarized his views in this way: "Do we still want foreign capital and technology? We certainly want these and moreover we must fully utilize them. The only thing is to do it over a longer period of time."[108] In addition to going about the task at a more measured pace, Chen cited the need to develop sources of foreign currency revenue. He agreed with foreign critics of Chinese capacity in this area. Chen then evaluated the various alternatives available to China:

> To rely on agricultural commodities, the potential is not great, and we must seek other routes. During the Central Work Conference, I saw material from the Tourist Bureau which claimed that by 1983 it could earn $3 billion. Is this easy to manage? I fear it is not. As to

[107] The April Work Conference had a broader agenda, addressing the Democracy Wall movement, personnel matters, ideological issues, and the incursion into Vietnam. We focus below only on the economic issues.

[108] From Chen Yun, "Readjust the National Economy; Develop in a Balanced Fashion," in *Zhonggong shiyi ju sanzhong quanhui yilai zhongyang shouyao jianghua ji wenjian xuanbian* (Changchun: People's Press, 1982), p. 76.

other resources, such as oil, American survey technology is high, so we should use American technology to undertake it. *Let us undertake oil development; this can be done quickly and effectively.* Compensation trade, co-production, and processing are all forms we can undertake. In sum, securing foreign currency must become a big topic for us.[109]

Chen's comments reveal he neither opposed an expansion of imports nor resisted cooperation with the United States in development of petroleum. However, he was concerned that cooperation proceed carefully, keeping risks at a minimum.

Personnel changes at the top accompanied the spring, 1979 economic retrenchment and departure from the neo-Maoist development strategy.[110] The net effect was to dilute the influence of the petroleum group. Chen Yun and Li Xiannian submitted a letter to the Party Center on March 14, 1979, suggesting the State Council establish a Finance and Economic Committee (FEC), to establish the orientation and policies in the economic sphere. On the same day, the Party Center accepted the suggestion and the nominees which Chen and Li had offered, thereby indicating that perhaps the matter had already been discussed. Chen and Li proposed that Chen chair the committee and Li become the deputy chairman. The pivotal job of Secretary General went to Yao Yilin, a long-time associate of Chen Yun and Li Xiannian and a student activist with Kang Shien at Qinghua in the 1930's. In essence, the FEC intruded on the role which Yu Qiuli and the SPC could be expected to play. Further, in June, the FEC established a "Research Group on Reform of the Economic Structure" to carry out studies on the economic reform.

The available information suggests, therefore, that the decision to enter into joint ventures on a risk basis did not occur when the petroleum group had the political initiative. To the contrary, it occurred when the authority of the SPC under Yu Qiuli was being curtailed through the creation of the FEC led by Chen Yun, Li Xiannian, and Yao Yilin. Nor does the evidence suggest that those such as Chen Yun who opposed the neo-Maoist development strategy of Hua Guofeng also opposed the risk contract. To the contrary, the slim evidence suggests they (and especially Chen Yun) found the risk contract and the foreign equity holdings in Chinese natural resources attractive because these forms of cooperation minimized Chinese financial obligations and offered maximum technol-

[109] *Ibid.*, pp. 78-79. Emphasis added.
[110] See Fang Weizhong, ed., *Jingji dashiji*, p. 621; Chen Yun, "Readjust," pp. 72-73; Zhou Taihe, ed., *Dangdai Zhongguo*, p. 171.

ogy transfer.[111] Driving the decision was the peaking of Daqing production and the perceived need to swiftly identify and develop new fields—both to maintain Chinese domestic supply and to provide a source for foreign exchange. More than any other factor, economic necessity drove policy forward. At the same time, the December, 1978 Party meetings had instilled a spirit of innovation and candid self-appraisal and an environment which facilitated bold decisions. Yet, the speeches and descriptions of the inner-Party meetings at this time reveal misgivings and quiet opposition to the policy of massive foreign imports and use of foreign capital. The concern was whether foreign capital and equipment would subvert China and deprive it of its independence. As so many times in the past, the petroleum group evidently had been able to offer a plausible solution to the problems which the top leaders perceived. The solution which the petroleum specialists offered—enter into risk contracts—had been quietly considered within MPI and CNOGEDC for years, and the foreign oil companies had been intensively educating these specialists about its virtues for nearly eighteen months. The petroleum specialists were finally able to sell the idea to even the skeptical top leaders, with whom they differed on many factional and policy grounds, because their solution met some pressing concerns of the skeptics. Here, in short, is an interesting instance of coalition building in Chinese politics, where some top leaders (Chen Yun, et al.) and a bureaucratic sector and its leaders (MPI, Yu Qiuli, et al.), can agree on a bold departure in policy *for different reasons*. As a result, the petroleum group was in an exposed position. They had every incentive to be tough negotiators over the precise terms of the joint venture, in order to reduce their vulnerability to criticism by the skeptics.

STAGE FIVE: ESTABLISHING A PARTNERSHIP WITH THE MULTI-NATIONALS, 1979-83

The policy process in the next stage differed significantly from the process we have analyzed thus far. To date, our study has concentrated on the interaction between the preeminent leader, the generalists, the economic specialists at the apex, and the leaders of the energy and especially petroleum bureaucracies. Now, our attention focuses on how the petroleum group sought to transform a broad mandate into specific practice.

[111] In addition to evidence already cited, see especially information about the April 5-28, 1979 Central Work Conference in Zhou Taihe, ed., *Dangdai Zhongguo*, p. 185; Fang Weizhong, ed., *Jingji dashiji*, p. 624, and Li Xiannian, "Speech at Central Work Conference," *Zhonggong shiyi ju*, pp. 109-147. These references do not mention risk contracts specifically, but they enumerate the concerns of the leaders at the time.

The story expands from the top levels to the ministerial levels and below. The relevant actors now include the bureaucrats—probably some of the officials who, acting as staff, originated the solutions which the petroleum group proposed to the top leaders. Now, we see the petroleum group as line officials, leading the drafters and negotiators of the contracts and establishing the organizations that would carry out the joint ventures with the foreign companies. To secure the cooperation of the pertinent ministries and provinces, they had to bargain and strike deals with officials in other Chinese agencies. Our analysis now extends to bureaucratic politics in China.

FROM FANGZHEN TO ZHENGCE

The next stage involved specifying the terms of risk contracts and negotiating the details of the joint ventures. The early 1979 Chinese decision to enter a risk contract and to permit foreign equity holdings in petroleum development established a general "orientation" (*fangzhen*); it did not address the details or define the precise policies (*zhengce*). These would be hammered out in the course of the negotiations. As explained in Chapter Four, this is a frequent phenomenon in Chinese politics. Acting either impetuously or, as in this case, on the advice of sectoral leaders, bureaucrats, and professionals with access to them, the top political leaders announce a bold initiative before its details have been decided or before its ramifications are well understood. In effect, the top political leaders move well beyond current bureaucratic practices. The publicity they give to their new orientation and goal becomes a tactic for generating support and creating a sense of certainty as to its realization. In subsequent months and years, the details are then added, and a range of specific issues are addressed which were not even perceived to exist at the time the bold initiative was proclaimed. During this process, a good deal of tugging and hauling occurs. Opponents of the initiative enter the fray, recommending implementational measures which, in effect, would undercut the new commitment. Various affected bureaucracies seek details which shape the policies in ways favorable to their interests. Meanwhile, the initiators of the policy must exercise their leverage to keep their decision from being eroded or subverted.

This process is often not well understood abroad. Our interviews suggest that foreign observers frequently assume that bold decisions have substantial bureaucratic undergirding to them, and therefore that the Chinese are prepared to move forward with dispatch. As a result, foreigners became impatient with what is an understandable and protracted effort to give substance and structure to the initiative.

The 1979-83 stage in our narrative illustrates this process. The early

1979 decision to enter into risk contracts for offshore oil exploration and development was made without either the top leaders or the bureaucrats fully appreciating the complexities or the consequences of their choice. The briefings which they had received in Beijing from the multinationals and the foreign consultants they had hired, however, had given them a general sense of the problems they would have to address. In four ways, this is not a "typical" case of how a leadership initiative acquires specificity. First, foreigners played a more important role in the process than usual. Second, whereas the leadership frequently is divided over bold initiatives, in this case there apparently was widespread agreement among the leaders that the initiative was necessary and proper. Third, the leaders, bureaucrats, and professionals educated themselves about the complex issues in an unusually methodical fashion. Finally, they were able to forestall activity until the details had been worked out. That is, the exploration stage did not begin until the contracts were signed, while in most other initiatives in China, the details are set as the policy is actually implemented.

The Issues

The decision to enter risk contracts created the need to address a wide range of issues.[112] Most important was the form of foreign participation. Essentially, the Chinese developed their own hybrid from three models: 1. *a joint venture arrangement*, in which the government awards a block to a company formed under its legal system to undertake the project. The company is a joint venture of foreign and domestic oil companies. The financing of the project is the responsibility of the joint venture. The involvement of a domestic corporation, especially if it is a state-owned entity, presumably helps to protect the interest of the host country and probably means some of the financial risk is borne by domestic financial institutions. (This is the Norwegian model.) The government derives its revenue through royalties and taxes on the joint venture; 2. *a risk-service contract*, in which the government creates a domestic oil company which obtains all oil in the event oil is discovered, and the foreign operator is paid for its exploration and development costs plus profit. The domestic oil company in turn makes arrangements with the foreign operator, which purchases and markets the crude abroad. (This is the Brazilian model.); 3. *a production-sharing contract*, in which foreign and domestic operators cooperate under contract to develop the petroleum

---

[112] Our discussion draws upon interviews with Western firms. See also Raymond Mikezell, *Petroleum Company Operations and Agreements* (Washington: Resources For the Future, 1984).

reserves, and production is shared among the foreign operators, the domestic oil company, and the government. (This is the Indonesian model.)

The key negotiating issues are different for each form of cooperation. Under the joint venture agreement, one of the key considerations in the negotiating process between the joint venture and the host government is the rate of taxation. Under the risk-service contract, the focus is on the rate of profit to which the foreign company is entitled and the amount of crude which it can or will purchase. Under the production sharing agreement, the big questions center around royalties which the government expects to be paid and the split in production between the foreign operator and the domestic partner. Also at issue is the portion of exploration costs which the foreign operator is entitled to recover during the production phase and the portion of exploration and development costs which the domestic parties are to provide. These three types of undertakings are abstract models, and in reality, the final arrangements can eclectically incorporate components from all three. As we will see, this is precisely what the Chinese did.

In addition to these big issues dealing with the form of cooperation, the allocation of production, and the finances, a large number of other issues had to be settled: To what extent would the survey, exploration, and development stages be linked? Would those who undertake the surveys have a prior claim on the right to explore and develop the plot? To what extent must the foreign operators avail themselves of domestic supplies? How much foreign technology was to be transferred and what obligations would the foreign operators have to train domestic personnel to run the operation? In case of disputes, what were the methods of arbitration and where would they be located? At what point would the obligations of the foreign company be completed in the exploration phase; that is, how many exploratory wells had to be dug, within what period of time, and to what depth, before the foreign company could terminate its effort? What factors would determine whether a field was commercial and merited development (such as total reserves in the field, daily rate of recovery, cost to bring into production)? To what extent would the contract indicate the responsibilities of the foreign operator to bring a field into production? Or, to what extent would the contract leave room for subsequent negotiations concerning the development and production phases?

The steps leading to the signing of the joint venture contract included the negotiations with the Japanese (1979-80); the undertaking of the seismic survey in the South China Sea by Western firms and the analysis of the data (1979-80); the drafting of the model contract (1979-82); and the actual negotiations (1982-83). The negotiations with Japan National

231

Oil Company and ELF Aquitane and CFP-Total of France for the Bohai set the pace. These contracts were signed in May, 1980. Chinese negotiations with Arco proceeded on a separate track, with a contract signed on June 4, 1981. The negotiations with the other multinationals—Exxon, BP, Texaco, Occidental, Pennzoil, and so on—for the South China Sea and South Yellow Sea followed a more protracted schedule. Compared to the Bohai, the South China Sea entailed greater expenditure, more difficult terrain, potentially larger reserves, and greater risk in that less was known about its geological formations. Following protracted and often difficult negotiations, contracts began to be signed in May, 1983 (with BP) and the parade of signing ceremonies concluded in December, 1983 (with Texaco-Chevron).

The Negotiations with Japan, July 1979-May 1980

The negotiations with JNOC which had been disrupted in mid-January resumed in July, 1979.[113] The fourth through seventh rounds occurred from July, 1979 to February 1980, with two separate agreements. During the sixth negotiation (November 22-December 7, 1979), the two sides agreed on the terms for cooperation in development of the south and west portions of the Bohai, while during the seventh round (January 28-February 6, 1980), the two sides agreed on cooperative development of the Chengbei field in the Bohai. The agreements encompassed a "risk" principle, but this had no significance for Chengbei, since the Chinese had already discovered oil in that locale. MITI and JNOC then established two different companies to develop the two blocks, the Japan-China Oil Development Company and the Chengbei Oil Development Company. On April 24, 1980, the Japanese established two separate companies to sign and implement each of the two contracts, consisting of JNOC, thirteen oil development companies, seventeen oil refinery companies, nine electric power companies, and eight steel companies. The refineries and electric companies shared an obligation to consume the product, while the steel companies expected to participate in supplying the ventures. The eighth to tenth negotiations from March 27, 1980 to May 28, 1980, included the newly formed companies and involved specifying the contract on the basis of the earlier agreements. CNOGEDC and the two Japanese operating companies signed the contracts on May 29, 1980, during the visit of Premier Hua Guofeng to Japan.

The contracts linked the survey, development, and production stages. The Chinese briefly attempted to separate the survey and development

[113] *Jetro Newsletter*, No. 16 and No. 18.

stages and to obtain the right to open the Bohai to international bidding after the survey data were available, as they did in the South China Sea. However, the Chinese accepted Japanese demands of linkage during the December, 1979 negotiations. Among the principal issues in the negotiations were financing of the development stage and the split of production. The Japanese agreed to pay for the survey exploration costs, estimated at $210 million. The two sides agreed that China would provide 51% of the development costs and the Japanese consortium would bear 49%. The issue was how to finance the Chinese portion, with the Chinese expecting a special, low interest, dollar-denominated Japanese loan. The Japanese desired the Chinese to avail themselves of a yen-denominated credit line at 6.5% interest which the Japanese Eximbank had already extended to China, but which the Chinese had not utilized extensively. In the December, 1979 negotiations, the Chinese conceded this point, but as a trade-off, the Japanese committed themselves to obtain low interest loans for their share of the costs. The Chinese had feared the Japanese would obtain high interest rate loans in Japan, with the interest charges coming at Chinese expense, as part of Japanese recoverable costs. As to production sharing, 42.5% of production was to be paid to Japan in kind, of which 39.85% was to cover the cost and 2.65% was for profit. The Chinese could sell additional oil at world market prices to repay their loans and to earn foreign exchange.

Although both Chinese and Japanese call their agreement a risk contract, in the eyes of American oilmen, the risk to JNOC was relatively low. In reality, the contract had the backing of a government-to-government agreement. Moreover, the Bohai had already been surveyed, and the likelihood of oil was great. (Indeed, commercial wells had already been drilled in the Chengbei field.) The total sums to be expended would not reach into the tens of billions of dollars. Finally, the Chinese were prepared to shoulder a substantial portion of the development costs (albeit on loan from Japan). The loans had government backing. The actual risk to the specially formed Japan-China Oil Development Company and the Chengbei Oil Development Company was quite limited.

The Seismic Survey, March 1979-June 1981

By mid-1979, the Ministry of Petroleum had accumulated a thick file of model or draft risk contracts. Several of its Vice Ministers and Deputy Ministers—for example, Zhang Wenbin, Qin Wencai, Li Tianxiang, Ma Wenlin, Zhao Zongnai, Zhao Shengzhen, You Dehua—had spent hundreds of hours in briefings on the differences between the Brazilian, Norwegian, and Indonesian models.

In early 1979, the Ministry of Petroleum entered into negotiations with several foreign oil companies—Phillips, Chevron, Texaco, Exxon, Mobil, Arco, Amoco—to carry out a group seismic survey of six large blocks in the South China Sea and two blocks in the Yellow Sea.[114] The Chinese obligated themselves, after the survey was completed and the data were analyzed, to select one-third of the surveyed area, divide it into blocks, and to offer the blocks for exploration and development on competitive bids. The negotiations for the surveys began in March, 1979, and contracts were signed from March through July. Many other companies then paid a fee to secure access to the seismic data, which the operators supplied to the Chinese, and to obtain the opportunity to bid for the right to explore and develop the blocks. The foreign companies obviously insisted that companies which did not carry out the surveys or pay a fee would not be eligible to bid. In the end, over 30 companies participated in this process.

The operating companies gave the analyzed results of their surveys to the Chinese twelve months after the start of the surveys. The Chinese also obtained all raw data—the digital tapes—and the companies that bought into the survey supplied their interpretations within eight months of receiving the processed data. The operating companies pooled and shared their data. The arrangement required and secured United States government and COCOM approval, since the Chinese received training in the sensitive, high technology art of interpreting seismic data. The surveys got underway in late summer, 1979, and all the required data went to the Chinese from mid-1980 to June, 1981. The data were massive, made all the more so because of the Chinese demand for a more dense survey than is usually carried out.

In effect, the Chinese obtained a free seismic survey of their offshore geological formations, at a cost to foreign oil companies of roughly $200 million. The companies provided one of the most extensive and intensive seismic surveys they had ever undertaken. In return, the companies obtained the right to bid on exploration and development of blocks, with little knowledge of the terms the Chinese would seek and no assurance their bids would be accepted. A major reason that the companies undertook this effort was their initial conviction that the area was very promising and was one of the last uncharted areas on earth. Their expectations had been aroused by the early ECAFE surveys and sustained by data

[114] In addition to interviews of officials from the operating companies, our account draws on Barnett, *China's Economy*, pp. 483-484; Ho and Huenemann, p. 166; Kim Woodard, "China and Offshore Energy," *Problems of Communism* (Nov.-Dec. 1981), pp. 32-45; and Kevin Fountain, "The Development of China's Offshore Oil," *China Business Review* (Jan.-Feb., 1980), pp. 29-31.

from some surveys which a survey ship had undertaken on behalf of one of the majors and which were circulating in the industry.

The major issues in the negotiations for the seismic survey included (a) the access of the foreign operators to seismic data which the Chinese had obtained from their own, prior geological surveys; (b) the right of the survey companies to participate in the bidding, that is, that those undertaking the surveys or paying for access to the data by a fixed date (initially late summer, 1979 and later set as December, 1979) would have exclusive rights to bid; (c) the rights of the companies and the Chinese to the seismic data; (d) the kind of survey to undertake; (e) the cost or prices the Chinese would charge for servicing the seismic ships; and (f) security issues. Each of the negotiations for the six surveys in the South China Seas proceeded somewhat differently, and not all these issues arose in all contract talks. The security issue arose, for example, for the westernmost surveys, which concerned areas under territorial dispute between Vietnam and China; the negotiations coincided with a period of military conflict between the disputants. The Chinese wanted American operators to conduct seismic operations in the disputed waters. One American negotiator recalled, "We said we would take financial risks but not political risks. We repeated this time and again. We asked for protection if we were working off Hainan, and the Chinese replied, 'No.' At that time, Vietnam was lobbing shells into Hainan, so we decided to pay the Chinese to conduct the survey work themselves, using their own crew and boats." The companies which actually undertook the surveys also sought to ensure that their activity improved their chances to bid successfully on blocks within the areas they surveyed. Finally, the foreign operators feared the Chinese would put up for bid the least attractive areas. The detailed seismic data would distinguish the more and less promising areas. The final agreement required the Chinese, when selecting the blocks put up for bid, to ensure one-third of the blocks were most attractive areas, one-third from the moderately attractive, and one-third from the least attractive.

The foreign operators did not find the Chinese approach unusual. A number of other countries (such as Norway and various African countries) had organized speculative surveys similar to the Chinese effort. However, in previous instances, the governments purchased the surveys as a service contract and then sold the information, thereby recouping their cost. In the Chinese case, perhaps reflecting the basis for the early 1979 decision to enter into risk contracts, the cost for the survey was immediately shifted to the foreign operators. In retrospect, other aspects of these negotiations foreshadowed the more complex and protracted negotiations over the exploration contracts. The Chinese sought to induce competition among the foreign operators and reduce their dependency upon any single operator by inviting several firms to undertake the surveys; but, in the end, the gambit was only partially successful, as all companies had roughly similar concerns and they all wished to have access to the total data and to be able to bid on all blocks. The Chinese sought to extract maximum benefit from the survey in terms of training, technology transfer, and acquisition of data. COCOM restrictions became a limiting factor, and the negotiations led to an easing of COCOM restrictions. The Chinese retained careful control over which companies obtained which survey areas, and they insisted in introducing non-American firms into the equation—such as bringing AGIP and BP into the Amoco survey block. Finally, the negotiations were under control of the Ministry of Petroleum. The Ministry of Geology, which had generated some of the Chinese seismic data and also had responsibility for seismic work, was not a partner to the agreement. From the outset, MPI had made the offshore oil program its project.

The Model Contract, 1979-1982

In effect, the seismic survey phase created a 24-month window from mid-1979 to mid-1981 to prepare for the actual negotiations. The Chinese used this time effectively, as did the oil companies. The two sides began to know each other, and where the personal chemistry permitted it, some feelings of respect, warmth, and friendship began to develop. As the seismic surveys began in 1979, the Chinese tentatively explored the possibility of also involving the multinationals in development of petroleum in the northwest. High ranking delegations from such companies as Texaco, Occidental, and Exxon visited Xinjiang and Qinghai provinces. The Chinese apparently probed whether the majors would be interested in simultaneous involvement in offshore and onshore cooperation, with the onshore activities to be financed with production from the offshore fields. None of the foreign companies proved receptive to the Chinese idea, and the approach was quickly and quietly shelved.

In effect, the Chinese wished to avoid the problems generated by each of the models they explored, and they sought to avail themselves of a source of revenue central to each model: royalty and taxation (Norway); taxation (Brazil); and production sharing (Indonesia). Those in the MPI responsible for formulating the Chinese approach did not wish to give the foreign operators any chance to earn ill-begotten or excessive income. At the same time, they recognized the need to offer the foreigners a suitably attractive package so that they would be willing to bid on the blocks when the Chinese offered them.

The Chinese proceeded methodically to identify what precisely the foreign companies sought. They did this through the drafting of a model contract which would serve as the basis for the negotiations with the foreign firms.

The Chinese established contact with the Norwegian government and the United Nations Center for Transnational Corporations (CTC), which provides counsel to developing countries concerning how to deal with foreign corporations. Both became consultants to the MPI. Apparently, the Chinese received conflicting information from their principal consultants in 1979-80. Responding to a Chinese invitation, a Norwegian delegation of government and corporate energy executives arrived in early spring 1979 to undertake a joint study of the Chinese energy situation. The invitation grew out of a September, 1978 trip to China by Norwegian Minister of Oil and Energy Bjartmer Gjerde. The spring, 1979 delegation included both petroleum and hydropower specialists. While the corporate executives inspected Chinese onshore and offshore operations, the government officials held a month-long series of intensive seminars on their experience in developing North Sea oil, in negotiating with foreign firms, and on the different ways to involve foreigners. They met with Kang Shien on the eve of his departure to the United States to initiate discussions on the seismic survey. The exchange led the Norwegian government to suggest to the Chinese that they enter into a formal consultancy agreement with Statoil, the Norwegian oil company.

The Chinese accepted the recommendation, and from 1979 through 1981, the relationship was intimate. The Statoil consultancy also gave the Chinese access to computers and software which they used to analyze the consequences of the Model Contract under varying assumptions and terms, but once the negotiations got underway, the Norwegians were no longer intimately involved. Many foreign oilmen believe the Norwegians provided the Chinese with advice to impose severe restrictions: to extract high royalty payments, and to shift the cost of exploration entirely to the foreign companies. One European source who knows a great deal about the MPI-Norway connection states, however, that the Norwegian government did not give the Chinese such advice. For example, when the consultations began, the Norwegians found that the Chinese were planning to subject petroleum equipment imports to high tariffs as a way of earning revenue from the foreign partners during the exploration stage. They dissuaded the Chinese of this idea, pointing out that the objective was to expedite the exploration phase so production could get underway swiftly.

While individual Norwegians privately offered a range of differing opinions, the leading Norwegian officials were acutely aware that the Chinese and Norwegian conditions differed dramatically and that the Norwegian model could not be easily transferred. Above all, the Norwegian joint venture approach grew out of a sophisticated legal system, with an accumulated body of corporate and tax laws into which a genuine joint venture arrangement could be nested. Further, they warned the Chinese that one danger of a very complicated contract was that, given the legal competence resident in the multinational oil companies, they would understand the contract better than the Chinese. Thus, the Norwegian contracts should have, on balance, impelled the Chinese toward the Indonesian model, which did not necessitate a complicated legal infrastructure. It was more suited to developing countries. But, the Chinese determination to reach for the most modern or the most advanced solution caused them to remain interested in the Norwegian model. The Chinese concluded that if a legal infrastructure was necessary to make the Norwegian model work, then they would create the legal infrastructure.

The United Nations CTC brought in consultants who explicitly argued against the Norwegian model and propounded the advantages in the Indonesian approach. It provided more incentive to the foreign operators to earn profits, and gave the host government a greater access to petroleum production. The conceptual difference, according to one informant, was that the Norwegian arrangement in the North Sea sought to keep the foreign operators under tight control and to guarantee government revenues from the outset, while the Indonesian model sought to harness the energies of the foreign operators, allowing them to earn more out of the belief the host government would also earn more.

Caught between these two approaches, and eventually persuaded that the Norwegian approach would not work in its entirety in China, the Chinese also examined other solutions, particularly the Brazilian model of a risk-service contract. To the uneducated, it appeared attractive, assuaging nationalistic feelings by creating at least the illusion that all production passed through the domestic oil company. However, by early 1980, the Chinese perceived its limitations as well. The Brazilian model demanded greater financial commitments by the host government than the Chinese wished to undertake, and it was not clear the foreign companies would accept its constraints. Further, the Chinese soon understood the Brazilian model entailed unnecessary cosmetic arrangements, in that a portion of production ends up being distributed abroad by the foreign operators. The Chinese had no interest in complicating their export arrangements. This combination of considerations inclined the

Chinese toward an eclectic solution, heavily influenced by both the Indonesian and Norwegian models, which the foreign companies found workable but perhaps unnecessarily ornate.

The Chinese became disenchanted with their United Nations consultancy when an early draft of the model contract (dated October, 1980), which they had first shared with private members of the UN team in strict confidence, surfaced in a well-known professional publication, the *Petroleum Concession Handbook*. The Chinese severed the consultancy relationship, but the Norwegians did not become the exclusive advisors as a result. Instead, the Chinese turned to others, and this included the foreign oil companies themselves. The multinationals reacted with alacrity to the draft of the model contract which appeared in the *Petroleum Concession Handbook*. Even before its appearance, CNOGEDC officials had begun to consult the foreign oil companies about clauses of concern to them, and the consultations intensified after the leak. Interviews with the officials of the multinationals indicate, as previously noted, that the Chinese confidentially whispered to at least four of the companies that it enjoyed a special status in Chinese eyes, that it alone was considered trustworthy and friendly. The Chinese in confidence showed several of the companies draft clauses or large sections of various drafts of the model contract. The foreign companies were asked to react, comment, and criticize the drafts. Each of the foreign companies maintained secrecy and believed it had earned Chinese respect and confidence. While the Chinese approach had obvious tactical advantages, it also facilitated a genuine give-and-take prior to the formal negotiations, and several companies devoted considerable time and thought to assisting the Chinese develop a model contract which would benefit all parties.

With the rupture in the UN consultancy, the Chinese began to draft and translate the model contract on their own. According to an American negotiator, the drafts shown to one company in early 1981 were "almost unintelligible. The English was so bad that it could hardly be read. It was very unclear what the Chinese were trying to do." Apparently, this draft was one subsequent to the leaked one. Its framework never changed, calling for a production-sharing contract (the Indonesian model) in which the foreign operators spent exploration money at risk and the Chinese had the right to participate in the development stage up to a level of 51%. The petroleum would then be divided on a predetermined basis. Virtually all other aspects of that draft did change. According to an informed American oilman (not from Exxon), from this time on, Exxon became a leader in the discussions. The Chinese, according to this source, saw Exxon as the largest of the oil companies: "It had an immense staff, and it could provide the Chinese with an educational course."

On the Chinese side, drafting the model contract was the responsibility of a special task force within MPI. Two key people in assembling the task force, according to an American with excellent access, were Shi Jiuguang and Zou Ming. Both were elderly technocrats with long experience in the industry. You Dehua and Zhao Shengzhen were also heavily involved. (We describe You and Zhao in the next section.) MPI drew people from other relevant ministries to put things together. The drafting process began in earnest in the second half of 1980, according to a Chinese official, and throughout 1981, consultations were held widely among the relevant Chinese agencies, culminating in a national meeting which lasted for a week in late 1981. The model contract went through eleven drafts, the result of considerable negotiation between the Foreign Investment Control Commission (FICC) and MPI.

Here is where the different missions of individual organizations discussed in Chapter Three came into play. FICC examined the contract to ensure it conformed with existing regulations and met the Chinese desire to import technology. It was concerned the model contract not weaken long-term trade agreements and conformed to the various principles to which China adheres in entering such agreements (such as, protection of national sovereignty and the unity of China). MPI is not charged with these missions; its mission is to discover and produce oil. These discussions between the FICC and MPI coincided with the period MPI was sharing portions of the draft with the multinationals. According to our Chinese source, the internal drafting process enabled MPI to secure a widespread consensus among the Chinese agencies as to the content of the contract. Both the Minister of Foreign Trade and Kang Shien, who formally became Minister of Petroleum in March, 1981, were kept informed of the drafting process. They were briefed after the initial draft and especially after opinions were secured from foreign firms. If there were complicated issues, then the MPI and the FICC appealed to higher levels. As a result of these extensive consultations, the FICC and its successor Foreign Investment Management Bureau at MOFERT were not deeply engaged in the subsequent contract negotiations. Its approval had been secured for the model contract on which these negotiations were based.

In early 1982, the Model Contract was in a final draft. In January, a Norwegian government delegation journeyed to Beijing on short notice to react to the draft. The Norwegians found the terms severe and the structure quite complex, an opinion they shared in an unusual meeting with a number of top level economic officials, including Yao Yilin and Kang Shien. Another round of consultations was then held with the favored foreign firms to test their reaction. While these firms complained about its restrictive terms, the Chinese concluded that the document provided an adequate basis for the negotiation.

CNOOC finally issued the 80-page-long model contract on May 10, 1982.[115] Forty companies responded to the Chinese invitation to participate in the bidding process. On that day, each firm picked up a locked suitcase that contained fourteen documents pertaining to the bidding process. The brand name embossed on the satchel, appropriately enough, was "Long March." The firms had 100 days—until August 17, 1982—to respond to the invitation and submit their bids for the 12 blocks in the Yellow Sea and the 31 blocks in the South China Sea. The firms paid $10,000 to be able to bid on each Yellow Sea block and $40,000 for each South China Sea block. Foreign bidders could combine into a consortium to bid on specific blocks.

The model contract attracted keen interest since, in absence of detailed Chinese law for many of the topics it addressed (such as taxation or investment protection), it filled the need of establishing a legal framework. Since it would apply to all foreign companies involved offshore, the model contract assumed a role similar to that of a legislative enactment. It called for cooperation over a life span of 30 years, broken down into three phases: exploration, development, and production. It established the basic structure of cooperation, charted the form of management organization for the joint ventures, detailed the obligations of the contracting parties, and stipulated the procurement procedures for the foreign operators. The Chinese retained the option of contributing up to 51% of the exploration costs. The model contract developed a complex formula for allocation of the crude petroleum: 17.5% of gross production to go to China as royalty and tax; 50% is deemed "cost recover oil" to compensate CNOOC and the foreign companies for operating costs; and 32.5% is designated "profit oil." The latter includes reimbursement for exploration costs (including interest payments). The division of "profit oil" between CNOOC and the foreign operators would depend on the size of the field and was subject to contract negotiations.

The Negotiations, August 1982-December, 1983

The deadline for bid submissions was August 17, 1982, by which date 40 bidders—20 individual companies and an equal number of consortia—

---

[115] The following paragraphs draw on Robert C. Godwin, Jr., "The Evolving Legal Framework," *The China Business Review* (May-June, 1983), pp. 42-44; Stephanie Green, "Offshore Business," *The China Business Review* (May-June, 1982), pp. 17-19; Michael J. Moser, "Offshore Oil Exploration and Development in China: The Current Regulatory Regime," in Moser, ed., pp. 186-194; Ho and Huenemann, pp. 167-171; and Ad. Ignatius, "China's Deal," *Petroleum News*, News Supplement (June, 1982).

submitted a total of 102 bids on 43 blocks.[116] The Chinese had convened a seminar in Beijing in June to answer questions about the model contract and to allay some of the concerns. As a result of the seminar and ongoing discussions with foreigners, the Chinese were hopeful that the negotiations could be completed expeditiously, with signings by the end of the year. The foreign operators, on the other hand, anticipated the negotiations would last well into 1983, and they proved correct. The Chinese obviously confronted a major challenge in absorbing and responding to the 102 proposals, and they had to organize negotiations, either simultaneously or in sequence, with the numerous bidders. The foreign companies began to be called back to Beijing in November to clarify their bids. CNOOC had concluded that some bids reflected evident reservations about the stability of China's opening to the outside, a nervousness reflected in the guarantees and assurances the firms were requesting. CNOOC officials stressed at this time (November-December, 1982) that, as Premier Zhao Ziyang had stated during the August, 1982 signing ceremony with Arco, the contract would have the force of law.

CNOOC completed its round of consultations in December, continued its evaluation and analysis of the bids in January-February, 1983, and entered into serious negotiations soon after the Spring Festival in mid-February. The Chinese evidently had hoped to carry out the negotiations in sequence, signing some contracts that set forth attractive precedents, after which they would move to the tougher cases. To this point, according to some foreign companies, the Chinese were approaching the negotiations with considerable confidence. However, oil prices were tumbling in late 1982-early 1983 which, combined with the tough features of the model contract, prompted all the majors to pursue the negotiations in a cautious and determined fashion. As a result, according to one source, CNOOC began to change its estimate of its bargaining leverage and its strategy, offering minor revisions in the model contract and deciding to foster greater competition among the bidders through a somewhat more protracted bidding process. The first contract finally was signed by a BP-led consortium in May, 1983, followed by two Occidental-led consortia on August, 1983; an Esso Exploration and Royal Dutch Shell consortium in August, 1983; the Idemitsu-led consortium in September, 1983; a Getty, Sun, and JNOC consortium in October, 1983; a Pennzoil consor-

[116] In addition to our interviews, this section is based on Ho and Huenemann, pp. 166-167; Kim Woodard, "The Drilling Begins," *China Business Review* (May-June, 1983), pp. 18-19; "Waiting for the Offshore Go Ahead," *Far Eastern Economic Review* (October 1, 1982), pp. 63-66; Teresa Ma, "Foreigners Too Would Like Some Offshore Business," *Far Eastern Economic Review* (August 25, 1983), pp. 61-63; "Oil Exploration Delayed in China," *The Financial Times*, March 4, 1983.

tium in November, 1983; a Phillips consortium in November, 1983; and, lastly, Texaco and Chevron in December, 1983. Each company or consortium paid a one million dollar signing fee. Toward the end of the negotiations, acting against earlier assurances that no forced marriages would be required, the Chinese insisted that several companies which had not bid together form consortia. Under this Chinese pressure, some of the American companies had to absorb companies from Europe and Latin America. An American whose company experienced this recalled, "The bid process seemed to be very politicized. They knew exactly who they wanted where. It was all political." Ambassadors in Beijing lobbied on behalf of their national oil companies—for example, Spain on behalf of Hispaniol—and induced the Chinese to insert their companies into consortia.

The negotiations and final contracts remain confidential matters between the foreign operators and the Chinese, and none of our informants demonstrated any inclination to be indiscreet. It is possible, however, to identify the major problems in the negotiations, to describe the Chinese negotiating team, and to assess the way the Chinese conducted the negotiations and the foreign reaction to the Chinese approach.

ISSUES IN CONTRACT NEGOTIATIONS

Ambiguities in the model contract had left several matters unsettled: the procedures for repatriation of profits, the legal status of CNOOC, the authority of the Joint Management Committees in everyday decision making, the responsibilities of the foreign firms to train Chinese and transfer technology, the wage rates to be paid Chinese employees, and the purchase of Chinese supplies. In addition, the model contract specifically left three major areas open for bid and negotiation: the work program, in which the foreign company specified its time schedule for exploration and development and the number of exploratory wells it would drill; the so-called "x factor" bid, that is, the portion of allocable profit oil which the foreign operator was prepared to share with the Chinese at different levels of production; and the contribution which the operator was prepared to make to China's offshore program or to other sectors of the Chinese economy. Finally, a set of issues arose which posed profound difficulties for the foreign operators and which challenged principles, fundamental policies, or deeply ingrained practices of the Chinese state. For example, their strong commitment to the principle of sovereignty made the Chinese reluctant to permit arbitration of disputes arising on Chinese soil to occur on foreign soil. Understandably, several foreign companies were reluctant to make themselves hostage to Chinese arbitration, and demanded international arbitration. The Chinese, in keeping with their cultural proclivities, preferred ambiguous clauses, while the foreigners tended to seek detailed clauses. Further, to the extent the detailed clauses departed from the model contract, CNOOC and MPI had to secure approval from the pertinent bureaucracies, a task the negotiators clearly were loath to undertake.

THE CHINESE NEGOTIATING TEAM[117]

The petroleum group assembled a skilled team to settle these issues in the contract negotiations. The Chinese personnel had the requisite personalities and skills to elicit the respect of the foreigners. You Dehua supervised three negotiating team heads: Sun Shujun, Tang Chengxu, and Shi Jiuguang. All were technically proficient. Tang had been trained as an engineer, Sun was a chemical engineer, while Shi was American trained and had, at some point in his distant past, worked in the oil business in southern California. (Shi, as noted above, had helped to organize the drafting of the model contract.) Each of these brought distinctive skills to the task. For example, technical points, such as the language of the contract, were handled by Shi Jiuguang. Sun had come to CNOOC from another ministry, according to an American negotiator, where she had done economic analysis. A native of Shanghai, she understood English and proved to be very bright. Several of our American informants believed that her substantive grasp grew noticeably through the negotiations and remarked on her ability to deal with Americans with toughness, candor, and competence. They sensed that her authority increased during the negotiations.

The chief negotiator You Dehua was born in Hebei in 1931 and was educated as a chemical engineer at Qinghua in the 1950's. One of his early assignments was in the Yumen oilfields, where he worked with Qin Wencai. Prior to 1966, he was assigned to the Sichuan gasfields and then to the Petroleum Design Institute in Chengdu, where he served as a janitor during the Cultural Revolution. After the Cultural Revolution, he served as a Deputy Manager of CNOGEDC and Deputy Director of the Foreign Affairs Bureau in MPI. Those positions gave him responsibility for foreign involvement in offshore oil development from at least February, 1978. He travelled with Tang Ke to Canada in 1974 and first visited the United States in 1979. He was the chief interlocutor of the Norwegian consultants in 1980-81. With the formation of CNOOC, You became its Vice President. While the portraits which our American in-

---

[117] This section draws largely on our interviews with American oilmen. Several companies kindly shared with us the biographical data they had gleaned about their interlocutors. In general, it is striking that the Chinese conveyed remarkably little information about themselves to these companies.

formants sketched of Chinese frequently varied considerably, their descriptions of You were remarkably consistent: businesslike, no-nonsense, tough, diligent, honorable, honest, intelligent, fair-minded, cautious, a clear defender of Chinese interests and viewpoints. You was self-taught in English, which he continued to study assiduously at home during the negotiations.

When CNOOC was established and the formal negotiations began, You supplanted Zhao Shengzhen as the chief interlocutor for American companies. In fact, Zhao initially was not named to any post at CNOOC, but many Americans had become familiar with him over the preceeding three years, and questions were asked about his absence both privately and in the Western press in spring, 1982. Perhaps as a result, he became a Vice President at CNOOC and played a role in the negotiations ancillary to that of You Dehua. Zhao, raised in a family of the intelligentsia, is a native of Zhejiang and a graduate of Qinghua University. He is fluent in English, having studied the language from age 10, and he took engineering courses in English at Qinghua before 1949. Zhang Wenbin brought Zhao to Daqing in 1959, where he served as a drilling engineer during the exploration and development stages. With training in Romania and fluency in French, Zhao was selected to travel abroad for MPI at an early date. From late 1963 to August, 1964, he spent a substantial portion of his time visiting Germany, Switzerland, Italy, Algeria, France, and the Netherlands. He travelled to Japan in the summer, 1966. By 1966-67, he was a planning engineer for CNOGEDC with evident responsibilities for purchase of foreign equipment. While he ceased public appearances during the Cultural Revolution, he was active again by 1972, when he became chief drilling engineer of the Ministry of Petroleum and Chemical Industries. By May, 1973, he was Deputy General Manager of CNOGEDC. By October, 1978, he was Deputy Director of the Foreign Affairs Bureau at MPI. Throughout the 1970's, he served as an advisor to the China National Technical Import Corporation, the body responsible for importation of petroleum equipment. He visited the United States first in June-July, 1977, as leader of a petroleum equipment survey group, and he returned in March, 1979 with Zhang Wenbin, during which discussions were held with several companies concerning offshore cooperation. He handled the negotiations for the seismic surveys and was the chief liaison officer in preparing the bidding package. Our informants tended to portray Zhao in similar terms: intellectually curious, urbane, sophisticated, cosmopolitan, direct, impatient, knowledgeable, outspoken, friendly, enthusiastic, independent-minded, clearly committed to cooperation with the outside world, and a bit of a maverick among Chinese bureaucrats.

Zhao Shengzhen had been at the forefront of the petroleum relationship with the United States from its inception. Yet, when the negotiations got underway, he yielded to You Dehua. The change from Zhao to You intrigued our American informants. Some believed the switch was due to the personality differences between the two. Several Americans believed Zhao was not as high ranking in the Party as was You Dehua. Others believed his ability to get along well with Americans may have, in the end, reduced Chinese confidence in him. Finally, some Americans believe Zhao may have made some errors in 1981, during the drafting of the model contract and the establishment of CNOOC. Whatever the reasons, the chief architect of the framework for the negotiations did not become the chief negotiator. The organizers of the exercise evidently saw advantage in disturbing the human relationships that had developed over the previous few years, while the complaints of the foreigners may have been a factor in reintroducing the architect into the equation.

The negotiating team included participants from related agencies, such as Finance and Customs, whose administrative jurisdiction extended to the clauses under negotiation (for example, tax or import procedures). These participants were subordinates to CNOOC leadership and usually just listened and took notes at the sessions. They had stronger roles behind the scenes.

FOREIGN IMPRESSIONS

While the Chinese displayed some internal differences during negotiating sessions, they did not comment about the negotiations to foreign firms outside the meeting room. Our American informants could recall few instances of their Chinese interlocutors violating discipline, and they recalled those moments vividly: an occasion when a subordinate telephoned his American counterpart to congratulate him for his curt departure from a meeting in which an obdurate Chinese began to raise uninformed questions about issues that had already been settled, or a few occasions when the Chinese team argued vigorously among themselves at the table. Yet, the Americans did sense that the chief Chinese negotiators from CNOOC spent more time negotiating with other Chinese than they did with the foreign companies. They were intermediaries between foreigners and the leadership—extending through CNOOC chief Qin Wencai to the very top—and the bureaucracies which would have to fulfill the contract commitments.

According to one American source, Tang, Sun, and Shi had very little authority. You Dehua could resolve most substantive, non-economic changes. Qin Wencai received matters involving substantive economic changes. Issues involving technology transfer, procurement and the preference clause, and repatriation of foreign currency all went outside CNOOC. Problems involving taxation went to the Ministry of Finance. Distribution of oil and settling the "x factor" went to MPI and possibly the State Council (with Kang Shien and SPC head Yao Yilin as the specialists). Another negotiator had this impression of the negotiating process:

> There were certain aspects of the contract for which CNOOC would have to go to another ministry over which it had no authority. The preference clause, for example, was not in its realm to resolve. Issues dealing with employment of Chinese workers involved many other ministries. CNOOC seemed to have good relations with the Ministry of Finance, which played a role in the negotiations. Ministry of Finance personnel were involved in tax and other aspects of accounting. They would attend negotiations to gather information and then go off and make decisions which CNOOC would then announce to the foreigners. MOFERT attended sessions dealing with contract terms.
>
> Several top leaders called the shots: They had the real clout. Several people at the highest levels were very much in favor of offshore development. There was also a lot of bureaucratic jealousy from other ministries over the money and resources being expended on offshore oil development. The whole process of the negotiation was one of starting and stopping, pushing and pulling. It was as if other ministries were trying to derail the car which the MPI was riding. The top leaders would then have to intervene to put the car back on the track.

In the final stages of each negotiation, according to another American, Tang Ke received a detailed briefing on the major points. He intervened to resolve remaining differences. His intervention proved decisive in at least two instances, and several American participants believe that his personal commitment to the process and the confidence the highest level officials had in him led him to instruct the CNOOC negotiators to yield on some sticking points. With agreement near, SPC Commissioner Yao Yilin, Kang Shien, and a very few unspecified others would then be briefed by CNOOC and MPI and endorse the contract for signature.

With the signing of the contracts from May to November, 1983, the negotiating was over and the drilling soon got underway. China and the outside world were about to embark on a distinctive effort in its modern history: Chinese and foreigners working as partners in a joint venture, within a framework established by the Chinese government.

Over four years had passed from the decision in early 1979 to permit foreign equity holdings in the development of China's offshore resources. Some foreign companies found the negotiating process painfully slow, but other observers believed that the Chinese had exhibited considerable capacity to learn and adapt to new conditions. Almost all foreign negotiators and consultants believed that, within the parameters the top leaders had set, the negotiations proceeded in an intelligent and admirable fashion. Our informants included the chief negotiators of all the major companies, and while many found the experience difficult and frustrating, all came away from their experience with considerable respect for the way the Chinese went about addressing the issues before them. This judgment was rendered both against an absolute standard of how intelligent oilmen would proceed under the circumstances and in comparison to how other developing countries had resolved similar issues.

Some Observations about the 1978-83 Negotiations

Our interviews and the narrative we have pieced together illuminate several important aspects of Chinese politics: the capacity of officials to learn and adjust; the effect of beliefs or ideology upon policy; the effect of foreign policy considerations upon the negotiations; and the relationship between domestic politics and policy outcomes.

A LEARNING CURVE

We earlier noted that the early 1979 decision was made largely out of necessity: to secure new sources of petroleum and foreign exchange at minimum expense. We also noted that the landmark decision went far beyond practices of the time or the ability of the organizations to implement them. The four years of discussions with foreigners—with the Japanese and the French in the Bohai; with Arco separately; and with the pack of companies through the seismic survey, model contract, and negotiating stages—enabled the Chinese to acquire some of the requisite understanding to host the foreign presence.

The object of our study—the officials of the energy industry—evolved considerably from early 1979 to late 1983. As one European who worked closely with them put it, "They came a very long way in a short time." From Kang Shien to the negotiators, the Chinese demonstrated a capacity to absorb complicated information, to learn, and to make increasingly complex choices. Any analysis of their beliefs must take into account their substantive grasp of the issue at hand. Behavior that analysts attribute to cultural inclinations—for example, the protracted pace of negotiations—is perhaps equally attributable to a sense of ignorance and of the need to master the issues before an agreement is reached. Moreover,

Chinese officials changed their positions as they became more knowledgeable. Our Western informants noted that some of their Chinese interlocutors learned more quickly than others, and a few were beyond hope. As a whole, these observers believed the Chinese learned more rapidly than any group in the developing world with which they had negotiated.

The implication is significant. Quite frequently, foreign analysts portray China's top leaders and bureaucrats in rigid and static categories. They give labels to the different contending schools (for example, "neo-Maoists," "eclectic modernizers," or "radical reformers"), and they portray the members of the particular school and the view of the school as unchanging.[118] The evolution of petroleum policy from 1978 to 1983, and especially from the early 1979 decision to enter into risk contracts to the late 1983 signing of the contracts, however, demonstrates that Chinese policy preferences cannot be cast in totally static, unchanging terms. Views change as the context changes, and the leaders become exposed to new phenomena and learn new facts. Obviously, some leaders are more flexible than others, but any satisfying portrayal of Chinese politics must take into account how the beliefs of the leaders evolve as their knowledge and understanding of their environment changes.[119]

THE EFFECT OF ATTITUDES AND BELIEFS

Yet, the Chinese did manifest certain core and deeply held values, beliefs, or ideological commitments that shaped their approach to the negotiations. From the outset, the Chinese were determined to remain the masters of their petroleum industry and to earn maximum revenues from the joint ventures. The process could have gone forward more rapidly if the Chinese were willing to trust the foreigners and to subordinate themselves on issues they did not understand. That, however, would have violated the spirit of the 1979 decision.

Several of our informants enjoyed special access to Chinese thinking: advisors from friendly foreign governments, consultants, and Chinese Americans. They report that MPI officials in 1979 expressed considerable apprehension about the big foreign oil companies. These officials re-

---

[118] The present authors have engaged in such analysis on many occasions. See, for example, Kenneth Lieberthal, "China and the Soviet Union: The Background in Chinese Politics," in Herbert Ellison (ed.), *The Sino-Soviet Conflict: A Global Perspective* (Seattle: University of Washington, 1982), pp. 3-28; and Michel Oksenberg and Steven Goldstein, "The Chinese Political Spectrum," *Problems of Communism* (March-April, 1974), pp. 1-13.

[119] For accounts which incorporate a learning theory, see Roderick MacFarquhar, *Origins*, and Frederick Teiwes, *Leadership*.

vealed both their sense of vulnerability and their mistrust of the companies with which they were dealing. The foreign companies perceived this attitude. As one negotiator recalled, "They are smart but they were afraid and this whole effort was alien to them."

A deep commitment to maintenance of sovereignty was not the sole concern which the Chinese exhibited. They also continually asked their foreign advisors about "international practice." MPI officials were neither nativists nor xenophobes. They clearly desired to negotiate a contract that met internationally accepted standards, demonstrated their competence to the world, and elicited international respect. The entire approach was characterized by an industriousness, seriousness, determination, honesty, and dignity which our informants contrasted with interlocutors they had encountered in many other developing countries.

Inquisitiveness was another persistent quality. One American described the Chinese as having "an insatiable appetite for knowledge," adding "They considered, to a greater or lesser degree, every type of contract." In no country had our American, British, and Japanese informants experienced as extensive effort by the host government to understand the issues at hand. As one consultant noted, with exasperation, "The problem was their numbers. As soon as one set of important officials learned the lessons, another group would appear who needed the same lesson."

Neither Marxism-Leninism nor Maoism intruded in the negotiations. Ideology in the sense of a rigid or dogmatic set of beliefs did not determine the outcome. As one negotiator put it, "I was expecting them to talk about political considerations, but I never saw ideology involved with anything." Rather, the Chinese searched for pragmatic solutions to specific problems. Yet, ideology did prevail in the sense that the top leaders and their negotiators at the MPI had certain very strong beliefs for which many had waged a revolution: to ensure Chinese independence and to regain its stature in world affairs. The result was a model contract that was severe in its demands on the foreign companies. At no point did the Chinese express hopes to the foreign companies that their cooperation would be enduring. Rather, the contracts were written carefully, with terminal dates included, envisioning that the purpose of cooperation was to enable the Chinese eventually to explore and develop their petroleum resources on their own.

The cooperation was instrumental to a nationalistic objective, hence the emphasis on technology transfer and training. Commenting on the contract his company signed, one particularly astute negotiator concluded, "To be precise, foreign companies do not have an equity position as it is defined in Western law. The foreign companies have no rights to the natural resources until it is extracted and above ground. The Chinese would have found it very difficult to allow foreigners in without this type of arrangement and without a partnership-type arrangement between the Chinese government and the foreign companies." This veteran negotiator continued, "The Chinese have veto rights with no equity (especially during the exploration phase, before they have contributed capital), and this exists nowhere else in the world. We tried to negotiate this out of the contract, but lost." The ethos in which the Chinese negotiators worked required that they fashion a method of cooperation which would extract the maximum amount of resources from their partner, and it was up to the foreigners to bargain vigorously to protect their interests.

Many of our informants described the avarice of Chinese organizations: "It is almost a national cause for the Chinese to get as much as possible out of the foreigners, whether this is fair or not. They go for the last drop of blood. The Chinese recognize that they need Americans, but they want to give just enough to whet the foreigners' appetites. We're always paying for everything." Yet, another veteran of the negotiations came to a similar conclusion: "Most of these Chinese will tell you certain things so that they get you where they want you to be. Then they will squeeze all the blood they can from you." The avarice, however, was for the benefit of one's organization. In these particular negotiations, at least, the Chinese exhibited what might be called bureaucratic avarice, rather than the forms of rapacity prevalent elsewhere: personal greed, familialism, or cronyism.

Yet, we are reluctant to ascribe this voraciousness entirely to nationalistic and anti-foreign impulses, for our research suggests Chinese organizations and individuals exhibit similar inclinations toward one another, unless the appetites are tempered by a sense of *guan-xi* and mutual obligations. That is, within Chinese society, those with wealth and resources are seen as fair game, and a deeply engrained objective is to enmesh them in relationships that will give one a claim on these resources. Thus, the negotiating process entailed an understandable search for all the mechanisms that would incorporate the entity (in this case, a foreign corporation) into a network of binding obligations. Rather than initially rooting the obligations primarily in human relations, however, the Chinese and foreigners sought to make them institutional and legal.

Once the formal links were established, the process of building personal relations began to unfold. As one of the more reflective American negotiators noted, "We have tried to work within their framework and understand them. They have come here and seen our operations, and we have begun to have mutual trust. Once we signed the contract, they became much more open. Before that we were not partners, and could not be together one to one. We were still negotiating at arm's length. Now we are partners." Several top American and Chinese officials now convincingly describe each other as friends, and when cancer struck one top Chinese energy official, the oil companies made arrangements for him to receive treatment in Houston.

EFFECT OF THE POLITICAL AND ECONOMIC SETTING

The leadership of the energy sector underwent considerable change from 1979 to 1983, and the petroleum group lost its dominance over national economic policy, although it retained its control over the energy sector. We already noted that the creation of the Finance and Economic Committee in the spring of 1979 began to dilute the control which the petroleum group had over the economy. While several members of the petroleum group were on the FEC (Yu Qiuli, Gu Mu, and Kang Shien), others who had no connection with it (Chen Yun and Yao Yilin) clearly had the leadership role. From June 16 to June 29, 1979, the FEC convened four meetings to discuss the controversial Baoshan Steel Project. The meetings recommended cutting the speed of construction and reducing the amount of foreign imports.[120] Baoshan came under attack again at the session of the National People's Congress convened from June 18 to July 1. Petroleum group members Yu Qiuli, Gu Mu, and Minister of Metallurgy Tang Ke had played such a pivotal role in Baoshan that their own reputation was inevitably implicated in these attacks.

By September, 1979, the FEC and not the SPC had the lead role in convening meetings concerning the 1980 and 1981 plans, and Chen Yun was enunciating basic economic policy.[121] At the November, 1979 National Planning Conference, the best that the Ministry of Petroleum could promise for the 1980 plan was that it would maintain production at 1979 levels. The accumulated resentment against the petroleum group for its earlier expansion and perceived arrogance was ready to be avenged. The occasion occurred during the August 30 to September 11, 1980, session of the National People's Congress. Prior to that, it appears, backers of the petroleum group may have attempted to stabilize their position. On March 17, 1980, the Standing Committee of the Politburo abolished the FEC and established a new group: the Finance and Economics Leadership Small Group with Zhao Ziyang as its head and Yu Qiuli, Fang Yi, Wan Li, Yao Yilin, and Gu Mu as its members. At the same time, a State Energy Commission was established with Yu Qiuli as its

---

[120] Fang Weizhong, ed., *Jingji dashiji*, p. 625.
[121] See Fang Weizhong, ed., *Jingji dashiji*, p. 634.

chairman.[122] The State Capital Construction Commission headed by Gu Mu called its second coordination meeting in Shanghai from June 10 to 15. Tang Ke attended. The tone of the meeting was quite positive, as the public report suggested: "Fairly rapid progress has been made. . . . Negotiations with foreign countries have been accelerated and all construction projects have been carried out smoothly. . . . The complex is preparing for production."[123]

These efforts failed to stem the tide, and the petroleum group came under increasing attack during the summer. Following a leak to the foreign press, on July 22 the *People's Daily* published a sensational story charging the MPI with covering up the sinking of an oil rig—the Bohai Two—during a storm in the Bohai on November 25, 1979. The disaster led to the loss of 72 lives. The MPI was accused of negligence at the time of the storm and then of seeking to hide the disaster. The article initially contained this sentence: "The capsizing demonstrates the long standing problems of MPI in its offshore explorations." However, RMRB editors deleted the sentence before publication. Next, unidentified leaders and bureaucrats in Beijing began to leak stories to the Hong Kong press. The target was Minister of Petroleum Song Zhenming. Quoting Beijing sources, a Hong Kong publication said, "His reckless approach and blind optimism in oil exploration were responsible for the serious imbalance of China's current drive to explore and extract oil. . . . Since there was only a 1.2% increase in China's oil output in the first half of this year, it has been predicted that production could even be curtailed in the next two years. This will put China in a fairly embarrassing position if its promised crude oil deliveries to foreign consumers fail."[124]

Tang Ke came under renewed attack for the Baoshan project at the NPC. In an unprecedented development, the delegates openly criticized Tang. While he responded to their criticisms and did not lose his position, the active and gregarious Minister then dropped from sight, making only three public appearances in 1981. The Bohai oil rig disaster also received considerable publicity during the NPC, as a result of which the Minister wrote a self criticism and lost his office. Kang Shien received a reprimand for the same affair. That the entire petroleum group was under pressure and that the Baoshan and oil rig affairs were used as a pretext was illustrated by the fate of Minister of Chemical Industries, Sun

[122] Fang Weizhong, ed., *Jingji dashiji*, p. 650. The establishment of the Energy Commission was not announced until August, 1980, by which time the political context had changed.

[123] Shanghai City Service, June 15, 1980, in FBIS, June 16, 1980, p. L-5.

[124] Shi Yiping, "Changes of Twenty Positions in the State Council," *Dongxiang*, No. 23 (August 16, 1980), pp. 4-6, in FBIS, August 21, 1980, pp. U1-2.

Jingwen, another of its members. He ceased to make public appearances after June, 1980. Although he received no criticism at the NPC, a communist controlled paper in Hong Kong revealed in early January, 1981 that Sun was to be replaced as Minister.[125] The usually reliable paper reported that two Vice Ministers were in serious political difficulty. For much of 1981, Sun was in the Tianjin Municipal Chemical Industry Bureau "solving practical problems and mapping production plans."[126] Sun formally lost his position as minister in March, 1982.

Thus, the evidence points unambiguously to a massive effort to remove the petroleum group from the commanding heights of the economic bureaucracies they had dominated since the early and mid-1970's. Yao Yilin took over the SPC from Yu Qiuli at the August, 1980 NPC; Yuan Baohua replaced Kang Shien at the SEC in March, 1981; and Gu Mu lost his directorship of the State Capital Construction Commission in May, 1981. However, the energy sector and especially MPI remained under the domination of the petroleum group. Kang Shien returned to head MPI in early 1981, and Tang Ke replaced him in April, 1982, when Kang, in effect, replaced Yu Qiuli as the top official in charge of the energy sector.

The institutional landscape also changed considerably from 1979 to 1983. A State Energy Commission under the leadership of Yu Qiuli sought to provide coherence and coordination to energy policy from August, 1980, when the body was established, to May, 1982, when it was abolished.[127] CNOGEDC managed the negotiations with foreign oil companies until the baton was passed to the newly created China National Offshore Oil Company on February 15, 1982. The foreign trade apparatus underwent several reorganizations, the Ministry of Finance experimented with several systems to manage central-provincial budgetary relations, and Guangdong and Fujian provinces acquired greatly expanded authority. Organizations such as China International Trust and Investment Corporation arose to aid foreigners seeking to do business in China. The government enacted numerous new laws, codes, and regulations affecting foreign corporations and employees in China.[128]

In short, the 1979-83 negotiations coincided with a period of major reorganization of the government bureaucracy. In addition, policies were unsteady, with a severe retrenchment ordered in late 1980. Further, Sino-American governmental relations encountered difficulties and ten-

[125] *Dagongbao* (English), January 29, 1981, p. 9.
[126] Beijing, New China News Agency, September 29, 1981, in FBIS, September 29, 1981, p. K-22. At this same time, Tang Ke was at Taiyuan Iron and Steel.
[127] Thomas Fingar, "Implementing Energy Policy."
[128] See Michael Moser, ed.

sion during 1980-82 over such issues as Taiwan, technology transfer, and Chinese textile exports to the United States.[129] A major analytical issue therefore presents itself. What was the effect of all this turmoil and change upon the negotiations? "Very little" is the evident answer. In contrast to our analysis of the stages from 1959 to 1979, when political and economic developments frequently and discernibly affected petroleum policy, we cannot identify clear instances when institutional changes, the reversals of the petroleum group, or economic conditions affected the negotiating process. The evidence suggests that a high level decision was made to insulate and protect the negotiations and to create a propitious climate for their successful conclusion.

In early 1982, for example, CNOOC head Qin Wencai went out of his way to stress that the tensions in Sino-American relations and the retaliations which China planned to undertake in response to US restrictions on PRC textile imports would not affect cooperation in petroleum development. Further, the top leaders of China made themselves readily accessible to the visiting CEO's of the multinational oil companies and of major drilling and tool companies. Deng Xiaoping and Li Xiannian met with such as Clifford Garvin of Exxon, Armand Hammer of Occidental, and Robert Anderson of Arco, on several separate occasions during the negotiation stage. Our Chinese sources indicated that these occasions were especially useful to MPI and CNOOC officials, for it gave them the opportunity to brief their leaders before the meeting on the state of progress. The Chinese counted on the American officials to make certain anticipated remarks, and the responses by Deng or another high level leader became a policy guideline which they could use internally to push the process forward. Another indication of the special status of these negotiations was the early assurance which the Chinese gave the oil companies that each contract would be a binding document entered into by an agent of the Chinese state and be treated, in effect, as a legal enactment. Thus, for example, the taxation arrangements in the contract took precedence over other Chinese tax laws.

Considerable political muscle had to be used to create this special, insulated environment. For example, the Geological General Administration, which became the Ministry of Geology in September, 1979, had previously played a leading role in conducting seismic surveys and carrying out test drillings in the Yellow and South China Seas. The Chinese navy, of course, also had major responsibilities and prerogatives in these waters as well. The intrusion of the multinational oil companies, with

[129] See Hong N. Kim and Jack L. Hammersmith, "US-China Relations in the Post-Normalization Era, 1979-1985," *Pacific Affairs* (Spring, 1986), pp. 66-91.

their understandable desire for non-interference and exclusivity, upset the previous division of labor and enhanced the domain of MPI and CNOOC—the partners of the foreign companies. In a sense, the multinationals and MPI/CNOOC became partners in creating their insulated environment.

The multinationals insisted that their negotiating partner enjoy special authority and rank. At one point in the formation of CNOOC, for example, a CNOGEDC official described the impending announcement of the formation of CNOOC to the executive of a company with which the Chinese had contact from the early 1970's and which MPI wished to be involved with in the offshore ventures. As this executive recalled the exchange, the Chinese stated that, "Tomorrow we will be introducing a new law our assembly is now considering to create CNOOC, authorizing it to enter into contracts." The American asked if the legislation gave MPI the authority to commit the Ministry of Foreign Trade, the Custom's Bureau, and other entities to the contract. The Chinese seemed stunned and asked, "What do you mean?" The American repeated earlier ideas concerning the authority this body should have. The Chinese then hurriedly left the meeting, and the American believes the legislation was withdrawn before passage for amendments to strengthen the authority of CNOOC.

MPI and its affiliates also used the drafting of the model contract to create a shelter for the actual negotiations. In effect, the drafting of the model contract enabled CNOOC to establish a general consensus among the many bureaucracies over agreeable terms before the actual contracts had to be submitted for the clearance process. MPI and CNOGEDC struck initial deals with the Ministry of Finance, the Customs Bureau, the Ministry of Machine Building, and so on, prior to the formal negotiations, thereby establishing an internally acceptable terrain under CNOOC and MOFERT control.

STAGE SIX: CREATING INTERFACE ORGANIZATIONS

Coinciding with the negotiations, the top leaders and MPI created an institutional infrastructure to enable China to move swiftly into the exploration stage once the contracts were signed. The underlying principle, embodied in the contracts, was that Chinese suppliers would enjoy preference in providing machinery, goods, and services to the joint ventures, as long as the indigenous source met the appropriate technical standards. Obviously, the objective was to require the foreign operating company to purchase as much of their required supplies in China as possible. In this way, proponents of the policy demonstrated their determination to extract maximum benefit for their nation from the joint ventures. This approach also enabled Beijing to secure enthusiastic support from the affected localities, since the exploration and development stages held promise of considerable foreign expenditures in their locales.

Four different sets of institutional arrangements were required, and each began to be detailed in the 1979-83 period. First, an organizational and legal apparatus was created to deal directly with the foreign oil companies. The China National Offshore Oil Company was formally established on February 15, 1982. We have already provided a profile of CNOOC in Chapter Three and discussed its role in organizing the negotiations. CNOOC then established four branches—the Bohai, South Yellow Sea, Nanhai East and Nanhai West—to be the operating companies in charge of supervising the joint venture contracts. Each of these branches then named Chinese personnel to the Joint Management Commissions which managed the actual implementation of the contract. This entire structure was rooted in the Offshore Development Regulations which the State Council promulgated on February 1-10, 1982.

Second, enterprises had to be created to provide the goods and services required by law. In the case of Nanhai West, which already had developed some capacity to service offshore exploration activities, the task was to improve and expand the existing capabilities. The onshore areas adjacent to the Bohai, South Yellow Sea, and the South China Sea had to create companies capable of providing helicopter service to the offshore rigs, sending supply boats to the rigs, providing mud and other essential supplies for the drilling process, and so on. In Guangdong, for example, CNOOC and the Guangdong government created the China Nanhai Oil Joint Services Committee in May, 1982. This company in turn began to create subsidiary joint ventures with other Chinese bureaucracies and/or foreign petroleum exploration supply firms such as Schlumberger, Zapata, or Racal Survey Company. Yet other Chinese ministries and corporations, such as the China Steamship Navigation Corporation, created their own subsidiaries and joint ventures in appropriate coastal cities. The joint ventures were necessary because the Chinese firms lacked the technology and experience to bid on the service contracts. All of this organizational activity created Chinese ventures which could acquire subcontracts to provide goods and services during the exploration process.

Third, localities—supply bases—had to be identified and developed from which the offshore activities could be supported. Several such bases began to be developed in Guangdong to serve the South China Sea operations, and similar bases were developed in Shanghai and Tianjin to serve the Bohai and South Yellow Sea operations.

Finally, since so much of the service activity would be provided through joint ventures, a legal regime had to be elaborated to entice the foreigners to form partnerships on Chinese soil. While the contracts with the multinationals had the force of law, this legal privilege arose out of the size and pioneering nature of the enterprise. For the rest, it would be far better to nest the joint ventures within an existing legal framework. The incentive to create this framework did not arise solely or even primarily from the petroleum sector. Rather, by early 1979, the top leaders had decided to seek foreign capital and technology in a wide range of industries by inviting foreign investment in China and offering foreign firms the opportunity to form joint ventures. In a manner probably analogous to the insulated environment they created for the petroleum specialists negotiating the risk contracts, the leaders gathered their legal specialists, who consulted widely abroad. They began to draft a torrent of legislation, which the State Council and Ministries began to pass. (A partial listing of these laws and regulations is in Table 5-3.)[130] Many obstacles confronted an effort which ran counter to certain deep-seated Chinese preferences for regulation of human relations through trust rather than law and for the resolution of disputes through mediation, with equity considerations paramount, rather than through adversarial proceedings, with judgments based on law. Nonetheless, progress began to be made.

Thus, by the time the contracts were signed in 1983, the foundations of an institutional infrastructure to host the joint ventures were being put in place. The politics surrounding the establishment of CNOJSC, Nanhai East, and Nanhai West involved central-provincial relations, a topic we address in Chapter Seven. At this point, we simply note that the MPI eliminated potential recalcitrance at the provincial and local levels by structuring the joint ventures to benefit the localities financially. The result was that by mid-1984, several coastal cities—especially in Guangdong—were enjoying an oil boom.

THE END OF AN ERA?

Drilling in the South China Sea under the first round of contracts proceeded in steady fashion in 1984-85. Arco had a major natural gas find in the Yinggehai south of Hainan Island which prompted protracted negotiations between Arco and CNOOC concerning the development of this field. Exxon-Shell, Texaco-Chevron, and Philips struck oil, but the size and commercial viability of the fields were not immediately evident.

---

[130] This table is derived from Moser, ed. See also Heilongjiang Legal Research Institute (ed.), *Jingji Fagui Xuanbian, 1977-1984* (Harbin: Study Press, 1984).

TABLE 5-3
Regulations Facilitating a Foreign Presence in China

Date	Law and Promulating Agency
July 8, 1979	Joint Venture Law—State Council
July 26, 1980	Measures for Registration of Joint Ventures using Chinese and Foreign Investment—State Council
July 26, 1980	Regulations on Labor Management in Joint Ventures— State Council
July 26, 1980	Provisional Regulations Concerning Use of Land for Construction by Joint Ventures—State Council
August 26, 1980	Regulations on Special Economic Zones in Guangdong— National People's Council Standing Committee
September 10, 1980	Income Tax Law of the PRC Concerning Joint Ventures— National People's Council
September 10, 1980	Individual Income Tax Law—National People's Council
September 20, 1980	Implementing Act for Joint Venture Law—State Council
October 30, 1980	Provisional Regulation Concerning the Control of Resident Representative Offices of Foreign Enterprises— State Council
December 14, 1980	Detailed Rules and Regulations for Implementation of Individual Income Tax Law—Ministry of Finance
December 14, 1980	Detailed Rules and Regulations for Implementing Income Tax Law Concerning Joint Ventures—Ministry of Finance
December 18, 1980	Provisional Regulations Governing Foreign Exchange Control—State Council
March 13, 1981	Provisional Measures for Providing Loans to Joint Ventures by the Bank of China—Bank of China
October 1, 1981	Provisional Measures of Customs Authorities Concerning the Supervision and Control of Imports and Exports Required in Cooperative Exploration and Development of Offshore Petroleum—General Administration of Customs
November 17, 1981	Provisional Regulations of Guangdong Special Economic Zones (SEZ) Governing Entry and Exit of Personnel— Guangdong People's Congress Standing Committee
November 17, 1981	Provisional Regulation of Guangdong SEZ Governing Labor and Wages—Guangdong People's Congress
November 17, 1981	Provisional Regulations Governing Land in Shenzhen SEZ's—Guangdong People's Congress
December 8, 1981	Circular Concerning Registration Procedures for Resident Offices of Foreign Enterprises—General Administration of Industry & Commerce
December 13, 1981	Income Tax Law Concerning Foreign Enterprises—National People's Council

TABLE 5-3   (cont.)

Date	Law and Promulating Agency
December 13, 1981	Economic Contracts Law—National People's Council
December 13, 1981	Foreign Enterprise Income Tax Law
January 30, 1982	Regulations on Exploitation of Offshore Petroleum Resources in Cooperation with Foreign Enterprises—State Council
February 21, 1982	Detailed Rules and Regulations for Implementing Foreign Enterprise Income Tax Law—Ministry of Finance
March, 1982	Provisional Regulations on Payment of Registration Fees by Joint Ventures—General Administration for Industry and Commerce
August 23, 1982	Offshore Environmental Protection Law—National People's Council Standing Committee
March 15, 1983	Measures Regarding Control of Registration of Long Term Representative Offices of Foreign Enterprises
August 1, 1983	Detailed Rules for Foreign Exchange Control—Foreign Exchange Control Administration
September 2, 1983	Revision of the Joint Venture Income Tax Law—National People's Council Standing Committee
January 28, 1984	Inspection Regulations for Import and Export of Commodities

The geological structure of the seabed in the South China Sea, many geologists concluded by 1985, may not permit the trapping of large oil pools, as in the Gulf of Mexico. At the same time, the drilling revealed that smaller pools exist in the area. The results, in short, did not fulfill the optimistic expectations of an oil bonanza which would finance China's foreign purchases. Yet, the findings were sufficiently promising to attract most oil companies to enter into the second round of bidding which commenced in late 1985. Exxon, Texaco-Chevron, and Philips all bid successfully for blocks adjacent to their discoveries. When one recalls the long history of exploration in the North Sea, Alaska, Libya, or Angola before the major finds were discovered, caution was warranted before writing off the South Sea effort.

Nonetheless, the gradual erosion in world oil prices from 1983 through 1985 and the precipitious drop in 1986 meant that proven reserves which would have been commercially viable at $20-25 per barrel were not profitable at $10-15. Thus on two counts, time did not work in the Chinese favor: the drop in price and the more sober assessments of the geological structures in the South China Sea. Consequently, the Chinese approached the second round of bidding in a more sober mood.

Moreover, they had learned more about the financial limits of their foreign partners. As a result, the negotiations proceeded in an expeditious and almost routine fashion.

Meanwhile, in 1985, the top leaders crossed another threshold when they decided to open ten coastal provinces to exploration and development through joint venture, risk contracts. A new organization, China National Oil Development Corporation, was established to handle the enterprise. Song Zhenming, the former Minister of Petroleum who resigned in the wake of the 1979-1980 oil rig disaster, became the head of the company, and foreign companies studied the possibilities. The Chinese envisioned a very different negotiating process for onshore exploration and development, eschewing both a model contract and a formal, protracted bidding process. One senses here, as in the second round of offshore negotiations, that the softening of world energy prices had a cumulative effect on Chinese thinking.

While our narrative focused on the involvement of the foreign oil companies in offshore exploration, foreign participation in onshore development of existing fields was also extensive in the late 1970's and 1980's. The extraction technology employed at Daqing in the 1960's resulted in the seepage of water into oil bearing stratum. Advanced technology was needed to prolong the life of the Daqing field and to retain efficient productivity at Daqang and Shengli. Equipment and supplies which permitted improved secondary and tertiary recovery of a field became of keen interest to MPI. World Bank loans were used to upgrade development and production techniques not only at Daqing and Shengli but at Zhongyuan as well, and, emphasis was given to exploiting the periphery of the Daqing field. These intensive efforts to improve production yielded results. Daqing production remained above 50 MMT per year, while estimates in the late 1970's and early 1980's were that its production would decline in the mid-1980's. Overall, production leveled off from 1978 through 1983, but substantial increases were registered in 1984 and 1985, largely as a result of improvements in existing fields.

Nonetheless, the common sense view which prompted the offshore efforts retained their essential validity into the mid-1980's. The bulk of Chinese production continued to come from the big three fields—Daqing, Shengli, and Daqang. At some point, unless major new fields were brought in, China would face major problems in sustaining production. Since offshore results lowered the previous expectations, the most attractive potential perceived to exist was in the northwest, where multinational corporations believe substantial deposits exist in three basins: Tsaidam, Dzungar, and Tarim. However, the cost to develop these resources, especially for the pipelines, would be enormous, and they would

TABLE 5-4
Petroleum Exports, 1975-1985[131]

Year	1 Total Prod. MMT	2 Crude Oil Exports MMT	3 Petroleum Product Exports MMT	4 Total Petr. Exports MMT	5 Domestic Availability of Crude	6 Total % of Pod. Exported
1975	77.1	9.9	2.1	12.0	65.1	15.6%
1976	86.9	8.5	2.0	10.5	76.4	12.1%
1977	93.6	9.1	2.0	11.1	82.5	11.9%
1978	104.5	11.4	2.2	13.6	90.9	13.0%
1979	106.2	13.4	3.0	16.4	89.9	15.4%
1980	105.6	13.3	4.2	17.5	88.1	16.6%
1981	101.2	13.8	4.6	18.4	82.8	18.2%
1982	102.1	14.7	5.8	20.5	82.6	20.1%
1983	106.5	14.8	5.1	19.9	86.6	18.7%
1984	114.3	21.9	5.7	27.6	86.7	24.1%
1985	124.8	29.0	6.0	35.0	89.0	28.0%

not be brought into production for sometime into the future. Exactly what fields would tide China over the inevitable reduction in production of the majors remained open to question.

Another aspect of the strategy of the 1970's—that revenue from growing increasing petroleum exports would be a reliable source of foreign exchange—also came unstuck as world oil prices dropped. Table 5-4 reveals in striking form the degree to which China came to depend upon petroleum exports and the extent to which increases in production were devoted to exports from 1975 to 1985. Column 4 details the rapid increase in the exports; 1980 exports of 17.5 MMT doubled to 35.0 MMT in 1985. As a result of the emphasis on exports, the domestic availability of crude petroleum varied from 82 to 90 MMT from 1977. In effect, all increases in production from 1977 through 1985 were exported. Consequently, as Column 6 demonstrates, the percentage of total production which was exported rose from 12%-13% in 1977-78 to 24%-28% in 1984-85.

Not surprisingly with this emphasis on exports, the foreign exchange earned from petroleum sales increased from one billion US dollars in

[131] This table is based on United States government data. This series varies slightly from the Chinese statistics used in Tables 1 and 2.

TABLE 5-4 (cont.)

7	8	9	10	11	12
Increase in Prod.	Increase in Exports	% of Increase in Prod. Exported	Foreign Exchange through Petr. Sales, $ Million	Total Exports (FOB) in $ Million	% of For. Exchange through Petr. Exports
6.3	4.9	78%	864	7,121	12.0%
9.8	−1.5	NA	775	7,266	10.7%
6.7	.6	19%	1,012	8,177	12.4%
10.9	2.5	23%	1,279	10,167	12.6%
2.3	2.8	122%	2,447	13,652	18.0%
−.6	1.1	NA	4,321	18,920	22.8%
−4.4	.9	NA	4,942	21,545	22.9%
−.9	2.1	NA	4,897	22,900	21.4%
4.4	−.6	NA	4,487	23,520	19.1%
7.8	7.7	99%	5,185	27,439	18.9%
10.5	7.4	70%	6,400	28,000 (est)	22.9%

1977 to 4.3 billion in 1980 and 6.4 billion in 1985. (See Column 10.) The data reveal a particularly significant surge in exports in 1984-85, and earnings increased from 4.5 billion to 6.4 billion in those two years. The performance was all the more significant since exports in several other vital categories, such as textiles, ceased their previous rapid growth.

Nonetheless, in two respects, the record was somewhat disappointing. First of all, even though the volume of exports doubled from 1980 to 1985, the value of exports rose by only 48%. We see here the consequence of declining oil prices during that time. Another reflection of declining oil prices is that the percentage of foreign currency earnings attributable to petroleum has remained at about 22% since 1980. (See Column 12.) If prices had remained at their 1980 level without affecting other aspects of policy, petroleum would have consisted of 30% of exports in value, instead of 22.9%. The dramatic surge in exports in 1984-85 becomes understandable; that was the only way to increase earnings as prices fell.

The adverse consequences of declining prices were intensified by the rapid drop in early 1986. By April, 1986, it was estimated that China would lose US $2-3 billion in export value, assuming the export levels of 1985 were maintained. These trends posed new, severe issues to the top leaders. Would they compensate for the loss in foreign revenue by increasing petroleum exports, by borrowing foreign capital, or by reducing imports? None of these choices were particularly appealing.

In broader perspective, the economic development strategy presaged in 1972-75 policies and pursued vigorously in the post-Mao era encountered increasing problems in 1984-85.[132] The strategy of 1978-1985 entailed increased foreign trade, administrative decentralization, decollectivization of agriculture, an increased role of the market place in the allocation of resources (and a concomitant restriction of the role of planning), and a shift away from traditionally favored industrial sectors to light industry. Significant institutional reforms were an integral part of the strategy both in agriculture and in industrial management. While the strategy yielded high growth rates, it also had several consequences which concerned the top leaders: government deficits, mounting foreign trade deficits, inflation, and high rates of capital construction.

By late 1985, the top leaders appeared divided over the causes of these problems. Some argued that the institutional changes—the reforms—were the source of the problem, while others argued that continued reform was the only way to surmount the problem. Such people advocated continued expansion of the market and price reform, as well as the introduction of capital, labor, and property (real estate) markets in China. In short, in the mid-1980's, as the Seventh Five Year Plan was being drafted, yet another debate erupted over the appropriate economic development strategy for China: whether to consolidate the gains of the past seven years or to embark on a second wave of reforms. Embedded in the debate was whether to expand the opening to the outside and to increase foreign borrowings at commercial interest rates.

The political situation was reminiscent of similar debates over development strategy in 1959-60, 1963-65, 1971-75, and 1977-79. But there was a noticeable difference this time. As this chapter has detailed, on each previous occasion, the petroleum group stepped forward, optimistic program in hand. A modified development strategy was hammered out in which petroleum was to be a prominent part of the solution. In fact, the strategy for development of petroleum was central to the entire economic strategy. But in the mid-1980's, the proposed solution was not likely to emanate from the petroleum sector.

The petroleum group itself had aged and scattered. It never recouped its losses from the 1979-1981 erosion in its influence. Yu Qiuli returned to the PLA, where he headed the Political Department in the military. This significant position removed him from direct responsibility for eco-

---

[132] Robert Dernberger (ed.), *China's Economy Looks Toward the Year 2000* (Washington: Government Printing Office, 1986).

nomic issues. Kang Shien recovered from his bout with cancer in 1985-87, but he shared responsibility for energy with Li Peng. Tang Ke was replaced as Minister of Petroleum in 1985, as was Gao Yangwen at Coal. Their successors were younger, with less political clout. The wave which the petroleum group rode so successfully—and helped create—had unmistakably crested.

The advocates of the 1979-1985 petroleum development strategy could mount a powerful argument for its essential success. The softening of world prices was likely to be an aberration. China was well positioned to take advantage of the inevitable rise in prices. Further, the negotiating acumen of the petroleum group at MPI and CNOOC secured a massive foreign investment of $1.7 billion from 1979 through 1985 for petroleum exploration in the South China Sea.[133] While the results did not meet expectations, a major natural gas field was discovered and three possibly commercial wells were struck. Further, petroleum exports did play a substantial role in financing China's increased imports. To a considerable extent, the pledges of the petroleum group—when discounted for the inevitable exaggeration of hopes—were redeemed.

However, this chapter has indicated that fulfilled promises do not guarantee that subsequent policy recommendations will be accepted. Credibility is helpful but not sufficient. The lesson from this chapter is that energy policies are adopted when the top leaders believe the proposed policies promise an attractive solution to the problems they perceive at the moment, make use of existing opportunities, support their ideological preferences and power needs (especially those of the preeminent leader), and are congruent with the organizational missions of the pertinent ministries. From this perspective, the petroleum sector occupied a different and less privileged position in the mid-1980's.

First, the Ministry of Coal demonstrated a very impressive record since the early 1980's. Production shot up, primarily through expansion of small-scale mines. The top leaders turned to MPI in the early 1960's, again during the Fourth Five Year Plan in the early 1970's, and in the late 1970's in part because of the problems with coal production. This is not to downgrade the importance of MPI; it continued to be a major source of central government revenue. But its prospects, in comparison to coal, seemed less promising in 1986-87 than at any point in the past generation. Further, top leaders have come to understand the high cost and long lead time for alternative means of generating electricity, hydropower and nuclear power. With the need to minimize domestic consumption of petroleum, it had become increasingly clear to the top lead-

<hr>

[133] *Asian Wall Street Journal*, January 6, 1986, p. 20.

ers that construction of coal-fired thermal plants would remain the basic means for increasing electric generating capacity. The economic development strategy for the late 1980's, therefore, was more likely to reflect the concerns of the coal-sector.

We have also seen the importance of the external environment in shaping energy and petroleum policy—the actual pressures and blandishment, the perceptions of top leaders concerning the dangers and opportunities, and their strategy for coping with their environment. To repeat, the Sino-Soviet dispute accelerated development of Daqing. The dangers arising from the Vietnam War in 1963-65 reenforced Mao's belief that the Daqing model of self-development merited nationwide emulation. Most important, the diplomatic breakthroughs in 1971-72 with the United States and Japan and the first easing of COCOM controls provided access to foreign petroleum equipment and technology. The role of Japan in stimulating the 1972-73 decision to export petroleum in a "steel for oil" deal and the 1978-79 decisions to accept foreign loans and enter into joint ventures was extremely important. So too, though in a different way, was the opportunity to use petroleum development as a way of consolidating Sino-American ties. Conversations from 1975 through 1978 between Deng Xiaoping and Li Xiannian on the Chinese side and such varied Americans as George Bush, Charles Yost, Cyrus Vance, Henry Jackson, James Schlesinger, and Robert Anderson placed cooperation in the energy sphere in a strategic context—as a way of signalling to the Soviet Union that China and the United States were forging an enduring and meaningful relationship. Moreover, several knowledgeable Japanese believe that strategic considerations led the Chinese to be particularly responsive to the Japanese overtures of the early 1970's as a way of countering possible Japanese involvement in development of Siberia. Soviet-Japanese cooperation on developing Siberian hydro-carbon reserves was a lively possibility in the early 1970's, and Mao and Zhou probably wished to forestall Japan from entering into constructive activities with China's bitter adversary while not having a similar stake in China's development. The longer-term consequence, Mao and Zhou may have feared, could be a Japanese tilt toward Moscow in the Sino-Soviet dispute.

These same observers believe a similar strategic calculus encouraged the Chinese in 1978-79 to draw Americans into South China Sea exploration. The formation of the Soviet-Vietnamese military alliance in 1978, the growing hostility between Beijing and Hanoi in 1977-78 and their 1979 border war, and the territorial disputes between Vietnam and China in the South China Sea provided incentives to involve American companies in the region. Finally, Chinese entry into the World Bank in

1981 provided new opportunities to acquire low interest loans and managerial assistance for upgrading onshore recovery techniques.

By the mid-1980's, the strategic calculus had changed. The two next evolutionary steps in China's turn outward for development of its petroleum reserves would be first to increase its foreign borrowing at commercial interest rates in order to finance improvements in secondary and tertiary recovery at existing sites and second to be willing to enter into production sharing, risk contracts for development of reserves in the northwest. But the external pressures and incentives were not as conducive to these two incremental steps to turn outward as the external environment was in the 1970's. We have already indicated the economic considerations that dictated caution. Further, the top leaders may have become less interested in the strategic benefits to be claimed from increased cooperation with the United States and Japan, as Sino-Soviet tensions and the immediate threat from Moscow subsided.[134] In addition, the public and private sectors in Japan and the United States probably were less interested in enticing China into closer economic cooperation than they were throughout the 1970's.

Nor were the domestic bureaucratic considerations the same. Going offshore with foreign firms was relatively easy. The existing system of bargains among the pertinent agencies could be relatively easily altered. The top leaders created an insulated environment for the negotiations, and the beneficiaries of the exploration stage far outweighed the losers. But as the subsequent two chapters demonstrate, a thorned thicket of ongoing bureaucratic arrangements exist onshore, and lodging joint ventures and new projects for natural resource development these would be much more nettlesome.

Finally, each step along the way came with the backing of the preeminent leader, and when he vacillated, as Mao did in 1973-75, or when his position eroded, as happened to Deng in 1980-82, the influence of his preferred policy makers in the energy sphere was immediately reduced. Moreover, divisions among the leaders induced caution, while consensus (as in early 1979) or weakness in the opposition (as in late 1972 and early 1973) facilitated bold departures. But in 1986-87, the top leaders appeared somewhat divided over whether to initiate the second wave of reforms, and Deng Xiaoping seemed more concerned with protecting the gains he had made to date than endorsing policies that would carry him into new and uncharted waters.

---

[134] Michel Oksenberg, "A Decade of Sino-American Relations," *Foreign Affairs*, Vol. 61, No. 1 (Fall 1982); Robert Ross, "International Bargaining and Domestic Politics," in *World Politics* (January, 1986), pp. 255-287.

Hence, our study appears to have covered an era in Chinese energy policy making that had·come to an end by 1986-87. The underlying dynamics of the policy making process which this chapter illuminates is likely to persist, though the political reforms are modifying that process. But the era in which petroleum industry and those who led it set the pace for the energy sector and the entire economy appears to have ended. Until world petroleum prices turn decisively upward and significant production increases in China can be secured from bringing new fields into production, solutions to energy issues will be shared among the Ministries of Petroleum, Coal, and Water Resources and Electric Power. The near monopoly of Petroleum has been broken.

· 6 ·

THE THREE GORGES DAM PROJECT

INTRODUCTION

The foregoing analysis of the petroleum sector embraced elements of the rationality and of the power struggle models. At each stage in the evolution of policy toward foreign involvement in China's petroleum development, Chinese officials related national means to national interests. Policy changed incrementally and in reasonable fashion. At the same time, key petroleum leaders—such as Yu Qiuli—used their success in this sector as a springboard to national political prominence. As a result, other officials began to perceive the existence of a "petroleum clique" that engaged in the political struggles among the top twenty-five to thirty-five leaders. Individual power considerations thus entered decision making in the petroleum sector. The handling of the Bohai Gulf oil rig disaster, for example, reflected political maneuvering as well as the merits of the tragic accident itself.

The Three Gorges dam project shares some of the characteristics that encouraged a rational approach in the petroleum sector. The project is amenable in many respects to technical analysis of construction and production possibilities and trade-offs. It is of such enormous scale and potential importance, moreover, that it has commanded the attention of national political figures and has remained on the national agenda since the 1950's. As petroleum, therefore, this project has not been submerged in the various ministries and provinces beyond the ken of the top coordinating bodies and officials who can assume a more national perspective.

But the Three Gorges dam project differs crucially from the petroleum sector in that it apparently never became a political weapon in the power struggles among the top political elite.[1] Although political leaders at the level of Zhou Enlai, Mao Zedong, and more recently Li Peng became directly involved in deliberations over the project, therefore, this did not produce gross distortions by bending technical considerations to the political needs of members of the top elite.

It is tempting, consequently, to analyze the Three Gorges project strictly in terms of the rationality model, but this would be incomplete and misleading. As the following analysis demonstrates, it is necessary

---

[1] This statement, as the entire analysis of the Three Gorges, is based on evidence pertaining to the period from the 1950's into 1986.

269

to blend in analysis of bureaucratic politics and of policy process to some extent in the 1950's and in major fashion since at least 1979-80 in order to understand the course of these deliberations. Unevenness in the availability of evidence for different periods clouds our understanding of the extent to which the situation itself evolved. Different bureaucracies adopted conflicting stances on the Three Gorges project at least as early as the mid-1950's, as detailed below. The evidence demonstrates, moreover, that at least since 1979 the top leaders have sought what Simon would term a "satisficing"solution to the issue—a compromise that would enable participants with widely varying interests and priorities to agree on some form of dam construction at the Three Gorges.

The evidence does not permit confident analysis of the pacing of the evolution of the system in the direction of increasing rights of bureaucracies to certain kinds of resources and prerogatives that the political elite would generally respect. But that evolution did occur, and to understand the deliberations over the Three Gorges in the 1980's (and probably for an indeterminate period of time before then), therefore, one must consider the missions and interests of the pertinent bureaucratic units.

This chapter first details the scope and importance of the dam and then reviews the key technical issues and trade-offs confronting dam construction. This review both highlights the technical complexity of the project *and* argues that even the best technical specialists cannot provide confident answers to all the major questions decision makers must pose. Therefore, a rationality model alone cannot guide decision making on the Three Gorges dam except in a rather loose sense. The ensuing actual history of the dam project provides evidence for three propositions: 1. that different bureaucracies right from the start provided the top leaders with very different assessments, based in each case on the mission and interests of the bureaucracy concerned; 2. that both major changes in the objective environment (such as the post Great Leap Forward economic depression) and bureaucratic cycles (such as the periodic consideration of each successive Five Year Plan) strongly influenced the ebb and flow of attention to this issue; and 3. that at least by the 1980's the top leadership proved unwilling to adopt a solution that violated the core interests of any of the major bureaucracies concerned, including the pertinent provinces.

This chapter concludes with a consideration of the probable effects of the Deng era reforms on deliberations on a huge project such as the Three Gorges dam. We feel the reforms very likely diminish the prospects that such a project will make the crucial transition from the planning stage to actual construction. Chapter Eight elaborates a broader the-

270

oretical explanation for this evolution of the Chinese system and examines some of the implications of this explanation.

In sum, the Three Gorges dam, like the petroleum development story, can be explained only in part through an application of a rationality model. In the Three Gorges case, this model need not be modified by power considerations at the top of the system. Rather, the Three Gorges dam brings to the fore the (possibly increasing) importance of bureaucratic interests, politics, and processes as necessary components in the explanation of decision making on major energy issues in the People's Republic of China.

THE DAM AS A NATIONAL CONCERN

The Three Gorges project is one of the boldest and most important construction projects ever contemplated in China. It promises to be the centerpiece of a multifaceted effort to control flooding in the middle reaches of the Yangtze (Changjiang) River. If undertaken, it would be an epic effort to tame a vast river and exert a telling influence on the spatial economy of China. The dam being contemplated at the Three Gorges would be unique. In size, it would dwarf any dam in the United States and exceed the Brazilian dam at Itaipu, the largest dam built to date. For example, a water level for the reservoir of 150 meters, which is the lowest normal water level stipulated in any 1980's plans, would produce a reservoir that would stretch for 247 miles from the dam. In addition, the dam would be unique for coping simultaneously with flood control, major hydropower generation, large amounts of shipping, and serious silt problems. The great size and the unprecedented complexity of tasks on a river with rapid changes in water level and high silt content give Three Gorges dam engineering, financial, and political challenges of dramatic scope.

The basic statistics about the Yangtze basin underscore the importance of the proposed dam. The Yangtze river is the longest in China (3,915 miles), and its drainage area covers about 20 percent of the area of the entire country. Mean annual flow through the Yangtze is roughly a trillion cubic feet of water. Some 35 percent of China's population—nearly 8% of the *world's* population—lives in the Yangtze basin, and they produce more than 40% of the country's agricultural output (including over 65% of the rice). The hydroelectric potential of the entire basin is estimated to total about 1,030 billion kWh of output per year. Current installed capacity is, however, only 29 billion kWh of output per year. The Three Gorges dam will have a generating capacity (according to the plan adopted in 1984 that calls for an installed capacity of 13,000 MW) of 64.9 billion kWh per year. In comparison, Gezhouba, the next largest hydropower project, will have an installed capacity of 2,715 MW when it is completed in 1989. The largest thermal power plant in China as of 1986, the Jianbi in Jiangsu province, has an installed capacity of 1,625 MW.[2]

While the Yangtze accounts for extraordinary percentages of China's population, production, and hydropower generation potential,[3] the potential for damage due to flooding is also exceptional. Most precipitation along the Yangtze comes from summer storms, and the basin is vulnerable to flood waters simultaneously cascading down the main stem in Sichuan and through the major tributaries that flow into the Yangtze from west of Wuhan (the Han River, which joins the Yangtze at Wuhan, and the Dongting Lake system). The last truly catastrophic flood occurred in 1870, when the total water volume spilling through the main channel reached 110,000 cubic meters per second. Smaller, very damaging floods in this century occurred in 1931, 1935, 1949, and 1954.[4]

The danger from flooding remains great: mid-1980's estimates are that an 1870-type flood could potentially breech the vital Jingjiang levee to the east of the Three Gorges. Should this occur during the night, over one million lives might be lost. Such a breech in the dike during the daytime could still result in more than a half-million deaths. For the inhabitants of Hubei and northern Hunan, few issues are of greater immediate importance than bringing this enormous flood threat under control.

The flood problem is, in a range of ways, primarily a rural issue. Wuhan and other cities are vulnerable to a flood of the 1870 type,[5] but they can be protected from lesser floods. Currently, this protection comes at the expense of peasants in the area, for it is achieved through a combination of dikes and flood diversion efforts. The latter utilize large tracts of densely populated farmland, at enormous cost to the peasantry. The Three Gorges dam would not by itself wholly relieve the threat of flood damage to the middle reaches of the Yangtze, but it would greatly reduce the use of flood diversion to cope with flood problems. The ben-

[2] Fujiko Kitani, "Electric Power in China," *China Newsletter*, No. 56 (May-June 1985), p. 14.

[3] The Yangtze contains about 42 percent of the combined hydropower potential of the Yangtze, Yellow, Huai, Hai, Pearl, Songhua and Liao rivers: *Xiandai Zhongguo shuili jianshe* (Beijing: September 1984).

[4] The 1931 flood inundated 8.5 million acres, that in 1935 flooded 3.8 million acres, the 1949 flood inundated 4.5 million acres, and the flood in 1954 inundated 7.9 million acres: U.S. Bureau of Reclamation (hereafter cited as USBR), Trip Report for April 30-June 12, 1981 trip to China, pp. II-4-5.

[5] That is, a flood where the volume of water cascading through the middle reaches of the Yangtze remains very large for a prolonged period of time.

efits to the peasants and small towns of northern Hunan and Hubei would be very great.[6]

The entire central and lower Yangtze region also suffers from an acute shortage of electric power, as does Sichuan province on the upper reaches of this great river. The power generated at the Three Gorges dam would greatly contribute to meeting the needs of this region (although Sichuan would receive less power from the dam than it would like).[7] In turning this into an area with adequate power, the dam would encourage industrial growth throughout the region from Hubei to Shanghai. Indeed, the provinces downstream from such a dam have much to gain from this project while, in many cases, suffering few if any losses.

The Three Gorges dam could also improve shipping capabilities between Wuhan and Chongqing, although this benefit is somewhat less certain. Ideally, the dam would permit a regulated water flow that will reduce the problem with shallow shoals between Yichang and Wuhan during the low water season. At the same time, if the maximum normal water surface is at least 180 meters high, the reservoir behind the dam would permit 10,000 ton tows to be pulled all the way to Chongqing (see map on following page).[8] Due to the very gentle flow of the river in the reservoir, moreover, the efficiency of the tugs would be greatly increased. Unresolved questions about potential silting, however, make these prognoses about the effects of the dam on navigation a matter of heated dispute. At best, the dam would open the port at Chongqing to the rich economy of central China. At worst, over a period of decades the dam might create navigational problems that could dwarf those currently experienced.

Overall, the Three Gorges dam is an exceptionally "lumpy" project, requiring huge commitments of funds and materials over a prolonged period before output will permit the state to begin to recapture its investment.[9] Its huge dimensions, enormous potential impact on the country's spatial economy, and dramatic implications for the lives of millions of residents in central China combine to make the Three Gorges project

[6] As explained below, dam advocates have consistently seen flood control rather than hydropower generation as the primary function of their project.

[7] In the 1984 plan for the Three Gorges, of the 13,000 megawatts of installed capacity, only 1,000 is allocated to serving Sichuan province. Almost all the remainder is to be supplied to Central and East China.

[8] Such tows will have to be disassembled to move through the dam locks and then be reassembled upstream.

[9] Mid 1980's plans would require ten years from the start of construction to the first generation of electric power. Even this decade-long lead time may well prove too short. In addition, at least another six years would be necessary before full power output is achieved.

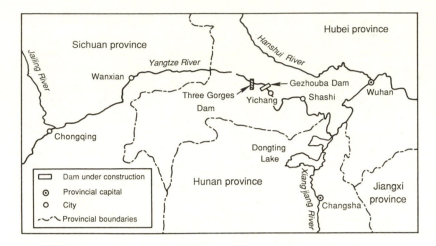

preeminently a national level issue that has repeatedly drawn the highest political elite into the decision-making process.

THE RATIONALITY MODEL AND ITS LIMITS

Chapter One discussed the implicit rational, problem-solving model of decision making employed by many Western scholars of China. A distinct but closely related matter is to ask the extent to which Chinese political leaders themselves actually employ rational approaches and criteria in reaching decisions on major issues. In many ways, the Three Gorges dam project seems well suited to such an approach.

The Three Gorges dam, like all dam projects, can be analyzed along a wide range of technical parameters. In this sense, it appears potentially more suited to decisions relating national goals and means than would decisions on more diffuse activities, such as the cultural or propaganda spheres. But two salient features of this major dam project limit the extent to which a rationality model can provide adequate guidance to the decision making process. First, the Three Gorges project involves a number of trade-offs. Politically, for example, for three reasons the project poses much more difficult challenges than the development of coal in Shanxi (a topic addressed in Chapter Seven): the huge number of refugees the project will create; the striking differences in the distribution of costs and of benefits among the affected units; and the very large number of bureaucratic and political units involved. In addition, as detailed below, there remain very important technical unknowns that can seriously affect the ultimate ability of the dam to meet its projected goals.

Indeed, although the Three Gorges project has been debated in the PRC since the mid 1950's, five core issues have remained unresolved throughout the long history of this project. The first two of these involve difficult trade-offs that ultimately must be made on the basis of tough political decisions. The latter three are rooted in inherent technical uncertainties. These core issues are:

1. To what extent should the Three Gorges be devoted primarily to flood control versus being more truly a multipurpose facility, and how should this relate to the optimum mix of efforts among the options of building the Three Gorges dam, strengthening the related dike system, building smaller dams on upstream tributaries, constructing thermal power stations, and developing various kinds of water storage facilities?
2. If the dam is built, how high should both the maximum normal water surface and the dam structure itself be? Note that "maximum normal water surface" is the height of the reservoir at the dam during the low water season. This, of course, need not be equal to the actual height of the dam itself, but it does dictate, among other things, the size and location of the population that will have to be moved permanently because of inundation. Hereafter, unless otherwise noted "dam height" actually refers to the maximum height of the normal water surface.
3. How much will the project actually cost, and how should the costs be met?
4. Can the silting problems be adequately anticipated and resolved, and what are the implications for transportation on the Yangtze?
5. Can other unprecedented technical issues in dam construction (such as finding appropriate material for cofferdam construction, solving problems of task coordination, and so forth) be satisfactorily handled so that the final project meets needed quality and safety standards?

Dam Functions and Priorities among Options

The YVPO has from the start considered flood control in the middle and lower reaches of the Yangtze as the core function of the Three Gorges project. The Yangtze basin has numerous large tributaries with complicated interrelationships, and the maximum safe channel capacity (SCC) below Yichang is far below the volume of water that can cascade through the river at peak flood periods.[10] In addition, the land level of the plains

---

[10] E.g., currently, the safe channel capacity of the Jingjiang reach from Jiangling to Jianli

areas of the middle and lower reaches is lower than the river water level during the high water season, making it very difficult to drain flooded farmland.

Thus, one major dam alone cannot achieve flood control on the Yangtze. The water volume and potential variability of flow defy an easy solution. Control must, therefore, result from a large number of inter-related efforts. Currently, there is a 30,000 km dike system in the middle and lower reaches of the Yangtze. To resolve the flood problem solely by raising the dikes would be too costly, although some work is being done to heighten and strengthen the key dikes. To help cope with flood waters that might breach these levees, a series of flood diversion and storage basins were created and are planned that make use of natural lakes and depressions that are kept empty until needed for flood diversion pur-poses. But this approach takes up valuable land in densely populated areas. Upstream flood control projects would permit a diminution in the scale of these diversion catchments.[11] The major sources of Yangtze flooding are the tributaries that join the river between Yibin and Yi-chang. An important part of any solution to the flood problem, therefore, is to construct dams at appropriate points along these tributaries. While over eighteen such dams have been proposed or are planned,[12] as of 1985 only three had actually either entered construction or been completed.[13] These smaller dams on the main river and the tributaries above Xiling Gorge are necessary parts of the overall solution to the flooding problem on the middle and lower reaches of the Yangtze. Many of them are them-selves in gorge areas that are suitable for substantial hydropower gener-ation, and each of them would cost only a small fraction of the cost for Three Gorges. Given China's enormous infrastructure needs in a wide range of areas, some officials pose the issue in terms of whether to build

(a distance of 113 miles) is 56,700 cubic meters per second (the SCC in this reach is actually decreasing due to siltation), and the capacity from Wuhan to Hukou is 70,000 meters per second. The 1870 flood reached a peak of 110,000 cubic meters per second at Yichang: USBR 1981 trip report, p. II-12. Indeed, every twenty years on the average a flood pours on the average of 72,300 cubic meters of water per second through the Three Gorges area: USBR Trip Report on June 21-July 19, 1984 trip, p. 78.

[11] The Dongting Lake also is part of this flood diversion scheme, but the size of this lake itself is decreasing alarmingly. The surface area of Dongting Lake has declined from 4,350 square km. to 2,740 square km. during the 1950's to 1970's: *Zhongguo shuili*, No. 2 (1981), p. 32.

[12] Two on the upper reaches of the Yangtze (most of which is called the Jinshajiang) east of Yibin, four on the Daduhe, one on the Minjiang, one on the Fujiang, four on the Jialing-jiang, one on the Qujiang, two on the Chishuihe, and three on the Wujiang.

[13] The Gongzui on the Dadu, the Wujiangdu on the Wujiang, and the Bikou on the Jialingjiang.

more of these smaller dams first and postpone the Three Gorges project (with its enormous investment costs, long payback period, and great technological complexity) until the economy itself has grown larger and more advanced.

In sum, with the imminent flood danger and the area's pressing need for additional electric power, a key issue is whether a dam with a ten-year lead time until initial power generation should be made the top priority for scarce investment funds. The alternative would be to build smaller dams and thermal power plants and also to upgrade ancillary flood control facilities, all of which could be done more quickly and less expensively. Even most opponents of the Three Gorges dam agree that at some point it will be appropriate to construct a major dam at the Three Gorges. The question is whether conditions make the 1980's the appropriate time to begin.

Dam Height and Reservoir Level

Dam height and reservoir level have also been major points of debate over the best mix of trade offs. These are somewhat separable issues, as the dam structure itself can be built to a greater height than will be the normal water level in the reservoir. The dam height obviously creates an upper limit on reservoir capacity. How high to make the reservoir during normal operations in the low water season (the "maximum normal water surface") will determine the amount of land that will be permanently inundated, the number of people displaced, and so forth. Power generation and flood control capabilities are also broadly related to dam height and policy toward reservoir size.

In some respects, a high dam is economical. For example, a 200 meter dam would yield a firm power output of 7,320 MW with an installed capacity of 25,000 MW and annual energy production of about 110 billion kWh. Direct investment per kWh would cost two-thirds of that of existing hydropower plants in China. In human terms, however, the high dam would be costly. The 200 meter dam would inundate 114,000 acres of farmland and require the relocation of at least 1.4 million people. A 185 meter dam, by contrast, would reduce installed power capacity to 20,000 MW with a significant reduction in generation and an increase in per unit cost of production. A 165 meter dam would have an installed capacity of only 13,000 MW. The smallest dam that has ever been considered is 140 meters, with a maximum normal water surface restricted to 128 meters. This would permit an installed power capacity of only 6,000 MW. This low variant would, however, require the inundation of only 11,000 acres of farmland and the relocation of 200,000 people.

Until 1980 serious consideration apparently was given primarily to dam heights of 190 meters or more, with a 200 meter dam evidently in favor in 1978-80.[14] With the Ministries of Water Conservancy and of Electric Power separated at the time, the Electric Power side tended to argue for a lower dam, while the Water Conservancy side generally included advocates of a higher dam.[15] Evidently, the electric power people preferred a lower dam for several reasons: 1. A 25,000 MW dam would utilize such large generator units that there was some technical question as to whether this dam would serve efficiently as a vehicle for meeting peak load demands on various power grids; 2. The investment required in a 200 meter dam would be so large as to affect the other power construction projects planned; and 3. With electric power in critically short supply as of 1980, too large a percentage of investment funds would be tied up in a project that would not come on line for at least ten years.[16]

For reasons that are not wholly clear, in 1983 the official maximum normal water surface was stipulated at the relatively low figure of 150 meters, with the dam structure itself to be built to a height of 175 meters. As explained below, this set of parameters was probably designed to obtain a reasonably broad consensus on constructing the dam, but these same parameters were subsequently called into serious question by provinces and central bureaucratic actors. Most of the critics argued for higher structures, while the lower parameters set in 1983 also had strong supporters. Thus, a consensus remains elusive on this critical set of issues through the mid-1980's.

Buried within the dam height and reservoir level debate are issues of enormous political consequence. Choices made directly affect the lives of millions of people, up to a million of whom could be forced to move from their ancestral homes to permit the dam to be built. The project also involves numerous administrative units and could drain investment from other highly desired projects, especially in Sichuan province. Dam projects always, moreover, distribute their blessings unevenly: in this case, the downstream provinces of Hubei, Hunan, Anhui, Jiangxi,

[14] See, e.g., Yang Xianyi, Wei Tingzhong, and Paul Chesen Chao "Three Gorge Dam, Why It Should Be Built," ENR (November 6, 1980), pp. 43-47; and "A Brief Introduction of the Three Gorge Project on the Yangtze River" (Yangtze Valley Planning Office: Feb. 1980) p. 10.

[15] The breakdown was not as neat as this, in that some officials in each ministry voiced the position attributed here to the other ministry. But most in each ministry assumed the positions described here.

[16] While the Three Gorges project has been seen as taking ten years before the first units come on line, other very large construction projects since the late 1960's have tended to take far longer than anticipated. This record may well have influenced the electric power officials' views toward the real time that Three Gorges would take to come on line.

Jiangsu, and Shanghai are the primary beneficiaries of flood control and power generation; Sichuan stands to gain electric power to a much lesser extent, and its flood control situation might actually be worsened, depending on the siltation effects discussed below. These dissimilar interests dictate the views on issues such as dam height and reservoir size adopted by the provinces affected.

Estimating Costs and Providing Financing

While the two previous issues essentially involve wide-ranging trade offs and thus are inherently political (in the broad sense of this term), the problems of estimating costs and providing financing for a project of this scope have proven to be matters of daunting technical complexity. Cost benefit analysis of the dam, for example, requires pricing such intangibles as the potential saving of human lives from catastrophic flooding. American government specialists who studied the Three Gorges project in 1981 recommended that a feasibility study typical of the United States Department of Interior Bureau of Reclamation be done to determine real costs and benefits. This recommendation fell on receptive ears, evidently in part because the Baoshan Iron and Steel Complex being constructed near Shanghai had just run into severe criticism over precisely the lack of appropriate feasibility studies. In 1982 the Ministry of Finance was asked to do a financial feasibility study, and the MWREP began working on the issues raised by the American specialists.

Nevertheless, this approach ran into some opposition, as reflected in an April 1982 article in the journal *Renmin Changjiang* (People's Yangtze). This article reviewed the lessons learned from the construction of the Danjiangkou dam on the Han River. Among its conclusions was the observation that, "You cannot use the cost estimates for the total project to measure whether a plan meets the principle of multi-purpose use, to judge a plan's quality." This is because different bases are used for computing the figures on flood control, power generation, and navigation, and thus the numbers are not really comparable. Also, different ministries have different priorities, and the financial calculus on a multi-purpose project would in any case depend on the actual and inherently unpredictable mix of uses and priorities once the project is completed.[17] As a result, producing a financial feasibility study became, ironically, a highly political and contentious effort, with different ministries arguing for different methods of cost accounting.

Studies dating back to the 1950's recognized the Three Gorges dam

---

[17] Hong Qingyu, "Dui Danjiangkou."

project would have a major impact on the development of industry in the entire region of the middle reaches of the Yangtze. Therefore, dam cost/benefit analyses must also take into account the possible influence of the dam on China's spatial economy. Further, the calculations cannot be undertaken in a vacuum. Costs must be compared to the alternatives, particularly for comparison with other sources of electric power. Coal-fired thermal plants would be the main competitor to the dam for the mid-Yangtze region, and calculating those costs requires estimating investments in transportation to bring the coal to the projected plants. The calculations involved in such analysis are enormously complex, and the task of obtaining economically meaningful cost/benefit data is made even more difficult by China's continuing use of administratively fixed prices to govern much of the production and use of many major commodities, including energy.

Potential costs could also be affected significantly if the dam were built in stages. Some proponents of the dam advocated constructing the dam to an intermediate height and generating power at that point. After funds accumulated from selling that power, according to this innovative and probably unrealistic suggestion, the dam would be completed at its full height. Arguments were advanced to utilize staged construction, the profits from the large dam downstream at Gezhouba that should be completed in 1989, and interest-free government investment funds to construct a 200-meter dam costing 12.5 billion yuan (including costs of relocation). This combination of measures would, it was asserted, make the total cost relatively easy to absorb.[18] Other estimates put total costs much higher and placed more emphasis on opportunity costs, the ultimate savings in building the dam at one swoop rather than in stages, and the real cost of capital (even if it is provided in the form of interest-free government grants) for constructing the dam. In sum, cost/benefit analysis was accepted (grudgingly, by some) in principle, but this task remained so complex and required so many judgments that the exercise still left many points of discussion unresolved.

Three key issues, moreover, dominate the cost/benefit calculation: 1. How high a dam will be built and what will the maximum normal water surface be? 2. How many refugees will the dam create? 3. What actions will be necessary to cope with the problem of siltation (discussed below)? As of 1985 there was still so much uncertainty surrounding each of these issues that financial planners were largely limited to a few very broad brush ideas. These included the recognition that the government would have to rely on loans as well as on outright grants to provide its

---

[18] *ENR*, April 1980, p. 47.

share of the funds necessary for the project and that some use of foreign funds would be required. The financial unknowns remained so large, though, that detailed financial planning was put aside until the three basic questions listed above could be settled. The Three Gorges dam opponents contended that it would be a number of years before China could afford to construct this dam.

The Siltation Problem

The potential silt problem at the Three Gorges site is severe, and sharp technical debate erupted over the adequacy of the models employed to study the effects of various dam heights on siltation. Complex currents, rapid and large-scale changes in water flows, and changing conditions along the upstream tributaries increase the uncertainty on silt issues.

The potential sedimentation problems are serious at three basic locales: the reservoir backwater, the damsite, and the area downstream of the dam. The mean annual suspended load is 520 million tons per year at the Three Gorges, and it is imperative both to maintain adequate reservoir volume and to keep open the navigation channel.[19] Opponents of the dam have raised a wide range of questions. Around the reservoir: Will it be possible to keep the Chongqing port clear if the reservoir backwater reaches Chongqing? Will silt accumulate where tributaries enter the reservoir, thus increasing the flood danger in these locales? These problems could arise because silt will begin to deposit in locales where the river will flow more slowly than it now does. At the dam site, issues arise over accumulation of silt behind the dam and how this will affect the estimated half-life of the dam, the pressure the base of the dam must withstand, and so on. Finally, downstream, might the reduced silt content of the water cause the river to lift sediment from the current channel there, thus over time causing alterations in that channel? Will different sediment flow in the Yangtze estuary near Shanghai change the marine biology of that area?

The debate over the silting issue is made more difficult by the long expected life of the dam, some 100 years. The technical complexities of making these projections are so great that any results generated leave much room for challenge and recalculation. While this debate rages, moreover, some argue that the silt problem is becoming more acute from denuding of forests and subsequent erosion in Western Sichuan. Silt projections must also take into account the effects that the construction of

[19] See United States Bureau of Reclamation 1984 Trip Report, pp. 51-53 for details. "Suspended load" is the amount of silt in the water that flows to the dam.

smaller dams on upstream tributaries might have—and this, in turn, demands that accurate assumptions be made about the timing and sequence of upriver dam construction.

Finally, the bitter experience with previously completed large dam projects that woefully underestimated silting problems further inflamed the debate over the potential silt problems at the Three Gorges project. The Sanmen Gorge dam on the Yellow River, built with Soviet assistance, suffered from the start due to its inability to cope with the enormous volume of silt carried by the Yellow River. As noted below, some critics of the Three Gorges project charged that initially this project would be known for the size of its refugee resettlement task, but after a period it would become notorious for the magnitude of the silt problem.

Other Unprecedented Problems

A final major problem concerns the technical feasibility of the dam construction itself. No single overriding technical issue clouds discussion of this project. Rather, many specific technical problems as yet have no solution, and their number and difficulty have aroused the concern of some design specialists. Naturally, detractors of the dam on other grounds may also seize on technical questions to strengthen their view.

Examples of such technical problems abound. For instance, cofferdam construction requires use of a blended material because of the lack of adequate natural material near the dam site. This blended material may not meet specifications for containing leakage at the depths required. Also, Chinese engineers have not designed and constructed cofferdams as deep as those required for the Three Gorges. On another matter, the Gezhouba project provided experience in constructing locks as long and wide as those required at Three Gorges, but the Ministry of Communications requested Three Gorges locks that are of unprecedented depth. This raises new and difficult technical issues. The karst rock and geological fault lines in the reservoir area, moreover, necessitate special studies on reservoir leakage and the effect of the reservoir on fault activity. Finally, the project requires sophisticated methods to achieve the optimum coordination among design, equipment purchases, material deliveries, and related activities for the construction schedule to be met. This involves computer modeling of the construction process in a way that has not previously been done in China.

None of these problems is inherently insurmountable. But each added a degree of uncertainty to the project plans. Each also highlights the importance of maintaining strict quality controls on all major aspects of Three Gorges construction—a requirement that has sometimes been dif-

ficult to meet in other Chinese dam projects, given the particular bureaucratic configuration that governs the allocation of responsibility for dam
project construction. China's administrative system does *not* give the
dam's designers direct control over the units that actually construct the
dam.[20]

The above five core issues alone indicate why a rationality model, with
assumptions about consistent goals, technical certainties, and measurable
trade offs, could not adequately explain decision making on the Three
Gorges dam. Since inherently political judgments must enter into the
decision making calculus the following section introduces the key bureaucratic units that have played significant roles in the history of deliberations on this project. As the subsequent investigation of the history
of the project from the mid-1950's to 1986 then details, each of these
units has tried to convince the pertinent leaders among the top twenty-
five to thirty-five of its own priorities and technical sophistication so as
to skew the ultimate political decisions on the project toward its own
preferences.

THE PERTINENT BUREAUCRACIES

From the vantage of the Center, the major bureaucratic actors on the
Three Gorges project are the: Yangtze Valley Planning Office; Ministry
of Water Resources and Electric Power; Ministry of Communications;
SPC; SSTC; pertinent Machine Building Ministries; the Ministry of Finance; Chongqing municipality; and the provinces along the Yangtze
from Sichuan to Shanghai. Not all of these have played equal or constant
roles. The following brief summarizes the core interests and perspective
of each organization.[21]

The *YVPO* as of 1985 had over 12,000 members. Established in Wuhan
in 1956 as a successor to the Yangtze Valley Planning Commission (itself
a successor to a similar KMT organization), the YVPO was responsible
both for an overall plan for development of the Yangtze and for the specific feasibility study and designs for Three Gorges.[22] The YVPO, headed
from its inception until the end of the 1970's by Lin Yishan, consistently

---

[20] Hurried construction work proved very costly in the work on other dams, as demonstrated for example, by the construction history of Danjiangkou: Hong Qingyu, "Dui Danjiangkou." Reportedly in late 1985 the cofferdam at Tianshengqiao collapsed due to leakage, with considerable loss of life.

[21] The sources for the following information are provided in the remaining sections of
this chapter. Some of this information is derived from interviews.

[22] The YVPO also designed the Gezhouba dam forty kilometers downstream from the
proposed Three Gorges site.

and vigorously supported construction of a high dam at Three Gorges whose major purpose would be flood control.[23] Lin and his organization repeatedly tried to launch construction of this dam. The YVPO until the 1970's was directly under the aegis of Premier Zhou Enlai. In the 1970's it became formally subordinate to the Ministery of Water Resources and Electric Power. At all times, however, it actually reported to the Ministry on routine matters and went directly to Premier Zhou only on major issues.

The *MWREP* is a hybrid, and the water resources people, primarily concerned with flood control, strongly advocated the Three Gorges dam. The electric power side, determined to bring new sources of power on line quickly and cheaply, believed Three Gorges was the wrong way to try to meet the country's pressing electric power needs. In addition, the water resources and the electric power people adopted different priorities on the optimal dam height and on dam management. Water resources officials generally preferred a higher dam structure and planned water surface levels based primarily on flood control considerations. Those in electric power sought somewhat lower levels to minimize costs and construction time, and they wanted water management attuned primarily to power generation needs. Putting these two ministries together did not eliminate these arguments but rather only contained them somewhat within one ministry. In the mid-1980's Qian Zhengying headed the combined ministry and strongly supported the Three Gorges dam project. Li Peng, former Minister of Electric Power and then the Vice-Premier responsible for Three Gorges planning, had a record as of 1980-81 of opposing this project.

Under the *Ministry of Communications* the Yangtze River Transport Bureau (*Changjiang hangwu ju*) was responsible for preserving continuous shipping capabilities on the Yangtze from Wuhan to Chongqing. This bureau and the ministry basically opposed the Three Gorges dam because they feared transportation disruptions during dam construction. They also believed that the silting problems from the dam could prove very pernicious. They thus, generally strongly criticized the plans put forward by the YVPO.

The *State Planning Commission* must play a central role in building the dam as it assumes responsibility for meshing the dam with national economic construction priorities and then must coordinate activities to construct the dam itself. Within the SPC, the Fuel and Power Bureau was directly concerned with the Three Gorges Project. Once the project

---

[23] This history is detailed below.

was put into the annual plan, the Key Projects Construction Bureau[24] would assume responsibility for coordinating the construction activities. While the SPC's advice on the dam must have been solicited at each stage since the 1950's, its actual views are known only for the period 1983-86. In early 1983 the SPC stated that the dam should be built but that a certain amount of additional work should first be done on resolving outstanding technical questions.

The *State Science and Technology Commission* helped to coordinate and carry out some of the technical studies related to the Three Gorges dam project. Its role in project activities apparently grew in the 1980's because of the increased national concern with the technical feasibility of proposed construction efforts. As of the mid-1980's, the SSTC and the SPC supervised and coordinated a wide range of technical studies on the dam at the request of the State Council.

Chongqing municipality had conflicting interests at stake. A normal water surface of at least 180 meters would permit 10,000 ton tows to reach Chongqing. The city saw this as its major potential benefit from the dam, for it would help integrate its economy with that of the rich middle and lower Yangtze areas.[25] At the same time, the dam posed drawbacks to Chongqing. Substantial parts of the city would be inundated by a 180 meter dam (although the municipality overall has been willing to sacrifice this older area for the benefits the dam would bring). There might also be major silting problems at the Chongqing harbor if the reservoir backwater extended to that locale. Even with these potential hazards, Chongqing strongly supported construction of the Three Gorges dam—providing that the dam would bring 10,000 ton tows to the city from the middle Yangtze. Chongqing's leverage was, moreover, probably strengthened in the early 1980's by reforms that greatly extended its boundaries and increased its status and power on budgetary issues.

While Chongqing was a consistent high dam supporter, populous *Sichuan province* fought the dam for most of the time since the 1950's. Until 1983-84, Sichuan faced the daunting burden of largely managing alone the resettlement of people displaced by the dam, which alone prompted its objection. In addition, Sichuan would stand to encounter potentially greater silting problems from the dam without realizing any

---

[24] This bureau, as noted in the section on the SPC in Chapter Three, formerly was a part of the State Capital Construction Commission.

[25] A somewhat lower normal water surface might actually be detrimental to Chongqing's economy. The smaller reservoir behind such a dam could permit Wanxian, to the East of Chongqing, to become the key port linking Sichuan to the middle Yangtze region, thereby robbing Chongqing of some of the business that it now captures.

flood control benefits from it. The province also was not slated to receive substantial hydropower benefits from the dam, because of the considerable distances from the dam itself to Sichuan's major industrial centers and the mountainous terrain across which the transmission lines would have to be constructed. From flood control, silting, and hydropower points of view, therefore, the provincial leaders' preference has been to build smaller dams on the tributaries of the Yangtze in Sichuan, thereby reducing the resettlement burden. As explained below, however, Sichuan's position changed somewhat after 1984, when the Center accepted in principle the idea of creating a new province to handle the resettlement and related issues.

Hubei and Hunan provinces were key dam supporters, with Hubei an especially vigorous advocate of the Three Gorges project. Both provinces would be the major beneficiaries of the flood control objectives and would receive significant hydropower benefits, too. Although the point is debatable, many also believe that the dam would improve navigation conditions between Yichang and Wuhan below the dam during the low water season by providing a controlled flow of higher water over the shallow shoals in this stretch.[26]

The remaining provinces on the Yangtze below the dam are *Jiangxi, Anhui, Jiangsu, and Shanghai.* The first three generally supported the dam, as they would receive some hydropower and flood control benefits without paying any real cost.[27] Shanghai itself had a somewhat more mixed view. It would receive some hydropower benefits and potentially some flood control benefits. The major changes in water flow and silt content that the dam would produce, however, could conceivably produce substantial changes in the marine biology of the Yangtze estuary. Shanghai voiced some concerns about the need to study this problem. But overall, the downstream provinces below Hubei and Hunan supported the dam.

This brief listing of the key actors and their basic interests prompts three additional comments. First, the list excludes what may be a very

[26] The Ministry of Communications, however, has suggested that the dam might further complicate navigation in this stretch for two reasons: 1. the water flow in the area is so complex that some silting problems may arise that have not been anticipated by the dam advocates; and 2. water discharges required by the hydropower function of the dam may run counter to optimal navigation needs. The Gezhouba dam is being built in part as a regulator dam to control the future water surges from the Three Gorges dam.

[27] There were some exceptions to this broad statement. E.g., at the beginning of the 1980's the Anhui Fisheries Bureau voiced alarm over the effect of the dam on the Yangtze sturgeon, which breeds upstream of the dam. The Bureau tried to make the dam promoters include a fish ladder as part of the dam design. The Bureau's concerns were, however, allayed by experiments that showed there are other ways to handle this issue.

important set of actors, the counties and prefectures that would be affected by the dam. The state structure gives these units resources with which to frustrate the desires of the dam proponents. Too little is known about the details of the positions these various units have taken, but this is likely to be a major (hidden) part of the Three Gorges story. The relevant local units include not only those that would be inundated by the reservoir but also those that would have to absorb the displaced populace. Submerging several counties and towns and moving the pertinent populations elsewhere also, of course, requires moving many officials and redividing power among local elites. Creating a new province to manage this issue highlights the degree to which these changes are political/administrative as well as social and economic. The web of affected interests—and the intensity of concern among those affected—is likely to have been and to remain a major factor in the dynamics of the decision making on the Three Gorges dam.

Second, "opposition" to construction of the dam may, of course, be more of a bargaining ploy than a firm position. The above stances of the various actors are based both on the actual record since the mid-1950's and on each unit's "objective" interests concerning costs and benefits. Their own evaluations of these interests may, however, adapt as the bargaining process creates new situations.

Finally, many of the above "actors" are themselves complex bureaucracies with a variety of interests. This is most obvious with the MWREP, but it is also true to a greater or lesser extent with each provincial government and central ministry. The policy positions in this chapter, therefore, in most cases only sketch in a very general way the view of each ministry or province, as far as it is known. Typically, the available data do not permit a more detailed analysis of the actual internal dynamics of handling the Three Gorges issue within these various units.

The above list indicates the wide ranging bureaucratic interests and views that have fed into the Three Gorges decision making. One additional piece of the decision making puzzle must be put in place, however, before looking in detail at the history of this project proposal: that is, the sequence of stages in the pertinent decision making process. While the concept of stages was introduced earlier, we now explore it in greater detail.

STAGES

The decisional process for any major construction project involves five major stages, and each stage involves a somewhat different set of bureaucratic units, a distinct set of issues, and therefore a distinctive political dynamic. To be sure, these stages can somewhat overlap, as has happened with the Three Gorges dam. The first stage involves setting long term goals or, in Chinese, *guihua*.[28] This stage brings forth overarching commitments to what may in many cases amount to little more than a wish list. The ten-year "plan" for the national economy adopted in March 1978 represents this type of exercise on a national scale.[29] Typically, relatively little debate occurs in this stage, as the goals are quite broad and are sufficiently distant in time that few people want to expend political capital in challenging the realism of *guihua*.

The second stage involves specific, concrete project[30] planning, in this instance *jihua*. Since the early 1980's, this requires a feasibility study that lays out basic specifications for the project and provides the basis for putting the project into the five year and the annual plans. Putting a project into the five year plan tentatively commits the government to a start-up time and triggers the ancillary long-term planning (regarding related railroad construction, cement production, and so forth) that may be necessary to make the project feasible. At this point, the investment funds are earmarked in principle for the project. Placing the project into the annual plan actually commits concrete funds and other resources to the effort during the coming year.

Five year plans are to a significant extent "rolling" plans, subject to frequent readjustment. But the inclusion of a major project in the five year plan is still important, as projects *not* included in it are unlikely to start up during the tenure of that plan.[31] Even when included, however, considerable additional effort and maneuvering may be required to have the project fully funded in the appropriate annual plan. This planning cycle helps to explain important dimensions in the history of the Three Gorges: this project was accepted as a long term goal (*guihua*) in the mid-1950's, and thereafter it inevitably had to be considered in the debate over each successive five year plan. Serious debate often accompanies the movement of a project from the *guihua* to the five year plan and the

[28] The standard translation of *guihua* is "plan," but *jihua*, also rendered as "plan," comes closer to the English equivalent.

[29] The full text of this plan is not available, but its key points are outlined in the Government Work Report delivered by Hua Guofeng to the First Session of the Fifth National People's Congress on February 26, 1978. The text of Hua's Report is in *Beijing Review*, March 10, 1978, pp. 7-40. The NPC formally adopted Hua's Report on March 5, 1978.

[30] In Chinese, *xiangmu*.

[31] As noted in Chapter Three, however, some funds were kept outside of the Seventh Five Year Plan (1986-90) for start up costs on major projects where agreement to initiate construction had not been reached as of the time the Plan was formally adopted in April 1986. According to knowledgeable Chinese officials, the Three Gorges Dam was one of these projects.

annual plan stages because competition for scarce investment funds is fierce.

The third stage is that of design, or *sheji*. The arguments at this stage are likely to be more technical. Opponents of a complex project may adopt positions on issues (such as the siltation and navigation problems in the Three Gorges case), however, that essentially use the "design" stage to stall a project by demanding technical alterations that add to the cost and complexity. Significant design alterations can force a project re-evaluation. Budget and time considerations became more important during the 1980's than previously, especially on projects for which the Chinese borrow money from abroad.

The fourth stage is construction, or *shigong*. Major activities shift to the construction corps, who differ bureaucratically from the planning and design organs. The task becomes one of mobilizing and coordinating the various relevant bureaucracies to complete work on time without sacrificing critical quality standards. This has been a particularly difficult stage in the Chinese major project cycle.

The fifth and final stage is utilization. Given the long lead times for major projects, key conditions (prices, demand for the product, etc.) often change in unanticipated ways by the time a project is brought on line. This may require that the original plans concerning the allocation of the project's results (electricity, etc.) be modified, and this in turn requires striking new balances among the pertinent actors.

The Three Gorges dam project is so large and controversial and has been under consideration for so long that it in fact has overlapped several of these stages simultaneously. In 1985, the project was in the design stage in the above cycle. Nevertheless, fundamental disputes that erupted early in the long term planning (*guihua*) stage—such as whether to build the Three Gorges dam before or after construction of smaller dams on tributaries to the Yangtze in Sichuan—still remained under dispute in the mid-1980's. The concrete planning (*jihua*) stage was formally completed in April 1984, when the State Council accepted the feasibility study for the project written by the Yangtze Valley Planning Office and stipulated that the project be made part of the Seventh Five Year Plan (1986-90) with actual construction beginning two years hence. But, as detailed below, this timetable was upset, and many of the issues characteristic of the concrete planning stage (economic feasibility, date for starting construction, technical feasibility, etc.) remained under sharp dispute. Still, design stage efforts proceeded apace as if the planning stages had been completed, and a preliminary design report was completed in 1985.

Thus, as of 1986 the Three Gorges dam project included elements characteristic of the long-term and concrete planning stages as well as of the design stage. The timetable for initiating the construction stage was set back and remained uncertain. This case study, therefore, focuses on only the initial stages of a major project. The concluding sections of this chapter raise some of the issues that should become important if actual construction begins.

THREE GORGES PROJECT HISTORY

Natural Disasters Prompt an Elite Initiative

Thoughts about constructing a large dam to control flooding on the Yangtze and to harness the river for hydropower generation date back at least to August 1923, when Sun Yatsen ordered an investigation of the possibilities at the Three Gorges after hearing that it had the potential to generate thirty million horsepower.[32] More serious planning began in the 1930's,[33] and a major study done under the leadership of the Bureau of Reclamation's Chief Design Engineer Dr. John L. Savage was undertaken at the end of WW II. These early planning efforts, however, occurred in an unstable political and economic environment that prevented marshalling the necessary resources to turn an ambitious idea into reality. The work in the 1940's involved the Chinese unit that in the 1950's became the YVPO, the key advocate of the Three Gorges project over the past three decades.[34] Some informal evidence suggests that the approaches developed through these early efforts contributed to the YVPO's subsequent thinking on the Three Gorges.

The Yangtze floods in 1949 and 1954 highlighted the importance of controlling this river, especially the devastating 1954 flood which evidently cost about 30,000 lives. Even before this natural catastrophe,

[32] *Water Resources of China,* JPRS, No. 32681 (November 2, 1965), p. 106. John Hersey has written an evocative short novel about a young Western engineer who travelled up the Yangtze to investigate the feasibility of building a dam at the Three Gorges. See his *A Single Pebble* (New York: Alfred A. Knopf, 1974). Hersey, who grew up in Tianjin, captures the age old dream of foreigners to transform China and, in Joseph Conrad fashion, the journey up the river becomes the metaphor through which the Westerner confronts his illusion.

[33] In 1933 three engineers from the Society of Engineers proposed a 420-foot dam at Huanglingmiao and a 42-foot high dam at Gezhouba: *Guangming ribao* (Beijing), July 1, 1956, and *Water Resources of China,* JPRS, No. 32681 (November 2, 1965), p.106.

[34] For summary information on Savage's study, see: *Changjiang sanxia shuili gongcheng jihua* (China: Ministry of Information, 1947). Good overall information on pre-1949 deliberations over a Three Gorges dam is available in: Daniel Michaels, "The Three Gorges Project in China's Modernization: Image and Reality," senior thesis in East Asian Studies, Princeton University, 1987, pp. 15-62.

however, Mao Zedong in 1953 had emphasized the importance of study-ing the Three Gorges at a time when the new regime began to focus on water resources nationally.[35] In 1954, the Chinese commissioned a major effort to devise a plan for the comprehensive utilization of the Yangtze.[36] This produced an intensive project to survey the Yangtze that com-menced during November 1955. At this time and indeed throughout the 1950's Soviet experts were intimately involved with China's dam plan-ning. The large Soviet involvement reflected the paucity of Chinese hy-draulic engineers and the extensive though not always relevant Soviet experience in hydroelectric projects.[37]

The over 1,000 man survey team mapped the Yangtze from late 1955 to 1957. On the Chinese side Li Baohua, Vice Minister of Water Re-sources and leader of the Party group in the Ministry, assumed leader-ship and the Yangtze Water Resources Committee's Planning Office managed the project. In November 1955 over twenty Soviet experts joined the team at China's request. The Soviet group was led by [Demi-teliyefu], an engineer who had been in charge of planning work on the [Anjiala] River in the USSR. Overall, this Sino-Soviet survey team sought to develop a master plan (*guihua*) for the siting of potential dams throughout the Yangtze and its tributaries to control and develop the entire basin.[38] The team, therefore, included specialists in planning, de-sign, geology, irrigation and drainage, shipping, hydropower, agricul-ture, and water resources.[39] This was, overall, a time of optimism in hy-droelectric dam construction in China. The Sanmen Gorge project was also on the drawing boards then.

The Soviet experts stayed with this effort in the field until September 1956. As of that August, a special sub-team began intensively studying the Three Gorges area to identify the best potential dam site, and focused especially on the distribution of granite and limestone formations. When the Soviet experts departed from the team, the hydrological studies of the upper reaches of the Yangtze were completed. The Chinese were doing similar studies of the middle and lower reaches and were analyzing

[35] *Water Resources of China*, JPRS, No. 32681 (November 2, 1965), p. 107.

[36] *Nanyang shangbao*, April 15, 1957. At the same time, in 1954 the Yangtze Water Resources Committee (*Changjiang shuili weiyuanhui*) recommended an intensive effort to work on the pertinent dikes, lakes, and marsh land: *Renmin ribao*, June 11, 1957.

[37] As noted in Chapter Two, Liu Lanbo and Li Rui, who were in charge of hydropower in China, spent four months in the Soviet Union in the winter of 1954-55 familiarizing themselves with Soviet hydropower experience. Li Rui, *Huainian shi pian*.

[38] Again, *guihua* indicates a long term, outline plan rather than a concrete, detailed pro-gram.

[39] Among the numerous sources that provide information on this survey effort are: *Ren-min ribao*, January 17, 1956; and *Zhongguo xinwen*, November 10, 1956.

cofferdams and temporary locks that would be built as part of the Three Gorges construction effort. In late summer, 1956, the Chinese felt that the first proposals of the Outline Plan would be ready in draft form by the end of that year.[40]

A Debate Emerges in the Bureaucracy

A sharp debate had already developed in the specialized Chinese technical media that spilled over into the general press in September 1956. While many individuals and units became involved in this discussion, two key protagonists who would continue to fight over the Three Gorges project into the 1980's had already squared off in 1956.[41] Li Rui, the former Vice Minister of Electric Power and an opponent of the project, cast the debate as a clash between the Yangtze Valley Planning Office, headed by Lin Yishan, and himself. Our account is not equally informed about the perspectives of the other central units—the Ministries of Communications, Finance, Machine Building, Electronics, and the State Planning Commission, State Science and Technology Commission, and so forth—that have played important roles in this project's history. Although we lack a detailed data base, a combination of documents and interviewing nevertheless permits a reasonably detailed reconstruction of the major issues and the history of the debate over Three Gorges, at least at the central level. The most enthusiastic and influential supporter of the project was Lin Yishan, a former member of the Fourth Field Army[42] who in 1949 had been put in charge of the Yangtze Valley Planning Committee in Wuhan and who then assumed leadership of the Yangtze Valley Planning Office when the latter was established in 1956.

Lin Yishan had no formal training in water management (he had concentrated on history in school), but over the years he nevertheless shaped the evolution of the YVPO and became a major force in water resources work on the Yangtze. By the 1960's the YVPO had its own university and employed thousands of people. Reflecting his success as an organization builder, Lin secured a large percentage of the young hydrologists and engineering geologists trained in the mid-1950's.[43] As of 1986, the

[40] *Ibid.*; *Hubei ribao*, October 4, 1956; and *Tianjin dagongbao*, September 1, 1956.

[41] A substantial portion of the data for the debate during the years before 1980 comes from one of these protagonists, Li Rui. *See* his *Lun Sanxia gongcheng* (Hunan: Hunan kexue jishu chubanshe, 1985).

[42] On the Fourth Field Army, see: William Whitson, *The Chinese High Command.*

[43] Of the approximately one hundred students trained in hydrology and in engineering geology in 1956, seventy were assigned to the YVPO. Meanwhile, other major projects lacked sufficient numbers of trained personnel: Li Rui, *Lun Sanxia*, p. 4.

YVPO had 12,000 staff members and occupied a major compound with many buildings for laboratories, computers, environmental protection work, administration, apartments for employees, and so forth.[44]

Just as Lin led the YVPO in advocating construction of a dam at the Three Gorges, Li Rui represented the hydropower interests in opposition to building the dam. Li spent the early 1950's in Hunan province. In 1952 he was transferred to Beijing to take charge of hydropower work at the Center. By the mid-1950's he was Vice-Minister of Electric Power and head of that ministry's General Bureau of Hydroelectric Construction.[45] When this ministry merged with the Ministry of Water Resources in February 1958 to form the Ministry of Water Resources and Electric Power, he became a Vice-Minister and retained that position until his purge at the Lushan Conference in 1959. Li also reportedly served for a time as Mao Zedong's secretary. Li and Lin first clashed over a potential dam at the Three Gorges in 1954, and the lines of argument that firmed up by late 1956 to a remarkable extent remained the core issues at stake into the 1980's—that is, decades after Li Rui's ouster at Lushan in 1959.

In 1954 Lin Yishan personally briefed Mao Zedong and Zhou Enlai on the efforts to conquer the 1954 flood, and the Ministry of Water Resources began planning for building a Three Gorges dam. Li Rui was then on his four-month study tour in the Soviet Union with China's Minister of Electric Power, and he quickly expressed doubt about China's ability to undertake such a long term project.[46] During the next two years, as Three Gorges planning progressed, the debate intensified.

In 1956 several organizational initiatives prepared the way for building a Three Gorges dam. As indicated above, the YVPO was established. This organ reported directly to Premier Zhou Enlai, who assumed overall charge of the Three Gorges project.[47] Li Rui claims that Zhou had doubts about the wisdom of Three Gorges from the beginning, and thus Zhou purportedly welcomed Li's relatively bold position against the dam in the face of the general enthusiasm for going ahead with the project.[48] During

[44] The YVPO also had branch offices in several other Yangtze cities and stationed people at experimental sites along the banks of the river.

[45] Li Rui, *Huainian shi pian*, p. 78; Wolfgang Bartke, *Who's Who*, p. 189.

[46] Li Rui, *Lun Sanxia*, p. 1.

[47] Zhou in fact reportedly "personally directed, examined, and approved the guiding principles and tasks of every stage of water resources work, the harnessing of every river and stream, and the construction of many major engineering projects": *Xiandai Zhongguo shuili jianshe, op. cit.*

[48] See, e.g., Li Rui, *Lun Sanxia*, pp. 2-3. That Li Rui is the sole source on Zhou's views is troubling, as Li may well in 1985 have been distorting views of the deceased premier to bolster his position.

1956, several different dam heights were discussed, ranging from 200 meters to 235 meters. The YVPO favored the 235 meter approach and saw the dam primarily in terms of its flood control potential.[49] The YVPO estimated that the survey and design work for the dam would take three years and the construction work another four years.[50] Lin published his basic views on this project in the ministerial journal *Zhongguo shuili*.[51] Li Rui critiqued this proposal in the September issue of the monthly publication *Shuili fadian*.[52]

Li's critique stressed the following points: The Three Gorges dam should not be devoted, as the YVPO advocated, wholly to flood control but rather should be planned as a multi-purpose project with hydropower and navigation considerations taken very much into account.[53] Even to prevent flooding, moreover, it makes little sense to rely on a single huge dam, as building a dam of sufficient height to accomplish this would create a reservoir that would flood the places (including half of Chongqing) where over two million people then lived. The costs of any such undertaking would overburden the national budget. Instead of first building this dam, therefore, the state should initiate other, smaller measures and turn to Three Gorges only when the national economy permitted.

The Ministry of Electric Power therefore advocated a staged approach to flood control on the Yangtze. Initially, the state should focus on raising and strengthening the dikes along the Yangtze,[54] developing catchment areas down-river from the Three Gorges by using lakes and depressions in the middle and lower reaches of the river,[55] and constructing smaller dams on key tributaries, especially on the main tributaries that feed into the Yangtze in Sichuan and on the Han River, whose waters combine with the Yangtze to menace Wuhan. At a later stage, when the economy had further developed, a dam could be built on the main channel of the Yangtze itself, although the measures taken during the first stage would have precluded the need for a dam as high as 235 meters. This sequential approach would also provide additional time in which to tackle the prickly technical issues that would have to be resolved before the Three Gorges dam could be built.

[49] The Ministry of Water Resources had responsibility for flood control. Hydropower generation, however, fell under the Ministry of Electric Power.

[50] From the technical information subsequently developed on a possible Three Gorges dam, it is clear with hindsight that these estimates were wildly unrealistic.

[51] Lin Yishan, "Guanyu Changjiang liuyu guihua ruogan wenti di shangtao," *Zhongguo shuili*, Nos. 5 and 6 (1956). This article ran 20,000 characters.

[52] The full text of this article is reprinted in Li Rui, *Lun Sanxia*, pp. 15-61.

[53] One major net effect of this would be to lower the dam height.

[54] As noted above, there are roughly 30,000 km. of such dikes.

[55] E.g., the Dongting Lake and low lying areas near it.

The technical issues identified in 1956 included: building larger locks than had ever been built before; minimizing disruptions in transportation during the course of construction of the dam (which in turn would demand new technologies in temporary locks)[56] constructing cofferdams that could withstand the unprecedented pressures and depths involved in a dam at Three Gorges; determining whether the base rock at the potential dam sites would prove suitable for such a dam;[57] developing the world's largest generators; and working out how to organize the construction of a dam of this extraordinary magnitude. All of these technical unknowns, according to the Electric Power Ministry's Li Rui, made the construction time schedule proposed by the YVPO quite unrealistic.

Before Li Rui's critique appeared, the issue emerged into the public domain via an article in *Renmin ribao* on 1 September 1956 that talked about the project as if it were about to begin. Li submitted a brief rebuttal to *Renmin ribao*, but Zhou Enlai reportedly prevented publication of this latter piece on the ground that he did not want this issue debated in public.[58] Opponents of the dam nevertheless quickly began to find media outlets for their views, and the newspapers soon acknowledged that sharp disagreement existed over the wisdom of building a dam at Three Gorges.[59]

The drafting process for the Yangtze River Development Plan provided the vehicle through which proponents of different perspectives advanced their views, with the statistics and projections put forward by different sides varying considerably. An article appearing in June 1957—just as the Hundred Flowers campaign was turning into an Anti-Rightist campaign—typifies the exaggerated arguments that were marshalled publicly against this project. This article asserted that the Three Gorges project would require more than ten billion yuan in direct investment in dam construction, plus another five to ten times that amount to build related industrial works, producing an overall total investment that could reach 250 percent of the entire investment in capital construction during the whole First Five Year Plan. A 235-meter high dam, moreover, would inundate some fourteen cities above Yichang, including a large portion of Chongqing itself. It would also inundate over 500 million acres of farmland. The electricity produced, however, would be more than China

[56] Later, this also involved the development of ship lifts.

[57] Subsequent investigations revealed that only a very small area of the Yangtze bed along this entire stretch has suitable base rock of almost solid granite. This condition characterizes only two places: Sandouping and Taipingxi.

[58] The only available source on Zhou's rationale is Li Rui, *Lun Sanxia*, p. 2.

[59] See, e.g., *Zhongguo xinwen*, October 20, 1956, and December 29, 1956; and *Nanyang shangbao*, April 15, 1957.

could effectively utilize for several decades. In addition, during the roughly 15-year construction cycle then anticipated for the Three Gorges, the middle and lower reaches of the Yangtze would remain subject to catastrophic flooding. Potential improvements to shipping on the Yangtze would not warrant this type of effort.[60]

Mass media articles attaching priority to the Three Gorges dam tended not to go into detail. Rather, they asserted that the Three Gorges project itself was pivotal in the historic effort to control the Yangtze. Beyond this, such articles elaborated upon the benefits to be derived from Three Gorges construction (including, in some instances, noting that this would allow water for irrigation to be diverted to the North China plain) without, typically, directly addressing the serious points being raised by the other side.[61]

The spate of articles that appeared in September 1956 to June 1957 inadvertently made clear that significant disagreements divided even those who opposed initial construction of Three Gorges dam, as nearly every article posited different priorities for what should be done before tackling the project. Nevertheless, the issue of whether or not to give first priority to Three Gorges dam construction in the Yangtze Plan evidently remained the key matter in dispute, and the inability to resolve this question produced back tracking on the date for submitting the Plan. During these months, the Three Gorges opponents, typically engineers (judging from the identifications of the authors who wrote against the Three Gorges for the public press), appeared to have the initiative—or at least they made their case(s) more powerfully in the many newspapers available in the West from that period.

Volatile national politics then began to buffet the Three Gorges debate. During the Hundred Flowers in early June 1957 key engineers who opposed giving priority to the Three Gorges were writing that the proponents of the Three Gorges dam were not taking technical issues seriously,[62] but the anti-rightist campaign unleashed that same month, which prompted an atmosphere of scorn for technical issues, provided an opportunity for the Three Gorges proponents to strike back. By early

[60] The author of this article, Lu Qinkan, represented hydropower interests in the Ministry of Electric Power. The article appeared in *Renmin ribao*, June 11, 1957, although it must have been written at the peak of the "blooming and contending" of the Hundred Flowers campaign. For a similar argument, see the article by Zhang Changling, Deputy Chief Engineer of the Water Resources and Power Construction General Administration, in *Zhongguo xinwen*, April 20, 1956. Zhang also notes, as do others, that the Three Gorges would require solutions to technical issues that go beyond anything yet accomplished anywhere in the world.

[61] *See*, for example, *Dagongbao* (Beijing), March 27, 1957.

[62] Lu Qinkan article in *Renmin ribao* (June 1, 1957).

September a *Changjiang ribao* article[63] smugly noted that the rightists—mostly engineers in the Yangtze Valley Planning Office—had capitulated. The anti-rightist campaign first struck this office in the last third of June. The "rightists" were accused of challenging Party leadership of technical work and of having sarcastically claimed that the Three Gorges dam would at best amount to a monument built for prestige alone. The dam, they had argued, simply would not work. It was in this atmosphere that the initial formal document, called the "Report on Major Points of the Outline Plan for Comprehensive Use of the Yangtze Valley [Discussion Draft]" (*Changjiang liuyu zonghe liyong guihua yaodian baogao [taolun gao]*),[64] from the survey work appeared.

No copy of this initial outline draft is currently available to foreign scholars, but it apparently signified that the tide had shifted in the direction of active preparations for construction of the Three Gorges dam. The "Report on Major Points . . ." circulated among the affected provinces for discussion starting in October 1957, while the Second Five Year Plan (1958-62) was being prepared. This coincided both with a general drift in national politics toward a more radical and mobilizational approach to economic work and with an evident weakening of Zhou Enlai and the State Council in economic decision making.[65]

In sum, virtually from the very beginning the proposal to build a high dam at the Three Gorges produced disputes that divided the flood control officials (led by Lin Yishan at the YVPO) from their hydropower counterparts (whose views are best known from the works of Vice Minister Li Rui at the Ministry of Electric Power). The division did not run solely along organizational lines, as the purge of YVPO engineers for opposing the dam demonstrated. But differences of perspective, linked logically to the differing organizational missions of the various concerned units, had become visible early on, and the issue went to the highest level political leadership for resolution.

Early 1958: The First Conditional Decision to Build the Dam

In January 1958 Mao Zedong personally sought briefings from the proponents and opponents of constructing the dam. Around the 18th, during a meeting of high level officials in Nanning, Mao asked both Lin

---

[63] September 2, 1957.

[64] *Ibid.*, and *Changjiang ribao*, October 27, 1957.

[65] See, e.g., the trenchant criticism of the State Council system in decision making that Mao Zedong voiced at the January 1958 Nanning Meeting: *Mao Zedong sixiang wansui*, pp. 145-154.

Yishan and Li Rui to make their cases orally to him. He then ordered each to write up his position and circulated the resulting documents to others at the Nanning conference. On 22 January at the conclusion of the Nanning Meeting, the Chairman convened a session to discuss the Three Gorges dam and the development of hydropower.

Mao had initiated this review at Nanning because he had continued to receive conflicting advice on the Three Gorges project even after the start of the anti-rightist campaign. The oral presentations on the 18th differed—Lin Yishan spoke for two hours, Li Rui for thirty minutes. Lin reportedly[66] argued in favor of a 200–210-meter dam that he estimated would cost seven billion yuan. He made his case in terms of navigation, hydropower, and the diversion of Yangtze water to the north as well as in terms of flood control, but flood control continued to provide the focus for his rationale. Lin reviewed the long history of Yangtze flooding and proclaimed that the Three Gorges dam alone could resolve this problem.

Li Rui disputed Lin on each issue, declaring that the Three Gorges dam could not resolve the flood control problem over the long run, that China at this point did not need the amount of electricity Three Gorges would generate, and so forth. Lin Yishan had not only lowered his preferred dam height (from 235 meters to 200-210 meters), but he had also stretched out somewhat the preparation and construction time. He suggested that actual construction begin in 1963, with completion in 1973. Li Rui asserted that even this timing remained unrealistic.

At the meeting on the 22nd, according to Li Rui, Mao predetermined the outcome by opening the meeting with a criticism of Lin Yishan for ideological confusion, lack of logic, and not having a basis for estimating that construction could begin in 1963. Bo Yibo and Hu Qiaomu also reportedly criticized Lin's paper. The final decision supported Li Rui's view that hydropower should be developed "as quickly as conditions permitted" (meaning the necessary conditions were still lacking).

While the Nanning Meeting should have ended the immediate debate on Three Gorges, the continuing national move to the left in the winter of 1957-58 kept the issue alive. Indeed, enthusiasm for the project grew during February 1958. It is not clear what relationship this bore to the decision on 11 February 1958 to merge the Ministries of Water Resources and of Electric Power. The merger threw together proponents and op-

---

[66] All of our detailed information on discussion of the Three Gorges comes from Li Rui, *Lun Sanxia*, pp. 3, 7-9, and thus may have a pro-Li Rui gloss. There is other independent evidence, however, that Three Gorges was a topic at the Nanning Meeting—see, e.g., *Water Resources of China*, p. 107. For a similar analysis of the effect of the anti-rightist campaign upon technical considerations in water resource management, see: Michel Oksenberg, *Policy Formulation in China*.

ponents of the project into a single unit where the power generation side would likely, over the long run, gain the upper hand over the water resources side.[67] Mao may, therefore, have ordered the merger at the conclusion of the Nanning Meeting so as to further dampen the bureaucratic impetus behind the Three Gorges project. But this is merely conjecture, and the politics of this merger remain obscure. It is possible, indeed, that supporters of Three Gorges promoted the merger as a gamble to bring the power generation people to heel in the context of growing enthusiasm for a radical leap forward in the economy!

Zhou Enlai seized the initiative in late February. He organized a boat trip through the Three Gorges for all the key advisors and decision makers on the project except Mao (Mao went by boat through the Three Gorges between 22 and 27 March 1958).[68] The roughly one hundred passengers included people from the relevant State Council ministries, from the pertinent provinces and municipalities, and also experts from the Soviet Union. Li Fuchun and Li Xiannian were on the voyage. On the boat, Zhou called on Li Rui to speak first at the initial meeting to discuss the dam project. When the boat reached Chongqing, Zhou then presided over a conference to draw up recommendations on the Three Gorges dam, and Soviet experts contributed their views at this meeting.[69] Zhou's report from this meeting provided the initial basis for discussion of the Three Gorges project at a meeting of high officials that began in Chengdu on February 28th.

At the Chengdu Conference, Zhou Enlai recommended criteria on Yangtze River Basin planning and on the Three Gorges dam.[70] Li Rui credits Zhou's efforts at this conference with being very important for having the meeting produce a decision that did not recklessly forge ahead with the Three Gorges project. The Chengdu Meeting issued a resolution entitled, "Opinion on the Three Gorges Water Resources Project and on the Outline Plan for the Yangtze Basin." This opinion declared that seven contradictory relationships would have to be worked out in order for the Three Gorges effort to proceed: long term and short term; main channel and tributaries; upper, middle, and lower reaches; large, medium, and small scale; flood control, power generation, irrigation and

[67] See the section of Chapter Three on the MWREP for an explanation of this premise.

[68] Dating of Zhou's trip is from: Gao Xia, "Jushi zhumu di Sanxia shuidian zhan," *Dili zhishi*, No. 4 (April 1985), p. 5; and *Zhou Enlai tongzhi shengping huodong nianbiao, 1898-1976* (Beijing: China Revolutionary Museum, 1980), pp. 55-56.

[69] Li Rui, *Lun Sanxia*, pp. 3-4, 11. On this meeting, see also: *Water Resources of China*, p. 107.

[70] Yang Xianyi, Wei Tingzheng, and Paul Cheshen Chao, "China's Three Gorge Dam Project on the Yangtze River," the full manuscript for an article that in edited form appeared in *ENR* (November 6, 1980).

drainage, and transport; hydropower and thermal power; and power generation versus power consumption (i.e., supply of and demand for power). Mao personally allegedly added the last three of these relationships.[71]

Particularly given the frenzied and euphoric environment during the March, 1958, Chengdu Conference, this meeting reacted relatively cautiously to the Three Gorges proposal. The conference evidently formally endorsed constructing the Three Gorges dam and concluded that about fifteen to twenty years would be required from exploration through construction. At the same time, this meeting cautioned that work should proceed only as conditions became ripe, and thus it set no deadlines.[72] The Chengdu Conference also concluded that the Three Gorges dam by itself could not fundamentally solve the flood problem on the Yangtze.[73]

Until the Chengdu Meeting, the major contention of the dam proponents had been that the project would enable a breakthrough in taming the Yangtze. The conclusion at Chengdu both that the dam alone could not resolve the major flooding problem and that the dam must be evaluated in terms of hydropower and navigation as well as flood control, therefore, undercut the most powerful argument the YVPO had used to date. This more complex analytical framework underlay the seven relationships noted above.

Thus, the Chengdu Conference formally ratified the Three Gorges project, but proposed envisioning it as a multi-purpose project for which technical issues and economic issues had to be resolved before construction could begin. It called for research on these problems within the context of a dam no more than 200 meters in height.[74] This meeting, in sum, produced a conditional decision: to build the dam but to make substantial efforts first to resolve key technical problems. According to Li Rui, Mao Zedong was sufficiently concerned over the technical difficulties and the magnitude of the project to adopt a cautious stance. At the same time, Mao *may* have decided to forge ahead in constructing the Danjiangkou dam on the Han River. If so, the Chairman probably desired to do something dramatic to save the Hubei peasants in the area from the scourge of almost biennial flooding of the Han that had been occurring. The Dan-

[71] Again, all pertinent information comes from Li Rui, *Lun Sanxia* (p. 10). No text of the resolution itself is available, and the documents available from the Chengdu Meeting do not discuss the Three Gorges project.

[72] The Resolution stated that, "Considering the long term economic development and technical conditions of the state, the Three Gorges Water Resources project should be built and can be built. However, it is necessary to wait until the preparatory work on important aspects has basically been completed before a final decision on building and on timing can be taken." Li Rui, *Lun Sanxia*, p. 3.

[73] Li Rui, *Lun Sanxia*, pp. 3-4.

[74] Li Rui, *Lun Sanxia*, p. 102.

jiangkou decision might also have reduced pressure on the Chairman for immediate action on the Three Gorges dam, for China obviously lacked the ability to put both of these huge projects into construction simultaneously.[75] As detailed below, the hasty Danjiangkou dam decision, based on inadequate planning, produced much subsequent waste and heartache.

There is a troubling anomaly between Mao's impetuous decision on Danjiangkou (and on many other matters that came up at the Chengdu Meeting) and his supposed caution on the Three Gorges issue. Li Rui claims that the Chairman recognized the validity of Li's own views, perhaps with the help of some additional counsel by Zhou Enlai. While this is possible, it is sufficiently out of character for Mao at the time that an alternative explanation merits consideration.

Namely, the two decisions on Three Gorges and Danjiangkou in 1958 possibly resulted from the Chinese equivalent of "ward politics." During his tour of Sichuan and Hubei provinces in early 1958, Mao dealt with two strong provincial leaders on this dam. Li Jingquan, the powerful head of Sichuan and an early and ardent supporter of Mao's Great Leap Forward, almost certainly strongly opposed the Three Gorges project. Wang Renzhong, who besides being a Long March cadre and the leader of Hubei was also a swimming partner of the Chairman,[76] likely lobbied for the dam. Mao may have found the dam appealing as a grand project to help the peasants but preferred not to ignore Li Jingquan's objections (supported by Zhou Enlai and others [77]). Mao may therefore have ordered early construction of Danjiangkou as a temporary sop to Wang Renzhong[78] while retaining a personal commitment (and enthusiasm) for construction of the Three Gorges dam. Zhou Enlai, by contrast, may have looked upon his responsibility for managing the subsequent technical studies to be done on the Three Gorges proposal as a vehicle for temporizing on actual construction of the dam.

1958-60: The Momentum Fades

Whatever the dynamics of the Chengdu Meeting, a May 1958 article suggested the new timetable for Three Gorges: "outline planning" to be

[75] Professor David M. Lampton has been helpful to our thinking on this issue.

[76] Tracey Strong and Helene Keyssar, "Anna Louis Strong: Three Interviews With Chairman Mao Zedong," *China Quarterly*, no. 103 (September 1985), p. 493.

[77] Including, possibly, Deng Xiaoping. Deng was a close friend of Li Jingchuan and was himself a native of Sichuan. As of early 1958 Mao was giving Deng strong support and had made him one of the few key generalists among the top 25 to 35 leaders.

[78] On Danjiangkou's subsequent record in reducing the flood threat to Hubei peasants, see: *Xiandai Zhongguo shuili jianshe.*

completed in 1959 and "initial [concrete] planning" to be finished in 1962. This article noted that some 4,000 to 6,000 people were already regularly involved in work on the Three Gorges.[79] At some point in 1958, also, the YVPO submitted a "Report on Major Points in the Initial Design of the Three Gorges Water Resources Project."[80]

For June 5-16, 1958, a major conference in Wuhan brought together 260 people from over eighty units to review the technical elements in the construction of the Three Gorges dam. The MWREP, the Chinese Academy of Sciences, the First Ministry of Machine Building, and the YVPO jointly prepared this conference. To judge from press reports, while confirming the desirability of building the dam, it stressed the enormous technical difficulties that had to be resolved for successful construction.[81] In any event, preliminary design work on the Three Gorges dam began in 1958, based on a presumed dam height of 190 to 200 meters. Lin Yishan took charge of the project, and Mao reportedly favored the effort.[82] Some initial physical preparations for the dam's construction reportedly began the following month, taking Sandouping as the dam site.[83] Activities concerning the eventual construction of the Three Gorges dam continued after mid-1958. Premier Zhou convened a meeting on the development of the Yangtze during the Beidaihe Conference in the last half of August 1958, and at this meeting he gave instructions concerning the Three Gorges proposal. Reportedly, these included support for Sandouping as the likely dam site.[84] One report indicates that by October 1958 a basic decision had been taken in favor of a 200-meter-high dam at the Sandouping site.[85] In the early 1980's, however, the Chinese indicated to American specialists that the Sandouping site was confirmed only in a 1960 report on site selection that had been drawn up on the basis of site visits by both Chinese and Soviet experts.

Parenthetically, the history of site selection reflects a recurring pat-

[79] The same article described the proposed dam as being 200 meters high with a generating capacity of 13.4 million watts: *Wenhuibao* (Shanghai), May 4, 1958.

[80] Gao Xia, "Jushi zhumu," p. 5. As noted above, the step from outline planning to actual design represents significant advancement along the decision line for a large project.

[81] On the conference, see: *Renmin ribao*, June 18, 1958 and Gao Xia, "Jushi zhumu," p. 5.

[82] *Xin guancha banyuekan*, June 16, 1958.

[83] *Water Resources of China*, p. 108.

[84] *Ibid.*, p. 107; and Gao Xia, "Jushi zhumu," p. 5. The Beidaihe Conference brought together the key leaders from all provinces, and thus Zhou may well have seized this opportunity to convene a separate caucus on a matter of such vital concern to the key provinces involved. At this meeting, Mao put Chen Yun and Li Xiannian in charge of water resource work for the coming year.

[85] *Water Resources of China*, p. 108.

tern. Formally resolved no later than 1960, the issue reappeared when the project moved high up on the national agenda again in the late 1970's. In several instances, formal decisions on this dam have been made, only to be opened again. Initiatives by Three Gorges promoters cause the opposition to coalesce and reverse the decision.

Thus, during 1958 the Chinese decided to begin construction of the Danjiangkou dam on the Han River. Although preliminary planning for the Danjiangkou dam began at the time of the major survey work on the Yangtze,[86] the decision to begin construction may have been primarily politically motivated. This hasty decision was, nevertheless, rationalized in part by noting that resolution of the technical issues at Danjiangkou could subsequently provide experience for the Three Gorges project. These issues were to have been addressed by 1960,[87] the year in which the first major feasibility study for the Three Gorges dam (begun in 1958) was scheduled for completion.[88] In 1970, as noted below, a similar rationale became part of the justification for beginning actual construction on the Gezhouba dam.

By late 1961, the costs of the accelerated and careless construction pace of the Great Leap years became clear at Danjiangkou. Work at that dam ceased upon discovery that substandard concrete had been used in the construction to that point. The national economic crisis growing out of the collapse of the Great Leap meant few resources were available to devote to the mammoth reconstruction job now needed to salvage the Danjiangkou project. Work on Danjiangkou resumed only in late 1964. Indeed, a decision was then made to build Danjiangkou in two stages. The first stage initially came on line in 1967, but this stage was not fully operational until 1973, long after the scheduled completion of the project.[89] Similar problems of inadequate planning, leading to major construction stoppages and large cost overruns, would subsequently plague the Gezhouba project, too.

Turning back to the Three Gorges proposal itself, during 1958-60 intensive research efforts involving many units probed technical questions related to the project. Reportedly, from the June 1958 meeting on technical questions until some point in 1960 over two hundred units and

[86] *Renmin Changjiang*, No. 4, 1982, p. 1.

[87] *Xinhua banyuekan*, No. 12 (1959), p. 79.

[88] Although specific evidence on this point is lacking, it is very likely that Lin Yishan and the YVPO opposed the quick decision in 1958 to build the Danjiangkou dam. Lin felt that the Three Gorges dam was critical to flood control work on the Yangtze, his chief concern. He may well have seen the Danjiangkou work as an ill-conceived diversion of scarce resources from the main project at hand.

[89] *Renmin Changjiang*, No. 4 (1982), p. 1.

roughly 10,000 scientific and technical personnel participated in related research. The only available comment on the results of this crash effort is that, "Fourteen major issues were resolved to varying degrees."[90]

The YVPO also tried to move the Three Gorges question from the long-term planning stage to an annual plan item for construction. Whereas in 1957-58 the discussion had taken place primarily in terms of the long-term plan (*guihua*) for the project, in 1960 the YVPO submitted a "Construction Proposal and Preparatory Construction Plan for the Three Gorges Water Resources Project" (*Sanxia shuili shuniu shigong fangan he shigong zhunbei jihua*). This momentum for moving the project from the research to construction stage was cut short in 1960, however, by the onset of the deep economic depression.[91]

In short, the period 1958-60 witnessed several efforts to mobilize the resources and technical know-how to go beyond the hedged decision of March 1958 and select a firm date for initiating dam construction. There is some evidence that momentum behind actual dam construction picked up during this period. For example, Li Rui was purged at the Lushan Conference in 1959.[92] Lin's YVPO continued to try to move the Three Gorges decision-making process ahead into the concrete planning and design stages. Nevertheless, technical problems remained, and the Danjiangkou project drained important resources from a potential early Three Gorges project construction effort.

The 1960 economic tailspin, moreover, provided dramatic evidence that the national situation was no longer "ripe" (in the terminology of the Three Gorges opponents) for undertaking a construction project of the magnitude of the Three Gorges dam. Soon thereafter, the folly of having undertaken the Danjiangkou dam without adequate planning also became obvious. The opponents of Three Gorges dam construction had continued to fight the dam even during the most intensive period of the Great Leap, and the changes in the national situation had by late 1960

[90] Gao Xia, "Jushi zhumu," p. 5.

[91] Gao Xia, "Jushi zhumu," p. 5.

[92] In one place, Li Rui suggests that he was purged for his stance at the Nanning Meeting and for related activities: Li Rui, *Lun Sanxia*, pp. 2 and 4. In another publication, however, he indicates that he fell because he was too close to Zhou Xiaozhou who in turn, according to Li, was the individual who persuaded Peng Dehuai to write his "letter of opinion" to Mao Zedong: Li Rui, *Huainian shi pian*, pp. 63-66. After his purge at Lushan, Li Rui was posted to a wilderness area in the North for two years. He returned to Beijing in late 1961 because of deteriorating health. After living "idly and alone" in Beijing for two years, in December 1963 Li became a cultural worker at a hydropower station in the Dabie Mountains. He made one brief visit back to Beijing in 1967. In the early 1970's, Li was imprisoned in the Beijing suburbs, but by 1976 he again labored in the Dabie Mountains. These biographical items are culled from *Huainian shi pian, passim*. Li was rehabilitated in 1979.

provided decisive supporting evidence for their continuing criticisms. The Three Gorges dam project moved to the back burner.

To summarize, during the 1950's the top political leaders received conflicting advice on the Three Gorges dam proposal from their water resources and their electric power experts, as well as from the various affected provinces. Nothing that occurred during these years seems to have changed the basic opinions of these bureaucratic officials regarding this dam, and these opinions generally conformed closely to those one would expect on the basis of the tasks and interests of the units themselves. At the apex of the system, Zhou Enlai managed the discussion, but Mao Zedong retained the power to decide the issue in whatever way he deemed fit. Mao decided against immediate construction of the Three Gorges dam, but his ill-conceived decision at the same time on the Danjiangkou dam suggests that he had the power (and the inclination) to override technical concerns in order to forge ahead with a project that could meet political objectives. That Mao decided against immediate construction of a high dam at the Three Gorges, therefore, may have reflected primarily Li Rui's personal closeness with the Chairman or other such idiosyncratic rather than systemic factors. Mao, as indicated above, may have decided in favor of the Danjiangkou dam on the basis of provincial politics. But the Chairman did not feel constrained by a need to protect the interests and resources of each of the major pertinent bureaucratic actors.

1960-78: Frustration for the Dam Proponents

During 1960-78 the Three Gorges dam proponents repeatedly tried to revive the momentum behind the project, especially during the preparatory period for each subsequent five year plan. They adjusted their arguments and approaches to the prevailing national priorities. Thus, they recommended building the dam in stages so as to provide for a relatively quick start-up of electrical power generation when in 1964 Mao decided that national security reasons dictated more rapid industrial development of the Southwest. The dam proponents also continued to do additional studies pertinent to eventual dam construction. But on balance the advocates experienced a period of nearly two decades of frustration. Their major initiatives were quashed by larger national events—the Cultural Revolution in 1966 (which produced such chaos that no project like the Three Gorges dam could be undertaken in 1966-68) and the Sino-Soviet war scare in 1969-70 (which caused the dam to be postponed because of the tempting target it might make for Soviet military planners). Only with the deaths of Zhou and Mao, the resurgence of the national econ-

305

omy, and the initiation of an all-out effort to achieve the "four modern-izations" could the Three Gorges dam be restored to a high place on the national agenda at the end of the 1970's.

No detailed information is available on discussion of the dam during 1960-63. Zhou Enlai opined to a visiting Vietnamese delegation in April 1961 that it would take "an historical period" to construct the dam at Three Gorges and that "this cannot be rushed and cannot be done in a casual way." Zhou, nevertheless, strongly affirmed that the dam would eventually be built.[93] In 1963, when hearing a briefing (*huibao*) on the Three Gorges project, Mao purportedly emphasized the importance of careful investigation of the long term silting problem.[94]

Additional studies took place during 1963-66. In the latter half of 1964 Mao decided that the Third Five Year Plan must provide resources for construction of the "third front" of industry in the Southwest to be available in case war with the United States materialized.[95] Lin Yishan recognized the resulting premium on electric power generation for the Southwest, and he therefore recommended a staged construction of the Three Gorges dam that would permit initial power generation after an investment of only 1.7 billion yuan. Premier Zhou handed this report over to the Ministry of Water Resources and Electric Power for study, and the Ministry rejected Lin's proposal.[96]

In 1966 the YVPO followed up with a "Report on Design Issues on the Yangtze Three Gorges" directly to Mao and the Party Center. This re-port suggested a staged construction of the Three Gorges dam, with the first stage at 115 meters, the second rising to 150 meters, and the final dam being built to 190-200 meters. This approach would permit the in-stallation and operation of generators long before completion of the final dam and would stretch out overall construction of the high dam without sacrificing the income that initial electrical generation would produce. This Report suggested that actual construction commence in 1968.[97] Many years later, American dam specialists were told that a decision in favor of a one-stage approach to the Three Gorges was taken in 1966. In

[93] Li Rui, *Lun Sanxia*, p. 10.

[94] *Ibid.* Since Mao heard this report in Wuhan, he was probably receiving a briefing from the YVPO, which is headquartered there.

[95] Fang Weizhong, ed., *Jingji dashiji*, p. 385.

[96] Recall that before the 1970's the YVPO was directly under Zhou and not under the MWREP. It may well be that by this time the anti-Three Gorges electric power people dominated the MWREP. This had certainly become the case by the late 1970's. Zhou's decision to send the YVPO report to the MWREP, therefore, may have been intended to torpedo the report. Information on the 1964 proposal comes from: Li Rui, *Lun Sanxia*, pp. 10-11.

[97] Li Rui, *Lun Sanxia*, p. 11.

the event, however, the Cultural Revolution quickly rendered the whole question moot, as the necessary organizational, financial, and technical conditions for commencing construction of such a massive project could not possibly have been put together during the chaos that ensued from late 1966 through 1968.

In 1969-70 Beijing tried to put the Chinese economy back together, and preparatory work for the Fourth Five Year Plan began.[98] In early 1969 China also faced major tasks in restoring political and social order and in preparing for what appeared to be a possible imminent outbreak of war with the Soviet Union. Two bloody border clashes had occurred in March, and Moscow issued only slightly veiled threats demanding immediate negotiations as the Chinese convened the Ninth Party Congress in early April.[99] Within this context, the Military Affairs Committee of the MWREP joined with the Hubei Provincial Revolutionary Committee[100] to call for two-stage construction of the Three Gorges dam, with the first stage at 150 meters and the final dam at 190-200 meters.[101] The first available responses from Mao came in September and October 1969. On both occasions, the Chairman said that war preparations precluded moving ahead on Three Gorges at that time.[102]

During 1970 Lin Yishan again tried to move Three Gorges from the *guihua* to the *jihua* stage. On April 24th he submitted a report to Li Desheng, Mao, and Zhou[103] entitled, "On the Issue of the Opportune Moment for Constructing the Key Water Resources Project at Three Gorges." This report argued that both need and capability made it timely to adopt the Three Gorges as a key construction project in the immediate future.[104] On 30 May, however, the MWREP itself submitted a very different suggestion: that work on a power station on the Qingjiang be stopped in favor of first building the Gezhouba dam on the Yangtze. The Wuhan Military District and the Hubei Provincial Revolutionary Com-

---

[98] Details on the five year plan preparatory work are in: Fang Weizhong, ed., *Jingji dashiji*, pp. 460-463.

[99] E.g., on April 11, Moscow called for negotiations to begin by April 14, or soon thereafter: *Pravda*, April 12, 1969.

[100] Hubei Province, as noted above, would be one of the largest beneficiaries of a high dam at Three Gorges.

[101] While this suggestion was submitted in April, it is not known whether it was prepared in time for the Ninth Party Congress or whether it was discussed at that Congress.

[102] Li Rui, *Lun Sanxia*, p. 11.

[103] It is not clear why Li Desheng was involved in this, but the wording of Li Rui's volume implies that Li Desheng was the primary recipient of this report. Li Desheng is originally from Hubei province and may have taken a special interest in this project.

[104] Lin must have had in mind the construction plan for the Five Year Plan that was then under consideration.

mittee supported this MWREP position in a formal joint report that in the final analysis served as the basis for the decision to move ahead first on Gezhouba. Gezhouba, according to this report, would be completed in 1975, at a total cost of 1.3 billion yuan. It would provide additional electricity for the development of western Hunan, western Hubei, western Henan, and eastern Sichuan provinces.[105] The MWREP added that during the following eight years, work on the Three Gorges could be finished.

In a letter to Zhou Enlai on December 27th Lin Yishan opposed this priority to Gezhouba construction. Gezhouba, like Danjiangkou before it, was seen in part as a testing ground for resolving key technical issues for Three Gorges, in this case especially problems concerning unprecedentedly large locks and certain silting questions.[106] Lin's December letter argued, instead, that China already had the technical wherewithal to build the dam at Three Gorges without first constructing Gezhouba.[107]

Zhou Enlai sided, on balance, with those who wanted to give priority to construction of Gezhouba. In his letter to Mao on the subject, Zhou emphasized military security (China should not build the Three Gorges dam until the international situation and China's anti-aircraft capability permitted it) and the need to acquire more experience. China decided in 1970 to begin construction of Gezhouba.[108]

As had been the case with the Danjiangkou dam, inadequate initial planning on a range of technical issues—transport, silting, and geology—plagued subsequent work on Gezhouba.[109] Work on Gezhouba had to be suspended in 1972 while redesign efforts took place. Zhou Enlai convened a three day meeting of the State Council on Gezhouba in 1972, at which the Premier sharply criticized the MWREP for mishandling work on the Yangtze and not properly summarizing experiences on the engineering problems that had been encountered at Danjiangkou. The 1972 redesign effort produced a large increment in both investment and the size of the Gezhouba construction force and pushed back the anticipated date of completion until 1981.[110] In reality, however, the Gezhouba dam experienced subsequent delays that moved the expected completion

[105] Fang Weizhong, ed., *Jingji dashiji*, pp. 471-472.

[106] Also, like Danjiangkou before it, the Center may have agreed to build Gezhouba as part of a strategy for bolstering support among Hubei provincial leaders.

[107] Construction of Gezhouba first would also complicate subsequent construction of Three Gorges because it would raise the water level considerably at the Sandouping site.

[108] Li Rui, *Lun Sanxia*, pp. 11-12.

[109] As noted above, the first stage of Danjiangkou came on stream only in 1973: *Renmin Changjiang*, No. 4 (1982), p. 1.

[110] Li Rui, *Lun Sanxia*, p. 12; Li Rui, *Huainian shi pian*, p. 74.

date to 1989. It incurred enormous cost overruns[111] and its work force grew to some 50,000 (including support personnel). It did, nevertheless, produce the necessary additional experience in the construction of locks of the length and width (although not necessarily of the depth) required for the Three Gorges project.

The issue of the appropriate dam site for Three Gorges arose again in 1972, possibly because of site problems that had been encountered at Gezhouba. Further studies examined the relative merits of the Sandouping and Taipingxi sites, and in 1978 a "Report on the Supplementary Design Stage for the Three Gorges Water Resources Project Site Selection" was completed. This report, in turn, led the State Council to entrust the Ministry of Water Resources to convene a May 1979 conference on dam site selection for Three Gorges.[112]

There is no record of renewed debate over the Three Gorges project during the planning for the Fifth Five Year Plan (1976-1980) in 1975-76. This probably reflected the fact that both the setbacks on Gezhouba and the continuing commitment to priority construction of that dam precluded any possibility of including the Three Gorges dam in this five year plan. That some preparatory work for Three Gorges continued during this period is, nonetheless, suggested by the fact that in 1976 a Bureau for the Protection of the Environment Against Pollution at the Three Gorges was established.

In sum, the period 1960-78 saw the Three Gorges proponents continue to try to turn the conditional decision of 1958 into an actual start-up date for the project. Unsettled national politics never permitted the sustained period of necessary stability to make this a realistic proposal.

During the period from the early to the late 1970's changes occurred that had potentially enormous significance for the Three Gorges project. Early in the decade, the YVPO lost its direct reporting relationship to Premier Zhou and became subordinate to the MWREP, reporting directly to its minister.[113] In 1976, both Zhou and Mao, who together had played decisive roles regarding actual Three Gorges dam construction, passed away.

[111] Gezhouba was originally budgeted for 1.3 billion yuan. As of 1984 the budget had grown to 4.0 billion yuan: Li Rui, *Lun Sanxia*, p. 103, and USBR 1984 Trip Report, p. 32. The final cost of the dam could climb still higher.

[112] Gao Xia, "Jushi zhumu," and information provided by the Chinese to American dam specialists. As explained below, in February 1979 the MWREP was again divided into separate Ministries of Water Resources and of Electric Power.

[113] Zhang Wenbi was the Minister in 1972-75, at which time he became the commander of the Zhejiang Military District. We have no information about his views on the Three Gorges project. In 1975 Madame Qian Zhengying became Minister, and in the 1980's Madame Qian emerged as one of the Three Gorges project's strongest proponents.

After Mao's death, events moved the Three Gorges project toward inclusion in the five year plan. Resumption of Gezhouba construction with the end (supposedly) in sight meant that the Three Gorges project could begin to return to center stage. Also, the general reestablishment of order during 1977-78 created a situation where the Chinese again had the potential organizational capabilities to construct a high dam on the Yangtze. In addition, the tremendous surge in construction and the December 1978 Third Plenum decision to give national priority to economic modernization highlighted the need for increased electric power generation to feed the appetite of China's growing industrial base.[114] This rapidly growing demand for electricity had mixed implications for the development of the Three Gorges dam, as the dam promised a quantum leap in electrical generating capacity—but only after at least ten years of mammoth investment at the cost of potential shorter term sources of electricity. Nevertheless, the general optimism associated with adoption of the ambitious ten-year plan in 1978 probably encouraged each ministry to push for its favorite major projects, and for the Ministry of Water Resources this included the Three Gorges dam.

1979: Dam Proponents Nearly Succeed

The Three Gorges project received serious attention in 1979 within the context of preparations for the Sixth Five Year Plan (1981-85). Nevertheless, the Three Gorges' reemergence in the midst of the 1979-80 general retrenchment suggests the possibility that Lin Yishan and MWREP Minister Qian Zhengying had obtained backing at the State Council and/or Politburo level—possibly from Wang Renzhong, who became a Vice Premier in December 1978[115]—for an effort to begin early construction of the dam. In February 1979 the MWREP again separated into individual Ministries of Electric Power and of Water Resources. As noted above, the electric power officials had generally been far less enthusiastic about the Three Gorges proposal than were the water resources officials, and yet the electric power side had dominated the combined ministry. Speculatively, the division of the MWREP thus may have sought to enhance

---

[114] For example, the major expansion and modernization of a steel plant in Wuhan in the mid 1970's had resulted in a modern facility that could run at full capacity only if it were able to use virtually all the electricity then available to all of Hubei province.

[115] Recall that Wang had headed Hubei province in the 1950's and was a strong supporter of the Three Gorges dam. Additional backing *may* also have come from Hua Guofeng, who had spent much of his career in Hunan Province, another potential major Three Gorges dam beneficiary.

the ability of the water resources people to encourage construction of Three Gorges dam.

A ministry is expected to speak with one voice when reflecting views to the State Council and its commissions. Qian Zhengying may have had to adopt ministerial positions against the dam as head of a combined ministry dominated by Three Gorges project opponents, and the YVPO under her would have been similarly handicapped. Dividing the ministry would at least give Qian (and the YVPO, which stayed with the Water Resources side) a better ability to make the case for the Three Gorges project. The new Water Resources Ministry became a part of the bureaucratic system led by the State Agricultural Commission. In February 1979 Wang Renzhong assumed leadership of this Commission.

A February 1979 proposal to the State Council on the organizational setup of the YVPO supports this conjectured linkage between the division of the MWREP and freer advocacy of the Three Gorges dam. Lin submitted his proposal on 11 February, and the newly rehabilitated Li Rui lost no time in sending the State Council leaders a very critical commentary on 5 March. Lin responded in kind, and the three documents were then collated into a July 1979 *Collection of Materials on the Three Gorges Question.*[116]

From Li Rui's response, it appears that Lin Yishan argued in support of: dividing the MWREP into its constituent ministries; building a high dam at the Three Gorges whose primary purpose would be flood control; and having the State Council put construction of this and other large dams under the direction of a Vice-Premier. Essentially, Lin's "Proposal" thus aimed at putting Three Gorges construction under a separate Ministry of Water Resources that would be answerable to a particular Vice-Premier (Wang Renzhong?).[117] Lin also cited the example of the US Bureau of Reclamation and the US Army Corps of Engineers to argue that the Ministry of Water Resources should sell to the Ministry of Electric Power the electricity generated by the Three Gorges dam.[118] Lin's

---

[116] Of these documents, only the rebuttal by Li Rui is available. The text is in: Li Rui, *Lun Sanxia,* pp. 100-105. Lin Yishan's February 11 proposal was entitled, "Guanyu Changjiang Liuyu Guihua Bangongshi jigou wenti de jianyi."

[117] Had electric power been the main purpose of the dam it seems possible that the project would have been handed over to the Ministry of Electric Power, which almost certainly would have doomed the Three Gorges dam proposal. On the Ministry of Electric Power's vocal opposition to the Three Gorges dam as of early 1979, see "Smaller Hydro Projects May Get Priority Over Huge Yangzi Gorge Plan," *The China Business Review* (July-August 1979), p. 58.

[118] Li Rui countered this particular point with the assertion that America's situation was totally different from China's and that this solution would create havoc in the financial and other pertinent bureaucratic systems.

proposal, in short, appears to have sought by organizational means to remove the Ministry of Electric Power from a direct role in decision making on the Three Gorges project and to use the resulting increment in power of the Water Resources officials to build a high dam primarily suited to flood control.

Li Rui's rebuttal cited Mao's and Zhou's insistence at the 1958 Chengdu Conference on limiting the height of the dam, making the dam a multi-use structure, and resolving all technical issues before beginning construction.[119] Li also argued in general for priority on multiple-use projects, regardless of the particular organizational arrangements. Consequently, as Li noted, the Ministry of Electric Power had already suggested formation of a Committee on the Multipurpose Utilization of River Valleys with membership representing the Ministries of Water Resources, Electric Power, Communications, Agriculture, Forestry, Aquatic Products, Environmental Protection (and, when necessary, relevant provinces and cities) under the unified leadership of the State Planning Commission. Li also caustically reviewed the cost overruns and other problems that had arisen with Gezhouba because it had been started without adequate preparation, and then noted that the disaster would have been larger by orders of magnitude had the central leadership in 1970 accepted Lin Yishan's position that the Three Gorges dam should be built immediately (rather than first building Gezhouba to gain experience).

Thus, Li Rui tried to block the immediate commencement of work on the Three Gorges dam by attacking Lin Yishan's suggested bureaucratic changes primarily on the ground that they would produce a dam too singly designed for flood control. Li also made an impassioned argument that the development of hydropower and the development of China's electrical power grids were inseparable—and therefore that the Ministry of Electric Power must have a key role in the construction of all major hydropower projects. Li's own proposal called for replacing the YVPO with a Yangtze Valley Planning Committee under the Ministry of Water Resources, with all authority over hydropower given to the Ministry of Electric Power. As noted above, Li also wanted the SPC to establish and lead a special committee to resolve the problems inherent in multi-use development of major river projects.[120] Thus, SPC head and Vice Premier Yu Qiuli, rather than the decidedly pro-Three Gorges Vice Premier Wang Renzhong, would effectively become the main leader responsible for Three Gorges project deliberations.

[119] Li noted acidly that Lin neglected to mention these facts in his "Opinion."
[120] The above paragraphs draw from Li Rui, *Lun Sanxia*, pp. 100-105.

Li Rui lost the argument. An early April YVPO report[121] to the State Council called for an early start on building the Three Gorges dam. On April 26, 1979, the State Council convened a meeting to discuss the Three Gorges dam issue, and it invited Lin Yishan and Qian Zhengying to participate. At this meeting, Lin, Qian, "and several vice-premiers" agreed that an early start should be made on the dam—specifically, that dam construction should begin in 1981 or 1982. The representative(s) from Sichuan province urged greater caution on the basis of the refugee, financial, and hydropower questions.[122] In May 1979 Lin Yishan convened a meeting to discuss site selection based on the premise that the dam would be included in the Sixth Five Year Plan and that construction would begin in 1981 or 1982.[123]

Up to this point in this narrative, the data available have permitted discussion only of major decision points and a few of the key actors in this drama. Beginning with the May 1979 site selection conference, however, the curtain begins to lift on a wider range of individuals and units that were brought into the pertinent deliberations. Unfortunately, there is no way to know to what extent these same units played a role in the deliberations of the 1950's to 1970's. Probably, a substantial and widespread bureaucratic involvement in this matter existed in the 1950's, but the key decisions on the issue were made by Mao—and the Chairman's most important advisor on it was Zhou Enlai. Mao and Zhou, moreover, retained the power to ride roughshod over the views of the affected bureaucratic units. Other slightly lower level leaders—Wang Renzhong, Li Jingquan, and so forth—became involved as advocates on one side or another, but they lacked either decision making or veto power on this issue. As of 1979-80, however, it appears that the evolution of the Chinese system had produced a wider range of participants—and that the participants increasingly felt free to articulate and defend their real views.[124]

The May 1979 meeting on site selection began around May 10th with all the participants visiting the possible sites (Sandouping and Taipingxi) by boat. Upon their return, they met in Wuhan until May 24th. The more than 200 participants included professors, specialists and technicians involved in water resources, hydropower, geography and earthquakes, shipping and communications, machine manufacturing, and en-

---

[121] Entitled: "Guanyu Changjiang liuyu guihua he Sanxia gongcheng huibao tigang": Li Rui, *Lun Sanxia*, p. 108. No full text is available.

[122] Zhao Ziyang headed Sichuan province at this time.

[123] Li Rui, *Lun Sanxia*, p. 12. Note that the site selection conference was a natural follow-up to the report on site selection that had been submitted in 1978, as noted above.

[124] This possibility is explored more thoroughly in our concluding chapter.

vironmental protection. A reference report prepared by three Xinhua reporters provides our major source of information on this meeting.[125] According to this report, the meeting could not reach a final agreement on site selection, but the discussion produced a number of important points.

First, "lingering fear" from earlier political troubles still kept many people from speaking their minds, according to the Xinhua report. Of those who did speak up, the YVPO representatives were the most enthusiastic supporters of making a quick start on the project. Indeed, the Xinhua report notes that a number of people at the YVPO had chosen careers in water resources in the first place only because they had been inspired by the dream of building a dam at the Three Gorges. The report also noted that quite a few experts and scientists at the meeting supported the idea of building such a dam "relying on our own strength" during their lifetimes.

But had conditions yet become "ripe" for such an undertaking? The YVPO and "comrades from some units" argued that after site selection, the final design study could be completed in the latter half of 1980 and construction of the dam could begin shortly thereafter. "Some representatives from central state organs and scientific research units," by contrast, felt that deficiencies in the YVPO's preparatory work demanded at least two or three more years of investigation before work could begin on the dam. In their opinion, to have the State Council issue an order to start construction based on the YVPO's reports and the "promises of a minister"[126] would be irresponsible.[127] But disagreement extended beyond this issue.

On the issue of a dam site, the YVPO and those who build protective engineering projects (*fanghu gongcheng*) favored the Taipingxi site; the shipping and construction departments favored the Sandouping site; and others felt that they lacked sufficient information to make a well-grounded decision. Regarding the flood control function of the dam, the YVPO's April report to the State Council had claimed (as the YVPO had been saying since the 1950's) that the Three Gorges dam would, "provide the key for basically resolving the flooding question on the Yangtze." Many technical people at the conference disputed this, arguing that at best the dam would provide protection for the area downstream as far as Wuhan. The region below Wuhan would not be well protected by the dam. The YVPO had also claimed that the Three Gorges dam would per-

---

[125] The text of this report is printed in: Li Rui, *Lun Sanxia*, pp. 106-113.

[126] Qian Zhengying?

[127] Li Rui, *Lun Sanxia*, p. 107.

mit transfer of Yangtze water to the North, but some at this conference argued that the power generation and transport requirements would not leave enough additional water to make this feasible. Some representatives raised a concern about possible effects on fish migration (especially of the Yangtze sturgeon, which migrates through the Three Gorges to spawn in Sichuan), but no experts attended from the relevant bureaus to speak to this issue.

Others voiced concern that the YVPO had not yet used experiments with physical models to study the silting and transportation problems. Potential silt-related difficulties might assume many forms: silt deposits could make it difficult to keep the harbor at Chongqing open, thus rendering useless one of the most important shipping benefits (the ability to get 10,000 ton tows up to Chongqing) promised from the project; the water action could deposit silt at the mouths of tributaries, creating an increased flood danger; and large grained silt would create severe friction against the parts of the dam, while finer silt would build up in locks and other areas near the dam. This was a matter of great concern to the representatives.

Other critics noted that China lacked the technology for the high voltage power transmission that the YVPO plan demanded and that the YVPO discussion of the refugee problem focused almost exclusively on the peasants, ignoring the problems of relocating the many urban dwellers who would lose their homes and livelihoods. The YVPO calculation that relocation costs for the 1.3 million people displaced by a 200-meter dam would be 3 billion yuan also, it was asserted, may have underestimated the true cost by one hundred percent.

Many of the criticisms of the YVPO plan came from the units most directly involved. For example the plan called for installing twenty-five 1,000-megawatt generators. But the Ministry of Electric Power and the First Machine Building Ministry pointed out that China could build only 300 MW generators and that the largest generators in the world were only 700 MW. Based on international experience, it would take a country typically about ten years to increase by 100 MW the size of the generators it could build. Also, the railway that would have to be built to the site would (according to the Ministry of Railways) take five years to construct, but the State Council deadline would allow far less time than this. The ship lift that the Ministry of Communications demanded in order to maintain navigation would be larger than any ever built, and this would not be feasible.

The Xinhua reporters submitted their *neibu* (internal) report to the central leadership, and upon reading it Li Xiannian reportedly issued a written instruction saying, "We should be cautious in handling the issue

315

of starting up work on the Three Gorges."[128] There is no concrete evidence to indicate whether Li and other top leaders simply were persuaded by the critical arguments raised at the conference—or whether the commitment to pragmatic economic growth and other changes in the system itself now made these leaders unwilling to ignore serious bureaucratic opposition to early construction of the Three Gorges dam. Developments during the ensuing years gave increasing credence to the latter explanation.

1979-82: The Momentum Slips Again

Li Rui maintained his drum beat of opposition to the Three Gorges dam with another written communication to "a central leading cadre" on 12 July 1979. In this, Li made the full case for building smaller dams on the tributaries and undertaking other related flood control work before starting construction of the Three Gorges dam. Li built his case on both economic and technical grounds. In mid-September Chen Yun added his own note of caution, as he sought to make his colleagues take a hard look at financial realities before undertaking too many mammoth projects. Chen argued that the state simply could not afford to have more than one or two huge investment projects in progress during any single five year plan.[129] Whether in response to these arguments or for other reasons, the State Council decided to assign the State Science and Technology Commission to convene a meeting of specialists in either late 1979 or early 1980 to thrash out the scientific aspects of the Three Gorges project.

For unstated reasons, however, the SSTC meeting did not in fact take place until 1983 (when it met under the aegis of the SPC, not the SSTC).[130] During these years, the SSTC was busily involved in working out national energy policy as a whole[131] and thus may simply have decided that a specific convocation on the Three Gorges dam would be premature before this larger framework had been fully articulated. It is also possible that the project simply lost momentum in the general move toward retrenchment that occurred in 1980. Wang Renzhong, as noted above, may have been able to provide high level support to this project

[128] Li Rui, *Lun Sanxia*, p. 13. Li Xiannian at that time was involved in a wide range of general economic issues.

[129] See Chen Yun's speech at a September 18, 1979 Report Meeting convened by the Finance and Economic Commission, in *Zhonggong shiyi ju sanzhong chuanhui*, vol. 1, p. 174.

[130] Li Rui, *Lun Sanxia*, p. 13.

[131] For details, see the section of Chapter Three on the SSTC.

when the retrenchement began in early 1979, but in August 1980 Wan Li replaced Wang as head of the State Agricultural Commission. Wang thus probably at this time lost his formal connection to the Three Gorges project.[132]

Relatively little information is available on the deliberations over the Three Gorges project during 1980-82. In early 1980, the United States began to become involved in the issue, as a team of American specialists spent three weeks in March inspecting the potential dam sites and receiving briefings on the plans for Three Gorges.[133] Some of these specialists decided that the dam was a very poor idea from economic, navigational, and security standpoints, and they communicated this conclusion to Minister Qian Zhengying in their report around March 20th. On April 3rd, several of these people were quoted in the American journal *ENR* as stating that the American delegation had successfully killed the Three Gorges project—a published assertion that reportedly so angered Minister Qian that she ordered a written rebuttal and redoubled her efforts to keep this project on line.[134]

A more constructive and potentially significant US visit took place on 30 April-12 June 1981, when a group representing the US Department of the Interior's Bureau of Reclamation held detailed talks with the Chinese about the Three Gorges dam and made appropriate site visits. This delegation gathered extensive information both on long term problems with which the proposed dam must deal and on the thinking—especially of the YVPO and the MWREP—on the Three Gorges project. The delegation also had talked with other relevant Chinese units, such as the Ministry of Communications.

This delegation adopted a generally positive attitude toward the Three Gorges dam but also encouraged the Chinese to undertake a Bureau of Reclamation type feasibility study that would realistically portray the various benefits and costs of each aspect of the proposed project—and of its possible alternatives. The delegation spent considerable effort in explaining how this type of study is done in the United States and felt it received high level assurances in China that a reasonably comparable ap-

[132] Wan replaced Wang because Wan was a stronger proponent of the agricultural reforms then underway, but as an unintended side effect this personnel change may have decreased the momentum behind the Three Gorges project. Wang retained an interest in the project and joined Zhao Ziyang and Li Peng on an inspection trip of the area in April, 1986. Xinhua Domestic, April 30, 1986, in FBIS, May 1, 1986, p. K-1.

[133] The Americans had gone to China as the first step in a five-year technology assistance program that Vice President Walter Mondale had signed with the Chinese in 1979.

[134] The original article appeared in ENR, April 3, 1980, pp. 12-13. The response ordered by Madame Qian was published in ENR, November 6, 1980, pp. 43-47.

proach would be taken to the Three Gorges project. For the first time since the 1950's, foreign ideas were again beginning to play an important role in the internal Chinese debate on this massive and controversial project.

The 1981 USBR delegation also recommended that the Chinese develop data for dam heights lower than the 200 meter structure then being planned so that Chinese leaders would have reliable information on a full range of options. It called for additional study of the siltation problem, more work on the environmental impact of the dam, further investigation of cofferdam construction and other technical problems, and construction of the dam at Sandouping rather than at Taipingxi. While agreeing with the YVPO that the Three Gorges project is essential for flood control on the Yangtze, this delegation concluded that, "Adequate planning has not been done to properly formulate the project and a feasibility investigation must be completed to determine both physical and economic feasibility." Even given the somewhat harsh wording of this conclusion, however, the overall tone of the visit and its report proved positive,[135] and the MWREP took the recommendations seriously.

The USBR's suggestion of a financial feasibility study produced both results and disputes. As noted previously, in 1982 the Ministry of Finance reportedly was asked for the first time to prepare a financial feasibility study for this project, a task that was still underway in 1984. The shock waves over the haste and lack of adequate planning concerning the Baoshan Iron and Steel Complex had by then reverberated through other areas, and thus the USBR's advocacy of a feasibility study fell on receptive ears at the national level.[136] Nevertheless, as noted above, an article in *Changjiang renmin* in April 1982 ostensibly about the history of the Danjiangkou dam argued against financial feasibility studies on major dam projects in general.[137]

In March 1982 the State Council announced mergers of several ministries and other bodies in order to facilitate changes in leadership and reductions in personnel. One such reorganization was to reconstitute the MWREP out of the Ministries of Water Resources and of Electric Power.

---

[135] E.g., the delegation viewed a feasibility study as potentially a good way to tilt the balance at the State Council in favor of Three Gorges dam construction. The quote is from the USBR Trip Report, p. 18.

[136] There is no evidence as of that time that such a study was under way, however. Curiously, a 1984 USBR team reported that the requirement for a feasibility study had been adopted for all large dam projects as of 1980: See, report of the June-July 1984 visit by the USBR, p. 68.

[137] No. 4, 1982, p. 1. In March 1983, however, Premier Zhao Ziyang stated that water resources work must henceforth give far higher priority to "stressing economic results": *Xiandai Zhongguo shuili jianshe.*

Knowledgeable Chinese have cited another reason for the re-creation of the MWREP. The constant disputes between the two separate ministries fell upon the State Council for settlement, and by putting the two ministries back together, the State Council effectively forced the newly reunited ministry to resolve disputes between electric power and water resource interests internally and reflect only the consensus view to higher levels.[138]

The merger created a delicate balance between power generation and water resources officials. Qian Zhengying, the former MWREP minister and a staunch advocate of the Three Gorges dam, became the new minister. Within a little over a year, Li Peng, the former Minister of Electric Power who had shown little affection for projects like Three Gorges dam in the past, had been promoted from Vice Minister of the MWREP to Vice Premier and assumed the energy portfolio at that level. In the process, the Three Gorges project shifted from the agricultural bureaucratic system to the energy system. By mid-1984, as explained below, the State Council formalized Li Peng's responsibility for this project.[139] Of the four MWREP Vice-Ministers as of mid-1984, two represented the electric power side (Li Daigeng and Zhao Qingfu) and the other two represented water resources (Li Boning and Yang Zhenhuai).[140]

During the remainder of 1982 the YVPO continued the feasibility study for the Three Gorges project, a task which it completed early the following year. This feasibility study assumed a dam height of 150 meters, which may have resulted in part from the recommendations of the USBR team.[141] The MWREP then submitted this study to the State Planning Commission.

1983-84: Another Conditional Decision
To Build the Dam

The SPC, in accordance with instructions given by the State Council, on 3-13 May 1983 convened a large meeting in Beijing to evaluate this study. It brought together over 350 participants who represented sixteen

[138] More details on this matter are presented in the section on the MWREP in Chapter Three.

[139] Note that the State Agricultural Commission was itself abolished at the same time that the MWREP was reconstituted in March 1982.

[140] Li Daigeng and Li Boning became vice-ministers in 1982. Zhao and Yang were promoted later.

[141] The team had not specified 150 meters as the ideal height but, as noted above, had argued for planning for possible dams lower than 200 meters. Unfortunately, no information is available on the process through which the YVPO feasibility study adopted a 150-meter level as the basis for its calculations.

State Council ministries and commissions, the provinces of Sichuan, Hubei, and Hunan, fifty-eight scientific research, design, and construction units and factories, and eleven higher level institutes and universities. The range of participants reflected the SPC's commitment by 1983 to soliciting views widely before deciding to go ahead with a major project.

The SPC meeting divided into specialized groups to consider the various aspects of the feasibility study, with individual groups concerned respectively with: overall planning (*guihua*); the electricity plan; shipping; large-scale electrical generator equipment; hydraulics; engineering; reservoir size; and environmental protection.[142]

A decision on dam height would affect the answers to virtually all the questions about siltation, shipping, reservoir size, relocation, and many other issues. Yao Yilin, who was then serving his last month as head of the SPC,[143] communicated the views of the "central leading cadres" on this issue, saying, "For more than twenty years the debate over the Three Gorges water resources project has concentrated mainly on the question of dam height. It is obvious and easy to understand that a higher dam will generate more electricity and provide more flood control benefits. But it will also inundate more, require more investment, and cannot obtain the approval of the masses on the upper reaches [of the Yangtze]. The State's financial strength also cannot bear it. But the relevant ministries and locales have not been reconciled to a low dam. We therefore have debated for many years without reaching a decision. If we continue to debate this issue, I believe that our own generation will not be able to accomplish anything on this. . . . I [therefore] propose to the conference that our examination work should be based on the 150-meter water resource proposal submitted by the YVPO. We should not again debate the dam height."[144]

It proved a harbinger of things to come that, while all conference participants formally supported the 150-meter proposed height, several voiced the opinion that a higher dam would be required at some point in the future. To Qinghua University Professor Huang Wenxi this meant that a higher capacity dam should be built now but that the water surface level be held to 150 meters until future requirements demanded that it be raised. The Nanjing Hydrology Institute's Hua Shiqian favored a plan to raise the dam structure itself in the future as the need required. Many others opposed this as being technically difficult and politically unpalat-

[142] Li Rui, *Lun Sanxia*, pp. 13 and 135.
[143] Yao had become head of the SPC in August 1980.
[144] Quoted in Li Rui, *Lun Sanxia*, pp. 135-136.

able to the people who would be living just above the 150-meter level in the coming years.[145]

Interestingly, delegates from Sichuan supported the 150-meter proposal—a posture that, as related below, Sichuan subsequently abandoned.[146]

The subgroups discussing environmental protection and the reservoir size concluded that the size of the relocation problem had been seriously understated. Delegates from Sichuan and Hubei (the two provinces that would have to handle the refugee issue) agreed with this assessment. These people also felt that the estimated budget required for relocation erred significantly on the low side: population growth had occurred in the region that would be inundated; and the newly adopted "responsibility system" in agriculture put additional pressure on the authorities to ensure that the peasants would not lose out financially with this forced move.

Regarding flood control benefits of the dam, experts from the Yellow River Water Resources Commission argued that the Three Gorges dam would not yield the full flood control benefits stipulated by the YVPO feasibility study. They were supported by, among others, representatives from the Hunan Agricultural Committee.

The Ministry of Communications made an extensive and multifaceted critique of the feasibility study's assertions that adequate navigation could be maintained during dam construction and that on balance the dam would improve shipping between Wuhan and Chongqing. The feasibility study made several assertions regarding potential shipping improvements: that better regulation of water discharge below the dam would avoid the current seasonal problem of shallow shoals between Yichang and Wuhan; that the reservoir would dramatically reduce the downstream current speed above the dam, thereby greatly increasing the efficiency of tugs; that the rapids and other dangerous areas above the dam would be eliminated; that greater water depth above the dam would permit much larger tows to be brought farther upstream;[147] and so forth.

---

[145] Some cited the difficult situation that had arisen when the Danjiangkou dam had been raised in several steps.

[146] Sichuan's preferred position had been not to build the dam at all. As of early 1983 the province probably felt that, since it would have to handle the bulk of the refugee problem, the smaller the dam the better. Alternatively, it is possible that the idea of creating a special province to handle the refugee problem—an idea discussed below—had already been broached. If so, Sichuan may have responded, at least at first blush, with qualified support for the dam.

[147] This would have to be done by breaking up tows into smaller barge components to get them through the locks and then reassembling them above the dam. Some literature has mistakenly asserted that the dam would permit 10,000 ton ships to reach Chongqing.

The Ministry of Communications disputed the underlying methodologies used to reach each of these conclusions and claimed that every one of them was false and misleading. The Ministry argued, indeed, that dam construction would seriously disrupt shipping and that post-construction shipping would become more difficult and costly than was the case before the dam was built.

Budget matters also received substantial—and critical—attention. The representatives of the Machine Building Ministry argued that the budget underestimated the Ministry's's costs by about 45 percent. The electric power people, likewise, felt the feasibility study seriously underestimated the costs of power transmission. Sichuan delegates argued against draining funds from water projects to build the Three Gorges dam (the key projects that would suffer were located on the Yangtze tributaries in Sichuan). Indeed, representatives of both Sichuan and the electric power industry argued that critical power shortages would occur in both Sichuan and the middle and lower reaches of the Yangtze if money were put into the Three Gorges dam in lieu of adequate investment in smaller power generation facilities (hydro and thermal) that could come on stream more quickly.

The conference, therefore, produced a mixed net assessment of the feasibility study. It affirmed that some parts of the YVPO report were satisfactory, but that other elements required substantial additional research. The study was better on the main project itself (e.g., direct costs of building the dam) but weak on important ancillary matters (relocation of people and enterprises, environmental effects, technical problems, and so forth). Overall, the economic aspects of the study were not covered adequately, and consideration of political and social issues was incomplete. Significantly, in virtually every known instance, the views expressed by the individual bureaucratic units at this conference conformed to those one would expect based on the unit's primary mission and ethos.

The Ministry of Communications recommended that the dam not be started until all of these issues had received adequate research attention, and the State Council's Technical Economics Research Center's Feasibility Research Specialized Group concurred. No text is available of the actual report on this meeting submitted to the State Council by the SPC,[148] but the meeting reportedly recommended that the State Council adopt

---

In reality, the lock size on any dam contemplated would limit single bottoms to less than 5,000 tons.

[148] Indeed, the above information again comes from Li Rui, *Lun Sanxia*, pp. 135-149, which provides far more detail than is related here.

the YVPO's feasibility study in principle.[149] The SPC agreed that the time had come to build the dam.

In late 1983 Qian Zhengying led an MWREP delegation to the United States and on this trip indicated her desire to have the USBR provide additional technical advisory services on the Three Gorges project in the future. Qian knew from previous advisory work done by the Bureau of Reclamation that the USBR basically supported construction of a dam at the Three Gorges, and thus she may have calculated that future USBR advice would, on balance, strengthen her hand internally in the Three Gorges debate.

The State Council itself took up the Three Gorges dam issue at a meeting in April 1984. This State Council meeting formally approved the YVPO's 1983 feasibility study and called for the construction of a dam of 175 meters in height with a maximum normal water surface of 150 meters, with the actual construction to begin in 1986, the first year of the Seventh Five Year Plan (1986-90). It divided the construction period into three phases: an initial three-year period of preparatory construction; an additional seven years at the end of which the first electricity would be generated by the dam; and a final six years until the entire power capacity of the dam (13,000 MW) would come on line. The State Council at this time called on the YVPO to do a preliminary design study, which would be completed in December 1984.[150] The State Council also asked that an environmental impact report be done, which was also scheduled for completion in 1984 but actually was finished in 1985.[151] Given the serious technical matters that had been raised at the SPC-sponsored May 1983 conference, the State Council instructed, in a manner very much reminiscent of the 1958 and 1979 actions on the dam, that the two-year period until 1986 be devoted to intensive research to answer the key technical unknowns. The State Council decision on maximum normal water surface level (of 150 meters) would provide the nec-

---

[149] Gao Xia, "Jushi zhumu," p. 5. Interviewing in China has supported important parts of Li Rui's reconstruction of this conference. His reconstruction does not, however, provide a basis for understanding why the SPC report basically endorsed the YVPO feasibility study. We lack the concrete data to pinpoint why the SPC adopted this position.

[150] This report would examine details of specifications for power plants, dam design, construction schedules, and so forth. The YVPO had already done much work pertinent to this report even prior to the State Council meeting, but in the final analysis the report was not in fact completed until the late summer of 1985. A final report—the Technical Design Report—would also have to be done to further refine the design work on the major engineering features.

[151] Considerable background work had already been done on this subject. In 1980 the YVPO itself set up its own environmental section in a separate building in its compound in Wuhan to work primarily on Three Gorges environmental issues.

essary baseline for these additional studies.[152] This element of the State Council action, therefore, was crucial to meeting the deadline set by the leaders for initiation of dam construction.

As of the summer of 1984, many Chinese bureaucrats thought that the National People's Congress meeting in the spring of 1985 would give final approval to construction of the Three Gorges dam, thus making it a key investment item in the Seventh Five Year Plan.[153] To oversee and coordinate the many studies that would have to be done in the ensuing two years, the State Council formalized Vice Premier Li Peng's responsibility for this issue by instructing him to set up an appropriate bureaucratic structure under his own aegis to handle these technical efforts. He established the Three Gorges "leadership small group" in mid-1984. During that summer, China also reportedly sought Japan's help in the potential construction of a $9 billion hydropower station at the Three Gorges site.[154]

1984-85: Another Loss of Momentum

In September 1984, only months after the April decision and before the Three Gorges project was formally made a part of the Seventh Five Year Plan, the central premise of the State Council decision—that there would be a maximum normal water surface of 150 meters—came under chal-

---

[152] Building the dam to 175 meters while having a maximum normal water height of 150 meters would increase the ability of the dam to cope with catastrophic flooding while minimizing the need to use flood diversion areas down stream. During the six-month flood season, the normal water surface would be reduced to 135 meters (and down to 130 meters, if necessary) in order to allow for additional flood water storage capacity, as necessary. A sliding scale—depending on the severity and longevity of a flood—of water release and increasing the water retention in the reservoir would be utilized according to a plan in an emergency. If necessary under this scheme, the water level in the reservoir would be allowed to rise to a maximum of over 170 meters for flood control purposes (although this would be required only in the case of a truly extraordinary flood). Generally, water discharges from the Three Gorges dam could be held within the 56,700 cubic meters per second safe channel capacity of the Jingjiang reach for floods of a "one in a hundred year" type (but not for floods of a "one in a thousand year" type). Permanent resettlement, however, would be demanded only of people who lived below the 150 meter maximum normal water surface. The others who lived between the 150 and 175 meter levels would simply be at risk of temporary resettlement. For details, see the 1984 USBR Trip Report, pp. 50-51 and 78.

[153] There was sentiment to submit this as a separate item to the NPC for discussion and approval so that in the future the dam would not be vulnerable to the same type of criticism by the NPC that the Baoshan Steel Complex had suffered several years earlier.

[154] Fujiko Kitani, "Electric Power in China," p. 17.

lenge.[155] Reportedly Chongqing, whose power the economic reform program enhanced, argued for a 180 meter maximum normal water surface—the minimum reservoir level that would permit tows up to 10,000 tons to be brought directly to the city's harbor.[156] A 180-meter level would in fact flood the lower portion of the city, but the municipality, which saw this transport capability as crucial to its long-term growth prospects, was willing to endure the necessary relocation and rebuilding effort.

The Ministry of Communications rapidly joined Chongqing in supporting the 180-meter proposal. Its basic strategy was evidently to support a dam that was so high (thereby causing so much trouble to build and finance) that the project would never be adopted.[157] Reportedly on the basis of some encouragement from Sichuan province, the Jiusan Society, which is one of the "democratic parties" consisting primarily of engineers, undertook its own study of the technical feasibility of the dam. That study highlighted severe technical problems with the project plans. The study circulated widely and had an impact at the State Council level.

In the spring of 1985 the NPC discussed the Three Gorges project and tabled it for further deliberation. The YVPO, as indicated above, completed its Preliminary Design and Environmental Impact Statements during the summer of 1985 and submitted them to higher levels in the fall. In the winter of 1985-86, however, national level economic considerations again intervened to prevent China from moving quickly to a decision to begin actual construction of the dam.

The Chinese economy encountered problems as major urban reforms were attempted beginning in late 1984. Too rapid growth created substantial shortages of capital and produced an alarming reduction in the country's foreign exchange reserves. As a result, the national leaders decided to refrain from any major new capital commitments during 1985-87. This effectively postponed a decision to start construction on the Three Gorges dam until late 1987, at the earliest.

[155] The remainder of this historical section is based primarily on interview data. Sources, therefore, cannot be cited. Most of the information presented has been verified with more than one source. Nevertheless, imputations of motivation and strategy, while reflecting the views of knowledgeable observers, may be wide of the mark.

[156] The 150 meter water level would leave the reservoir over one hundred miles shy of Chongqing.

[157] The Ministry of Communications also demanded redundant and, in the view of some technical specialists, excessive facilities to take care of shipping problems during the dam construction period. This demand for "gold plating" could be aimed at making the project too expensive to build. The YVPO was so anxious to garner support for the dam, though, that it acceded to the Communication Ministry's temporary lock and ship lift requests.

Although actual construction did not move forward in 1986, numerous additional studies of silting, transportation, and other issues were still under way during that year. These generally assumed a 150-meter maximum normal water surface level. As previously noted, however, that water level was called into question and as of early 1986 was itself a topic of serious debate.

Although an enormous amount of study and deliberation had been done over the previous nearly three decades regarding the Three Gorges dam, therefore, the situation in 1986 was broadly analogous to that in late 1958-61: the leaders had decided to build the dam but felt constrained by general economic problems and wanted additional technical studies completed first so as to clarify the options. One of the core premises of these studies, the maximum normal water surface, remained in sharp dispute, and most other outcomes would depend on the decision made on this core issue. Those in charge of overseeing the technical studies on the Three Gorges dam hoped to have the normal water surface issue resolved by the winter of 1986-87. Since the actual water level chosen would likely exceed 150 meters, studies conducted in 1987 would then adjust previous findings accordingly.

Continuity and Changes

To be sure, despite this continuity, a great deal changed during 1958-1986: potential dam heights dropped considerably; the extensive design and feasibility work made initial plans more likely to conform closely to actual outcomes; environmental concerns received increasing attention; more sophisticated methods were developed and applied for studying problems such as silting; and so forth. Also, the objective economic environment changed: the Central and East China economies as of the late 1990's would be ready to absorb all the power generated as the Three Gorges dam came on line. Had the dam been constructed much earlier, the economy of the region would not have effectively utilized its electrical power during its initial years.

The substance of some problems also changed: the immediate regional shortage of electricity grew more pressing; the amount of silt in the Yangtze itself increased substantially; the size of the population in the areas to be inundated increased; and so forth.

Perhaps the most important change, however, was more subtle than any of the above issues. That change concerned the power of the pertinent bureaucratic interests in the decision making over the Three Gorges dam proposal. We therefore turn to the strategies and approaches of the major institutional actors as of the conclusion of this case study in 1986.[158]

THE STATE OF PLAY IN 1986

As of 1986, the preparatory stage of construction on the Three Gorges almost certainly could not begin for another two years.[159] Should the economic situation not stabilize satisfactorily by late 1987, the policy against beginning new construction on a project the size of the Three Gorges would likely be further extended. Even if work began around early 1988, the phase involving intensive investment expenditures would fall into the Eighth rather than the Seventh Five Year Plan.[160] As of 1986, three key matters beyond the many technical issues noted in the above historical presentation remained unresolved—and many bureaucratic units had established relatively clear positions on two of these.

First was the fundamental issue of the maximum normal water surface. Everything else—the inundated land area, refugee relocation problem, silting dynamics, power generation, flood control, financing, and so forth—would depend on this decision, and the studies in 1986 generally assumed that the YVPO feasibility report's 150-meter height would be honored. In reality, however, options under serious consideration during 1986 ranged from 150 to 190 meters, with very strong partisans in favor of virtually every height between 150 and 180 meters. Chongqing favored a 180-meter maximum normal water surface, and the Ministry of Communications, perhaps for quite different reasons, agreed.

Sichuan province reportedly also sought a 180-meter dam.[161] Previously, Sichuan had opposed the Three Gorges dam altogether or, as of 1983, supported a 150-meter dam (so as to minimize refugees) if a structure had to be built at all. Sichuan was also very much concerned that the cost of the project not be taken out of funding for other hydropower

[158] Here and elsewhere, comments on strategies of major institutional actors reflect the considered opinion of knowledgeable individuals about the basic viewpoints of these institutions. This does not imply that every person in the unit agreed with the unit's position or even that the unit articulated this position in a formal document.

[159] Some relatively marginal work was already under way, such as running electrical lines and constructing access roads to the site. This, however, differed from an actual start-up of the initial construction phase.

[160] As previously noted, China decided to establish a fund outside of the Five Year Plan investment pool to tap for start-up costs on the Three Gorges or on any of several other major investment projects on which agreement had not been reached as of the start of the Seventh Five Year Plan.

[161] Some knowledgeable Chinese officials assert that this was Sichuan's position, while others say that this is not true.

developments in the province. The major cost increment in going from 150 to 180 meters, however, is not in dam construction. Rather, it is in refugee resettlement, as the number of refugees involved roughly triples with this 30-meter increase in maximum normal water surface. Sichuan's reported change of heart on the maximum normal water surface issue evidently stemmed, therefore, from an important change in the way the refugee issue would be handled. Instead of making this a task primarily of Sichuan and Hubei provinces (with the former bearing much of the burden), a new province called Three Gorges Province (*Sanxia sheng*) was proposed. This new entity would assume the entire responsibility for refugee resettlement. Under this new approach to the refugee issue, Sichuan's opposition to the dam softened.

Wanxian, the largest city along the Yangtze between Yichang and Chongqing, would benefit most from a normal water surface below 180 meters. At 150 meters the city is about half submerged, and at 160 meters still more urban land is lost. Nevertheless, the major parts to be inundated are from the old sections of the city, and Wanxian municipal officials anticipated a bonanza from a dam with a normal water surface of 160 meters or so. The state would funnel in substantial funds for new building and relocation above the inundation line.[162] More importantly, Wanxian would then become the key port for Sichuan's trade with central China.[163] A normal water surface of 180 meters would, of course, move the major Sichuan port to Chongqing and cause irreparable losses to Wanxian.

Other parties also harbored their own preferences on the maximum normal water surface issue. The MWREP itself inclined toward a 160-meter level, while the YVPO preferred 170 meters. The provinces downstream from the dam, however, generally wanted 150 meters, presumably because they would like the dam built quickly and the lower height would make this both politically and technically more feasible. As of early 1986, the State Council had entrusted the SPC and the SSTC to provide studies to further elucidate the costs and benefits at each level.[164]

[162] These comments on Wanxian reflect the views of key officials in the city. A normal water surface of 160 meters, however, would still leave Wanxian in serious danger of virtually total inundation when major flood waters cascaded down the Yangtze. As previously noted, the plan to contain these waters would permit the water level just behind the dam to rise to just over 170 meters.

[163] It would require only a small extension of existing rail facilities to link the Wanxian port with a trunk line going into the Sichuan interior.

[164] The SSTC in turn set up a special unit, the Three Gorges Science and Technology Office (*Sanxia keji bangongshi*) to focus on this matter, and the SPC may also have organized a special body to handle work related to the Three Gorges project. Reportedly, the Ministry of Communications, Ministry of Machine Building and the Ministry of Electronics also established special units to deal with the Three Gorges project. The YVPO also

The second major unresolved question concerned when to begin actual construction of the dam. Even in the face of the State Council decision of April 1984, debate continued over the best sequence for undertaking the following tasks: building the Three Gorges dam; building smaller dams on the tributaries to the Yangtze in Sichuan; enhancing thermal power capacities for the region; and undertaking other measures, such as improving the dike system, to alleviate somewhat the flood danger. The major problem here remained the extraordinarily long construction time before the Three Gorges dam could be completed. Electricity needs for the whole area continued to grow rapidly in the face of acute shortages. In addition, the Han—Yangtze plain, with the city of Wuhan at its eastern terminus, would face serious danger of catastrophic flooding until major additional efforts at flood control were completed. There remained, therefore, a wide range of opinion about the wisdom of putting major resources into the construction of the Three Gorges dam as a first investment priority.

Sichuan province still wanted to give priority to building smaller dams in the province. For a number of these smaller dams, significant preparatory work had already been done, and they could be completed and generating electricity within 5 to 7 years. Prior construction of these dams would also help to alleviate the flooding and silting problems with which the Three Gorges dam must deal. The MWREP, the YVPO, and the provinces below the proposed Three Gorges dam, by contrast, wanted to begin Three Gorges dam construction as quickly as possible. The State Science and Technology Commission appeared to favor moving cautiously until the important technical issues could be resolved. The attitudes of the other major institutional actors on this matter as of 1986 are not available, and a number of them may have had no strong preferences. The Ministry of Communications preferred that the Three Gorges dam not be constructed at all.

The third basic question concerned finances. Serious consideration of this issue was, however, essentially postponed until the issues of dam height and time to begin construction could be settled. There was, though, some serious thought given to financing the resettlement effort without draining state coffers. The actual amount needed remained unknown for several reasons: the dam height and reservoir size would have an enormous impact on this;[165] there was no agreed methodology for

---

continued work on this issue. The resulting reports were to be coordinated by Li Peng's leadership small group, formed for this purpose. Li would then report the recommendation reached to the State Council itself for a final decision on the dam height.

[165] The resettlement issue was of great importance because of cost as well as because of the political and social instability that could ensue if it were handled improperly. For ex-

determining actual costs; sharp debate continued about the actual number of refugees that would be created at any given maximum normal water surface;[166] and potential methods of financing (and their costs) would depend in part on the time frame during which the resettlement occurred.

As of 1986, therefore, various studies and consultations remained incomplete. Each pertinent bureaucratic unit tended to persist in pursuing its core task and to assume a posture on the Three Gorges dam project that reflected its understanding of the dictates of this task. Eventually, the various studies and recommendations would be put together by the leadership small group headed by Vice Premier Li Peng, and this group would then recommend appropriate action to the State Council Standing Committee. This recommendation, in theory, should not concern *whether* to build the Three Gorges dam, as that had already been decided in principle. Rather, the recommendation would concern how *high* the dam should be and *when* to begin construction.

Finally, against the background of this overview of three decades of deliberations on this project, it bears noting that if the dam construction actually commenced, a new constellation of forces would come into being to shape the development of the effort. First, a new bureaucratic unit would be created to exercise control over both the YVPO (the design organ) and the construction crews. Since both these units are of equal bureaucratic rank, neither could issue binding orders to the other. Given the size of the project and its long duration, moreover, much would still have to be worked out during construction to achieve the continuing cooperation necessary to build the dam on schedule and on budget. Management of the refugee, navigation, communications, employment, and related problems would require enormous ongoing efforts to sustain a consensus in an evolving situation.

CONCLUSION: THREE GORGES AND THE POLICY PROCESS

Evaluation of the history of the Three Gorges dam proposal is complicated by a marked unevenness of data. Too much of the above history has had to rely on sources produced by opponents of the project. Too

---

ample, it is estimated by some that at 170 meters maximum normal water surface the cost of resettlement would equal half of the entire cost of the project.

[166] This issue is complicated both by a lack of adequate census data and by differences of opinion about the size of the secondary relocation problem—i.e., the problem of moving people who currently occupy land to which inhabitants of flooded towns will have to be moved. Observers generally agreed that the YVPO's figures for the size of the refugee problem were too low, perhaps by as much as forty percent or more.

little is known about various institutional actors in the debate before the late 1970's. In addition, some very important potential actors—such as the military, which typically contributes large construction forces to such projects[167]—are simply beyond the reach of the research materials available. Thus, there is always a danger that generalizations based on the above history reflect more the biases in the data than the real world of decision making on the Three Gorges project. Nevertheless, on balance this case study provides more detail, with more sources for at least partial corroboration, than is typically available on development projects in the PRC, and thus we will treat the above story as sufficiently complete to permit broader generalizations.

The long history of the Three Gorges project makes clear that this issue came to the fore during the preparatory stage for each subsequent Five Year Plan once the project itself had been accepted as a long-term goal in the mid-1950's. It cropped up in late 1957-early 1958, again in late 1964-66, also during 1969-70, in 1979-80, and in 1984-86. Five Year Plans have a somewhat ephemeral quality to them in many respects. Most have not been sustained to completion. Nevertheless, this study of the Three Gorges project history demonstrates that Five Year Plan drafting mobilizes forces to do battle over major projects that are high on the priority lists of powerful bureaucratic units. Thus, during the late 1950's through the 1970's, the Five Year Plans remained important in nurturing a cycle of decision making, even if the plans themselves typically succumbed to political upheavals. In preparing for each Five Year Plan, the question concerning Three Gorges was whether to move the project from being on a long-term wish list to actually scheduling the start-up of construction during the ensuing five years. Within this context, there were also specific changes that bear mention.

First, the reasons why actual construction of the Three Gorges dam never began shifted over time. The deep economic depression that began in 1960 sidetracked the 1958 decision to build the dam once some technical issues had been resolved. The effort to put the dam back on the planning agenda in late 1964 continued into early 1966, at which time the outbreak of the Cultural Revolution precluded progress on any project of this magnitude. The attempt in 1969-70 to put the dam into the new Five Year Plan ran into national security objections based on the war

---

[167] The Hydropower Command (*shuidian silingbu*) under the PRC Armed Police commanded by General He Yi operated in the mid 1980's under the dual leadership of the PLA and the MWREP. The PLA controlled administrative matters in this unit, while the MWREP took charge of substantive tasks for it. This construction force normally constructed dams in more remote areas, but under the reforms of the mid 1980's it acquired the right to bid on other projects, too.

scare with the Soviet Union. In 1979-80, the momentum behind starting up construction appears to have fallen victim to the general retrenchment that was carried out then. And the 1984-86 effort encountered problems stemming from two causes: a general economic retrenchment, especially after mid-1985; and the systemic changes that have resulted from the evolution of the system and the economic and political reform effort to date. As explained below, the reforms have simultaneously increased the importance of obtaining a consensus and made it more difficult to do precisely this.

In addition, the water resources officials headed by Lin Yishan modified their rationales for building the dam to meet changing circumstances. Their main rationale in 1958 was to achieve a decisive breakthrough in flood control. In the mid-1960's their approach shifted in the direction of producing additional electricity to support Mao's desire for constructing a "third line" of industry in Southwest China for security reasons. By the late 1970's, though, flood control again became the central focus, as Lin tried to pry the project out of the bureaucratic bailiwick of his opponents in the electric power industry.

A long-term look at the history of the Three Gorges project also reveals some important continuities and trends. The two key continuities are those of basic issues and of bureaucratic positions. The parameters of the debate on the Three Gorges dam remained remarkably constant over the thirty-year discussion of this project reviewed above. So did the positions of the pertinent bureaucratic (including provincial) units.

Three trends also emerge from the above historical overview. These are: the diminishing role of a single leader; the widening range of bureaucratic actors who play significant roles in decision making on this project; and the increasingly central and complex roles that foreigners played in the developments concerning Three Gorges project decision making. All of these trends are intricately bound up with China's adoption of the four modernizations and the related economic and political reforms since the late 1970's. We, therefore, deal with them in the context of these larger developments.

Four Modernizations and the Three Gorges Dam

The adoption of the four modernizations policy in the 1970's led to a commitment to increase the country's GNP fourfold by the end of the century. Mid-1980's estimates indicated that this task would require that by the year 2000 China be able to generate 240 million kilowatts of electricity. The Three Gorges dam could at best contribute less than 15 million of these kilowatts. This urgent energy situation created strong incentives to adopt policies that would provide maximum electrical generating capacity at minimum direct cost and with the shortest possible lead time—that is, to build thermal plants rather than massive hydroelectric facilities.

Other considerations, though, diminish the allure of thermal plants. Thermal power poses troublesome environmental problems, especially given the high percentage of China's power generation that is fueled by coal. Major new thermal power facilities also require new rail construction and other additional efforts that affect comparative cost calculations.

On balance, the mid-1980's pressures to increase electrical output at the least short-term cost evidently weighed against start-up of construction of the Three Gorges dam. In the coal sector, as explained in Chapter Seven, similar pressures produced an increased emphasis on development of local coal facilities, even though over the long run greater investment in major central mines would probably have been a wiser strategy. Quick payoffs for minimum investment appear, then, to have become the preferred way to meet the ambitious four modernizations goals.

Although the four modernizations policy highlighted the critical importance of adding to electrical power generation capabilities, this did not necessarily make it more likely that a dam at the Three Gorges would be seen as a good investment strategy. Indeed, as explained below, the economic and political reforms that accompanied the four modernizations policy made it more likely that shorter term solutions to China's energy and flood control needs would receive priority.

Economic Reform and the Three Gorges Dam

The *four modernizations* stipulate a set of goals in industry, agriculture, science and technology, and national defense. The *economic reforms* provide the structural and policy changes to achieve these goals. As with the modernization goals themselves, the economic reform measures significantly affected the context and dynamics for policy making concerning the Three Gorges dam. Chapter Eight examines systematically the implications of the reforms for China's policy process. The current section focuses more narrowly on the effects of the reforms on decision making concerning the Three Gorges dam.

The economic reform measures are very complex and cannot be summarized accurately in a few general paragraphs. Indeed, competing goals within the reform movement on occasion produced policies not readily compatible with each other. Nevertheless, some basic ideas lie at the heart of the reforms, one of which is the notion that it is possible to develop a more pragmatic and efficient policy process.

Several important initiatives grew from this notion. First, the reformers recognized the dangers to rational decision making when one man can dominate the system, as Mao Zedong did. They thus stressed the need to diffuse authority so that an extensive consultative process would precede each major decision. An accompanying very marked reduction in political coercion aimed, in part, at encouraging relevant people to contribute their views in a more forthright manner in this consultative process. This portion of the reform effort attempted to strengthen the role of pragmatic vetting of issues in the pertinent bureaucracies so as to circumscribe the latitude allowed to any one top leader.

A second reform principle touted increased use of economic criteria and of economic forces in economic policy decision making. This dimension of the reforms created some tension with the first, as the first put issues into a bureaucratic arena where economic analysis traditionally took a back seat to considerations of need, capabilities, and bureaucratic requirements. This tension produced different adaptations in various sectors of the Chinese economy. In the energy sector, major projects stayed fundamentally within the bureaucratic nexus, and the economic evaluations of them remained secondary. Continuing pressures worked, however, to increase the role of economic criteria in reaching decisions in this arena.

While China reduced its reliance on strong personal leadership to override disagreement and push policies forward, the country did not at the same time develop an adequate legal system to resolve basic disputes among bureaucratic units. The desire to avoid imposing solutions on recalcitrant bureaucracies from the top within the executive—combined with the lack of a non-executive body capable of adjudicating contentious issues—enhanced the need for consensus building within the executive branch itself. Put differently, top leaders in the 1980's generally refused simply to override the strongly held views of major bureaucratic units. The only viable solution, in this situation, was for bureaucracies in conflict to seek a working consensus.

Other aspects of the reform movement also indirectly affected decision making on the Three Gorges dam. For example, investment funds were made available outside the plan to encourage enterprises to seize some initiative in developing their production capabilities. Beijing's ability to mobilize resources for the Three Gorges project was not completely undercut by these financial reforms, but the dam would now have to be built in a more competitive domestic economic environment—with fewer resources directly controlled from the Center—than was the case in previous decades.

The reform movement also made foreign economic institutions actors on the scene. China turned to the outside world not only for advanced technology and equipment but also for funds themselves. This increased the leverage of the Center (through its brokering of outside funds) and subjected Beijing to potentially important demands emanating from the international economic arena.

Other aspects of the reform movement also affected the Three Gorges project. For example, the rural economic reforms provided guarantees to peasants that effectively increased potential resettlement costs above what they would have been a decade earlier. Inflation—a spinoff of price reforms—also increased potential costs of the project.

On balance, nevertheless, the three most consequential reforms in terms of impact on the Three Gorges project decision making were: the diminished role of personal leadership and greater importance of consensus building among affected bureaucratic (including political/territorial) units; the greater utilization of feasibility studies and economic analysis; and the "open" policy with its potential for access to foreign funds and expertise.

With regard to the first of these, in the 1950's the effort to start construction on the Three Gorges primarily required gaining the acquiescence of Mao Zedong. Numerous bodies became involved in the series of consultations and studies before the issue went to Mao personally. In this sense, China in the 1950's had a highly consultative system. But even basic failure to forge a consensus among the contributing units would not stand as a serious obstacle in the way of a decision by Mao to build the Three Gorges dam. Thus, in 1958 there was systematic disagreement between the electric power and the water resources people on the dam, with the positions of other pertinent units unknown. Nevertheless, a decision by Mao at Nanning and Chengdu to start dam construction would have produced an effort to forge ahead, regardless of the strength of the opposition.

The situation in the 1980's had changed. If before 1986 Deng Xiaoping, Hu Yaobang, and Zhao Ziyang had backed the project fully, it would probably have been put into the Seventh Five Year Plan. But the very top leaders would be unlikely to take this type of stance on a major issue when there remained basic disagreement among the key bureaucratic actors involved in the project.[168] The YVPO, itself the strongest supporter

[168] As noted in Chapter Seven, there is evidence that Deng personally promoted the Pingshuo joint venture with Occidental Petroleum over the dissent of major bureaucratic

of the Three Gorges dam, therefore, bent over backwards in the 1980's to accommodate the wishes of others. It lowered the prospective maximum normal water surface to 150 meters to meet the concerns of Sichuan over refugees and to encourage downstream provinces to believe that the dam could be built and brought on line relatively quickly. It also agreed to the Ministry of Communication's demands for both temporary locks and large ship lifts to take care of the shipping issue during dam construction. All of this reflected the YVPO's recognition of the importance of building broad-based support for its Three Gorges proposal. At the same time, while it appears to be the case that one leader alone will not ride roughshod over the relevant bureaucracies in putting such a project on line, it is also very likely that no major project can be carried out without the enthusiastic support of one of the very top leaders.

The dynamics of consensus building in China of the mid-1980's were partially revealed by the reactions of some of the key units to the YVPO's strategy. Both Chongqing and the Communications Ministry, as noted above, opted for a 180-meter maximum normal water surface, albeit for somewhat different reasons. The fact that they continued to make this case even in the wake of the April 1984 State Council decision in favor of a 150-meter dam suggests that they assumed that the top leadership would not forge ahead on this major project without having formed a consensus among the key units.

Indeed, even a relatively crude and unsophisticated attribution of basic interests to the key bureaucratic (including provincial) units involved in this story provides a remarkably good predictor of the actual positions on the Three Gorges project that these units adopted. All the provinces below the dam supported the effort, while Sichuan generally either opposed it or tried in other ways to lessen the chances the dam would be built. The water resources people supported it, while both electric power and communications bureaucracies dissented. The interesting phenomenon here is the degree to which bureaucracies acted on the basis of their perception of their own tasks, varying their strategies as the situation evolved but not changing their basic concerns about the project. The "reform" climate in the country, moreover, *de facto* encouraged these bureaucracies to articulate and fight for their positions.

Having noted above the increasing importance the reforms place on financial analysis, the Three Gorges case nevertheless demonstrates that the quality of economic analysis for such projects remained relatively

---

actors involved. This, however, worked out in such a way that probably made it less likely that either Deng or other top leaders would follow a similar strategy on a major energy project in the future.

poor. Decisions remained confined to a bureaucratic arena where physical needs and capabilities assumed more weight than did economic cost/benefit analyses. In April 1984, for example, the State Council approved this project even though the Ministry of Finance's study of it had not been completed. The YVPO's feasibility study paid relatively scant attention to economic analysis. Indeed, as foreign experts in the 1980's looked at the work done on this project over the previous twenty years, they were impressed both by the comprehensiveness of the physical planning and by the paucity of pertinent economic analysis. The domestic economic reforms, therefore, did not by the mid-1980's introduce economic analysis into decision making on the Three Gorges dam in a serious fashion.

China's "open" policy toward the outside world did, however, introduce significant new factors into decision making on the Three Gorges dam. Foreign expertise was brought to bear on this project during the 1980's in a range of ways. For example, the US Bureau of Reclamation provided technical expertise to the YVPO and the MWREP on a contract basis. Brazil actively promoted its own expertise, based on construction of the Itaipu Dam, and Zhao Ziyang's November 1985 visit to Brazil included substantial discussion of this issue. China tried to entice both Japan and Canada into active involvement in the Three Gorges project. All of this, moreover, took place while the project remained a highly contentious issue in China. In fact, the Chinese received different advice from various foreign sources—to the extent that each side in the domestic debate at times cited "its" foreign specialists in support of its own view. De facto, international bureaucratic alliances, such as that between the MWREP/YVPO and the USBR, formed on this issue.

The potential need to go abroad for financing for this project also carried with it several important implications. First, it would almost certainly require that the Chinese do more detailed and rigorous financial feasibility work and cost/benefit analysis than was previously thought necessary. In addition, China's taking out hard currency loans on a long-term basis would create new and urgent pressures to keep the project on its construction schedule, as compounding interest would drive up the costs of any significant delays dramatically. Finally, given the size, complexity, and highly controversial nature of this project within China, foreign involvement on a substantial scale could present potential political issues of a unique nature if the project were to fall seriously short of expectations—especially because foreigners might have to become increasingly involved in actual project construction management to preserve any possibility of having this complex effort completed on schedule.

In sum, the economic reforms exerted a mixed impact on the Three

Gorges project. In some ways, these reforms produced a more technically sophisticated, pragmatic approach to the dam. At the same time, the further diffusion of authority, the resulting stress on reaching consensus among bureaucratic units, and the more competitive domestic economic situation within China impeded Beijing's ability to make a firm decision on the project and to build it on schedule. The "open" policy introduced the international economic arena into the equation but did not simplify the decision making on the Chinese side. While the reforms thus encompassed measures for more rational decision making, they also enhanced the importance of a satisficing approach to problem solving by leaders and bureaucrats alike.

The trends noted above based on the economic reforms and this project's history appear to portend more pragmatic decision making on major new energy projects in the future than has been the case at times in the past. They also highlight, though, that economic analysis remains a relatively underdeveloped facet of this process, that bureaucratic relationships and procedures structure a large part of the dynamics (and therefore the substance) of the issue, and that the system may be moving toward a point where the stress on consensus is making it extraordinarily difficult to build controversial, large new projects when smaller alternatives with faster payoffs are available.

· 7 ·

CENTRAL-PROVINCIAL AND INTERAGENCY RELATIONS
IN ENERGY DEVELOPMENT

Our case studies tracing cooperation with the outside world in petroleum development and planning for construction of the Three Gorges dam focused primarily on politics at the Center. Our chapters on the elite and the energy bureaucracies also concentrated on the national level. Only our chapter on bureaucratic processes briefly dwelled on provincial and local levels. We now shift our focus to the provincial levels and below, probing the nature of central-provincial and local, interagency relations, first by presenting an overview of the situation and then detailing how Shanxi province deals with the Center and is structured internally in the exploitation of its rich coal resources and how Guangdong and locales under its jurisdiction have become involved in offshore petroleum exploration and development.

Our information illustrates a number of important features of bureaucratic politics at the local levels. First, to repeat a theme introduced in earlier chapters, interagency relations entail constant negotiations, bargains, and deals. One provincial official whom we encountered briefly on a plane summarized the situation this way: "No unit or individual lets you have something strictly according to regulations. Rather, you must have *guanxi* or you come up with nothing. This is true everywhere but especially in the South. The *guanxi* does not refer to old school ties and so on. Rather, the *guanxi* is based on interest—strictly a you scratch my back and I scratch yours situation. The exchange of goods and favors seals the deal. This situation is pervasive because that is the way things are done at higher levels, and until they do things differently, nobody else will change." Our data do not permit a definitive portrayal of how these bargains are struck, but they suggest the importance of this insight. Our material on the Antaibao open-pit coal mine is particularly suggestive in this regard.

Further, interagency competition and rivalry are key features of bureaucratic practices at lower levels. Our data on Guangdong and South China Sea petroleum development highlight this dimension of local politics. The search for revenue, the tendency to expand beyond original missions, and the search for security through multiple activities are endemic practices at lower levels.

Both the Shanxi coal and Guangdong petroleum cases highlight the

339

ambiguities and looseness of the system. Jurisdictions are poorly delin-eated, and many bureaucratic struggles at lower levels arise because the higher levels frequently give vague directives or charge more than one local agency with the same responsiblity. The overlapping jurisdictions of CNOOC, Nanhai West, Nanhai East, and China Nanhai Offshore Joint Services Corporation (CNOJSC), for example, engender constant problems of coordination, competition, and jealousy. Further, organiza-tions spawn subordinate units to undertake activities in new or reward-ing areas. This prompts an enormous proliferation of institutions, as var-ious parent units seek to obtain a piece of the action. There is no shortage of bureaucratic entrepreneurship in post-Mao China, though frequently the requisite competence is lacking, and outside observers find it difficult to ascertain which of the new organizations are substantial and which are essentially organizations in name only.

The ambiguity and the looseness in the system, however, may be a deliberate tactic of the Center to build a broad coalition in support of its policies. By not specifying the precise beneficiaries of a new policy or project and by offering hunting licenses to a large number of potential participants, the Center may stimulate additional support. For example, we will note below that neither in the case of South China Sea oil and gas nor of Antaibao coal did the Center specify how the natural resource, domestic revenue, and foreign currency would be allocated before the development projects would get underway. Guangdong and Shanxi provinces cooperated in confidence that they would profit directly, with the exact split to be discussed later. All the actors then had an incentive to assist the project in ways which strengthened their claims once the project came on stream.

Finally, the chapter specifies the effect of the opening to the outside world upon bureaucratic behavior at the local level. In particular, the thirst for foreign currency, the rise of personnel capable of working ef-fectively with foreigners, and the benefits which accrue through a foreign connection are all demonstrated in our interview materials from Shanxi and Guangdong.

CENTRAL-PROVINCIAL RELATIONS

The provinces and directly ruled cities (Tianjin, Beijing, and Shanghai) vary enormously in size, population, climate, topology, and level of eco-nomic development.[1] Many Chinese provinces are the size of countries:

[1] For discussions of provincial variation in China, *see* Robert M. Field, Nicholas Lardy, and John Emerson, "Industrial Output by Province in China, 1949-73," *China Quarterly*,

Sichuan, over 100 million people; Henan and Shandong, 75 million each; Jiangsu and Guangdong, 61 million each. Some have large concentrations of non-Han, minority peoples, while others are nearly pure Han. Mountain ranges define the boundaries of some provinces, with the core of such provinces defined by a set of river valleys. Hunan, Jiangsi, Shanxi, and Sichuan are examples. Others lack well-defined natural boundaries. Some have a well-defined sense of cultural and historical distinctiveness (such as Guangdong or Shanghai), while others either have a less well-defined provincial identity (Jilin and perhaps Henan) or, due to their topography and linguistic considerations, embrace distinctive cultural subunits of great longevity (Fujian or Anhui). Some correspond to relatively self-contained, natural economic systems (Sichuan); others are part of a larger, natural economic region (Hubei in Central China or Hebei as part of the north China plain); and others fall into more than one natural commercial system (Zhejiang, Inner Mongolia or Shaanxi).[2]

With such diversity, generalities about provinces and their relations with the Center are not easily made. In fact, every province has a distinctive relationship with the center. Before identifying the factors which shape the nature of a province's ties to the Center, however, let us sketch the general structure of the province, the sources of central control, and the bases of provincial autonomy.

The Political Structure of the Province

The basic structure of provincial level units mirrors that of the Center. A small group of provincial officials presides over a bureaucratic struc-

No. 63 (September, 1975), pp. 409-434; Robert M. Field, Kathleen McGlynn, and William Abnett, "Political Conflict and Industrial Growth in China: 1965-1977," *Chinese Economy Post-Mao*, Vol. 1, Joint Economic Committee (Washington: U.S. Government Printing Office, 1978), pp. 239-284; David M. Lampton, "The Roots of Interprovincial Inequality in Education and Health Services in China Since 1949," *American Political Science Review* (June, 1979), pp. 459-477; Nicholas Lardy, *Agriculture in China's Modern Economic Development* (London: Cambridge Press, 1983); Robert Roll and K. C. Yeh, "Balance in Coastal and Inland Industrial Development," *China: A Reassessment of the Economy*, Joint Economic Committee (Washington: U.S. Government Printing Office, 1975), pp. 81-93; and Ross Terrill, *Flowers on an Iron Tree: Five Cities of China* (Boston: Little, Brown and Company, 1975).

[2] The writings of G. William Skinner suggest the political significance of this variation; See his "Marketing and Social Structure in Rural China," *Journal of Asian Studies*, No. 24, Vol. 1 (November, 1964), pp. 3-44 (Part I); No. 24, Vol. 2 (February, 1965), pp. 195-288 (Part II); No. 24, Vol. 3 (May, 1965), pp. 363-400 (Part III); G. William Skinner (ed.), "Cities and the Hierarchy of Local Systems," *The City in Late Imperial China* (Stanford University Press, 1977), pp. 275-352; and "Presidential Address: The Structure of Chinese History," *Journal of Asian Studies*, Vol. XLIV, No. 2 (February, 1985), pp. 271-292.

ture which, to a great extent, duplicates the national level. In this group of provincial officials, the first among equals is the First Party Secretary, with the Governor (or Mayor in Beijing, Tianjin and Shanghai) and the commander of the military region or district headquartered in the provincial capital also crucial individuals. A rough division of labor exists among the three, with the Party Secretary usually more responsible for ideology, personnel assignments, rural policy, and the running of campaigns to achieve specific objectives through *ad hoc* organizations and mobilization of the populace. The governor has primary jurisdiction over economic matters and education, while the military commander obviously is concerned with the PLA and its diverse activities within a province (extending to economic and cultural activities which the PLA undertakes). He also can become involved in public security matters.

The relative importance of the members of this triumvirate depends upon the force of their personalities, the strength of their organizations in the province, and the situation in the national capital. During the Cultural Revolution and its aftermath, for example, when Minister of Defense Lin Biao rose to the pinnacle of power and nearly half of the top 25 to 35 leaders in Beijing came from the PLA, the military region or district commander was the leading official in many provinces. In such areas as Xinjiang, Xizang (Tibet), and Heilongjiang, where PLA forces are based in large numbers and where PLA veterans have developed extensive state farms, the provincial military commander retains an influential role. In the 1980's, with the efforts to separate the Party from the government at lower levels, to create identifiable spheres of responsibility for government leaders, and to select vigorous, younger, better educated and technically proficient governors, many holders of that office became quite significant and influential.

Looking over the shoulders of this triumvirate are a few elders who long led the province. Some date to the revolutionary era and served in the communist forces that operated in the province in the 1930's and 1940's. Some are non-Party dignitaries—intellectuals and businessmen—who were prominent before 1949 and whose connections in the locality are deep. Such people frequently were in disgrace from the mid-1950's or mid-1960's to Mao's death, but in the 1980's they were restored to honored posts to help revitalize the province by resuscitating atrophied, traditional practices. Finally, the elders include officials who led the province through the 1950's to the Cultural Revolution and returned in the 1970's. As the younger provincial leaders take over the reigns of power, these elders play crucial roles in advising their successors—many of whom were recently transferred to the province—on how to get things done.

The First Party Secretary and his associates, as at the Center, include several functional specialists. They hold such positions as Party Secretaries, Vice Governors, and members of the Provincial Party Committees. They are responsible for different sectors of the bureaucracy: agriculture, finance and trade, industry and communications, education, culture and ideology, and so on.

Next come the provincial bureaucracies. Each of the principal or "comprehensive" economic agencies at the Center—SPC, SEC, SSTC, and MOF—have identifiable subordinate units in every province. However, the table of organization at the provincial level does not precisely parallel the structure at the national level. For example, while most provinces have separate planning and economic commissions, some combine the functions of these two national bodies within a single provincial agency which receives professional guidance (*yewu guanxi*) from both by the SPC and SEC in Beijing. Or, even though the national State Capital Construction Commission was abolished in 1982, not all provinces immediately followed suit. Nor did all provinces emulate the Center in its merger of water resources and electric power. Within the Party, while the Central Committee has not established a department in charge of rural policy (instead, establishing a Rural Policy Research Center), many provinces have a CCP Rural Work Department.

The provincial structure of line ministries depends upon their internal organization and the extent of their activities in the particular province. For example, the highly centralized Ministry of Petroleum leads its oil fields directly, and its provincial-level agencies do not appear to be important actors in the exploration, development, and production process. The Ministry of Petroleum has extensive operations in several coastal provinces: Heilongjiang (Daqing), Liaoning (Liaohe), Hebei (Dagang and Shengli), Shandong (Shengli), Henan (Zhongyuan), which it manages directly. Its activities in Qinghai and Xinjiang in the west and Sichuan are coordinated by the Northwest China Petroleum Administration and the Southwest China Petroleum Administration respectively. But, where MPI has yet to discover extensive reserves, it is not an important actor on the local scene.

Similarly, the Ministry of Coal has more intimate links to provinces that have large coal mines (Liaoning, Hebei, Shanxi, Jiangsu, and so on) than to areas with scattered deposits only suitable to small mining operations. In the case of Shanxi coal, so extensive and differentiated are its deposits that the province as of 1984 had three provincial-level coal agencies, each with extensive activities, different responsibilities, and distinctive relations with the Ministry of Coal. Provinces, in short, do not host the full panoply of bureaucracies that crowd the space of Beijing.

Provincial departments and their subordinate agencies at city, county, and township levels both are agents of their superior bodies and also are entrepreneurial units in their own right. That is, a provincial department manages activities on behalf of the central ministry and can undertake activities on its own. For example, a provincial education department helps to supervise the universities (if any) within the province that are designated "key point" and are directly led by the central State Education Commission. It also cultivates various types of universities directly under its leadership, and it may encourage its subordinate education bureaus at lower levels to develop their own universities.

A bewildering range of state-run enterprises coexist within a province: some are centrally run and look to the Center for their financing; others are led directly by the province; and yet others are the creatures of local governments. The administrative rules governing these different types of enterprises are different: how they fit into the state plan and secure their inputs; how they obtain investment funds; what approvals they must secure to do business abroad or with foreigners; how they obtain foreign currency or purchase foreign equipment. Further complicating this picture, each type of enterprise—center, provincial, and local—was undergoing sweeping reforms of its supervisory system in the mid-1980's.

Provincial Leaders

The top leaders of China's provinces and large cities deserve closer scrutiny, for the roles they play are crucial to the effective functioning of the system.[3] The top provincial leaders are responsible for implementing and giving coherence to the diverse policy guidelines that cascade from above. They must achieve a degree of coordination in the implementation of policy, since the sum of the directives from the huge and diverse central bureaucracies demand more in commitments than the province can really sustain. Moreover, the central directives frequently are vague and contradictory. Provincial leaders perforce must determine which directives are really serious and merit priority attention and which can safely be discarded. They must combine the new directives with their

[3] For other discussions of the roles of provincial leaders, *see* David Goodman, "The Provincial First Party Secretary in the People's Republic of China, 1949-1978: A Profile," *British Journal of Political Science*, Vol. X, no. 1 (1980); Peter Moody, "Policy and Power: The Career of T'ao Chu, 1956-66," *China Quarterly*, No. 54 (April-June, 1973), pp. 267-293; David Goodman, *Centre and Province in the PRC: Sichuan and Guizhou, 1955-1965* (Cambridge: Cambridge University Press, 1986), especially pp. 1-24 and 177-195.

own on-going programs. Their latitude of choice in complying with central directives as a result becomes considerable.

At the same time, provincial officials are expected to represent their territory at the Center. The top 25 to 35 officials look to their provincial officials for indications as to whether their policy preferences can be implemented. The top leaders consider their local officials to be a major source of information. They expect their provincial leaders to deliver revenue and material resources to the Center and to ask for allocations from the Center. Within limits which vary over time and according to the province, the central leaders count on their provincial leaders being the spokesmen of the interests and needs of their localities—as long as their primary loyalty is to the Center.

Provinces and their lower levels are rated in their performance of central commands. The crude accolades are "advanced" or "model" units, while the pejorative label is "backward." In fact, the designations can be more precise and numerical, at least at the county level. In effect, provinces and counties have report cards: for example, excellent in implementation of agricultural policy, average in education and public health, and weak in maintenance of public order. Since local leaders do not command sufficient resources to attain "excellent" ratings across the board, they choose in what areas they will pursue excellence and what, as a strategic choice, they will deliberately neglect. This entails risk, since the neglected area may become a crucial concern to the top leaders; as a result, provincial leaders select their priorities with the interests of the top leaders in mind.[4]

Enormous variation exists in the motivations and behavior of top provincial officials. Some apparently see themselves as agents of the Center: enforcers of the priority policies of the top 25 to 35 officials. Not infrequently, these agents are precisely that. They have been dispatched to a laggard province to whip it into shape: to put an end to factional strife, to improve performance, to show some pet policies of central leaders can produce dramatic results, turning the province into a showcase, and so on.[5] Or, a particular leader or faction may have assigned the individual to advance its particular interests in the province. On other occasions,

[4] This information is based on 1981 interviews in Jin county, Hebei province, and with Hebei officials in Shijiazhuang.

[5] Examples would include the dispatch of Li Dazhang to Guizhou in 1965, Wang Dongxing to Jiangxi in 1958, and Yang Shangkun and Xi Zhongxun to Guangdong in 1978. On Li Dazhang, see Goodman, *Centre and Province*, p. 134. On Wang Dongxing, see Parris Chang, "The Rise of Wang Tung-hsing: Head of China's Security Apparatus," *China Quarterly*, No. 73 (March, 1978), p. 127.

the role of "central agent" is self-selected.[6] Provincial secretaries or governors become particularly enthusiastic supporters of national policies, appearing more Catholic than the Pope. They attach themselves to particular contenders for power at the Center, either out of ideological preference or personalities.[7] They achieve national acclaim by surpassing targets, achieving the sought results in record time, and so on.[8] Their motivation can be self-serving, seeking rapid promotion, or they may genuinely believe in the top leaders and their policies. Alternatively, national policies actually may coincide with the interests of the province.[9] Whatever the reason, the result is the same: the provincial leaders turn their province into a pace-setter. Agents of the Center fly high while the top leaders they serve prosper and the policies succeed. They may indeed be promoted. But the course is risky, for if their patrons falter or the policies prove disasterous, the provincial enthusiasts usually fall also.

Other provincial leaders give greater weight to advancing the interests of their locality, hastening its economic development, hoarding resources for its benefit and extracting maximum benefits from the Center.[10] Frequently, this can be done openly and vigorously at the annual planning and financial conferences, when each province strikes its balance with the Center in terms of the obligations each pledges to fulfill toward the other in the coming year. In the day-to-day operations, the top provincial officials seek the resources necessary to fulfill the formal and informal contracts they have made. Unlike line ministries in Beijing, each of which has a designated top leader responsible for it, provinces lack a spe-

[6] The classic example is the assignment of Mao Yuanxin, the nephew of the Chairman, to advance the cause of the Cultural Revolutionaries in Liaoning in the mid-1970's. See Galen Fox, *Campaigning for Power in China During the Cultural Revolution Era, 1967-1976*, Ph.D. thesis (Princeton University, 1978), pp. 218 and 314.

[7] A prominent example is the support Shanghai officials Zhang Chunqiao and Yao Wenyuan provided Jiang Qing in 1963-65. See Parris Chang, "Shanghai in Chinese Politics: Before and After the Cultural Revolution," in Christopher Howe (ed.) *Shanghai: Revolution and Development in an Asian Metropolis* (Cambridge: Cambridge University Press, 1981), pp. 66-90.

[8] The frequently cited examples are Wu Zhipu in Henan during the Great Leap Forward, Nan Ping in Zhejiang during the early 1970's, and Xiang Nan in Fujian. On Wu, see Parris Chang, *Power and Policy*. On Nan Ping, see Galen Fox, *Campaigning for Power*, p. 112.

[9] This could help explain the pace-setting roles of Wan Li in Anhui in promoting agricultural reform and of Zhao Ziyang in Sichuan concerning industrial reform in 1978-80. Both Wan and Zhao implemented reform policies that had received enthusiastic support in these provinces years earlier. See David Goodman, *Centre and Province*, p. 194. On Wan Li in Anhui, see David Zweig, "Context and Content in Policy Implementation: Household Contracts and Decollectivization, 1977-1983," in David Lampton, ed., *Policy Implementation*, pp. 255-284. On Zhao in Sichuan, see David Shambaugh, *The Making of a Premier: Zhao Ziyang's Provincial Career* (Boulder: Westview, 1984).

[10] Numerous knowledgeable informants stressed this point in interviews.

cific top leader who officially handles its portfolio at the highest councils of the state. Nonetheless, each province comes to look to one or two top officials as its unofficial representative in the capital. The official may be one whose ministry is particularly active in the province. Thus, Shanxi officials look to the Minister of Coal and the top leaders in charge of coal as their patrons. Further, officials among the top 25 to 35 officials may have long served in a particular province as a First Secretary or Governor, he may have led guerrilla forces in the province and/or he may hail from the province. Available evidence suggests that many top central leaders feel some special responsibility toward provinces with which they have had such ties, though they are cautious and constrained in advancing the cause of their locality. Provincial level officials then cultivate relations with their potential patrons at the Center.[11]

In addition to serving as "central agents" and "provincial defenders" who act on behalf of their provinces, provincial officials have a third objective: to survive. Provincial leaders who have mounted the dangerous tiger world of Chinese politics know they cannot dismount without being devoured. For some, the primary purpose has become to hang on, neither defending their province nor acting for the Center but rather reconciling conflicting pressure in order to survive. These are the cautious provincial leaders who sufficiently comply with current policies to get by but who do enough foot dragging to be able to prove, when policies change, that their compliance was unenthusiastic. Their concern is that in appearance, they comply with the Center, while in reality, they permit diversity in implementation to placate their constituencies. They seek neither to be pace-setters nor laggards. They seek to shift responsibility to superiors in Beijing and to subordinates at lower levels. Their goal is to be average, thereby keeping expectations about their future performance within attainable bounds. They accumulate and hide resources from superiors and subordinates to provide a margin of safety and to insulate their level from uncertainties in their environment. It is the unusual provincial leader who does not, over the long haul, succumb to the temptation to pursue the security of such mediocrity.

Sources of Central Control

What, it might be asked, are the precise instruments through which the Center maintains control over top provincial officials? In part, the answer

---

[11] Thus, for many years, Ye Jianying retained special links to Guangdong, Li Xiannian to Hubei, Deng Xiaoping to Sichuan, and Peng Zhen to Shanxi. These leaders did not solely protect their old haunts. They also used their links to demand more from their base. But the relationship could be utilized by provincial leaders in case of need.

is to be found in the triumvirate arrangement. The Center does not depend upon the loyalty of a single official. It enjoys alternate access routes into the province. Further, the Center retains control over the appointments and dismissals of First Party Secretaries, Governors, and military commanders, as well as several of their key subordinates.[12] The Center, in short, determines the careers of provincial leaders. This does not mean the Center has unbridled initiative. It evidently seeks to select provincial leaders who are likely to be welcomed by at least a portion of the provincial apparatus and have some skills and experience relevant to the situation. The appointment and removal of provincial officials on occasion appears to have involved a protracted negotiation. Still, the ultimate authority resides in Beijing.

Beijing also retains direct control over certain mobile military forces, which it can deploy in an extreme instance of defiance by provincial officials.[13] (Only one such known instance has occurred in the 36-year-history of the PRC, when the leaders of Wuhan and Hubei resisted central orders during the Cultural Revolution and forcefully detained emissaries from the Center. The revolt was quickly quelled.)[14] The Center can and has transferred military units to ensure that loyal units are stationed in potentially sensitive locales. Central-provincial politics are played out, in short, against the backdrop of effective central control over elite army, navy, and air force units. Provincial officials confront the Center essentially stripped of an ability to resist through force. (Nor do we wish to imply that they would wish such force to be at their disposal. This would mean a disunity of their country they do not seek.)

The Center also controls the propaganda apparatus, and while the Center has relaxed this control considerably in the post-Mao era, still, Beijing largely determines the ideological tenor of the country and shapes the cultural environment in which provincial officials work.[15]

Finally, the Center controls key economic resources which provinces need to meet their output targets. Electricity, a high percentage of petroleum, somewhat over 50% of coal, and a significant percentage of metals

---

[12] For a discussion of the personnel management system in China, see Melanie Manion, "The Cadre Management System, Post-Mao: The Appointment, Promotion, Transfer, and Removal of Party and State Leaders," *China Quarterly*, No. 102 (June, 1985), pp. 203-233.

[13] See Harvey Nelsen, *The Chinese Military System*, especially chapters 2 and 4.

[14] Thomas Robinson, "The Wuhan Incident."

[15] No single work fully captures the scope of the propaganda apparatus. It not only encompasses the print and broadcast media, but also includes the school system, the social science academies (and, before the Cultural Revolution, the natural science academies), parts of the public health system, and numerous other bodies.

are allocated by the Center.[16] The Center has attempted to retain control over the major transportation systems—air, rail, and water—by subdividing the systems into regional bureaus that do not coincide with individual provinces. As an indication of the province's dependence in these economic matters, each province maintains a large office in Beijing which has as one of its prime functions ensuring that Beijing supplies these needed commodities. Moreover, provinces must deposit their funds in the centralized People's Bank. On more than one occasion, the central government—facing a deficit—simply requisitioned these deposits. Nominally, the Center "borrowed" the money, but at no interest and with no promised date of repayment. The unified state budget, through which somewhat less than 50% of investment expenditures are now allocated, also gives the Center limited leverage on the provinces.

These mechanisms of control are imperfect. They prevent rebellion and unyielding defiance, and at a minimum guarantee the Center a major role in shaping what occurs within the province. But, they do not establish the automatic dominance of the Center over the province.

Provincial Autonomy

Provinces enjoy certain inevitable sources of strength. We do not refer here to the grants of authority bestowed by the Center and also retrievable by it, such as in the allocation of foreign currency or the right to enter into joint ventures. Rather, we refer to certain immutable aspects of the system. Among these, stemming from the sheer size of the country and the numbers of the people involved, are control of land and people. The great bulk of personnel assignments must be made at provincial and local levels. Disposition of land, too, is a local matter. Custom and cultural considerations may be the main factor here. The fact is that the law of eminent domain and the concept of unfettered and immediate state access to subsurface minerals are not well developed, and basic level units largely control land use. Villages cannot easily be commanded to surrender their land, and the process of identifying appropriate compensation can be protracted, as the difficulties over the Three Gorges project in this regard reveal. Moreover, while somewhat less than 50% of investment comes from the state budget, somewhat over 50% is under control of provincial-level enterprises and local units. This practice, the cumulative result of temporary grants of authority to local levels, has grown through the years and has become deeply embedded in the fiscal

---

[16] The First Party Secretary of one province once told a leading American politician that the Center's control over electric supply was its single greatest source of leverage over him. Inadequate supply meant he could not meet plan targets.

system. It gives provinces and localities the financial capacity to depart from the Center.

Another source of provincial leverage is its intermediate position in the hierarchy.[17] The Center cannot reach directly into the nation's 750,000-1,000,000 villages, over 2,000 counties, or hundreds of thousands of enterprises. In the final analysis, it must go through the province to reach the local levels. The provincial level is a gatekeeper guarding and providing access to the local levels. The Center, in the end, cannot reach the object of its rule without the cooperation of the provincial level, and provincial leaders know how to turn their pivotal position into a source of influence and constraint on the Center.

These sources of provincial strength are insufficient to establish provincial independence or autonomy. What we see is that both Center and province command resources that the other needs, with the balance-of-power between the two in the Center's favor. The situation establishes the basis for a bargaining relationship between the two, with the province a necessary ally so that the Center can reach the local levels. Over time, as our research and the secondary literature suggest, the balance may have gradually shifted somewhat in the province's favor, though the trend line has been interrupted by periods of significantly increased or circumscribed central control.[18]

Variation

The precise balance between Center and province varies from province to province. What factors determine the balance between the two? This is a very complex and subtle issue. We have already noted one crucial ingredient—the specific individuals involved, the characteristics of the provincial leaders and their personal connections at the Center. A second factor is the strength of the Center and particularly of the preeminent leader among the populace. That is, is the Party apparatus sufficiently widespread and effective at the grass roots, are the mass media capable of reaching into rural households directly, and is the respect for the Center

---

[17] This is the major theme of David Goodman, *Centre and Province.*

[18] At least, from the 1960's into the mid-1970's, most analysts stressed the essential compliance and subordination of provincial officials to Beijing. See Victor Falkenheim, "Continuing Central Predominance," *Problems of Communism*, Vol. 21, No. 4 (1972), pp. 75-83; and Frederick Teiwes, *Provincial Leadership in China: The Cultural Revolution and its Aftermath* (Ithaca: Cornell University, 1974). And for works which stress the ability of central officials to enforce their demands into the 1960's, see Ezra Vogel, *Canton under Communism* (Cambridge: Harvard University Press, 1969); David Goodman, *Centre and Province*; and Nicholas Lardy, *Economic Growth and Distribution in China* (Cambridge: Cambridge University Press, 1978).

sufficiently great that the Center can bypass the province and elicit a response directly from the local levels and the populace? The Center's ability to reach directly to the grass roots varies considerably from province to province (as it has over time).

Clearly, center-provincial relations are affected by the level of economic development and the revenue flow between the two. But exactly how this works is unclear. If a provincial-level unit receives subsidies from the Center, does this mean it has successfully exercised leverage? Or, does the subsidy mean the Center feels more able to interfere in the administration of the province? Does a province or municipality which is a net contributor to the central budget secure increased influence as a result, or does the transfer already reveal subservience to the Center? What is cause and what the effect? The existing evidence—and it is quite slim—suggests that revenue-producing areas both have a greater claim upon the Center and are the object of tighter control by the Center. The wealthier, revenue-producing areas thus have a more intimate relationship with the Center, which paradoxically means they are under closer scrutiny and have greater opportunity to influence policies of concern to them.

A third factor affecting center-provincial relations is proximity to Beijing and ease of transportation to the Center. While airplane transportation and telecommunications have brought all provincial capitals into easy reach from the Center on important issues, still Beijing's presence noticeably diminishes as one moves physically away from it. A number of provincial capitals have special overnight train service to Beijing and convenient return trains timed with the work day in the national capital. Changchun in Jilin, Shenyang in Liaoning, Jinan in Shandong, Taiyuan in Shanxi, Hefei in Anhui, Shijiazhuang in Hebei, and Zhengzhou in Henan are the principal capitals within Beijing's easy range. But by the time one gets to the periphery—Guangzhou, Guangdong; Fuzhou, Fujian; Nanning, Guangxi; Kunming, Yunnan; Guiyang, Guizhou; Chengdu, Sichuan; or Ulumuqi, Xinjiang—Beijing seems much more remote. Shanghai, Wuhan, and Xian occupy the intermediate space in this regard. With the exception of Guangdong and Sichuan, the more remote areas are also less wealthy, so that the Center also has somewhat diminished interest in them except in two crucial respects. National security considerations dictate a military concern with their defense; and they have substantial unexploited natural resources. For example, the prospects of Xinjiang oil and Yunnan coal make those provinces interesting to the respective ministries.

Another factor, related to transportation networks and proximity to Beijing, has to do with the natural commercial flows in and out of the province and the roles played by the provincial capital in regional and national economic systems. Guangzhou, Wuhan, Shanghai, and Shenyang in particular are at the hubs of large regional commercial networks, and the capitals of nearby provinces look to these cities as markets and sources of supply. Hangzhou and much of Zhejiang, Hefei and much of Anhui, Nanjing and much of Jiangsu, and Nanchang and a portion of Jiangxi, for example, are part of the Shanghai or lower Yangtze natural economic region. These and other provinces maintain offices in Shanghai as well as Beijing. Provinces on the North China plain look to Beijing as both their political and, along with Tianjin, their economic center. Provincial capitals which are simultaneously the seats of large economic regions approach the Center with a sense of importance that further encourages a bargaining relationship. Yet other provincial capitals look to Beijing as their political leader while looking to another city to satisfy some of its economic needs. A measure of autonomy and choice is therefore created.

Post-Mao reforms encourage commercial centers to go outside administrative channels and to establish direct ties with localities through investment, contracts to purchase above quota production, and so on. As a result, this dimension of central-provincial relations has become more evident.

A final factor is the role of the province in earning foreign exchange, particularly as a producer of manufactured goods or as a port. (That Shandong, Hebei, and Heilongjiang are sources of petroleum exports does not appear to have substantially accrued to their benefit, however.) In order to encourage exports, Beijing permits provinces to retain a portion of the foreign exchange they earn, with the portion varying over time and place. Provinces that have greater access to foreign currency, such as Guangdong and Fujian, obviously enjoy increased autonomy, but through its control of provincial foreign currency accounts in the Bank of China, the central government does have leverage over the situation. (To circumvent this central control, apparently some local units seek to accumulate their foreign currency in cash or to deposit their money in Hong Kong.)

Summary

We have portrayed central-provincial relations neither in terms of central dominance nor provincial autonomy. Rather, interdependence characterizes the relationship, with the balance generally in favor of the Center. However, the precise balance and reasons for it vary from province to province. The essence of central-provincial relations is a complex bargaining relationship, with the leaders of each capable of extracting resources or other values they seek in exchange for goods at their command. Throughout this discussion we have noted that energy in its various forms is an important source of leverage and a resource each is willing to pay a premium to obtain from the other. Our first case seeks to capture the complicated organizational, budgetary, and material allocation balances struck between Shanxi and the Center in the development of its coal resources. We then show how Guangdong, recognizing the perceived need of the Center to explore and develop the South China Sea on a joint venture basis, exacted a price for its cooperation, and the Center, acknowledging its dependence on this cooperation, structured the offshore operation so that Guangdong would benefit from the foreign presence.

CENTRAL-PROVINCIAL RELATIONS AND THE DEVELOPMENT OF SHANXI COAL

The development of the extensive coal deposits in the Shanxi coal basin vividly illustrates the complexities of central-provincial relations and of provincial-local relations as well. It is probably impossible for an outsider to grasp the intricacies of the deals that have been struck or to understand the process through which the bargaining occurs. Our limited data are derived from two brief visits to Taiyuan, the capital of Shanxi province, trips into two large coal mines outside Taiyuan (East and West mines), six interviews with a handful of Shanxi coal officials, and five discussions with several officials in the national coal ministry. This does not permit a detailed grasp of the situation. Our purpose, however, is a more limited one: to demonstrate the extent to which bargaining is at the heart of central-provincial relations. Further, our evidence reveals that the outside observer cannot easily conclude how the participants perceive their interests. There is no easily identified, objective set of "provincial interests" which Shanxi officials pursue and defend. These interests are defined within a particular set of regulations, bureaucratic structures, transportation facilities and financial and technological constraints. Thus, the development of Shanxi coal is not the product of a single, rational blueprint but rather the cumulative result of many disjointed decisions by the bureaucracies, taken over a period of thirty years and more.

We develop these themes by examining several aspects of Shanxi coal: the bureaucratic structure as of 1984; the arrangements for transportation of coal; the bargains over development of Pingshuo and Jincheng;

and the perceptions of Shanxi officials concerning development of their province.

Structure of the Shanxi Coal Bureaucracy: Summer, 1984

LARGE MINES

Coal production in Shanxi province in 1983 totalled 160 million metric tons. Of this total, 67 MMT came from seven very large mines: Datong, Xishan, Fenxi, Lu'an, Jincheng, Xuangang, and Yangquan. From 1970 through 1983, these seven large mines were under the management of the Shanxi Provincial Coal Department (*meitan ting*), but investment, provision of equipment, and the *total* allocation of their coal production were directly under the control of the Ministry of Coal. Provincial management meant that the province supplied working capital, was responsible for administrative and many personnel decisions, and received the profits of these mines as its revenue. In 1984, these seven mines reverted to the direct control of the Ministry of Coal, and the previous Provincial Coal Department became a dispatched organ (*paichu jiguan*) of the Ministry of Coal and acquired the name "Shanxi Coal Management District" (*meitan guanli qu*). This change, which on the surface would appear to have entailed *recentralization*, in fact was intended to facilitate *decentralization* of authority. When responding to requests from mine managers to undertake innovations, for example, the previous Provincial Coal Department had to obtain approval from its provincial comprehensive agencies (such as the Shanxi Planning Commission) and from the central Ministry of Coal. Thus, when the manager of a large-scale mine such as Datong referred matters to the Provincial Coal Department, it in turn had to obtain approvals from higher units in Beijing and Taiyuan. As one official explained, "The local mine manager had hardly any autonomy, and the approval process was very slow. In many matters, a mine manager had to obtain approval from four or five agencies before he could undertake an innovation." However, the new dispatched office of the Center was not directly under control of the province and had the latitude to act on behalf of the Ministry. As a result, the apparent recentralization—placing the seven mines under the Shanxi Coal Management District of the MCI—enabled mine managers to obtain a swifter response and required fewer approvals to his requests. (The change also had budgetary implications for the province which we describe below.)

LOCAL MINES

Five types of local mines were managed by the Shanxi Local Coal Management Bureau (*difang meitan guanli ju*). This bureau—the LCMB—

had 209 mines under its jurisdiction, producing 39 million metric tons. The five types of mines included:

1. Seven large, state-run mines that were jointly managed by the LCMB and the municipal (*shi*), special district (*diqu*), or county (*xian*) levels. These seven mines produced a total of nearly 10 MMT in 1983, were under the national unified coal allocation system, and shipped all of their production outside the province. The administration of these seven mines was very complicated. In terms of their technology, investment, and allocation of production, these seven mines were in fact directly led by MCI. However, in terms of their finances and personnel decisions, they were under municipal, special district, or county jurisdiction. Working capital was provided by the local government, although the sum to be provided was stipulated by the MCI. The LCMB led these seven mines on behalf of MCI, and provided supplementary guidance on behalf of the province. The profits from these seven mines were split between the province and the locality.

2. Other state-run mines at the municipal, special district, and county levels which receive their investment funds from within the province. A negotiated portion of their planned production remained in the province, and another planned portion was sold outside the province by Shanxi and its sub-units.

3. Large collective mines which were jointly managed by the LCMB and the collective (the commune). These mines received their investment funds from the state, which was the reason for LCMB involvement. These mines appeared on the organizational chart under the jurisdiction of the Shanxi Number Two Light Industry Department (*dier qinggongyeh ting*), the agency charged with supervising those commune level enterprises which received funds from the state. But since the Department had no expertise in coal, actual guidance was provided by the LCMB.

4. Four mines run by the legal (*sifa*) system. The Provincial Labor Reform Bureau (*laogai ju*) ran these mines, and the workers were undergoing "labor reform." In other words, these mines used prison labor. The LCMB handled the business side of these mines.

5. Mines run by the military. These mines were owned by the PLA and their output met the needs of the military. Their administrative matters were handled by the PLA, and the LCMB had professional relations (*yewu guanxi*) with them (referring, e.g., to

technical issues, equipment decisions, survey and design, and so on).

The third major category of mines were the township and market town (*xiang zhen*) mines. These mines, also called "collective" mines, were run by communes, brigades, and their successor organizations, and more recently by individuals. Shanxi had over 3,000 mines of this type, producing somewhat over 50 MMT of coal in 1983—substantially more than the five types of mines under the LCMB. The Shanxi Township Enterprise Management Bureau (*xiangzhen qiye guanli ju*) managed these mines; the Bureau was the same rank as the LCMB. Previously all local mines had been managed within one bureau, but in 1979 they were split into two, to permit some specialization in the management of the two types of mines: one semi-mechanized using state investments and the other primitive, labor intensive, and funded outside the state budget.

Coal Resource Management Commission

Before 1984, according to the formal regulations, the Provincial Coal Department (the department which supervised the seven large, modern mines) decided on the allocation of Shanxi coal reserves among potential claimants and developers—center, local, and collective. The decisions were based on the size of the reserves and the capital and technology needed to develop them. Other fields had been reserved by the Center—via the Provincial Coal Department—for provincial and local development when exploitation would make sense. Although one provincial official claimed, "The province was poor because it was not able to develop its own coal," in reality many collective and even some local mines were opened without securing proper approvals. The reason for provincial poverty had more to do with the low price of coal and poor transportation than the inability of the province and lower units to open new mines.

To bring some order and rationality to provincial coal development, as well as to ensure Shanxi would get its fair share of provincial coal, in early 1984 the province established the Coal Resources Management Commission (CRMC—*Meitan ziyuan guanli weiyuan hui*). Its appearance on the scene roughly corresponded with the transfer of the seven large mines to central control and the transformation of the Shanxi Coal Department under provincial control to the Shanxi Coal Management District under MCI. The previously ineffectively used power of the Coal Department to decide on the development of coal fields was lodged—*at the initiative of the provincial authorities*—in the new Coal Resources Management Commission.

The provincial government assigned three tasks to the CRMC: 1. to develop a comprehensive plan for development of coal deposits throughout the province; 2. to set relevant regulations for the development of coal; and 3. to decide which level—center, local, or township—can develop coal reserves in a particular region. The CRMC claimed all new mines must be approved by this commission. Most of our informants noted that great problems and contradictions exist in deciding which level of government should develop coal, so the provincial government finally decided to establish the CRMC to decide the issue. It became the provincial organ for implementing Shanxi policy in coal. As its officials explained, "We resolve the contradictions. We must approve everything. Exploitation of all coal resources in this province must pass through this commission."

While formally established on January 1, 1984, the CRMC had begun its work in August, 1983, in the guise of a provincial leadership small group. One of its first actions was to develop a map detailing the proven coal reserves in the entire province and also indicating at that point which of three levels—center, local, or collective—should develop the various reserves. Prior to the establishment of the CRMC, no consolidated map of this sort apparently existed. The map was not widely available and was considered secret, although each county in the province knew about the portion of the map pertinent to its work.

The CRMC was headed by Vice Governor Yan Wuhong, and its deputy head was Tian Zibing, formerly the head of the Provincial Coal Department. The CRMC had eleven members, including officials from the Shanxi Planning Commission, Shanxi Economic Commission, the Local Coal Management Bureau, and the Township Enterprise Management Bureau. Major issues were studied and decided by the 11-member committee, while daily issues were handled by the 15-member staff office drawn from the Provincial Coal Department, the Provincial Coal Design Institute, the Provincial Coal Geological Survey Corporation, and the Provincial Coal Science Research Institute. This agency was established without formal central approval, although the MCI was informed. Reflecting the jealous guarding of privileges that come with rank, we were told that "A central level ministry is not involved in approving the structure of a provincial level government body. You must remember that a ministry and the province are equal in level."

Upon learning of the establishment of the CRMC, Minister of Coal Gao Yangwen came to Shanxi to say that the ministry wanted to dispatch a work team to Taiyuan to work with the new committee. Shanxi provincial leaders refused. The presence of such a team from the Center would have had considerable stature. Gao then proposed that the CRMC be subject to dual leadership of MCI and the province. While the details apparently were still being negotiated during the summer of 1984, Gao's proposal was likely to be accepted, since the province required MCI cooperation to obtain investment funds for the seven mines under the jurisdiction of the LCMB. The Center, MCI, and Gao also had incentive to welcome the creation of the CRMB. Namely, it could help shut mines that had been illegally or inappropriately opened in areas which the Center wished to develop through large scale tunnel or open-pit mining. Without provincial cooperation, the Center would be stymied in its efforts to reserve certain deposits for its exploitation.

Prices, Taxes, and Transportation of Coal

The bargain between the Center and Shanxi over coal was hammered out along several dimensions: the allocation of provincial revenue between Beijing and the province; prices and subsidies; and access to transportation. As seen from Taiyuan, the bargain was very much in favor of the Center, which got cheap coal from Shanxi to fuel thermal plants, to power railroads, and to stoke blast furnaces in the steel mills.

Nonetheless, the Center did seek ways to throw bones to Taiyuan. Over the years, the parameters of the exchange had become somewhat ingrained, and changes in one dimension of the exchange resulted in adjustments in other dimensions of the relationship. This was evident in the reduction of the sum Shanxi paid to the Center in the annual revenue transfer as a result of the loss in revenue which Shanxi suffered through changes in the financial system.

REVENUE SHARING

We have already noted that all coal from fourteen mines—seven under the jurisdiction of the MCI Shanxi Coal Management District and seven under the LCMB—was transported out of the province for sale in other areas. The cost of production for coal from these mines generally was 13 to 14 *yuan* per ton. When loaded on a train, the state purchase price was roughly 17.5 *yuan*. In addition, the province received two *yuan* per ton for all coal shipped by rail as a surtax payment. In the past, these large mines transferred all their profits to the provincial government. Under the new revenue system, the mines no longer remitted all profits to the province. Instead, they retained their profits and paid a tax (*ligai shui*). In the case of the 14 large mines in Shanxi, 55% of this tax went to the Center, and 45% remained in the province, with a portion going to the provincial level and another portion to lower levels. The split of the 45% varied from mine to mine, depending on the ownership of the mine. The 55%-45% split was negotiated on an industry-wide basis, and the split varied considerably from industry to industry. For example, a higher portion of the textile *ligai shui* went to the province. The introduction of the *ligai shui* tax led to a formal loss of provincial revenue from coal. The Center then devised a way to compensate Shanxi for this loss in revenue, namely to reduce the amount which the Center collected in revenue from Shanxi. Prior to 1984 and the introduction of the *ligai shui* system, Shanxi province transmitted a substantial portion of its total revenue to the Center, the precise sum being set through negotiations held annually. In the early 1980's, this was set at around 20% of its total revenue with Shanxi retaining 80%. With the transfer of the seven large mines to MCI and with the introduction of the *ligai shui*, the Center allowed Shanxi in 1985 to keep 97.5% of its provincial revenue.

PRICES

The administered price for coal from the large mines averaged about 17.5 *yuan* per ton. Beginning in 1981, once the coal was on a railroad car, the Center paid the province a subsidy of 10 *yuan* per ton.[19] Presumably, this served as an incentive to the mines and local officials to actually load the coal from these mines on the cars and ship it out of the province, rather than diverting the empty cars to small, locally run mines, where the cost of production was less and the revenue remained in the province. The average cost of coal from unmechanized, labor intensive, small mines frequently was between 4-9 *yuan* per ton, considerably less than the cost from the mechanized, large mines. The temptation, therefore, was to ship inexpensive coal produced in locally run mines.

Shanxi provincial government set the price for coal produced by local mines within the plan. It kept these prices low within the province, to ensure that coal remained within the financial reach of the poor peasants who inhabited the province and that local industries availed themselves of cheap coal. Since the price of coal was higher outside the province, considerable incentive existed to export coal from Shanxi. In short, coal prices in the province exhibited little rationality but rather resulted from bureaucratic decisions. There was no uniform structure of price, the profit margins varied enormously from mine to mine, and the price of coal jumped dramatically as soon as it was placed on a coal car headed out of the province.

[19] We received contradictory information as to whether this 10 *yuan* subsidy was paid for coal from all fourteen large mines or just the seven mines under the provincial control of the LCMB.

TRANSPORTATION

Before tracing the implications of this situation, we must sketch the transportation situation in the province. In a word, the coal-rich province sorely lacks means for transporting the coal out of the province. Only three railroad lines connect the province to its major coal customers to the east and south. The rail system was used at full capacity, and it was not sufficient to move the amount produced in the province.[20] In 1983-84, roughly 60% of production left the province by rail, 10% was trucked out, and 30% was used within the province—with a good portion of coal consumed within the province also shipped by rail.

The major impediment to rapid development of Shanxi coal was the inadequate transportation network. The 14 large state mines had first access to the railways. Local mines came next, and the collective mines had lowest priority. There was, in fact, considerable competition for access to the railways. Beginning in December, 1983, the newly established Coal Transport and Sales Corporation (*meitan yunxiao zonggongsi*) assumed responsibility for implementing the allocation and transport plan for coal. The state plan for the allocation of coal was quite detailed, as was the transportation plan. This plan stipulated how many empty cars the Beijing Management Bureau of the Ministry of Railways was to supply the Shanxi Railway Subbureau for each time span, and the Coal Transport and Sales Corporation (CTSC) supervised the subdivision of these cars. According to one official with long experience in the Ministry of Railways, in spite of the efforts of the planners, the plan usually was not fulfilled. The real value of an empty coal car was quite high, given the difference in price between unloaded and loaded coal. Corruption and a black market in empty coal cars was the result. Not infrequently, empty cars were intercepted en route to the mine head. According to this official, diversion occurred even in the mine field, for example, with empty cars being diverted in such mines as Datong or Fenxi. (The plan allocates the empty cars to large mines, but the mines are responsible for delivering the empty cars to the mine heads.) The cultivation of personal relations and side deals therefore frequently were undertaken between the planned suppliers and consumers to ensure plan fulfillment.[21]

Not surprisingly under these circumstances, disruptions in coal sup-

[20] The capacity could be expanded through use of more powerful locomotives, larger coal cars, and improved loading facilities.

[21] The irrational price system also helps explain the shortage in coal cars. The Ministry of Railways runs the coal car manufacturing plants. The same plants manufacture and repair cars. According to the administered prices, it is much more profitable to manufacture new cars than to repair old cars. Therefore, the plants concentrate on turning out new cars, while allowing cars in disrepair to accumulate.

ply—or at least the fear of disruption brought on by inadequate inventories—plagued the Chinese economy. The SEC in Beijing and the Shanxi Economic Commission played vital roles through the mid-1980's in alleviating coal shortages. (The situation altered somewhat after coal production began to increase substantially in the mid-1980's. The price of above-quota coal and coal produced in small mines was allowed to float upward and reflect supply and demand, and a significant portion of coal production no longer was allocated according to state plan.)

Thus, despite or more accurately because of its vast coal deposits, Shanxi province suffered from the failure of the Center to expand rail transportation into the province and from the low price of coal. As one Shanxi official explained,

> Shanxi suffered from too low a price for coal. Eighty-six to eighty-seven percent of the province's railroad capacity is utilized exclusively to transport coal. Shanxi has the capacity to expand into other products, but we cannot get the goods moved by rail because of the national needs for coal. Investment by the Center has enabled coal production to grow very fast. This has tied up the rail system and suppressed the growth of other industries. We give the Center a lot and get back little.
> Coal prices are held down because of the role of coal in the national economy. If we raise the coal price, then we would get inflation throughout the economy, and state expenses will go way up. The profit in coal, therefore, is not high. The price is not as high as the value. Shanxi has proposed raising coal prices to the Center, but the Center is [instead

using financial subsidies to help make up the difference to the province.]

OFFSETS

In sum, according to both provincial officials and many economists at the Center, the Center dominated the exchange, but it did provide Shanxi with some side payments. These subsidies included the 2 *yuan* per ton subsidy for each ton shipped out of the province, the 10 *yuan* subsidy for each ton of coal from large mines when loaded on the train, and the investments allocated to the province, especially to the seven mines under the Local Coal Management Bureau.

Another part of the bargain was the access to rail transport which the Center guaranteed to the province under the State Plan. The fourteen mines for which all production was exported by rail according to the plan produced roughly 79 MMT in 1983. The total shipped out of the province was 106 MMT. Thus, 27 MMT or about 25% of the total exported from the province by rail came from mines under the jurisdiction of the LCMB and the Township Enterprises Management Bureau. These exports did not receive the 10 *yuan* per ton subsidy. The province decided on the allocation of this 25% of the total coal exported by rail. The distribution of this coal did not require Central approval, although its shipment had to fit into the national rail transport plan. In theory, the price for this coal was fixed, but in fact it was a negotiated price. Other provinces sent representatives to Shanxi to buy this coal; a sufficient national demand existed that Shanxi did not need to send salesmen elsewhere to identify buyers.[22] Some of this coal was swapped on a barter basis for commodities needed in the province. This system began in the 1950's. The percentage of coal that fell under this arrangement has varied over time, and the percentage was fixed each year when Shanxi and the Center negotiated their exchanges for the coming year. The profit which Shanxi earned became part of the provincial revenue.

Development of New Mines: The Cases of Jincheng and Antaibao

The complexity of central-provincial relations and the bargains that are struck are revealed in the way new mines are approved. The cases of Jincheng and Antaibao illustrate the point.[23]

JINCHENG

This large field extends over three counties and one municipality, and its reserves are estimated to total 8 billion tons. In 1984, Jincheng consisted of three separate large underground complexes, and it was one of the seven mining areas recently placed under direct central control. Under MCI instructions, the Hanxing Coal Mine Design Institute in Hebei

---

[22] For example, in the mid-1980's, Jiangsu province needed 24 million tons of coal each year, but the Center only supplied 16 million tons through the plan. Individual local units in Jiangsu therefore dispatch thousands of buyers to Shanxi and other coal producing provinces to purchase coal—often paying 150 or 160 *yuan* per ton. See Kazuo Yamanouchi, "The Chinese Price System and the Thrust of Reform," *China Newsletter*, No. 60 (January-February, 1986), p. 4.

[23] These cases are derived from interviews. Additional references to central-local tensions and bargains over coal development can be found in the Chinese press. See for example: "Bravely Lift Heavy Burdens," *Shanxi Ribao*, April 10, 1981, p. 1, translated in *JPRS China Report—Economic Affairs*, No. 143 (June 16, 1981), pp. 42-43; "Dispute over Resources Resolved," in *Shanxi Ribao*, May 12, 1981, p. 2, translated in *JPRS China Report—Economic Affairs*, No. 148 (July 6, 1981), pp. 39-40; "Shanxi Governor Solves Mine Building Dispute," Xinhua Domestic Service, June 27, 1983, in FBIS, June 28, 1983, pp. R4-5.

province developed a comprehensive design for the development of the entire field. The institute proposed to develop six additional centrally run mines within the field with a productive capacity of 22 million tons per year. On November 19, 1983, the MCI convened a meeting at Jincheng to unveil the development plan prepared by the Design Institute and to elicit opinions. Attending the meeting were representatives from the SPC in Beijing, the Jincheng Coal Mine Administration, the Shanxi Coal Department, and the provincial coal resources leadership small group (the predecessor of the Coal Resources Management Commission). Except for the latter, all other attendees had received a copy of the proposal. At this meeting, the leadership small group asserted that the six new mines would have little benefit for the three counties and the municipality affected. Representatives from these localities supported this viewpoint. When the provincial leadership small group presented its views, the MCI representative from Beijing and the Hanxing Design Institute vociferously disagreed, while the localities warmly supported the provincial spokesman. The dispute was very heated, according to one participant.

In any case, the meeting did not constitute a decisional body, as the SPC had to issue the formal approval. The representatives of the SPC therefore returned to Beijing knowing that Shanxi did not approve of the MCI plans. The MCI in fact, though, simply forwarded the original Hanxing project design to the SPC, and chose not to highlight provincial opposition. However, the SPC in turn sent a cable and telephoned to ascertain the precise provincial position. Then, in March, 1984, the Shanxi CRMC sent a formal report to the Design and Approval Bureau in the SPC. So, the SPC received two reports—one the Hanxing plan transmitted by the MCI with its approval and the second the Shanxi report. In the end, according to Shanxi officials, the SPC agreed with the provincial report and approved the development of four additional mines under central control while authorizing the remaining portions of the field to be reserved for local development.

THE ANTAIBAO JOINT VENTURE WITH OCCIDENTAL

In March, 1982, Occidental Petroleum agreed to undertake a feasibility study for development of an open pit mine at Antaibao in the Pingshuo coal field of Shanxi province.[24] The rough framework was for Occidental to obtain 60% and the Chinese 40% of the anticipated production of 15 million tons per year. After Occidental had regained its investment, Oc-

---

[24] This section draws on interviews with coal mining, banking, and financial officials in Beijing and Shanxi province and knowledgeable Americans.

cidental would sell 40% of production on the world market and China would have 60% of production for its domestic use or for export. The subsequent negotiations over the exact terms of the joint venture were protracted and difficult. Our purpose here is not to recount the history of the tortuous negotiations; through Bank of China loans to Occidental, the Chinese ended up financing a much higher percentage of the total costs than they had initially anticipated. Nor is our purpose to explicate how this particular joint venture was structured and how the Chinese approached the negotiations.[25] Rather, our purpose here is to illuminate central-Shanxi relations in the carving out of the Antaibao reserves for exploitation by the Center through a joint venture agreement.

Pingshuo is a large coal field in northern Shanxi, a southwest extension of the huge Datong mining area. Pingshuo has 12.7 billion tons of reserves. The Shenyang Design Institute (SDI) developed plans from 1960 to 1966 for exploiting the Pingshuo field. It concluded that the optimal development of the field would occur through 12 medium sized modern mines, several of which would be in the Antaibao portion of the Pingshuo field. The SDI completed its plan on the eve of the Cultural Revolution, but in 1970, the top leaders in Beijing adopted policies to encourage the rapid development of small-scale coal mines under provincial, special district, county, and commune guidance. Moreover, during the Cultural Revolution, there simply was no money or technical ability to develop the twelve modern mines envisioned in the SDI plans. With the emphasis on small-scale mines from 1970 on, some of the best locations for modern mines at Pingshuo began to be developed by local governments as underground mines. In addition, new technologies and equipment on the world market enabled exploitation of the coal field through open-pit mines on a scale much larger than originally envisioned. As a result, by the mid- and late 1970's, the original plan of development formulated by the SDI was outdated, and a new plan was drafted in 1977-78 calling for development of three large open pit mines at Pingshuo involving foreign participation. This plan was based on a pre-feasibility study which the MCI undertook in 1975-76.

The new plan called for development of a large open pit mine at Antaibao before 1985, with an estimated 450 million tons of reserves. The second and third mines each had reserves of about 400 million tons, and

---

[25] On both counts, the Pingshuo project differed substantially from the South China Sea projects. In essence, Occidental did not enter into a risk, equity contract. And MCI did not prepare as meticulously for this negotiation as MPI did. MCI apparently did not systematically explore patterns in the financing and management of open pit coal mine projects aimed at the export markets. It did not develop a model contract, nor did it invite bids for the Antaibao project.

these were to be developed in subsequent five year plans. The three large open pit mines were to be developed by the Center, and the plan preserved substantial portions of the Pingshuo field for provincial development as well. In effect, the Ministry of Coal assigned parts of the Pingshuo field to the province and lower levels for development, and in exchange preserved the core of the field for development by the Center through the three open pit mines.

The Shanxi Coal Resources Management Commission, already described above, assumed responsiblity for protecting Antaibao and the other two sites for development by the Center. At Antaibao, ten small-scale coal mines were already in operation by the mid-1970's, with shafts and tunnels already dug. The Shanxi CRMB shut these mines, with Beijing providing compensation to the local government units that had developed these mines. Also as part of the deal, the Center reiterated its commitment to assign portions of the Pingshuo field to the province and promised to provide investment funds to assist in development of those portions of the field under provincial control. As a Shanxi official explained, "The Center found it harder to halt the exploration and development at Antaibao by local governments than the province." Describing why the province acceded to the demands of the Center, the provincial bureaucrat indicated, "It was necessary for the province to halt this development because Occidental and Mr. Hammer signed a contract to develop Pingshuo."

Left unsaid was Deng Xiaoping's widely known strong personal backing of the project. Indeed, as early as the summer of 1978, Deng encouraged visiting Americans to explore the possibility of developing open pit coal mines in China. He personally extended an invitation to Armand Hammer during the Vice Premier's February, 1979 visit to Houston, Texas, which Hammer swiftly accepted. Acting against the advice of detractors within their respective organizations, Deng and Hammer provided the initiative to sign the contract. As world coal prices dropped through the early 1980's, the commercial viability of the project became somewhat suspect, and Occidental found it difficult to meet its commitment to obtain foreign financing for the project. The 1982 Occidental feasibility study, which built upon the 1977-78 MCI study, was based on $50 per ton steaming coal, but by 1984, world prices had dropped below $40 per ton. In 1984, Deng yielded to Occidental pressures for concessions in the 1982-83 agreements, and the Bank of China stepped into the financing breach, presumably with the encouragement of Deng Xiaoping. Deng seemed eager to make this project a showcase of Sino-foreign cooperation. In sum, the central-provincial deals struck over this project enjoyed the total support of the preeminent leader—an aspect of the project absent in the Three Gorges deliberations but also present in the South China Sea joint ventures.

Shanxi had reasons to be concerned about the joint venture at Antaibao other than its possible loss of this resource to central control. Specifically, with railroad transportation out of the province already heavily committed to shipment of coal from the fourteen mines under the unified distribution plan, the province had legitimate reason to fear that the export of Antaibao coal would utilize coal cars previously available for provincial coal. Bargains appear to have been struck to alleviate this provincial and subprovincial concern. First, decisions to undertake the projects were accompanied by decisions to expand the rail capacity from the Datong region to Qinhuangdao, the harbor from which Antaibao coal would be shipped to Japan, southeast Asia, and other foreign markets. These improvements were financed in part by a loan from Japan. Second, the Datong-Taiyuan trunk line runs within 20 km. of Antaibao. The Center financed the entire construction of the spur line to the mine. (One of our sources said the China National Coal Development Corporation financed construction of the spur line; another source said the Ministry of Railways paid the full cost of the 20 km. spur.) Third, access to the spur was not limited to Antaibao coal. Rather, local mines in the area were allowed to build their own lines to the new spur, with the cost of the feeder lines shouldered by the province. Previously, local mines in this area moved their coal via truck. Thus, Shanxi shared in the increased rail capacity which Antaibao necessitated and stimulated. Finally, contracts for construction of the spur line were let on bids—a new method for selection of the construction firm in China. Although the 14th Construction Company of the Ministry of Railways—a central level company—won the bid against a unit from the Ministry of Metallurgy, many Shanxi local companies obtained subcontracts to undertake a lot of items in the project, for example, in civil engineering and in supply of services.

Shanxi also derived benefit from the financing and revenue arrangements. The province would earn revenue from a land tax on Antaibao and would retain 10% of the tax on profits paid by the Antaibao corporation. The revenues from the product tax (*chan pin shui*) and the natural resource tax paid by the Antaibao corporation also would be split between the province and the Center. Most significantly, the Antaibao project is a joint venture between the China National Coal Development Corporation and Occidental. As to the financing, CNCDC organized "Party A"—the Chinese side—to provide $200-300 million for the project, while Occidental and the Bank of China became "Party B," committed to investing over $400 million.[26] "Party A" consisted of the Ministry of Coal, the China International Trust and Investment Corporation, and Shanxi province. CNCDC credited Shanxi province with a 5% share in the total contribution of Party A. The 5% was calculated as the value of the provincial contribution to the venture: the land. The province did not put up any currency. Through this calculation, Shanxi province would get 5% of the profit accruing to the Chinese side. Presumably, since a substantial portion of the coal would be exported, the profit would include access to some foreign currency.

As a result of the many trade-offs, Shanxi officials expressed hope but some uncertainty that the development of Pingshuo would accrue to the provincial benefit. In response to a question as to whether the province would have gained more revenue if the field had remained under total Shanxi control, one provincial-level informant replied:

> Not necessarily. The full utilization of the coal resources through an open pit mine will be more productive than had the coal been mined through shaft mines, and hence will yield more revenue. The issue is how the coal from Pingshuo will be distributed, and that has not yet been fully decided. If the coal produced at Pingshuo is transported to other provinces, then the effect on provincial revenue is not yet clear. But if thermal plants are associated with the mine and electricity is generated at the mine head, then this will be conducive to the economic development of both Beijing and Shanxi province. So the effect will be to enhance the revenue base of the province.
> Two huge coal-fired thermal plants are now being built which will use coal from Pingshuo, one near Pingshuo and another one in Datong. This will enable the province to bring electricity to the southern portion of the province, where water is more abundant but electricity is in short supply. In short, opening of the Pingshuo coal field

[26] Three supposedly knowledgeable Chinese sources gave us three different figures for the contribution of "Party A": $200 million; $240 million; and $300 million. The *China Daily* gave a figure of $250 million. (*China Daily*, December, 1984.) The discrepancies are explainable, since the contract specified the contributions of Party A in terms of the goods and services it was to supply: offices, construction of the substructure (for example, construction of the railway within the mine and of dams to divert water), and so on. Most of these items would be purchased with Chinese currency; only a small amount required foreign currency. While the contract attached a US dollar figure to each of the goods and services Party A was to contribute, fulfillment of the contractual obligation depended on providing the specified good or service. If Party A could meet its obligation at less than the estimated cost, it pocketed the profit; if its actual cost exceeded the estimates, it absorbed the loss. Similarly, Party B was obligated to provide specific goods and services, with the bulk being the actual equipment.

will help the economic development of the southern part of the province.

Further, the quality of Pingshuo coal is different. It has high volatility, is low in ash and sulfur content, and is low in phosphorous. It makes very good steam coal. Using this coal will free up other coal which Shanxi is currently obligated to deliver, and further, through the two thermal plants now under construction, Shanxi will become an even greater supplier of electricity to other regions, especially Hebei, Beijing, and Tianjin. By supplying electricity rather than building more coal-fired thermal plants in those localities which would burn Shanxi coal, we will have more coal that the province can ship by rail for its own allocation. What must be understood is that the management of economic development is like playing on a chess board, and the calculation of the effect of a project upon provincial revenue is complicated.

There are two final points. Pingshuo will employ many people from the province. Finally, it must be remembered that Antaibao will come at no cost to the province. The Center is bearing the investment costs.

Our description of the complex central-provincial deal over the Antaibao joint venture and Pingshuo development more generally captures but the tip of the iceberg. Doubtlessly, the actual tradeoffs were even more intricate and extended to employment of personnel at the mines, access to the foreign currency to be earned from the exported coal, and so on. Further, as the quotation above reveals, construction of the mine began before the full deal had been struck, as the actual allocation or use of Antaibao coal would only be set after production begins. The vignette suggests that the bargains between Center and province are subject to constant renegotiation and adjustment as the situation changes.

The Pingshuo case also reveals the difficulty which the outside observer faces in assessing whether a province will welcome a particular project. One cannot automatically assume, for example, that a province seeks to increase its revenue base or resists the transfer of administrative responsibility over natural resource development from its sphere to the Center. One must also ascertain in such instances what additional responsibilities may devolve onto the province when its revenue base expands or what side payments are made when it surrenders jurisdiction over a source of revenue. As a Shanxi official explained, "The province does not necessarily prefer provincially or locally developed mines. It really depends on the site—the thickness of the seams, the quality of the coal. Views depend on which level of government can effectively develop the coal and which level has the financial resources to finance the development."

Another Shanxi official explained that more generally, "Provinces usually welcome a project which the Center wishes to build and for which the Center provides the investment funds. Some issues do arise, of course. For example, the province or local governments must spend money on providing a commercial network, schools, cultural facilities and so on. It must guarantee food supplies to the new industrial project. However, the Center pays for other infrastructure services which have more general use, such as railways. When the Center decides to locate a big project in a province, there is inevitably considerable negotiation between the Center and province." The official then explained that the greatest concern of provincial officials usually was with the spatial consequences of the project: Would the project benefit the region within the province to which the provincial leaders were then assigning primacy? Shanxi officials exhibited this concern over Pingshuo when they hoped electricity generated from its nearby thermal plants would be available to help develop the southern portion of the province. Hence, according to our Shanxi informants—and our Guangdong data point in the same direction—the geographical distribution of the benefits from a Beijing-funded and managed project is a major concern of provincial officials.

Thus, as one Shanxi official disclosed, "A particularly contentious issue in centrally-initiated projects is the actual site selection—where the project will be located within the province." The reaction of a province to a major project therefore depends on its configuration: where it is located, how it affects the political needs and long-term development plans of provincial officials, what the financial package entails, what burdens the project adds or removes from provincial shoulders, and what employment opportunites it provides. The joint venture at Antaibao reflects how the project was structured to alleviate many of Shanxi concerns in order to secure the necessary cooperation of provincial officials, with some other potentially contentious issues simply postponed.

The Structure of Center-Shanxi Relations in Coal

Where and how were the deals struck between Shanxi and the Center? Our data do not permit a definitive response to this fundamental question, but we can at least identify the institutional mechanisms or "arenas" in which the issues were addressed in 1983-84. The channels reflected the hierarchical levels and processes we detailed in Chapters Two and Three: 1. personal interventions by the top leaders; 2. *ad hoc* coordinating committees and groups which act in the name of the State

Council and which in fact are staffs of the top leaders; 3. bureaucratic mechanisms centering on MCI, the SPC, and the SEC; and 4. the annual economic, planning, and finance conferences. We have already noted the personal involvement of Deng Xiaoping in the Antaibao project, and we have indicated that the top leaders responsible for the economy and energy—Zhao Ziyang, Li Peng, and at an earlier stage Kang Shien—provided the ultimate courts of appeal in disputes between ministries and Shanxi. Also, Shanxi depended heavily upon the Ministry of Coal to act on its behalf among the top leaders. When Gao Yangwen was Minister, his apparent high standing with the top leaders, as well as the connections of Vice Minister Kong Xun, proved beneficial to Shanxi on issues where MCI and Shanxi had the same viewpoint. Long-time economic specialist among the top leaders Bo Yibo, a native of Shanxi and guerrilla leader in the region, also took a particular interest in Shanxi affairs.

The top leaders did not have enough time to resolve all central-provincial disputes, however, and they therefore turned to trusted aides to conduct studies and mediate the issues for them. Veteran economic official Ma Hong, for example, played an important role in assisting the top leaders address various problems related to Shanxi coal. Using his bases in the Chinese Academy of Social Sciences and in several small research centers in the State Council in 1981-82, Ma Hong and his aides carried out several studies and convened several meetings concerning the development of the Shanxi coal basin.

When Premier Zhao Ziyang received a report on this activity, he instructed his associates (including Ma Hong) to broaden the geographic scope of the plan to include the entire coal basin which extends to Henan, Hebei, Shanxi, and Inner Mongolia. He also instructed that the scope be extended to include downstream uses of coal, such as methanol, and to analyze how coal could be used to establish Shanxi as an industrial base. The final report totaled over a million words, with a 50,000-word summary.

The State Council then formed a Shanxi Coal Base Development Office (SCBDO) to provide the necessary coordination and to secure implementation of the plan. The SCBDO is an example, in form, of the coordinating committee established in the Zhongnanhai as a link between the top leaders and the commissions and ministries that Chapter Two discussed. As with many other such committees, its composition suggested that while technically under the State Council, in reality it operated within one of the Commissions, in this instance the SPC.[27] Guo Hong-tao, a deputy director of the SPC, was named head of the office. It had 10

---

[27] Recall that similarly the Offshore Rig Leadership Small Group was under the SEC.

to 12 members, including a Vice Governor of Shanxi and representation from the SPC and such ministries as Coal, Railways, and Communications. The SCBDO members travelled frequently to Taiyuan. In addition, at the request of Shanxi province, the SCBDO established a team (*zu*) in Shanxi. The team had a designated manpower ceiling of ten people, though in August, 1985, only six worked in the office. A key liaison figure between the SCBDO in the Zhongnanhai and its Taiyuan group, Guo Qingan, resided in Taiyuan but was in charge of Shanxi affairs for the SCBDO. With one foot in Beijing and another in Taiyuan, Guo Qingan played a key bureaucratic liaison role. The Shanxi group of the SCBDO was given the rank of a dispatched office (*paichu jiguan*) of the State Council and therefore ranked above the provincial planning commission. The group utilized the staff office (*bangongshi*) of the provincial planning commission. Herein is the reason Shanxi welcomed the group in the province. Instructions issued under its command had greater weight than orders from the provincial planning commission. There were too many Central agencies in Shanxi for the Shanxi government to be able to coordinate them. The staff in the SCBDO group in Taiyuan were Shanxi people, and they utilized their rank as a State Council dispatched office to coordinate the work of various central agencies in Shanxi. In particular, in addition to enforcing the long term development plan, the SCBDO and its group in Shanxi arranged logistical support for the development of coal and assisted in hastening development of industries necessary to utilize the coal effectively.

Organizing the South China Sea Effort

We now turn to Guangdong province and the institutional measures initiated from 1980 through 1985 to accommodate the Western presence. Our narrative sketches the principal organizations created to implement the contracts and service the offshore activities: Nanhai West, Nanhai East, the Joint Management Committees under their control, China Nanhai Offshore Joint Services Corporation, and other joint venture service companies. Through the detail we provide, we seek to capture the salient characteristics of central-provincial relations and of interagency relations at lower levels.

Nanhai West

ORIGINS

On May 16, 1983, CNOOC announced the formation of four regional oil companies to undertake oil exploration and other work for foreign companies exploring and developing China's offshore oil. The four companies included Nanhai West Petroleum Company based in Zhanjiang. Nanhai West assumed the task of working with foreign companies with blocks in the Beibu Gulf, the Yingge Sea, and areas in the South China Sea west of the Pearl River mouth. It also would provide services on contract to foreign firms throughout the South China Sea.

Nanhai West was not a new organization especially created to work with the foreigners. Rather, it grew out of the South China Sea Branch of the China Petroleum Corporation and had been engaged in petroleum exploration and development for a number of years. The Ministry of Geology pioneered offshore exploration in the Yingge Sea south of Hainan Island in the 1960's, an exercise which produced considerable optimism.[28] Then, in 1973, the Chinese began land-based offshore drilling in the South China Sea, using the small Paracel islets as the base. Following the importation of a digital seismic prospecting vessel and jack-up drilling platform from Singapore in 1975, exploration in the waters around Hainan intensified.[29] The South China Sea Branch required a base to service its offshore activities, which it established in Zhanjiang in western Guangdong in 1973. (For the politics surrounding the establishment of the base, see Chapter Four.) Zhanjiang, a natural harbor located on the Liuzhou peninsula, had once been a French treaty port, serving as a northern base of operations to check piracy in the South China Sea. By the 1980's, it was the headquarters of the South China naval fleet and its extensive wharf facilities were used for commercial shipping in grain, oil, and machinery to and from western Guangdong and Guangxi province.

From 1973 on, the South China Sea Branch gradually grew. Its leaders and technicians came from oil and gas fields throughout China, with two large groups coming from the natural gas field in Sichuan and from Huabei. At the time, according to one foreign observer, Zhanjiang was considered a hardship post, and it did not necessarily attract eager and able volunteers at the outset. According to Chinese and Americans who claim familiarity with the politics of Nanhai West, the organization could be subdivided into clusters of higher officials and people they brought with them from a particular field. Thus, there was a Sichuan group, a Daqing group, and so on. What was lacking at the higher levels of Nanhai West was Cantonese. While ordinary laborers came from the province, the top leaders came from outside the province, and the organization gave the impression of being an outpost of Mandarin speakers. By early 1980, the

[28] See Guo Shuisheng and Chen Weihuang, "Vast Vistas in Yingge Sea Oil Exploration," *China Oil*, Vol. 2, No. 2 (Summer, 1985), pp. 46-49.

[29] We see here the consequences of the 1973-75 turn outward, described in Chapter Five.

organization had 6,000 employees, and in mid-1984, it had grown to 11,000 employees.

From 1973 to 1984, the total investment of the Ministry of Petroleum in its Zhanjiang operation was 800 million RMB. Before 1980, the bulk of this was for infrastructure, and after that date, most expenditures were for exploration in the Yingge Sea and Beibuwan. The entire sum came from the Ministry of Petroleum in Beijing; none of the investment funds came from Zhanjiang municipality or Guangdong province.

The formation of Nanhai West, in a sense, detracted from both the responsibility and stature of the previous South Sea Branch. It lost a portion of its territorial domain to the newly created Nanhai East. While retaining its formal level as a "bureau" (ju), instead of reporting directly to a Vice Minister of Petroleum, Nanhai West was under the jurisdiction of CNOOC. And it no longer was in charge of offshore development; the foreign oil companies would share in the task and in the profit. There is little indication, however, that the Nanhai West organization opposed the turn to the outside world. Some of their personnel had already dealt with foreigners at other oil and natural gas fields. They also understood the technological imperatives and capital requirements that necessitated cooperation with the multinational oil companies. And, as this section illuminates, the cooperation with the outside world offered financial, technological, and career benefits. Foreign observers sense, however, that the South China Sea Branch did not welcome the creation of CNOOC, its being made subordinate to CNOOC, or the formation of Nanhai East.

TASKS

In summer, 1984, its leaders portrayed Nanhai West as having four tasks, with separate parts of the organization responsible for each task. First, it cooperated in the exploration and development of offshore petroleum with Western companies in a zone from 108 degrees to 113 degrees 10' longitude east. (Nanhai East claimed responsibility for the area from 113 degrees 10' to 118 degrees.) Its first cooperative venture, even before its creation as Nanhai West, began in 1980 with Total of France. It initiated work with Arco in 1983, and by 1984, it was cooperating with eight different foreign ventures drilling in nine blocks. These ventures had a total of 22 foreign companies. (We describe below how the cooperation actually was organized.) The bulk of Nanhai West personnel responsible for this activity, especially the personnel of the joint management committees, were newly assigned to Zhanjiang in the early 1980's. According to a Hong Kong based PRC official, over 200 came from Chongqing.

Its second task was to provide offshore services. It used its Zhanjiang base for this, and also built new bases on Hainan Island and in the Shenzhen special economic zone north of Hong Kong. Nanhai West had two seismic vessels, one seabed coring and survey vessel, four drilling rigs, and material supply vessels. Nanhai West also managed navigation positioning installations at fourteen spots along the entire Guangdong coast, including the area from 113 degrees 10′ to 118 degrees, for which Nanhai East was responsible offshore. The Zhanjiang base included wharfs, storage areas, machine repair shops, office buildings, a computer processing center, fuel and water tanks, and supply depots for mud, cement, and barelyte.

The third task was to undertake onshore survey and exploration activities. In mid-1984, these included seismic surveys in the Liuzhou peninsula and drilling activities in the Fushan area of northern Hainan and in the Sanshui area near Guangzhou. Finally, typical of all such large organizations in China, Nanhai developed its own support network for its employees: housing, kindergarten, schools, commercial and food stores, restaurants, barbershops, and so on. Zhanjiang municipality received no budgetary appropriation to provide these facilities for its new inhabitants, and the responsibility for serving the employees passed to the employer. Its responsibilities in the offshore petroleum sphere—undertaking and servicing offshore exploration and development activities—necessitated extensive cooperation with foreign firms after 1983, and the adjustments for Nanhai West did not come easily. In fact, many foreign firms described Nanhai West as a difficult partner in such areas as contract adherence, financial charges, and safety.

COMMUNICATIONS WITH OTHER AGENCIES

Although transportation and communication facilities were being improved, the Nanhai West base was somewhat isolated physically, across the bay from the old and new towns, naval base, and wharves of Zhanjiang. Overcrowded, small ferries chugged irregularly across the bay. Lorries, vans, bicyclists, and pedestrians competed for the limited space, assuming the sea was sufficiently calm to permit the gangplanks to be lowered onto the steeply sloping pier and the ferrymen were not breaking for lunch. The local airport had no radar, and air service to Guangzhou was uncertain for much of the year. No helicopter service linked the Nanhai base to the airport or hotel complex in Zhanjiang city, with the result that foreign operators had to battle the ferry lines to get to their headquarters. Telecommunications from Nanhai West were limited and, as of 1984, foreign firms found the facilities antiquated. Nanhai West managed the telecommunication facilities from the base to Zhanjiang city across the bay, and from there to Guangzhou, the responsibility passed to the China Nanhai Oil Joint Services Company. In fact, the

Zhanjiang base was so isolated in 1983-84 that several of the foreign companies had established more efficient communication links from other spots in the province to their offshore operations. The main reason Occidental, Texaco, Pennzoil, Arco and others had established offices in the Nanhai complex was to have effective communication with their Chinese operating partner. The joint venture arrangement, in other words, required the foreigner to have a presence and cooperate with the indigenous operator.

The physical setting and communication facilities underscored the remoteness of Nanhai West in the early days of its cooperation with foreign oil companies, naturally raising questions about its relations with Beijing and about coordination with the Chinese bureaucracy. The foreign operators complained about the inability or reluctance of Nanhai West to share information with CNOOC headquarters in Beijing. It is not clear whether the communication problems were due to technological inadequacies or the desire to hoard information. Many foreign observers thought the latter was the more likely reason. Even within Nanhai West, these observers noted, information frequently was hoarded within a division. No matter what the reason, the foreign firms ended up serving as one bridge between Nanhai West and CNOOC, and they routinely passed information to both organizations out of recognition that the superior and subordinate did not always adequately share their data.

> For example, one foreign operator noted: There is a severe lack of communication among Chinese organizations—CNOOC, Nanhai West, Nanhai East, and Guangdong. Indeed, there is even lack of communication between lower levels and the leadership of some of these organs. For example, we brought in a key set of environmental equipment. When the equipment arrived on the rig, we literally had representatives from CNOOC, Nanhai East, Nanhai West, and Guangdong on the rig itself to witness the arrival of the machinery. We signed all the forms and handed over all the pertinent data at that time. We subsequently received a separate request from CNOOC for its own copy of the data. In sum, each subunit on the Chinese side hoards information and husbands its own authority.

Efforts were made to overcome such barriers, however. The head of the Nanhai West, Wang Yan, travelled to Beijing four to five times a year for various meetings, and Nanhai West maintained a liaison office in the Ministry of Petroleum compound in Beijing, staffed by five people. Nanhai West also dispatched personnel to Beijing for special purposes, such as sending specialists to represent it at the second round of bidding in 1985. Occasionally, high level officials visited Nanhai West. Kang Shien and Gu Mu, for instance, both had visited the base. (On the other hand, neither Yu Qiuli nor Li Peng had travelled to the facilities.) CNOOC also routinely dispatched teams to check conditions. All these mechanisms did not eliminate the great gap between Beijing and Zhanjiang, however.

SUMMARY

To conclude, then, Nanhai West started as an offshore petroleum exploration and development company, and in typical Chinese fashion, had to develop its own upstream capability to service its activities and its own institutions to provide for its employees. All this activity was financed totally by the Ministry of Petroleum. The signing of the joint venture contract prompted a reorganization, with the South Sea Branch losing a portion of its domain to the newly created Nanhai East. Further, it created a new division to deal with the foreign companies. With its 11,000 employees, it was—as one Western observer put it—the largest oil company in the world with no production. All of its revenue came from Beijing. The attraction of the Western connection was the possibility of foreign revenue. The service portion of the organization sought to secure contracts from the offshore activities. Further, Nanhai West anticipated that it would share in a portion of revenue that MPI and CNOOC would obtain from any production of petroleum and natural gas. (The split among MPI, CNOOC, and Nanhai West had not been set as of 1984 and would be decided after production began.) Moreover, Nanhai West personnel enjoyed enhanced career opportunities through the foreign ties. Many personnel received training in Houston, Los Angeles, and other sites beginning with the seismic surveys. Those working with the foreign firms on the joint management committees and their subordinate units believed their careers would flourish, should their particular joint venture culminate in production.

Nanhai East

CREATING NANHAI EAST

The organization implementing the contracts in the eastern portion of the South China Sea contrasted sharply with Nanhai West. With no prior history, it was created solely as an operating company. It did not have nor did it seek to develop a capacity to service the offshore rigs. With headquarters in Guangzhou, it looked to various service companies in Guangzhou, the Shenzhen special economic zone, and Hong Kong. These companies (described below) were either indigenous, joint ventures, or foreign owned.

The reasons for the creation of Nanhai East remain somewhat obscure. Some uncertainty as to its jurisdiction—and possibly an indication of Nanhai West dissatisfaction—is that the boundary delineating the jurisdiction between the two was moved slightly eastward on two occasions, reducing the scope of Nanhai East. The location of Nanhai West at remote Zhanjiang certainly explains the need to establish an office in Guangzhou to oversee the joint ventures in the eastern portion of the province. Chinese officials assert Nanhai East was created because Nanhai West simply did not have the capacity to manage all the contracts in the South China Sea. But this does not explain why the old South China Sea Branch did not establish a subbranch in Guangzhou subordinate to its Zhanjiang headquarters. Our Chinese informants were unable to shed light on this issue, but knowledgeable foreign observers offered three hypotheses. First, were the Guangzhou office to be subordinate to Zhanjiang headquarters, its rank would be at the *ke* (section) level, and that would be too low for the unit in the bureaucratic world of Guangzhou. Its head would not have adequate access to provincial and municipal offices. Further, CNOOC may have seen some advantage in not being reliant upon a single subordinate agency; such an agency may have accumulated sufficient resources that it would have been even more difficult to control. Finally, by creating a Nanhai East without its own service capabilities and therefore without incentive to direct service contracts to its agencies, greater opportunity may have been created for Guangzhou-based suppliers. In short, the creation of Nanhai East may have appealed to Guangdong and Guangzhou authorities, as it increased their capacity to profit directly from the offshore activity. Unfortunately, our data do not enable us to select from among these alternative explanations. Indeed, all factors may have been involved in the decision to establish Nanhai East, with different people supporting its creation for different reasons. For our purposes, what is important is the range of bureaucratic considerations which were involved in structuring the institutions for hosting the Western presence.

The result of having two operating companies was to create problems of coordination for the foreign oil companies. While these problems subsided somewhat with the passage of time, in 1984-85 the foreign operators reported on minor, annoying problems and petty jealousies in working with the two. Oil companies such as Exxon with blocks in both sectors had to deal with two joint management committees. Transfer of rigs from one block to another entailed administrative difficulties. And the foreign oil companies found the different administrative styles and competence of the two organizations, as well as their reluctance to share information with one another, vexing. As in the case of communications

377

between Nanhai West and CNOOC, the foreign operators played a role in facilitating communications between Nanhai East and Nanhai West.

STRUCTURE OF NANHAI EAST[30]

The company had somewhat over 600 employees in mid-1984 and nearly 850 in October, 1985. They were grouped into fourteen functional departments and seven joint management committees in charge of implementing contracts with seven foreign operators in eight blocks. The fourteen departments included: 1. comprehensive management; 2. economic planning; 3. foreign liaison; 4. exploration and development (which reviewed the exploration plan for each block, the location of wells, the logging and testing program, etc.); 5. operations (which gave professional guidance to the Chinese representatives on the JMC's and monitors compliance with the marine environment protection law, safety laws, and similar regulations); 6. procurement (which reviewed the procurement and import plans and assists the operators in clearing customs); 7. engineering (which supervised construction work, including review of designs and inspection of completed work); 8. finance (which audited accounts, supervises tax collection, and assisted the operators in such areas as insurance, currency transactions, and bank accounts); 9. labor and personnel department; 10. technical development training (which supervised implementation of the training programs and technology transfer that the contracts require of the foreign operators); 11. research center (which carried out geological studies of the Pearl River Basin and of the contract blocks); 12. Shenzhen work (which facilitated the activities of the foreign operators in Shenzhen); 13. living service (which provided logistical support to company employees); and 14. capital construction.

Of the 600 employees, somewhat over 70 were devoted to the JMC's. The bulk of the personnel were involved in staff work and scientific research. About 200 were involved in interpretation of geological data, so that Nanhai East could present its independently developed and informed viewpoint about the explorations. The Nanhai East staff consisted of geologists, physicists, petroleum engineers, and so on. They came mostly from onshore petroleum fields, such as Daqing, Huabei, Shengli, Liaohe, and so on. Not many were Cantonese, and not many were transferred from the South Sea Branch in Zhanjiang. Seventy percent of the employees were engineers, with most claiming over 15 years of experience. The organization was built quickly. The Cadre Department of MPI sent people to various oil fields to select and transfer staff on a priority basis.

---

[30] In addition to interviews, this section draws on "Nanhai East Oil Company," *China Oil*, Vol. 1 (Summer, 1984), pp. 140-142.

Over one-third of the employees were Chinese Communist Party members, and the Nanhai East Party Committee made sure they supported policy. Whether a Party branch existed on a rig depended upon the number of Party members on the rig. Party life for rig hands was handled by the Party Committees from the original units of the workers. Since many workers came from Nanhai West—such as the workers on their boats—the Nanhai West Party Committee organized their CCP activities. Thus, Nanhai West had a reach into the operations under the administrative supervision of Nanhai East. The Nanhai East Party Committee, as Nanhai West, was under the dual leadership of the Guangdong and CNOOC Party Committees. However, since the bigger issues went to CNOOC, they were "mainly" led by the CNOOC CCP Committee. That Committee articulated the responsibility of cooperating with foreigners.

As the leaders of Nanhai East explained, "In building this organization, we have *not* sought to create our own 'total' society, with our own hospitals, schools, services, buildings, and so on. Rather, we use existing facilities in Guangdong and instead of offering our own capabilities to the offshore operations, we use a bidding system to determine who will provide the logistical services for the offshore operations." The difference between Nanhai East and Nanhai West in definition of the organizational mission could not be phrased more clearly. And this led to a different view of the role of the local governmental units. In contrast with Nanhai West, where the leaders were unfamiliar with the development plans of Zhanjiang municipality and made little reference to them, the Nanhai East official volunteered this observation: "We need support from various departments in the Guangdong and Guangzhou governments."

RELATIONS WITH GUANGDONG PROVINCIAL APPARATUS

Nanhai East was an agent of the central government. Its budget came entirely from CNOOC. Its officials considered their mandate to be nothing less than the law of the state. From their perspective, Premier Zhao Ziyang had stated that the joint venture contracts which Nanhai East implemented had the force of law. Thus armed, Nanhai East officials sallied forth to elicit the cooperation of local agencies. Nanhai East officials considered themselves part of the provincial level economic system and had contacts with all relevant departments. The leading bodies, Nanhai East officials explained, were the Foreign Economic Commission, the Economic Commission, the Planning Commission, the Construction Commission, the Personnel Bureau, the Public Security Bureau, and the Foreign Affairs Office. No *ad hoc* coordinating committee had been established within the provincial government to bring together all the units involved in the South China Sea operation.

The main operational agencies in the provincial government with which Nanhai East dealt were: 1. the Customs Service; 2. the Port Authority (*kouan bangongshi*), a provincial coordinating agency which integrated health, immigration, customs, and similar activities in all Guangdong ports; 3. the Sea Security Headquarters (*haishang anquan zhihuibu*), a central organ directly under the State Council involved with sea security matters; 4. the bank; 5. the Border Control (*bian fa*), which involved immigration forces; 6. the Navy, which had to be kept informed for purposes of safety at sea; and 7. the Foreign Affairs Office, which managed the diplomatic dimension.

Nanhai East officials believed they generally had elicited the support of provincial officials. They attributed this support to several factors. First, the Center—the CCP and the State Council—had made its policy very clear: it favored the policy of opening to the outside. Guangdong authorities understood this. Second, Guangdong historically had special insights into dealing with foreigners and was enthusiastic about renewing contact with the outside world. Third, the province was deficient in energy and hoped to lay claim to any portion that might be produced. Finally, Guangdong profited from the material, human, and transportation support which the operators needed. Such activities as providing supply boats, helicopters, communications, and weather forecasts were organized by the province. This stimulated the Guangdong economy.

DIVISION OF LABOR WITH CNOOC

Nanhai East, in sum, was responsible for implementing the risk contracts: securing office space for the operators, making sure communication systems were adequate, providing liaison with appropriate Chinese agencies, and so on. It represented and protected the Chinese interest in the exploration and development of the blocks awarded in the bidding process. Where the contract was ambiguous, the issue went to CNOOC. And under the contract and under internal procedures, several specific matters had to go to CNOOC for approval in any case. These included the operating budget, the work program, and foreign procurements. These plans were submitted to CNOOC through Nanhai East, and CNOOC then investigated and approved the plan. CNOOC had its own set of geologists and data analysis center which enabled it to render an independent judgment of Nanhai East recommendations. Foreign operators therefore had to retain contact with both levels. The foreign companies also took their complaints and problems with Nanhai East to Beijing for resolution.

For example, in the drilling of a particular well, the foreign operator might have decided to abandon the effort as clearly futile. Under the contract terms, the foreign firms reserved the right of final decision on this issue. But the Chinese side might disagree with the decision. The role of Nanhai East was to monitor the situation, and if its geologists were dissatisfied, Nanhai East expressed its view in the joint venture's JMC. Since the foreign operator's opinion was likely to prevail in the JMC, the issue might be referred for further discussion between CNOOC and the foreign operator in Beijing. Nanhai East had the technological capacity to assist the Chinese representative on the JMC, while CNOOC possessed a similar capability to inform its negotiators in Beijing. If CNOOC decided it was important to continue drilling, it would renegotiate the contract, adjusting the x-factor (the sliding portion going to the foreign operator, depending on the rate of production).

As with Nanhai West, in the first two years of operation, communications between Nanhai East and CNOOC were not always effective. For example, one Western operator[31] put it this way:

> Both Nanhai East and West have been adamant in demanding that no information be sent directly to Beijing. CNOOC then communicated to me—not via either of the operating companies—to insist that blind copies of all information be sent directly to CNOOC in Beijing. I did not want to run the risk of sending blind copies, so I began to provide an additional copy for CNOOC with everything that I sent to Nanhai East and Nanhai West, and I asked them to be sure to forward these additional copies to CNOOC. As it turns out, they did not send this material on. This spring (of 1984), CNOOC head Qin Wencai came down to Guangzhou, and at a meeting where all of us were present, he told Nanhai East and Nanhai West that to save time, copies of all data henceforth should be sent directly from me to CNOOC. We have done this since then.

With the 1985 promotion of Nanhai East head Wang Tao to become Minister of Petroleum, problems of communication between CNOOC and Nanhai East greatly eased, and by October, 1985, the complaints of foreign operators about lack of coordination had greatly diminished.

Joint Management Committees

The implementation of the joint venture contracts occurred within the organizational framework of joint management committees. A separate

---

[31] This informant is *not* the same as the one quoted above concerning Nanhai West and CNOOC.

committee of ten to fifteen members existed for each contract governing the activity in a particular block. Each JMC was chaired by a Chinese appointed either by Nanhai East or Nanhai West. CNOOC monitored the appointment process. The Deputy Chairman of the JMC was a representative from the lead foreign operating company and was based either in Zhanjiang or Guangzhou. The JMC met quarterly or semi-annually to review work plans, service contracts, expenses, and analysis of previous works. Interviews with each of the foreign companies revealed that no two JMC's worked exactly the same. Such factors as the personalities of the Chinese and Americans and the distinctive corporate philosophies came into play. For example, Exxon, BP, Arco, Pennzoil, Occidental, Texaco, and Total have very different management styles—the number of people they assign to a foreign operation, the length of assignment before rotation, the extent to which they are willing to share confidences and bring their foreign partners into the operation, the degree of autonomy they give to their local representatives, the degree of ambiguity they are willing to tolerate in agreements, and their patience and willingness to adapt to local conditions. Our Chinese informants were sensitive to these differences and were willing to comment upon them. Unfortunately, the need to protect the confidentiality of our sources precludes detailing our findings.

From the vantage point of the foreigners, too, some Chinese JMC heads appeared to enjoy the total confidence of their superiors at Nanhai East or Nanhai West and had considerable autonomy, while others were on a tighter leash. Some Chinese seemed to like dealing with foreigners, while others appeared quite distrusting and nativistic. Another factor was that Nanhai West clearly was a more difficult parent body than Nanhai East, since it placed pressure on its JMCs to award service contracts to Nanhai West suppliers. As a result of these considerations, some JMCs appeared to work very smoothly, while others were more acrimonious. For some, the quarterly JMC meeting was routine, and the decisions made at lower levels were rapidly ratified. There was not enough business to use up the three hours allotted to the meeting. For others, the JMC quarterly meeting was a serious and lengthy affair, with the minutes carefully checked since each side felt the other would seek to interpret agreements to its advantage.

The JMC structure varied somewhat, but in general, most JMCs established joint technical committees (JTC), joint procurement committees (JPC), and a secretariat for handling daily liaison. Routine consultations took place at this level. With offices either in Guangzhou or in the Nanhai West compound in Zhanjiang, the foreign companies had immediate access to the Chinese members of their JTC's, JPC's and secretariat.

The most contentious issues by far pertained to contracting for services, where foreign firms felt the pressures were excessive to use indigenous services when the cost and quality were not competitive with foreign offers. The preference clause gave Chinese bidders some advantage, but Western firms believed the bidding system was unfairly rigged, and they cited many examples to prove it.

With the passage of time, the process worked increasingly smoothly, and by the end of 1985, many of the early difficulties had eased, mutual trust had begun to be established, and operational routines had been created. By that time, the first round of drilling was nearing an end, and the second round of bidding was underway.

China Nanhai Oil Joint Services Company

CNOJSC was formally established on May 1, 1982, as a joint venture between CNOOC and Guangdong province.[32] Its initial capital was 100,000,000 RMB, with 50% of the investment coming from each partner. In fact, the concept of CNOJSC antedated its formation by over a year, and it was really the creation of MPI and Guangdong. Just as the origins of Nanhai East and West can be traced to the production-sharing formula of China's risk contract with the foreign oil companies, the need for CNOJSC is to be found in the preference clause of the contract. Having successfully demanded that the joint ventures purchase indigenous supplies and services, the Chinese then had to organize themselves to seize the opportunity. With Nanhai East and West as the interface organizations leading the foreign companies to Chinese suppliers, at least according to its officials, CNOJSC was envisioned as the organization that would create the Chinese suppliers.[33] And it would do so for the financial benefit of Guangdong province. Its antecedents appropriately enough perhaps can be traced to the compradore merchants who first appeared in Guangzhou in the nineteenth century, and to some extent, its capitalistic style and bureaucratic entrepreneurship echo corporate be-

[32] The State Economic Commission approved the charter of the corporation. One Chinese informant told us the SEC was involved because CNOJSC was *intended* to improve Chinese management practices, a task that falls under the SEC mandate. We remain puzzled by this explanation, however, since the purposes of CNOJSC in fact only tangentially dealt with management. Perhaps more to the point may be the SEC mandates for securing implementation of the plan, providing interagency coordination, and mediating interagency disputes. These concerns were all important in CNOJSC's creation.

[33] We will see below that in September 1983, Beijing decided not to give CNOJSC the exclusive license in this regard.

havior of late Qing and the Republican period.[34] In particular, bureaucratic avarice, the proliferation of paper organizations, the severe undercapitalization, the exaggerated expectations, the overcommitment, and an inadequately trained manpower base plagued CNOJSC in its early days and recalled similar problems along the China coast in the 1800's. At the same time, CNOJSC exhibited admirable talents which also were reminiscent of the past: flexibility, adaptability, a capacity to learn and innovate, and an ability to create a complex organization with remarkable rapidity.

The table of organization of CNOJSC was very complicated. A ten-member Board of Directors met once or twice a year in Guangzhou. Its Board members came from CNOOC, Nanhai East and West, and the Provincial Planning Commission, Economic Commission, and Foreign Economic Commission. Its Chairman, Yang Guoqing, was head of the Guangdong Capital Construction Commission, while its highly respected vice chairman, Zhong Yimin, came from CNOOC and was considered one of the chief organizational architects of China's offshore efforts. Board members were not highly active, and the general manager and his chief deputies bore the chief responsibility. They were longtime officials in Guangdong and brought a provincial perspective to their job.

As of late 1984, CNOJSC consisted of nearly 40 departments and companies. These had over 1,000 employees, of which 600 were personnel belonging to CNOJSC. These sub-units consisted of the following types of organizations:

— six staff departments at company headquarters (personnel, finance, foreign liaison, and so on), with 120 employees;

— three wholly owned, but independently managed companies, namely the Manpower Company (which supplied personnel such as typists, secretaries, and drill workers to the joint ventures and which ran training programs on their behalf); the Daily Living Services Company (which supplied daily necessities to the rigs and company personnel); and the Material Supply Company (which supplied mud, cement, and other drilling materials);

— four companies whose staffs were from other agencies but which had a "professional relationship" with CNOJSC and reported to the general manager (a Helicopter Company staffed by the CAAC South China Sea Branch; Meterological Service Company, by the Guangdong Meterology Bureau; Shipping Com-

[34] See John K. Fairbank, *Trade and Diplomacy on the China Coast* (Cambridge: Harvard University Press, 1953), and Albert Feuerwerker, *China's Early Industrialization* (Cambridge: Harvard University Press, 1958).

pany, by the Provincial Department of Communications; and Diving and Standby Company, by the Guangdong Salvage Bureau of the Ministry of Communications);

— two companies that were joint ventures in which CNOJSC was the majority owner (a communications company with the Guangdong Post and Telecommunications Bureau and a venture with the Hong Kong Mei-shi Investment Company to build a large office and housing complex in Guangzhou);

— over ten joint venture subsidiaries of the above nine companies, all with such foreign partners as Jardine-Matheson, Seahorse, or Santa Fe. In effect, the nine companies listed above sought out or responded to foreign companies that desired Chinese partners with whom to cooperate in securing the offshore business. Examples included the Nanlian Food Company (a joint venture of Jardine Consolidated Catering Services and the Daily Living Service Company), or the Yue-Xin Helicopter Service Company, a joint venture of the Helicopter Company and Singapore Airtrust Group;

— a wholly owned base in Shenzhen Special Economic Zone (SEZ);

— two joint venture bases in Zhanjiang and Sanya, a town on Hainan Island. CNOJSC planned for the Sanya base to have hotels and office space for the foreign companies, manage communication facilities, and provide space for the activities of the various CNOJSC operations (such as berthing space for supply ships and helicopter pads); while in Zhanjiang, CNOJSC became a partner in the hotel-apartment complex on the Nanhai base.

— six joint ventures in which CNOJSC was the minority stockholder, including bases in the Zhuhai and Shenzhen SEZs.

According to a knowledgeable American observer, CNOJSC did not contribute money to attain its equity position in most of these joint ventures. Rather, the partner saw CNOJSC participation as useful or necessary to be able to bid successfully on the service contracts. In essence, then, Guangdong was earning revenue from the exploration stage with a minimum investment of 50 million RMB in CNOJSC. The arrangement echoes Shanxi having acquired an equity position in Pingshuo without having invested in the project. When the Chinese partner did have to put up cash, the funds were secured on loan from the Bank of China, while the foreign firms secured funding from such foreign banks as Chemical Bank and the Mitsubishi Bank.

CNOJSC received an exemption from usual Chinese regulations, and the joint ventures could retain a portion of their profits. In addition, from

1982 to 1984, CNOJSC was allowed to retain the remaining portion of the profits and not pay tax or remit a portion of its profits to the Center. It did have to give a portion of its foreign exchange earnings to the state, split between the Center and the province, and it also retained a portion. CNOJSC was not exempt from payment of provincial taxes, however, and Guangdong collected the usual commercial, import, and industrial taxes.

That CNOJSC was really an agent of the province can be seen in yet one other way. It tilted purchases toward Guangdong rather than other parts of China. As its spokesman explained, "Guangdong can service many of the new activities. So, we will try to use the provincial capacity as much as possible. Only if Guangdong cannot make the item or provide the service, then we will go to Beijing and Shanghai. But we will also try to raise the technical level of Guangdong to meet the competition."

At the outset, the creation of a new and significant company like this created several problems at the local level. First of all, while much of the activity was located in Guangzhou, the municipal level government did not benefit greatly. Rather, the provincial level was the main beneficiary. As a result, Guangzhou eventually withdrew its cooperation from CNOJSC. Initially, it planned a joint venture base with CNOJSC, but by late 1984, Guangzhou established its own, small version of CNOJSC. Second, so attractive did the prospects of CNOJSC appear in 1983-84 that most Chinese bureaucratic partners wanted to transfer or assign more cadres to the joint ventures than CNOJSC needed. While foreign observers found CNOJSC somewhat bloated in staff by mid-1984, from the CNOJSC perspective, it had expended considerable effort to keep its manpower totals as trim as they were. Third, the equity contribution of Chinese partners in joint ventures frequently was in the form of equipment, not money. Considerable differences arose as to the worth of the contribution and hence of the percentage equity due each Chinese bureaucracy. Such disputes were resolved by the provincial governor.

Finally, from the vantage of our many Western sources, their most vexing problems were the lack of coordination and jealousies among CNOJSC, Nanhai East, and Nanhai West, the exorbitant charges, and occasionally rigged bidding processes.[35] Almost all the foreign oil companies had their lore of bureaucratic delays, rivalries, and skullduggery. For example, some JMCs demanded use of Chinese data analysis centers when they clearly did not possess the requisite ability, with the end result that a portion of the data were analyzed twice—by a Chinese firm

[35] In addition to our interviews, this paragraph draws on *The Asian Wall Street Journal*, November 23, 1983, and June 3, 1983.

and by the home office in the States. Or, in addition to the CNOJSC joint venture helicopter company with the Civil Aviation Administration of China (CAAC), the Chinese navy formed a competing joint venture helicopter company. This brought together the navy, the Petroleum Helicopters, Inc. of Louisiana and other foreign entities. One JMC awarded its transport contract to the latter joint venture, only to find that CAAC controlled takeoff and landing rights for civilian aircraft. Frequently, CAAC refused to give permission for takeoffs to the navy joint venture. The matter was finally ironed out through a meeting at higher levels.

Yet it would be a distortion to concentrate upon these serious bureaucratic problems. With several exceptions of accidents—particularly the capsizing of an exploration ship during a typhoon, with possibly preventable loss of lives—the first round of drilling proceeded with few untoward incidents. And on balance, the foreign operators felt the bureaucratic environment was no more difficult than in many other countries. The costs were substantially higher, but corruption at the outset was not a major problem.

The real danger by late 1984 was that the Chinese—and CNOJSC—had developed a far more elaborate system than they needed. CNOJSC was building four bases for offshore operations. Grandiose projects were proceeding to build accommodations for a few thousand foreigners. The assumption had been that the offshore oil development and production phase was in the offing. By late 1984, however, the question for CNOJSC was what to do, since it was becoming clear no immediate offshore oil bonanza would in fact materialize.

Other Organizations

Although CNOJSC was established as the primary organization to foster services for offshore activity, it in fact did not retain a monopoly. We have already noted that Nanhai West was a natural rival, and no clear division of labor existed between them. In addition, other Chinese competitors soon appeared on the scene. The helicopter service which the navy offered was but one example. Another was the creation by Guangzhou municipality of its own service company which intended to build a housing and office complex for the foreign oil companies.

Untangling the various organizations involved in developing the Shekou and Chiwan bases in the Shenzhen SEZ is particularly difficult. There, the China Merchant Steam Navigation Company (CMSNC) played a crucial role, managing the Shekou base and investing in the Chiwan base. CMSNC was the Hong Kong outpost of the Ministry of Communications, and it became involved because of the harbor and shipping dimensions of the bases. Both Nanhai West and CNOJSC established separate operations in Shenzhen. The frenzied pace of organizational activity from 1982 to 1985 reflected the desire of many agencies to participate in the growth of the special economic zone, particularly in the event of substantial offshore production.

In fact, the proliferation of companies—though bewildering to the foreign companies which had expected an orderly institutional landscape in China—meant that the foreign operators actually confronted competing Chinese suppliers. In the final analysis, Beijing could not, or more likely did not wish to, create monopoly suppliers. An internal Chinese directive specified the five areas in which Chinese or Chinese-foreign enterprises could bid for contracts: supply boats, helicopters, telecommunications, rig positioning, and operation of logistics bases.[36] An Offshore Rig Leadership Small Group under Fan Muhan at the State Economic Commission was established precisely to provide some coordination and to monitor competition in the rig area.

The competitive aspect can be attributed to a September, 1983 decision in the Premier's office.[37] The JMC of the British Petroleum joint venture awarded a contract for supply boats to two subsidiaries of the Ministry of Communications. CNOJSC and Guangdong officials appealed the contract, contending the two winning bids were not CNOJSC subsidiaries. The decision by Premier Zhao upholding the JMC decision deliberately encouraged competition. As CNOOC head Qin Wencai stated, "We encourage competition. It is state policy."

Competitors can combine and cooperate, however, and that happened as well. CNOJSC and the CMSNC subsidiary of the Ministry of Communications became partners along with Nanhai West, the Bank of China, and the China Resources Company of Hong Kong in China Offshore Oilfield Services (COOS). The company brought together five major actors in Guangdong. This Hong Kong based company pursued business in three areas: foreign procurement, travel services for foreign companies engaged in offshore exploration and production, and shipping. COOS opened its doors with a capitalization of five million Hong Kong dollars, later raised to thirteen million. To judge from its publicity, the organization seemed a potentially significant actor. The reality was less grandiose. As of 1985, it was located within the CNOOC branch office in Hong Kong. It had two managers, one from the Bank of China and one from China Merchant Steam Navigation. Its two deputy managers were from CNOOC and China Resources. It had no general man-

[36] *The Asian Wall Street Journal*, November 23, 1983.

[37] This is based on interviews and *The Asian Wall Street Journal*, November 23, 1983.

ager because the five partners could not agree who should head the organization. The lessons would seem to be that organizations—as policies—can exist in name well before the reality comes into effect. And for competitors to combine in joint ventures does not necessarily end the rivalry.

What one senses is a cultural talent for rapidly creating organizations to fill voids and seek potential profit. Indeed, this talent may exist to an excess. For, by 1985, it was clear that an excessive organizational capacity had been created for the reserves that had been discovered to date.

Conclusion

This chapter has provided the evidence for portraying central-provincial relations as a bargaining process, albeit with the Center enjoying more resources to strike deals in its favor. But we have also demonstrated that individual bureaucratic units have the capacity to pursue strategies which reduce control by superiors and which enable them autonomously to survive challenges and expand.

Developments at CNOOC and CNOJSC in 1985-86 further underscored this theme. Both CNOOC and Guangdong responded to the discovery of a major natural gas field off Hainan Island in ways stemming from their organizational ethos and mission. The response of CNOOC was to ensure that it would be involved in the development and distribution of the natural gas. CNOOC established a company to purchase and distribute the natural gas from an Arco-CNOOC joint venture which Nanhai West would manage. This obviously placed CNOOC in an exposed position. First, CNOOC had to negotiate a development agreement with Arco at a time when natural gas prices dropped precipitously, and its initial agreement left it—as Arco—exposed to further erosion in natural gas prices. Second, CNOOC had to placate Guangdong. Guangdong was not particularly happy with this development. The availability of natural gas as an energy feedstock affected existing plans to expand energy supply through the nuclear power plant at Daya Bay, hydropower from the Red River, and coal-fired thermal plants. But Guangdong authorities knew CNOOC must reach an accommodation with them in order to be able to distribute the gas in the province. Once again, we see the leverage that accrues to a province vis-à-vis Beijing simply because its cooperation is essential to complete projects in a timely fashion.

In 1985-86, CNOJSC had to respond to unmet expectations. Deprived by Beijing of a monopoly position as a supplier, hemmed in by Nanhai West, the Guangzhou base, and China Merchant Steam Navigation, and victim of modest yields in the offshore drilling, it adopted a strategy to diversify and reduce its dependence on the oil business. It largely abandoned efforts to establish a position in Zhanjiang, other than a joint venture hotel it was constructing with Nanhai West. The appointment of a new leader, Wang Jie, who formerly was head of the Maoming refinery, signalled an interest in becoming involved in downstream production activities. CNOJSC made tentative plans to build a small refinery in Shenzhen should oil be produced offshore. More to the point, CNOJSC opened a trading company in Hong Kong with import capabilities. It attempted to become more of a Guangdong development authority, seeking to develop property in the Guangzhou area and to develop an industrial area in the Shenzhen SEZ near its Chiwan base. It formed three additional wholly owned companies in 1985 to diversify its activities: 1. a commerce and industry service company to open hotels and shops; 2. a construction and development company; and 3. a credit and trade service company.

As a CNOJSC spokesman put it, "We will never forget our main task of supporting the South China Sea oil effort, but we are also developing diversified enterprises. We are becoming a multi-purpose economy." The projects and joint ventures CNOJSC had in mind were local, not national, and thus only the Guangdong SEC and not MOFERT in Beijing needed approve these projects. CNOJSC also sought to become involved in Hainan. Having established a base early on in Sanya, it hoped to build a hotel there for the Arco personnel. It had similar plans for Zhuhai, the SEZ north of Macao, where it began building harbor facilities and living accommodations for foreigners. According to the CNOJSC official, "These various bases are being developed in a way that can be used for other purposes if offshore oil does not yield good results. We are consciously developing in a multi-purpose way so as to provide insurance."

Both CNOOC and CNOJSC in 1985-86, as Nanhai West in 1981-85 or the Shanxi coal mining bureaucracies in the 1980's, demonstrated their resiliance and adaptabilty. The objective environment and the policies of the Center shape the parameters in which local organizations work, but skilled bureaucrats at the provincial level and below know how to respond and survive in their world. Two major conceptual issues arise from this situation: What were the underlying dynamics that produced the "mature" bureaucratic state which this and our previous chapters portrayed? And, given the slothfulness and inefficiency endemic to this "mature" bureaucratic state, can the winds of reform blowing in almost all communist countries in the 1980's produce systemic results? We turn to these questions in our concluding chapter.

· 8 ·

SOME IMPLICATIONS FOR
COMPARATIVE COMMUNIST STUDIES

Thus far, our analysis has focused on China, and we have drawn on the literature on organizational theory and on other political systems to help illuminate the *Chinese* policy process. Now, we employ our findings for comparative purposes. Our research only superficially traced changes in the Chinese system. While Chapters Five and Six charted the evolution of policies on the Three Gorges project and the turn outward for offshore petroleum development, otherwise our data primarily capture the system of the 1980's. Our information does suggest that bureaucracies were less fragmented and the policy process less consultative and protracted in the early Mao era, and other monographic literature points even more strongly in the same direction.[1] Our study, nevertheless, does not permit a careful reconstruction of the evolution of bureaucratic structures and processes since the 1950's.

Further, we focus on only one bureaucratic sector in China, and we cannot confidently say other sectors in China—much less other one-party, non-market, bureaucratic systems—exhibit the same characteristics. We are sometimes aware that in the social sciences, grand theories are proposed on the basis of a relatively narrow study such as this one, with the generalizations proven increasingly inaccurate and misleading as the years pass.

Rather than pursuing more sweeping comparisons, due to the quality of our data and the narrowness of our topic we prefer to stay closer to home and explore the ability of our findings to enhance understanding of other Soviet-type systems. We recognize that our study potentially has more general relevance. It is worthy of note that the writings on the American executive branch seem so germane, and our study also is a reminder of some ubiquitous phenomena in the way leaders must interact with and are constrained by the bureaucratic structures they lead. Nonetheless, we eschew the temptation to use our data for the comparative politics of all bureaucratic systems.

We explore the significance of our findings for comparative communist studies at three levels. First, our study has implications for the research

---

[1] See, e.g.: Ezra Vogel, *Canton Under Communism*; and H. Franz Schurmann, *Ideology and Organization*. These researchers, however, were unable to observe and interview bureaucrats in China.

agenda on bureaucracy in Soviet-type[2] systems. Second, our data suggest that key issues which have garnered much attention in comparative communist studies in recent years deserve to be rethought. We examine two of these—how authority is allocated within bureaucracies (usually referred to as the centralization-decentralization issue) and how interests are represented (usually debated as the applicability of Western interest group theory). Our findings point to some important ways to reshape the ways in which these issues have been debated in the secondary literature. Third and much more speculatively, our analysis of the critical importance of the bureaucratic arena in China's policy process leads us to examine two of the "big" conceptual questions in comparative communist studies: What explains the seemingly similar path of all communist systems from mobilization regimes to bureaucratic states? And what are the potentialities, the obstacles, the inducements, and the constraints upon the reform of these systems? The rest of the chapter explores each of these topics, casting our findings in a comparative framework.

New Items on the Research Agenda on Bureaucracy in Soviet-Style Systems

We from the start recognized the importance of the bureaucratic arena in our study of China's energy sector decision making, but we initially had little understanding of just what should be asked about this sphere. Through this research, we have gained an appreciation of the utility both of pursuing a case study approach and of exploring some particular facets of the bureaucratic world of China's officials. We present these insights systematically in this section with the object of encouraging comparable research on other Soviet-type systems.

Case Studies of Specific Decisions

Nearly a decade ago, Professor Zvi Gitelman admonished his colleagues in a symposium on interest groups in socialist countries, "We desperately need systematic and detailed descriptions (*horribile dictu*) and analyses of contemporary political processes in Eastern Europe. Were we to get these . . . we would learn a great deal about interest groups, among other things. We have discussed the nature of groups long enough. . . .

[2] "Soviet-type systems" refer to the USSR and those countries that consciously copied the USSR in creating their state structures and developing their general approaches to industrialization in the late 1940's and early 1950's: Poland, Czechoslovakia, Hungary, the German Democratic Republic, Bulgaria, Albania, Romania, and China.

We [now] have no choice but to leave the study and the symposium for the library and the field."[3]

Although Gitelman's call for study of policy processes was persuasive, surprisingly little research has been done on the detailed history of specific decisions, from initial idea through adoption and implementation. Several important research benefits flow, we believe, from such case studies (versus the more typical studies of the evolution of broad policies—education, agriculture, foreign policy—debated at the elite level). First, every decision has a history that the participants recall and that affects perceptions and strategies. Starting at the genesis of a particular initiative—rather than focusing on the period when the initiative became highly visible because top leaders took it up—may identify the forces pushing the issue onto the national agenda and shaping the outcome. Second, the study of a specific project or policy encourages the scholar of politics to become knowledgeable about the technical substance of the particular matter under consideration. Only in this way can the interplay among elite, bureaucracies, and objective considerations be understood. Substantive concerns—costs, technologies, uncertainties, trade-offs—are important in shaping outcomes. All too often, political analysts have downplayed the importance of the substantive issues at stake because they have not mastered the issues themselves. Our case studies suggest the history of the Three Gorges dam project cannot be traced without background knowledge of Yangtze River hydrology, and the strategies and sentiments of leaders in petroleum and coal development can be deciphered only through acquaintance with the technologies involved. Finally, a focus on a specific project or decision often enables the researcher to identify a wider range of pertinent players and explain their involvement in the issue. In brief, examination of one narrowly defined policy or one project reduces the research effort to a scale that permits deeper probing into how the system actually functions.

The Terminology of Bureaucracy

Research into specific decisions has in turn made us acutely sensitive to the need to understand the bureaucratic system through the terms and distinctions employed by the participants. We leave the research convinced that one cannot fully interpret the nuances of bureaucracy without viewing it in the categories its participants employ. For example, the distinction between a broad policy initiative (*fangzhen*) and a specific pol-

---

[3] "Comment" in the symposium on "Pluralism in Communist Societies: Is the Emperor Naked?" *Studies in Comparative Communism*, XII, No. 1 (Spring 1979), p. 38.

icy decision (*zhengce*) is critical to Chinese officials, as is the difference between a long-term indication of policy priorities (*guihua*) and the concrete prioritizing that has short-term policy ramifications (*jihua*). Yet, the former terms are typically both rendered as "policy" in English, while the latter are usually both translated as "plan." The politics and processes governing each differ considerably (as explained in Chapters Four, Five, and Six). Our discovery of the rich Chinese vocabulary and refined distinctions for different types of leadership relationships helped open our eyes to the fragmented nature of authority. In short, sensitivity to the nuances of terminology and an effort to understand what each term means *to the cadres in the system* are important in constructing a realistic understanding of politics and processes in Soviet-type systems. One important issue, for comparative purposes, is whether all Soviet-style systems employ the same linguistic distinctions.

The Chinese differentiate the specificity and force of formal authority along a number of gradations that are reflected in their bureaucratic terminology. To recall one example, there is a key difference between a superior unit having "leadership relations" (*lingdao guanxi*) with its subordinate and its having "professional relations" (*yewu guanxi*). The former implies a substantial degree of direct control, while the latter does not, but organizational charts obscure these distinctions. In other socialist countries, does a similar variety of terms exist for various types of relationships and forms of leadership, coordination, etc.? If so, what are the full implications of each term in the minds of the officials who serve in the system? Enquiries about bureaucratic terminology can yield a rich harvest of insights about how officials view the distribution of authority in the system. Where possible, such enquiries ideally should be made concerning both Party and government relationships.

The Formal Structure of Authority

Our research indicates that in the Chinese case, formal structures of authority include more than is usually conveyed by organization charts. For example, we noted the reach which various Commissions have into Ministries through the functionally specific bureaus (finance, production, planning, science and technology, and so on) within the Ministries. We portrayed the bewildering array of jurisdictions over the Shanxi coal fields, and found that different administrative units within the same mine district might be led by different levels of government: production by the Center and personnel by the province. We found two instances in Shanxi where seeming efforts to increase Beijing's authority in management of coal were in reality intended to facilitate local autonomy.[4] We even found that not all Party committees in units are led exclusively by their territorial Party committees. For example, the Nanhai East Party Committee looked to the CCP committee of the CNOOC for its basic leadership. Given the importance of the formal lines of authority in establishing organizational identities, vulnerabilities, and responsibilities, researchers must ferret out which agencies exercise what formal leverage over what other agencies in competition with yet what other agencies.

Basic Building Blocks

Some units and subunits in any system exhibit great continuity and are the basic bureaucratic building blocks of the system. In China, for example, the bureaus in State Council ministries and commissions have displayed enormous continuity in staff and operations over the decades, even as ministers, vice ministers, and indeed ministerial boundaries have changed frequently and dramatically. Thus, bureau level units involved in a particular issue may become complex policy communities with considerable continuity over time, despite seemingly major governmental reorganizations. Focusing solely on the ministerial level and above may yield a very misleading view of the debates and processes. Researchers must seek to identify the basic bureaucratic building blocks in each system.

Organizational Ethos

We have learned the importance of asking about each unit's goals or "mission" and its organizational ethos (or "ideology"). In China, these differ considerably among units, as the summary of the core goals and ethos of each pertinent bureaucracy in Chapter Three details. Relatedly, does the unit under study believe that it has an identifiable constituency? What are the behavioral consequences of the unit's ethos and goals?

The Policy Rhythm

It is important to identify the pertinent temporal cycles or rhythms (e.g. agricultural cycles, budgetary meetings, personnel reviews, etc.), and to remain sensitive to how these structure and influence decision making. Put differently, researchers must ask what are the key *recurrent* proc-

[4] We refer to the 1984 change of the Shanxi Provincial Coal Department to a dispatched organ of the Ministry of Coal Industry and to the State Council's establishment of a Shanxi Coal Base Development Office, both analyzed in Chapter Seven.

esses, if any, that influence behavior and outcomes? The Three Gorges project case study, for example, observed that the advocates of the dam generally timed their periodic initiatives to the preparations for each successive five year plan, and their strategies were oriented to this larger policy cycle. But does the same recurrent process (e.g., the annual plan cycle) have similar repercussions for the policy process in a range of different issue areas? Relatedly, how do different recurrent cycles—such as periodic meetings of top leaders versus the agricultural cycle—influence each other? In short, what are the periodic rhythms of the policy process that structure activities, and what effects do those periodic events have?

Trends In Structure

Finally, these dimensions of a system change over time. It is tempting to apply insights generated from interviewing and analysis in the mid-1980's to earlier periods, but this is likely to produce quite misleading results. Thus, to reiterate, an important question is: how have structures and processes evolved and how confidently can this assessment be made?

Only through answers to these sets of questions can the researcher develop a textured analysis of bureaucratic structures and understand some of the sources of behavior they generate. A level of detail is required which the current secondary literature on communist systems for the most part lacks.

CORE ISSUES IN COMPARATIVE COMMUNIST STUDIES

The results of the detailed bureaucratic analysis we have done in this study potentially speak to a wide range of issues in the literature on comparative communist studies. To illustrate the applicability of this type of case study research to basic questions that have been debated in the comparative communism literature, we examine two such issues. In each case, our research provides a basis for recasting the issue for future research purposes.

Bureaucratic Structure and the Representation of Interests

In the late 1960's, in reaction to the previous leader-dominated view, Western scholarship began to ask how popular interests and opinions were represented in Soviet-type systems. While some analysts had focused on particular sectors of the populace,[5] Gordon Skilling was among the first to investigate the emergence and conduct of interest groups.[6] His notion that quasi-autonomous groups legitimately articulated and pursued their interests in the political system challenged the dominant totalitarian model of Soviet studies in the 1950's and early 1960's. This seminal work sparked a flurry of publications, largely conceptual, on the representation of interests in socialist systems. Debates ensued concerning the nature and definition of interest groups, potential points of access of these groups to the political system, and the ways in which Marxist-Leninist political systems could manage their relations with these groups.[7] Most of this work took place, however, with only a thin empirical base, and the research efforts soon bogged down, as the limited ability of autonomous groups to set the agenda and influence policy became evident.[8]

The next step came with the application of corporatist theories of the state to communist systems. This theory developed around the notion that in many political systems it is the state that decides which groups should be permitted interest representation and that legitimizes that representation through the granting of a deliberate representational monopoly within their respective categories. In exchange, the groups have to operate within boundaries determined by the state and through leaders either chosen or approved by the state. The state thus understands society to be comprised of groups with various interests, and the state itself determines which of those interests are to be treated as legitimate and what organizations can "represent" those interests.[9] While corporatism was developed primarily to deal with various types of Western political systems, attempts were made to apply it to communist systems to better

[5] E.g., Jeremy Azrael, *Managerial Power in Soviet Politics* (Cambridge: Harvard University Press, 1966) on managers; and Moshe Lewin, *Russian Peasants and Soviet Power* (London: George Allen and Unwin, 1968) on peasants.

[6] Gordon Skilling, "Interest Groups and Communist Politics," *World Politics* (April 1966), pp. 435-451.

[7] See, for example: A.H. Brown, "Pluralistic Trends in Czechoslovakia," *Soviet Studies* (April 1966), pp. 453-472; Joel Schwartz and William R. Keech, "Group Influence and the Policy Process in the Soviet Union," *American Political Science Review* (September 1968), pp. 840-851; Andrew Janos, "Group Politics in Communist Society: A Second Look at the Pluralistic Model," in Huntington and Moore (eds.), *Authoritarian Politics In Modern Society* (New York: Basic Books, 1970); and William Odom, "A Dissenting View on the Group Approach to Soviet Politics," *World Politics* (July 1976), pp. 452-567.

[8] For a very sound overview of this literature and its problems, see the symposium on "Pluralism in Communist Countries: Is the Emperor Naked?" pp. 3-38.

[9] The major theorist of corporatism is Phillipe C. Schmitter. See, for example, his, "Still the Century of Corporatism?" in Frederick B. Pike and Thomas Stritch (eds.), *The New Corporatism* (Notre Dame: University of Notre Dame, 1974), pp. 85-131.

understand how the latter deal with interests.[10] The fit between corporatism and the literature on socialist politics remained, however, uneasy at best.[11]

There has all along been a central paradox in the conceptualization of socialist systems in the Western literature. On the one hand, these are systems whose defining characteristics include extraordinary control from the political apex. No legal boundaries constrain the power of the highest political leaders, and officials at lower levels are constantly exhorted to place national concerns over parochial ones. On the other hand, good decisions in ruling complex societies require that the leaders receive advice from numerous quarters, each of which elucidates in a forceful and rigorous way some approach to a major problem. How to balance the need for what might be termed "parochial" advice with the desire for centralized control has remained a major operational problem for communist political leaders. How to conceptualize this balance has been a continuing problem for scholars (and practitioners).

This volume suggests that the Chinese leaders recognize neither the legitimacy of interest groups among the population nor the "right" of the populace to press the government and Party with their demands.[12] Rather, the Chinese feel that the officials themselves—often, it seems, at the highest levels—must identify the problems to be given formal recognition and, depending on the nature of the problem, be either managed or solved. The leaders then create or assign an organization to deal with the issue they have identified. In theory, then, the tasks of Chinese bureaucracies are defined not in terms of a particular social or economic group which they represented but rather in terms of the problems and issues that prompt their creation and justify their continued existence.

Hence, the Chinese system is structured, at least in the 1980's, in the expectation that each organization will vigorously pursue its assigned task (rather than some vague national consensus position). In other words the Chinese (at least in the era of Deng Xiaoping) have recognized and accepted within ill-defined bounds the phenomenon of goal displacement.[13] Policy advocacy is thus built into the state structure through the

---

[10] See, for example, Valerie Bunce and John Echols III, "Soviet Politics in the Brezhnev Era: 'Pluralism' or 'Corporatism?' " in Donald R. Kelley (ed.), *Soviet Politics in the Brezhnev Era* (New York: Praeger Publishers, 1980), pp. 1-26.

[11] Nina Halpern reviews the pertinent literature in her *Economic Specialists*.

[12] Andrew Nathan finds the sources for this attitude in cultural notions about the fundamental harmony of interests between the people and the rulers. See: Andrew Nathan, *Chinese Democracy* (New York: Alfred A. Knopf, 1985). See also Victor Falkenheim, *Citizens and Groups*; and Lucian Pye, *Dynamics*.

[13] "Goal displacement" means putting the priorities of an individual unit above those of the national system as a whole.

assigning of responsibilities and resources to various bureaucracies whose major purpose becomes surviving and pursuing their tasks. The Chinese leaders, for example, *de facto* incorporate peasant interests in flood control by assigning the Ministry of Water Resources to manage flood control.[14] That ministry may in the course of its work consult with the affected public to a greater or lesser degree. Regardless of the extent of any such consultation, however, the flood control "interests" are addressed in the decision-making process by this ministry *because of its designated task*. The same dynamic can be seen in many other areas of Chinese policy making. High level recognition of environmental problems in the late 1970's, for instance, led to the organization of a State Council Environmental Protection Office.[15]

This approach to the representation of interests is not described in the literature on other socialist systems. Some scholars have used variations of Skilling's approach and essentially searched for the resources that unofficial groups acquire to pressure the Party and government. The corporatist literature, as noted above, makes a useful contribution in calling attention to the more active role of the state in authoritarian societies in determining which groups' interests might be considered "legitimate." For broad social groups, moreover, some scholars have argued that communist systems create "mass organizations" (trade unions, women's federations, youth leagues, writer's associations, professional groups, etc.) whose initial purpose is to transmit official policies to the affected groups and to preempt any autonomous group formation, but which eventually, to a limited extent, begin to advance the interests of their members. (The Chinese also have mass organizations, but these have been used more to convey the Party's views to the pertinent memberships than as a major means for bringing problems to the attention of the Party leaders.)[16] Some top leaders in China and elsewhere have sought to turn some mass organizations into bodies that more realistically represent the interests of their members,[17] but these have not produced any profound change in such organizations as instruments of mobilization.

In sum, the research on other socialist countries primarily has ex-

[14] As detailed in Chapters Three and Six, when this ministry merged with the Electric Power Ministry to form the Ministry of Water Resources and Electric Power, the flood control and power generation agencies within the ministry struggled against each other because each continued to pursue vigorously its own task.

[15] This was established in 1978.

[16] The most thorough treatment of the Chinese case is in James Townsend, *Political Participation*, pp. 145-173.

[17] For example, the Chinese in 1985 for the first time permitted the writers to elect to the leadership of the Writers Association people of their own choice.

plored representation of interests either by seeking to identify the influence which relevant autonomous groups have on the leaders or which the mobilization organizations begin to exert on the leaders.[18] Neither of these inquiries has yielded much evidence of popular influence on governance, with the result that the "top down," leaders-in-control portrayal of the system remains dominant.

The Chinese case suggests another possibility merits study: that the leaders reject the concept of representation of the interests of any given group, but that they embrace the idea of resolving problems they have identified through the creation and/or tasking of organizations to deal with those problems. The problems targeted by the leaders may, of course, *de facto* embrace a portion of the interests of particular social groups. The Chinese case thus points to the incorporation of what might be termed "partial interests" into organizational missions through the purposeful design of the leaders. Our data, therefore, suggest neither a totally "top down" control image of the system nor a "bottom up" representation image is appropriate. This bureaucratic encapsulation of partial interests through the assignment of organizational tasks posits a more complex relationship between elite and mass and raises a new analytical problem: that is, how do the leaders become aware of the issues that demand attention?[19]

In China, the issue should be phrased as: how do the leaders who create organizations and assign tasks become aware of and convinced that new issues demand bureaucratic attention? Unfortunately, our research does not allow an answer to this important question. The role of intellectuals, especially those with some personal connections to top leaders, possibly becomes critical here,[20] as, obviously, are such major shocks as natural disasters that focus leaders' attention on underlying problems. Thane Gustafson's pathbreaking work on the Soviet Union suggests that on energy issues some scientists caught the attention of a politician who could then carry the issue to the political system.[21] More work must be done on this in the Chinese case as in the Soviet Union and Eastern Europe.[22]

---

[18] In the corporatist variant, the leaders still recognize that various groups have interests, but the political leaders play a more active role in determining the scope and modalities of the representation of such interests in the polity.

[19] This issue is skillfully handled in the American context in John W. Kingdon, *Agendas*.

[20] As explained in Chapter Three, for example, Chinese scientists in 1979-80 called the leaders' attention to the energy crisis, perhaps leading to the creation of an Energy Commission under the State Council.

[21] Thane Gustafson, *Reform in Soviet Politics* (New York: Cambridge University Press, 1981).

[22] Nina Halpern has made initial progress on this in her examination of the role of economic experts in China's policy making: *Economic Specialists*.

The Chinese situation in fact may not be replicated in other socialist systems. In Hungary, for example, non-governmental environmental organizations established largely by disaffected individuals apparently have seized the initiative on the environmental question.[23] While bureaucratic encapsulation of partial interests is not the only approach to the identification and handling of "interests" in the socialist world, it nevertheless may be the most common way and thus represents an approach to "interests" and their "representation" that deserves further empirical work.

The Allocation of Authority in a Soviet-Type System

Few concepts are as vague and subject to multiple interpretations as centralization and decentralization.[24] These are the usual categories employed for organizing analysis of distribution of authority among various levels in a Soviet-type system. This study suggests a more complex way of analyzing the issue is needed. At all times, the higher levels have important resources and sources of authority that give them considerable initiative. But without winning the active cooperation of lower level units, the higher levels are likely to find that they encounter difficulties and obstructions (rarely overt but usually devastatingly effective) that blunt their initiatives. Thus, rather than characterizing the socialist systems simply as "centralized" or "decentralized," it may be more realistic to examine the zoning of decision making authority, the allocation of resources, and the various bargains that upper and lower levels strike in order to advance particular initiatives.

Research on negotiations and bureaucratic exchange in other socialist systems might reveal the types of resources that provide leverage to various units. This in itself would make studies of the policy process more realistic than the simplistic notions of highly centralized—or decentralized—sectors. Often the local territorial Party committee is the key body able to mobilize local resources, and this may help to explain the considerable leverage that the local Party officials clearly have in the theoretically top-down Soviet system.[25] A concern with bargaining processes

[23] We thank Denise Wydra for this information.

[24] Frederic Pryor provides ten different definitions of this duality in his *Property and Industrial Organization in Communist and Capitalist Nations* (Bloomington: Indiana University Press, 1973), pp. 281-287.

[25] See Jerry Hough, *The Soviet Prefects* (Cambridge: Harvard University Press, 1969). Hough views the local Party chiefs as playing vital, helpful roles in the system. Alexander Yanov, *The Drama of the Soviet 1960's* (Berkeley: Institute of International Studies, 1984) sees them more as tyrannical local leaders who simply insist on having the final say in everything, regardless of their level of competence. Both, however, stress the leverage of Party cadres in the basic level of territorial Party committees.

also may help to direct research toward the long term development both of a policy decision and of its implementation. The key questions in this regard are not so much when a decision was made but rather what balances were potentially upset by a decision and how—and to what extent—the affected units were brought on board.

EXPLAINING THE EVOLUTION OF BUREAUCRATIC STRUCTURES AND PROCESSES IN COMMUNIST SYSTEMS

We now go beyond a careful use of our findings to join, in more speculative fashion, other analyses of the evolution of communist systems. The importance of bureaucratic structures in explaining policy process and the degree to which bureaucracies constrain and shape the choices of the top leaders are not surprising or new findings to observers of Soviet-style systems. They frequently have dwelled on and sought to explain the triumph of bureaucracy in such regimes. Richard Lowenthal offered one elegant interpretation in his classic article, "Development Versus Utopia in Communist Policy."[26] Lowenthal argued that the utopian ideology of revolutionary leaders proves unsuitable to the task of economic development, and that gradually a transformation in the priorities of the leaders (from utopia to modernization) accompanies an evolution from the mobilization system of the revolutionaries to more stable, bureaucratic rule in the post-revolutionary era.[27] Another explanation for the triumph of state bureaucracy focuses on the combination of its control over productive resources and the absence of a free market in socialist systems. This combination enables the bureaucrats to control access to sources of privilege, with their resulting emergence as a "new class" intent on perpetuating its privileges.[28] Yet a third explanation is that new revolutionary regimes face national security dangers that necessitate the creation of a strong bureaucratic state capable of resisting these external threats. Domestically, potentially subversive collaborationists must be denied autonomy and freedom to establish links with the external foes.[29]

[26] In Workshop on the Comparative Study of Communist Systems, *Change in Communist Systems* (Stanford: Stanford University Press, 1970), pp. 33-116.

[27] For a distinctive and insightful analysis of this same basic issue see: Barrington Moore, Jr., *Soviet Politics—The Dilemma of Power* (New York: Harper and Row, 1965).

[28] Richard Kraus, *Class Conflict in Chinese Socialism* (New York: Columbia University Press, 1981); and Milovan Djilas, *The New Class* (New York: Frederick A. Praeger, 1957). Ralph Dahrendorf, in his *Class and Class Conflict in Industrial Society* (Stanford: Stanford University Press, 1959), provides a subtle and complex analysis of the tendency of the managerial class to assume ownership-like control over industrial organizations.

[29] Some advocates of this explanation have been political practitioners. For example, Stalin, in his report to the Eight Party Congress of the CPSU on March 10, 1939, stated, "It

These admittedly powerful theories thus seek to explain the emergence of a bureaucratically dominant state due to the growing irrelevance of the utopian revolutionary ideology; the nature of class and class conflict in non-market societies; and the foreign environment. Each of these approaches provides distinctive insights into the expanding importance and power of bureaucracies in non-market developing countries, and each theory details the consequences of these developments for society. None of them, however, proceeds to detail the implications of the structure of a mature Soviet-style state—that is, a bureaucratically dominant but fragmented system with a protracted, disjointed policy process characterized by bargaining and consensus-building. This structure itself affects both policy process and substantive outcomes. This argument thus requires tracing the evolution of state bureaucracies, their changing linkages to the top leaders, and the consequences of this evolution for policy processes and outcomes in socialist systems. Our findings hint at an organizational behavior explanation for the evolution of such states which merits explication and refinement through comparative and historical study. We posit several overlapping stages in the evolution of such states: initial centralization; erosion of control; response by the leaders; response by the agencies; and the emergence of a mature system.

Initial Centralization

The top leaders of a new communist regime seek to establish a highly unified, centralized structure of authority. Since the new regime inherits some bureaucracies from the previous regime—the tax collection bureaus, the communication agencies, the banks, and so on—the degree to which effective central control is imposed initially may be less than is apparent to the outside observer. Further, the top leaders preside over organizations which propelled them to power but which in the course of the revolution may have acquired a measure of autonomy and independent bases of power. For these as well as ideological considerations, the

---

is sometimes asked, . . . Why do we not help our socialist state to die away? . . . These questions show that these comrades . . . do not understand present day international conditions, have overlooked the capitalist encirclement and the dangers it entails for the socialist country. [They also underestimate the extent to which capitalist countries] send spies, assassins and wreckers into our country and are waiting for a favorable opportunity to attack it by armed force." Quoted from Bruce Franklin, *The Essential Stalin* (Garden City: Doubleday, 1972), pp. 379-380. Some scholars have also used the security environment as one explanation of the development of a strong state apparatus following a revolution. Theda Skocpol, for example, considers the international context as an important variable both in creating revolutionary situations and in shaping their outcomes. See her: *States and Social Revolutions* (Cambridge: Cambridge University Press, 1979).

new leaders soon after coming to power attempt to eliminate bureaucratic opposition and independence and establish mechanisms for sustaining their command.

Erosion of Control

Four factors soon begin to erode the control mechanisms they have employed. First, the leaders must subdivide the tasks of governance and arrange for a division of labor in the bureaucracy. Different agencies are charged with particular responsibilities. Goal displacement occurs, as bureaucrats attach increasing importance to their specific missions and neglect overarching national goals. The net result is a flattening of bureaucratic hierarchies and the emergence of a bargaining system within the governing bureaucracies.

DIVISION OF LABOR

As in the Soviet Union, a core organizing principle of the Chinese system is the division of labor according to functional task. The Soviet experience strongly shaped the basic organizational principles of the Chinese Communist Party since the early 1920's and the organization of the Chinese government after 1949. The Soviet approach itself evolved from the division of labor advocated by Lenin for Party work in *What Is To Be Done* (1902). With regard to personnel assignments, by 1922 the Soviet Party staffing procedures accepted the specialization of labor as necessary, and subsequent initiatives by Stalin effectively accentuated this development.[30] Foreign scholars have not systematically traced Soviet thinking about the organization of the state, and thus the origins of the ideas that informed the Stalinist approach to the division of labor in governance of the country remain obscure. But, as indicated above, China imported this organizational framework during the early years of the People's Republic.

The specialization of bureaucratic function poses inevitable risks to the leaders. The bureaucracies require new personnel who are less likely to share fully the values and goals of the revolutionary leaders. More fundamental is the tendency for individuals in various specialized bureaucracies to evaluate national needs from the perspectives of their own bureaucratic unit.[31] The tension between what the Chinese term

[30] Jeremy Azrael, "The Internal Dynamics of the CPSU," in Samuel Huntington and Clement Moore (eds.), *Authoritarian Politics*, pp. 261-283.

[31] In China, at least, this tendency has been strengthened by the practice of having most individuals spend their entire careers in one functional bureaucratic system: Barnett,

"departmentalism" (*benwei zhuyi*) and the adoption of a "comprehensive" (*quan mian*) perspective easily grows.

PROLIFERATION OF AGENCIES

Next in the process of eroding control is the consequence of proliferating agencies. Newly established Soviet-type regimes particularly exhibit this tendency, since they typically seek to undermine and take over all loci of administrative and political power formerly outside of the formal political structure[32] and radically to transform the society through active control over the entire economy, educational system, and other areas that are autonomous or semi-autonomous in other societies.[33] Inevitably, the revolutionary leaders become aware of new problems and create additional agencies to address them. As the tasks of governance become more complex and the awareness of difficulties grows, bureaucracies proliferate and segmentation occurs, leading to problems of inadequate monitoring and coordination. As the range of issues which leaders seek to manage expands, the natural tendency is toward increased bureaucratic specialization. New organs are continually created to keep the span of control of each individual organ within reasonable bounds.

THE FLATTENING OF HIERARCHIES

To an extent, the revolution enabled the leaders to reallocate resources; few precedents existed to guide budgetary allocation, personnel assignments, and so on. But gradually, patterns emerged concerning allocation of funds, resource flows, access to privileges, and so on. Lower level officials began to acquire a proprietary attitude toward the resources they had received. Rigidity and fragmentation set in.

This last tendency—that units acquire a sense of "right" to resources—is easily overlooked. Reference to land rights in Chinese cities elucidates this issue. During the 1950's, government and Party bureaucracies, military units, factories, schools, and other urban units acquired use rights to the land they occupied (and often to other land as well). These "rights" were not formalized in contractual form, and no land market was allowed to develop. Rather, each unit simply acquired the use of "its" land rent-free and in perpetuity. Units could transfer their land to another unit but could not openly sell it. Therefore, land became

---

Cadres, Bureaucracy and Political Power in Communist China; and Paul Wong, *China's Higher Leadership In the Socialist Transition* (New York: The Free Press, 1976).

[32] See, for example: Kenneth Lieberthal, *Revolution and Tradition*.

[33] *See*, Kenneth Jowitt, *Revolutionary Breakthroughs and National Development: The Case of Romania, 1944-1965* (Berkeley and Los Angeles: University of California Press, 1971).

a commodity to be bargained—even the state rarely simply commandeered land without first engaging in protracted negotiations over the land and/or other benefits to be provided to the displaced individuals and agencies.

Land thus became a permanent resource of each urban unit that had it, although this was not a resource protected by law or recognized as something conferred by "right." In similar fashion, bureaucratic units have acquired resources that by custom cannot easily be confiscated against their will. These include, *inter alia*, a basic operating budget of at least the size of the previous year's allocation and a degree of control over certain resources such as physical property, personnel, programs, and rule-making authority in certain areas.[34]

As bureaucratic units have acquired some control over resources, the organizational hierarchy has operationally become "flattened," to borrow a term from organizational theory. That is, units at all levels of the national hierarchy have acquired control over resources that enable them to bargain with their superiors rather than to simply accept the chain-of-command of formal organization charts. The absence of markets for allocating resources, moreover, has further contributed to the flattening of bureaucratic hierarchy. Upper level units (and units in different functional sectors) have no source of supply other than the bureaucracies with which they are dealing—there is no market from which the required resources can be obtained. Formally subordinate units enjoy enhanced ability to bargain with their "superiors."

A BARGAINING SYSTEM EMERGES

Finally, unable to obtain resources they seek in the marketplace, bureaucrats seek to obtain guaranteed sources of necessary supply through exchange of resources under their command. Networks develop of officials, bound by mutual obligations and patron-client ties. Informal means for facilitating inter-agency and inter-personal cooperation and exchange make the formal system work. A system of bargaining develops. To translate their policy pronouncements into reality, the top leaders must use their limited leverage and weave their policies and projects into the existing web of bureaucratic exchanges through a protracted process of negotiations and consensus building.

Our case studies of the politics of energy development highlighted this phenomenon. Bargaining occurred not only because of the overwhelming complexity of the issues and organs but also because numerous units

---

[34] An extensive literature discusses bureaucratic control of resources as a form of property. See especially Frederic Pryor, *Property and Industrial Organization*.

acquired some *de facto* leverage that could be utilized in negotiations among bureaucratic units. To be sure, the prevailing norms affected the ends officials sought in striking bargains, and the official rules and structure of formal authority substantially affected the dynamics of bargaining. But the need of upper levels to bargain to *secure compliance from subordinate units* with their initiatives—as well as to bargain with people in a different bureaucratic hierarchy on the same level of the national bureaucracy—is central to the system. A key research topic is whether other Soviet-type systems have evolved along similar lines.

The Leaders Respond

The willful leaders at the apex find these trends vexing and frustrating, and they therefore embark upon periodic efforts to make the bureaucracy more responsive to them. In short, the top leaders are not powerless in the face of the growing bureaucratic constraints upon their power, and particularly vigorous ones such as Stalin and Mao seek means to check the fragmentation of the system.

The Soviets almost from the start utilized a variety of means to prevent specialization from too deeply affecting the perspectives of officials. They, for example, have tried to inculcate Communist Party officials with a "comprehensive" perspective and have them monitor the administrative organs of the state. The problem then became one of finding a balance that permitted the Communist Party hierarchy to supervise the state organs closely without themselves succumbing to the "departmentalism" that they were supposed to limit. This dilemma has defied a totally satisfying solution.[35]

Other measures have included: periodic amalgamations of specialized bureaucracies into super agencies with broader mandates (each such move has led in turn to re-differentiation over the ensuing years);[36] occasional efforts to shift the major organizational principle from functional task to territorial coordination (but these have always produced such strong manifestations of "localism" that they have led to recentral-

---

[35] At the height of the Stalin era the "national" perspective became synonymous with meeting Stalin's own demands. Terror largely replaced Party supervision as the means for enforcing this: Seweryn Bialer, *Stalin's Successors* (Cambridge: Cambridge University Press, 1980), chapter 1. Khrushchev sought in the late 1950's to reestablish the Party's role as a core national institution that would prevent the state agencies from becoming parochial.

[36] In the Soviet Union under Stalin, for example, the number of ministries changed as follows: 18 in 1936; 59 in 1947; 48 in 1949; 51 in 1952; 25 in 1953; Merle Fainsod, *How Russia Is Ruled*, rev. ed. (Cambridge: Harvard University Press, 1963), p. 393.

izing measures rather quickly);[37] and purging and punishing individuals for a "departmental" deviation (which has run so counter to many of the other incentives in the system that it has produced defensive moves to encapsulate the unit rather than engendering the "comprehensive" perspective sought by the leaders).[38] Bureaucratic growth and division of responsibility according to functional task thus create an insoluble tension in the system.

Mao Zedong, more than most leaders, deeply believed that officials should and could be virtuous generalists with the correct "orientation" and commitment.[39] In this, Mao drew from traditional Chinese bureaucratic ideals as well as from the experiences of the long struggle for power through which he led the Chinese Communist Party. Mao therefore proved more willing than most leaders to adopt increasingly drastic measures to cope with the goal displacement that so characterized the bureaucratic development that he witnessed after 1949.

Mao at one time or another adopted each of the measures that had been used in the Soviet Union.[40] He used the Party to monitor the government, and then used the army to supervise both Party and government. He experimented with many different ways of subdividing the tasks of rule. He adopted a basically territorial approach during the initial stage of the Great Leap Forward. Repeatedly, he sought to punish officials who seemed too narrowly specialized in their outlooks. And ministerial amalgamation and redifferentiation characterized the Maoist era.[41]

But Mao also went beyond these techniques. Increasingly, he turned to what can only be described as deinstitutionalization to solve the problem. This began with Mao's use of political campaigns that effectively circumvented normal bureaucratic channels and practices to accomplish tasks.[42] Some of these campaigns actually targeted bureaucratic behavior

[37] See, for example, the evolution of policy toward the sovnarkhozy (which represented a dramatic shift to territorially-based administration of the economy under Khrushchev) in: Alec Nove, "Economic Policy and Economic Trends," in A. Dallin and Thomas B. Larson (eds.), *Soviet Politics Since Khrushchev* (Englewood Cliffs: Prentice Hall, 1968), pp. 73-110.

[38] On the formation of defensive alliances of factory managers, Party secretaries and KGB chiefs in units, see: Jeremy Azrael, *Managerial Power.*

[39] See: Martin Whyte, "Bureaucracy and Modernization in China: The Maoist Critique," *American Sociological Review* (April 1973), pp. 149-163.

[40] Harry Harding has traced this history in his *Organizing China.*

[41] For additional information on these points, *see:* H. Franz Schurmann, *Ideology and Organization;* and James Townsend, *Politics in China* (Boston: Little, Brown and Company, 1974).

[42] See: Gordon Bennett, *Yundong: Mass Campaigns in Chinese Communist Leadership* (Berkeley: Center for Chinese Studies, 1976); Charles P. Cell, *Revolution at Work: Mass Campaigns in China* (New York: Academic Press, 1977); and Michel Oksenberg, "The Chinese Policy Process and the Public Health Issue."

itself as the focus for change.[43] Mao also supported efforts to chasten bureaucrats by sending them "down" for periods of manual labor, often in the countryside.[44] This immersion in the "real" world of China was intended to cleanse the bureaucrats of their officious and narrow ways of thinking, instilling instead a renewed commitment to general social goals. As the results of this "sending down" (*xiafang*, in Chinese) proved inadequate, Mao sanctioned still more drastic measures. Ultimately, these led to the direct attacks on bureaucratic authority, massive purges of officials, and the virtual destruction of many bureaucratic units during his most momentous political campaign, the Cultural Revolution. At all times, Mao combined these measures with very heavy doses of political study to impress his values and priorities on Chinese officialdom.

It is unclear how effective Mao was in inhibiting bureaucratic specialization and goal displacement. The limited evidence suggests that "departmentalism" had become a vexing problem by the mid-1950's. For example, the State Council found that legislation which various ministries drafted in the mid-1950's quite consistently reflected ministerial interests and viewpoints.[45] By the end of the 1970's, legislative activities revived and a number of ministries refused even minimally to consult with their counterparts when drafting new legislation.[46] The increasing ferocity of Mao's combat against these tendencies suggests that the Chairman felt he was losing the battle. He vainly challenged unconquerable pressures for stability, for routine, and for the devolution of resources to various bureaucratic units virtually as a matter of right.

Agencies Respond

To counter these efforts and reduce their vulnerability to the vagaries of the top leaders, administrators seek self-sufficiency. They try to obtain guaranteed sources of supply necessary to the success of their mission, to create excess capacity and add people to the payroll, and to accumulate inventories so as to protect themselves from their external environment. They hoard information, feign compliance, cultivate patrons at higher levels, and expand their mandate. Over time, in short, they learn to blunt the weapons of control of the top leaders.

[43] See Harry Harding, *Organizing China*, and Frederick Teiwes, *Politics and Purges in China*.

[44] See: Rensaleer Lee III, "The Hsia-fang System: Marxism and Modernization," *China Quarterly*, no. 28 (October-December 1966), pp. 40-62.

[45] Wu Daying, et al., *Zhongguo shehuizhuyi lifa wenti* (Qunzhong chubanshe, 1984).

[46] Yang Hong and Wang Jinzhong, "Yao jiaqiang jingji lifa gongzuo," *Renmin ribao*, May 14, 1981.

A Mature System Emerges

The arenas of decision proliferate as organizations which allocate resources come to exist at all levels of the system. The arena in which an issue is decided affects the outcome, since different arenas incorporate distinctive sets of values, interests, and resources. Specific issues, moreover, may move from one arena to another. External impulses—changes in foreign affairs, natural disasters, demographic changes, economic development, or public opinion—are thus increasingly filtered through specialized bureaucracies. The top political leaders, directly exposed to such external impulses in the early days of a revolutionary regime, become somewhat insulated and buffered from changes in the social, economic, or security environment. The fragmented bureaucracies, the staffs, and coordinating bodies therefore exert a growing influence on policy outcomes. To be sure, the leaders retain substantial resources with which to push their initiatives. They can create new organizations, open the country to international currents, and in other ways generate pressures to move the system in the directions they please. But while the top leaders remain very important in a mature Soviet-type system, they are constrained by the bureaucratic evolution of the system they have created. The mature Soviet type system, to repeat, is a bureaucratically dominant but fragmented system with a protracted, disjointed policy process characterized by bargaining and consensus building.[47]

As noted above, our data do not enable us to validate this bureaucratic structural portrayal of the evolution of Soviet-type systems. Rather, our study of the Chinese system of the 1980's suggests that this tentative interpretation merits scrutiny through further research on China and other socialist systems. Insofar as this interpretation is valid, of course, understanding bureaucratic structures and processes becomes increasingly important to analysis of decision making (even at an elite level) in maturing communist systems.

THE CAPACITY FOR REFORM

Our interpretation of the bureaucratic structural evolution of Soviet-type systems raises important questions about the process and potentialities of the various reforms that have gripped East Europe since the late

---

[47] Many scholars have noted that the increasing complexity of the economy—and the resulting necessary evolution from extensive to intensive economic growth—sharply limit the options of the top leaders. We do not argue with this. Rather, we simply note that this complexity has an administrative dimension that is also of great importance for understanding the dynamics of mature Soviet-type systems.

1960's, China since the late 1970's, and the Soviet Union itself in the mid-1980's. All these reforms sought greater use of technical expertise, some expansion in the economic decision making authority of both enterprises and lower administrative levels,[48] a reduction in the scope of mandatory planning, some readjustment of prices and of exchange rates to reflect internal supply and demand and international prices, greater openness to the international Western economy (including imports of both foreign capital and foreign technology), a weakening of central control over foreign trade and increased authority of individual ministries, local governments, and enterprises to engage in foreign trade, and a grudging abandonment of previous attitudes toward foreign trade (of importing only what cannot be produced at home and exporting only that which is necessary to pay for imports).[49] These and related changes seek increased economic efficiency and improved quality (including making better use of new technologies) through reduction in the role of state administration in the economy. Different countries have, of course, implemented these ideas to widely varying extents.[50]

How have these reforms affected the structural characteristics of a Soviet-type system? In the Chinese case, as the Three Gorges and the Shanxi coal development issues demonstrate, the reforms appear to have further flattened bureaucratic hierarchies both by increasing the resources available to local units and altering in the atmosphere in which inter-unit bargaining and consensus building take place. Indeed, in broad terms the reforms tend to reduce the resources available to central leaders to discipline bureaucracies so as to achieve major regime goals. In China, for example, the reform-oriented top leaders are reluctant to employ the tools that Mao and his colleagues once wielded to overcome bureaucratic lethargy and resistance—political campaigns, ideological broadsides, suppression of dissent, purges of recalcitrant individuals, deification of the top leader, and so forth. In their effort to encourage empirical analysis and legitimate debate, the political leaders have eschewed political coercion, especially in matters of economic policy making.

[48] Janos Kornai, *Dilemmas and Contradictions* (Cambridge: MIT Press, 1986).

[49] On traditional communist foreign trade practice, *see*: Alexander Eckstein, *Communist China's Economic Growth and Foreign Trade* (New York: McGraw-Hill, 1966).

[50] The East Europeans have already produced a significant literature concerning reform, although the best of these writings focus on economics rather than politics. See especially the insightful writings of Janos Kornai, many of whose ideas are summarized in his *Contradictions and Dilemmas*. On the initial Soviet reforms, see: Timothy Colton, "Approaches to the Politics of Systemic Economic Reform in the Soviet Union" (Paper prepared for Conference on Soviet Economic Reform, Airlie House, Virginia, January 29, 1987); and Edward A. Hewitt, "Reform or Rhetoric: Gorbachev and the Soviet Economy," *The Brookings Review*, vol. 4 (Fall 1986).

More fundamentally, the reforms have scattered further resources (such as foreign exchange) among bureaucratic units and have emboldened units overtly to articulate and defend their own perspectives. The reformers encourage units to state their views and to marshall supporting evidence for their positions so that the final decision will be reasoned. One consequence is that the bureaucracies have increased opportunity to advance their departmental causes. Here is the behavioral consequence of requiring feasibility studies before launching energy projects.

Avoidance of major mistakes might be one outcome of this increased debate. Other outcomes, however, include providing a greater mantle of legitimacy for each unit to marshall arguments in favor of its own perspective on issues and to push those arguments very strongly. This situation makes theoretical sense, given the relationship between units, tasks, and interests outlined above. At the same time, though, it may make units less willing to compromise on issues of concern to them.[51] The sharp diminution in political coercion associated with the reforms, moreover, may encourage various units to stick to their positions and prevent a consensus from forming because they recognize that stubbornness will more likely pay off than be punished. In sum, the reforms may make it less likely that the system will make major mistakes—but also less likely that it will be possible to achieve the consensus necessary to pursue major projects that affect a wide range of units and interests.

Relatedly, the reforms have increased the amount of money that is available for various units to undertake activities outside of the state plan. This has created a wider range of potential opportunities for units to use their resources for their own purposes instead of having few opportunities other than state-mandated activities. The further fragmentation of authority growing out of the reforms has, therefore, contributed to the very extensive consultative process that, as detailed throughout this study, characterizes decision making on large energy projects.

The reforms complicate this consultative process, moreover, in that they promote changes not only in procedure but also in values. Economic units, for example, are instructed to place greater value on efficiency and on measuring tasks and accomplishments in monetary terms. The previous values, such as maximizing employment and preserving particular networks of relationships, are no longer to have priority. Inevitably, some units seize upon these changes more rapidly than others, and these

[51] These issues may only partly relate to unit tasks. They may also include preserving the unit's resources and its network of relations with other units. See Chapter Four and Kelley, "Toward a Model of Soviet Decision Making."

units become both promoters of reform and increasingly out of step with other parts of the bureaucratic system. The net result is a period of growing uncertainty, as units become less able to gauge the reactions that their various initiatives will produce in the affected bureaucracies. This lack of underlying agreement on values, then, complicates the bargaining among units in different bureaucratic hierarchies, as various units find it more difficult to judge the mix of responses that their initiatives will engender.[52]

At an enterprise level, moreover, the reforms do not go far enough to create a system where behavior is truly disciplined by market forces.[53] When in financial difficulty, the rational enterprise manager will still turn first to the state to alter relationships in a way that will enable his firm to survive and prosper. The reforms do, however, reduce in more than a trivial way the intrusion of the very top level leaders into economic decision making. The net result—reform rhetoric about the market notwithstanding—is that the dynamics of bureaucratic behavior assume a larger role than before the reforms in determining policy process and policy outcomes. There is a contradiction here, however, in the fact that the reforms imply, overall, a major redistribution of power and resources among those very same bureaucracies. Naturally, in this process the bureaucracies that stand to gain from the new procedures, priorities, and distribution of resources become strong advocates of further reform efforts.

Our study of decision making in the energy sector suggests that the reforms have further flattened hierarchies and thereby potentially made it more difficult to bring about a major redistribution of resources and power among those hierarchies. A very large number of units have essentially acquired an enhanced ability to use both policy (such as a stress on feasibility studies) and new resources (such as access to bank loans) to enhance their ability to resist demands from the Center. The consequences, paradoxically, may be a more empirically based process of policy making (more discussion of technical issues, fuller vetting of questions, a more deliberate pace of decision making), but the policy outcomes (in efficiency, quality, redistribution of resources, etc.) may not accord with the aims of reform.

Our analysis thus highlights the irony that partial reforms of mature Soviet-type systems produce, *inter alia*, obstacles to reform. Such reforms provide ample opportunity for threatened bureaucracies to acquire

---

[52] There is ample treatment of this problem in the theoretical literature on decision making. See, for example, Thomas Schelling, *The Strategy of Conflict*, p. 16.

[53] This is true even in Hungary, as Kornai has shown; *See* his *Contradictions and Dilemmas*.

new resources to protect themselves. A blitzkrieg-type reform, to borrow Samuel Huntington's apt phrase, could potentially circumvent this problem, but this type of initiative would require more political momentum at the top than any reformist leadership has been able to muster.[54] The closest approximation to blitzkrieg-type reform occurred in Hungary, and even this could not be carried through to completion.[55]

The top leaders do not, however, lose all initiative once a partial reform gets underway—our statements about the devolution of power to the bureaucracies has been cast in relative, not absolute, terms. There are, indeed, three types of initiatives beyond simply making a case for their policies that leaders of incremental reforms can take to further their cause.

First, they can create organizations with a vested interest in the reforms themselves. The reform leaders, at least in China, retain their ability to foster the development and tasking of new organizations. Drawing on our study of Chinese energy policy, for example, the creation of the China National Offshore Oil Corporation produced a bureaucratic entity that would fight hard to enhance collaboration with international companies to explore for and develop China's offshore oil resources. The China International Trust and Investment Corporation, created as a part of the reform effort, has also become a powerful force on the Chinese scene in support of the country's opening to the international economy of the West.[56] Since Chinese organizations pursue their tasks with a vengeance, in short, these tasks, properly shaped, can be made to serve the cause of reform. Many old organizations, however, are already so deeply enmeshed in networks of relations and arrangements that reformers find it too difficult to reorient their work.[57]

The international arena provides the second resource available to the reform leaders. On the economic side, foreign firms create pressures for a more fully developed legal system, for direct access to end users, for more information about economic performance, for a larger cadre of officials who can speak foreign languages and understand international practices, and so forth. These international pressures can thus become

[54] Samuel Huntington, *Political Order in Changing Societies* (New Haven: Yale University Press, 1968), pp. 346-347.

[55] Kornai, *Dilemmas and Contradictions.*

[56] See, for example, *Far Eastern Economic Review* (May 7, 1987), pp. 118-123.

[57] The reforms do, nevertheless, conform to the interests of some of the old organizations, and these can become strong advocates of the reform effort. In addition, it is occasionally possible to win old organizations over to new tasks (e.g., the Chinese reformers successfully tasked the SEC with technical renovation and industrial management reform). But the most powerful previous organizations—such as the state planning agencies and the heavy industry ministries—typically are more the targets of the reformers than their allies.

major driving forces for reform. The pressures, moreover, extend beyond the production system itself. Foreign life styles, foreign literature, and foreign political processes all become objects of interest and (often) envy. These popular and elite feelings drive the system toward greater reform. There is a danger here that elite alarm over foreign cultural and economic influence will precipitate an anti-reform, conservative reaction. On balance, however, the international arena must be counted as a resource that skillful leaders can use to promote the cause of continuing, incremental reform.

Increasing the use of market mechanisms in the domestic economy is a third resource available to the reformers. "Incremental" reform by its very nature means that the economy will not be transformed at one step into a market system. Nevertheless, leaders can use a growing role for the market as a source of pressure for ever greater reform. In the Chinese case, the major step in this direction took the form of decollectivization of agriculture (what the Chinese call the development of "the responsibility system in agriculture"), primarily during 1979-84. The development of this huge internal market created a range of pressures to spread the use of the market into the urban economy. The very success of the rural market reforms, moreover, generated momentum that could be used by the reform leaders to promote their urban reform initiatives. Internal markets by themselves are not sufficient to ensure the continuing spread of domestic economic reform, but to the extent they can be created by fiat, they can under the right conditions contribute to the energy sustaining incremental reform.

We thus conclude with a complex picture. Our analysis of mature Soviet-type systems explains the importance of bureaucratic practices in determining outcomes even in the face of incremental reforms that seek to reduce the roles of the governing bureaucracies. The reforms themselves, we believe, contribute to the further flattening of bureaucratic hierarchies and reduce the ability of the leaders to change this situation. An incremental strategy concentrated solely on changes within the administrative system, therefore, cannot be effectively sustained. But the leaders still retain other important resources. If the top leaders remain determined, they can utilize international forces and domestic markets— and can create new bureaucracies with vested interests in reform—to sustain an effort that is itself generating obstacles to further reform. The jury is still out on whether this wider ranging set of strategies can successfully produce a reform breakthrough in a mature Soviet-type system.

BIBLIOGRAPHY OF SOURCES
CITED IN THE TEXT

"A Brief Introduction of the Three Gorge Project on the Yangtze River." Wuhan: Yangtze Valley Planning Office, Feb. 1980.

Ahn, Byung-joon. *Chinese Politics and the Cultural Revolution*. Seattle: University of Washington Press, 1976.

Akagi, Akio, and Morihiko Sato. "Taching Oil Fields and China's Industrial Technology." *Shizhen* (Nature), May 1974, pp. 62-73, translated in *Translations on the People's Republic of China* No. 305 (JPRS 64466, April 2, 1975).

Allison, Graham. *Essence of Decision: Explaining the Cuban Missile Crisis*. Boston: Little, Brown and Company, 1971.

"An Analysis of China's Economic Situation during the Period of Ten Years of Internal Disorder," *Jingji yanjiu* (Economic Research), No. 1 (January, 1984), pp. 23-31, translated in FBIS, March 7, 1984.

"A Record of Talk at the Spring Festival," Feb. 13, 1964, in *Mao Zedong Sixiang Wansui* (Long live the thought of Chairman Mao). NP, ND.

Axelrod, Robert. *The Evolution of Cooperation*. New York: Basic Books, 1984.

Azrael, Jeremy. "The Internal Dynamics of the CPSU," in Samuel Huntington and Barrington Moore, eds. *Authoritarian Politics in Modern Society*. New York: Basic Books, 1970, pp. 261-283.

Azrael, Jeremy. *Managerial Power in Soviet Politics*. Cambridge: Harvard University Press, 1966.

Bachman, David. *Chen Yun and the Chinese Political System*. Berkeley and Los Angeles: University of California Press, 1985.

Bachman, David. *To Leap Forward: Chinese Policy-Making, 1956-57*. Ph.D. thesis. Stanford University, 1984.

Barnett, A. Doak. *Cadres, Bureaucracy, and Political Power in Communist China*. New York: Columbia University Press, 1967.

Barnett, A. Doak. *China's Economy in Global Perspective*. Washington: Brookings, 1981.

Barnett, A. Doak. *The Making of Foreign Policy in China: Structure and Process*. Boulder: Westview Press, 1985.

Barnett, A. Doak. *Uncertain Passage*. Washington: Brookings, 1974.

Barnett, A. Doak and Ralph Clough, eds. *Modernizing China*. Boulder: Westview, 1986.

Bartke, Wolfgang. *Who's Who in the People's Republic of China*. Armonk: M. E. Sharpe, 1981.

Baum, Richard. "Revolution and Reaction in the Chinese Countryside: The Socialist Education Movement in Cultural Revolutionary Perspective." *China Quarterly* No. 38 (April-June, 1969), pp. 92-119.

Baum, Richard and Frederick C. Teiwes. *Ssu-Ch'ing: The Socialist Education Movement of 1962-1966*. China Research Monograph, No. 2. Berkeley and Los Angeles: University of California Press, 1968.

Bennett, Gordon. *Yundong: Mass Campaigns in Chinese Communist Leadership*. Berkeley and Los Angeles: University of California Center for Chinese Studies, 1976.

Bialer, Seweryn. *Stalin's Successors*. Cambridge: Cambridge University Press, 1980.

Bower, Joseph. "Descriptive Decision Theory from the 'Administrative' Viewpoint," in Raymond Bauer and Kenneth Gergen, eds. *The Study of Policy Formulation*. New York: The Free Press, 1968, pp. 103-148.

"Bravely Lift Heavy Burdens." *Shanxi Ribao* (Shanxi daily) April 10, 1981, p. 1, translated in JPRS *China Report—Economic Affairs*, No. 143 (June 16, 1981), pp. 42-43.

Brown, A. H. "Pluralistic Trends in Czechoslovakia." *Soviet Studies* (April 1966), pp. 453-472.

Bunce, Valerie and John Echols III. "Soviet Politics in the Brezhnev Era: 'Pluralism' or 'Corporatism?' " in Donald R. Kelley, ed. *Soviet Politics in the Brezhnev Era*. New York: Praeger Publishers, 1980, pp. 1-26.

Burns, John. *Chinese Peasant Interest Articulation: 1949-1974*, Ph.D. thesis. New York: Columbia University, 1978.

Cell, Charles P. *Revolution at Work: Mass Campaigns in China*. New York: Academic Press, 1977.

Chan, Leslie. *The Taching Oilfield: A Maoist Model for Economic Development*, Contemporary China Papers No. 8. Canberra: ANU Press, 1974.

Chang, Parris. *Power and Policy in China*. University Park: Pennsylvania State University, 1976.

Chang, Parris. "The rise of Wang Tung-hsing: Head of China's security apparatus." *China Quarterly* No. 73 (March, 1978), p. 127.

Chang, Parris. "Shanghai in Chinese Politics: Before and After the Cultural Revolution," in Christopher Howe, ed. *Shanghai: Revolution and Development in an Asian Metropolis*. Cambridge: Cambridge University Press, 1981, pp. 66-90.

Changjiang sanxia shuili gongcheng jihua (Plan for the Yangtze Three Gorges Key Water Resources Project). China: Ministry of Information, 1947.

Chao, Kang. *Agricultural Production in Communist China, 1949-1985*. Madison: University of Wisconsin Press, 1970.

Chen, Yun. "Readjust the National Economy; Develop in a Balanced Fashion." in *Zhonggong shiyi ju sanzhong guanhui yilai zhongyang shouyao jianghua ji wenjian xuanbian* (Selection of important central speeches and documents since the Third Plenum), vol. 1. Changchun: People's Press, 1982.

China Coal Industry Yearbook. Hong Kong: Economic Information and Agency, 1985.

China Revolutionary Museum. *Zhonghua Renmin Gongheguo quanguo renda, zhongyang he difang zhengfu, quanguo zhengxie lijie fuzeren renminglu*

418

(Directory of Responsible Personages of the NPC, Central and Local Governments, and the CPPCC). Beijing: People's Daily Press, 1984.

"China's Taching Oilfield." *Current Scene* Vol. VI, No. 16 (September 17, 1968).

"Chou Enlai Speech to Rebels of the Departments of Industry and Communications." *Hongse zaofanbao* (Red Rebel Paper) February 19, 1967, in *SCMP Supplement*, No. 238 (November 8, 1968).

Chu Chi-lin. "China's Skyrocketing Oil Output." *Peking Review*, No. 23 (August 5, 1958), pp. 9-11.

Clarke, Christopher. "China's Third Generation." *China Business Review* (March-April 1984).

Cohen, Jerome. *The Criminal System in the People's Republic of China*. Cambridge: Harvard University Press, 1968.

Cohen, Michael D., James G. March, and Johan P. Olsen. "A Garbage Can Model of Organizational Choice." *Administrative Science Quarterly* (March 1972), pp. 1-25.

Colton, Timothy. "Approaches to the Politics of Systemic Economic Reform in the Soviet Union." Paper prepared for Conference on Soviet Economic Reform, Airlie House, Virginia, January 29, 1987.

Crozier, Michel. *The Bureaucratic Phenomenon*. Chicago: University of Chicago Press, 1964.

Cyert, Richard M. and James G. March. *A Behavioral Theory of the Firm*. Englewood Cliffs, N.J.: Prentice-Hall, 1963.

Dahrendorf, Ralph. *Class and Class Conflict in Industrial Society*. Stanford: Stanford University Press, 1959.

Dalton, Melville. *Men Who Manage*. New York: John Wiley, 1959.

Daqing. Beijing: People's Fine Arts Press, 1970.

Daqing gongshe (Daqing Commune). NP. ND.

"Daqing Oilfield Achieves High Standards" (Beijing: NCNA English, September 29, 1969). *Translations on Communist China* No. 74 (JPRS 49030, October 10, 1969), pp. 33-34.

Denny, David. "China's On-Land Oil and Gas Organizations." *The China Business Review* (January-February, 1985), pp. 30-36.

Dernberger, Robert, ed. *China's Economy Looks Toward the Year 2000*. Washington: Government Printing Office, 1986.

Dernberger, Robert. "The Resurgence of 'Chung-hsueh wei-t'i, Hsi-hsueh wei-yung' in Contemporary China: The Transfer of Technology to the PRC." Paper prepared for Conference on Technology and Communist Culture, Villa Serbelloni, August 22-28, 1975.

"Dispute over Resources Resolved." *Shanxi Ribao* (Shanxi daily) May 12, 1981, p. 2, translated in JPRS *China Report—Economic Affairs*, No. 148 (July 6, 1981), pp. 39-40.

Dittmer, Lowell. "Bases of Power in Chinese Politics: A Theory of Analysis of the Fall of the Gang of Four." *World Politics* (October 1978), pp. 26-60.

Dittmer, Lowell. *Liu Shao-ch'i and the Chinese Cultural Revolution: The Poli-

tics of Mass Criticism. Berkeley and Los Angeles: University of California Press, 1975.

Djilas, Milovan. *The New Class.* New York: Frederick A. Praeger, 1957.

Domes, Jurgen. *China After the Cultural Revolution: Politics Between Two Party Congresses.* London: C. Hurst and Company, 1976.

Domes, Jurgen. *The Government and Politics of the PRC: A Time of Transition.* Boulder: Westview Press, 1985.

Dong, Xusheng. "Zhongguo weilai: liu Su pai yu liu Mei pai de bodou" (China's future: The struggle between the returnees from the Soviet Union and the returnees from America). *Zhongguo zhi chun* (China's spring) (November 1985), pp. 10-16.

Donnithorne, Audrey. "China's Cellular Economy: Some Economic Trends Since the Cultural Revolution." *China Quarterly* No. 52 (October-December 1972), pp. 605-619.

Donnithorne, Audrey. *China's Economic System.* New York: Praeger Publishers, 1967.

Donnithorne, Audrey and Nicholas Lardy. "Comment: Centralization and Decentralization in China's Fiscal Management." *China Quarterly* No. 66 (June, 1976), pp. 328-354.

Downs, Anthony. *Inside Bureaucracy.* Boston: Little, Brown and Company, 1967.

Dui Daqing jingyan de zhengzhi jingji xue gaocha (The Political Economy of the Daqing Experience). People's Press, 1979.

Eckstein, Alexander. *Communist China's Economic Growth and Foreign Trade.* New York: McGraw-Hill, 1966.

Fainsod, Merle. *How Russia Is Ruled.* Rev. ed. Cambridge: Harvard University Press, 1963.

Fairbank, John K. *Trade and Diplomacy on the China Coast.* Cambridge: Harvard University Press, 1953.

Fairbank, John K. *The United States and China.* Fourth edition, enlarged. Cambridge: Harvard University Press, 1983.

Falkenheim, Victor, ed. *Citizens and Groups in Contemporary China.* University of Michigan: Center for Chinese Studies, forthcoming.

Falkenheim, Victor. "Continuing Central Predominance." *Problems of Communism* Vol. 21, No. 4 (1972), pp. 75-83.

Falkenheim, Victor. *Provincial Administration in Fukien, 1949-1966.* Ph.D. thesis. New York: Columbia University, 1972.

Fang Weizhong, ed. *Zhonghua Renmin Gongheguo jingji dashiji* (Economic Chronology of the PRC). Beijing: Chinese Social Sciences Press, 1984.

Feuerwerker, Albert. *China's Early Industrialization.* Cambridge: Harvard University Press, 1958.

Field, Robert M., Nicholas Lardy, and John Emerson. "Industrial Output by Province in China, 1949-73." *China Quarterly* No. 63 (September, 1975), pp. 409-434.

Field, Robert M., Kathleen McGlynn, and William Abnett. "Political Conflict and Industrial Growth in China: 1965-1977." *Chinese Economy Post-Mao* Vol. 1. Joint Economic Committee. Washington: US Government Printing Office, 1978, pp. 239-284.

Fingar, Thomas. "Implementing Energy Policy: The Rise and Demise of the State Energy Commission," in David M. Lampton, ed. *Policy Implementation in the People's Republic of China*. Berkeley and Los Angeles: University of California Press, 1987.

Fingar, Thomas. "Overview: Energy in China," in Robert Dernberger, ed. *China's Economy Looks Toward the Year 2000*. Washington: Government Printing Office, 1986, Vol. 2, pp. 1-21.

Fountain, Kevin. "The Development of China's Offshore Oil." *China Business Review* (Jan.-Feb., 1980), pp. 29-31.

Fox, Galen. *Campaigning for Power in China During the Cultural Revolution Era, 1967-1976*. Ph.D. thesis. Princeton: Princeton University, 1978.

Franklin, Bruce. *The Essential Stalin*. New York: Doubleday, 1972.

Fried, Morton. *Fabric of Chinese Society: A Study of the Social Life of a Chinese County Seat*. New York: 1969.

Gao, Xia. "Jushi zhumu de Sanxia shuidian zhan" (The Three Gorges Hydropower Station that is the focus of world attention). *Dili zhishi* (Geographic knowledge) No. 4 (April 1985), pp. 5-6.

Glassman, Joel. "Change and Continuity in Chinese Communist Education Policy." *Contemporary China* Vol. 2, No. 2 (September, 1978), pp. 847-890.

Godwin, Robert C., Jr. "The Evolving Legal Framework." *The China Business Review* (May-June, 1983), pp. 42-44.

Goldman, Merle. *China's Intellectuals: Advise and Dissent*. Cambridge: Harvard University Press, 1981.

Goodman, David S. *Centre and Province in the PRC: Sichuan and Guizhou, 1955-1965*. Cambridge: Cambridge University Press, 1986.

Goodman, David S., ed. *Groups and Politics in the People's Republic of China*. Armonk, N.Y.: M. E. Sharpe, 1984.

Goodman, David S. "The Provincial First Party Secretary in the People's Republic of China, 1949-1978: A Profile." *British Journal of Political Science* Vol. X, No. 1 (1980).

Green, Stephanie. "Offshore Business." *The China Business Review* (May-June, 1982), pp. 17-19.

Griffith, William. *Albania and the Sino-Soviet Rift*. Cambridge: MIT Press, 1963.

Guo, Shuisheng and Chen Weihuang. "Vast Vistas in Yingge Sea Oil Exploration." *China Oil* Vol. 2, No. 2 (Summer, 1985), pp. 46-49.

Gustafson, Thane. *Reform in Soviet Politics*. Cambridge: Cambridge University Press, 1981.

Halpern, Nina. *Economic Specialists and the Making of Chinese Economic Policy, 1955-1983*. Ph.D. thesis. Ann Arbor: University of Michigan, 1985.

Halpern, Nina. "Policy Communities, Garbage Cans, and the Chinese Economic Policy Process." Unpublished manuscript, 1984.

Halpern, Nina. " 'Scientific Decision Making': The Organization of Expert Advice in Post-Mao China." Unpublished ms.

Hama, Katsuhiko. "Systemic Reforms and Financial Problems—The 'Investment Fever' Mechanism." *China Newsletter* No. 47 (November-December 1983), pp. 7-14.

Hao, Mengbi and Duan Gaoran, eds. *Zhongguo gongchandang liushi nian* (Sixty years of the CCP). Beijing: PLA Press, 1984, Vol. two.

Harding, Harry. "From China With Disdain: New Trends in the Study of China." *Asian Survey* (October 1982), pp. 934-958.

Harding, Harry. *Organizing China.* Stanford: Stanford University Press, 1981.

Harrison, Selig. *China, Oil, and Asia: Conflict Ahead.* New York: Columbia, 1977.

He Jianzhang and Zhang Zhiye, eds. *Zhongguo jihua guanli wenti* (Problems in the management of Chinese planning). Beijing: Chinese Social Sciences Press, 1984.

Heilongjiang Legal Research Institute, ed. *Jingji Fagui Xuanbian, 1977-1984.* Harbin: Study Press, 1984.

Henderson, Gail and Myron Cohen. *The Chinese Hospital.* New Haven: Yale University Press, 1984.

Hersey, John. *A Single Pebble.* New York: Alfred A. Knopf, 1974.

Hewitt, Edward A. "Reform or Rhetoric: Gorbachev and the Soviet Economy." *The Brookings Review* vol. 4 (Fall 1986).

Ho, Samuel and Ralph Heunemann. *China's Open Door Policy.* Vancouver: University of British Columbia Press, 1984.

Hong Qingyu, "Dui Danjiangkou shuili shuniu ruogan wenti de kanfa" (Views on certain issues on the Danjiangkou key water resources project). *Renmin Changjiang* (People's Yangtze) No. 4. 1982.

Hough, Jerry. *The Soviet Prefects.* Cambridge: Harvard University Press, 1969.

Huntington, Samuel. *Political Order in Changing Societies.* New Haven: Yale University Press, 1968.

Ignatius, Ad. "China's deal." *Petroleum News* news supplement, June, 1982.

Janos, Andrew. "Group Politics in Communist Society: A Second Look at the Pluralistic Model," in Samuel Huntington and Clement Moore, eds. *Authoritarian Politics in Modern Society.* New York: Basic Books, 1970. pp. 204-238.

"Ji Li Peng" (Remember Li Peng). *Liaowang* (Outlook) (November 20, 1983), pp. 6-8.

Jowitt, Kenneth. *Revolutionary Breakthroughs and National Development: The Case of Romania, 1944-1965.* Berkeley and Los Angeles: University of California Press, 1971.

Kao, Michael Ying-mao, ed. *The Lin Piao Affair: Power, Politics and Military Coup.* White Plains, N.Y.: M. E. Sharpe, 1975.

Kao, Michael Ying-mao. *The People's Liberation Army and China's Nation Building.* White Plains, N.Y.: International Arts and Sciences Press, 1973.

Kasumigaseki Society. *Gendai Chugoku jimmei jiten, 1982* (Biographical Dictionary of Contemporary China). Tokyo: Konan Shoin, 1982.

Kelley, Donald R. "Toward a Model of Soviet Decision Making: A Research Note." *American Political Science Review* vol. 68 (1974), pp. 701-706.

Kim, Hong N. and Jack L. Hammersmith. "US-China Relations in the Post-Normalization Era, 1979-1985." *Pacific Affairs* (Spring, 1986), pp. 66-91.

Kingdon, John W. *Agendas, Alternatives, and Public Policies.* Boston: Little, Brown, 1984.

Kitani, Fujiko. "Electric power in China." *China Newsletter* No. 56 (May-June 1985), p. 14.

Klein, Donald and Anne B. Clark. *Biographical Dictionary of Chinese Communism, 1921-1965.* Cambridge: Harvard Press, 1971.

Klein, Donald. "Sources for Elite Studies and Biographical Materials on China," in Robert Scalapino, ed. *Elites in the People's Republic of China.* Seattle: University of Washington Press, 1962. pp. 609-656.

Kornai, Janos. *Dilemmas and Contradictions.* Cambridge: MIT Press, 1986.

Kraus, Richard. *Class Conflict in Chinese Socialism.* New York: Columbia University Press, 1981.

Kuo, Chi. "Foreign Trade: Why the 'Gang of Four' Created Confusion." *Peking Review* vol. 20, no. 9 (February 25, 1977).

Lampton, David M. "Chinese Politics: The Bargaining Treadmill." *Issues and Studies* vol. 23, no. 3. 1987. pp. 11-41.

Lampton, David M. *Health, Conflict, and the Chinese Political System.* Ann Arbor: University of Michigan's Center for Chinese Studies, 1974.

Lampton, David M. *Paths to Power.* Ann Arbor: University of Michigan Center for Chinese Studies, 1986.

Lampton, David M., ed. *Policy Implementation in the People's Republic of China.* Berkeley and Los Angeles: University of California Press, 1987.

Lampton, David M. *The Politics of Medicine in China: The Policy Process, 1949-1977.* Boulder: Westview Press, 1977.

Lampton, David M. "The Roots of Interprovincial Inequality in Education and Health Services in China Since 1949." *American Political Science Review* (June, 1979), pp. 459-477.

Lardy, Nicholas. *Agriculture in China's Modern Economic Development.* London: Cambridge Press, 1983.

Lardy, Nicholas. *Economic Growth and Distribution in China.* Cambridge: Cambridge University Press, 1978.

Lardy, Nicholas. "Reply." *China Quarterly* No. 66 (June, 1976), pp. 340-354.

Lardy, Nicholas and Kenneth Lieberthal, eds. *Chen Yun's Strategy for China's Development.* Armonk: M. E. Sharpe, 1983.

Lee, Chae-Jin. *China and Japan: New Economic Diplomacy.* Stanford: Hoover Institution, 1984.

Lee, Hong Yung. *The Politics of the Chinese Cultural Revolution.* Berkeley and Los Angeles: University of California Press, 1978.

Lee, Rensaleer III. "The Hsia-fang System: Marxism and Modernization." *China Quarterly* No. 28 (October-December 1966), pp. 40-62.

Lewin, Moshe. *Russian Peasants and Soviet Power*. London: George Allen and Unwin, 1968.

Lewis, John Wilson. *Leadership in Communist China*. Ithaca: Cornell University Press, 1963.

Lewis, John Wilson. *Political Networks and the Chinese Policy Process*. Stanford: Northeast Asia-United States Forum on International Policy, 1986.

Li, Chengrui. "An Analysis of China's Economic Situation during the Period of Ten Years of Internal Disorder." *Jingji Yanjiu* (Economic research) No. 1, January, 1984, pp. 23-31, translated in FBIS, Vol. I, No. 46 (March 7, 1984), esp. p. K-8.

Li, Rui, ed. *Huainian shi pian* (Ten Articles of Commemoration). Beijing: People's Press, 1983.

Li, Rui. "It is Necessary to Develop Hydropower on a Priority Basis." *Renmin Ribao* March 6, 1980.

Li, Rui. *Lun Sanxia gongcheng* (On the Three Gorges Project). Hunan: Hunan Science and Technology Press, 1985.

Lieberthal, Kenneth. "Beijing's Consumer Market." *China Business Review* (September-October 1981).

Lieberthal, Kenneth with James Tong and Sai-cheung Yeung, *Central Documents and Politburo Politics in China*. Ann Arbor: University of Michigan Center for Chinese Studies, 1978.

Lieberthal, Kenneth. "China and the Soviet Union: The Background in Chinese Politics," in Herbert Ellison, ed. *The Sino-Soviet Conflict: A Global Perspective*. Seattle: University of Washington, 1982, pp. 3-28.

Lieberthal, Kenneth. "The Great Leap Forward and the Split in the Yenan Leadership," in John K. Fairbank and Roderick MacFarquhar, eds. *The Cambridge History of China*. Vol. XIV. Cambridge: Cambridge University Press, 1987.

Lieberthal, Kenneth. *A Research Guide to Central Party and Government Meetings in China, 1949-75*. White Plains: International Arts and Sciences Press, 1976.

Lieberthal, Kenneth. *Revolution and Tradition in Tientsin, 1949-52*. Stanford: Stanford University Press, 1980.

Lin, Yishan. "Guanyu Changjiang liuyu guihua ruogan wenti de shangtao" (Discussion of certain problems in the Yangtze basin plan). *Zhongguo shuili* (China water resources), Nos. 5 and 6 (1956).

Lindblom, Charles E. "The Science of Muddling Through." *Public Administration Review* (Spring 1959), pp. 79-88.

Ling, H. C. *The Petroleum Industry of the People's Republic of China*. Stanford: Hoover Institution Press, 1975.

Liu, Suinian, et al. *Liushi niandai guomin jingji tiaozheng de huigu* (Recollection of the economic readjustment of the 1960's). Beijing: Finance and Economic Press, 1983.

Ludlow, Nicholas. "Gezhouba On the Yangzi." *The China Business Review* (May-June 1980), pp. 11-15.

Ludlow, Nicholas H. "Three Gorges Project: Harnessing the Yangzi." *China Business Review* (May-June 1980), pp. 16-21.

Luo, Long. "Project Approval," MOR *China Newsletter* (April-May 1987), pp. 6-7.

Ma, Teresa. "Foreigners Too Would Like Some Offshore Business." *Far Eastern Economic Review* (August 25, 1983), pp. 61-63.

MacFarquhar, Roderick. *The Origins of the Cultural Revolution*. 2 vols. New York: Columbia University Press, 1974 and 1983.

McCormick, Barry. *Political Reform in Post-Mao China: Democracy and Due Process in the Leninist State*. Ph.D. thesis. Madison: University of Wisconsin, 1985.

Manion, Melanie. "The Cadre Management System, Post-Mao: The Appointment, Promotion, Transfer, and Removal of Party and State Leaders." *China Quarterly* No. 102 (June, 1985), pp. 203-233.

Mao Zedong sixiang wansui (Long live Mao Zedong Thought). 1969.

March, James G. "Bounded Rationality, Ambiguity, and the Engineering of Choice." *Bell Journal of Economics* (Autumn 1978), pp. 587-608.

March, James G. and Johan P. Olsen, eds. *Ambiguity and Choice in Organizations*. Bergen: Universitetsforlaget, 1976.

March, James G. and Herbert A. Simon, *Organizations*. New York: John Wiley, 1958.

Meisner, Maurice. *Mao's China: A History of the People's Republic of China*. New York: Free Press, 1977.

Michaels, Daniel. "The Three Gorges Project in China's Modernization: Image and Reality." Senior thesis in East Asian Studies. Princeton: Princeton University, 1987.

Mikezell, Raymond. *Petroleum Company Operations and Agreements*. Washington: Resources For the Future, 1984.

Mills, William. "Generational Change in China." *Problems of Communism* (November-December 1983).

Min, Yu. "The Daqing Oil Field Developed Under the Direction of the Thought of Mao Zedong." *Hongqi* (Red Flag) No. 13 (December 6, 1965), translated in *Survey of China Mainland Press*, No. 505 (January 3, 1966).

Ministry of Petroleum Industry. "Zhongguo shiyou gongye de jueqi" (Rise of China's petroleum industry), in *Guanghui de chengjiu* (Glorious achievements). Beijing: People's Press, 1984.

Minnick, Kathryn. "The Development of Chinese Nuclear Energy Policy." M.A. Thesis. Ann Arbor: University of Michigan Center for Chinese Studies, 1987.

Moody, Peter. "Policy and Power: The Career of T'ao Chu, 1956-66." *China Quarterly* No. 54 (April-June, 1973), pp. 267-293.

Moore, Barrington, Jr. *Soviet Politics—The Dilemma of Power*. New York: Harper and Row, 1965.

Moser, Michael, ed. *Foreign Trade, Investment and the Law in the People's Republic of China.* Oxford: Oxford University Press, 1984.

"Nanhai East Oil Company." *China Oil.* Vol. I (Summer 1984), pp. 140-142.

Nathan, Andrew. *Chinese Democracy.* New York: Alfred A. Knopf, 1985.

Nathan, Andrew. "A Factionalism Model for CCP Politics." *China Quarterly* No. 53 (January-March 1973), pp. 34-66.

Nathan, Andrew. *Peking Politics, 1918-1923.* Berkeley and Los Angeles: University of California Press, 1976.

Naughton, Barry. "The Decline of Central Control Over Investment in Post Mao China," in David M. Lampton, ed. *Policy Implementation in the People's Republic of China.* Berkeley and Los Angeles: University of California Press, 1987.

Naughton, Barry. "The Economy of the Cultural Revolution: Military Preparation, Decentralization, and Leaps Forward." Paper prepared for the "New Perspectives on the Cultural Revolution" Conference, Harvard University, May 15-17, 1987.

Nelsen, Harvey. *The Chinese Military System: An Organizational Study of the People's Liberation Army.* Boulder: Westview Press, 1977.

Nie Rongzhen huiyi lu (Reminisces of Nie Rongzhen). Beijing: Liberation Army Press, 1984.

Nove, Alec. "Economic Policy and Economic Trends," in Alexander Dallin and Thomas B. Larson, eds. *Soviet Politics Since Khrushchev.* Englewood Cliffs, N.J.: Prentice Hall, 1968. pp. 73-110.

Odom, William. "A Dissenting View on the Group Approach to Soviet Politics." *World Politics* (July 1976), pp. 452-567.

Oi, Jean Chun. *State and Peasant in Contemporary China: The Politics of Grain Procurement.* Ph.D. thesis. Ann Arbor: University of Michigan, 1983.

Oksenberg, Michel. "The Chinese Policy Process and the Public Health Issue: An Arena Approach." *Studies in Comparative Communism* (Winter, 1974), Vol. VII, No. 4, pp. 375-408.

Oksenberg, Michel. "A Decade of Sino-American Relations." *Foreign Affairs* Vol. 61, No. 1 (Fall 1982).

Oksenberg, Michel. "Economic Policy-Making in China: Summer 1981." *China Quarterly* No. 90 (June 1982), pp. 165-194.

Oksenberg, Michel. "The Literature on Post-1949 China: An Interpretive Essay," in John Fairbank and Roderick MacFarquhar, eds. *The Cambridge History of China* Vol. 13, Part One. Cambridge: Cambridge University Press, 1987.

Oksenberg, Michel. "Methods of Communication Within the Chinese Bureaucracy." *China Quarterly* No. 57 (January-March 1974), pp. 1-39.

Oksenberg, Michel. "Occupations and Groups in Chinese Society and the Cultural Revolution," in *The Cultural Revolution: 1967 in Review.* Michel Oksenberg, et al., eds. Ann Arbor: University of Michigan, Center for Chinese Studies, 1968, pp. 1-39.

Oksenberg, Michel. *Policy Formulation in China: The Case of the 1957-58*

Water Conservancy Campaign. Ph.D. thesis. New York: Columbia University, 1969.

Oksenberg, Michel. "Sources and Methodological Problems in the Study of Contemporary China," in A. Doak Barnett, ed. *Chinese Communist Politics in Action*. Seattle: University of Washington Press, 1969.

Oksenberg, Michel and Steven Goldstein. "The Chinese Political Spectrum." *Problems of Communism* (March-April, 1974), pp. 1-13.

Onate, Andres. "Hua Kuo-feng and the Arrest of the 'Gang of Four,' " *China Quarterly* No. 70 (September, 1979), pp. 540-565.

Perkins, Dwight. *Market Control and Planning in Communist China*. Cambridge: Harvard University Press, 1966.

Perry, Elizabeth and Christine Wong, eds. *The Political Economy of Reform in Post-Mao China*. Cambridge: Harvard University Press, 1985.

"Pluralism in Communist Societies: Is the Emperor Naked?" *Studies in Comparative Communism* XII, No. 1 (Spring 1979).

Preparatory Office of the China Three Gorges Project Development Corporation. "A Brief Account of (*sic*) Three Gorges Project" (March 1986).

Pryor, Frederic. *Property and Industrial Organization in Communist and Capitalist Nations*. Bloomington: Indiana University Press, 1973.

Pye, Lucian. *The Dynamics of Chinese Politics*. Cambridge: Oelgeschlager, Gunn, and Hain, 1981.

Pye, Lucian. *The Spirit of Chinese Politics*. Cambridge, Mass: MIT Press, 1968.

Renmin shouce (People's Handbook). Beijing: Dagongbao Press, 1964.

Rice, Edwin. *Mao's Way*. Berkeley and Los Angeles: University of California Press, 1972.

Robinson, Thomas. "The Wuhan Incident." *China Quarterly* No. 47 (July-September, 1971), pp. 413-438.

Roll, Robert and K. C. Yeh. "Balance in Coastal and Inland Industrial Development." *China: A Reassessment of the Economy*, Joint Economic Committee. Washington: U.S. Government Printing Office, 1975, pp. 81-93.

Rosen, Stanley. *Red Guard Factionalism and the Cultural Revolution in Guangzhou*. Boulder: Westview Press, 1981.

Ross, Lester. *Environmental Policy in China*. Bloomington: Indiana University Press, forthcoming.

Ross, Robert. "International Bargaining and Domestic Politics," in *World Politics* (January, 1986), pp. 255-287.

Schelling, Thomas C. *The Strategy of Conflict*. Cambridge: Harvard University Press, 1960.

Schmitter, Phillipe C. "Still the Century of Corporatism?" in Frederick B. Pike and Thomas Stritch, eds. *The New Corporatism*. Notre Dame: University of Notre Dame, 1974. pp. 85-131.

Schram, Stuart, ed. *Authority, Participation and Cultural Change in China*. Cambridge: Cambridge University Press, 1973.

Schram, Stuart. *Mao Tse-tung: A Political Biography*. New York: Simon and Schuster, 1966.

Schurmann, H. Franz. *Ideology and Organization in Communist China*. 2nd ed. Berkeley and Los Angeles: University of California Press, 1968.

Schwartz, Benjamin. *Communism and China; Ideology in Flux*. Cambridge: Harvard University Press, 1968.

Schwartz, Joel and William R. Keech. "Group Influence and the Policy Process in the Soviet Union." *American Political Science Review* (September 1968), pp. 840-851.

Shambaugh, David. *The Making of a Premier: Zhao Ziyang's Provincial Career*. Boulder: Westview Press, 1984.

Shi, Yiping. "Changes of Twenty Positions in the State Council." *Dongxiang* (Trends) No. 23 (August 16, 1980), pp. 4-6, in FBIS, August 21, 1980, pp. U1-2.

Shirk, Susan. *Competitive Comrades*. Berkeley and Los Angeles: University of California Press, 1982.

Shirk, Susan. "The Politics of Industrial Reform," in Elizabeth Perry and Christine Wong, eds. *The Political Economy of Reform in Post-Mao China*. Cambridge: Harvard University Press, 1985.

Simon, Herbert A. *Administrative Behavior*. 2nd ed. New York: Macmillan, 1957.

Simon, Herbert A. "A Behavioral Model of Rational Choice," in *Models of Man: Social and Rational*. New York: John Wiley, 1957, pp. 241-260.

Skilling, Gordon. "Interest Groups and Communist Politics." *World Politics* (April 1966), pp. 435-451.

Skinner, G. William. "Cities and the Hierarchy of Local Systems." G. William Skinner, ed. *The City in Late Imperial China*. Stanford University Press, 1977, pp. 275-352.

Skinner, G. William. "Marketing and Social Structure in Rural China." *Journal of Asian Studies* No. 24, Vol. 1 (November, 1964), pp. 3-44 (Part I); No. 24, Vol. 2 (February, 1965), pp. 195-288 (Part II); No. 24, Vol. 3 (May, 1965), pp. 363-400 (Part III).

Skinner, G. William. "Presidential Address: The Structure of Chinese History." *Journal of Asian Studies* Vol. XLIV, No. 2 (February, 1985), pp. 271-292.

Skocpol, Theda. *States and Social Revolutions*. Cambridge: Cambridge University Press, 1979.

"Smaller Hydro Projects May Get Priority Over Huge Yangzi Gorge Plan." *The China Business Review* (July-August 1979), p. 58.

Soeya, Yoshi. *Japan's Postwar Economic Diplomacy with China: Three Decades of Non-Governmental Experience*. Ph.D. thesis. Ann Arbor: University of Michigan, 1987.

Solinger, Dorothy J. *Chinese Business Under Socialism*. Berkeley and Los Angeles: University of California Press, 1984.

Solomon, Richard. *Mao's Revolution and the Chinese Political Culture*. Berkeley and Los Angeles: University of California Press, 1971.

State Statistical Bureau, ed. *Zhongguo tongji nianjian* (China Statistical Yearbook). (Beijing: Chinese Statistical Press, 1983).

Stavis, Benedict. *Making Green Revolution: The Politics of Agricultural Development in China, Rural Development Monograph*, No. 1. Ithaca: Cornell University Press, 1974.

Stavis, Benedict. *The Politics of Agricultural Mechanization in China*. Ithaca: Cornell University Press, 1978.

Steinbruner, John D. *The Cybernetic Theory of Decision: New Dimensions of Political Analysis*. Princeton: Princeton University Press, 1974.

Strong, Tracey and Helene Keyssar. "Anna Louis Strong: Three Interviews With Chairman Mao Zedong." *China Quarterly* No. 103 (September 1985).

Stuermer, John. "The Foreign Exchange Situation." *China Business Review* (January-February 1986), pp. 14-17.

"Summary of Central Work Symposium," December 20, 1964, in *Mao Zedong sixiang wansui* (Long Live the Thought of Mao Zedong), (n.p., n.d.).

Suttmeier, Richard P. *Research and Revolution: Scientific Policy and Societal Change in China*. Lexington, Mass.: Lexington Books, 1974.

"The Taching Oilfield: Triumph and Troubles." *China Topics* YB 533 (August 15, 1969).

Tang, Tsou. "Prolegomenon to the Study of Informal Groups in Chinese Communist Party Politics." *China Quarterly* No. 65 (March, 1976), pp. 98-114.

Tanner, James. "Promise of Finds Draws Oil Firms to China." *Wall Street Journal*, October 19, 1978.

Taylor, Donald W. "Decision Making and Problem Solving," in James G. March, ed. *Handbook of Organizations*. New York: John Wiley & Sons, 1959.

Terrill, Ross. *Flowers on an Iron Tree: Five Cities of China*. Boston: Little, Brown and Company, 1975.

Teiwes, Frederick C. *Leadership, Legitimacy, and Conflict in China*. Armonk, N.Y.: M. E. Sharpe, 1984.

Teiwes, Frederick C. *Politics and Purges in China*. Armonk, N.Y.: M. E. Sharpe, 1979.

Teiwes, Frederick C. *Provincial Leadership in China: The Cultural Revolution and its Aftermath*. Ithaca: Cornell University, 1974.

Townsend, James. *Political Participation in Communist China*. Berkeley and Los Angeles: University of California Press, 1967.

Townsend, James. *Politics in China*. Boston: Little, Brown and Company, 1974.

United States Bureau of Reclamation, Trip Report for April 30-June 12, 1981 trip to China.

United States Bureau of Reclamation, Trip Report for June-July 1984 trip to China.

United States Government. *Appearances and Activities of Chinese Communist Officials*. 1966.

United States Government. *Directory of Chinese Communist Officials*. 1963.

Vogel, Ezra. *Canton under Communism*. Cambridge: Harvard University Press, 1969.

Vogel, Ezra. "From Friendship to Comradeship." *China Quarterly* No. 21 (January-March 1965), pp. 46-60.

"Waiting for the Offshore Go Ahead." *Far Eastern Economic Review* (October 1, 1982), pp. 63-66.

Walder, Andrew G. *Communist Neo-Traditionalism: Work and Authority in Chinese Industry.* Berkeley and Los Angeles: University of California Press, 1986.

Walker, Jack L. "The Diffusion of Knowledge, Policy Committees, and Agenda Setting," in John E. Tropman et al. *New Strategic Perspectives on Social Policy.* New York: Pergamon Press, 1981.

Water Resources of China. JPRS, No. 32681 (November 2, 1965).

White, Gordon. *Party and Professionals: The Political Role of Teachers in Contemporary China.* Armonk, N.Y.: M. E. Sharpe, 1981.

White, Lynn. "Workers Politics in Shanghai." *Journal of Asian Studies* No. 36 (November, 1976), pp. 99-116.

Whiting, Allen. *The Chinese Calculus of Deterrence.* Ann Arbor: University of Michigan Press, 1975.

Whiting, Allen. *Chinese Domestic Politics and Foreign Policy in the 1970s.* Ann Arbor: University of Michigan Center for Chinese Studies, 1979.

Whitson, William. *The Chinese High Command: A History of Communist Military Politics, 1927-71.* New York: Praeger, 1973.

Whitson, William, ed. *The Military and Political Power in China to the 1970's.* New York: Praeger Press, 1972.

Whitson, William. "Organizational Perspectives and Decision Making in the Chinese Communist High Command," in Robert Scalapino, ed. *Elites in the People's Republic of China.* Seattle: University of Washington Press, 1972.

Whyte, Martin. "Bureaucracy and Modernization in China: The Maoist Critique." *American Sociological Review* (April 1973), pp. 149-163.

Wong, Paul. *China's Higher Leadership In the Socialist Transition.* New York: The Free Press, 1976.

Woodard, Kim. "China and Offshore Energy," *Problems of Communism* (Nov.-Dec. 1981), pp. 32-45.

Woodard, Kim. "The Drilling Begins." *China Business Review* (May-June, 1983).

Woodard, Kim. *The International Energy Relations of China.* Stanford: Stanford University Press, 1980.

Workshop on the Comparative Study of Communist Systems. *Change in Communist Systems.* Stanford: Stanford University Press, 1970.

World Bank. *China: Long-Term Development Issues and Options.* Washington, DC: Johns Hopkins University Press, 1985.

World Bank. *China: Socialist Economic Development, The Energy Sector.* Annex E. Washington: World Bank, June 1, 1981.

Wu, Daying, et al. *Zhongguo shehuizhuyi lifa wenti* (Problems in China's socialist legislation). Masses Press, 1984.

Xiandai Zhongguo shuili jianshe (Contemporary China's water resources construction). Beijing: September 1984.

Xu, Jinqiang. "Basic Experience in Revolutionizing Daqing Oil Field." *Jingji yanjiu* (Economic Research) No. 4 (April 20, 1956), in *SCMM*, No. 538 (August 22, 1966), pp. 8-27.

Xu, Yi and Chen Baosen, eds. *Caizheng xue* (Finance). Chinese Finance and Economics Press, 1984.

Xu, Yi and Chen Baosen. *Zhongguo de caizheng, 1977-80* (China's Finance, 1977-80). Beijing: People's Press.

Yamanouchi, Kazuo. "The Chinese Price System and the Thrust of Reform." *China Newsletter* No. 60 (January-February, 1986).

Yang Guanghan, *et al. Mishu xue yu mishu gongzuo* (secretarial study and secretarial work). Beijing: Guangming Daily Press, 1984.

Yang, Hong and Wang Jinzhong. "Yao jiaqiang jingji lifa gongzuo" (Economic legislative work should be strengthened). *Renmin ribao* May 14, 1981.

Yang, Xianyi, Wei Tingzheng, and Paul Cheshen Chao, "Three Gorge Dam: Why It Should Be Built." ENR (November 6, 1980). Also, the longer original manuscript for this article.

Yanov, Alexander. *The Drama of the Soviet 1960's*. Berkeley: Institute of International Studies, 1984.

Yao Mingli. "The Past, Present, and Future of Daqing, China." *China Oil* Vol. 2, No. 1 (Spring, 1985).

Zagoria, Donald. *The Sino-Soviet Conflict, 1956-1961*. Princeton: Princeton University Press, 1962.

Zhonggong dangshi dashi nianbiao (A chronology of major events in the history of the CCP). Beijing, People's Press, 1981.

Zhonggong shiyi ju sanzhong chuanhui yilai zhongyang shouyao jianghua ji wenjian xuanbian (Selection of important central speeches and documents since the Third Plenum). Vol. 1. Changchun: People's Press, 1982.

Zhongguo dui wai jingji maoyi nianjian, 1984 (1984 Yearbook of Chinese Foreign Economic Trade). Beijing: Chinese Foreign Trade Press, 1984.

Zhongguo gongchandang lizi zhongyao huiyi ji (A collection of historically important meetings of the Chinese Communist Party). Shanghai: People's Press, 1983.

Zhongguo tongji nianjian 1984 (Chinese statistical annual, 1984). Beijing: Chinese Statistical Press, 1985.

Zhongyang Caizheng Fagui Huibian (Central Finance Legal Compendium, 1956 and 1957). Beijing: Finance Press, 1957.

Zhongyang he zhongyang lingdao tongzhi guanyu shehuizhuyi minzhu, shehuizhuyi fazhi he renmin daibiao dahui zhidu de lunshu (Commentary of the center and the leadership comrades on socialist democracy, socialist legality, and the people's congress system). Beijing: Standing Committee of Beijing Municipal Assembly, 1984.

Zhou Enlai tongzhi shengping huodong nianbiao, 1898-1976 (Chronological table of Comrade Zhou Enlai's lifelong activities, 1898-1976). Beijing: China Revolutionary Museum, 1980.

Zhou, Taihe, ed., *Dangdai Zhongguo de jingji tizhi gaige* (Reform of the Economic Structure of Contemporary China). Beijing: Social Sciences Press, 1984.

Zweig, David. *Agrarian Radicalism in China: 1968-78; The Search for a Social Base*, Ph.D. thesis. Ann Arbor: University of Michigan, 1983.

PERIODICALS

Asian Wall Street Journal. Hong Kong.
Beijing Review (formerly called *Peking Review*). Beijing.
Changjiang ribao (Yangtze daily).
China Business Review. Washington.
China Daily. Beijing.
China Pictorial. Beijing.
Dagongbao. Beijing.
Dagongbao. Hong Kong.
ENR News, The McGraw-Hill Construction Weekly. New York.
Far Eastern Economic Review. Hong Kong.
Financial Times. London.
Fujian ribao (Fujian daily).
Guangming Ribao (Brightness Daily).
Hongqi (Red flag).
Hongse gongjiao (Red industry and communications).
Hongse zaofanbao (Red rebel paper).
Hubei ribao (Hubei daily).
Jetro China Newsletter.
Jinggangshan (Jingkang Mountain).
Nanyang shangbao (Southeast Asia Commercial Bulletin).
New York Times.
Petroleum News.
Pravda.
Renmin Changjiang (People's Yangtze).
Renmin ribao (People's Daily). Beijing.
Shuili shuidian jishu (Water Resources and Hydropower Technology).
Shijie jingji daobao (World Economic Journal).
Shiyou Kantan (Petroleum Survey).
Shuili Fadian (Hydropower).
Sichuan Ribao (Sichuan daily).
South China Morning Post. Hong Kong.
Tianjin dagongbao (Tianjin Impartial Daily).
Wenhuibao. Shanghai.
Wen Wei Po. Hong Kong.
Xin guancha banyuekan (New observation semimonthly).
Xinhua banyuekan (New China semimonthly).
Zhengming (Contention). Hong Kong.
Zhongguo shuili (China water resources).
Zhongguo xinwen (China news).

INDEX

Adjustment Office, 146
AGIP, 236
Akira, Matsuzawa, 218, 222
Alcoa, 49
Amoco, 234, 236
Anderson, Robert, 220, 255, 266
Antaibao coal mine, 339, 362, 363-369;
   Deng Xiaoping's involvement in, 370
anti-rightist campaign, 295
Arco, 86, 125, 126, 219-222, 232, 234, 242,
   255, 258; South China Oil project, 373,
   375, 382, 389, 390
Aspen Institute, 220
authority, allocation of, 135; cellular nature of, 135, 136; center/locale competition for, 138, 140; evolution of, in communist states, 34; fragmentation of, 22,
   23, 25, 137, 138, 142, 151, 158-160;
   horizontal function of, 141; relations/
   competition for, 139; structure of, 27,
   135; vertical function of, 141

Bank of China, 32, 64, 75, 91, 112, 116,
   117, 125, 133, 134, 140, 155, 165, 218,
   223; description, 120-128; financing
   projects, 133, 365; Foreign Exchange
   Funds Department, 122, functions, 120-
   123; Second Credit Department, 122;
   South Sea Oil Project, 385, 388; struc-
   ture, 121
Baoshan Iron and Steel Works, 49, 50, 109,
   216, 223; financing of, 112
Barnett, A. Doak, 5, 12
Beidaihe conference: Three Gorges project,
   302
Beijing Electric Power Administration, 53
Beijing Petroleum Research Institute, 174
Beijing Power Supply Bureau, 53, 54
Beijing University, 188
Bethlehem Steel, 49
Bjartmer, Gjerde, 237
Bohai Gulf Oil Rig Incident, 49, 253, 269
Bo Yibo, 37; State Economic Commission
   and, 190, 298, 370

British Petroleum, 222, 236, 242, 382, 388
Bureau for the Protection of the Environment Against Pollution, 309
Bureau of Fisheries, 98
bureaucracy: continuity and change in,
   154, 155; integration of, 151-153; personal ties (*guanxi*) and, 155-157; Soviet
   style, 391-393
bureaucracy, Chinese: characteristics of,
   394-396
bureaucratic behavior, 229; strategies of,
   161-167
bureaucratic rank, 24; among government
   organizations, 142, 143; individual stature and, 145-148; leadership relations
   and, 148, 149, 394; party organization
   and, 144; professional/business relations
   and, 149, 355, 394; protection of, 150,
   151
bureaucratic reform, capacity for, 410-415
bureaucratic specialization: 404-405; opposition to, 408, 409
bureaucratic structure: 34; evolution of,
   402-410; policy process and, 16-19
Bush, George, 213, 266

Capital Construction Commission, 154
Center (*zhongyang*), 24, 32, 138, 335, 344,
   345, 413; local relations and, 33; role in
   policy process, 26, 27; South Sea oil
   project and, 380. *See also* Chinese Com-
   munist Party; Politburo; State Council;
   Zhongnanhai
Central Committee, *see* Chinese Commu-
   nist Party
central documents, 153
Central Energy Research Society, 159
central-provincial relations, 339-353;
   Shanxi coal mines and, 369-371; South
   Sea Oil Project and, 371-389
Central Work Conferences, 29, 152
CFP-Total, 232
Changjiang renmin, 318
Changjiang ribao, 297
Chemical Bank, 385